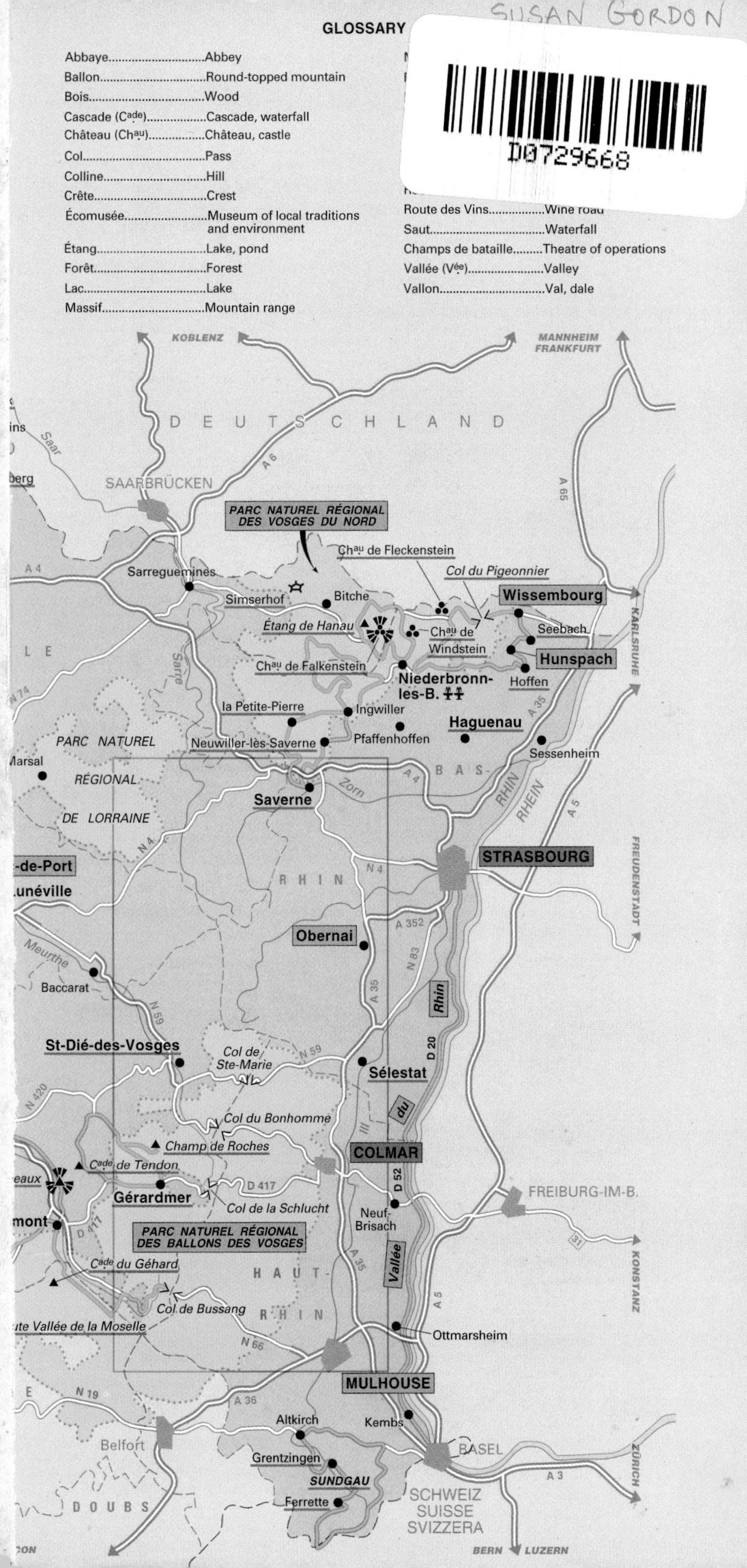

SUSAN GORDON
D0729668
GLOSSARY
Abbaye..........Abbey
Ballon..........Round-topped mountain
Bois..........Wood
Cascade (Cade)..........Cascade, waterfall
Château (Chau)..........Château, castle
Col..........Pass
Colline..........Hill
Crête..........Crest
Écomusée..........Museum of local traditions and environment
Étang..........Lake, pond
Forêt..........Forest
Lac..........Lake
Massif..........Mountain range
Route des Vins..........Wine road
Saut..........Waterfall
Champs de bataille..........Theatre of operations
Vallée (Vée)..........Valley
Vallon..........Val, dale
KOBLENZ
MANNHEIM
FRANKFURT
DEUTSCHLAND
SAARBRÜCKEN
Saar
A 6
A 65
PARC NATUREL RÉGIONAL DES VOSGES DU NORD
Chau de Fleckenstein
Col du Pigeonnier
A 4
Sarreguemines
Simserhof
Bitche
Wissembourg
Étang de Hanau
Chau de Windstein
Seebach
Hunspach
KARLSRUHE
Chau de Falkenstein
Niederbronn-les-B.
Hoffen
Sarre
N 74
la Petite-Pierre
Ingwiller
A 35
Haguenau
PARC NATUREL
Neuwiller-lès-Saverne
Pfaffenhoffen
Sessenheim
RÉGIONAL
DE LORRAINE
Saverne
Zorn
A 4
BAS-
RHIN
RHEIN
A 5
N 4
STRASBOURG
FREUDENSTADT
Lunéville
RHIN
N 4
A 352
Obernai
Meurthe
N 83
Baccarat
A 35
Rhin
N 59
D 20
St-Dié-des-Vosges
Col de Ste-Marie
N 59
Sélestat
N 420
Col du Bonhomme
du
Champ de Roches
COLMAR
Cade de Tendon
D 417
D 52
Gérardmer
Col de la Schlucht
FREIBURG-IM-B.
Neuf-Brisach
D 417
PARC NATUREL RÉGIONAL DES BALLONS DES VOSGES
31
KONSTANZ
Cade du Géhard
HAUT-
A 35
Vallée
A 5
Col de Bussang
RHIN
Ottmarsheim
N 66
MULHOUSE
N 19
A 36
Altkirch
Kembs
Belfort
BASEL
ZÜRICH
Grentzingen
A 3
SUNDGAU
DOUBS
Ferrette
SCHWEIZ
SUISSE
SVIZZERA
BERN
LUZERN

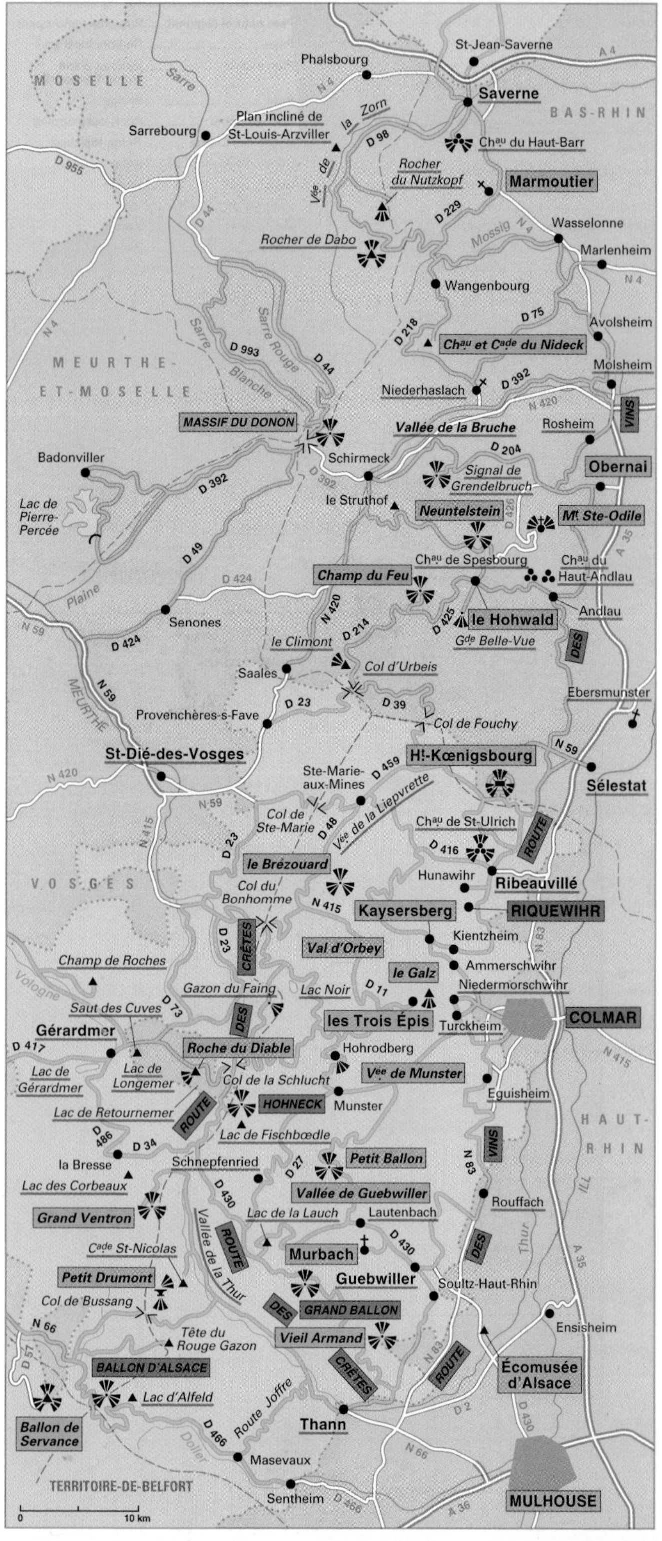

St-Jean-Saverne
Phalsbourg
MOSELLE
Saverne
BAS-RHIN
Plan incliné de St-Louis-Arzviller
Sarrebourg
Chau du Haut-Barr
Rocher du Nutzkopf
Marmoutier
Wasselonne
Rocher de Dabo
Marlenheim
Wangenbourg
Avolsheim
Chau et Cade du Nideck
Molsheim
MEURTHE-ET-MOSELLE
Niederhaslach
MASSIF DU DONON
Vallée de la Bruche
Rosheim
VINS
Badonviller
Schirmeck
Obernai
Signal de Grendelbruch
Lac de Pierre-Percée
le Struthof
Neuntelstein
Mt Ste-Odile
Chau de Spesbourg
Chau du Haut-Andlau
Champ du Feu
Andlau
le Hohwald
Senones
Gde Belle-Vue
le Climont
DES
Col d'Urbeis
Saales
Ebersmunster
Provenchères-s-Fave
Col de Fouchy
Ht-Kœnigsbourg
St-Dié-des-Vosges
Sélestat
Ste-Marie-aux-Mines
Vée de la Liepvrette
Col de Ste-Marie
Chau de St-Ulrich
ROUTE
le Brézouard
Hunawihr
Ribeauvillé
VOSGES
Col du Bonhomme
Kaysersberg
RIQUEWIHR
Kientzheim
CRÊTES
Val d'Orbey
Ammerschwihr
Champ de Roches
le Galz
Niedermorschwihr
Gazon du Faing
Lac Noir
Saut des Cuves
les Trois Épis
COLMAR
Gérardmer
Turckheim
Roche du Diable
Hohrodberg
Lac de Gérardmer
Lac de Longemer
Col de la Schlucht
Vée de Munster
Eguisheim
Lac de Retournemer
HOHNECK
Munster
HAUT-RHIN
Lac de Fischbœdle
la Bresse
Schnepfenried
Petit Ballon
Lac des Corbeaux
Vallée de Guebwiller
Rouffach
Grand Ventron
Lac de la Lauch
Lautenbach
Vallée de la Thur
Cade St-Nicolas
Murbach
Petit Drumont
Guebwiller
Soultz-Haut-Rhin
Col de Bussang
GRAND BALLON
Ensisheim
Tête du Rouge Gazon
Vieil Armand
BALLON D'ALSACE
Écomusée d'Alsace
Lac d'Alfeld
Route Joffre
Thann
Ballon de Servance
Masevaux
TERRITOIRE-DE-BELFORT
Sentheim
MULHOUSE
0
10 km

ALSACE
LORRAINE
CHAMPAGNE

R. Mattès/MICHELIN

Chief Editor	Cynthia Clayton Ochterbeck

THE GREEN GUIDE ALSACE LORRAINE CHAMPAGNE

Editor	Gaven R. Watkins
Contributing Writers	Lisa Pasold, Natasha Edwards
Production Coordinator	Natasha G. George
Cartography	Alain Baldet, Michèle Cana, Peter Wrenn
Photo Editor	Lydia Strong
Proofreader	Jonathan P. Gilbert
Layout & Design	Ute Weber and John Higginbottom
Cover Design	Laurent Muller and Ute Weber

Contact Us:

The Green Guide
Michelin Maps and Guides
One Parkway South
Greenville, SC 29615
USA
☎1-800-423-0485
www.michelintravel.com
michelin.guides@us.michelin.com

Michelin Maps and Guides
Hannay House
39 Clarendon Road
Watford, Herts WD17 1JA
UK
☎01923 205240
www.ViaMichelin.com
travelpubsales@uk.michelin.com

Special Sales:

For information regarding bulk sales, customized editions and premium sales, please contact our Customer Service Departments:

USA	1-800-432-6277
UK	01923 205240
Canada	1-800-361-8236

One Team ...
A Commitment to Quality

There's just one reason our team is dedicated to producing quality travel publications—you, our reader.

Throughout our guides we offer **practical information**, **touring tips** and **suggestions** for finding the best places for a break.

Michelin driving tours help you hit the highlights and quickly absorb the best of the region. Our descriptive **walking tours** make you your own guide, armed with directions, maps and expert information.

We scout out the attractions, classify them with **star ratings**, and describe in detail what you will find when you visit them.

Michelin maps featured throughout the guide offer vibrant, detailed and easy-to-follow outlines of everything from close-up museum plans to international maps.

Places to stay and eat are always a big part of travel, so we research **hotels and restaurants** that we think convey the essence of the destination and arrange them by geographic area and price. We walk you through the best shopping districts and point you towards the host of entertainment and recreation possibilities on offer.

We **test**, **retest**, **check and recheck** to make sure that our guidebooks are truly just that: a personalized guide to help you make the most of your visit. And if you still want a speaking guide, we list local tour guides who will lead you on all the boat, bus, guided, historical, culinary, and other tours you shouldn't miss.

In short, we remove the guesswork involved with travel. After all, we want you to enjoy exploring with Michelin as much as we do.

The Michelin Green Guide Team

PLANNING YOUR TRIP

INTRODUCTION TO ALSACE LORRAINE CHAMPAGNE

SYMBOLS

- Tourist Information
- Hours of Operation
- Periods of Closure
- A Bit of Advice
- Details to Consider
- Entry Fees
- Especially for Children
- Tours
- Wheelchair Accessible

CONTENTS

DISCOVERING ALSACE LORRAINE CHAMPAGNE

HOW TO USE THIS GUIDE

Orientation

To help you grasp the "lay of the land" quickly and easily, so you'll feel confident and comfortable finding your way around the region, we offer the following tools in this guide:

- Detailed table of contents for an overview of what you'll find in the guide, and how it is organized.
- Map of Alsace, Lorraine, Champagne at the front of the guide, with the Principal Sights highlighted for easy reference.
- Detailed maps for major cities and villages, including driving tour maps and larger-scale maps for walking tours.
- Map of 11 Regional Driving Tours, each one numbered and color coded.
- Map showing places to stay plus a map of the wines of Champagne.

Practicalities

At the front of the guide, you'll see a section called "Planning Your Trip" that contains information about planning your trip, the best time to go, different ways of getting to the region and getting around, basic facts and tips for making the most of your visit. You'll find a calendar of popular festivals, driving and themed tours, and suggestions for outdoor fun. Information on shopping, sightseeing and activities for kids is also included.

WHERE TO STAY

We've made a selection of hotels and arranged them within the cities, categorized by price category to fit all budgets *(see the Legend on the cover flap for an explanation of the price categories)*. For the most part, we selected accommodations based on their unique regional quality, their regional feel, as it were. So, unless the individual hotel or bed & breakfast embodies local ambience, it's rare that we include chain properties, which typically have their own imprint. If you want a more comprehensive selection of places to stay, see the red-cover **Michelin Guide France**.

WHERE TO EAT

We thought you'd like to know the popular eating spots in Alsace, Lorraine and Champagne. So we selected restaurants that capture the regional experience—those that have a unique regional flavor and local atmosphere. We're not rating the quality of the food per se. As we did with the hotels, we selected restaurants for many towns and villages, categorized by price to appeal to all wallets. If you want a more comprehensive selection of dining recommendations in the region, see the red-cover **Michelin Guide France**.

Attractions

Principal Sights are arranged alphabetically. Within each Principal Sight, attractions for each town, village, or geographical area are divided into local Sights or Walking Tours, nearby Excursions to sights outside the town, or detailed Driving Tours—suggested itineraries for seeing several attractions around a major town. Contact information, admission charges and hours of operation are given for the majority of attractions. Unless otherwise noted, admission prices shown are for a single adult only. Discounts for seniors, students, teachers, etc. may be available; be sure to ask. If no admission charge is shown, entrance to the attraction is free.
If you're pressed for time, we recommend you visit the three- and two-star sights first: the stars are your guide.

STAR RATINGS

Michelin has used stars as a rating tool for more than 100 years:

★★★ Highly recommended
★★ Recommended
★ Interesting

SYMBOLS IN THE TEXT

Besides the stars, other symbols in the text indicate sights that are closed to the public ; on-site eating facilities ; also see ; breakfast included in the nightly rate ; on-site parking ; spa facilities ; camping facilities ; swimming pool ; beaches ; and expect long lines/queues .
See the box appearing on the Contents page and the Legend on the cover flap for other symbols used in the text.
See the Maps explanation below for symbols appearing on the maps.
Throughout the guide you will find peach-coloured text boxes or sidebars containing anecdotal or background information. Green-coloured boxes contain information to help you save time or money.

Maps

All maps in this guide are oriented north, unless otherwise indicated by a directional arrow. The term "Local Map" refers to a map within the chapter or Tourism Region. See the map Legend at the back of the guide for an explanation of other map symbols. A complete list of the maps found in the guide appears at the back of this book.

Addresses, phone numbers, opening hours and prices published in this guide are accurate at press time. We welcome corrections and suggestions that may assist us in preparing the next edition. Please send your comments to:

Michelin Maps and Guides
Hannay House
39 Clarendon Road
Watford, Herts WD17 1JA
UK
travelpubsales@uk.michelin.com
www.michelin.co.uk

Michelin Maps and Guides
Editorial Department
P.O. Box 19001
Greenville, SC 29602-9001
USA
michelin.guides@us.michelin.com
www.michelintravel.com

Ardennais horses
S. Sauvignier/MICHELIN

MICHELIN DRIVING TOURS

The following is a brief description of each of the driving tours shown on the map on the inside back cover.

1 THE ARGONNE REGION AND FOREST

200km/120mi starting from Ste-Menehould

Located at the border of Champagne and Lorraine, the Argonne region has its own distinctive geographic characteristics. The hilly, wooded land is a lovely place for long walks or cycling trips; horseback riding and off-road biking are also great ways to enjoy the natural setting.

Ste-Menehould is a good starting point for such adventures. The terrain is rewarding and constantly changing with ridges and plateaux and deep rivers in narrow gorges.

Break your journey at the Château de Braux-Ste-Cohière, home to the Champagne-Argonne cultural association, which sponsors many events and festivities to promote the region, and home to an interesting regional museum.

The conflicts that have ravaged the Argonne at different times have left their scars and trenches from the First World War are still visible in the forest outside Varennes, at the historic site of Haute-Chevauchée.

2 THE GOLDEN TRIANGLE

120km/72mi starting from Reims

Between Reims, Châlons, Épernay and Château-Thierry, the vineyards stretch along the sunny hillsides. Villages seem to float and bob like ships on a sea of green in summer months.

The "gold" in this tour is bottled and bubbly. Many fine cellars await you in the regions of the Montagne de Reims, the Marne Valley and the Côte des Blancs. The vintners will welcome you and tell you all about the methods behind the magic. Some have even set up interpretation centres and museums devoted to the fine art of Champagne-making. Of course, you will want to taste a little (go easy if you're driving), and no doubt you can be persuaded to pick up a few bottles to take home.

3 BRIE CHAMPENOISE

165km/100mi starting from Provins

Between the regions of Île-de-France and Champagne, the landscapes of Brie are adorned with historic old towns set along the rivers and streams like the beads of a necklace. Nogent-sur-Seine, Villenauxe-la-Grande, Montmirail and Verdelot are al good places to stop and take in the sights or have a meal.

The jewel in this setting is Provins, a medieval city standing on a hilltop that has been occupied since Roman times. You can easily spend a very pleasant afternoon strolling along the high ramparts and in summer there are all sorts of activities here including a jousting tournament and falconry demonstrations.

While Provins is famed for its red roses, the gardens at Viels-Maisons are famous for their myriad varieties of fragrant flowers, herbs and shrubs. The park is a feast for the senses, divided into gardens both formal and "English-style".

4 THE LAKES OF THE DER REGION

170km/102mi starting from Brienne

If you're the outdoor type then you'll no doubt enjoy this excursion. Whether you prefer the peace and quiet of secluded natural sites for observing wildlife or fishing, or you would sooner join in lively sports and games at the beaches and recreation areas, there's a place for you.

Swimming, boating and fishing are just some of the activities on the agenda on the large lake at Der-Chantecoq. Birdwatchers will want to bring along their binoculars to study the many species of migratory waterfowl, (including the *grue cendrée,* grey crane.) The Maison de l'Oiseau et du Poisson, with exhibits on the local ecosystem, is a good place to stop before setting out to observe the inhabitants of the lake and its shores.

As you drive around the region, notice the local half-timber style of architecture, which extends to its churches. Farther north, the Forêt de l'Orient is a lovely wood that also has several lakes devoted to recreational uses. The Parc de vision animalier in the eastern part of the Regional Nature Park, includes hides where with a bit of quiet patience you can observe animals in their natural state.

The Lac d'Orient is a bird sanctuary, but also offers opportunities for scuba diving, sailing and swimming; the road that runs around it is a pretty drive. Anglers and canoeists should visit the Lac du Temple, whereas the smaller Lac Amance is reserved for motorised craft.

5 CHAMPAGNE: FROM BAR TO BAR

225km/135mi starting from Troyes

The title is not meant to encourage you to drink and drive (far from it...). In fact it is a reference to the region known as the Côte des Bars. The towns of Bar-sur-Aube and Bar-sur-Seine derive their names from the old Celtic word *barr,* signifying summit. This route passes through beautiful landscapes of vineyards, forest and fields. The town of Riceys is the only commune in all France to produce three wines labelled *appellation d'origine contrôlée,* including the delightful rosé for which it is best known. Children will enjoy an afternoon at the Kids Nigloland amusement park.

6 ARTS AND CRAFTS IN HAUTE-MARNE

200km/120mi starting from Langres

Begin your journey in the old town of Langres, and enjoy the view from the ramparts.

Carry on to Fayl-Billot, where there is a national school of wickerwork, and look for a basket to put the rest of your souvenirs in. There are a number of artisans who give demonstrations in their shops.

S. Sauvignier/MICHELIN

La Côte des Blancs, near Cramant

In Bourbonne-les-Bains, you may be tempted to ease your aches and pains in a warm mineral water bath or go for a massage. In Nogent, the Musée de la coutellerie is devoted to the cutlery trade, and includes an old-fashioned workshop with a large wheel dating from the 18C.

7 REMEMBERING TWO WORLD WARS

272km/163mi starting from Verdun

Begin this drive in Verdun. Although the First and Second World Wars are an ever more distant memory for older travellers, and may seem like ancient history to the young, this tour brings the events that rent Europe asunder into sharp focus and reminds one and all of the absurd tragedy of war.
Verdun is famous for its fortifications and as the site of numerous battles, but the peaceful old town is well worth a visit, too. In the national cemetery, there is a memorial to seven unknown soldiers, and the Douaumont ossuary is the resting place of soldiers who once fought under different colours. The fort and the "bayonet trench" are startling reminders of the violence of the First World War.
The once-vaunted, later taunted Maginot Line (built to stop the Germans in the Second World War but in fact easily circumvented by them) is still marked by several forts and defensive works: Fermont Fort and its military museum, the Immerhof defensive works, the Zeiterholz shelter and Fort Guentrange.
In Longwy, you can stop to admire the works of enamel artisans, and in Thionville the Château de la Grange is worth seeing.
Continue the tour of military installations at Hackenberg, impressive in its size. In the busy city of Metz, visit the cathedral and the old town.
Complete the tour via Briey, where the visionary architect Le Corbusier built one of his *cités radieuses,* and Étain, entirely rebuilt after 1918.

8 BETWEEN MEUSE AND MOSELLE

261km/157mi starting from Metz

This drive leads you between the banks of the two rivers, and through different periods of French history. Begin in Metz, where the past is associated with wars and religion, but also with culture and fine architecture (Metz is especially lovely at night under the many lights installed to accentuate the features and proportions of buildings).
In Pont-à-Mousson, the old abbey dates from the 18C. Nancy is the former capital of the dukes of Lorraine. The beautiful monuments and public squares are evidence of its rich cultural and artistic heritage.

R Mattès/MICHELIN

Vologne Valley from the Roche du Diable

R Mattès/MICHELIN

Strasbourg – La Petite France

Vaucouleurs and nearby Domrémy-la-Pucelle are forever linked to the most famous of all French heroines, Joan of Arc. Born in Domrémy, the simple peasant girl first took her quest to the governor of Vaucouleurs, whose condescension did nothing to dissuade her fervour.

Commercy is reputed to be the best source of the soft cakes favoured by Marcel Proust, madeleines. On your way back to Metz, visit the Château de Stanislas, the old town of Bar-le-Duc and the 17C church in St-Mihiel.

9 SPA RESORTS IN THE VOSGES

219km/131mi starting from Vittel

The French are very fond of their spa treatments, or cures, which are prescribed for a variety of ailments. In addition to the therapeutic values of the waters, the spa experience improves overall health and well-being in other ways, such as enabling patients to take a break from medication, reducing stress, improving sleeping and eating habits and encouraging outdoor exercise. A full course of treatment generally runs for three weeks, but some spas offer short stays for a quick programme of revitalisation. Most of these resorts are well equipped to entertain *curistes* and their families, often with casinos, racetracks, facilities for tennis and golf, and they are usually located in pleasant and accessible natural settings. This tour takes you through Vittel, Contrexéville, Bourbonne-les-Bains, Luxeuil-les-Bains), Plombières-les-Bains and Bains-les-Bains, which combined, seem to treat just about every ailment known to man! For information on spa treatments, contact the local tourist office or log on to www.thermes-de-france.com.

10 THE VOSGES FOREST

377km/226mi starting from St-Dié

Put on your walking shoes as you leave St-Dié and head out to the enchanting hills and dales of the beautiful Vosges forest.

After visiting the cathedral and cloisters in St-Dié, head to the old town of Senones. The Donon range begins here, defining the border of Alsace and Lorraine and providing wonderful views of the Vosges mountains. There are several good walks to take starting from Schirmeck. By way of contrast the former concentration camp of Struthof is open to visitors interested in this tragic chapter of the history of the Second World War.

For more strenuous outdoor excursions, you could climb the Neuntelstein peak,

discover the Hohwald or (in season), ski on the slopes at Champ du Feu.
Ste-Marie-aux-Mines is the ancestral home of the Pennsylvania Dutch, where you will find fabric displays in the textile museum which echo Amish designs.
Travel the high passes on the Route des Crêtes, including Col du Bonhomme and Col de la Schlucht. Stop at Munster to taste its eponymous cheese, then it's on to the Petit Ballon and the Markstein ski resort. From the Grand Ballon, the view is panoramic.
Thann is at a lower altitude, and you can admire the church there before climbing to the highest point in the range, the Ballon d'Alsace.
Around St-Maurice-sur-Moselle and La Bresse there are many ski areas. In Gérardmer, you can ski in winter, or take a pedal boat out on the lake in fine weather.

11 THE ALSATIAN WINE ROAD

277km/166mi starting from Strasbourg

Begin your wine tour in the European capital of Strasbourg. The city has long been an economic, cultural and intellectual magnet for the region and is now becoming a city break in its own right.
At nearby Haguenau you can trace the fortifications of this historic town.
Bouxwiller, once the home of princes and princesses, seems to huddle for warmth at the base of Mt Batsberg, a legendary haunt of sorcerers and witches. Then it is on to Saverne to visit the marina and château.
The wine begins flowing in earnest in Molsheim where the nearby hillsides are covered in Riesling grapes.
Obernai is a lovely wine-growing town surrounded by vineyards. Climb to the top of Mont Ste-Odile for a visit to the old convent – this is one of the most popular tourist attractions in Alsace. Some come for the view (all the way to the Black Forest on a clear day), others for sacred inspiration, while many more are drawn by the mystery of the "pagan wall" Iron-Age fort.
The city of Barr is awash in celebration during the Wine Fair, though at any time of year you can enjoy the local Sylvaner and Gewürztraminer wines. Following along the wine road, you will pass by the ruins of Andlau Abbey, guarded by a stone bear. The fortifications of Sélestat, storks' nests and a castle at Ribeauvillé mark your route as you continue to the village of Riquewihr, the capital of Riesling.
Kaysersberg is another picturesque hamlet; it seems to have sprung straight off the pages of a book of fairy tales with its ruined medieval castle, half-timbered houses, pots of bright geraniums and fortified bridge. Continue through charming Niedermorschwihr and the towers of Turckheim on the way to the city of Colmar. This is the capital of the wine-growing region; the old town and the area known as la Petite Venise are particularly attractive. Return to Strasbourg by way of the Rhine Valley.

WHEN AND WHERE TO GO

When to Go

CLIMATE

In Alsace, Lorraine and Champagne, weather patterns vary appreciably with the landscapes. The Ardenne uplands are known for heavy precipitation, low clouds, fog and frost; a bleak climate which may partially explain why this area has one of the lowest population densities in Europe. The lower plains of Champagne form part of the Paris Basin and share its milder climate; temperatures occasionally drop below freezing between November and March; the hottest days are in July and August.

In Alsace, comparable variations can be observed between the plain and the Vosges mountains. The average annual temperature in Colmar, for example, is 10.3°C/50.5°F, while the Grand Ballon (the highest summit) averages just 3°C/37.4°F. Prevailing winds arrive from the west or southwest, carrying rain and snow. When these weather systems run up against the Vosges, they result in precipitation, leaving the eastern plain fairly dry. Colmar holds the record for the lowest annual rainfall in France.

While the uplands are generally wetter and cooler throughout the area, visitors travelling on mountain roads may experience a curious phenomenon of temperature inversion, which occurs when atmospheric pressure is high. At such times, while thick mist swathes the plain, the mountains bask in bright sunlight; temperatures may be 10°C/50°F higher than in the valley below. The luminosity and extensive views are uniquely magnificent.

SEASONS

Visitors will enjoy the **summer** months for holidays, but other seasons have their own charms. In the **autumn**, the vineyards and forests are rich with colour and harvest time livens up the villages, as the cool evening air brings red to your cheeks. Hunting season in the Ardenne Forest opens in November. **Winter** resorts in the Vosges are especially attractive to cross-country skiers and snowshoe enthusiasts, who appreciate the largely unspoiled beauty of the forest, and the traditional mountain villages; many areas have satisfactory downhill runs as well, and are equipped with snow-makers. The main resorts are Le Bonhomme (700m/2 297ft), La Bresse-Hohneck (650m/2 133ft), Gérardmer (750m/2 461ft), Saint-Maurice-sur-Moselle (560m/1 837ft) and Ventron (630m/2 067ft).

WHAT TO PACK

As little as possible! Cleaning and laundry services are available everywhere. Most personal items can be replaced at reasonable cost. Try to pack everything in one suitcase and a tote bag. Porter help may be in short supply, and new purchases will add to the original weight. Take an extra tote bag for packing new purchases, shopping at the open-air market, carrying a picnic, etc. Be sure luggage is clearly labelled and old travel tags are removed. Do not pack medication in checked luggage, but keep it with you.

WEATHER FORECAST

National forecast:
☎32 50 *(0.34€/min).*
Information about the weather is also available online at:
www.meteofrance.com

Themed Tours

HISTORY

Routes historiques are heritage trails mapped out by the Fédération Nationale des Routes Historiques (www.routes-historiques.com). These guide motorists to towns, villages, châteaux, manors, abbeys, parks and gardens of architectural and historical interest. Among others, they include the **Route Historique des Marches de Lorraine**, running through the Moselle, the Meuse and the Vosges, and the **Route du Patrimoine Culturel Quebécois** in the Champagne region, retracing the history of the French who settled in Québec.

TOURIST ITINERARIES

In the areas covered by this guide, there are numerous *routes touristiques* plotted out for motorists who wish to explore a particular aspect of the area. The best-known routes in Alsace are the **Route des Crêtes**, running along the ridge of the Vosges from the Col du Bonhomme to Thann, and the **Route des Vins**, or wine road, both described in this guide.
Motorists will notice many other itineraries signposted in the region: for example, the **Route du Rhin** from Lauterbourg to St-Louis along the River Rhine, the **Route de l'Amitié** from Paris to Munich, taking in the Lorraine region, both sides of the Vosges, Strasbourg, the Black Forest etc, the **Route du Cristal**, with visits to the principal crystal works in Lorraine and the **Route des Potiers**, featuring the pottery workshops of Soufflenheim and Betschdorf.
In Champagne-Ardenne, you may like to take the **Route Touristique du Champagne** through the Marne, Aisne and Aube *départements*, the **Route des Légendes de Meuse et Semoy, Route des Fortifications** or the **Route des Forêts, Lacs et Abbayes**, to name but a few.

CULTURAL HERITAGE

Focusing more specifically on the cultural heritage of the Champagne region are the **Route des Églises à Pans de Bois**, specialising in timber-framed churches and the **Route de la statuaire et du Vitrail**, taking in stained glass and religious sculpture in the Aube département.

The **Route romane d'Alsace** offers a choice of some 120 sites from the more prestigious to the lesser known ones.
The **Route de la Musique en Lorraine; route des Orgues en Moselle,** takes visitors across the Moselle département where a wealth of organs can be seen and heard (some 20 concerts are organised during the holiday season).

TRADITIONS AND NATURE

Routes gastronomiques

As you may expect, these itineraries are dedicated to unearthing regional culinary specialities, cheeses, beers, trout, *choucroute* etc.
These and other special itineraries are the subject of brochures that can be found in most local tourist offices.

Parcs et jardins de Haute-Marne

Every summer, some 20 parks and gardens throughout the département welcome visitors: a brochure is available from tourist offices and further information can be obtained by applying to **Conseil d'architecture, d'urbanisme et d'environnement**, ☎03 25 32 52 62.

"Jardins sans Frontières"

This scheme, launched in late 2000, presents a selection of themed gardens in the Moselle département and across its borders into the neighbouring Sarre and Luxemburg. Information is available from the **Comité Départemental du tourisme de la Moselle**, 1 rue du Pont-Moreau, ☎03 87 65 96 40.

Animal parks

There are many animal parks in the region, some offering entertainment in the form of shows and demonstrations, many keeping their animals in semi-captivity:

- **Parc Animalier de St-Laurent**, near Charleville-Mézières (several tours available), ☎03 24 57 39 84.
- **Parc Animalier de la Bannie**, near Bourbonne-les-Bains, ☎ 03 25 90 14 80.

- **Parc de Vision Animalier in the Forêt d'Orient Nature Park**, ☎ 03 25 43 81 90.
- **Parc Animalier de Ste-Croix, Lac de Madine**, ☎03 87 03 92 05.
- **Centre de Réintroduction des Cigognes (storks) et des Loutres (otters) in Hunawihr**, ☎ 03 89 73 72 62.
- **Jardin des papillons exotiques** (butterfly conservatory) in Hunawihr, ☎03 89 73 33 33.
- **Montagne des Singes** (monkey mountain) in Kintzheim, near Sélestat, ☎03 88 92 11 09.
- **Volerie des Aigles** (eagle aviary) in Kintzheim, ☎03 88 92 84 33.
- **Zoo and Botanical Gardens** in Mulhouse, ☎03 89 31 85 10.
- **La Pépinière (plant nursery), gardens and zoo** in Nancy.
- **Tropical Aquarium** in Nancy, ☎03 83 32 99 97.
- **Les Naïades Aquarium** in Ottrott, ☎03 88 95 90 32.
- **Zoo de l'Orangerie**, opposite the Palais de l'Europe in Strasbourg.

WINE AND BEER COUNTRY

Roaming the vineyards

In Alsace, the **Route des Vins** carries travellers from Marlenheim to Thann, linking up the charming little wine-growing villages of the region and incorporating the seven officially recognised *(appellation d'origine contrôlée)* grape varieties in the area.

A number of small towns have waymarked tracks winding through the heart of the vineyards, punctuated by information boards explaining work on the vines and the different grape varieties. These *sentiers viticoles* can be found in Soultzmatt, Westhalten, Pfaffenheim, Eguisheim, Turckheim, Kientzheim, Bennwihr-Mittelwihr-Beblenheim-Zellenber-Riquewihr-Hunawihr (Grands Crus itinerary), Bergheim, Scherwiller, Dambach-la-Ville, Epfig, Mittelbergheim, Barr, Obernai, Dorlisheim, Molsheim, Traenheim, Dahlenheim and Marlenheim.

Information about wine in general is available from the following:

- **Maison des Vins d'Alsace**, *12 avenue de la Foire-aux-Vins (north of the town), 68012 Colmar Cedex, ☎03 89 20 16 20; www.vinalsace.com; open weekdays 9am-noon and 2-5pm*. This organisation publishes a number of brochures on the wines of Alsace, including a guide-directory with details of wine cellars open to the public.
- The **Espace Alsace Coopération** (☎ 03 89 47 91 33), in Beblenheim, on the wine route, has a good selection of regional wines produced by Alsace's 18 different cooperatives, along with other local products to taste.
- The castle in Kientzheim (☎ 03 89 78 21 36) houses the **Musée du Vignoble et des Vins d'Alsace**, with exhibits explaining various aspects of vines and wines. It also has a monumental winepress.

In the Champagne region, take the **Route du Champagne**, where many signposts indicate the way to vineyards, Champagne houses and cooperatives.

For novices and enthusiasts who would like to learn more, there are a number of courses available:

IN ALSACE:

- **Centre de Formation, Lycée Viticole**, 8 Aux-Remparts, 68250 Rouffach, ☎03 89 78 73 07.

IN CHAMPAGNE:

- **Comité départemental du tourisme de l'Aube**, 34 quai Dampierre, 10000 Troyes, ☎03 25 42 50 00. A brochure lists wine-growers who offer wine-tasting courses.
- **Chambre d'agriculture de la Marne**, Complexe agricole du Mont-Bernard, route de Suippes, BP 525, 51009 Châlons-en-Champagne Cedex, ☎03 26 64 08 13. Several wine-growers offer half-day wine-tasting courses.
- **Institut international des vins de Champagne**, contact Yves Richardot, Villa Bissinger, 15 rue Jeanson, 51160 Ay, ☎03 26 55 78

78. Courses offer wine-tasting, gastronomy and tour of various cellars.

Wine Festivals

Harvest festivals are held in October throughout Alsace; other celebrations take place from April to October:

April	**Ammerschwihr**
1 May	**Molsheim**
Ascension	**Guebwiller**
Mid-July	**Barr**
4th weekend in July	**Ribeauvillé**
1st half of August	**Colmar**
1st weekend in August	**Turckheim**
Last weekend in August	**Eguisheim**
September	**Riquewihr**

Breweries

Guided tours are available at the following:

- **Heineken**, 4 rue St-Charles, 67300 Schiltigheim, ☎03 88 19 57 55; free guided tour by appointment only.
- **Kronenbourg**, 68 route d'Oberhausbergen, 67000 Strasbourg, ☎03 88 27 41 59; free guided tour, booking essential.
- **Schutzenberger**, 8 rue de la Patrie, BP 182, 67304 Schiltigheim, ☎03 88 18 61 00; free guided tour on Tue and Thu at 2.30pm by appointment only.
- Monks on the Web. If you love Trappist beer and would like to know more about how it is made, take a virtual tour of the abbey where Chimay is brewed: *www.chimay.be*.

LOCAL CRAFTS AND INDUSTRIES

A brochure is published by the regional chamber of commerce (*☎ 03 26 69 33 40*) to help you to discover the people and trades of the region; information is also available from the Comités départementaux du tourisme *(see addresses in Planning Your Trip: Know Before You Go)*. For instance free guided tours are offered by PSA Peugeot-Citroën, Météo France or La Poste as well as by small traditional businesses such as the slipper and carpet factories in Sedan (*information from the CDT des Ardennes, ☎03 24 56 06 08)*.

COOKERY COURSES 

A number of restaurant owners in Alsace offer cookery courses with accommodation. They are usually held in winter:

- **Hôtellerie du Pape**, 10 Grande Rue, 68420 Eguisheim, ☎ 03 89 41 41 21.
- **Hôtel-restaurant Alsace Villages**, 49 rue Principale, 67510 Obersteinbach, ☎03 88 09 50 59.
- **Hôtel-restaurant Aux Deux Clefs**, 50 Grand'Rue, 68600 Bisheim, ☎03 89 72 51 20.
- **Ferme-auberge, Madame Fuchs**, 22 rue de l'École, 67670 Waltenheim-sur-Zorn, ☎ 03 88 51 64 57

KNOW BEFORE YOU GO

Useful Websites

www.franceguide.com
The **French Government Tourist Office (FGTO) / Maison de la France** site is packed with practical information and tips for those travelling to France. The home page has a number of links to more specific guidance, for American or Canadian travellers for example, or to the FGTO's London pages.

www.FranceKeys.com
A useful portal that takes you straight in to the individual regions, tourist boards, leading hotels and sights.

www.fr-holidaystore.co.uk
This travel agency site is useful for planning the details of your trip, whether it's camping, holiday homes or specialist holidays, and full details of getting around the country.

The **French Travel Centre in London** has gone on-line with this service, providing information on all of the regions of France, including updated special travel offers and details on available accommodation.

For travellers doing The Grand Tour

www.visiteurope.com
The **European Travel Commission** provides useful information on travelling to and around all European countries, with links to commercial booking services (including vehicle hire), rail schedules and weather reports.

For travellers from the USA

www.ambafrance-us.org
This website of the **French Embassy in the USA** providies information including geography, visiting France, France-US relations, culture, news and business-related information. It offers special pages for children, and pages devoted to language study and travel.

Tourist Offices

FRENCH TOURIST OFFICES ABROAD

For a complete list of all 31 Maison de la France/France National tourist offices abroad visit http://english.pidf.com/page/p-891.

Australia – New Zealand

- **Sydney** 25 Bligh Street – level 22 NSW 2000 Sydney. ☎(02) 9231 5244. Fax (02) 9221 8682.

Canada

- **Montreal** – 1800 Avenue McGill College, Montreal QC H3A 3J6. ☎(514) 288-4264. Fax: (514) 845 4868.

Ireland

- **Dublin** – 10 Suffolk Street, Dublin 2. ☎(01) 635 1008. Fax: (01) 679 0814.

South Africa

- **Illovo** – 196 Oxford Road, 1st Floor Oxford Manor 2196. ☎00 27 11 880 80 62. Fax 00 27 11 770 16 66.

United Kingdom

- **London** – **Maison de la France** – 178 Piccadilly, London W1J 9AL, ☎020 7399 3500. Fax: 020 7493 6594.

United States

- **East Coast** – **New York** – 444 Madison Avenue, 16th Floor, NY 10022-6903, ☎(212) 838-7800 – Fax: (212) 838-7855.
- **Los Angeles** – 9454 Wilshire Boulevard, Suite 715, Beverly Hills, CA 90212-2967. ☎(310) 271 66 65.
- **Chicago** – 676 North Michigan Avenue 60611 Illinois. ☎(312) 751 78 00. Fax (312) 337 6339.
- **Miami** – 1 Biscayne Tower, ste 2 South Biscayne Bld FL 33131 Miami ☎(305) 373 8177. Fax (305) 373 5828.

LOCAL TOURIST OFFICES

Visitors may also contact local tourist offices for more precise information, and to receive brochures and maps. The addresses and telephone numbers of tourist offices in the larger towns are listed after the symbol ℹ in the *Discovering Alsace* section of the guide. Below, the addresses are given for local tourist offices of the *départements* and *régions* covered in this guide.

Départements

Address enquiries to the **Comité Départemental du Tourisme (CDT)**:

- **Ardennes** – 4 place Ducale, BP 419, 08000 Charleville-Mézières. ☎03 24 55 69 90. www.ardennes.com
- **Aube** – 34 quai Dampierre, 10000 Troyes Cedex, ☎03 25 42 50 00. www.aube-champagne.com
- **Bas-Rhin** – 7 place des Meuniers, 6700 Strasbourg. ☎03 88 75 56 56. Visit www.tourisme67.com for a list of all tourist offices in Northern Alsace.
- **Haute-Marne** – place du General de Gaulle, Chaumont 52000. ☎03 25 03 80 80. www.tourisme-hautemarne.com.
- **Haut-Rhin** – Maison du Tourisme de Haute-Alsace, 1 rue Schlumberger, BP 371, 680067, Colmar Cedex, ☎ 03 89 20 10 68. www.tourisme68.asso.fr.
- **Marne** – 13bis, rue Carnot, BP 74, 51006 Châlons-en-Champagne Cedex, ☎03 26 68 37 52. www.tourisme-en-champagne.com
- **Meurthe-et-Moselle** – 48 rue du Sergent-Blandan, BP 10065, 54062 Nancy Cedex, ☎03 83 94 51 90. www.cdt-meurthe-et-moselle.fr
- **Meuse** – 33 Rue des Grangettes, 55000 Bar-le-Duc, ☎03 29 45 78 40. www.tourisme-meuse.com
- **Moselle** – Hôtel du Département, 1 rue du Pont-Moreau, BP 11096, 57036 Metz Cedex 1, ☎03 87 37 57 80. www.cdt-moselle.fr
- **Vosges** – 6 place Saint-Goëry, BP 304, 88008 Épinal. ☎03 29 82 53 32. www.tourismevosges.fr

Regions

- **Alsace** – 20A, rue Berthe Molly BP 50247, 68005 Colmar cedex. ☎03 89 24 73 50. www.tourisme-alsace.com.
- **Lorraine** – Abbaye des Prémontrés, BP 97, 54700 Pont-à-Mousson Cedex. ☎03 83 80 01 80. www.crt-lorraine.fr.
- **Champagne-Ardenne** – 15 avenue du Maréchal-Leclerc, BP 319, 51013 Châlons-en-Champagne Cedex. ☎03 26 21 85 80. www.tourisme-champagne-ardenne.com.

International Visitors

EMBASSIES AND CONSULATES IN FRANCE

- **Australia Embassy**
  4 rue Jean-Rey, 75724 Paris. ☎01 40 59 33 00. www.france.embassy.gov.au
- **Canada Embassy**
  35 avenue Montaigne, 75008 Paris. ☎01 44 43 29 00. www.amb-canada.fr
- **Ireland Embassy**
  12 avenue Foch, 75116 Paris. ☎01 44 17 67 00.www.embassyofirelandparis.netfirms.com
- **New Zealand Embassy**
  7ter rue Léonard-de-Vinci, 75116 Paris. ☎01 45 01 43 43. www.nzembassy.com/france
- **South Africa Embassy**
  59 quai d'Orsay, 75343 Paris. ☎01 53 59 23 23. www.afriquesud.net
- **UK Embassy**
  35 rue du Faubourg-St-Honoré, 75383 Paris. ☎01 44 51 31 00. Fax: 01 44 51 32 324.
- **UK Consulate**
  18 bis, rue d'Anjou, 75008 Paris. ☎01 44 51 31 00. Fax: 01 44 51 31 27. (Consulates also in Bordeaux, Lille, Lyon, Marseilles).

- **USA Embassy**
  2 avenue Gabriel, 75382 Paris.
  ☎01 43 12 22 22.
  www.amb-usa.fr.
- **USA Consulate**
  2 rue St-Florentin, 75001 Paris.
  ☎01 42 96 14 88.
- **USA Consulate**
  15 avenue d'Alsace, 67082
  Strasbourg. ☎03 88 35 31 04
  Fax: 03 88 24 06 95.
  (Consulate also in Marseille)

ENTRY REQUIREMENTS

Passport

Nationals of countries within the European Union entering France need only a national identity card. Nationals of other countries must be in possession of a valid national **passport.** In case of loss or theft, report to your embassy or consulate and the local police.

Visa

No **entry visa** is required for Canadian, US or Australian citizens travelling as tourists and staying less than 90 days, except for students planning to study in France. If you think you may need a visa, apply to your local French Consulate.
US citizens should visit *http://travel.state.gov.* and download the booklet *Safe Trip Abroad,* which provides useful information on visa requirements, customs regulations, medical care etc for international travellers. US passport application forms can also be downloaded from here. General passport information is available by phone from the **Federal Information Center** (☎800-688-9889).

CUSTOMS REGULATIONS

Visit the **Customs Office (UK)** website for the full range of duty-free allowances at www.hmrc.gov.uk.
For **US Customs** allowances, visit *www.customs.ustreas.gov).*
Residents from a member state of the European Union are not restricted with regard to purchasing goods for private use; the allowances for alcoholic beverages and tobacco are listed in the chart opposite.

HEALTH

First aid, medical advice and chemists' night service rotas are available from local chemists/drugstores *(pharmacie)* identified by the green cross sign. All prescription drugs should be clearly labelled; it is recommended that you carry a copy of the prescription.
It is advisable to take out comprehensive insurance coverage as the bill for medical treatment in French hospitals or clinics must be paid by the patient.
Nationals of non-EU countries should check with their insurance companies about policy limitations. Reimbursement can then be negotiated with the insurance company according to the policy held.

British and Irish citizens should apply to the Department of Health and Social Security **before travelling** for for a **European Health Insurance Card (EHIC),** which entitles the holder to urgent treatment for accident or unexpected illness in EU countries.
American citizens concerned about travel and health can contact the International Association for Medical Assistance to Travelers, which can also provide details of English-speaking doctors in different parts of France (☎716-754-4883. www.iamat.org).

Duty-Free Allowances	
Spirits (whisky, gin, vodka etc)	10 litres
Fortified wines (vermouth, port etc)	20 litres
Wine (not more than 60 sparkling)	90 litres
Beer	110 litres
Cigarettes	3200
Cigarillos	400
Cigars	200
Smoking tobacco	3 kg

- **The American Hospital of Paris** is open 24hr for emergencies as well as consultations, with English-speaking staff and is accredited by major insurance companies (63 boulevard Victor-Hugo, 92200 Neuilly-sur-Seine. ☎01 46 41 25 25. www.american-hospital.org).
- **The British Hertford Hospital** is just outside Paris (Levallois-Perret, 3 rue Barbès. ☎01 46 39 22 22. www.britishhospital.org).

Accessibility

The sights described in this guide that are easily accessible to people with reduced mobility are indicated in the admission times and charges section by the symbol ♿ *(see individual sights in the Discovering Alsace sections of the guide).*

On TGV and Corail trains operated by the national railway (SNCF), there are special wheelchair slots in first-class carriages available to holders of second-class tickets. On Eurostar and Thalys, special rates are available for accompanying adults. All airports are equipped to receive physically disabled passengers.

For more information visit www.access-able.com. For museum access contact La Direction, Les Musées de France, Service Accueil des Publics Spécifiques, 6 rue des Pyramides, 75041 Paris Cedex 1. ☎01 40 15 80 72.

The **Michelin Guide France** and the **Michelin Camping France** guide indicate hotels and campsites with facilities suitable for physically handicapped people.

GETTING THERE & GETTING AROUND

By Plane

Various international and other independent airlines operate services to **Paris** (Roissy-Charles de Gaulle and Orly airports) and there are regular air links to **Strasbourg** International Airport, **Basel-Mulhouse** (EuroAirport) and **Metz-Nancy-Lorraine** Airport from Paris and a host of other, mainly European, cities. There is a shuttle bus service into Strasbourg every 30min from Monday to Friday, and as planes arrive on weekends (journey time of 30min). The shuttle service from EuroAirport to Mulhouse train station also takes 30min. Metz-Nancy-Lorraine airport is situated between Metz and Nancy. The Aérolor shuttle runs from the airport to Metz (30min) or Nancy (40min) train stations.

Contact airline companies and travel agents for details of package tour flights with a rail or coach link-up, as well as fly-drive packages.

By Ship

There are numerous **cross-Channel services** (passenger and car ferries, hovercraft) from the United Kingdom and Ireland. The rail shuttle through the Channel Tunnel (**Le Shuttle-Eurotunnel**. ☎08705 35 35 35 www.eurotunnel.com) takes just 35min from Folkestone to Calais. For details, apply to travel agencies, or to:

- **P & O Ferries** ☎08705 980 333. www.poferries.com
- **Brittany Ferries** ☎0870 9076 103. www.brittany-ferries.com
- **Irish Ferries** ☎08705 17 17 17. www.irishferries.com
- **Seafrance** ☎0871 663 2546. www.seafrance.fr

By Train

Eurostar runs via the Channel Tunnel between **London** (St Pancras from November 2007) and **Paris** (Gare du Nord) and London and **Lille** (☎0870 518 6186. www.eurostar.com).
From Paris (Gare de l'Est), the French national railways **SNCF** (www.sncf.fr) operates an extensive service to the region. In summer 2007, SNCF launched its **TGV Est Européen** (High Speed East European service) on the Paris-Metz-Luxembourg line, and the Paris-Nancy-Strasbourg line, reducing the journey time from Strasbourg to Paris to under 2 hrs 30 mins.
Eurailpass, Flexipass and **Saverpass** are travel passes which may be purchased in the US. Contact your travel agent or **Rail Europe** (☎1-888-667-9734. www.eurail.on.ca) or **Europrail International** (☎1-888-667-9731. www.raileurop.com.us). In the UK ☎08705 848 848.
There are numerous discounts available when you purchase your tickets in France, from 25-50% below the regular rate. These include **discounts** for using senior cards and youth cards (cards that must be purchased, and showing your name and a photograph), and lower rates for 2-9 people travelling together (advance purchase necessary). There are a limited number of discount seats available during peak travel times, and the best discounts are available during off-peak periods.
Tickets bought in France must be validated (*composter*) by using the orange automatic date-stamping machines at the platform entrance (failure to do so may result in a fine).
The French railway company SNCF operates a telephone information, reservation and prepayment service in English (French time). In France call ☎08 92 35 35 39. You may also order and pay for tickets to be sent to your home address on the SNCF website (www.sncf.fr).

©Eurostar

Eurostar

By Coach / Bus

For information about travelling anywhere in Europe by coach, visit **www.eurolines.com**. ☎08705 808 080 (UK office). ☎01 49 72 57 80 (Paris office).

By Car

PLANNING YOUR ROUTE

The area covered in this guide is easily reached by motorways and national routes. **Michelin map 721** indicates the main itineraries as well as alternate routes for avoiding heavy traffic during busy holiday periods, and gives estimated travel times. **Michelin France Tourist & Motoring Atlas** details French motorways, indicating tolls, rest areas and services along the route; it includes a table for calculating distances and times. The latest Michelin route-planning service is available on the Internet at **www.ViaMichelin.com**. Travellers can calculate a precise route using such options as shortest route, route avoiding toll roads, Michelin-recommended route, and gain access to tourist information (hotels, restaurants, attractions). The service is available on a pay-per-route basis or by subscription.
The roads are very busy during the holiday period (particularly weekends in July and August) and, to avoid traffic congestion, it is advisable to follow the recommended secondary routes (signposted as *Bison Futé – itinéraires bis*). The motorway network includes rest areas *(aires de repos)* and petrol stations *(stations-service)*, usually with restaurant and shopping complexes attached, around every 40km/25mi.

DOCUMENTS

Driving Licence

Travellers from other European Union countries and North America can drive in France with a valid national or home-state **driving licence**. An international driving permit is useful because the information on it appears in nine languages. A permit is available (US$15) from the **National Automobile Club** (☎1-800 622 2136. www.nationalautoclub.com) or contact your local branch of the American Automobile Association.

Registration papers

For the vehicle, it is necessary to have the registration papers (logbook) and a nationality plate of the approved size.

INSURANCE

Certain motoring organisations (AAA, AA, RAC) offer accident insurance and breakdown service schemes for members. Check with your insurance company with regard to coverage while abroad.

ROAD REGULATIONS

In France the minimum driving age is 18. Traffic drives on the right. All passengers must wear **seat belts**. Children under the age of 10 must ride in the back seat. Headlights must be switched on in poor visibility and at night; use side-lights only when the vehicle is stationary.
In the case of a **breakdown**, a red warning triangle or hazard warning lights are obligatory. In the absence of stop signs at intersections, cars must **give way to the right**. Traffic on main roads outside built-up areas (priority indicated by a yellow diamond sign) and on roundabouts has right of way. Vehicles must stop when the lights turn red at road junctions and may filter to the right only when indicated by an amber arrow.
The regulations on **drinking and driving** (limited to 0.50g/l) and **speeding** are strictly enforced: usually by an on-the-spot fine and/or confiscation of the vehicle.

Speed limits

Although liable to modification, speed limits are as follows:

- toll motorways *(autoroutes)* 130kph/80mph (110kph/68mph when raining);
- dual carriageways and motorways without tolls 110kph/68mph (100kph/62mph when raining);
- other roads 90kph/56mph (80kph/50mph when raining) and in towns 50kph/31mph;
- outside lane on motorways during daylight, on level ground and with good visibility – minimum speed limit of 80kph/50mph.

Parking Regulations

In built up areas there are zones where parking is either restricted or subject to a fee; tickets should be obtained from the ticket machines (*horodateurs* – small change necessary) and displayed inside the windscreen on the driver's side; failure to display may result in a fine, or towing and impoundment. Other parking areas in town may require you to take a ticket when passing through a barrier. To exit, you must pay the parking fee (usually there is a machine located by the exit – *sortie*) and insert the paid-up card in another machine which will lift the exit gate.

Tolls

In France, most motorway sections are subject to a toll *(péage)*. You can pay in cash or with a credit card (usually Visa or Mastercard).

CAR RENTAL

There are car rental agencies at airports, railway stations and in all large towns throughout France. European cars have manual transmissions; automatic cars are available in larger cities only if an advance reservation is made. Drivers must be over 21; between ages 21-25, drivers are required to pay an

Rental Cars – Central Reservation in France	
Avis	☏08 20 05 05 05. www.avis.com
Europcar	☏08 25 82 54 57. www.europcar.com
Budget	☏08 25 00 35 64 www.budget.com
Hertz	☏01 47 03 49 12. www.hertz.com
SIXT-Eurorent	☏ 08 20 00 74 98
National-CITER	☏ 01 45 22 77 91

extra daily fee; some companies allow drivers under 23 only if the reservation has been made through a travel agent. It is relatively expensive to hire a car in France; Americans in particular will notice the difference and should make arrangements before leaving, take advantage of **fly-drive offers** when you buy your ticket, or seek advice from a travel agent, specifying requirements. There are many on-line services that will look for the best prices on car rental around the globe.

MOTORHOME RENTAL 

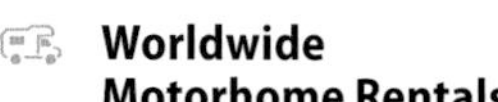

Worldwide Motorhome Rentals
Offers fully equipped camper vans for rent. You can view them on the company's web page.
☏888-519-8969 *US toll-free.*
☏1-530-389-8316 *outside the US.*
www.mhrww.com

PETROL/GASOLINE

French service stations dispense:
- *sans plomb 98* (super unleaded 98)
- *sans plomb 95* (super unleaded 95)
- *diesel/gazole* (diesel)
- *GPL* (LPG).

Gasoline is considerably more expensive in France than in the USA. it is usually cheaper to fill the tank after leaving the motorway; check the large hypermarkets on the outskirts of town.

WHERE TO STAY AND EAT

For Hotel and Restaurant selections, see the Address Books within the Discovering Alsace sections of the guide.

Where to Stay

Included in this guide are descriptions of selected accommodations for the region, found in the Address Books within the Principal Sights. The Legend at the back of the guide explains the symbols used in the Address Books. We have reported the prices *(for double occupancy)* and conditions as we observed them, but of course, changes in management and other factors may mean that you will find some discrepancies. Please keep us informed of any major differences you might encounter.

Use the **map of Places to stay** that follows to identify recommended places for overnight stops. For an even greater selection, use the **Michelin Guide France** with its famously reliable star-rating system and descriptions of hundreds of establishments all over France. The **Michelin Charming Places to Stay** guide contains a selection of some 1 000 hotels and guesthouses at reasonable prices.
Be sure to book ahead to ensure that you get the accommodation you want, not only in tourist season, but year round, as many towns fill up during trade fairs, arts festivals, etc. Some places require an advance deposit or reconfirmation. Reconfirming is especially important if you plan to arrive after 6pm.

For further assistance, **Loisirs Accueil** (www.loisirsaccueilfranc.com) is a booking service that has offices in some *départements* – contact the tourist offices listed above for further information or visit the website.
A guide to good-value, family-run hotels, **Logis et Auberges de France** (www. logis-de-france.fr) is available from the French Tourist Office, as are lists of other kinds of accommodation. **Relais & Châteaux** provides information on booking in luxury hotels with character ☎00800 2000 0002 (UK), 1-800 735 2478. www.relaischateaux.

ECONOMY CHAIN HOTELS

If you need a place to stop en route, these lodgings can be useful, as they are inexpensive *(typically less than €35 for a double room)* and generally located near the main road. While breakfast is available, there may not be a restaurant; rooms are small, with a television and bathroom. Central reservation numbers:

- **Akena** – ☎01 69 84 85 17. www.hotels-akena.com
- **B&B** – ☎172 365 106 (French only, premium-rate). www.hotel-bb.com
- **Mister Bed** – ☎01 46 14 38 0. www.misterbed.fr
- **Villages Hôtel** – ☎03 80 60 92 70. www.villages-hotel.com

The hotels listed below are slightly more expensive but offer more amenities and services. Central reservation numbers:

- **Louvre Hotels (Campanile, Premiere Class, Kyriad)** – ☎0825 003 003 (in France). ☎33 1 64 62 46 00. www.envergure.fr
- **Ibis** – www.ibishotel.com

COTTAGES AND BED AND BREAKFAST

The Maison des Gîtes de France is an information service on self-catering accommodation in France. *Gîtes* usually take the form of a cottage or apartment decorated in the local style where visitors can make themselves at home, or bed and breakfast accommodation *(chambres d'hôtes)* that consists of a room and breakfast at a reasonable price.
Gîtes de France publishes a booklet on bed and breakfast accommodation *(chambres d'hôte)* that includes a room and breakfast at a reasonable price. Visit www.gites-de-france.fr for details of all properties and offices in Alsace, Lorraine and Champagne, or in the UK, **Brittany Ferries** ☎08705 561 600. www.brittany-ferries.com.
The Fédération Française des Stations Vertes de Vacances, ☎03 80 54 10 50. www.stationsvertes.com (*French only*), is able to provide details

S. Sauvignier/MICHELIN

Bed and Breakfast at the Château de Châtel

of accommodation, leisure facilities and natural attractions in rural locations selected for their tranquillity. For **Bed & Breakfast:** ☎0871 781 0834 (UK office), www.bedbreak.com offers numerous properties in Alsace, Lorraine and Champagne.

FARM VACATIONS

The guide *Bienvenue à la ferme* is available from the Assemblée Permanente des Chambres d'Agriculture. ☎01 53 57 11 44. www.bienvenue-a-la-ferme.com. It includes the addresses of over 5 000 farmers providing guest facilities. *Bienvenue à la ferme* farms are vetted for quality standards and can be identified by the yellow flower that serves as their logo.

ACTIVE HOLIDAYS ACCOMMODATION

Travellers on active holidays, such as hiking, cycling, climbing, skiing and canoeing might like to visit www.gites-refuges.com.

HOSTELS, CAMPING

To obtain an **International Youth Hostel Federation** card (there is no age requirement, and there is a senior card available too) contact the IYHF in your own country for information and membership applications (US ☎202 932 2300; UK. ☎01707 324 170; Canada ☎613-273 7884; Australia ☎61-2-9565-1669. www.iyhf.org.) which you may use to reserve rooms as early as six months in advance.
The main youth hostel associations in France is the **Ligue Française pour les Auberges de la Jeunesse** (☎ 01 44 16 78 78. www.auberges-de-jeunesse.com).
There are numerous officially graded **camp sites** with varying standards of facilities throughout the region. The **Michelin Camping France** guide lists a selection of camp sites. The area is popular with campers in the summer months, so it is wise to reserve in advance.

Where to Eat

Included in this guide are descriptions of selected places to eat in the region (*see the Address Books in the* Discovering Alsace *sections of the guide*). The Legend at the back of the guide explains the symbols used in these Address Books. Use the **Michelin Guide France**, with its famously reliable star-rating system and descriptions of hundreds of establishments all over France, for an even greater choice. If you would like to experience a meal in a highly rated restaurant from the Michelin Guide, be sure to book ahead.
In the countryside, restaurants usually serve lunch between noon and 2pm and the evening meal between 7.30-10pm. It is not always easy to get something to eat in between those two meal times, a snack in a café or a brasserie may fill the gap.
in Alsace **winstubs and brasseries** are two very traditional types of eating house. *Winstubs* were created by the Strasbourg wine producers to promote their wines and provide a convivial setting in which to order a carafe of Alsatian wine to accompany a choice of different local dishes. For those who prefer beer, *brasseries* offer the opportunity to taste food from the region accompanied by a glass of beer brewed on site.
Fermes-auberges (farm-inns) may or may not offer overnight accommodation, but they do serve farm produce and local speciality dishes. The tradition of serving country fare to travellers is centuries old in the Hautes-Vosges, where dairy farmers were known as *marcaires*. The *repas marcaire* proposed by many farms usually includes a *tourte de la vallée de Munster* (deep-dish pie with smoked pork, onions and garlic), followed by a blueberry tart. The *Guide des Fermes-auberges* in the Haute-Alsace is available from the **Association des Fermes-auberges du Haut-Rhin**. (☎03 89 20 10 68; www.bienvenue-a-la-ferme.com).

Places to stay

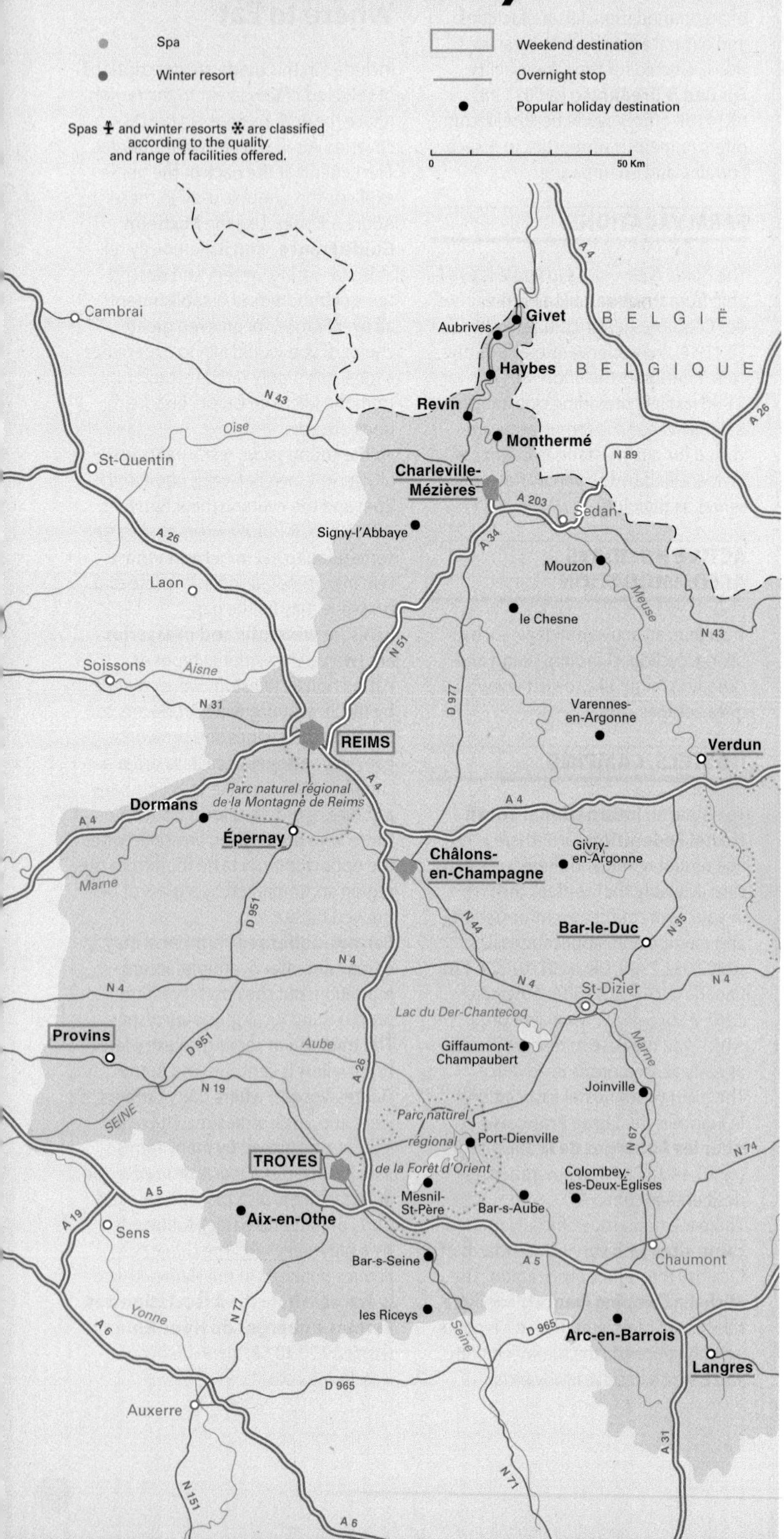

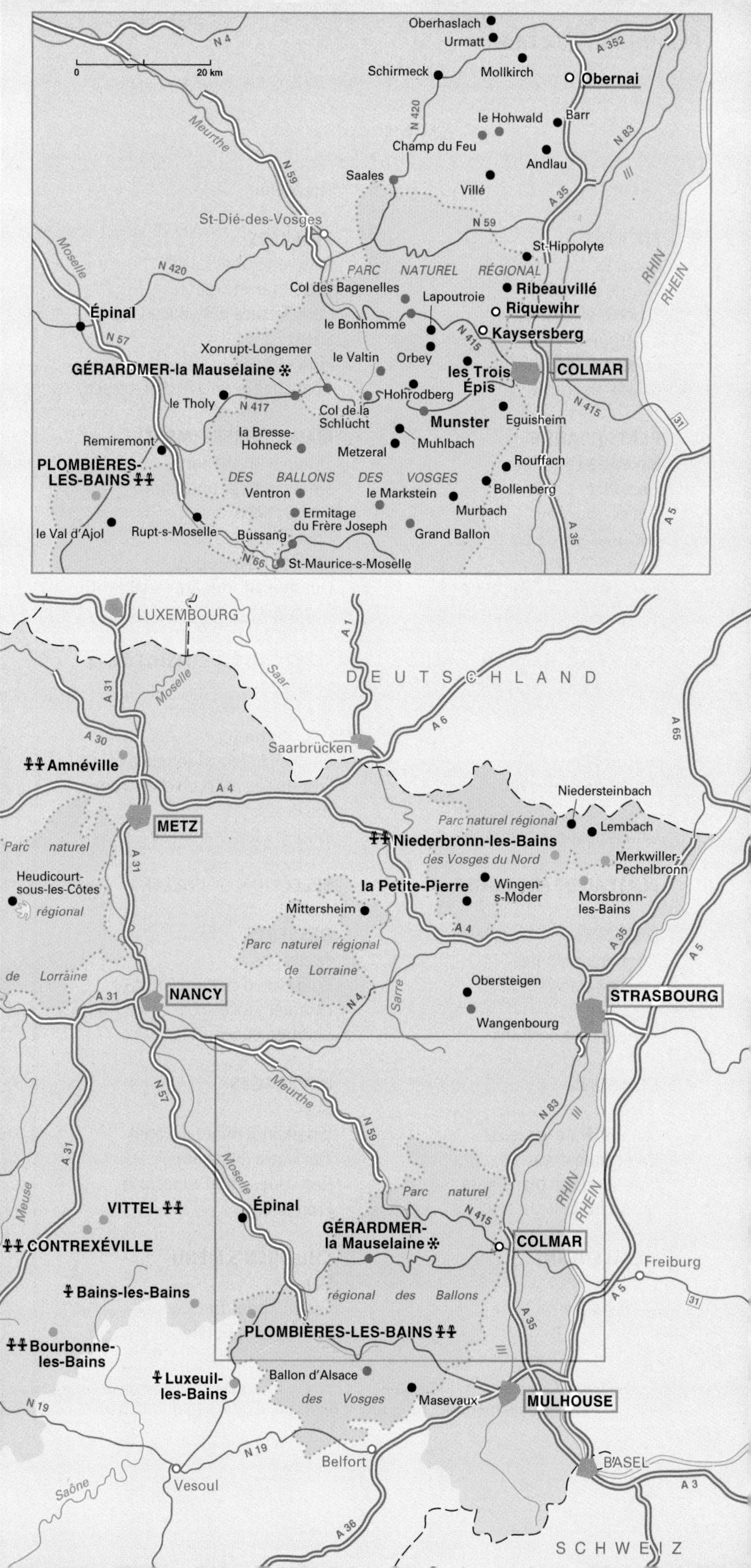

0
20 km
Oberhaslach
Urmatt
Schirmeck
Mollkirch
Obernai
Barr
le Hohwald
Champ du Feu
Andlau
Saales
Villé
St-Dié-des-Vosges
N 59
St-Hippolyte
PARC NATUREL RÉGIONAL
Col des Bagenelles
Lapoutroie
Ribeauvillé
Riquewihr
Kaysersberg
le Bonhomme
Épinal
Xonrupt-Longemer
le Valtin
Orbey
GÉRARDMER-la Mauselaine
les Trois Épis
COLMAR
le Tholy
Col de la Schlucht
Hohrodberg
Munster
Eguisheim
la Bresse-Hohneck
Metzeral
Muhlbach
Remiremont
PLOMBIÈRES-LES-BAINS
Rouffach
DES BALLONS DES VOSGES
Ventron
le Markstein
Bollenberg
Murbach
Ermitage du Frère Joseph
le Val d'Ajol
Rupt-s-Moselle
Bussang
Grand Ballon
St-Maurice-s-Moselle
Meurthe
Moselle
RHIN
RHEIN
LUXEMBOURG
DEUTSCHLAND
Saar
Saarbrücken
Amnéville
METZ
Niedersteinbach
Parc naturel régional
Lembach
Niederbronn-les-Bains
des Vosges du Nord
Merkwiller-Pechelbronn
Parc naturel régional
Heudicourt-sous-les-Côtes
la Petite-Pierre
Wingen-s-Moder
Morsbronn-les-Bains
Mittersheim
Parc naturel régional de Lorraine
de Lorraine
Obersteigen
NANCY
Wangenbourg
STRASBOURG
Sarre
Parc naturel
VITTEL
Épinal
GÉRARDMER-la Mauselaine
COLMAR
CONTREXÉVILLE
Freiburg
régional des Ballons
Bains-les-Bains
PLOMBIÈRES-LES-BAINS
Bourbonne-les-Bains
Ballon d'Alsace
Luxeuil-les-Bains
des Vosges
Masevaux
MULHOUSE
Belfort
BASEL
Vesoul
Saône
Meuse
SCHWEIZ

MENU READER

La Carte	The Menu
ENTRÉES	**STARTERS**
Crudités	Raw vegetable salad
Terrine de lapin	Rabbit terrine (pâté)
Frisée aux lardons	Curly lettuce with bacon bits
Escargots	Snails
Cuisses de grenouille	Frog's legs
Salade au crottin	Goat cheese on a bed of lettuce
PLATS (VIANDES)	**MAIN COURSES (MEAT)**
Bavette à l'échalote	Sirloin with shallots
Faux filet au poivre	Sirloin with pepper sauce
Côtes d'agneau	Lamb chops
Filet mignon de porc	Pork fillet
Blanquette de veau	Veal in cream sauce
Nos viandes sont garnies	Our meat dishes are served with vegetables
PLATS (POISSONS, VOILAILLE)	**MAIN COURSES (FISH, FOWL)**
Filets de sole	Sole fillets
Dorade aux herbes	Sea bream with herbs
Saumon grillé	Grilled salmon
Coq au vin	Chicken in red wine sauce
Poulet de Bresse rôti	Free-range roast chicken from the Bresse
Omelette aux morilles	Wild-mushroom omelette
PLATEAU DE FROMAGES	**SELECTION OF CHEESES**
DESSERTS	**DESSERTS**
Tarte aux pommes	Apple pie
Crème caramel	Cold baked custard with caramel sauce
Sorbet: trois parfums	Sherbet: choose 3 flavours
BOISSONS	**BEVERAGES**
Bière	Beer
Eau minérale (gazeuse)	(Sparkling) mineral water
Une carafe d'eau	Tap water (no charge)
Vin rouge, vin blanc, rosé	Red wine, white wine, rosé
Jus de fruit	Fruit juice
MENU ENFANT	**CHILDREN'S MENU**
Jambon	Ham
Steak haché	Ground beef/beefburger
Frites	French fried potatoes

Well-done, medium, rare, raw = *bien cuit, à point, saignant, cru*

GOURMET GUIDE

Alsace-Lorraine boasts a number of production sites, gastronomic itineraries, fairs and other events that particularly appeal to the gourmet traveller. Among those that have been awarded the special distinction of *site remarquable du goût* are the Kronenbourg and Météor breweries for their beer, the sugar festival in the Erstein area (last weekend in August), the fried carp route in the Sundgau, the wine road in Alsace, the Kugelhopf (a local cake) festival in Ribeauvillé (first fortnight in June) and the cheeses of Cornimont (Munster, Géromé and Bargkass).
In Champagne-Ardenne, a number of chefs offering local recipes or products have formed a special group and display a sign with a chef's hat on a red background at the entrance to their establishments. In Ardenne, those who offer at least three or four specialities from the region display a blue-and-red sign.
For information on local specialities, see Regional Cuisine in the Introduction.

TIPPING

In French restaurants and cafés, a service charge is included. Tipping is not necessary, but French people often leave the small change from their bill on their table, or where service has been good, about 5% for the waiter.

WHAT TO SEE AND DO

Outdoor Fun

WATER SPORTS

The entire region covered by this guide is dotted with lakes, canals and rivers, providing many opportunities for recreational activities.

Fishing

The **Fédération de Pêche** or angling union (www.unpf.fr *French only*) is a good source of information for local fishing. You need to buy a permit, or *Carte de pêche,* and familiarise yourself with national and local regulations. Permits and information are available at tourist offices and in cafés and bars near popular fishing spots.

Canoeing-kayaking

This sport is popular on the majority of rivers in the Champagne and Ardenne regions. The more challenging courses are on the Blaise, Saulx, Rognon and Aire. Gentler waters are the Meuse (at Sedan), the Aube and the Marne. The **Fédération Française de Canoë-kayak**, 87 quai de la Marne, BP 58, 94344 Joinville-le-Pont, ☎01 45 11 08 50. www.ffck.org (*French only*) co-publishes map 1M905, *Water Sports in France*, with watercourses classified by level of difficulty.
In the Aube, canoeing or kayaking can be practised on the Seine, Aube and Ource rivers or the lakes of the Forêt d'Orient. Information can be obtained from local tourist offices.

Bases de loisirs are signed recreational areas with sports and recreation facilities (picnic areas, trails, etc.)

D. Hée/MICHELIN

Waymarked footpaths

Stepping Smart

Choosing the right equipment for a hiking expedition is essential: flexible hiking shoes with non-slip soles, a rain jacket or poncho, an extra sweater, sun protection (hat, glasses, lotion), drinking water (1-2l per person), high energy snacks (chocolate, cereal bars etc), and a first aid kit. Of course, you'll need a good map (and a compass if you plan to leave the main trails). Plan your itinerary well, keeping in mind that while the average walking speed for an adult is 4kph/2.5mph, you will need time to eat and rest, and some hikers may not keep up the same pace. Leave your itinerary with someone before setting out (for example, an innkeeper or fellow camper).

Respect for nature is a cardinal rule and includes the following precautions: don't smoke or light fires in the forest, which are particularly susceptible in the dry summer months; always carry your rubbish out; leave wild flowers as they are; walk around, not through, farmers' fields; close gates behind you.

If you are caught in an electrical storm, avoid high ground, and do not move along a ridge top; do not seek shelter under overhanging rocks, isolated trees in otherwise open areas, at the entrance to caves or other openings in the rocks, or in the proximity of metal fences or gates. Do not use a metallic survival blanket. If possible, position yourself at least 15m/15yd from the highest point around you (rock or tree); crouch with your knees up and without touching the rock face with your hands or any exposed part of your body. A car is a good refuge, as its rubber tyres ground it and provide protection for those inside.

HIKING

There is an extensive network of well-marked footpaths in France for rambling *(la randonnée)*. Several **Grande Randonnée (GR)** trails, denoted by the red-and-white horizontal marks on trees, rocks, and in town on walls, signposts etc, go through the region. Along with the GR, there are also the **Petite Randonnée (PR)** paths, which are usually blazed with blue (2hr walk), yellow (2hr 15min-3hr 45min) or green (4-6hr) marks.
To use these trails, get the *topoguide* for the area published by the **Fédération Française de Randonnée Pédestre** (☎01 44 89 93 90; www.ffrandonnee.fr, *French only*). Some English-language editions are available. Another source of walking maps and guides is the **Institut Géographique National** (www.ign.fr).

Le Club Vosgien

Founded in 1872, this is the oldest hikers' association in France (☎ 03 88 32 57 96; www.club-vosgien.com (*French only*) and also the largest, with over 34 000 members. The hikers have joined forces to protect natural and historic sites, and maintain the marks on around 16 500km/ 10 000mi of trails. The club sponsors a quarterly publication, *Les Vosges,* and publishes detailed maps and guides to paths on the Lorraine plateau, in the Jura mountains of Alsace, in the Vosges and on the Alsatian plain. Check with local tourist offices for the dates of scheduled group rambles.

Grande Randonnée trails

- **GR 2** – Across the Pays d'Othe, through a hilly landscape and along the River Seine.
- **GR 5** – From the border of Luxembourg to the Ballon d'Alsace, through the Lorraine Regional Nature Park.
- **GR 7** – Across the Vosges from the Ballon d'Alsace to Bourbonne-les-Bains, and continuing into the region of Burgundy.
- **GR 12** – A section of European footpath no 3 (Atlantic-Bohemia), cutting across the French and Belgian Ardennes.
- **GR 14** – Follows the Montagne de Reims through vineyards and forest, then continues across the chalk hills of Champagne to Bar-le-Duc before turning towards the Ardennes.
- **GR 24** – The loop starts at Bar-sur-Seine and goes through the Forêt d'Orient Regional Nature Park, vineyards and farmland.

- **GR 53** – From Wissembourg to the Col du Donon, through the northern Vosges Regional Nature Park.
- **GR 654** – Links Northern Europe to Santiago de Compostela via Rocroi, Signy-l'Abbaye and Reims.
- **GR 714** – From Bar-le-Duc to Vittel, linking GR 14 and GR 7.
- **GR 533** – Sarrebourg to the Ballon d'Alsace.

CYCLING 

For general information concerning France, contact the **Fédération Française de Cyclotourisme** (☎01 56 20 88 88; www.ffct.org. *French only*). Off-road and mountain bike (VTT in French) enthusiasts can contact the **Fédération Française de Cyclisme** (☎01 49 35 69 24; www.ffc.fr *French only*) and request the *Guide des centres VTT. The IGN (see Hiking)*

Lake/ reservoir	Nearest town	Acreage	Swimming	Boating	Fishing
Alfeld	Kirchberg	25	🏊	⛵	🐟
Amance	Troyes	1 236211	🏊	⛵	🐟
Bairon	Le Chesne	297	🏊	⛵	🐟
Blanc	Orbey	7270	–	–	🐟
Blanchemer	La Bresse	1423	–	⛵	🐟
Charmes	Langres	487	🏊	⛵	🐟
Corbeaux	La Bresse	2523	–	⛵	🐟
Der-Chantecoq	Vitry-le-François	11 861	🏊	⛵	🐟
Folie	Contrexéville	25	🏊	⛵	🐟
Gérardmer	Gérardmer	284	🏊	⛵	🐟
Gondrexange	Sarrebourg	1 730902	🏊	⛵	🐟
Hanau	Falkenstein	44	🏊	⛵	🐟
Lauch	Le Markstein	27	–	⛵	🐟
Liez	Langres	717	🏊	⛵	🐟
Longemer	Gérardmer	188	🏊	⛵	🐟
Madine	Hattonchâtel	2 718	🏊	⛵	🐟
Mouche	Langres	232	–	–	🐟
Noir	Orbey	35	–	–	🐟
Orient	Troyes	5 6836 177	🏊	⛵	🐟
Pierre Percée	Badonviller	692988	🏊	⛵	🐟
Retournemer	Gérardmer	14	–	–	–
Temple	Troyes	4 522	–	–	🐟
Vieilles-Forges	Revin	371	🏊	⛵	🐟
Vert	Hohrodberg	556	–	–	–
Vingeanne	Langres	487492	🏊	⛵	🐟

offers Map 1M906, *Mountain bike and cycle touring in France*.
Regional tourist offices (Comité départemental du tourisme, see *Know Before You Go*) can provide information on special mountain-bike itineraries in their area, and local tourist offices usually have a list of cycle hire firms. Regional associations and mountain bike centres include:

- **Ligue régionale de cyclotourisme**,12 rue de la Lune, 10000 Troyes. ☎03 25 70 68 31.
- **Lac du Der-Chantecoq**, Maison du Lac, 51290 Giffaumont-Champaubert. ☎03 26 72 62 80.

A free brochure published by the **Parc naturel régional des Ballons des Vosges** (*Échappées en VVT*) describes 12 mountain-bike itineraries; it is available from local tourist offices.

HORSEBACK RIDING 

The **Comité National de Tourisme Équestre**, 9 boulevard MacDonald, 75019 Paris, ☎01 53 26 15 50, publishes an annual brochure entitled *Cheval Nature, l'Officiel du tourisme équestre en France.* It lists all the possibilities for riding by region and *département.* Also access: www.terre-equestre.com.

Alsace

- **Délégation au tourisme équestre.** ☎03 89 24 43 18. www.tourisme-alsace.com/fr/randonnees-equestres.
- **Comité départemental de tourisme équestre du Bas-Rhin**, 4 rue des Violettes, 67201 Eckbolsheim. ☎03 88 77 39 64.

Lorraine

- **Comité départemental de tourisme équestre de la Meuse,** M.François Sepulchre, Grande-Rue, 55290 Biencourt-sur-Orge. ☎03 29 75 94 26.
- **Comité départemental de tourisme équestre de Moselle**, M. Gérard Collignon, 53 rue Principale, 57940 Volstroff. ☎03 82 56 85 12.
- **Comité départemental de tourisme équestre des Vosges**, Marie Vandekerkhoue, 1 rue de l'Usine, 88220 Uzemain. ☎03 29 30 73 50.

Champagne-Ardenne

- **Association de Champagne-Ardenne pour le Tourisme Équestre (ACATE),** 3 impasse Bionnerie, 51170 Ville-en-Tardenois, ☎03 26 61 88 96.
- The **Conseil Général des Ardennes** produces a topographical guide, *Les Ardennes à cheval,* showing 330km/205mi of bridle paths; it is available from the Hôtel du Département, 08011 Charleville-Mézières. ☎03 24 59 60 60.
- The **Relais de la Largue**, 3 rue Ste-Barbe, 68210 Altenach, ☎03 89 25 12 92, organises seven-day trips in Sundgau and the Alsatian Jura by pioneer-style covered wagon, with overnight accommodation in good standard hotels or *gîtes*.

HUNTING

The Ardenne Forest, thick and sparsely populated, is a good place to hunt deer and wild boar. For more information, contact the **Fédération départementale des chasseurs des Ardennes,** ☎03 24 56 07 35; the **Fédération départementale des chasseurs de l'Aube**, ☎03 25 80 72 88; or the **Union Nationale des Fédérations Départementales des Chasseurs,**☎01 43 2 7 85 76; www.chasseurdefrance.com.
One-day and weekend hunting parties are organised on the estate of the **Maison Forestière de Germaine** in the hamlet of Vauremont, 5 rue de la Croix-Verte, 51160 Germaine, ☎03 26 51 08 27, including hunting from an observation tower, in a 400ha/988-acre park, or in a 1 200ha/2 970-acre wooded area.
In the Ardennes the **Pavillon du Territoire du Sanglier** (Office de Tourisme des 3 Cantons. ☎03 24 29 79 91) offers introductions to wild boar hunting.

GOLF

Golf is growing increasingly popular in France, and the area covered in this guide is well equipped with courses, particularly Lorraine, where both regular players and novices are welcome. The Comité Régional du Tourisme *(see Know Before You Go)* publishes a brochure-map with all of the addresses and services available, including nearby lodging. The **Golf Pass Lorraine** gives access to 18 golf courses in the region (four 27-hole courses, ten 18-hole courses and four 9-hole courses). For information, contact the **Ligue Lorraine de Golf de Champagne-Ardenne,** 6 place du Roi-Georges, BP 60552, 57009 Metz Cedex 1; ☎03 87 55 05 68; www.golf-lorraine.com. A good general website is www.golfinfrance.com.

SKIING 

The Vosges mountains are perfect for skiers. In the pine forests, gentle landscapes unfold between 600m/1 968ft-1 400m/4 600ft. Resorts offer downhill and cross-country trails, snowboarding, biathlon, ski jumping, snowshoeing, dogsledding, toboggan riding or simply peaceful walks through the wintry countryside. Downhill skiers have 170 lifts to choose from and many stations are equipped with snow-making machines and lighting for night skiing, notably Gérardmer, La Bresse, Le Markstein and Lac Blanc. Schnepfenried is appreciated for the panoramic view of the crests forming the blue line of the Vosges. Cross-country skiers can enjoy more than 1 000km/621mi of marked and groomed trails.

For information and reservations, contact local tourist offices, or visitwww.skifrance.fr for the latest update on snow conditions; some sites also list available accommodation.

Spas

The Vosges mountains on the Lorraine side and the region of Lorraine itself are especially blessed with natural spring waters that have given rise to spa resorts. The Alsatian side of the range also has its share of resorts. None of the waters are sulphurous, but all other types of spring water are found and used in treating various chronic affections.

MINERAL SPRINGS AND HOT SPRINGS

Natural springs result when water filters through permeable layers of the earth's surface until it meets resistance in the form of an impermeable

R. Mattès/MICHELIN

Cross-country skiing at Champ de Feu

layer of rock. The water flows along this impenetrable layer until it breaks through to the open air, and the water surges forth.

A mineral spring can be water surging forth in the same way, or water rising from deep within the earth, collecting mineral substances and gases with therapeutic properties as it flows towards the surface. Hot springs produce water which hits the air at a temperature of at least 35°C/95°F. Springs are found in zones where the earth's crust is fairly thin, where boulders have been thrown into place by eruptions or cracking. Hot springs are found along the Lorraine plateau fault line or near crystalline mountain ranges and outcrops.

Water, water everywhere

Water from mineral or hot springs is usually unstable, and contact with the air changes its properties. This is why its therapeutic virtues are best enjoyed at the source. Spa therapy is based on this principle.

The two geographic zones in the Vosges, the "plain" to the west and the "mountains" to the east and south-east, have different types of springs, each with its own specificity.

Cold springs

The plain is dominated by cold springs, water which has filtered through the earth's crust and re-emerges enriched with calcium and magnesium and, in some cases, lithium and sodium.

The best-known resort in the area is certainly **Vittel;** the waters were reputed in Roman times, then forgotten, only to be rediscovered in 1845. In 1854, the Bouloumié family began actively promoting and marketing the spring water.

Vittel and the neighbouring spa at **Contrexéville** treat kidney and liver ailments and Vittel also specialises in metabolic diseases. In conjunction with therapeutic activities at the spa, the water is bottled for sale, and many tourists visit the plants each year (with Évian, it is one of the world's largest bottling operations).

Hot springs

The springs found in the mountainous region are quite different. Of volcanic origin, their properties depend less on mineral content than on temperature and radioactivity.

Also known to the Romans, who appreciated warm springs, as did the Celts and the Gauls, these waters have a long-standing reputation. **Plombières**, with 27 hot springs, some of which reach 80°C/176°F, is reputed for the treatment of rheumatism and enteritis. **Bains-les-Bains** is a spa specialising in the treatment of a number of heart and artery disorders, whereas **Luxeuil-les-Bains** treats gynaecological ailments.

A relatively recent arrival on the scene is **Amnéville**, where *curistes* come to relieve the symptoms of rheumatism and respiratory problems, using the therapeutic waters of the St-Éloy spring, which emerge at 41°C/106°F. **Bourbonne-les-Bains**, located on the border of Lorraine and Champagne, boasts warm, radioactive water with a slight chlorine content. Louis XV created a military hospital on the site, for the treatment of soldiers with shot-wounds. Today, the spa is prescribed for the purposes of healing bones, arthritis, rheumatism and respiratory problems.

In Alsace, **Niederbronn-les-Bains** is recognised for the treatment of digestive and kidney afflictions and arteriosclerosis. **Morsbronn-les-Bains** is a small spa specialising in rheumatic disorders.

HYDROTHERAPY AND TOURISM

The benefits of spa treatments were rediscovered in the 18C to 19C. At that time, "taking the waters" was reserved for wealthy clients with time to spare. Today, the French national health system recognises the therapeutic value of many spa treatments, and patients' stays are provided for, all or in part, by different social welfare organisations. Treatment occupies only part of the day, so spas offer their guests many other activities to pass the time pleasantly — sports, recreation and various forms of entertainment. More often than not, the beautiful natural settings provide the opportunity for outdoor excursions.

Besides the traditional courses of treatment, which usually last three weeks, many resorts offer shorter stays for clients with a specific goal in mind, such as stress relief and relaxation, fitness and shaping up, giving up smoking, losing weight etc.

The **Association des Stations Thermales Vosgiennes** publishes a brochure, *Vosges thermales,* with information on Bains-les-Bains, Contrexéville, Plombières and Vittel.

To obtain a copy, write to BP 332, 88008 Épinal.

You can also get information by contacting the following:

- **Union Nationale des Établissements Thermaux**, 1 rue de Cels, 75014 Paris, ☎01 53 91 05 75; www.france-thermale.org *(French only)*
- **Chaîne thermale du Soleil/ Maison du thermalisme,** 32 avenue de l'Opéra, 75002 Paris, ☎01 44 71 37 00; www.sante-eau.com *(French only)*

The spas and their specialities

- **Amnéville:** rheumatic disorders, post-traumatic injury treatment and respiratory problems. Open: February to December.
- **Bains-les-Bains:** cardiovascular ailments, rheumatic disorders, post-traumatic injury treatment. Open: April to October.
- **Bourbonne-les-Bains:** rheumatic disorders, osteoarthritis, respiratory ailments, bone fractures. Open: March to November.
- **Contrexéville:** kidney and urinary problems, excess weight. Open: April to October.
- **Luxeuil-les-Bains:** phlebology, gynaecology. Open: March to November.
- **Morsbronn-les-Bains:** rheumatic disorders, post-traumatic injury treatment. Open: year round.

J.-P. Clapham/MICHELIN

Roman baths at Bains-les-Bains

- **Niederbronn-les-Bains:** rheumatic disorders, post-traumatic injury treatment, physical rehabilitation. Open: April to December.
- **Plombières-les-Bains:** Digestive ailments, nutritional problems, rheumatic disorders, post-traumatic osteo-articular therapy. Open: April to October.
- **Vittel:** Liver and kidney ailments, rheumatic disorders, post-traumatic injury treatment, nutritional problems. Open: February to December.

Activities for Children

This region has a lot to offer children, from having fun in leisure parks such as Nigloland to visiting zoos, safari parks, aquariums, museums and castles. (*see Sightseeing*).

Throughout the *Discovering Alsace* sections of the guide, places and activities particularly suited to children are denoted by the symbol Kids.

Calendar of Events

Regional tourist offices publish brochures listing local festivals and fairs and details of forthcoming events are to be found on websites.

Nearly all places hold festivities for France's National Day (14 July), and many organise events on 15 August, also a public holiday.

MUSIC

MARCH—MAY

Épinal — Festival of classical music. ☎03 29 35 11 63. www.office-tourisme-epinal.com

ASCENSION (odd numbered years)

Nancy — International festival of choir singing (5 000 choristers). ☎03 83 27 56 56. www.chantchoral.org

MAY

Vandœuvre-lès-Nancy — Musique Action, festival of contemporary music and theatre. ☎03 83 57 52 24.

JUNE

Strasbourg — Music festival. ☎03 88 15 44 66. www.strasbourg.fr

JUNE—AUGUST

Reims — Summer music festival. ☎03 26 36 78 00. www.flaneries.com. Jazz and classical music. **Châlons-en-Champagne** — rock, jazz, blues and world music festival. ☎03 26 68 47 27. www.musiques-ici-ailleurs.com (*French only*).

JUNE—SEPTEMBER

Fénétrange — International festival of music and gastronomy. ☎03 87 07 54 38. www.festival-fenetrange.org (*French only*).

JULY

Colmar — International music festival. ☎03 89 20 68 97. www.festival-colmar.com

St-Dizier — Music festival: pop, rock, world. ☎03 25 07 31 31. www.ville-saintdizier.fr (*French only*).

LATE SEPTEMBER—EARLY OCTOBER

Strasbourg — Musica, international contemporary music festival. ☎03 88 23 46 46. www.festival-musica.org (*French only*).

MID-OCTOBER

Nancy — Nancy Jazz Pulsations. ☎03 83 35 40 86. www. nancyjazzpulsations.com. Jazz and world music.

CULINARY AND WINE FESTIVALS

SATURDAY OR SUNDAY FOLLOWING 22 JANUARY

In all wine-growing towns — St Vincent festival, honouring the patron saint of wine-growers.

THURSDAY BEFORE EASTER

Les Riceys — Grand Jeudi wine fair. ☎03 25 29 15 38.

LATE APRIL

Rethel — Boudin Blanc festival. ☎03 24 38 03 28.

JUNE

Revin — Bread festival. ☎03 24 40 20 91.

1ST WEEKEND IN JUNE

Ribeauvillé — Kugelhopf festival. www.ribeauville.net

LAST WEEKEND IN AUGUST

Erstein — Sugar festival. ☎03 88 98 14 33.

LATE AUGUST-EARLY SEPTEMBER

Metz — Mirabelle festival: Flower-decorated floats, parade and fireworks. ☎03 87 55 53 76. www.mairie-metz (*French only*).
Geispolsheim — Choucroute festival. www.ville-geispolsheim.fr

SEPTEMBER

Baccarat — Pâté Lorrain festival.

2ND SUNDAY IN SEPTEMBER

Pays d'Othe — Cider festival. ☎ 03 25 46 75 00. www.paysdothe.fr

3RD WEEKEND IN SEPTEMBER

Brienne-le-Château — Choucroute de Champagne festival. www.ville-brienne-le-chateau.fr ☎ 03 25 92 86 64.

OCTOBER

Renwez — Mushroom festival. ☎03 24 54 82 66 or 03 24 54 93 19
Launois-sur-Vence — Ardenne festival of food and drink (3rd weekend). ☎03 24 54 43 06. www.paysdeccretes.com (*French only*).

OTHER EVENTS

FEBRUARY

Gérardmer — Fantasy film festival. ☎03 29 60 98 21. www.gerardmer-fantasticart.com

MARDI GRAS (MARCH-APRIL)

Strasbourg — Carnival. www.ot-strasbourg.com

LAST SATURDAY IN MARCH

Châlons-en-Champagne — Carnival. ☎03 26 65 17 89. www.chalons-en-champagne.net

WEDNESDAY BEFORE EASTER

Épinal — Champs Golots festival: Children float illuminated boats on the pool near the town hall. www.office-tourisme-epinal.com

APRIL

Gérardmer — Daffodil festival: Parade floats decorated with daffodils. ☎03 29 63 12 89 or 03 29 60 60. www.ville-gerardmer.fr (*French only*).

APRIL—NOVEMBER

Provins Storming the ramparts (—June).
Eagles on the ramparts (— Oct).
Jousting tournament (—Nov).
☎01 64 60 26 26.
www.provins.net

MAY

Grand Jardin de Joinville — Plants and gardens festival (early May). ☎03 25 94 17 54. www.legrandjardin.com (*French only*).
Parc naturel de la Forêt d'Orient — Water sports festival. ☎03 25 41 53 19.
Château-Thierry — Jean de la Fontaine festival of music theatre and dance. ☎03 23 83 10 14. www.festivaljeandelafontaine.com (*French only*).

WHITSUN

Wissembourg — Opening of the annual fun fair (until the following Sunday). Folk dancing, parade of traditional costumes, horse races. ☎03 88 94 10 11. www.ot-wissembourg.fr (*French only*).

2ND HALF OF JUNE

Châlons-en-Champagne — Furies Festival of street theatre and circus. ☎03 26 65 90 06. www.festival-furies.com (*French only*).

2ND SUNDAY IN JUNE

Reims — Fêtes Johanniques historical pageant and folklore festival. ☎03 26 77 45 25. www.reims-fetes.com (*French only*).

2ND AND 3RD WEEKEND IN JUNE

Provins — Medieval festival. Sound and light. ☎01 64 60 16 77. www.provins.net

3RD SUNDAY IN JUNE

Saverne — Rose festival. ☎03 88 71 21 33. www.roserai.saverne.fr (*French only*).

MID-JUNE—MID-AUGUST

Verdun — Musiques & Terasses rock and pop music. ☎03 29 84 50 00. www.musiques-terrasses.com (*French only*).

SUNDAY AFTER 14 JULY

Seebach — Streisselhochzeit (Traditional customs festival plus rock and pop music). ☎03 89 94 70 94. www.uas.fr (*French only*).

LATE JULY—EARLY AUGUST

Chambley, near Metz — Biennale Mondiale de l'Aérostation, the world's second-largest international balloon festival. On odd-numbered years. ☎03 87 64 08 08.

JULY-AUGUST

Vendresse — Open-air theatre plus sound and light show at the Casine Château. ☎03 24 35 44 84 or 03 24 56 67 76.

2ND SATURDAY IN AUGUST

Sélestat — Corso Fleuri, flower-decorated floats on parade. www.selestat-tourisme.com. ☎03 88 58 85 75.

14 AUGUST

Gérardmer — Music and light show, dragon boats and fireworks over the lake. ☎03 29 27 27 27. www.ville-gerardmer.fr (*French only*).

LAST WEEKEND IN AUGUST

Haguenau — Hops festival, world folklore festival. ☎03 88 73 30 41.
Eguisheim — Wine-growers festival. www.ot-eguisheim.fr

LAST SUNDAY IN AUGUST

Provins — Harvest festival. ☎01 64 60 26 26. www.provins.net

1ST SATURDAY IN SEPTEMBER

Ribeauvillé — Fête des Ménétriers or Pfifferdaj (minstrels): Historical parade, wine flows freely. ☎03 89 73 20 04.

SEPTEMBER, (even numbered years).

Troyes — 48-hour vintage car rally. ☎03 25 40 86 99.

LATE OCTOBER—EARLY NOVEMBER

Troyes — Nuits de Champagne. Major choral festival (inc rock pop, folk and blues bands). ☎03 25 72 11 65. www.nuitsdechampagne.com

DECEMBER

Throughout Alsace and Lorraine
— St-Nicolas Feast.
☎03 29 27 27 27.
Christmas markets.

FEAST OF ST. NICHOLAS

The legend of St Nicholas
St Nicholas, bishop of Myra in Asia Minor in the 4C, is known for offering a dowry to three impoverished girls. He is also said to have prevented the execution of three unjustly accused officers. Perhaps because of images relating to the number three, he has also been associated, since the 12C in France, with the miraculous resurrection of three young children who had been cut up and set to cure by a butcher.
These different legends have created a popular figure who, on the night of 5 December, distributes gifts to good children in the countries of northern Europe (Lorraine, Germany, Belgium, the Netherlands, Switzerland).

Fête de la St-Nicolas
The Feast is celebrated either on the eve of or on the 6 December, or sometimes the following Saturday or Sunday. Many towns in Lorraine have celebrations, especially St-Nicolas-de-Port (torchlight procession in the basilica), Nancy (parade and fireworks), Metz (musical parade), and Épinal (floats in a parade).

Shopping

OPENING HOURS

Most of the larger shops are open Monday to Saturday from 9am to 6.30 or 7.30pm. Smaller, individual shops may close during the lunch hour. Food shops — grocers, wine merchants and bakeries — are generally open from 7am to 6.30 or 7.30pm; some open on Sunday mornings. Many food shops close between noon and 2pm and on Mondays. Bakery and pastry shops sometimes close on Wednesdays. Hypermarkets usually open until 9pm or later.
People travelling to the USA cannot import plant products or fresh food, including fruit, cheeses and nuts. It is acceptable to carry tinned (canned) products or preserves.

VALUE ADDED TAX

There is a Value Added Tax in France *(TVA)* of 19.6% on almost every purchase (some foods and books are subject to a lower rate). However, non-European visitors who spend more than €175 (including VAT) in a single shop on the same day can get the VAT amount refunded. Usually, you fill out a form at the store, showing your passport. Upon leaving the country, you submit all forms to customs for approval (they may want to see the goods, so if possible don't pack them in checked luggage). The refund is usually paid directly into your bank or credit card account, or it can be sent by mail. Big department stores that cater to tourists provide special services to help you; be sure to mention that you plan to seek a refund before you pay for goods (no refund is possible for tax on services). If you are visiting two or more countries within the European Union, you submit the forms only on departure from the last EU country. The refund is worthwhile for those visitors who would like to buy fashions, furniture or other fairly expensive items, but remember, the minimum amount must be spent in a single shop (though not necessarily on the same day). For full details visit www.douane.gouv.fr.

Sightseeing

TOURIST TRAINS (CHEMINS DE FER TOURISTIQUES)

In Alsace steam and diesel locomotives offer visitors a charming ride through the countryside.
(All services operate regularly at weekends in the summer, see their websites for timetables).

At the southern end of the Route des Crêtes, you can enjoy a ride along the **Vallée de la Doller** from Cernay to Sentheim *(10 Rue de la Gare, Sentheim ☎03 89 82 88 48. www.train-doller.org/vallee_doller.htm)*, travel aboard the **forest train** from Abreschviller to Grand Soldat in the Massif du Donon *(☎03 87 03 71 45 http://train-abreschviller.fr)* or take a combined boat and steam train trip along the **Rhine** between Neuf-Brisach and Baltzenheim *(2 rue de la Gare, Volgelsheim. ☎03 89 71 51 42. http://cftr.evolutive.org)*. In Champagne-Ardenne, the **Train touristique de la Forêt d'Orient** (*departure from Port-Mesnil. ☎03 25 41 20 72*) offers its passengers a charming ride through the regional nature park. The **Autorail Touristique de Wassy/Train touristique de la Blaise et du Der** runs north from Wassy to Éclaron or south from Wassy to Dommartin-le-Franc and Doulevant-le-Château *(http://cfbd.site.voila.fr)*.
The **Train touristique du Sud des Ardennes** (cour de la Gare, Attigny, ☎03 24 38 26 79. http://cftsa.free.fr/ steams down part of the Aisne Valley from Attigny to Challerange, passing through Vouziers (31km/19mi); or from Attigny to Amagne-Lucquy (9.5km/6mi).

Draisines

In the past, pedal cars, handcars and trolleys (known collectively as draisines) were propelled by railroad workers maintaining or inspecting the track. Today, this mode of locomotion can be used to explore the **Vallée de la Mortagne**. Energetic travellers can pedal along 20km/12mi of otherwise unused railways, starting from Magnières, west of Baccarat (☎03 83 72 34 73. www.trains-fr.org/unecto/valde-mortagne).
Similarly in the **Vallée de la Canner,** you can pedal the 11km/6.8mi from Vigy to Budange (☎03 87 77 92 18).

FROM ABOVE

- **Balloon rides** – For a unique view and memorable experience, consider a hot-air balloon ride:
- **Aérovision** – 4 rue de Hohrod, 68140 Munster, ☎03 89 77 22 81. www.aerovision-montgolfiere.com *(French only)*.
- **Pôle aérostatique Pilâtre de Rozier** – 6 place du Temple, 57530 Courcelles-Chaussy, ☎03 87 64 08 08. www.pilatre-de-rozier.com
- **Flights in light aircraft** – Flights in small planes are arranged by the Aéroclub du Sud Meusien, Aérodrome des Hauts de Chée Conde en Barrois. ☎03 29 77 18 30. www.ac-sud-meusien.net *(French only)*.
- **Helicopter flights** – Flights on the outskirts of Nancy are offered by Proteus Hélicoptères: Aéroport de Nancy-Essey, ☎03 83 29 80 60. Flights over the Lac du Der-Chantecoq start from Vauclerc airport, ☎03 26 74 28 18.

EXCURSIONS TO NEIGHBOURING COUNTRIES

The region is bordered by Germany to the north and east, Switzerland to the south-east, Belgium and Luxembourg to the north.
Visitors to Alsace will naturally be drawn to the other side of the River Rhine and such lovely towns as Freiberg, Belchen and Baden-Baden in the Black Forest. Consult the **Green Guide Germany** for tourist information, and the **Michelin Guide Deutschland** for hotels and restaurants.
Basel, in Switzerland, is also a popular tourist destination, especially at carnival time. The three days before the beginning of Lent mark the only Catholic ceremony to have survived the Reformation; a festival of parades and costumed revelry. The **Green Guide Switzerland** is useful for visiting Basel and the surrounding region. The **Michelin Guide Switzerland** makes it easy to choose where to spend the night and to find a special restaurant.
The Ardennes Forest covers most of the Belgian provinces of Luxembourg, Namur and Liège and part of the Grand Duchy as well as the French *département*. The valley of the River

S.Sauvignier/MICHELIN

River cruise

Meuse meanders to the North Sea by way of **Dinant**. This picturesque town is just 60km/37mi from Charleville-Mézières. Travellers can enjoy local honey cakes known as *couques*, baked in decorative wooden moulds, and may like to take advantage of a boat trip on the river (board in front of the town hall). Carry on to **Bouillon,** nestled in a bend of the River Semois and dominated by its medieval fortress. **Chimay** is known for its castle, but is also a familiar name to beer-lovers; the Trappist monks have their brewery at the abbey of Notre-Dame-de-Scourmount, just a few miles south of the town. Round off the excursion with a stop at **Orval Abbey**, in the Gaume Forest. Founded in 1070 by Benedictines from Calabria in southern Italy, it became one of Europe's wealthiest and best-known Cistercian abbeys. The tour includes a short film on monastery life, and a visit to the ruins dating from the Middle Ages to the 18C. From Dinant to Orval, the distance is 99km/61mi.

For further information, see the **Green Guide Belgium** and the **Michelin Guide Benelux.**

RIVER AND CANAL CRUISING

There are numerous navigable waterways in the region, where you can enjoy a cruise or hire your own boat. **Voies Navigables de France** (www.vnf.fr), can provide information on travelling the waterways, or you may like to contact the regional tourist office for information (*see Know Before You Go*).

Nautical maps guides and services

- **Éditions Grafocarte-Navicarte**, Champagne Ardenne in English; order online, www.guide-fluvial.com.
- **Éditions du Plaisancier,** 43 porte du Grand-Lyon, 01700 Neyron, ☎04 72 01 58 68; e-mail jacquartth@wanadoo.fr.

Self-skippered holidays

The following hire fleet agencies and bases offer boats accommodating two to eight people:

- **Ardennes Nautisme** – Bases: Pont-à-Bar and Namur (Belgium). ☎03 24 27 05 15. http://gb.ardennes-fluvial.com.
- **Crown Blue Line** – Bases: Boofzheim, Hesse, Saarbrück-enHesse, ☎0870 770 6301 (UK office). www.crown-blueline.com.
- **Locaboat Plaisance** – Bases: Anseremmes-Dinant, Pont-à-Bar,

Lutzelbourg. ☎03 86 91 72 72. www.locaboat.com.

- **Nicols** – Base: Saverne. ☎02 41 56 46 56, www.nicols.com.

Cruises

These can last a few hours to two week travelling along the Rhine, Moselle, Sarre, Neckar, Main, Danube, Meuse, Marne or Seine.

The brochure *Lorraine au fil de l'eau* contains information on boat trips in the area and can be obtained from the **Comité Régional du Tourisme de Lorraine** (*see Know Before You Go: Local Tourist Offices*).

CroisiEurope-Alsace Croisières, (www.croisieurope.com. ☎03 88 32 49 96), offers many trips out of Strasbourg. From March to December, you can tour the city while enjoying lunch or dinner on a boat leaving from quai Finkwiller, in the care of **Bateaux Touristiques Strasbourgeois,** 15 bis rue de Nantes, 67100 Strasbourg, ☎03 88 84 10 01. www.bateauxstras bourgeois.

Take a trip on the **River Marne** aboard the *Champagne-Vallée* (☎03 26 55 23 36. www.champagne-et-croisiere.com) leaving from Cumières. The barge, *La Quiétude,* offers day cruises on the Seine (☎03 36 62 27 47 28. http://bathotel.free.fr).

For a cruise on the River Meuse, try **Merganser itineraries,** 46 rue de Warnécourt, BP 11, 08000 Prix-les--Mézières, ☎01992 550 616 (UK office). www.bargedirect.com/mergitin2007.htm.

BIRDWATCHING AND NATURE PARKS

Birdwatching

The many lakes in Champagne-Ardenne attract a sizeable feathered population. Part of the **Lac de Bairon** has been set aside as a **bird refuge** and includes a nature discovery centre in Boult-aux-Bois (☎ 03 24 30 08 74; www.ardennesmaisonsnature.com). So too has part of the Lac d'Orient in the Forêt d'Orient Nature Park (information from the Maison du Parc in Piney, ☎03 24 43 81 90; www.pnr-foret-orient.fr). The **Lac du Der-Chantecoq**, ☎03.26.72.54.47 (LPO, Ligue pour la protection des oiseaux) http://champagne-ardenne.lpo.fr/ and nearby ponds have observatories and discovery trails. Here, the **Ferme aux Grues** is devoted to cranes, their migratory habits, how to observe them and conservation measures. The **Maison de l'Oiseau et du Poisson** is devoted to birds and fish and has exhibits and displays explaining the lake's ecosystem. More information on the area's bird population is available from the Musée du Pays du Der, 51290 Sainte-Marie-du-Lac-Nuisement, ☎03 26 41 01 02; www.museedupaysduder.com (*French only*).

Nature parks

There are five regional nature parks in the region described in this guide:

Two in Champagne-Ardenne, the **Parc naturel regional de la Montagne de Reims** (between Reims in the north and Épernay in the south) and the **Parc naturel regional de la Forêt d'Orient** (east of Troyes).

Three in Alsace-Lorraine, the **Parc naturel regional des Ballons des Vosges** (west of the Rhine between Sélestat in the north and Mulhouse in the south), the **Parc naturel regional des Vosges du Nord** (west of the Rhine, between Wissembourg in the north and Saverne in the south) and the **Parc naturel regional de Lorraine** split into two sections situated east and west of the Metz-Nancy motorway.

They are all described in the *Discovering Alsace* section of the guide. For wemsites and contact details visit www.gites-refuges.com/parcs.htm.

Nature conservatories

Devoted to the safeguard of natural sites, they organise nature discovery tours:

- **Conservatoire des sites alsaciens,** Maison des espaces naturels, Écomusée, 68190 Ungersheim, ☎03 89 83 34 20; http://csa.cren.free.fr (*French only*).

- **Conservatoire des sites lorrains**, 7 place Albert-Schweitzer, 57930 Fénétrange, ☏03 87 03 00 90; www. cren-lorraine.com (*French only*).

Books

HÉLOÏSE AND ABÉLARD

Latin scholars can enjoy the beautiful **Letters** written by these medieval lovers and thankfully there are also various modern translations available. Although their authenticity has sometimes been called into question (they may have been improved by scribes who came after), there is no denying the beauty and profound humanity of sentiment that rings true in all ages. **Peter Abélard**, by Helen Waddell, was first published in 1933 and has had over 30 reprints (Constable and Co Ltd, 1968). This slim volume is a novel but reads like a true account, moving in its simplicity.

- **Stealing Heaven: the Love Story of Héloïse and Abélard,** by Marion Meade (Soho Press, 1979), tells the story from a woman's perspective. This sensuous historical novel of epic proportions is an immersion in 12C France.
- **Abelard: A Medieval Life**, by M. T. Clanchy (Blackwell Publishers 2000). This is the first new work to come out on Abelard in 30 years. The author paints a vivid and clear portrait of the 12C scientist (master of Latin, logic and philosophy), monk and controversial theologian. The book defends a new concept: it was Heloise who inspired many of Abelard's most profound ideas.

POETS FOR EVERY PURPOSE

- **The Complete Fables of La Fontaine,** edited and with rhymed verse translation by Norman B. Spector (Northwestern University Press, 1988). No verse is unturned in this collection, which presents the French text opposite its translation, keen wit intact. Illustrated children's editions and paperback editions of the Fables are also available.
- **Paul Verlaine**, a seminal Symbolist and critical author, left an extensive body of work. Readily available in translation (ie by Jacques LeClerque, Westport Conn., Greenwood Press, 1977) are such famous books as *Songs Without Words, Yesteryear and Yesterday, The Accursed Poets* and *Confessions of a Poet.*
- **One Hundred and One Poems by Paul Verlaine: A Bilingual Edition,** translation Norman R. Shapiro (University of Chicago Press, 1999) presents exciting new translations of works spanning the poet's entire life.
- **Arthur Rimbaud** got quite a few stanzas out before putting down his pen at age 20. His best-known works available in translation include *A Season in Hell* and *The Drunken Boat.* **Rimbaud and Jim Morrison: the Rebel as Poet,** by Wallace Fowlie (Duke University Press, 1994), was inspired by a letter written to the author by the Doors' founder and lead singer, thanking him for publishing his translations of Rimbaud. The illustrated volume is a twinned tale exploring the symmetry of two lives and the parallels between European literary tradition and American rock music.
- **Rimbaud: A Biography,** by Graham Robb (Norton & Company, 2001) takes a long look at the volatile youth, the outrageous behavior and the poetic genius of Rimbaud and his influence on contemporary cultural icons such as Bob Dylan and other rebellious artists who have rallied to his call for "derangement of the senses."

THE RAVAGES OF WAR

- **The Franco-Prussian War: The German Conquest of France in 1870-1871,** by Geoffrey Wawro (Cambridge University Press,

2003), is a concise account of a war that violently changed the course of European history. The author analyses innovative tactics, weaponry, logistics and organisation as well as the characters of the leading generals, from the bloody battles at Gravelotte and Sedan to the last murderous fights on the Loire and in Paris.

- **The Debacle** by Émile Zola (translated by LW Tancock, Penguin, 1972) takes place during the Franco-Prussian War of 1870 and describes the tragic events of the defeat at Sedan as well as the uprising of the Paris Commune. The author carried out extensive research (arms, strategy, tactics) to produce this remarkably factual novel depicting the battle and its aftermath.
- **The Pity of War** by Niall Ferguson (London, Allen Lane, 1998). This radical, readable reassessment of the powers driving nations and individuals into the terrible conflict of the First World War focuses on life in the trenches.
- **A Balcony in the Forest**, by Julien Gracq (translated by Richard Howard, London, Harper Collins, 1992), is set in the Ardennes Forest in the winter of 1939-40, during the so-called Phoney War. Following a winter of solitude and contemplation of nature, a young officer on the Maginot Line must face attacking Panzer divisions.
- **A Time for Trumpets: The Untold Story of the Battle of the Bulge,** Charles B. MacDonald (NY, Morrow, 1984). The author was one of the 600 000 American soldiers who fought against Hitler's vanguard troops in the mists and snow of the Ardennes Forest on 16 December, 1944 – Germany's last desperate gamble and the turning point of the war.
- **Memoirs of Hope: Renewal and Endeavour**, Charles de Gaulle (NY, Simon and Schuster, 1971). Written in Colombey-les-Deux-Églises, the General's memoirs also include descriptions of the landscape of the Champagne region beyond the windows of his study.
- **Alamo in the Ardennes**: The untold story of the American soldiers who made the defense of Bastogne (the linch-pin in the Battle of the Bulge) possible by John C. McManus, John Wiley & Son, 2007).

WORDS ON WINE

Among the many books on wines of the region: *The Wines of Alsace* (Tom Stevenson, London, Faber and Faber, 1994); *Touring In Wine Country: Alsace* (Hubrecht Duijker, 1996); Oz Clarke's Wine Companion Champagne and Alsace Guide (David Cobbold, 1997) *Alsace Wines* (Pamela V Price, London, Sotheby Publications, 1984).

Michelin Guides

The Wine Regions of France (2007) An in-depth guide to the wine-producing regions of France.

... ON CHAMPAGNE

The Wine Lover's Guide to Champagne and North East France (Michael Busselle, NY, Viking, 1989). *The Glory of Champagne* (Don Hewitson, London, MacMillan, 1989). *Champagne for Dummies* (Ed McCarthy, 1999). *Tom Stevenson's Champagne & Sparkling Wine Guide* (Tom Stevenson, 2002), *Champagne: How the World's Most Glamorous Wine Triumphed Over War and Hard Times* (Don Kladstrup and Petie Kladstrup, 2005). *Champagne for the Soul: Celebrating God's Gift of Joy* (Mike Mason, 2006).

...AND ON FOOD

The Pâtissier: Recipes and Conversations from Alsace, France (Susan Lundquist, Hossine Bennara, and Frederic Lacroix, 2006). *Champagne Cookbook: Add Some Sparkle to Your Cooking and Your Life* (Malcolm R. Hebert, 2007).

USEFUL WORDS & PHRASES

Architectural Terms

See Introduction: Architecture.

Sights

abbaye	abbey
beffroi	belfry
chapelle	chapel
château	castle
cimetière	cemetery
cloître	cloisters
colombage	half-timbering
cour	courtyard
couvent	convent
écluse	lock (canal)
église	church
fontaine	fountain
gothique	Gothic
halle	covered market
jardin	garden
mairie	town hall
maison	house
marché	market
monastère	monastery
moulin	windmill
musée	museum
pan de bois (en)	timber-framed
parc	park
place	square
pont	bridge
port	port/harbour
porte	gateway
quai	quay
remparts	ramparts
romain	Roman
roman	Romanesque
rue	street
statue	statue
tour	tower

Natural Sites

abîme	chasm
aven	swallow-hole
barrage	dam
belvédère	viewpoint
cascade	waterfall
col	pass
corniche	ledge
côte	coast, hillside
forêt	forest
grotte	cave
lac	lake
plage	beach
rivière	river
ruisseau	stream
signal	beacon
source	spring
vallée	valley

On the Road

car park	parking
diesel	diesel/gazole
driving licence	permis de conduire
east	Est
garage (for repairs)	garage
left	gauche
LPG	GPL
motorway/ highway	autoroute
north	Nord
parking meter	horodateur
petrol/gas	essence
petrol/gas station	station essence
right	droite
south	Sud
toll	péage
traffic lights	feu tricolore
tire	pneu
unleaded	sans plomb
west	Ouest
wheel clamp	sabot
pedestrian crossing	passage clouté

Time

today	aujourd'hui
tomorrow	demain
yesterday	hier
winter	hiver
spring	printemps
summer	été
autumn/fall	automne
week	semaine
Monday	lundi
Tuesday	mardi
Wednesday	mercredi

Thursday	jeudi
Friday	vendredi
Saturday	samedi
Sunday	dimanche

Numbers

0	zéro
1	un
2	deux
3	trois
4	quatre
5	cinq
6	six
7	sept
8	huit
9	neuf
10	dix
11	onze
12	douze
13	treize
14	quatorze
15	quinze
16	seize
17	dix-sept
18	dix-huit
19	dix-neuf
20	vingt
30	trente
40	quarante
50	cinquante
60	soixante
70	soixante-dix
80	quatre-vingt
90	quatre-vingt-dix
100	cent
1000	mille

Shopping

antiseptic	antiseptique
bank	banque
baker's	boulangerie
big	grand
bookshop	librairie
butcher's	boucherie
chemist's/ drugstore	pharmacie
closed	fermé
cough mixture	sirop pour la toux
cough sweets	cachets pour la gorge
entrance	entrée
exit	sortie
fishmonger's	poissonnerie
grocer's	épicerie
newsagent	maison de la presse, marchand de journaux
open	ouvert
pain killer	analgésique
plaster (adhesive)	pansement adhésif
post office	poste
pound (weight)	livre
push	pousser
pull	tirer
shop	magasin
small	petit
stamps	timbres

Food and Drink

beef	bœuf
beer	bière
butter	beurre
bread	pain
breakfast	petit-déjeuner
cheese	fromage
chicken	poulet
dessert	dessert
dinner	dîner
duck	canard
fish	poisson
fork	fourchette
fruit	fruits
glass	verre
grape	raisin
green salad	salade verte
ham	jambon
ice cream	glace
ice cubes	glaçons
jug of water	carafe d'eau
jug of wine	pichet de vin
knife	couteau
lamb	agneau
lunch	déjeuner
meat	viande
mineral water	eau minérale
mixed salad	salade composée
orange juice	jus d'orange
plate	assiette
pork	porc
red wine	vin rouge
salt	sel
sparkling water	eau gazeuse

spoon	cuillère
still water	eau plate
sugar	sucre
tap water	eau du robinet
turkey	dinde
vegetables	légumes
water	de l'eau
white wine	vin blanc
yoghurt	yaourt

Personal Documents and Travel

airport	aéroport
credit card	carte de crédit
customs	douane
passport	passeport
platform	voie, quai
railway station	gare
shuttle	navette
suitcase	valise
train/plane ticket	billet de train/ d'avion
wallet	portefeuille

Clothing

coat	manteau
jumper	pull
raincoat	imperméable
shirt	chemise
shoes	chaussures
socks	chaussettes
stockings	bas
suit	costume/tailleur
tights	collant
trousers	pantalon

Useful Phrases

goodbye	au revoir
hello/ good morning	bonjour
how	comment
excuse me	excusez-moi
thank you	merci
yes/no	oui/non
I am sorry	pardon
why	pourquoi
when	quand
please	s'il vous plaît

- **Do you speak English?**
  Parlez-vous anglais?
- **I don't understand**
  Je ne comprends pas
- **Talk slowly**
  Parlez lentement
- **Where's...?**
  Où est...?
- **When does the ... leave?**
  À quelle heure part...?
- **When does the ... arrive?**
  À quelle heure arrive...?
- **When does the museum open?**
  À quelle heure ouvre le musée?
- **When is the show?**
  À quelle heure est la représentation?
- **When is breakfast served?**
  À quelle heure sert-on le petit-déjeuner?
- **What does it cost?**
  Combien cela coûte-t-il?
- **Where can I buy a newspaper in English?**
  Où puis-je acheter un journal en anglais?
- **Where is the nearest petrol/gas station?**
  Où se trouve la station essence la plus proche?
- **Where can I change travellers' cheques?**
  Où puis-je échanger des travellers' cheques?
- **Where are the toilets?**
  Où sont les toilettes?
- **Do you accept credit cards?**
  Acceptez-vous les cartes de crédit?
- **I need a receipt**
  Je voudrais un reçu

BASIC INFORMATION

Communications

Most public phones in France use prepaid phone cards *(télécartes)*, rather than coins, and many telephone booths accept credit cards (Visa, Mastercard/Eurocard). *Télécartes* (50 or 120 units) can be bought in post offices, branches of France Télécom, *bureaux de tabac* (cafés that sell cigarettes) and newsagents and can be used to make calls in France and abroad. Calls can be received at phone boxes where the blue bell sign is shown; the phone will not ring, so keep your eye on the little message screen.

Emergency numbers	
Police:	**17**
SAMU (Paramedics):	15
Fire (Pompiers):c	18

NATIONAL CALLS

French telephone numbers have 10 digits. Paris and Paris region numbers begin with 01; 02 in north-west France; 03 in north-east France; 04 in south-east France and Corsica; 05 in south-west France.

INTERNATIONAL CALLS

To call France from abroad, dial the country code (33) + 9-digit number (omit the initial 0). When calling abroad from France dial 00, then dial the country code followed by the area code and number of your correspondent.

To use your personal calling card	
AT&T	☎ 0-800 99 00 11
Sprint	☎ 0-800 99 00 87
MCI	☎ 0-800 99 00 19
Canada Direct	☎ 0-800 99 00 16

International Dialling Codes *(00 + code)*			
Australia	☎ 61	New Zealand	☎ 64
Canada	☎ 1	United Kingdom	☎ 44
Eire	☎ 353	United States	☎ 1

- **International Information:** US/Canada: 00 33 12 11
- **International operator:** 00 33 12 + country code
- **Local directory assistance:** 12
- **Toll-free numbers** in France begin 0 800 to 0 805.

Minitel

France Télécom operates a system offering directory enquiries (free of charge up to 3min), travel and entertainment reservations, and other services (cost per minute varies). These small computer-like terminals can be found in some post offices, hotels and France Télécom agencies and in many French homes. 3614 PAGES E is the code for **directory assistance in English:** turn on the unit, dial 3614, hit the *connexion* button when you get the tone, type in "PAGES E", and follow the instructions on the screen.

CELLULAR PHONES

In France these phones have numbers that begin with 06. If you are bringing your own mobile phone to France from outside Europe you may wish to check with your phone provider whether it will work and what the cost will be. From inside Europe it will almost certainly work, though if you intend making many calls, it pays to do your homework on researching the various tariffs available. If you are staying in France for a while and/or intending using your phone frequently, it may well pay you to either fit a French SIM card into your phone (check that you can do this with your own phone company) or more simply buy a cheap French pay-as-you-go phone and simply top it up with prepaid *mobicartes*.

Electricity

In France the electric current is 220 volts. Circular two-pin plugs are the rule. Adapters and converters should be bought before you leave home; they are on sale in most airports.
If you have a rechargeable device (video camera, lap-top computer, battery charger), read the instructions carefully. Sometimes these items only require a plug adapter; in other cases you must use a voltage converter as well or risk ruining your device.

Public Holidays

Public services, museums and other monuments may be closed or may vary their hours of admission on the following public holidays:

1 January	New Year's Day *(Jour de l'An)*
	Easter Day and Easter Monday *(Pâques)*
1 May	May Day *(Fête du Travail)*
8 May	VE Day *(Fête de la Libération)*
Thursday 40 days after Easter	Ascension Day *(Ascension)*
7th Sunday-Monday after Easter	Whit Sunday and Monday *(Pentecôte)*
14 July	France's National Day *(Fête de la Bastille)*
15 August	Assumption *(Assomption)*
1 November	All Saint's Day *(Toussaint)*
11 November	Armistice Day *(Fête de la Victoire)*
25 December	Christmas Day *(Noël)*

National museums and art galleries are closed on Tuesdays; municipal museums are generally closed on Mondays. In addition to the usual school holidays at Christmas and in the spring and summer, there are long mid-term breaks (10 days to a fortnight) in February and early November.

Mail/Post

Post offices open Mondays to Fridays, 8am to 7pm, Saturdays, 8am to noon. Smaller branch post offices often close at lunchtime between noon and 2pm and in the afternoon at 4pm.

Postage via air mail to

- **European Union and domestic:**
  ✉ letter (20g) 0.53€
- **Rest of the world**
  ✉ letter (20g) 0.90€

Stamps are also available from news agents and tobacconists.
Stamp collectors should ask for *timbres de collection* in any post office.
Poste Restante (General Delivery) mail should be addressed as follows: Name, Poste Restante, Poste Centrale, post code of the *département* followed by town name, France. The *Michelin Guide France* gives local post codes.

Money

CURRENCY

There are no restrictions on the amount of currency visitors can take into France. Visitors carrying a lot of cash are advised to complete a currency declaration form on arrival, because there are restrictions on currency export.

NOTES AND COINS

Since 17 February 2002, the **euro** has been the only currency accepted as a means of payment in France, as in the other European countries participating in the monetary union. Old notes in French francs can be exchanged only at the Banque de France until 2012.

BANKS

Although business hours vary from branch to branch, banks are usually open from 9am to noon and 2pm to 5pm and are closed either on Mondays or Saturdays. Banks close early on the day before a bank holiday. A passport is necessary as identification when cashing travellers cheques in banks. Commission charges vary and hotels usually charge more than banks for cashing cheques.

CREDIT CARDS

Visa is the most widely accepted credit card, followed by Mastercard; other cards, credit and debit (Diners Club, Plus, Cirrus, etc) are also accepted in some cash machines. American Express is more often accepted in premium establishments. Most places post signs indicating which card they accept; if you don't see such a sign and want to pay with a card, ask before ordering or making a selection. Cards are widely accepted in shops, hypermarkets, hotels and restaurants, at tollbooths and in petrol stations. Before you leave home, check with the bank that issued your card for emergency replacement procedures.

Note: As part of a more intense effort to prevent identity theft, some credit card companies will place a hold on your account if it is used abroad. It is a good idea to notify your card carrier of your itinerary before you travel, in order to prevent any disruption in service.

Carry your card number and emergency phone numbers separate from your wallet and handbag; leave a copy of this information with someone you can easily reach. You must report any loss or theft of credit cards or traveller's cheques to the French police who will issue you with a certificate (useful proof to show the issuing company).

American Express ☏ 01 47 77 72 00
Visa ☏ 0 800 901 179
MasterCard ☏ 01 45 67 84 84
Diners Club ☏ 0 810 314 519

At most ATM machines, 24-hour hotline numbers are posted.

DISCOUNTS

Significant discounts are available for senior citizens, students, young people under the age of 25, teachers, and groups for public transportation, museums and monuments and for some leisure activities such as the cinema (at certain times of day). Bring student or senior cards with you, and bring along some extra passport-size photos for discount travel cards.
The **International Student Travel Confederation** (www.isic.org), global administrator of the International Student and Teacher Identity Cards, is an association of student travel organisations around the world.
ISTC members collectively negotiate benefits with airlines, governments, and providers of other goods and services for the student and teacher community, both in their own country and around the world. The non-profit association sells international ID cards for students, under 25-year-olds and teachers (who may get discounts on museum entrances, for example).

PRICES AND TIPS

Since a service charge is automatically included in the prices of meals and accommodation in France, it is not necessary to tip in restaurants and hotels. However, if the service in a restaurant is especially good or if you have enjoyed a fine meal, an extra tip (this is the *pourboire,* rather than the *service)* will be appreciated. Usually 1.50 to 3.50 euros is enough, but if the bill is big (a large party or a luxury restaurant), it is not uncommon to leave 7 to 8 euros or more.

As a rule, the cost of staying in a hotel and eating in restaurants is significantly higher in Paris than in the French regions. However, by reserving a hotel room well in advance and taking advantage of the wide choice of restaurants, you can enjoy your trip without breaking the bank.

Restaurants usually charge for meals in two ways: a *menu* that is a fixed-price menu with 2 or 3 courses, sometimes a small pitcher of wine, all for a stated price, or *à la carte,* the more expensive way, with each course ordered separately.

Cafés have very different prices, depending on where they are located. The price of a drink or a coffee is cheaper if you stand at the counter *(comptoir)* than if you sit down *(salle)* and sometimes it is even more expensive if you sit outdoors *(terrasse).*

Time

France is 1hr ahead of Greenwich Mean Time (GMT). France goes on daylight-saving time from the last Sunday in March to the last Sunday in October.

When it is **noon in France**, it is	
3am	in Los Angeles
6am	in New York
11am	in Dublin
11am	in London
7pm	in Perth
9pm	in Sydney
11pm	in Auckland
In France "am" and "pm" are not used but the 24-hour clock is widely applied.	

CONVERSION TABLES

Weights and Measures

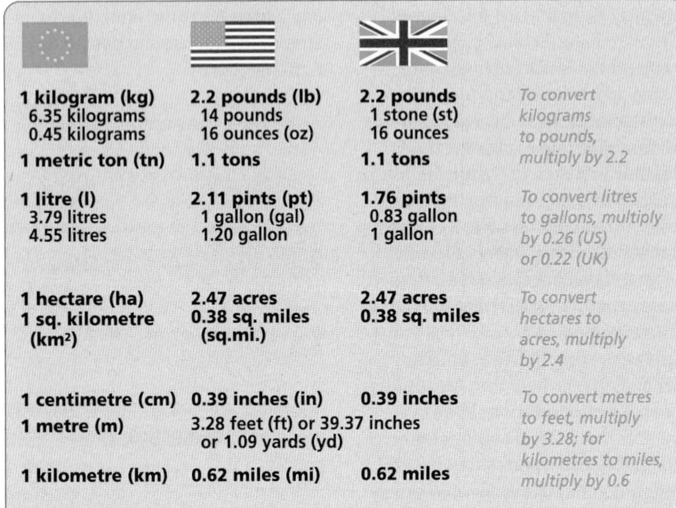

EU	US	UK	
1 kilogram (kg)	**2.2 pounds (lb)**	**2.2 pounds**	*To convert kilograms to pounds, multiply by 2.2*
6.35 kilograms	14 pounds	1 stone (st)	
0.45 kilograms	16 ounces (oz)	16 ounces	
1 metric ton (tn)	**1.1 tons**	**1.1 tons**	
1 litre (l)	**2.11 pints (pt)**	**1.76 pints**	*To convert litres to gallons, multiply by 0.26 (US) or 0.22 (UK)*
3.79 litres	1 gallon (gal)	0.83 gallon	
4.55 litres	1.20 gallon	1 gallon	
1 hectare (ha)	**2.47 acres**	**2.47 acres**	*To convert hectares to acres, multiply by 2.4*
1 sq. kilometre (km²)	**0.38 sq. miles (sq.mi.)**	**0.38 sq. miles**	
1 centimetre (cm)	**0.39 inches (in)**	**0.39 inches**	*To convert metres to feet, multiply by 3.28; for kilometres to miles, multiply by 0.6*
1 metre (m)	3.28 feet (ft) or 39.37 inches or 1.09 yards (yd)		
1 kilometre (km)	**0.62 miles (mi)**	**0.62 miles**	

Clothing

Women	EU	US	UK
Shoes	35	4	2½
	36	5	3½
	37	6	4½
	38	7	5½
	39	8	6½
	40	9	7½
	41	10	8½
Dresses & suits	36	6	8
	38	8	10
	40	10	12
	42	12	14
	44	14	16
	46	16	18
Blouses & sweaters	36	06	30
	38	08	32
	40	10	34
	42	12	36
	44	14	38
	46	16	40

Men	EU	US	UK
Shoes	40	7½	7
	41	8½	8
	42	9½	9
	43	10½	10
	44	11½	11
	45	12½	12
	46	13½	13
Suits	46	36	36
	48	38	38
	50	40	40
	52	42	42
	54	44	44
	56	46	48
Shirts	37	14½	14½
	38	15	15
	39	15½	15½
	40	15¾	15¾
	41	16	16
	42	16½	16½

Sizes often vary depending on the designer. These equivalents are given for guidance only.

Speed

KPH	10	30	50	70	80	90	100	110	120	130
MPH	6	19	31	43	50	56	62	68	75	81

Temperature

Celsius (°C)	0°	5°	10°	15°	20°	25°	30°	40°	60°	80°	100°
Fahrenheit (°F)	32°	41°	50°	59°	68°	77°	86°	104°	140°	176°	212°

To convert Celsius into Fahrenheit, multiply °C by 9, divide by 5, and add 32.
To convert Fahrenheit into Celsius, subtract 32 from °F, multiply by 5, and divide by 9.

NB: Conversion factors on this page are approximate.

World Heritage List

In 1972, The United Nations Educational, Scientific and Cultural Organization (UNESCO) adopted a Convention for the preservation of cultural and natural sites. To date, more than 150 States Parties have signed this international agreement, which has listed over 500 sites "of outstanding universal value" on the World Heritage List. Each year, a committee of representatives from 21 countries, assisted by technical organisations (ICOMOS – International Council on Monuments and Sites; IUCN – International Union for Conservation of Nature and Natural Resources; ICCROM – International Centre for the Study of the Preservation and Restoration of Cultural Property, the Rome Centre), evaluates the proposals for new sites to be included on the list, which grows longer as new nominations are accepted and more countries sign the Convention. To be considered, a site must be nominated by the country in which it is located.
The protected **cultural heritage** sites may be monuments (buildings, sculptures, archaeological structures, etc.) with unique historical, artistic or scientific features; groups of buildings (such as religious communities, ancient cities); or sites (human settlements, examples of exceptional landscapes, cultural landscapes) which are the combined works of man and nature of exceptional beauty. Natural heritage sites may be a testimony to the stages of the earth's geological history or to the development of human cultures and creative genius or represent significant ongoing ecological processes, contain superlative natural phenomena or provide a habitat for threatened species.
Signatories of the Convention pledge to co-operate to preserve and protect these sites around the world as a common heritage to be shared by all humanity, and contribute to the **World Heritage Fund**. The Fund serves to carry out studies, plan conservation measures, train local specialists, supply equipment for the protection of a park or the restoration of a monument, etc.
Some of the most well-known places which the World Heritage Committee has inscribed include: Australia's Great Barrier Reef (1981), the Canadian Rocky Mountain Parks (1984), The Great Wall of China (1987), the Statue of Liberty (1984), the Kremlin (1990), Mont-Saint-Michel and its Bay (France – 1979), Durham Castle and Cathedral (1986).

UNESCO World Heritage sites included in this guide are:

Place Stanislas, Place de la Carrière and Place d'Alliance in Nancy

The temporary residence of a king without a kingdom – Stansislas Leszcynski – is an example of an enlightened monarchy responding to the needs of the public. Constructed between 1752 and 1756 by a brilliant team under the direction of the architect Héré, this project illustrates a perfect coherence between the desire for prestige and a concern for functionality.

Strasbourg, Grande île

The historic centre of the Alsatian capital lies between two arms of the River Ill. The district occupied by the Cathedral, four ancient churches and the Palais Rohan recalls the typical medieval city plan, and shows the evolution of the city from the 15C to the 18C.

Cathedral of Notre-Dame, former Abbey of Saint-Remi and Palace of Tau, Reims

The Cathedral, its sculpted decorations embellishing the Gothic architecture, is a masterpiece. The former abbey has conserved its beautiful 9C nave where the holy anointing of the kings of France was first carried out by St Remi. The Tau Palace was almost entirely reconstructed in the 17C.

Provins

This beautiful fortified medieval town has a lively summer programme of activities which recreate historic activities such as jousting and falconry.

Hunawihr
R. Mattés/MICHELIN

INTRODUCTION TO ALSACE LORRAINE CHAMPAGNE

NATURE

This guide covers three of France's 22 *Régions* (the largest type of administrative district): Alsace, Lorraine, and Champagne-Ardenne. Each Region is made up of départements (numbered 01 to 96 alphabetically – their numbers are used as identification on automobile number plates and in postal codes). Thus, Alsace includes Bas-Rhin (67) and Haut-Rhin (68); Lorraine is made up of Meurthe-et-Moselle (54), Meuse (55), Moselle (67) and Vosges (88); Champagne-Ardenne includes the Ardennes (08), Aube (10), Marne (51) and Haute-Marne (52). The French *départements* were created in 1790 and generally given the name of the main river within their territory. The country is further divided into *arrondissements*, which are split into cantons, and finally communes, which are managed by an elected mayor. There are 36 556 mayoralties in France.

Regions

The easternmost portion of the area covered in this guide is the **Alsatian plain**. Barely 30km/19mi in width, it stretches, north to south, over 170km/106mi. The border with Germany is traced by the Rhine, which forms an alluvial basin with the River Ill; a porous, friable blanket of marl and loam deposits, consisting predominantly of silt (known as *loess*). At the southern end, the pebbly soil of the **Sundgau** region links it to the Jura range.

Like a wall on the other edge of the narrow plain, the **Vosges** mountains rise abruptly, running parallel to the Rhine for the whole length of Alsace. This ancient range formed by folding movements of the earth 300 million years ago is made of crystalline rock (granites, porphyries) and ancient sedimentary rock, mostly sandstone. At the southern end, the mountain tops have distinctive, rounded shapes locally known as *ballons*. The glaciers left behind high mountain lakes. To the north, the lower altitude has resulted in a thicker sedimentary crust, and a forest cover.

The western slope of the range is more gradual than the Alsatian side. The geological history of the **Ardennes** uplands is a complex one, the result of intense folding, faulting, uplifts and denudations, with some of the older strata of rock thrust above the younger. The highest point of the plateau in France is the Croix de Scalle (502m/1 647ft), on the border with Belgium. The Meuse flows through deeply entrenched meanders between the tip of the French Ardennes, Givet, and Charleville-Mézières. The rugged **Argonne** Forest is drained by the River Aisne.

The region of **Champagne** is part of the Paris Basin, a vast bowl-like formation

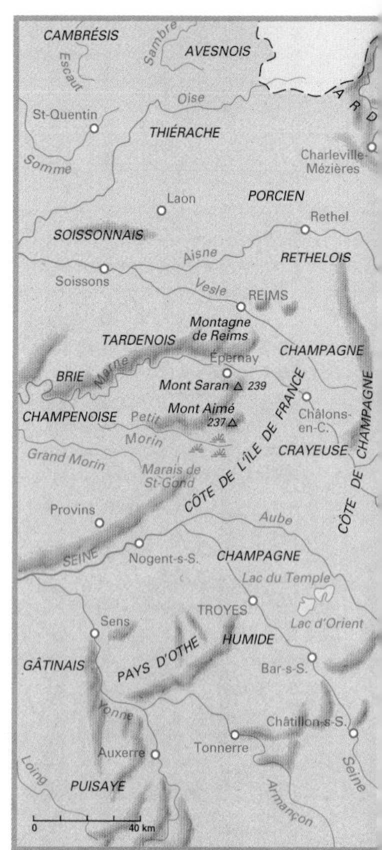

contained by the Ardennes and the Vosges (north and east) and the Morvan and Massif Armoricain (south and west). The landscape has been shaped by a series of concentric layers, one on top of the other in diminishing size, like a stack of saucers, with the oldest and smallest on top. The **Lorraine** plateau marks the eastern rim of the basin.

Land Formation

THE VOSGES AND ALSACE

Primary (Palaeozoic) Era

About 560 million years ago, France was covered in water. The earth's crust underwent a great upheaval and the so-called "Hercynian folds" pushed up the bedrock of the Vosges and what is now the Black Forest, constituting a crystalline massif dominated by granite.

Secondary (Mesozoic) Era

This era began about 200 million years ago. The Vosges, planed down by erosion, were surrounded by the sea which filled the Paris Basin at different periods. At the end of the Secondary Era, the range was covered in water; sedimentary soils (sandstone, limestone, marl, clay and chalk) piled up on top of the primitive bedrock.

Tertiary Era

About 65 million years ago, a tremendous folding of the crust of the earth brought out the Alps. In reaction to this movement, the old Hercynian hills slowly lifted up. In the first phase, the Vosges and the Black Forest reached an altitude of nearly 3 000m/9 843ft.

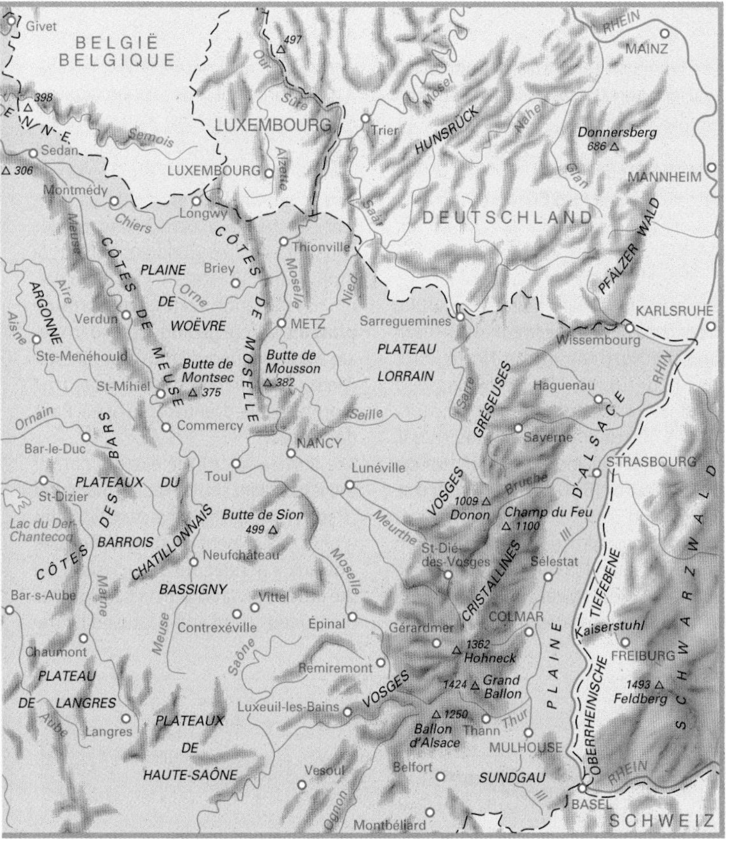

In the second phase, the central zone, unbalanced by the upheaval, collapsed inward. This sunken area was to become the Alsatian plain, separating the Vosges from the Black Forest, and explaining the symmetry of the structure and relief found between the two areas.

Quaternary (Glacial) Era

The earth underwent a global cooling period some two million years ago. Glaciers covered the southern Vosges. Descending slowly, they widened the valleys and steepened the slopes, gouged the rock and left hollows that were later filled with water (Lac Noir, Lac Blanc). When the climate warmed, the accumulated earth and stones carried by the glaciers were finally deposited in formations known as moraines, some of which created natural dams and lakes (Lac de Gérardmer). Since the glaciers retreated, rainwater, rivers and streams have further eroded the Vosges. The old stone peaks have been laid bare in the south, whereas the northern end of the range, preserved from the harshest glacier aggression, has retained a thick sandstone mantle.

ARDENNES: HERCYNIAN HISTORY

At the end of the Palaeozoic Era, the European continent was subject to a period of mountain-building resulting from the collision between the African and the North American-North European continent. The Hercynian belt extends in Western Europe for more than 3 000km/1 860mi from Portugal, Ireland and England in the west through Spain, France (Brittany, Massif Central, Vosges and Corsica), and Germany (Black Forest, Harz) to the Czech Republic in the Bohemian Massif. Analyses of the rocks and geological structures found in these zones indicate that they are the result of the seabed spreading, subduction of the oceanic crust and plate collision. The lateral compression of the upper layers of the earth pushed accumulated sediment upward, bringing ridges of hard, old rocks together like the jaws of a clamp.

Thus, the Ardennes uplands emerged around 550 to 220 million years BC. Spreading over the countries of France, Germany and Belgium, the region has been eroded over time until it now appears as a mostly flat plain. The River Meuse has marked a course through the very hard stone, revealed in the dramatic canyon-like walls of dark rock through which it winds (*see Meanders of the MEUSE)*. Near Givet, the river valleys widen as the water passes over bands of shale and limestone.

LORRAINE AND CHAMPAGNE

These two regions form the eastern part of the **Paris Basin**. At the end of the Primary Era, and into the early Tertiary Era, this vast depression was a sea. A great variety of sedimentary deposits – sandstone, limestone, marl, clay, chalk – piled up 2 000m/6 562ft deep. By the middle of the Tertiary Era, the water began to drain from this wide "saucer," whereas the rim, in particular to the east and south-east, rose under the effects of Alpine folding. Erosion worked to flatten out the land, creating the **Lorraine plateau**, where geology served to create a homogeneous landscape; greater diversity of soil composition created the more diversified landscapes of the **Pays des Côtes.**

The illustration of the eastern part of the Paris Basin shows the formation of cuestas (côtes). The characteristic of this type of escarpment is a steep cliff on one side and a gentler dip or back slope on the other. This landform occurs in areas of inclined strata and is caused by the

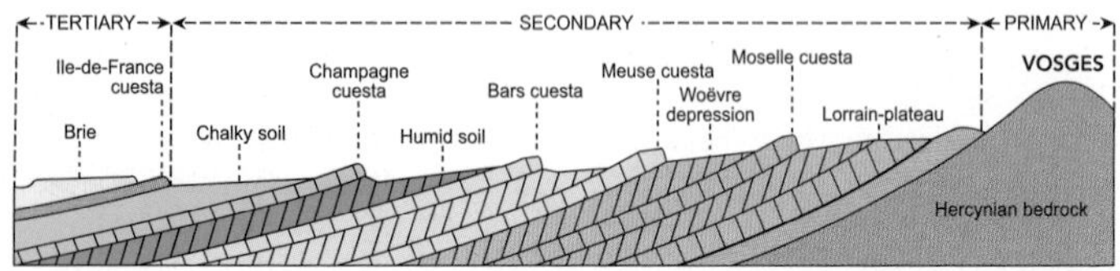

manner in which different types of soil and rock react to weathering and erosion. Here, the resistant layers (limestone) surmount softer layers (clay, marl). Running water works a channel in the hard layer until it reaches the more porous zones below. The softer areas are washed away and leave a depression, which is hemmed in by the abrupt rise of the hard rock (the front de côte or steep face); the softer surface slopes back at a gentle angle. This back slope, protected from wind, is characterised by loose, fertile soil whose chalky layers below the surface help the soil warm up quickly in the spring. These areas are ideal for cultivating vineyards.

The Champagne region is made up of many small pays, areas with distinct climates and soils. **Champagne crayeuse** refers to the chalky soil which gave the region its name (etymological descendent of "calcareous plain"). This zone forms a circle with a circumference of about 80km/50mi, with Paris near the centre. The **Brie and Tardenois plateau** is crossed by rivers (the Marne, the two Morins and the Seine); impenetrable marl holds in humidity, whereas siliceous limestone forms the upper layer. The Barrois is another plateau, crossed by the valleys of the Saulx and the Ornain, home to the towns of Bar-le-Duc and Ligny-en-Barrois. It extends into the **Côte de Bars**, where the vineyards of the Aube département grow.

Between the Champagne and Bars cuestas lies the region known as **Champagne humide**, a verdant and well-watered area of woodlands, pastures, and orchards. The creation of the lake-reservoirs in the **Der-Chantecoq** and **Orient** forests have further transformed the lay of the land, where the heavy, clay rich soil is more suited to grazing than cultivation.

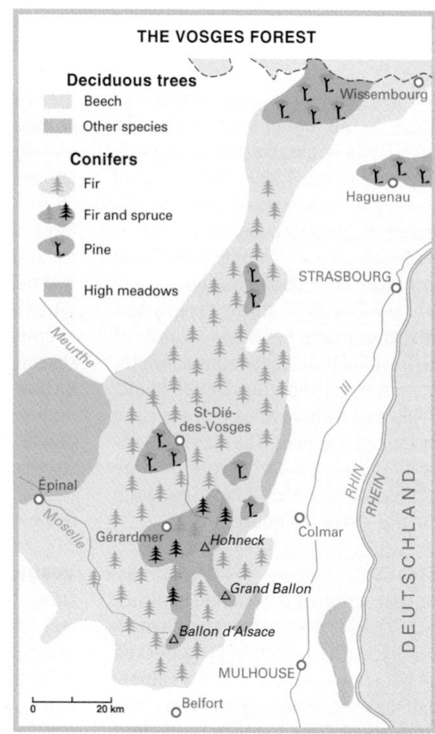

Forests and Wildlife

ALSACE AND THE VOSGES

The Vosges mountains are particularly lovely for the forest cover, which changes subtly according to altitude, orientation and the composition of the soil. The southern part of the range is known as *Vosges cristallines*, in reference to the granite content of the high mountains. The ballons and other summits are rounded, with moderate slopes on the western side. Facing the Alsatian plain, however, the rocky faces appear sharper and steeper. The River Bruche marks the separation with the *Vosges gréseuses* – the "sandy" northern end. The range diminishes in altitude and the red sandstone so prevalent in the construction of castles and churches has also sculpted the landscape. The forest blanketing the whole hilly area is sometimes a harmonious mixture of species, and sometimes dominated by a single species, creating a variety of colours and distinctive woodland environments.

Facing the region of **Lorraine**, the lower hills of the north are exposed to the wet western winds, and dominated by beech trees. Firs grow at an altitude of 400m/1 312ft. In the higher southern peaks, Scotch pine grow above 700m/2 297ft. Beyond 1 000m/3 280ft, conifers yield to deciduous varieties, including beech, maple and mountain ash. On the highest ridge tops, there are no trees at all, just low brush and bilberry bushes.

On the warmer slope facing the **Alsatian plain**, firs begin to grow at 600m/1 968ft. Just above the vineyards, groves of chestnut trees can be found; in the past their wood was used to stake out the grape vines. The warm, dry climate is congenial to spruce. A large population of oak flourishes in the Harth Forest, east of Mulhouse.

Storks

No discussion of the wildlife in Alsace would be complete without the mention of storks. These stately, long-necked creatures are symbolic of the region, and believed to bring good luck.

Each spring, their return is awaited anxiously. After years of decline (due to hunting in their winter habitat in Africa, and accidents involving high-voltage electric lines), the population seems to be stabilising and the gracious birds are once again a common sight. It is estimated that about 200 couples now live in Alsace, some year-round. The migrating storks come to roost, typically atop chimneys, in the month of March. Storks are voiceless, or nearly so, but announce their presence by clattering their bills loudly. The male arrives first, and begins work on a large platform of twigs and vines. The circular nest is refurbished yearly, and may weigh up to 500kg/1 100lb for 2m/6.5ft in diameter. Most nests are under 1m/3ft high, but exceptionally they may reach double that height.

When the chosen mate has arrived, the couple produce three to six eggs in a season, which hatch after 36 days of incubation by both parents. Generously nourished with insects, larva, lizards, newts, mice, moles and snakes, baby storks grow quickly; they begin testing their wings at about four weeks and are flying one month later.

Vosges lakes

On each side of the crest of the Vosges, many lakes add to the pleasure of an excursion to the mountains. The largest is Gérardmer (115ha/284 acres), on the Lorraine side; one of the region's most popular winter resorts is located along its banks. The deepest lake is Lac Blanc (71m/233ft), on the Alsatian side.

The lakes were created by the glaciers that once covered the range, hundreds of centuries ago. Most are found at high altitudes, in bowl-like formations with steep waterfront terrain (Lac des Corbeaux, Lac Noir, Lac Blanc, etc). Many of them are now used as reservoirs,

B. Kaufmann/Michelin

Lac Blanc

particularly useful for meeting the needs of textile plants when water is in short supply.
Other lakes, in the valleys, were formed by glacier deposits, moraines, which retain or deviate waters. Gérardmer and Longemer are such lakes.

ARDENNE

The French Region of Ardenne is the south-west margin of the larger Ardennes highlands and the adjacent lowlands in the Meuse and Aisne valleys. The thick, apparently impenetrable forest has been the scene of battles since the French Revolution. In addition to the sandstone, limestone and quartzite found in neighbouring regions, the Ardenne is famous for the blue slate quarried there. The oldest sections of the forest are majestic with hardwoods such as oak, beech and yellow birch; younger growth includes European white birch and willows. The variety of soil quality has a strong influence on the height of trees: on the plateau a mature oak may yield only a dozen logs for the fire; an ash further south in the Signy-l'Abbaye area may climb more than 30m/110ft.
Game is abundawnt in the Ardennes forest, where hunting is popular. The region's emblematic animal is the wild boar, sanglier. The wild population has returned from the brink of extinction thanks to better management. There is also a limited hunting season (two to six weeks, depending on the district) on the plains, for pheasant, partridge and hare. Each hunting permit is delivered with tags which the hunter must affix to the animals captured. Deer are now found only in animal parks; few escaped the devastation of the Second World War, however, the population has been restored thanks to the Belval animal reserve. Things have changed considerably since the days of Charlemagne: on 8 December 799, the Emperor and his party bagged two bison, two aurochs, 46 boar, 28 stags and a wolf, using spears, bows and arrows.

S. Sauvignier/MICHELIN
Wild Boar

ARGONNE

The southernmost part of the French Ardenne is wooded and hilly, more temperate in every way than the highlands. The massif is a natural barrier between Champagne and Lorraine, about 65km/40mi long and 15km/10mi wide, rarely exceeding 200m/650ft in altitude. The Aire and Aisne river systems cut deep valleys through this region which has been of great strategic importance. Beech groves are common on the slopes, and it is not unusual to see regal chestnuts atop the crests. Shrubs, berry bushes and reeds provide shelter for birds and other creatures; bluebells, lungwort and daffodils grow wild on the

Beech

Spruce

Scotch pine

Fir

M. Janvier/MICHELIN

Big Bad Wolf

The Ardennes Forest extends over the present-day borders of Belgium and Luxembourg; for many local inhabitants, being an *Ardennais* is more significant than being French or Belgian. At the end of the 19C, the thick forest was the perfect environment for smuggling cheap coffee and tobacco into France. Dogs were trained to make runs at night, and "Little Red Riding Hoods" carried innocent baskets for "Grandmother" while they stuffed their underclothes with contraband. Notorious customs officers, known as *noirs* because of their black uniforms, developed the habit of thoroughly searching any young lady found alone in the forest and were generally despised as predators by the native country folk.

forest floor. Some species have migrated to the area from other regions of France, including heather from Brittany; specialists may look out for a non-indigenous blue lily from England, a souvenir from soldiers of the First World War.

Bird sanctuaries and other animal reserves are found around many of the region's lakes and nature parks. There are numerous discovery trails and nature centres where visitors can learn more about the environment, the flora and fauna of the region.

HISTORY

Time Line

PREHISTORIC INHABITANTS

Human settlements in Champagne and the Ardenne had developed into small villages by the Neolithic Era (4500-2000 BC). By the Bronze Age (1800-750 BC), the region had already established what would become a long tradition of metal working.

BC 58-52 — Roman conquest. In Champagne and Ardenne, the people lent their support to Ceasar's troops. In Alsace, the Germanic tribes were forced to retreat to the east of the Rhine.

27 — Under Emperor Augustus (27BC-14AD), Champagne was part of the province of Belgium. A sophisticated civilisation developed under the *Pax Romana;* villas were built, trading centres grew and roads improved communication. The area's thermal springs were appreciated for their curative powers.

CHRISTIANITY AND MONARCHY TAKE ROOT

AD 69-70 — Following the death of Nero, the Roman Empire weakened. Assembly held in Reims.

3-5C — Missionaries travelled the region; Germanic invasions: Alemanni, Vandals and Huns successively carried out raids.

486 — The regions of the Meuse and Moselle came under the control of the Merovingian king Clovis, establishing a Frankish kingdom. While the **Franks** were not numerous, they became the ruling class of the territories conquered.

498 — St Remi persuaded Clovis to convert on Christmas Day.

511 — Death of Clovis. Champagne was divided into incoherent parcels, constituting several small kingdoms.

683 — The duke of Étichon, father of St Odile, ruled Alsace. After his reign, the land was divided into Nordgau and Sundgau, each ruled by a count.

774 — Charles Martel seized church property for the secular state. At the same time, the region was organised into parishes, and the power and authority of the church grew stronger; a balance of powers developed.

800 — The title of emperor was revived and conferred upon **Charlemagne**. The **Holy Roman Empire** was a complex of lands in Western and Central Europe ruled by Frankish then German kings for 10 centuries (until renunciation of the imperial title in 1806). The empire and the papacy were the two most important institutions of Western Europe through the Middle Ages.

816 — Louis I, (known as The Pious and also The Debonair), son of Charlemagne and Hildegarde the Swabian, was crowned emperor in Reims by Pope Stephen IV; a forceful French monarchy began to take shape.

817 — Louis I, in accordance with his father's will, divided Charlemagne's realm among three sons from his first marriage: Bavaria to Louis the German, Aquitaine to Pepin, and Lothair he named co-emperor and heir.

829 — Louis' second marriage to Judith of Bavaria had produced a son (Charles the Bald), to whom he granted the realm then known as Alemannia. From this time on, the sons formed and dissolved alliances, overthrew their father twice, and territories were passed back and forth or seized outright by the brothers who continued fighting for decades after their father's death.

839 — With Pepin dead, another attempt at partition divided the empire between Lothair and Charles, with Bavaria left in the hands of Louis the German. The following year, Louis I died.

843 — Under the Treaty of Verdun, Lothair received *Francia Media* (today, parts of Belgium, the Netherlands, western Germany, eastern France, Switzerland and much of Italy); Louis the German received *Francia Orientalis* (land east of the Rhine); Charles received *Francia Occidentalis* (the remainder of present-day France). This treaty marked the dissolution of Charlemagne's empire, and foreshadowed the formation of the modern countries of Western Europe.

870 — Lothair left the land of Lotharingia (Greater Lorraine) to a son (Lothair II) who died without a legitimate heir. By the Treaty of Meersen, Charles received western Lorraine and Louis the German saw great expansion of his territories west of the Rhine. The region today known as Alsace remained separate from the rest of the French kingdom for the next seven centuries.

911 — Louis IV died, the last of the east **Frankish Carolingians**. The many dukes controlling the feudal states in the region elected Conrad, duke of Franconia, as successor; he was followed by Henry (918) and thus began more than a century of **Saxon** rule in the region.

959 — Lotharingia was divided into two parts: Upper Lorraine (Ardennes, Moselle Valley, Upper Meuse Valley) and Lower Lorraine (northern part of the realm, including parts of modern Belgium and the Netherlands).

late 9C and 10C — Raids by Northmen destabilised Charles' reign; power struggles continued as rival dynasties emerged and the feudal system took hold of the people. In France, the Carolingian dynasty waned.

THE MIDDLE AGES

987 — Hugues Capet was crowned, the first of 13 French kings in the **Capetian** dynasty, which lasted until 1328.

11C — The domains of Tardenois, Château-Thierry, Provins, Reims, Châlons and Troyes, through marriage agreements, came under the authority of the counts of Blois (the king's immediate vassals, but also his most dangerous rivals).

1098 — Robert de Molesmes founded the abbey at Cîteaux.

25 June 1115 — Clairvaux Abbey was founded by St Bernard.

1125-52 — Thibaud II, count of Blois, strengthened the economy by creating sound currency and cashing in on trade between Italy and the Netherlands. Communication routes improved, many trade fairs (Lagny, Provins, Sézanne, Troyes, Bar-sur-Aube) were the meeting place for Nordic and Mediterranean merchants.

1015 — On the site of a temple to Hercules, a Romanesque cathedral was begun in Strasbourg. St Bernard said Mass there in 1145, before it was destroyed by fire.

1152 — French King Louis VII repudiated Eleanor of Aquitaine, who later married Henry Plantagenet, bringing western France under the English crown. For three centuries, the French and English remained "hereditary enemies."

1176 — The new cathedral at Strasbourg was begun, inspired by the Gothic style.

1179-1223 — Philippe Auguste reigned as the "king of France" rather than the "king of the Franks."

1210 — Construction started on the cathedral at Reims.

1284 — The brilliant court and unified counties of Champagne joined the French crown with the marriage of Jeanne, Countess of Champagne and Navarre, to Philippe le Bel.

1337 — Beginning of the Hundred Years War.

14C — In Alsace, 10 cities formed the Decapole, to resist the excesses of the feudal system; gradually these cities (Strasbourg, Colmar, Haguenau, and others) freed themselves from their overlords.

1429 — Joan of Arc, aged 17, led the French armies to victory over the English at Orléans, thus opening the way for the coronation of Charles VII at Reims.

1434 — **Gutenberg** settled in Strasbourg and formed a partnership with three local men for the development of a secret invention. Their association ended acrimoniously in a court of law; in 1448, in Mainz, his printing press saw the light of day.

1480 — The Upper Duchy of Lorraine (Lower Lorraine was no longer a unified duchy) united with Bar and Vaudémont, and became known simply as Lorraine.

THE RENAISSANCE

Late 15C — After a century of strife in Champagne, trade flourished anew during the reign of Louis XI.

1507 — In St-Dié, the *Cosmographiae Introductio*, a work by several scholars, first gave the name America to the continent discovered by Christopher Columbus, in honour of the navigator Amerigo Vespucci.

1515-59 — Uprisings against the house of Austria in Mézières, Ste-Menehould, St-Dizier and Vitry.

1525 — The revolt of peasants *(Rustauds)* ended with their massacre in the town of Saverne.

1562 — The massacre at Wassy signalled the beginning of the Wars of Religion in Champagne, which devastated the region for the following century.

THE UNIFICATION OF LORRAINE AND ALSACE WITH FRANCE

1552-53 — Henri II occupied Metz, Toul and Verdun, defeating Charles V.

1572 — The St Bartholomew's Day massacre undermined the power of Protestants in the regions of Champagne and Ardenne.

1635-37 — An outbreak of plague in Lorraine killed half of the population; the Thirty Years War, plague and famine ravaged the entire region.

1648-53 — The period was marked by serious unrest caused by the far-reaching peasant revolt known as *La Fronde*, and persistent Spanish offensives in Champagne.

1678 — The Nijmegen peace agreement confirmed the unification of Alsace and France.

1681 — Louis XIV revoked the independence of Strasbourg.

1738 — **Stanislas Leszczynski**, former king of Poland, father-in-law of Louis XV, was named duke of Lorraine.

1766 — After the death of Stanislas, Lorraine was definitively annexed by France.

REVOLUTION AND THE TRANSFORMATION OF EUROPE

1785 — Napoleon Bonaparte became an officer of the French army.

1789 — The French Revolution toppled the king, proclaimed the rights of man and destroyed the Ancien Régime.

1791 — Louis XVI and his family were arrested in Varennes-en-Argonne.

1792 — Rouget de Lisle sang the *Marseillaise*, the future French national anthem, in Strasbourg.

1794 — Near Saverne, Chappe's telegraph began operation.

1798 — Mulhouse, the last independent town in Alsace, united with France.

1799 — Napoleon instituted a military dictatorship and named himself First Consul.

1804-15 — Napoleon had himself crowned emperor after victories in Austria and Russia, and successfully consolidated most of Europe as his empire until about 1810. The revived Allied coalition and his defeat at Waterloo led to his final exile.

1814-15 — The Congress of Vienna reorganised Europe after the Napoleonic Wars. It began in September 1814, 5 months after Napoleon's first abdication, and completed its "Final Act" just before Waterloo and the end of the Hundred Days of his return to power.

1815-71 — France was ruled by a limited monarchy, with the exception of a brief republican period (1848-52).

1870-71 — At the end of the Franco-Prussian War, Alsace and part of Lorraine were in German hands.

1885 — Pasteur administered the first rabies vaccine to a young Alsatian shepherd.

1906 — Captain Dreyfus, a native of Mulhouse, was reinstated and

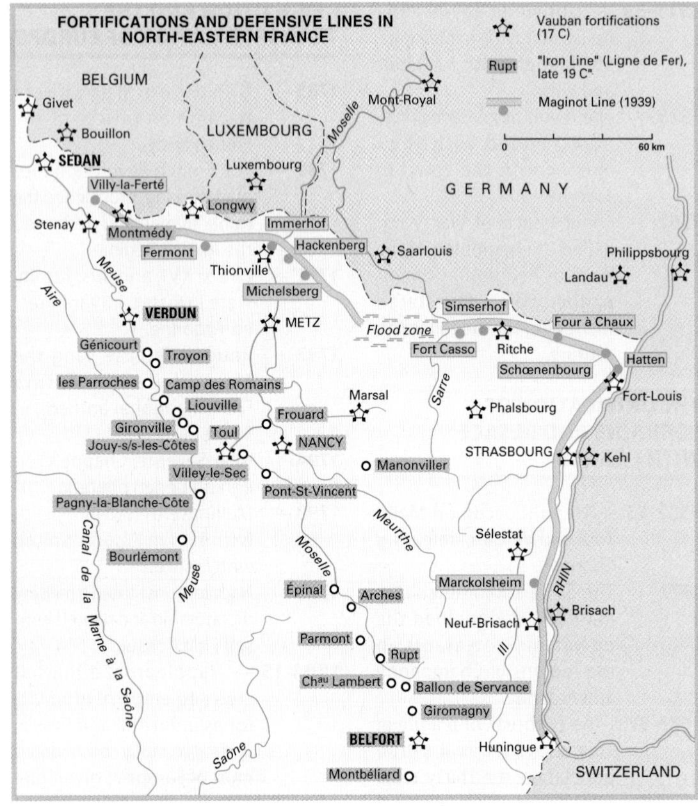

decorated with the Legion of Honour, the conclusion of the scandalous "affair" of 1894.

THE WORLD AT WAR

1914-18 — The violent conflicts of the First World War lasted four years; at the end, Alsace and Lorraine were once again in French territory.

1928 — Construction of the Grand Canal of Alsace.

1930-40 — Construction of the Maginot Line.

1940-44 — Germany invaded France; Alsace and Lorraine occupied.

Late 1944 — Lorraine liberated by French and Allied armies.

1945 — Final German retreat from Alsace, Armistice signed in Reims.

1949 — The Council of Europe established headquarters in Strasbourg.

1952 — Dr Albert Schweitzer, of Kaysersberg was awarded the Nobel Peace Prize.

1963 — Canalisation of the River Moselle.

1962—99 — The decline of the area's traditional heavy industries, notably Mines and metalworks meant some 178 000 workers left the region to find employment elsewhere.

1974 — Works were completed on the Rhine in Alsace, with the inauguration of the hydroelectric plant at Gambsheim.

1976 — Paris-Metz-Strasbourg motorway opened.

1977 — The Palais de l'Europe (European Economic Community) buildings were inaugurated in Strasbourg.

1991 — Creation of ARTE *(Association Relative à la Télévision Européenne)*, a joint Franco-German TV station based in Strasbourg.

1993 — Strasbourg confirmed as the seat of the European Parliament.

1995-96 — Nuclear power plant Chooz B begins operating on the Meuse.

1999 — Total solar eclipse observed in Reims.
1 500th anniversary of the baptism of Clovis.
The striking New European Union Parliament Louise Weiss building opens in Strasbourg.

2001 — Provins, Town of Medieval Fairs, is placed on the UNESCO World Heritage List.

2004 — Closure of potassium mines with loss of 2 000 jobs.

2007 — The new high-speed TGV Est Européen train service (operating at a maximum speed of 320 kph) cuts train times between Strasbourg and Paris from 4 hrs to 2 hr 20 mins. As train speeds increase further the journey time will be less than 2 hrs.

The Franco-Prussian War

From July 1870 to May 1871, the war also known as the Franco-German War came to mark the end of French hegemony on the continent and formed the basis for the Prussian Empire.

Napoleon III's ambitious plans appeared to Prussian chancellor Otto von Bismark as an opportunity to unite northern and southern German states in a confederation against the French. Within four weeks, French troops had been effectively bottled up in the fortress at Metz. The rest of the army, under Marshal Mac-Mahon and accompanied by Napoleon, was surrounded and trapped at Sedan on 31 August. By 2 September, they had surrendered.

French resistance fought the desperate odds under a new government of national defence, which had assumed power and deposed the emperor on 4 September 1870, establishing the Third Republic. With Paris under siege, negotiations were stalled while Bismarck demanded Alsace and Lorraine. Léon Gambetta, a provisional government leader, organised new armies after escaping from Paris in a balloon. Despite their valiant efforts, and the Paris insurrection which declared the independence of the **Commune de Paris**, capitulation was at hand. The Treaty of Frankfurt was signed on 10 May 1871: Germany annexed all of Alsace and most of Lorraine, with Metz; France had to pay a heavy indemnity. Thus French influence on German states came to a halt and the Prussian domination of Germany was ensured. For the next 40 years, until the First World War, an uneasy peace held sway as further consequences were felt: the papacy lost power and Italian troops entered Rome; the Russian government repudiated the Treaty of Paris and began an aggressive campaign in Eastern Europe.

The First World War (1914-18)

The Germans planned a six-week campaign to conquer France by way of an invasion of Belgium and a northern attack, bypassing France's solidly defended eastern flank. Once victory in France had been achieved, the plan called for transporting German troops to the Russian front, where the northern giant would be beaten in a few short months.

AUGUST-SEPTEMBER 1914

French troops crossed the border on 7 August and entered Mulhouse the following day, but had to withdraw to Belfort under the enemy's counter-attack. On 19 August, after grim combat, Mulhouse was captured anew and the Germans retreated towards the Rhine. Preparing an offensive, the French took

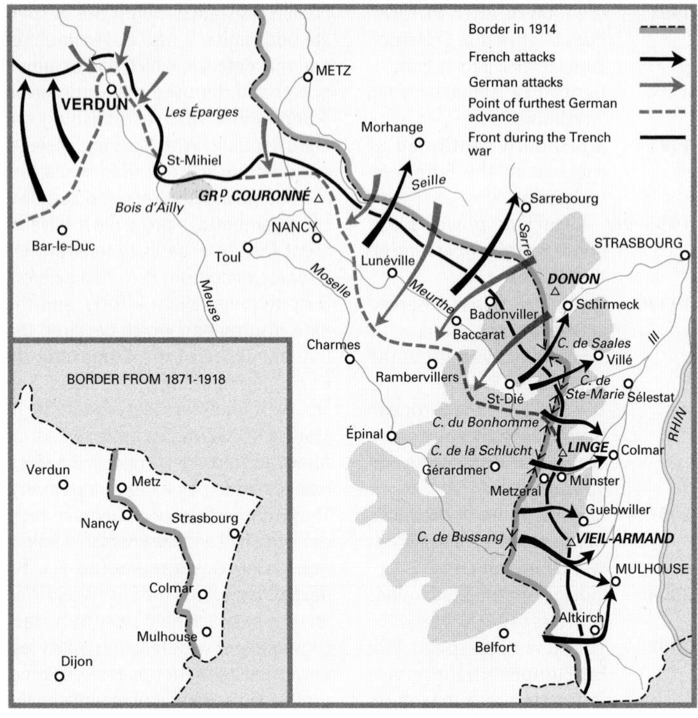

control of mountain passes in the Vosges. Meanwhile, on 14 August, the First and Second French Armies had penetrated occupied Lorraine. An assault launched on 20 August was met with such a violence of firepower that the French troops were decimated, and forced to pull back to the Meurthe. The defensive line between Badonviller and Nancy formed a funnel shape, with the town of Charmes at the narrow end. The Germans took advantage of this position to attack Charmes, but met with resistance. From 26 August to 9 September they brought their force to bear on the eastern front, the line of the Vosges towards upper Meurthe and on to Nancy. Yet German commander **Moltke** spread his infantry too thin, and hesitation cost him the **Battle of the Marne** (5-10 September 1914) along with his military command. Marshal **Von Kluck** pushed the German troops towards the Seine. For the French, **Joffre** and **Gallieni** attempted a bold attack on the German's right flank. Four thousand reinforcement troops were carried to the front in the famous **Marne taxis**. British soldiers were able to drive into the opening thus created in the German line, forcing a retreat as far as the Aisne Valley. A terrible war of attrition settled in along the front from the Jura mountains to the North Sea, through the heart of Alsace and Lorraine.

TRENCH WARFARE (1915-18)

After the Battle of the Marne the German position stabilised along the pre-war border in Lorraine, the Vosges and Alsace. Fierce localised combat pitted the armies against each other as they strove to take and hold strategic positions (Les Éparges, Ailly woods, Le Linge, Le Vieil-Armand). In February 1916, the Germans concentrated their efforts on Verdun; the stakes were high as the site became a giant battlefield which was to determine the outcome of the war.
The **Second Battle of the Marne** began with a German incursion in June 1918; Foch led the French forces in powerful resistance. Under pressure from all sides,

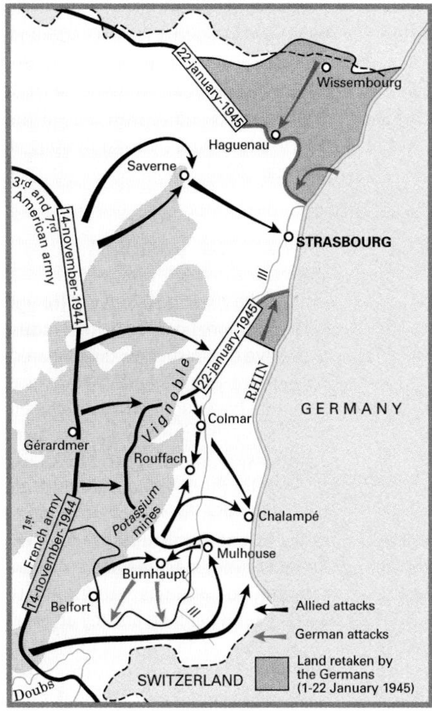

the Germans fell back to the so-called Hindenburg Line. On 26 September of the same year, Marshal **Foch** launched a general offensive which finally brought about German defeat and the Armistice of 11 November 1918, executed at Rethondes.

The Second World War (1939-45)

The Second World War was in ways a continuation of the disputes left unresolved at the end of the First World War. France expected that if another war occurred, it would resemble the last one, and so built up a continuous defensive front, the Maginot Line, which also responded to the very low demographics of the eastern regions of France after the first war. This siege mentality, coupled with the old guard's refusal to modernise offensive and defensive weapons or to develop new strategies, proved poor preparation for the onslaught to come.

In May 1940, a German offensive drove the Dutch to surrender within days. Meanwhile, armoured units made their way through the supposedly impenetrable Ardennes Forest – simply bypassing the Maginot Line, France's illusory defence. By 20 May, the Germans had reached the coast. Not until D-Day, 6 June 1944 was the Norman peninsula wrested from German occupation by American, British and Canadian troops.

As the Allies advanced to liberate France however, on December 16, 1944 the Germans launched the **Ardennes Offensive**, better known as the **Battle of the Bulge**. Their plan was to split the British and American lines (causing a bulge on the battle map, which gave the popular title) then encircle and destroy them. During one of the coldest snowiest winters the area had known this came to be one of the fiecest battles of the war, fought between half a million Germans, 600 000 US troops and around 55 000 British. It was one of the greatest tank battles ever with each side losing around 800 machines. By the time it finished a month later on January 15 1945, with victory for the Allied Forces, there were 100,000 German casualties (killed, wounded or captured), and 81,000 American casualties, including 23,554 captured and 19,000 killed — the bloodiest campaign the USA had ever fought up to that point. The Battle of the Bulge was also renowned for its brutality, culminating in the **Malmedy Massacre**, when around 86 American soldiers were murdered — the worst atrocity committed against American troops during the war in Europe.

With the last major Axis offensive overcome the Allied armies raced eastward and northward: Paris was liberated on 25 August; Verdun at the end of the month. Nancy and Épinal followed in mid Sep-

tember. The fierce German defence did not yield in Metz until 22 November.
On 1 January 1945, the Germans rallied and re-occupied Strasbourg. Eventually the Wehrmacht was forced over the last bridge still under its control, at Chalampé, on 9 February.
German capitulation was marked by the signature of the Armistice at Reims on 7 May 1945.

European Peace and Unification

On 9 May 1950 Robert Schuman (a former French foreign minister, born in Alsace-Lorraine) proposed the idea of the European Coal and Steel Community (ECSC). Schuman's declaration was inspired by Jean Monnet's idea of "building Europe" step by step. Six States laid the foundations: Belgium, France, Germany, Italy, Luxembourg and The Netherlands. By 1993, the Member States numbered 12, and the Treaty on European Union came into force.
The **European Union**, founded to promote peace and economic stability, freedom of movement, and a unified approach to problems of security, defence, and social welfare, operates through Parliament, which meets in **Strasbourg**, but also other bodies: the Commission makes proposals for European legislation and action; the Council of the European Union is made up of one minister for each Member State government and for each subject; the European Council decides broad policy lines for Community policy and for matters of foreign and security policy and justice; the Court of Justice is the supreme court of the European Union.
Among the main aims of the Union, the goal of a single European currency is becoming a reality in many countries. The euro is now the currency used by banking and financial institutions in most EU nations, and entirely replaced French francs, along with the currencies of other participating nations, in the year 2002.

Diversification

See also The Region Today. Although their traditional coal and steel industries have diminished or disappeared, both Alsace-Lorraine and Champagne-Ardennes have successfully diversified, so much so that the former is the third wealthiest region in France. In Alsace, agriculture (high-value crops include hops and tobacco), cars (PSA Peugeot-Citroen), chemicals (Rhône-Poulenc) metal casting, machine and tool construction, oil and gas refining, boat-building and banking are key areas, as well as tourism. In Lorraine interesting vestiges of traditional industries that have survived include glass-making at Baccarat, violin-making at Mirecourt, and high quality ceramics at Longwy, Lunéville and Sarreguemines.
Champagne-Ardennes meanwhile has retained its metallurgic and textile industries. Lacoste shirts, for example, are made in Troyes, and in the Nogent Basin some 2 000 workers are employed producing fine cutlery, surgical instruments and tools. The area has long been famous for its gastronomy and wine production, and tourism is now a vital part of the economy with much of it based around the famous eponymous sparkling wine — rare is the trip made to Champagne without at least one visit to its world-famous *caves*.

ART AND CULTURE

ABC of Architecture

Religious architecture

I. Ground plan of a church

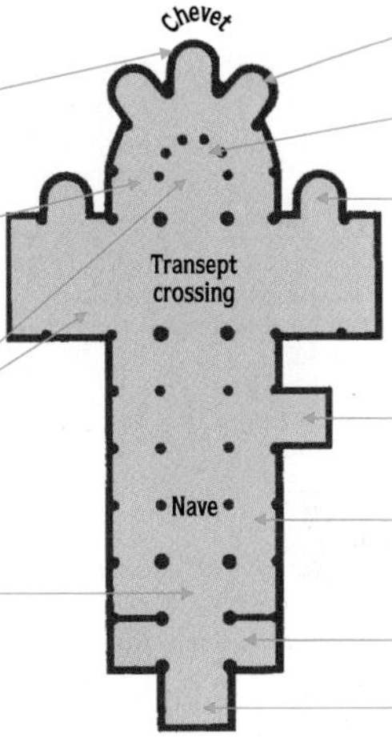

Axial chapel: in churches which are not dedicated to the Virgin this chapel, in the main axis of the building, is often consecrated to the Virgin (Lady Chapel)
Ambulatory: in pilgrimage churches the aisles were extended round the chancel, forming the ambulatory, to allow the faithful to file past the relics
Chancel, nearly always facing east towards Jerusalem
Arm of the transept, often extending outward
Bay: transverse section of the nave between two pillars
Chevet
Transept crossing
Nave
Radiating or apsidal chapel
Sanctuary
Transept chapel
Side chapel
Side aisles
Narthex
Porch

II. Cross-section of a church

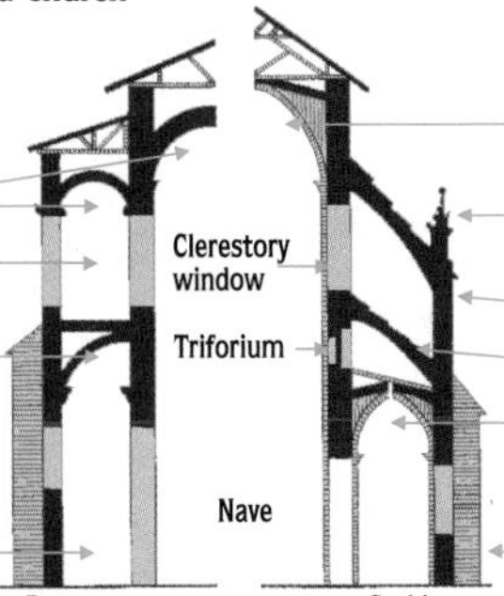

Barrel vault
Tribune or gallery
Half-barrel vault
Aisle
Clerestory window
Triforium
Nave
Romanesque
Gothic
Pointed vault
Pinnacle
Pier of a flying buttress
Flying buttress
Pointed vault
Buttress

III. MÉZIÈRES – Notre-Dame-de-l'Espérance Basilica (15 C)

Keystone pendentive: characteristic of late or Flamboyant Gothic period, embellishments, added in the Renaissance
Lierne: a short, intermediate rib
Tierceron: an intermediate rib between the main ribs
Diagonal rib
Transverse arch: reinforcing arch under a vault
Transverse rib
R. Corbel

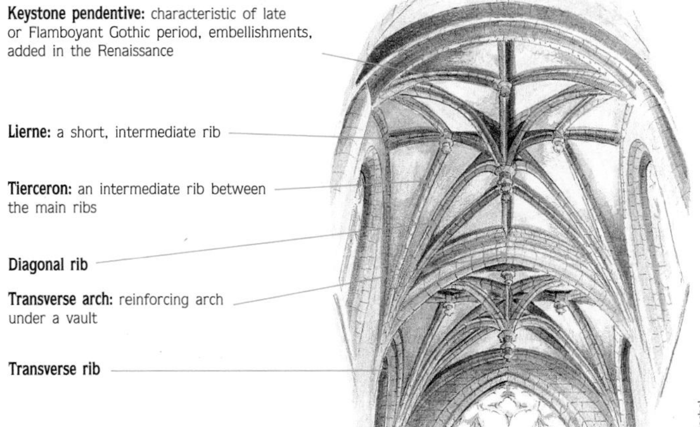

IV. MARMOUTIER – Romanesque façade of St-Étienne (*c*1140)

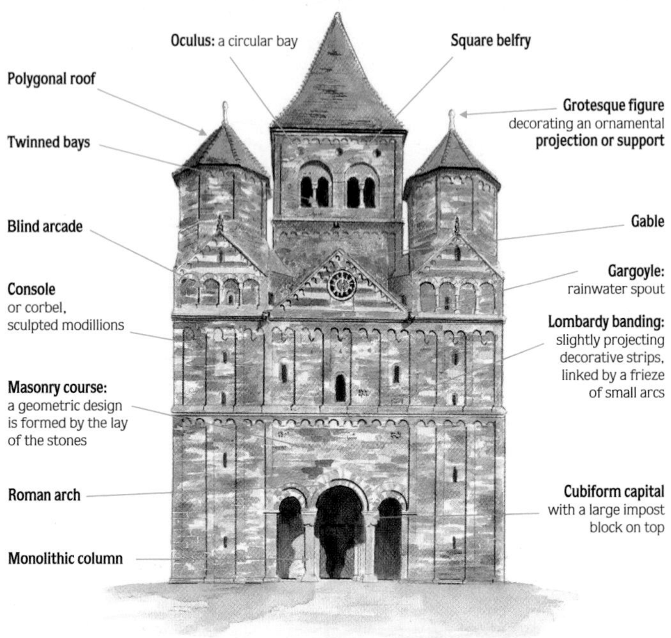

V. REIMS – Chevet of the cathedral (1211-1260)

The cathedral in Reims can be compared to Chartres. Both are great works of Gothic architecture, which reached an apogee in Champagne and the Ile-de-France region between the late 12C and mid-13C.

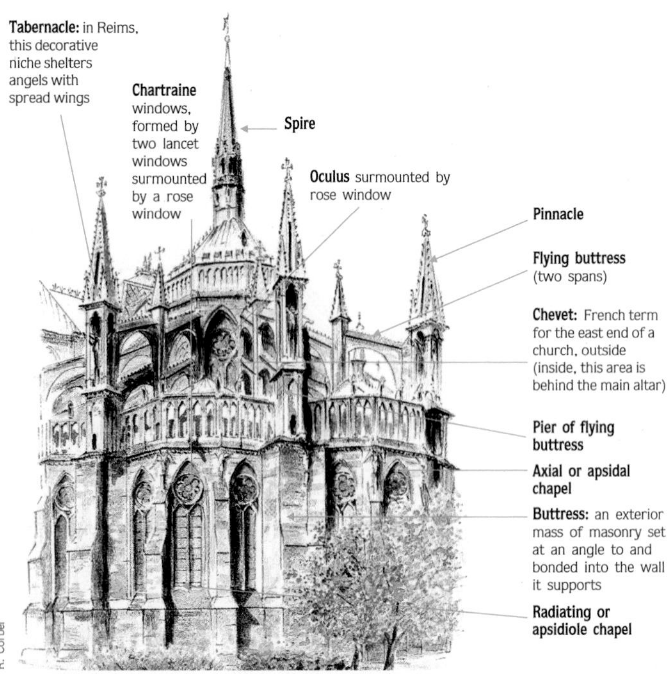

VI. Strasbourg – Central façade of Notre-Dame cathedral (12-15C)

The abundant detail of Flamboyant Gothic is evident in the central doorway, richly sculpted and crowned with openwork gables.

VII. MOUZON – Interior of the Abbey church (1195-c1240)

The elevation of the nave embraces four storeys (arcades, gallery, Triforium, clerestory windows), typical of primitive Gothic art (second half of the 12C).

Sexpartite vault, ribbed vault whose lateral triangles are bisected by an intermediate transverse rib producing six triangles within a bay

Clerestory window

Trefoil arch

Blind Triforium: series of simulated openings between the large arcades and the clerestory windows

Corner piece: between the arch and its frame

Engaged column, partly embedded in or bonded to the wall

Crocket capital

Shaft of a column: between the base and the capital

Tribune: upper gallery where small groups can convene

Nave

Keystone

Cell or **Quarter** segment or part of the vault defined by the groins (1) or ribs (2)

Transverse arch

Apse: the eastern end of a church behind the main altar (interior). Compare to chevet

Canopy

Chancel

Main arcade: separates the nave from the aisles

VIII. THANN – Choir stalls in St-Thiébaut (14C-early 16C)

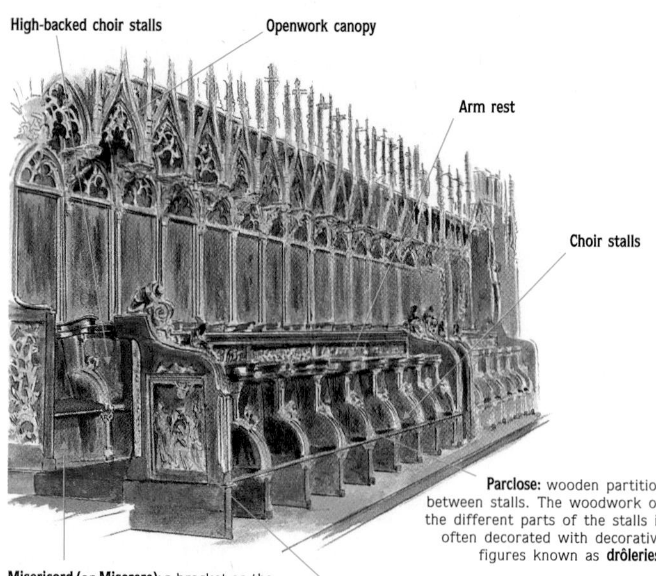

R. Corbel

Civil architecture

IX. SAVERNE – Katz House (1605-1668), no 76, Grand'Rue

Half-timbered houses, numerous in Alsace, illustrate the skill of local carpenters, especially between the 17-19C.

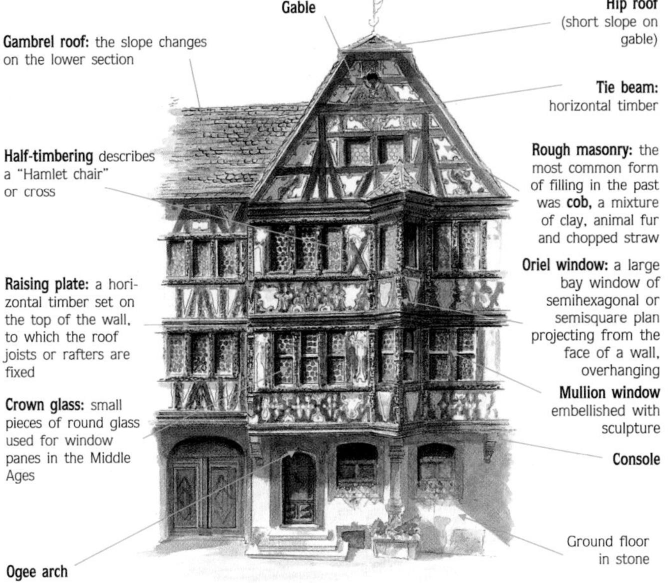

X. LUNÉVILLE – Château (18C)

Also known as "Petit-Versailles", this château was designed by the architect Germain Boffrand.

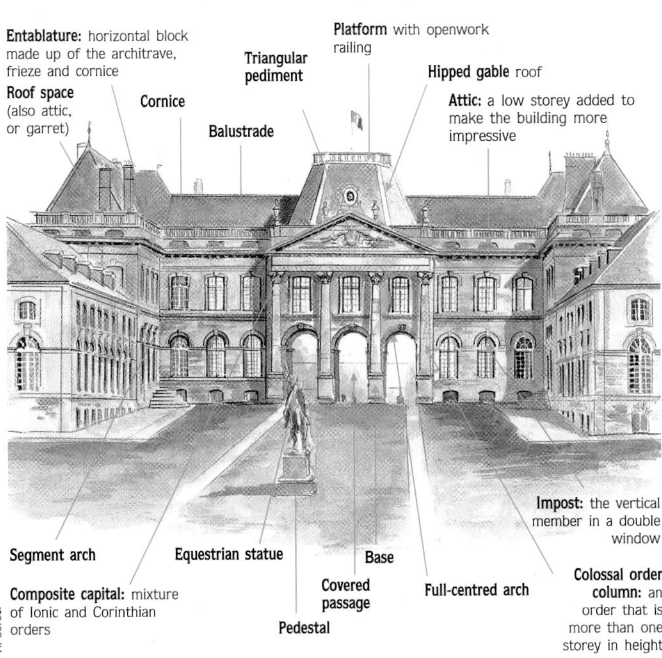

R. Corbel

XI. CONTREXÉVILLE – Thermal springs gallery and pavilion

The design expresses the architectural eclecticism typical of spa town; neo-Byzantine style predominates.

Drum embellished with decorative brick designs
Cupola: metal frame is pierced to let light in
Doric capitals
Concentric peristyle
Circular pavilion above the spring
Large **bay windows**
Gallery-portico
Fluted columns with mosaic embellishments

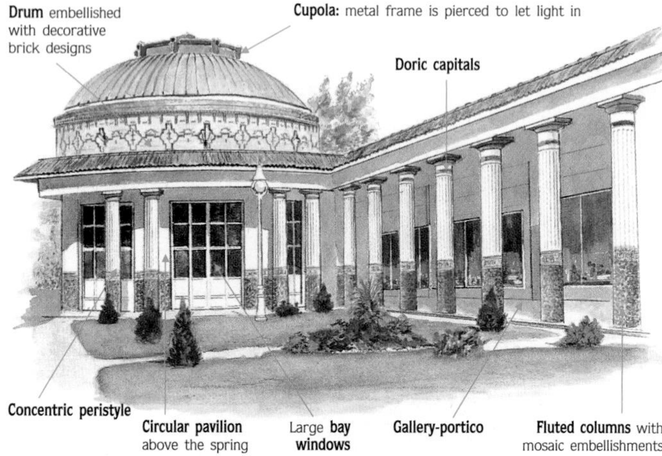

Military architecture

XII. HAUT-KOENIGSBOURG – Feudal castle rebuilt in the early 20C

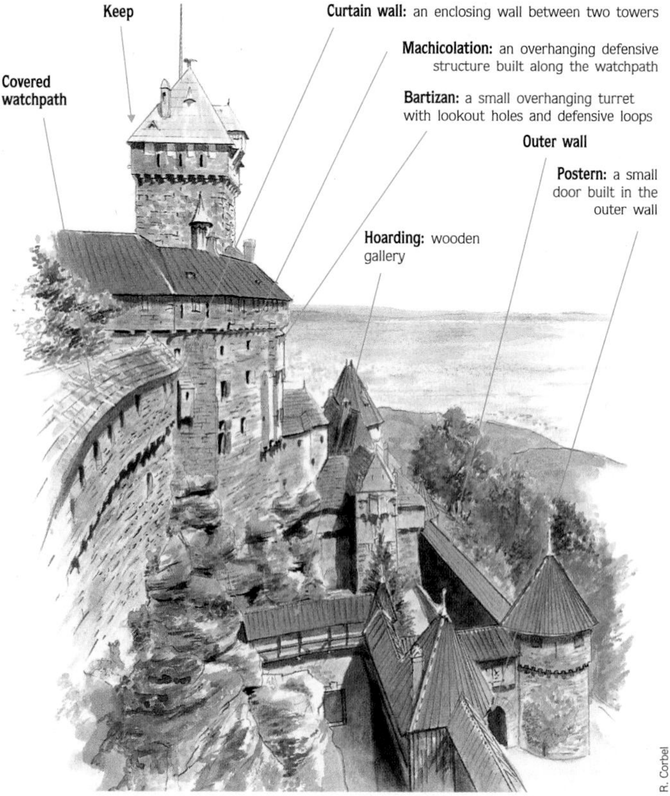

Keep
Curtain wall: an enclosing wall between two towers
Machicolation: an overhanging defensive structure built along the watchpath
Covered watchpath
Bartizan: a small overhanging turret with lookout holes and defensive loops
Outer wall
Postern: a small door built in the outer wall
Hoarding: wooden gallery
R. Corbel

XIII. NEUF-BRISACH – Stronghold (1698-1703)

The polygonal stronghold was developed in the early 16C, as firearms became more common in warfare: the cannon mounted on one structure covered the "blind spot" of the neighbouring position. This stronghold was built by Vauban, opposite the formidable Breisach, handed back to the Hapsburgs under the Treaty of Ryswick (1697).

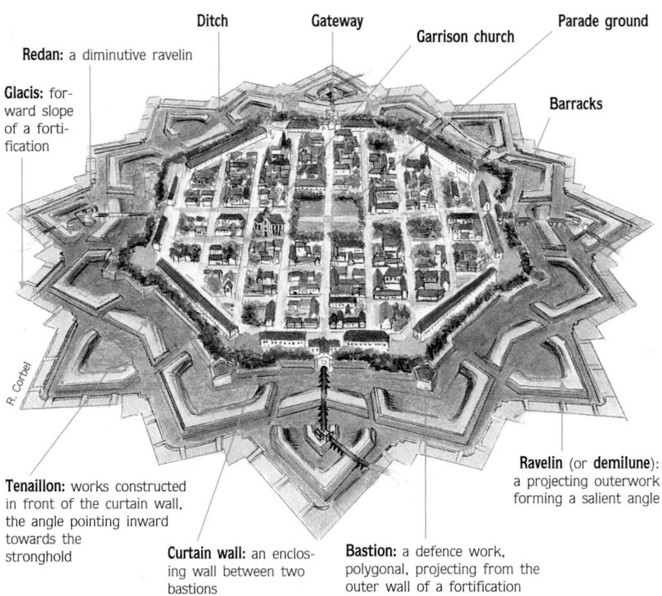

Other architectural terms used in this guide

Ashlar Hewn masonry or squared stones lain in regular courses, as distinguished from rubble work.

Bailey Space enclosed by the outer walls of a castle (also: *ward*).

Barbican Outwork of a medieval castle, often with a tower, defending a gate or bridge.

Bartizan An overhanging battlemented corner turret, corbelled out; sometimes as grandiose as an overhanging gallery (illustration XII).

Battlements Parapet of medieval fortifications, with a walkway for archers, protected by merlons, with embrasures between them.

Buttress Vertical mass of masonry built against a wall, so strengthening it and resisting the pressure of a vaulted roof (illustration II).

Clerestory Upper stage of an elevation, consisting of a range of tall windows (illustration VII).

Crenellation The low segment of the alternating high and low segments of a battlement.

Donjon French term for the castle *keep* (illustration XII).

Glacis A bank sloping down from a castle which acts as a defence against invaders; broad, sloping naked rock or earth on which the attackers are completely exposed (illustration XIII).

Machicolation In medieval castles, a row of openings below the projecting parapet though which missiles could be rained down upon the enemy.

Merlon The high segment of the alternating high and low segments of a battlement.

Portcullis A heavy timber or metal grill that protected the castle entrance and could be raised or lowered from within to block passage or to trap attackers.

Postern Gate A side or less important gate into a castle; usually for peacetime use by pedestrians (illustration XII).

Rustication Worked ashlar stone with beveled edges defining conspicuous joints.

Wicket Person-sized door set into the main gate door.

Architecture in Alsace

RELIGIOUS ARCHITECTURE

Romanesque churches

In Alsace, Carolingian influences persisted longer than elsewhere in France; the flowering of Romanesque art took place in the 12C, lagging a century behind the rest of the country.

Exterior

Most of the churches in Alsace are small or modest, and laid out in the form of a Latin cross with short lateral arms. The 11C church at Ottmarsheim still shows the Carolingian polygonal ground plan, inspired by the Palatine chapel in Aix-la-Chapelle (Aachen).

Among the distinctive local features, **tours lanternes** (lantern towers) are found above the transept crossing (Ste-Foy in Sélestat is a good example). **Belfries**, both square and round, often rise from the angle made by the main body of the church (chancel and nave) and the transept crossing. The western façade, with or without a porch, is flanked by belfries several storeys high.

The east end culminates in a semicircular apse; flattened chevets (Murbach) are the exception. The side walls, gables, apse and façade are embellished with Lombardy banding, slightly projecting decorative strips linked by a frieze of small arcs.

Interior

The architecture is ascetic; arcading and bays without decorative moulding are surmounted by a wall, with one or two windows that flare open wider on the inside. The chancel is not ringed by an ambulatory. Vaulting was not used until late in the 12C.

The main supports are Romanesque arches that shape the ribbed vault. They rest on thick rectangular pillars flanked on four sides by engaged columns. The side aisles are covered with groined vaulting formed by the intersection of the long vault of the side aisle and the transverse vaults.

Decoration

The spare decoration is mostly found on doorways, in plain geometric patterns; only the church at Andlau has any interesting sculptures.

The **capitals**, the wide upper portion of columns supporting arches, are an important part of the architectural style. Ribs from more than one vault can rest on a single pillar. In Alsace, the Romanesque churches usually have very simple, cubic capitals, with little variety of sculpted forms – a few rare figures and some foliage.

Gothic churches

Gothic art in Alsace reached a rare degree of perfection: the cathedral in **Strasbourg** is proof enough. Many Gothic buildings, civil and religious, went up between the 13C and the 14C: in **Colmar**, the Unterlinden cloisters, St-Martin Church, the Koifhus (Customs House); in Wissembourg, St-Pierre-St-Paul; St-George in Sélestat, to name a few.

At the end of the 15C, Flamboyant Gothic appeared on the scene in **Thann** (St-Thiébaut) and Strasbourg (St-Laurent doorway on the cathedral).

During the 16C, while the Renaissance was influencing civil architecture, religious buildings remained true to the Gothic spirit. The churches in **Ammer-**

R. Mattès/MICHELIN

Flamboyant Gothic doorway, Avioth basilica

schwihr (16C) and **Molsheim** (16C-17C) reflect this well.
Traces of the **Renaissance** are more evident in charming private residences and admirable public buildings.

Classical style

In the 17C, a long period of trials and warfare halted nearly all construction of new civil and religious buildings. Under French authority, Alsace rebuilt and embellished monasteries. Yet there are a few churches dating from this time, including St-Pierre in **Colmar** (Regency style), and Notre-Dame in **Guebwiller**, built by the abbots of Murbach on a strict Classical design.
Baroque influences are apparent in the abbey church at **Ebersmunster**, lavishly decorated with sculptures, mouldings and frescoes.

R. Mattès/MICHELIN

Place Kléber, Strasbourg

CIVIL ARCHITECTURE

Town halls

As early as the Middle Ages, Alsatian towns sought a degree of independence. Town halls were built to serve the municipal authorities, a symbol of power and an illustration of architectural preferences of the times.
The lovely town halls in **Ensisheim, Mulhouse** (the covered porch was inspired by Swiss buildings), **Obernai, Rouffach, Kaysersberg, Molsheim** and **Guebwiller** as well as the old town hall of Strasbourg (today the Chamber of Commerce), testify to the intensity of local politics.

Bourgeois and princely manors

Picturesque places like **Riquewhir, Kaysersberg**, the Petite France district of **Strasbourg** and Petite Venise in **Colmar** have a rich architectural heritage of traditional 16C-17C private residences. Overhanging elements mark the façade, and the upper storeys culminate in sharp points; both stone and wood are used as building materials.
During the Renaissance, many amusing details were added: fancy gables, wooden galleries around towers, wrought-iron work, sculpted or painted wooden panelling on the façade. The two most distinctive features of Alsatian manors built in the 15C and during the Renaissance are the gables and the oriel windows.
Gables perch ornately atop buildings. In Strasbourg, the Maison de l'Œuvre Notre-Dame is topped with a gable mounting squarely upwards like a set of stairs; in Colmar, curling scrolls adorn the sloping sides of the gable on the Maison des Têtes.

Oriel windows

These large bay windows with semi-hexagonal or semi-square plans project from the façade, creating an overhang, as on the Maison des Têtes. The oriel window provides a break in the uniformity of a façade and creates a lively play of light and shadow. For a building located on a narrow street, it can be a precious source of light, and a good vantage point for watching the comings and goings of the town. Prestigious residences built for the powerful lords, prelates and financiers in the 17C – once the devastating Thirty Years War was past and Alsace was in the hands of Louis XIV – and the 18C are distinguished by the increase in French influence on the banks of the Rhine. While 18C residences do not have the imaginative style of Renaissance houses, they are admirable for their graceful balconies, delicate corbels and elegant

R. Mattès/MICHELIN

Montmédy

bay windows, as well as the fine quality of stone.
The luxurious palaces of the Rohan family, in **Strasbourg** and **Saverne**, are splendid examples of Classical architecture.

MILITARY ARCHITECTURE

All along the Vosges hillsides, rising above the plain of Alsace, the vestiges of ancient fortresses and feudal keeps mark the horizon.
More recent vestiges also interest the visitor: magnificent ramparts built and renovated by Vauban; German defences put up between 1870 and 1914; concrete pillboxes and armoured towers from the above and below-ground works that made up the **Maginot Line**; numerous forts and blockhouses left from the Second World War.

Defensive castles

Sentinels in times of war, all of these castles have kept their proud bearing, even those that are little more than an isolated keep or a lone wall crumbling under moss. The reconstitution of the Haut-Kœnigsbourg Castle, by the order of Kaiser Wilhelm II, was controversial from the outset. Still today, some prefer the romantic reverie of ruins to the academic demonstration of a pristine reconstruction.

Medieval walled cities

In the Middle Ages, towns and cities built fortifications to defend themselves from both feudal lords and enemies from abroad. A city would build a ring of protective walls, with strategically located towers and just a few gateways that could be closed up and protected. These gateways still stand in many towns (Porte Haute), and towers (Tour du Diable, Tour des Sorcières) mark the line of the old fortified wall.

Architecture in Lorraine

RELIGIOUS ARCHITECTURE

Romanesque churches

The churches in Lorraine are mostly basilicas, often simplified to the extreme. The smaller churches have only a nave, a chancel and an apse. The doors are crowned with a semicircular tympanum, and the façades are sparsely decorated. Ribbed vaulting is common in Romanesque building; it was introduced in Lorraine in the last third of the 12C. Towers are generally square, and placed atop the square formed by the transept.
Among the most characteristic churches of this period, one is in Mont-Devant-Sassay; part of Notre-Dame de Verdun is also a good illustration of this style.

Gothic churches

Lorraine was slow moving from Romanesque to Gothic architecture.
In **Toul** and **Metz**, the cathedrals bear the marks of French influence. Indeed,

they were designed by masters who had already worked in Champagne and Île-de-France, the cradle of the French Gothic style.

The links between Lorraine and France were numerous at that time, and French predominance was felt in many fields: students from Lorraine travelled to the University of Paris; the famous trade fairs in Lorraine made it an economic centre; the dukes of Lorraine were well aware of the ambitious plans of the Capetian kings next door.

Other Gothic edifices worth citing: **Avioth**, where the great ambulatory of the church was frequented by pilgrims, St-Étienne in **St-Mihiel** and the basilica of **St-Nicolas-de-Port**, whose magnificent façade was completed in the 16C.

Renaissance

The most significant works from this period are the Chapelle des Évêques in the cathedral at **Toul** and the church at **St-Gengoult**.

CIVIL ARCHITECTURE

Renaissance

The monumental doorway of the old ducal palace at Nancy, so finely wrought, dates from the 16C. Few châteaux from the period are still standing, but those at **Louppy-sur-Loison, Cons-la-Grandville** and **Fléville** are worth seeing.

Classical architecture

The 18C was the heyday of this style. Although there was a pronounced taste for French styles, the traditional Italian influence remained present. Robert de Cotte designed the Château de la Grange and the Verdun bishopric in this style.

Germain Boffrand, a student of Jules Hardouin-Mansart, superintendent of buildings for the French king, drew the plans for Lunéville Château, the "Versailles of Lorraine," for the benefit of Duke Leopold. He also built the lovely Château d'Haroué. But the most impressive examples of Classical architecture are found together in the city of **Nancy**. When he was granted the duchy of Lorraine in 1737, former Polish king Stanislas Leszczynski undertook a plan to beautify his new capital. In particular, he called on Boffrand's disciple, **Emmanuel Héré**, and a metalwork craftsman from Nancy, **Jean Lamour**. Their work still shines on place Stanislas (on the UNESCO World Heritage List), the Arc de Triomphe and place de la Carrière. The ensemble constitutes one of the masterpieces of European urban architecture.

MILITARY ARCHITECTURE

Many defensive castles were erected in the Middle Ages. Today most have been reduced to ruins, or mere vestiges remain: Prény, Sierk, Tour aux Puces (Thionville), Châtel-sur-Moselle.

Few of the former fortified towns have kept all of their walls, exceptions being **Montmédy** and **Neuf-Brisach**. Often, it is only the gateways which have remained.

Architecture in Champagne-Ardenne

RELIGIOUS ARCHITECTURE

Romanesque churches

As in Lorraine, most of the works dating from the Carolingian period have disappeared. Of the many sanctuaries built in the 9C, only the chancel of the abbey at Isle-Aumont remains.

Architecture in the year 1000

A period of reconstruction followed the Norman and Hungarian invasions. The East Frankish Ottonian Empire (962-1002) had a strong influence on contemporary artistic style at the time.

Churches from the early 11C often look like big basilicas, with sturdy framework allowing for many openings to provide light; there are towers outside, and galleries and sometimes an ambulatory inside. The interior decoration is usually very simple, based on geometric patterns.

Three churches in Champagne illustrate this style: Notre-Dame in **Montier-en-Der** (rebuilt in 1940), St-Étienne in **Vignory** and St-Remi in **Reims**. St-Étienne is one of the most remarkable monuments in the region because it has

Ph. Gajic/MICHELIN

Reims Cathedral

changed so little over time. St-Remi, on the other hand, has been renovated many times, and yet the Romanesque elements are easily recognisable, in particular the sculpted capitals adorned with foliage and figures.

End of the 11C and 12C

The traditions of the year 1000 continued to grow through the 11C, while at the same time, Gothic influences from the neighbouring Île-de-France were making inroads. Romanesque architecture from this period is mainly represented by a few buildings around Reims and in the Ardenne. Covered porches are common, and because of this are often referred to as *porches champenois*. The Carolingian influence is apparent in the plain decorative effects: capitals and cornices are embellished with rows of geometric designs, palmettos, and notched patterns.

Romanesque traces in vestigial monastic buildings hint at the great beauty that must have been there: the cloisters of Notre-Dame-en-Vaux at **Châlons-en-Champagne**, the doorway of St-Ayoul in **Provins**, and the chapter house in St-Remi in **Reims**.

The birth of Gothic

Gothic art originated in the Île-de-France in the 12C and quickly spread to the Champagne region, where manpower and financing made construction possible. The primitive Gothic style has echoes of the Romanesque: the use of embellished decoration was restrained and structures remained simple. Experimentation was taking place, too, with the building of the abbey church at **Mouzon**, Notre-Dame-en-Vaux in **Châlons-en-Champagne**, St-Quiriace in **Provins**, and the abbey church at **Orbais**, where the architect Jean Orbais designed a remarkable chancel that served as a model for Reims Cathedral. The chancels of Notre-Dame in **Montier-en-Der** and St-Remi in **Reims,** which date from the origins of Gothic art, have a distinctive feature: columns stand in the ambulatory at the entrance to the side chapels, and support ribs of both chapel and ambulatory vaults, forming an elegant and airy colonnade.

The apogee of Gothic art

The golden age of the great cathedrals was the **13C** and **14C**; brilliantly lit by vast bays and vivid rose windows, they are covered in delicately carved sculptures.

When the cathedral at **Reims** was built, architects were already seeking to lighten the walls and interiors with immense bays: St-Amand-sur-Fion, the cathedrals at Châlons and **Troyes** and in particular St-Urbain show the accomplished fruits of their labours.

Decline

Gothic architecture then moved into its Flamboyant period (15C-16C), just before it began to wane. The over-abundance of decorative elements tended to mask the essential lines of the buildings. In the Champagne region, the basilica of Notre-Dame de l'Épine is the best example.

The Renaissance (16C)

Most of the architectural achievements of the Renaissance concern civil construction, but a few churches which were enlarged or renovated are worth mentioning: St-André-les-Vergers, Pont-Ste-Marie, Les Riceys, Auxon and Bérulle. Many beautiful windows and statues were produced in Troyes during this period.

CIVIL ARCHITECTURE

Gallo-Roman vestiges

Although not many major monuments are still intact, there are some very interesting vestiges. In **Reims**, remains of the ancient urban settlement include a triumphant arch, the Porte Mars, and a cryptoporticus; in **Langres**, a gateway stands. In **Andilly-en-Bassigny**, archaeological research has uncovered a villa complete with its baths. Museums in Troyes, Reims, Nogent-sur-Seine and Langres have extensive collections.

The Renaissance

Italian influence brought about a major change in style, notable for a renewed interest in forms from ancient civilisation: columns and superimposed galleries lend grandeur to monuments of the period. Niches, statues and medallions are set into the façades; pilasters frame the bays (**Joinville Château** and Renaissance manors in **Troyes** and **Reims**).

Classical architecture

In the Ardennes region this style is best represented by the masterpiece in the Henri IV-Louis XIII style, place Ducale in **Charleville**. There are many similarities with the famous place des Vosges in Paris.

In the 18C, the construction of large urban squares on the Classical model was popular in France. In Paris, place Louis-XV (now place de la Concorde) inspired similar works in **Reims** (place Royale) and **Châlons-en-Champagne**, where the town hall is further evidence of the Parisian influence.

MILITARY ARCHITECTURE

Located on the French border, the Ardennes still boasts a few fortifications, including the impressive château of Sedan, the largest in Europe, which was built between the 15C and the 18C. There are fortified churches in the Thiérache region, dating from the 16C and 17C; a few traditional fortifications erected by Vauban; the **Villy-la-Ferté** fort was part of the Maginot Line.

Most **fortified churches** were built up at the end of the 16C and early 17C to serve as refuges. The region, neighbouring both The Netherlands under Spanish rule and the Prussian Empire was rocked by incessant warfare.

Vauban

Sébastien le Prestre de Vauban (1633-1707) took inspiration from his predecessors, and in particular from **Jean Errard** (1554-1610) of Bar-le-Duc, who published a treatise on fortifications in 1600. Able to learn his lessons from the many wars of siege that occurred in his century, Vauban promoted fortifications in the countryside. Vauban's system is characterised by bastions which function with advanced ravelins – projecting, arrow-shaped outworks – all surrounded by deep ditches. One of the best examples of his work is in **Rocroi**. Taking advantage of natural obstacles, using materials found nearby, he also sought to bring some beauty to his fortifications, by bestowing monumental stone entrances upon them. On the northern front in the Ardennes Forest, he set up a system known as Pré carré. This consisted of two lines of strongholds located near enough to one another to prevent enemy passage, and to offer help in the case of attack. Although most of these fortified places are in today's Flanders and Hainaut regions, the Ardennes was defended by the **Charlemont** fort on the front lines, and by Rocroi, **Mézières** and **Sedan** on the rear lines.

The Maginot Line

Devised by War Minister Paul Painlevé and his successor, **André Maginot** (1877-1932), this line of defensive fortifications was under study by 1925. It includes a series of concrete works placed at the top of a hill or on the hillside all along the north-eastern border from the Ardennes Forest to the Rhine. The fort of **Villy-la-Ferté** is a good example of the defensive architecture of the line. Unfortunately for the French, this stronghold was without troops at the crucial moment, which meant that the resistance of May-June 1940 was pathetically futile.

Besides the famous series of fortifications, the Maginot Line today also has a series of museums and tourist facilities; a tour is both easy to undertake and educational. *See Ligne MAGINOT in the Exploring the Region section.*

Sculpture and Stained Glass

ALSACE

The finest examples of **sculpture** in Alsace are found in the embellishment of churches: statues, low-relief sculptures and funerary monuments. The most famous sculptor to come from Alsace was **Auguste Bartholdi**, from Colmar, who made the Belfort Lion (a copy can be found in Paris, place Denfert-Rochereau) and what may be the world's best-known statue, the Statue of Liberty which stands in New York Harbour.

B. Kaufmann/MICHELIN

Gothic doorway, Metz Cathedral

Some of the more remarkable **religious sculptures** in the region are found in **Andlau** on the church porch. In the 13C, Gothic artists had a field day on the cathedral of Strasbourg (low-relief sculpture of the Death of the Virgin, the Angels' Pillar); the 14C statuary shows a more fluid style (Virtues and Vices, Wise and Foolish Virgins).

The doorway of St-Thiébaut in **Thann** and St Laurent's doorway in Strasbourg Cathedral illustrate the opulent art of the Flamboyant period (15C). **Hans Hammer** carved the pulpit in Strasbourg Cathedral, which is often referred to as lace tatted from stone.

The best examples of **funerary sculpture** are also found in **Strasbourg**, in St-Thomas's Church: the tomb of Bishop Adeloch (12C), in the form of a sarcophagus, and the tomb of Marshal Maurice de Saxe.

The proudest piece of **sculpture in wood** is no doubt the Issenheim altar in the Unterlinden Museum in Colmar. The paintings are by Grünewald, but some of the glory must go to **Nicolas de Haguenau**, who carved the gilded statues of saints Anthony, Augustine and Jerôme; Sébastien Beychel crafted the lower section which shows Christ in the midst of his Apostles.

Beautiful carved screens and altars are also on view in **Kaysersberg, Dambach** and **Soultzbach-les-Bains**. Elsewhere, there is a profusion of pulpits, organ lofts, and choir stalls **(Marmoutier, Thann)**, which demonstrates the skill and artistry of local artisans.

The windows in **Strasbourg Cathedral** date from the 12C, 13C and 14C, and although they have been damaged over time, they are remarkable in number.

LORRAINE

Romanesque decoration of churches was often rather awkward. The doorway of Mont-Devant-Sassey, dedicated to the Virgin Mary, is in fact an inferior reproduction of statuary in Reims. A better example is Notre-Dame in **Verdun** where the Lion's Door is carved with a Christ in Majesty surrounded by symbols of the Apostles; though some find it lacks elegance, it does have its own original beauty.

In the 16C, **Ligier Richier**, working in **St-Mihiel,** brought new life to the art of sculpture, and his influence is felt throughout Lorraine.

Many mausoleums were embellished with **funerary art** between the 16C and the 18C. Perhaps the most remarkable example of Richer's work is in St-Étienne church (*see Bar-le-Duc*); known as the Tormented Soul, the skeletal figure with one arm raised high, adorns the tomb of René de Chalon. Richier also sculpted the tomb of Philippa de Gueldre in the Église des Cordeliers in **Nancy**; the tomb of René II in the same church is by Mansuy Gauvain. In Notre-Dame-de-Bon-Secours, the tomb of Stanislas and the mausoleum of his wife Catherine Opalinska are the work of Vassé and the Adam brothers, respectively.

St-Étienne Cathedral in **Metz** was built between the 13C and the 16C. The church has been called God's lantern because of the many stained-glass windows. The oldest date from the 13C, and the most recent are contemporary, including some designed by painter Marc Chagall. Other modern stained-glass windows of interest can be found in the church at **St-Dié**. In **Baccarat**, St-Rémy Church has windows made of crystal.

CHAMPAGNE-ARDENNE

Gothic **sculptures** on buildings are made in fine-grained limestone, which is easy to carve, and are both ornamental and figurative. The **Ateliers de Reims** workshops were especially productive in the 13C, and the masterpieces produced there are visible on Reims Cathedral. The famous smiling angel is a good illustration of the delicate mastery of sculptors from the Reims School. During the **14C-15C**, while the Hundred Years War raged artists favoured funerary art such as *gisants* (recumbent figures) and monumental sepulchres showing scenes from the Passion of Christ.

The first half of the 16C was an exceptionally creative time for sculptors in **Troyes,** as styles segued from Gothic to Renaissance. The treatment of draped fabric and folds in clothing, of embroideries and jewels shows extraordinary attention to detail. Facial expressions suggest a range of emotion, and in particular give an impression of sweetness, sadness or timidity. The great master of this type of sculpture created the statue of St Martha in Ste-Madeleine Church (Troyes), the Pietà in **Bayel** and the Entombment in **Chaource**. The Flamboyant altar screen in Ste-Madeleine is from the same period.

The emergence of the Italian style is also evident in St-Urbain, where a statue of the Virgin Mary holding grapes has graceful posture and a gentle expression, marking a departure from Gothic Realism. As of 1540, such manneristic, refined representations had completely invested the Troyes School of Sculpture, and put an end to its distinctive appearance. Churches installed many works by **Dominique Florentin**, an Italian artist who married a native of Troyes and settled there, training students in his workshops.

Some works in **stained glass** have survived the wars, pollution and the 18C practice of replacing coloured windows with milky white ones (to make it easier to read the liturgy).

The **13C** saw the creation of the windows in the chancel of Troyes Cathedral as well as those of Notre-Dame in **Reims** (apse and rose on the façade), a few in St-Étienne in **Châlons-en-Champagne** and finally the great windows of **St-Urbain in Troyes**, which are most typical of the era. Very colourful, they portray solitary characters (bishops) in the high panels, whereas the lower panels, more easily studied by visitors, illustrate the lives of the saints or episodes from the Life of Christ. The compositions are enlivened by complex backgrounds and the expressive attitudes of the figures; some panels tell us something about the daily life of the time.

In the **16C**, painting on glass became popular and many pieces were ordered for donations to churches (the donor's name or likeness often appearing thereon). Cartoons (basic drawing patterns) made it possible to reproduce the same image over and over, which explains the wealth of windows in the small churches of the Aube region. Some of the artists' names are known to us today: Jehan Soudain, Jean Verrat, Lievin Varin. Early in the 16C, colours exploded on the scene, as can be seen in the spectacular upper windows in **Troyes Cathedral**, which were installed between 1498 and 1501. In these windows the contours of the drawings are clearly defined and the technical prowess is evident in engraving, pearling, brushed *grisaille* which creates a three-dimensional illusion, and inlays of different coloured glass as used in the stars.

As of 1530, polychrome effects were abandoned by the masters in favour of grisaille – tones of a single colour – on white glass with golden yellow and blood red highlights. Italian influence is found in the evolution of the drawings. The architectural backgrounds were inspired by the Fontainebleau School.

In the 17C, the tradition of stained-glass craft continued in Troyes with **Linard Gontier**, who brought back polychrome windows with a new technique of enamelling on white glass, which produced bright hues. He is considered the master of monumental compositions, with works such as the Mystical Press, in Troyes Cathedral. He was also an exceptional miniaturist and portraitist, working in *grisaille*.

R Mattès/MICHELIN

Traditional pottery, Soufflenheim

Decorative Arts and Painting

MEROVINGIAN TREASURES

The Merovingian period refers to the first dynasty of Frankish kings founded by Clovis and reigning in France and Germany from about 500 to 751. Recently, art historians have become more interested in works from this often neglected time. In the Champagne-Ardenne region, a trove of funerary objects has been uncovered in the many necropolises that once served local communities. In the archaeological museum in **Troyes**, the tomb of Pouan, a prince, reveals much to us about the artistic temper of the times.

Gold and silver work was highly prized. The decorative items on view in the museums include **fibulae** (clasps resembling safety pins), belt buckles, parts of shields, and sword handles. The eastern influence is obvious in the designs, in particular the fantastic animal turning its head to look back. Styles and techniques were also adapted by Germanic invaders. The rarity of precious metals led to a preference for gold and silver beaten into fine sheets or pulled into threads; other metals were also substituted for a precious effect, including copper, tin and bronze.

Arms made during the Merovingian period are another illustration of the prowess of metalwork masters. Various metals, always high quality, were juxtaposed in the forging process. They were welded together and hammered. The layered structure thus created was both resistant and elastic. The most common arms were long double-edged swords, axes and the *scramasax*, a sort of sabre with one cutting edge.

In addition to metalwork, a speciality of Germanic regions, some sculptural works have also survived. In Isle-Aumont, a set of sarcophagi shows the evolution of style between the 5C and the 8C.

ALSACE

In the 15C, great **painting** began to appear in Alsace, with the arrival in

Colmar of **Gaspard Idenmann**, creator of a Passion inspired by the Flemish style, now on view in the Unterlinden Museum. Another Colmar resident, **Martin Schongauer**, painted the magnificent Virgin in the Rose Bower *(in the Église des Dominicains,* *see COLMAR)*. Students under his direction painted a series of Passion works (also in the Unterlinden), and created other remarkable works, such as the Buhl altar screen. The great German artist **Matthias Grünewald** painted the high altar of the Antonite Church in Issenheim. This screen sets a Crucifixion of fearful realism against exquisite figures of the Annunciation and a Heavenly Choir. Some excellent portraitists (Jean-Jacques Henner) were Alsatian, as were a number of draughtsmen, engravers and lithographers, including **Gustave Doré**, who was from Strasbourg.

In the realm of **decorative arts**, Alsatian craftsmen excelled in woodwork, ironwork, tinsmithing and working precious metals. They have a reputation as skilled watch and clock makers, as the astronomical clock in Strasbourg Cathedral proves.

Ceramics made the **Hannong** family, creators of the "old Strasbourg" style, eminent for generations; their production is on view in the Strasbourg Museum. In the second half of the 19C, Théodore Deck of Guebwiller brought new ideas to ceramic arts and refined techniques.

LORRAINE

The region, with its wealth and as a cosmopolitan crossroads, produced many painters, miniaturists and engravers over the centuries. Some achieved fame beyond the local area. Arts in the 17C were imprinted with the influence of **Georges Lallemand**, a native of Nancy who established himself in Paris in 1601; **Jacques Bellange**, master of Mannerism; **Claude Deruet**, official court painter par excellence; **Georges de la Tour**, known for his remarkable candlelight and torchlight effects incorporating deep black nights; **Claude Gellée**, a landscape painter; **Jacques Callot**, a great draughtsman and engraver (most of his works are shown in the museum of the history of Lorraine in Nancy).

In the 19C, **Isabey** was the leading painter of miniature portraits, and one of the favourite painters of Imperial society, alongside **François Dumont**, from Lunéville.

Mention must be made of **Épinal**. In the 18C and 19C, this town specialised in the production of pretty coloured prints, which were sold around France by street vendors. The pictures became so well known that it is common nowadays to use the expression *image d'Épinal* to refer to any simplistic or naive representation of life.

Ceramic production in Lorraine was mostly centred around **Lunéville** and **Sarreguemines**; enamellers settled around Longwy.

Crystal

Lorraine has several famous crystal manufacturers, including those in **Baccarat, Daum** and **Saint Louis**. This activity was able to develop, especially in the 16C, thanks to the abundance of wood (to stoke the fires), water and sand in the region. Today, in addition to traditional glassware, as appreciated by the royal and imperial courts of Persia, Russia, Germany and Italy, these venerable companies produce objects designed in contemporary styles by Salvador Dali and Philippe Starck, among others.

ART NOUVEAU AND THE 20C

At the end of the 19C, a movement to rehabilitate decorative arts and architecture, known as **Art Nouveau**, came to the fore. It is easily recognisable by its use of long, sinuous lines, often expressed in the shapes of vines and tendrils, flower stalks, butterfly wings and other curvaceous natural forms.

In France, the first works to appear were in Nancy, made by **Émile Gallé**; he produced glassware inspired by the patterns and forms of nature. His work was hailed at the Universal Exhibitions of 1884, 1889 and 1900 in Paris. Soon a group of artists working in various media (glass, wood, ceramic, engraving and sculpture) had gathered around him. Among them were **Daum, Majore-**

R Mattès/MICHELIN

Palais des Droits de l'Homme, Strasbourg

lle, Vallin, Prouvé, and together they formed the **École de Nancy.**

Between 1900 and 1910, the influence of the Nancy School became apparent in local architecture (about 10 years behind decorative arts). Nancy is now, with Brussels, Vienna and Paris, one of the great centres of Art Nouveau architecture in Europe.

The second half of the 20C saw some **architectural achievements** in the larger towns: the Tour de l'Europe in Mulhouse (1966); the Tour Altea in Nancy (1974); the Palais de l'Europe (1977). In Strasbourg the striking landmark **Palais des Droits de l'Homme** (European Court of Human Rights, 1995) by Richard Rogers, was followed by the **European Parliament building** (1997) which houses the largest debating chamber in Europe.

The most famous artist of the 20C to come from the region was **Jean (or Hans) Arp** (1887-1966) born in Strasbourg. A leader of the avant-garde, he produced sculptures, paintings and poetry. In Paris, he was acquainted with Modigliani, Picasso and Robert Delaunay He sought refuge in Zurich during the First World War, and while there became one of the founders of the Dada movemen. A fine collection of Arp's works and other modern and contemporary art works are assembled in the Musée d'Art Moderne et Contemporain in Strasbourg.

Traditions and Folklore

ALSACE

Both the mountains and the plain are rich in local colour, and legends abound in Alsace. Of course, visitors today are not likely to see women wearing distinctive, bow-shaped black headdresses, unless there is a local heritage *fête* in progress. But the preservation of so much architectural patrimony – a miracle considering the strife and wars that long plagued the region – provides a setting that vividly evokes the past.

Some local traditions do persist, in particular those associated with saints' feast days. Each village celebrates the feast day of its patron saint, **la fête patronale**, also known as *messti* (Bas-Rhin), and *kilwe* or *kilbe* (Haut-Rhin) in local dialect. Folk dancing and traditional costumes enliven the festivities. Ribeauvillé has held its especially popular fair in early September for centuries.

Many seasonal traditions would seem very familiar to a visitor from the United Kingdom or North America: brightly lit and sparkling trees, red and green ribbons, gingerbread men, and markets full of "stocking-stuffers" in December; carnival celebrated with doughnuts; Easter which brings a rabbit who hides coloured eggs in the garden.

Legends often surround lakes, rivers, and the romantic ruins of castles.

There are religious legends as well, often remembered in traditional ceremonies like the one held in Thann every 30 June, when three pines are set afire. While the realm of legend sometimes reflects aspects of reality and history, the advantage here is that good always conquers and evil is inevitably punished. The characters in these legends are knights and ladies, monks and beggars, saints and demons, gnomes and giants.

The most famous legend in Alsace may be the story of **Mont Ste-Odile**. The patron saint of Alsace (Odilia, Ottilia and other variations are found) was the daughter of Duke Adalric; she founded a nunnery on a mountain around the year 700 and was its first abbess. From these historical facts, a legend has grown, which recounts the birth of a blind Odile, rejected by her father, and spirited away to safety by her mother. By this account, Odile, now a beautiful young woman, was baptised by St Erhard, her uncle, and miraculously recovered her sight. Her father decided to marry her off, despite the girl's religious vocation, and he pursued her through the forest as she ran from the fate he had devised for her. Suddenly, a rock opened up and enfolded her, protecting Odile from the duke. From that rock, a sacred spring came forth. Adalric got the message and built her a convent instead.

Many pilgrims came to visit the holy woman. It is said that, upon encountering a sick man dying of thirst, Odile struck the ground with her cane and brought forth a spring. The man drank and was cured; many people came to pray at the site and wash their eyes with the curative water. Odile's intercession is still sought after by those with diseases of the eye.

LORRAINE

The traditional emblem of Lorraine is the **Croix de Lorraine**, a cross with two horizontal arms, the shorter one above the longer. It appeared on coins minted by the dukes of Lorraine, was made famous by General de Gaulle who took it for his personal standard, and is found on everything from biscuit tins to postage stamps. Its origins can be traced to the kingdom

R Mattès/MICHELIN

"How beautiful is our Alsace"

of Hungary, which used such a cross as its coat of arms. When the Árpád dynasty expired, a series of Angevin kings came to power, beginning with Robert of Anjou (1308-42). Ultimately, René II inherited the title from the dukes of Anjou and brought the emblem to his duchy of Lorraine. In 1477, the cross blazed on banners rallying the people to the Battle of Nancy, and from that time on it has been known as the Lorraine Cross.

St Nicholas has also held a special place in the hearts of the people of Lorraine since the days of the Holy Roman Empire. With his bishop's mitre and backpack full of toys, he travels Lorraine on the night of 5-6 December. The patron saint of the region is celebrated in all the towns and villages with festive lights and parades. The beautiful Flamboyant church of St-Nicolas-de-Port was the site of many pilgrimages; the town was once one of the liveliest in Lorraine.

CHAMPAGNE-ARDENNE

In this region, as elsewhere in France, recent years have seen a renewed interest in ancestral traditions, including religious and pagan festivities and activities related to daily life in the countryside.

Carnival costume parades are coming back in style in many towns and villages where the custom had nearly died out. Around the textile centre of Sedan, costumes were commonly made from canvas sacks used to hold spools of yarn; five or six people would climb into one and march along broadside. Near Mézières, carnival-goers stick their heads through the rungs of a horizontal ladder draped with white cloth and pop out one or several burlesque faces at a time. Popular games are blindfold races, horseshoe throwing, and wheelbarrow races, with the loser buying a round at the nearest café.

At nightfall, the crowd gathers round for the bonfire. A procession through the streets bears a sort of scarecrow who, from village to village, may be named Nicolas, Christophe, Joseph or Pansard, and may be dressed as a ragged beggar or a bridegroom. As the carnival figure burns and sparks fly up, dancing and singing mark the end of the festive day. In some places, the ashes from the fire are believed to have special powers, or bring good luck, especially to young couples.

Although Mardi Gras is associated with the Christian rite, the carnival has well-documented pagan origins and is clearly associated with chasing out winter and preparing for spring.

A funny tradition still observed in villages is the May Day *charivari*. Young rascals band together on the eve of 1 May and spend the dark night going from house to house, where they quietly make off with anything that isn't nailed down or locked up: ladders, barrows, benches, rakes. The whole lot is then piled up on the main square, where everyone gathers the next morning, to laugh or complain according to temper, and to recover the goods.

Literature

LITERATURE IN ALSACE-LORRAINE

In this border region, literary tradition has three expressions: French, German and dialect. German works represent the oldest, most prestigious tradition. The **Renaissance, Humanism** and the **Reform** marked the golden age of Alsatian literature. Gutenberg worked on developing his printing press in Strasbourg before getting it up and running in Mainz. The wonderful collection of the Humanist library in Sélestat is testimony to the regional attachment to the written word. The German author Goethe lived in Strasbourg in 1770-71, a memorable time because it marked the beginning of the so-called *Sturm und Drang* (storm and stress) movement. This style of literature exalted nature, feelings and human individualism, and was strongly influenced by the ideas of French author Jean-Jacques Rousseau, and by the works of Shakespeare, which had just been translated.

The **20C** was marked by the upheavals of war. German literature was still most prevalent, but by the end of the First World War, numerous works had been published in dialect, certainly in response to the need to express cultural identity in a region caught in the middle

The Legend of the Lac du Ballon

Long ago, a green meadow lay like an emerald in the blue velvet folds of the Vosges Forest, below the majestic Grand Ballon. The field belonged to a man who earned his living making charcoal, a *charbonnier*. A covetous bourgeois from the Guebwiller Valley tried to buy the field, and when the collier refused, he bribed a local judge into forcing the forfeit of the land.

The proud new owner arrived with a fancy golden wagon to cut the fragrant hay, and he passed by the collier's simple dwelling with a smug, victorious grin. The wronged man shook his fist, and called on Providence to render the justice that the courts of law had denied him.

Suddenly, a menacing gloom came over the sky and a violent storm erupted in the high mountains, followed by a downpour so heavy it cut off all sight like a thick dark curtain. When the light returned, a round lake appeared in the place of the field, its deep waters covering the bourgeois, his wagon and horses.

As you gaze on the lake, remember the French proverb: *Charbonnier est maître chez soi* (even a charcoal-burner is master in his own house). Every man's home is his castle.

of a terrible power struggle. Between the wars, the French language got a foothold and today it is the language most commonly heard and used.

CHAMPAGNE: CRADLE OF FRENCH LITERATURE

In the **12C**, Champagne was home to many authors writing in the emerging French language. Bertrand de Bar-sur-Aube is reputed to have composed *Aimeri de Narbonne*, the best-known chapter of the ballad of William of Orange (later to inspire Victor Hugo). Chrétien de Troyes (c 1135-c 1183) wrote tales of chivalry based on the legends of Brittany, including the characters Lancelot and Perceval. The search for the Holy Grail and the Crusades inspired Geoffroi de Villehardouin (1150-1213), who wrote about his adventures in History of the Conquest of Constantinople. Another medieval bard, Jean, Sire de Joinville, described travelling to Egypt with St Louis (1309). The Count of Champagne, Thibaud IV, crowned king of Navarre in 1234, preferred to pen poetry, whereas his countryman Rutebeuf entertained with biting satires of the church, the university and tradesmen.

A major figure from the 17C was **Jean de la Fontaine**, celebrated for his *Fables*. Born into a bourgeois family in Château-Thierry, he married a local heiress in 1647, but separated from her 11 years later. An outstanding feature of his character was his life-long ability to attract wealthy patrons, thus freeing himself from the pedestrian worries of earning a living so he could devote his time to writing 12 books of fables and other works. The first collection of six books is based on the Aesopic tradition, whereas the second takes its inspiration from East Asian stories. His use of animal characters is a light-hearted ploy for expressing the everyday moral experience of humankind; his poetic technique has been called the exquisite quintessence of the preceding century of French literature. La Fontaine's *Fables* continue to form part of the culture of every French schoolchild, and his reputation has lost none of its glow.

The **18C** brought bold thinkers to the fore, none more so than **Voltaire** (pseudonym of François-Marie Arouet). Upon his return to France after a two-year exile in England, Voltaire found refuge in Champagne in the château of Mme du Châtelet in Cirey-sur-Blaise. They lived a life both studious and passionate, translating Newton, conducting experiments in their laboratory, travelling and frequenting high society. She died in childbirth in 1749, ending their complex relationship of 15 years, and leaving her lover bereft.

Voltaire's most famous work is probably *Candide* (1758), a satirical masterpiece on philosophical optimism.

The **19C** and **20C** produced two figures whose memory has been perpetuated by modern-day songwriters and film directors: **Paul Verlaine** and **Arthur Rimbaud.**

Verlaine was born in Metz in 1844, Rimbaud 10 years later in Charleville. The older poet was from a comfortable background, the well-educated son of an army officer; the younger was raised in poverty by his mother and yet distinguished himself as a gifted student. After graduating with honours from the Lycée Bonaparte, Verlaine became a clerk in an insurance company, then a civil servant. His early work was published in respectable literary reviews; he married and had a son. During the Franco-Prussian War, he was the press officer for the Paris insurgents of the *Commune*. Meanwhile, Rimbaud, a restless and despondent soul, lived on the streets of the capital in squalor, reading everything he could get his hands on – including the poetry of Baudelaire (considered immoral by the cultural establishment at the time) and works on the occult – and shaping his own poetic philosophy.

In 1871 the two met, moved to London and carried on a scandalous affair. While Verlaine vacillated between decadent thrills and anguished repentance, Rimbaud was seen as his friend's evil helmsman on their *Drunken Boat*. In 1873, a violent quarrel in Brussels ended with Rimbaud shot in the wrist and Verlaine in prison for 18 months. Rimbaud, both distraught and exhilarated, feverishly

Rimbaud

completed *A Season in Hell:... As for me, I am intact, and I don't care.*

By his 20th birthday, Rimbaud had given up writing and turned to gunrunning in Africa. In 1891, his right leg was amputated, and he died the same year. He has been cited as an inspiration by many, in particular the Beat poets, Jim Morrison, Bob Dylan and Patti Smith.

Verlaine, released from prison, became a devout Catholic and moved to England where he taught French. In 1877, he returned to France and began writing the series of poems to be published as *Sagesse* (Wisdom – or perhaps, simply "wising up"). Further heartbreak (the deaths of a favourite student and the poet's mother) and a failure to reconcile with his wife drove Verlaine back to drink, but sympathetic friends encouraged him to continue writing and publishing, and supported him financially. His significant body of work marks a transition between the Romantic poets and the Symbolists.

The Last Word ...

Can you identify the quotes below?

Here is a hint...half are from the pen of Voltaire, and the others are morals from the *Fables of La Fontaine.*

In this best of all possible worlds ... all is for the best.

Better to suffer than to die: that is mankind's motto.
The secret of being a bore is to tell everything.
People who make no noise are dangerous.
Love truth, but pardon error.
It is a double pleasure to deceive the deceiver.
History is no more than a portrayal of crimes and misfortunes.
We heed no instincts but our own.
Thought depends on the stomach, but in spite of that, those who have the best stomachs are not the best thinkers.
A hungry stomach cannot hear.
I disapprove of what you say, but I will defend to the death your right to say it.
The opinion of the strongest is always the best.

Answer: The first is Voltaire, the second La Fontaine, the next one is Voltaire, and so on, in alternation.

Joan of Arc, heroine for all time

No discussion of the history of Lorraine, the Vosges or Champagne would be complete without some mention of Joan of Arc (Jeanne d'Arc), a country girl whose achievements were a decisive factor in awakening a national consciousness in France. The subject of a wide array of books, films and plays, Joan officially attained sainthood in 1920. However, her canonisation did not put an end to speculation on the divine (or perhaps delusional?) nature of the voices that guided her. She remains an enigma.

Born c1412 in Dorémy, on the border of the duchies of Bar and Lorraine (now in the Vosges département), Joan began life as the daughter of a tenant farmer of modest means and good reputation. According to the transcript of her trial, "at the age of 13, she received a voice from God, guiding her, and this voice came to her around noon, in the summer, in her father's garden." Joan believed that God spoke to her through the "voices" of Saint Michael, Saint Catherine and Saint Margaret.

The French crown was then in dispute between the Valois king (the "Dauphin" Charles) and the Lancastrian English king Henry VI (allied with the duke of Burgundy). The villagers of Dorémy were under constant threat from the Burgundians, and had little love for Henry. Charles needed to reach Reims to be crowned in the cathedral and reign legitimately, but Reims was deep in enemy territory.

Joan, possessed of remarkable courage and drive, made the dangerous journey to Chinon to speak to the Dauphin. Charles, 25 years old at the time, had known only war and intrigue, and was unable to reconquer his kingdom or make a peace agreement with the Burgundians. In a legendary confrontation, Charles, unsure and receiving contradictory counsel, made Joan wait several days before allowing her to enter the castle. He then disguised himself as an ordinary member of the court. However Joan was not fooled an instant, knelt before him without hesitation and said that she wanted to go to battle with the English and accompany him to Reims for his coronation. While Charles vacillated, Joan pressed on. She led attacks on Orleans, Beaugency and Patay, inspiring French troops and routing the English. Soon the mere sight of Joan's standard at the gates of a town was enough to make loyalties waver; thus Joan brought the Dauphin to Reims. She also wrote to the Duke of Burgundy, urging him to make peace with the legitimate monarch.

In 1430, when the Duke of Burgundy laid siege to Compiègne, Joan entered the town under cover of night and twice repelled the enemy. Protecting her rear guard to the last, Joan was unhorsed and captured. Charles, deep in his endless negotiations with the Burgundians, did nothing to seek her release. The Duke accepted an offer of 10,000 francs from the University of Paris, controlled by English partisans, to turn the young prisoner over to be tried – not for offences against the Lancastrian monarchy, but for heresy. Indeed, Joan's manner of direct discourse with her God threatened the powerful church hierarchy; proving her a heretic could also bring discredit on Charles. For five months, she was imprisoned in the harshest conditions, persecuted by her accusers, and her faith constantly called into question. Finally, her tormentors turned Joan over to the secular arm of justice, in order that she be condemned to death. On May 30, 1431, she was burned at the stake; witnesses to her death agreed that she died a faithful Christian.

Ruling as Charles VII, the new sovereign obtained a posthumous reversal of her sentence, perhaps more out of a perceived need to justify his coronation than a sense of justice. Despite his rather apathetic, indolent character, Charles VII made significant financial and military reforms which strengthened the French monarchy, and began to reunify the kingdom.

On 24 June, 1920, the French parliament declared a national festival in honour of Joan, held the second Sunday in May. She became, and remains, a symbol of the French spirit.

THE REGION TODAY

The Economy

ALSACE

This region has become a symbol of the transnational European economy. For the past 30 years, regional development has centred around this theme. Strasbourg, seat of the Council of Europe, was one of the first "Eurocities" on the continent. Mulhouse has expanded its commercial activities through close ties with the cities of Basel and Fribourg across the Rhine. Because of its history, language and traditions, Alsace is able to develop privileged trading partnerships with the bordering nations of Germany and Switzerland. The valley of the River Rhine, long a significant communications corridor, has contributed to regional prosperity. As early as the 8C-9C, boats left Strasbourg for the North Sea, where they sold wine to the English, Danish and Swedish. Steam ships made their appearance in 1826. But it was the construction of the Canal d'Alsace, begun in 1920, which modernised navigation on the Rhine, at the same time harnessing the considerable energy resources provided by the river between Basel and Strasbourg. A strong local policy for encouraging investment has made Alsace the second most dynamic region in France for capital growth, the third wealthiest, and of 160 regions in the European Union, Alsace is ranked 13th for prosperity.

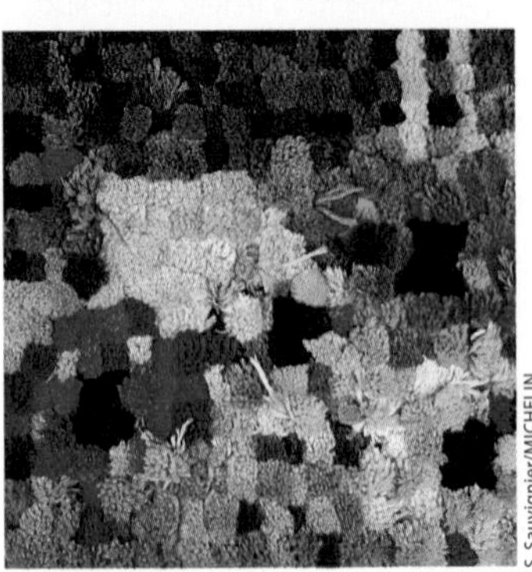

S. Sauvignier/MICHELIN

Textile colour chart

The fertile plain of Alsace could be used for growing many different crops, but the long strip at the foot of the Vosges is used almost exclusively for the cultivation of grapes: 14 566ha/36 212 acres. All of the wines are bottled in the region of production (almost 150 million bottles), and represent more than 18% of total French still white wine production. This activity involves 7 000 wine-growers. Grapes make up more than half of overall crop production in the region (40% of total agricultural output). On the domestic market, one-third of still white AOC wines consumed in France is from Alsace. The export market takes up 25% of the yearly production (about 40 million bottles).

LORRAINE

Its reputation as an industrial leader has been tarnished since its most brilliant period in the late 19C. First the textile crisis, then the decline of the **steel industry** and the closure of **coal mines** pushed the area into a deep economic slump. Local policy makers have had to work overtime to find innovative solutions for recovery. These include the creation of "technopoles" in Metz and Nancy, districts zoned for the development of high-tech industries. Subsidies have been allotted to areas around the Meuse Valley, Longwy and Thionville for similar development projects.

Diversification is slowly making inroads where heavy industry once dominated: manufacture of synthetic fabrics for tyre manufacture, paper products, service industries and tourism are expanding. Lorraine is also involved in joint development projects with its neighbours in Germany and Luxembourg.

Around 2 000 new jobs were created in Hambach for the manufacture of the innovative Smart Car. A collaborative effort, the mixed diesel/electric or petrol automobile has the design pedigree of Swatch and the motoring quality imprint of Mercedes.

Farms in Lorraine are France's leading producers of rape seed, used for making cooking and salad oil; the flowering plants make bright yellow fields. The region actively promotes "quality labelling" of agricultural products, including beef, cheese and eggs. Wood and wood-processing operations (parquet flooring, panelling, furniture etc) also account for a significant share of French production.

CHAMPAGNE

Clearly the most important export (20% of total) for this region is its namesake, sparkling wine. But it should be noted that in recent years, an accumulation of stock and subsequent lowering of prices have pushed leading traders to rethink their marketing philosophy. Related economic activities include bottling and processing plants and farm machine manufacture. The "Packaging Valley" association brings together 250 businesses specialising in packaging products and processes.

Agriculture, shored up by government subsidies, has also made steps towards increased profitability through diversification. Milk products have taken on an important role; the region produces 25% of all the ice cream in France (mostly in Haute-Marne). Research is underway on the chemical components of natural substances, used in non-food products: biological fuels from rape seed, alcohol and ethanol from sugar beets, paper products and adhesives from wheat starch. Research is carried out in a European institute, the Agropôle, in Reims.

The textile industry offers employment to a significant number of people in Champagne-Ardenne, especially in Troyes and the Aube département. Among the world famous manufacturers of knitted goods are Absorba, Petit Bateau, Lacoste (from Saint-Dizier and Troyes), Dior and Benetton. Some 35% of all French socks and 58% of infant layettes are made here.

Arriving at the spa ...

PROTET S.A.

... Leaving the spa

ARDENNE

Foundry and metalworks are leading sources of employment, and many automobile and appliance makers place orders with local plants (Citroën, Ford, Électrolux, General Motors, BMW, Porsche). Various industries related to automobile equipment have also set up shop (automotive textiles, safety parts, machine tools), as well as plants producing parts for high-tech projects such as Ariane rockets, TGV trains, Airbus, Rafale fighter jets and the Channel Tunnel. More recently plastics have taken off, in some instances replacing metal parts and devices, and also in the packaging field.

Most of the businesses in Ardenne are small and medium-sized firms engaged in subcontracting. The network of companies is supported by the CRITT (Regional Centre for Technology Transfer) in Charleville-Mézières, which works in research and development of new and rare materials, microanalysis, non-destructive controls, thermic and thermionic treatments and other highly specialised testing. In an immense effort to revitalise the region after the damage of the Second World War and the decline of heavy industry, the government offers significant fiscal advantages to companies choosing to locate in Ardenne. Their employees benefit from the exceptionally clean and quiet natural environment and the transport network that puts them no more than a few hours away from major European capitals.

Tourism has become an important economic factor in all of the regions covered in this guide. Local authorities have sought to enhance and promote the value of the many historic towns and sites, natural resources and recreational opportunities they provide. Improvements in the **transportation network** have helped this effort, most notably the launch of the new high-speed **TGV Est Européen** train service in June 2007 which begins operating at a maximum speed of 320 kph. This has slashed journey times bringing the region withn commuting distance of Paris: for example, Reims, *was* 1hr 35 mins, *now* 45 min; Nancy, *was* 2 hr 45 mins, *now* l hr 30 mins; Strasbourg, was 4 hrs, *now* 2 hr 20 mins. And as train speeds increase further (the TGV Est Européen has recorded the world-record conventional train speed of just under 575 km/hr!) the journey time will be even shorter; for example Paris-Strasbourg will eventually be cut to 1 hr 50mins.

International airports in Strasbourg and Basel-Mulhouse also provide connections to European capitals. The network of autoroutes is dense and practical, and has also recently been augmented, making it easy to reach the area by car, from the north or south. The waterways have adapted to tourism as well, and there are many possibilities for short trips and longer cruises through the countryside. Major investments around the region have stimulated the development of golf courses, marinas and water sports recreation areas, trails for walking, riding and cycling, and various mountain sports resorts. Many tourists also enjoy a stay at one of the spas – especially after enjoying the fine wines and hearty cuisine of the region (*see Planning Your Trip for more details on spas*).

M. Roche/Musée de Châlons-en-Champagne

Exhibit in the town museum in Châlons-en-Champagne

Life in the Countryside

VILLAGES

Most of the people living outside main urban centres live fairly close to their neighbours in villages. This has been the custom since the first settlers arrived. Rather than a response to a perceived need for protection, this pattern is more likely a result of communal farming and forestry techniques.

In **Alsace,** the houses in a village are generally detached from one another, and may even be facing in different directions. Some villages are little more than a group of farmhouses around a belfry. Traces of a more glorious past may remain: a ruined castle rising above the roof line, a lovely church in an otherwise unremarkable place. In any case, one of the most conspicuous features of the Alsatian village is the care the inhabitants take to keep their doorways swept, windows sparkling, and geraniums in bloom.

In **Lorraine**, the houses in the village are generally attached, and stand along both sides of the street in an orderly row. Often, there is an entranceway wide enough to accommodate a tractor or wagon, and a smaller doorway into the building itself. The large entrance opens onto the farmyard, and often the farm extends far back beyond the main house, with the usual collection of buildings and equipment scattered about. Nowadays, most inhabitants reserve the small front yard for a flower garden.

On the dry plain of **Champagne**, sizeable villages grew up around fresh water springs, often quite far from one another. While the streets are narrow and confined, through an open gate you might glimpse a spacious courtyard with neatly kept buildings holding presses and other equipment needed to maintain and harvest grapes. In the southern part of the region, around Bar-sur-Aube, Bar-sur-Seine, Langres and the Blaise Valley, villages can be seen from afar as the buildings are predominately made of bright white limestone. In the Argonne Forest, the linear look of houses lined up along the road is reminiscent of neighbouring Lorraine.

HOUSES AND FARMS

While houses and farms in rural Alsace have many things in common, there are also many subtle differences from one area to another. Gables, the colour, shape and type of timbers, and the materials, patterns and embellishments used to fill in the frame, all vary from north to south. In the vineyard region, the ground floor, in stone, is used for pressing grapes and storing wine. An outside stair leads to the living areas above. The Écomusée (*see entry heading*) is a good place to see various building techniques.

In a typical Lorraine village, the older buildings have gently sloping roofs covered with a kind of hollow tile. The traditional farmhouse held the living area, barn and stables under one roof. The limestone walls are coated to preserve the mortar joints.

The **Champagne** region is home to many wine-growers. Their houses are typically low, made of millstone, local chalkstone or brick. In **"dry" Champagne**, the farmyards are generally bordered by the living area (facing the street), the barn (facing the fields) and other buildings for animals. In the south-east, half-timbering appears, filled in with blocks of chalkstone or cob covered with plaster. In the greener or **"wet" Champagne**, timbers are cut from pine and poplar, held with cross beams and daub, or earthen bricks. Around **Troyes**, brick is commonly used in decorative patterns between the timbers. A traditional dwelling in the **Argonne** Forest has a dark brick façade on the ground floor and a roughcast plaster storey above. The flat tiles of the roof extend out over the sides of the house.

photo en habillage

The region of **Ardenne** is rich in schist and quartzite stone, often used for building; the blue slate quarried here is of excellent quality. These materials make the houses rather gloomy looking. To defeat the rigours of winter, all of the farm buildings are close together, making for a single, long building, in contrast to the rectangular courtyard with outbuildings seen in more clement neighbouring areas.

Regional Cuisine

ALSACE-LORRAINE

Charcuteries

Ham and Strasbourg sausages are featured in the classic *assiette alsacienne*, an array of pork meats; but *foies gras* (fattened livers) hold pride of place. This delicacy has been appreciated since the Roman era; in 1778 a young local chef, Jean-Pierre Clause, created the prototype goose liver *pâté en croûte* (wrapped in a crust). Today there are over 40 variations on his theme on sale in local delicatessens.

In Lorraine, traditional dishes are loaded with butter, bacon and cream. **Potée** is a pot roast made with salt pork and sausages, white cabbage and other vegetables. Of course, **Quiche Lorraine** is famous fare: a creamy pie made with beaten eggs, thick cream and bacon bits. Pâté from Lorraine is made from veal and pork.

Choucroute

Strasbourg is the capital of this cabbage-based speciality made with white Alsatian wine. The savoury white cabbage is heaped with sausages, pork chops, bacon and ham, and on special occasions a bit of partridge, a few crayfish or a truffle find their way in.

Fish and fowl

Chicken dishes are popular in Alsace, and menus often list *coq* and *poularde* (pullet hen), served with mushroom and cream sauce; local *coq au vin* is made with Riesling wine. Local fish recipes are eels stewed in wine sauce (matelote), fried carp, pike and salmon.

Les marcaireries

Dairy farmers and cheesemakers in the Vosges are known as *marcaires*.

Traditionally, they take their herds up to the high pasturelands (chaumes) on 25 May (the old feast day of St Urbain), and bring them down again on 29 September. Nowadays, farms that serve country fare to travellers may be called by the more usual French name of *ferme-auberge*, but the local traditions remain the same.

Munster and Géromé

The perfect way to polish off an Alsatian meal is with one of these two cheeses, which are only made in the Vosges. Munster is an unpasteurised, soft fermented cheese, which many enjoy with a dash of cumin.

On the Lorraine side, Géromé – a word in dialect which means "from Gérardmer" – also has a long-standing reputation. It is made with unheated whole milk to which rennet (for solidifying) is added immediately. The cheese is aged for four months in a cool cellar until the crust turns russet and the interior is creamy.

Pastries

There are as many different tarts in Alsace as there are fruits to make them with. Any chef is proud to pull a perfect **Kugelhopf** out of the oven, a delightful puff of flour, butter, eggs, sweetened milk, raisins and almonds. Other special desserts are *macarons de Boulay* (dainty biscuits of egg whites and almonds), *madeleines de Commercy* (soft, buttery cakes), and *bergamotes de Nancy* (hard sweets flavoured with citrus rind).

Waffles (gaufres) were traditionally made at carnival time in irons forged with unique designs, both religious and profane. Hot waffles sprinkled with sugar or dripping with chocolate are still a popular treat, but the old-fashioned irons are now rare collector's items. **Meringues** were first served in France at the table of Duke Stanislas, in Nancy.

Beer

Breweries abound in Alsace (Schiltigheim, Strasbourg, Hochfelden, Obernai, Saverne); Stenay is home to the Beer Museum; the Brewery Museum is in St-Nicolas-de-Port. Beer has always been made from the same elements: pure water, barley, hops and yeast. Barley transforms into malt, giving colour and flavour; hops provide the bitterness. Each brewery cultivates its own yeast, which gives each brand its distinctive taste.

Beer has been enjoyed since Antiquity: Egyptians called it liquid bread; Hippocrates defended its use as a therapeutic medicine. Today, beer production starts with the reduction of malt to flour, the addition of water, and heating at a low temperature. While the mixture is stirred, the starch contained in the grain turns to sugar. In another tank, non-malted grain such as corn is prepared in the same way. The two tanks are mixed into a **mash**, which is filtered to become the **stock** or **wort**. The hops are added to the **wort kettle** where the mixture is heated, then filtered again. Fermentation takes place at temperatures between 5-10°C/40-50°F. Pasteurisation makes the final product more stable, and industrial chilling enables year-round production. Beer leaves the brew house and has yeast added to it, which turns the sugar into alcohol over two weeks, in large tanks kept at low temperatures. The yeast is removed after maturation: a final filtration and it's ready for the bottle.

CHAMPAGNE-ARDENNE

Champagne

Savoury sauces, rich meats and fresh produce are the ingredients of fine cuisine in the region. Sauces made with Champagne garnish many recipes for chicken, pullet, thrush, kidneys, stuffed trout, grilled pike, crayfish and snails. Smoked ham and sausage are used in **potée champenoise**, a popular dish at grape harvest time, served with mounds of fresh cabbage, a vegetable which is at its prime in the fall. Brenne-le-Château has its own recipe for *choucroute*, Troyes is celebrated for its *andouillettes* sausage and Ste-Menehould is famous for dishing out pigs' trotters and mashed potatoes.

In the pays d'Othe region, sometimes called little Normandy, apple orchards, though less numerous today than in the past, still produce fruit for making sparkling cider, however it is now more of a hobby than an industry.

Ardenne

The isolation of this region has contributed to the conservation of local traditions. The cuisine is hearty and fortifying, based on natural products found in the wooded hills. Game and fish are prominent on the menu: young boar, venison, rabbit with sauce *chasseur*; woodcock and thrush roasted in sage leaves or served *en terrine* with juniper berries; rich pâtés of marinated veal and pork meats. Smoked ham cured over juniper or broomwood and *boudin* sausages are on display in local charcuteries.
Salads made with fresh wild greens are flavoured with *crétons* or *fritons*, local terms for crunchy bacon bits. A menu offering plain country fare may feature *baïenne*, a satisfying dish of potatoes, onions and garlic.

Cheese

South of Troyes, the region has specialised in the production of creamy cheeses such as Chaource, which are only slightly aged. This cheese has been served at the best tables since the 12C. It can be enjoyed within five days after it is set out (frais) or may be left to firm up for about 20 days (fait). Firmer cheese may be covered with a thin film of white mould. Some other regional cheeses are varieties of **Cendré**, with a powdery dusting of grey ash (Châlons-en-Champagne, Les Riceys and the Marne Valley). **Maroilles** is a fragrant cheese from Thiérache that is usually enjoyed at harvest time. Mostafait is a white cream cheese blended with butter and tarragon. **Rocroi** is from the town of the same name; **Igny** shares its name with the Trappist monastery that produces it; **Troyen** is a regional cheese that resembles Camembert.

Pastries

At carnival time, doughnuts are a festive treat, variously known as *frivoles* or *fiverolles* or *crottes d'âne* (donkey droppings!). At Easter, little tarts (dariolles) are filled with a flan mixture made from milk and eggs. Gingerbread is still made with a reliable recipe from the 13C.
In Reims, many varieties of delicate biscuits are served with Champagne: *massepains, croquignols, bouchons*.

©Martina Frietsch/SXC

Quiche Lorraine

In the Ardennes region, crêpes are called *vautes* or *tantimolles*; hard sugar biscuits are served with coffee; soft cakes served at wedding banquets were sometimes baked with a silver ring inside, for luck. Blueberry pie is delicious in the summer, and at Christmas time there are many sorts of seasonal sweets, including little red candy animals.

Wine and Champagne

VINS D'ALSACE

The vineyards of Alsace stretch from Thann to Wissembourg, over about 100km/60mi, but the main area to explore starts just south of Marlenheim, where travellers join the famous **Route des Vins**. The route meanders through a sea of grape vines and many wine-growing villages; everything is devoted to the production of wine. The most exciting time to visit is certainly the autumn, when the harvest is in full swing and the leaves are vivid red. The eastern foothills of the Vosges are well exposed, and the climate is sunny and mild.

Varieties

The wines of Alsace are identified, not by geographical area, but by grape variety. **Riesling** is a bright star in the constellation of white grape varieties. Most of the wine produced in the valley of the River Rhine is made from these grapes, which create a sophisticated, subtle bouquet.
Gewürztraminer is a heady, fragrant wine with an intense bouquet.

The wine to choose if you wish to quench a thirst is **Sylvaner**, dry and light, with a fruity note.

Pinot blanc wines are generally considered well-balanced, with a fresh and supple character.

Pinot gris, also called **Tokay Pinot gris**, is a distinguished grape which produces opulent, full-bodied wine.

The flavour of fresh grapes has a strong presence in **Muscat d'Alsace**.

The only red variety is **Pinot noir**. These grapes have grown in popularity in recent years, and go into fruity rosé or red wines marked by a cherry aroma and taste. The red wines are firmer and more complex than the rosés.

Edelzwicker is the name given to the only wine made from a blend of varieties, including the less noble Chasselas.

Vin d'Alsace is an Appellation d'Origine Contrôlée, and is always bottled in the region of production. It is generally served in a round glass with a thin green stem. Most Alsace wines are best when fairly young (one to five years after harvest), and should be chilled.

Before a meal, a sparkling Crémant or sweet Muscat is a good apéritif; Sylvaner goes well with assorted cold cuts served as a starter. Riesling or Pinot accompany fish, fowl, meats and, of course, choucroute. Flavourful cheeses and desserts do well with the rich aroma of Gewürztraminer.

Eaux-de-vie

Cherries, mirabelles and raspberries are used to make sweet liqueurs: kirsche in the Vosges, *quetsch* and mirabelle in Lorraine. Clear raspberry liqueur is served in a large glass to increase the pleasure of the aroma. The musée des Eaux-de-vie in Lapoutroie shows how such liqueurs were traditionally made.

CHAMPAGNE

A long and prestigious past

When Roman soldiers arrived in the Champagne region, grapes were already cultivated on the slopes. The first bishops of Reims encouraged this activity; vineyards flourished around monasteries and the many travellers attending trade fairs or coming to the royal court boosted sales. Even the popes favoured Champagne, starting with Urbain II, a native of the region. During the Renaissance, Pope Leo X had his own vineyard to keep him supplied. St Bernard, in Clairvaux, introduced the arbanne stock, which created the basis for Côte des Bars vintages.

Champagne has been called the "nectar of the gods" and the "wine of kings". Henri IV, impatient with the Spanish ambassador's recitation of his master's aristocratic titles, interrupted him by saying, "Tell His Majesty the King of Spain, Castille and Aragon that Henri, lord of Ay and Gonesse, is master of the greatest vineyards in the world...".

At that time, Champagne was a still wine with only a hint of sparkle. That sparkle caught the eye of **Dom Pérignon**, who carefully studied the wine's characteristics and developed blending. The popularity of Champagne grew throughout the centuries, admired and imbibed by kings and their courts and figures of romance such as Mme de Pompadour and Casanova.

Political revolutions came and went, but Champagne remained. Napoleon was a faithful client, and Talleyrand plied the participants at the Congress of Vienna with Champagne in hopes of gaining a better settlement. The Prince of Wales, the future Edward VII, speaking of the Most Honourable Order of the Bath, is reputed to have said, "I'd rather have a bath of Champagne".

The vineyards

The vineyards cover about 30 000ha/74 130 acres, in the *départements* of Marne, Aube and Aisne. The most famous areas of production are the Côte des Blancs, the Marne Valley and the Montagne de Reims, where the great vintages originate. The grapes grow half way up the limestone slopes, above the chalky bedrock and in the sandy clay soil of the Côte de l'Île de France. The only varieties allowed are Pinot noir, Pinot Meunier and Chardonnay; the vines are planted close together and pruned low.

A delicate process

Champagne is created through a series of carefully executed steps which take place in the vineyards and in the cellars, where a steady temperature of about 10°C/50°F must be maintained.

Harvest

In October, bunches of grapes are picked and set down in flat trays; they are then sorted and carried to the press.

Pressing

The entire grapes are pressed, which results in a white must, even when dark grapes are used. Only the juice obtained by the first pressing (about 2 550l/660gal from 4 000kg/8 800lb of grapes) is used to make true Champagne wine.

Fermentation

The juice is stored in barrels or vats and fermentation is underway by Christmas.

Vintage and blend

In the spring, the maître de chais creates the vintage by blending different still wines, produced by various vineyards in various years. Each Champagne house has its own vintage that respects quality standards. Blendings include wines from the Montagne de Reims (hearty, full-bodied), the Marne Valley (fruity, aromatic wines), the Côte des Blancs (fresh, elegant wines) and the Côte des Bars. Red and white grapes are used in proportions that may vary but are generally about 2/3 to 1/3. Blanc de Blancs sparkling wine is made with only white grapes. Exceptionally, although ever more frequently, Champagne labels bear the vintage year, when the blending includes only wines of the same year.

Second fermentation and foam

The second fermentation is brought about by adding sugar and selected yeasts to the wine. The wine is drawn and put in very thick bottles that withstand pressure. Under the effects of the yeast (in the form of powder collected from the grape skins), the sugar is transformed into alcohol or carbonised into gas which, when the bottle is uncorked, creates foam. The bottles are set on racks in a cellar for 15 months to three years and sometimes more.

Settling and removing sediment

Over time, a deposit forms and must be eliminated. It is forced to settle in the bottle neck by storing the bottles at an angle, upside down. Each day, one person alone gives a slight turn (1/8 rotation) to as many as 40 000 bottles, and adjusts them for gradually increasing verticality. After five or six weeks, the bottle is fully vertical and all of the sediment has settled around the cork. The cork is then removed and the sediment with it. This process is called *dégorgement*. The bottle is topped off with more of the same wine, which may have had sugar added to make the final product sweeter.

Magnum: 2 bottles
Jeroboam: 4 bottles
Rehoboam: 6 bottles
Methuselah: 8 bottles
Salmanazar: 12 bottles
Balthazar: 16 bottles
Nebuchadnezzar: 20 bottles

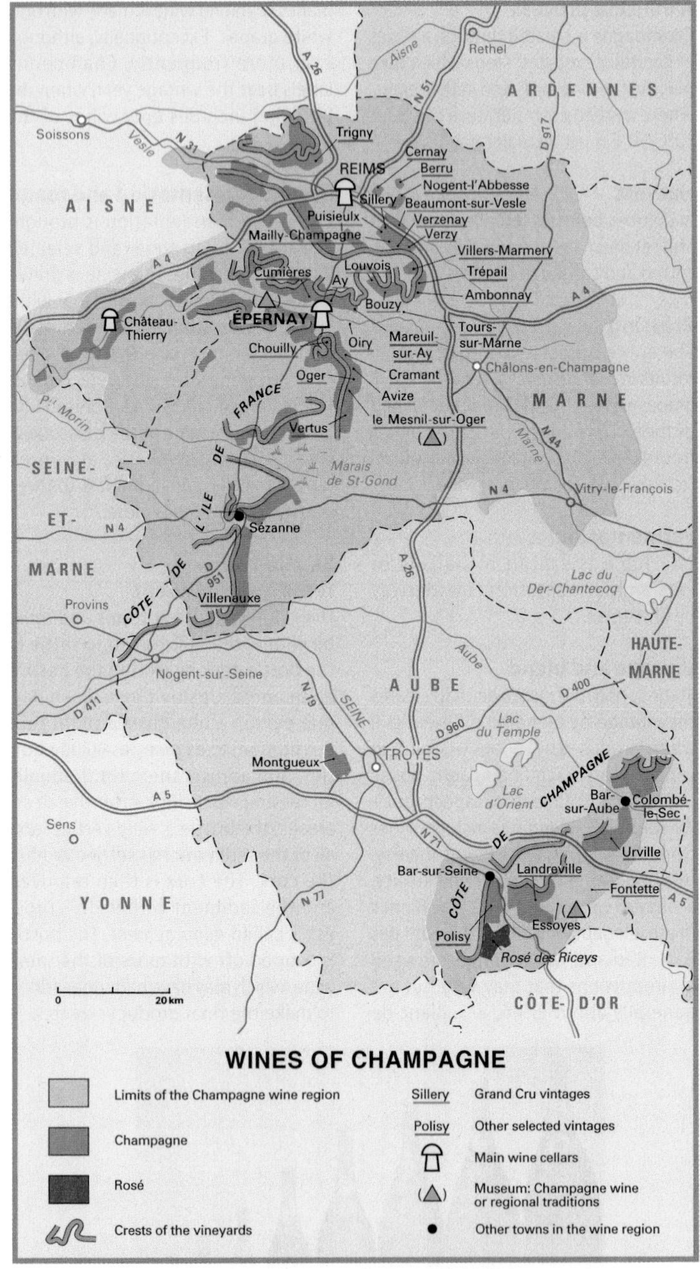

Finishing

The corks need to be wired down to contain the pressure of the gas within; then the bottle can be labelled and shipped. Champagne that is already three or four years old will not improve any more in the bottle and should be consumed. Champagne comes in many sizes – one is sure to be right for your party!

A Merry Widow

Veuve Clicquot-Ponsardin is one of France's best-known and best-selling brands of Champagne. The eponymous origin is indeed a Grande Dame, Nicole-Barbe Ponsardin. In 1798, she married François Clicquot in a Champagne cellar (the churches had not yet been restored for worship after the Revolution); he left her a widow eight years later. Twenty-seven years old, with a baby daughter and almost no experience in the trade, she took over the family Champagne house, and ran the business until her death in 1866.

She revolutionised the art of blending (assemblage) when she developed the technique known as *remuage*. Previously, the wine had to be decanted into new bottles after the second fermentation, an inefficient process that was necessary to remove the sediment, but which reduced precious effervescence. Nowadays, using her technique, the bottles are twisted and tilted so that the dregs settle around the cork, which can then be popped open briefly. A small bit of wine is removed (dégorgement), then the bottle is quickly topped off.

"Champagne," wrote Madame de Pompadour, "is the only wine which leaves a woman beautiful after drinking it. It gives brilliance to the eyes without flushing the face." Good news for merrymakers!

Marketing

Nearly 120 Champagne houses, mostly family-owned, and many dating back to the 18C, produce 70% of all Champagne shipped, with the remaining 30% in the hands of récoltants-manipulants, who blend their own wine; there are a few cooperatives as well. Financial backing is necessary for successful operations, because Champagne must be stored – and cared for – for an average of three years before it can be marketed, and thus involves keeping a lot of stock on hand. Every year, more and more Champagne leaves the region for sale elsewhere. In 1995, over 246 million bottles were shipped. Just a decade later in 2005, champagne sales are thought to have topped 300 million bottles world-wide, Production of the region's sparkling wine accounts for around four percent of total French wine production, but because of its value generate about 33% of France's earnings from wine exports.

Wrought-iron entrance to Stanislas Square, Nancy
R. Mattès/ MICHELIN

DISCOVERING ALSACE LORRAINE CHAMPAGNE

AMNÉVILLE

POPULATION 9 314

MICHELIN LOCAL MAP 307: H-3

Lying at the heart of the Coulange Forest, covering 500ha/1236 acres, this former industrial town became an important spa following the discovery of ferruginous water at a temperature of 41°C/105.8°F; today it is a lively resort with good tourist facilities, including a splendid fitness centre, Thermapolis. Children will rejoice in the Walibi-Schtroumpf leisure park nearby.

- **Orient Yourself:** Amnéville is situated 5km/3mi from the A4 motorway (exit 35), along D 953 and is 10min from Thionville and 15min from Metz by A 31, exit 37 (Mondelange).
- **Don't Miss:** The splendid fitness centre, Thermapolis *(see Sports & Recreation in the Address Book)* and of course the zoological park.
- **Organising Your Time:** It's best to begin with the zoo and the aquarium. If you are travelling with children, make sure you save time for nearby Walibi-Lorraine.
- Kids **Especially for Kids:** Children will love Amnéville Zoo, and will demand to visit the Walibi-Lorraine theme park. Older children might enjoy the motorbike and bicylce museum.

Sights

Parc zoologique d'Amnéville★★

Apr-Sep: 9.30am-7.30pm, Sun & holidays 9.30am-8pm; Oct-Mar: 10am to nightfall. €18 (children: €13). 03 87 70 25 60. www.zoo-amneville.com.

Kids About 600 animals representing almost 110 different species roam around in pens spread over a forested area covering 8ha/20 acres.

The zoo is committed to international programmes intended to protect endangered species. Educational shows, including the excellent Parrot's Jungle, add further interest to the visit.

Kids Located 300m/328yd from the zoo, the **Aquarium** (*Jul-Aug: 10am-7pm; Sep-Jun: 2-6pm, Sat 10am-7pm, Sun and holidays 10am-7pm. Dec 25. €9 (children: €6.50). 03 87 70 36v81. www.aquarium-amneville.com)* offers species of fish and underwater life-forms from the Caribbean, Australian rivers, African Lakes and the Amazon Valley. Several species of sharks share a huge tank.

R. Mattès/ MICHELIN

In France, a "Smurf" is a "Schtroumpf"

Parc d'Attraction Walibi-Lorraine★

3km/1.9mi S of Amnéville. Easter to Oct. Enquire for times and charges. 03 87 51 90 52. www.walabi.com.

Kids This 42ha/104-acre leisure park offers visitors of all ages a journey with Walibi, the friendly kangaroo, and the Schtroumpfs, the famous blue characters from Peyo's comic strip.

There is a wide choice of shops, snacks and restaurants, as well as several shows, so visitors can easily spend a whole day in the park.

Attractions include the **Odisséa**, a buoy tossed about among rapids, and the Waligator which splashes 12m/39ft down a waterfall. For the more daring, there is the **Comet Space** or the **Sismic Panic**. But will you be brave enough to face the **Vengeance de Gargamel**, which will propel you 55m/60yd upwards in two and a half seconds?

Address Book

For coin ranges, see the Legend on the cover flap.

PRACTICAL INFORMATION

Tourist office – *2 r. du Casino, 57360 Amnéville,* ☎*03 87 70 10 40– www.amneville.com*

WHERE TO EAT

⊖⊖ **La Forêt** – *In the Bois de Coulange leisure park – 2.5km/1.5mi S of Amnéville –* ☎*03 87 70 34 34 – resto.laforet@wanadoo.fr – closed 26 Jul-9 Aug, 23 Dec-7 Jan, Sun evening and Mon.* This popular restaurant in the Bois de Coulange leisure centre is surrounded by trees, and its dining room and terrace are pleasantly arranged with cane furniture and plants. The cooking is good, too.

WHERE TO STAY

⊖⊖ **Hôtel Orion** – *In the Bois de Coulange leisure park – 2.5km/1.5mi S of Amnéville –* ☎*03 87 70 20 20 – accueilhotel@wanadoo.fr – closed 27 Dec-2 Jan and Sun Nov-Apr – 44 rooms –* ☕ *€7 – restaurant* ⊖⊖. This spa resort hotel offers simple, identical rooms with rendered walls and cane furniture. A modern building offering practical, inexpensive accommodation.

SPORTS & RECREATION

Centre thermal St-Éloy – ☎*03 87 70 19 09 – Feb-Dec.* The St-Éloy spring is rich in salt, calcium and magnesium – and naturally heated to 41.2°C/106°F. This modern spa recommends its waters for treating rheumatic disorders, post-traumatic injuries and respiratory problems.

Thermapolis – *Av. de l'Europe –* ☎*03 87 71 83v50 – www.thermapolis.com – Closed during Sep, 23-25 and 31 Dec, 1 Jan.* This is the place to rediscover your vitality and sense of well-being. Bubbling pools, Turkish baths, hot marble surfaces. 2-hr or 3-hr admission, or membership available.

Base de loisirs du bois de Coulanges – *1 r. Tigre –* ☎*03 87 70 25v60 – www.zoo-amneville.com – Apr-Sep, daily 9.30am-7.30pm (Sun and holidays until 8pm); Oct-Mar daily 10am-dusk – €18 (children: €13).* Sports and recreation park with swimming pool, Olympic ice rink, an 18-hole golf course, a casino, show area, monorail tobogganing over 290m/317yd and a zoo.

Musée de la Moto et du Vélo

♿ *Centre Thermal et Touristique –* ⏲ *May-Sep: 1-7pm; Oct-Apr: daily except Mon 1:30pm-6pm.* ⏲ *1 Jan and 25 Dec. €5 (children: €3).* ☎*03 87 72 35 57.*

Kids This museum houses more than 200 bicycles and motorbikes, the oldest dating from 1895. Some are rare, like the motorbike of an English parachutist (1943) weighing only 43kg/95lb.

ANDLAU★

POPULATION 1 654

MICHELIN LOCAL MAP 315: I-6 – ALSO SEE ROUTE DES VINS

This small flower-decked town, nestling in the green valley of the River Andlau, is in the heart of Riesling country, with three famous vintages produced nearby.

Orient Yourself: Andlau lies at the foot of the Champ du Feu, along D 425 or 4km/2.4mi south of Barr along the Route des Vins.

Sights

Église St-Pierre-et-St-Paul★

⏲ *Jun-Sep: 10am-2pm and 2pm-6pm* ☎*03 88 08 93 38.*

The church is a fine example of 12C architecture (though the upper part of the steeple dates from the 17C) with an extraordinary carved **doorway**★★.

R. Mattès/ MICHELIN

The vineyard surrounds Andlau

Inside, the **chancel**, situated above the 11C **crypt**★, has impressive 15C stalls.

Excursion

Epfig
6km/3.7mi SE along D 253 and D 335.

Drive through the village and follow D 603 towards Kogenheim.

Situated east of the village, above the Rhine Valley, the **Chapelle Ste-Marguerite** (*Guided tour by request; contact Mme Schaeffer, ☎03 88 85 50 39*) was built in the 11C and 12C. According to legend, it was used by a congregation of nuns; the ossuary remains a mystery.

Address Book

PRACTICAL INFORMATION

Tourist office – *5 r. du Gén.-de-Gaulle – ☎03 88 08 22 57. www.andlau.fr*

WINE-TASTING

André Durrmann – *11 rue des Forgerons – ☎03 88 08 26 42. www.durmann.fr.st – 9am-7pm by appointment – closed 2nd fortnight Aug and Sun.* Instructive tours of the estate.

Marcel Schlosser – *Domaine du Vieux Pressoir, 5-7 rue des Forgerons – ☎03 88 08 03v26 – www.isasite.net/marcel-schlosser – Mon-Sat 9am-noon 1.30-6pm, Sun and holidays by appointment.* Tour of the cellars; wine tasting; sale of wine.

Gérard Wohleber – *14 rue du Mar.-Foch – ☎03 88 08 93 36. www.espace-wohleber.com – 8am-noon and 1-7pm.* In magnificent restored 1549 house.

ARGONNE★

MICHELIN LOCAL MAP 307: B/C 3/4

The Argonne region is a geographical entity of rolling hills and forests situated on the border of Champagne and Lorraine. The valleys separating the scenic hills have long been used as pathways by invaders.

Orient Yourself: The Argonne region spans three *départements*: Ardennes, Marne and Meuse.

A Bit of History

In 1792, Prussian troops were held up here after the fall of Verdun, which enabled Dumouriez to get his own troops ready in Valmy and to stop the enemy as it came out of the Argonne passes. During the First World War, the front line actually split Argonne in two. Fierce fighting took place near the Vauquois and Beaulieu heights.

Driving Tour

77km/48mi – Allow one day

Clermont-en-Argonne

Clermont is picturesquely situated on a wooded hillside above the Aire Valley; the top of the hill reaches 308m/1010ft, the highest point in the Argonne region.

The former capital of the county of Clermontois belonged in turn to the Holy Roman Empire, to the bishopric of Verdun, to the county of Bar and to the duchy of Lorraine before being joined to the kingdom of France in 1632. The **Église St-Didier** (*Tours by advance appointment; 03 29 87 41 20 or enquire at the presbytery, no 20 opposite the church*), dating from the 16C, is adorned with two Renaissance doorways.

Take the path on the right of the church and follow the shaded alleyway leading to the tip of the promontory: the view extends across the Argonne Forest and the plateau carved by the Aire Valley (*viewing table*).

Leave Clermont-en-Argonne on D 998 towards Neuvilly-en-Argonne. From Neuvilly, follow D 946. In Boureuilles, take D 212 on the right towards Vauquois. As you enter Vauquois, follow the surfaced path on the left, which leads to the hillock. Leave the car and climb along the footpath to the top of the hill.

Butte de Vauquois

No charge for visit of above-ground area. Guided tour of underground installations (2hr) 1st Sun of the month 9.30am-noon. 1, 8 May and National Heritage Day: 10am-5pm. €3. 03 29 80 73v15.

Between 1914 and 1918, there was fierce fighting on both sides over this hill. .

Return to D 38 which leads to Varennes-en-Argonne.

St-Didier church

Varennes-en-Argonne

This small town, built on the banks of the River Aire, is famous as the place where Louis XVI was arrested when he tried to flee France with his family during the Revolution. The royal coach was stopped by a handful of soldiers at 11pm on 21 June 1791.

The **Musée d'Argonne** (*Jul-Aug: 10.30pm-noon 3pm-6pm; Apr-Jun and Sep: Sat-Sun and holidays 3-6pm; Nov 1 to Easter; €4; 03 29 80 71 14*) features Louis XVI's arrest, arts and crafts of the Argonne region, and mementoes from the First World War (underground fighting and the American intervention).

Bear legend

The abbey was founded in 880 by Richarde, the wife of Emperor Charles le Gros (the Fat). According to legend, Richarde had a vision telling her to build a convent on the spot where she would meet a female bear building a shelter for her young. She met the animal in the forest and built the convent there; from then on, a live bear was kept at the convent and passing bear-leaders were always given free lodging and food. A hole in the paving of the crypt of St-Pierre-et-St-Paul Church is said to mark the very spot indicated by the bear; it is guarded by the pre-Romanesque stone statue of a bear!

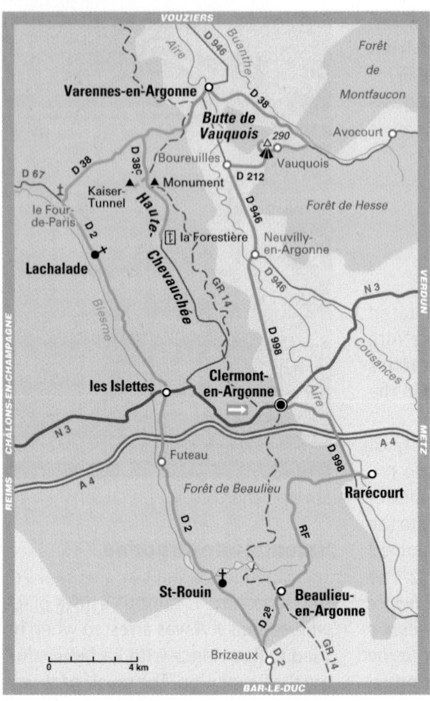

The **Mémorial de Pennsylvanie** is dedicated to American soldiers who died in 1918.

There is a lovely view of the River Aire and the surrounding countryside.

Return to D 38 then turn left onto the Haute-Chevauchée road.

Haute-Chevauchée

May-Sep: (guided tour 1hr) Sun and holidays 2-6pm; Mar-Apr and Oct-Nov: first Sun of the month 2-6.30pm. €3.50. 03 29 88 42 22.

This is one of the main sites of the First World War yet the road offers a pleasant walk through the forest to the **Kaisertunnel** and the Forestière military cemetery.

Return to D 38 and continue to Four-de-Paris, then take D 2 to Lachalade.

Lachalade

The village is overlooked by the imposing silhouette of a former Cistercian abbey. The 14C **church** looks oddly proportioned, owing to the fact that it is reduced to two bays.

Continue towards Les Islettes.

Les Islettes

This village was famous for its tileries, glassworks and earthenware factories.

Beyond Futeau, D 2 goes through the Beaulieu Forest.

Ermitage de St-Rouin

St Roding (or Rouin), a 7C Irish monk, settled in Argonne and founded a monastery which preceded the Beaulieu Abbey. Today, under the canopy formed by the trees, stands a concrete chapel designed by Father Rayssiguier, a disciple of Le Corbusier.

Continue along D 2 and turn left towards Beaulieu-en-Argonne.

Beaulieu-en-Argonne

Of the important Benedictine abbey which once stood here, only a few walls

Address Book

WHERE TO STAY

For coin categories, see the Legend.

Hostellerie de l'Abbaye *– 7 Grande-Rue – 55250 Beaulieu-en-Argonne – 03 29 70 72 81 – closed 2 Nov-14 Mar – 8 rooms – €5 – restaurant*. This establishment in the main street of the village houses the local café, a small number of well-maintained rooms and a simple restaurant. Unpretentious, family atmosphere. Lovely view of the Argonne and the surrounding mountain forests.

CALENDAR

Pilgrimage Once a year, on the Sunday after September 17, an important pilgrimage takes place at 3pm to the Ermitage de St-Rouin.

remain apart from the huge 13C **winepress**★ (Mar-Nov: 9am-6pm).

From Beaulieu-en-Argonne take the forest road running alongside the winepress building (on the left), continue straight on beyond the Trois Pins crossroads then turn right to Rarécourt.

Rarécourt

The **Musée de la Faïence** (*Late jun-early-Sep: 10am-noon, 2-6.30pm; €4 (under 12 free); 03 83 56 95 40*) is housed in a 17C-18C fortified building.

From Rarécourt, return to Clermont-en-Argonne along D 998.

BASILIQUE D'AVIOTH★★

MICHELIN LOCAL MAP 307: D-1

This magnificent church, situated in the centre of a remote village near the Belgian border, includes an unusual monument, the Recevresse, intended to receive offerings from pilgrims.

Visit

Basilique Notre-Dame

Allow about 30min. May-Sept: guided tours (45min) Mon-Sat 3pm-5pm; Oct-Apr: by appointment. €3.20. Night-time guided tours possible Jul-Aug. 03 29 88 90v96.

The discovery of a statue of the Virgin Mary, believed to have been sculpted by angels, led to a pilgrimage during the early 12C and to the construction of the basilica.

Exterior

The **west doorway** arching is decorated with 70 figures, and Christ's Passion is depicted on the lintel. The **south doorway** is dedicated to the Virgin Mary and to Christ's childhood.

Left of the south doorway stands **La Recevresse**★, a small yet elegant edifice in Flamboyant style decorated with fine tracery work.

Interior

The basilica includes a walkway (unusual in this region) and an ambulatory; radiating from it are shallow chapels fitted between the buttresses which happen to be inside the church according to a Champagne practice. Restoration work has brought to light 14C and 15C paintings and frescoes over the chancel screen and vaulting.

Worth noting in the chancel is the 14C high altar decorated with symbols of the four evangelists. To the left of the altar, one can see the ancient statue of **Notre-Dame d'Avioth**, carved out of lime c 1110 and resting on a 15C stone throne. Note also the 14 polychrome statues placed high against the pillars of the east end . The gothic tabernacle on the right of the altar dates from the 15 C. The elegant pulpit dates from 1538 and is carved with Renaissance motifs.

R Mattès/MICHELIN

La Recevresse

BACCARAT

POPULATION 4 746

MICHELIN LOCAL MAP 307: L-8

This small town lying on both sides of the River Meurthe is famous for its crystalworks founded in 1764.

- **Orient Yourself:** Baccarat is half-way (60km/37.3mi) between Nancy and Gérardmer on N 59.

A Bit of History

Crystalworks

In 1764 King Louis XV allowed the bishop of Metz to revive an ancient glass-making tradition; in 1817 the glassworks were turned into crystalworks and since 1828, the works have been supplying kings, presidents and the international jetset, including Tsar Nicholas II, who commissioned a 3.85m/12.6ft tall candelabrum. There was a time of great prosperity at the beginning of the 19C and again in the 1950s after the sombre period marked by two world wars. The workers' district comprised several long buildings. Glassworkers lived near the crystalworks because they had to run to the factory as soon as the bell rang signalling that the crystal had melted.

Address Book

For coin ranges, see the Legend on the cover flap.

PRACTICAL INFORMATION

Tourist office – *2 rue Adrien-Michaut, ☎03 83 75 13 37 – www.ville-baccarat.fr*

WHERE TO EAT

Le Wagon du Pré Fleury *– 54129 Magnières – 15km/9.3mi W of Baccarat, Bayon direction on D 22 – ☎03 83 72 32 58 – http://wagon-restaurant.free.fr – closed Jan, Sun evening and Mon.* This restaurant has a rather unlikely setting, in an old railway carriage and its station! It is run by a former industrial designer and saddler and is pleasantly decorated in a slightly old-fashioned style. Regional cooking. Nearby attractions include fishing, walking and pedal-propelled railcars.

SHOPPING

Cristal de Baccarat – *2 r. des Cristalleries – ☎03 83 76 60 01. www.baccarat.fr– Open Daily 9.30am-12.30pm and 1.30-7pm, Sun and holidays 10am-12.30pm and 2.30-7pm – closed Dec 25 and Jan 1.* Each item made here bears a specific mark only available from certain agents. Boutiques selling individual items and gallery display.

SPORTS & RECREATION

Draisine – *Val de Mortagne, former railway station – 54129 Magnières – ☎03 83 72 34 73 – val-montagne@wanadoo.fr – Apr and Sep 2-6pm; May-June 9am-noon, 2-7pm; July-Aug 9am-12pm, 1.30-7pm; Oct-Mar by arrangement – 10€/hr – 4 people.* The Draisine was formerly used by workers as a means of transport for maintaining and overseeing the train tracks. Nowadays it is used to explore the Mortagne Valley as you pedal along an old railway stretching for 20km/12.4mi from Magnières (13km/8mi West of Baccarat).

Kids **Fraispertuis City** – *50 r. de la colline des Eaux – 20km/14.5mi S of Baccarat on D 935, D 435 and D 32. – 88700 Jeanménil – ☎03 29 65 27v06 – www.fraispertuis.city.fr – July-Aug daily 10am-6.30pm; Apr, May, June, Sep 10am-6pm – 12€ (no charge children under 1m/3.3ft).* Over twenty rides and attractions on a Far West theme (the adventure river, the Grand Canyon and the Far West train and two new attractions since 2004, Los Sombreros and Old America) can be enjoyed by children and adults alike at this theme park. Restaurant facilities on site.

Today, the high-tech crystalworks use a special furnace that fines down the melted mixture, and 38 highly qualified craftsmen have been nominated "best workers in France". *Crystalworks not open to the public.*

Sights

Musée du Cristal

Apr-Oct: 9.30am-12.30pm, 2-630pm; Nov-Mar: 10am-12pm, 2-6pm. 1 Jan, 25 Dec. €2.50. 03 83 76 61 37. www.baccarat.fr

Located in the mansion which once belonged to the crystalworks' founder, the museum displays antique and contemporary pieces: 19C opalines, agates, millefiori paperweights, plain, cut or carved glasses, and table sets ordered by sovereigns and heads of states. In the last room, the various techniques and tools used are illustrated: work under heat, cutting, carving and the gilding process.

Église St-Rémy

Built in 1957, the church has an unusual roof with large awnings. The steeple, a 55m/180ft pyramid, stands beside the church. The interior decoration, which consists in a huge low relief made up of concrete elements and **stained-glass panels**★ in Baccarat crystal (more than 50 different colours), illustrates the creation of the world. The tabernacle and christening font lit by two stained-glass windows depicting the Twelve Apostles are also noteworthy.

Excursions

Deneuvre

Excavations, carried out between 1974 and 1986 south of this village adjacent to Baccarat, led to the discovery of a 2C Gallo-Roman sanctuary once dedicated to Hercules, which has been reconstructed in a museum.

J.-P. Clapham/ MICHELIN

Window in St-Rémy church

Les Sources d'Hercule

May-Sep: 10am-noon, 2-6pm; Oct: 2-5pm; Mar-Apr: Sat-Sun 2-5pm and daily during school holidays. Nov-Feb. €3.50. 03 83 75 22 82.

In the entrance hall there are explanations, maps, plans and models dealing with the discovery of the site. Three pools were at the disposal of those who wished to perform their ablutions; over centuries of use, the ex-voto offerings (usually figurines of Hercules) piled up around the springs.

Fontenoy-la-Joûte

6km/3.5mi W. In this typically stretched-out Lorraine village, 18C semi-detached houses have been turned into bookshops, and Fontenoy has become a **book village** (*a big fair is held the last Sun of the month, Apr-Sep; 03 83 71 53 25. http://levillagedulivre.free.fr*) with some 15 bookshops, a first-class bookbinder and a printing house.

BALLON D'ALSACE★★★

MICHELIN LOCAL MAP 314: J-6

The Ballon d'Alsace belongs to the crystalline part of this range where granite predominates and the massif is clad with dense forests of spruce and fir trees; ravines are pleasantly cool and the heights are covered with pastures dotted with Alpine flowers. The massif owes its name to its rounded shape, although ballon could be derived from the name of the Celtic god Bel as there is some evidence that the peak was used as a solar observatory in Celtic times.

- **Orient Yourself:** The Ballon d'Alsace is the highest peak (alt 1 250m/4 101ft) of the Massif du Ballon d'Alsace situated at the southern end of the Vosges mountain range. The walking path begins in front of the Ferme-Restaurant, situated off D 465 *(see Ballon d'Alsace below)*; be prepared for frequent fogs in this region.
- **Don't Miss:** The panorama from the viewing platform on the mountain (a 30min round-trip hike).
- **Organising Your Time:** Allow 2 hours for the 38km/23.6mi driving tour itself. The tour takes in several interesting attractions as well as specific hikes. Add another 3 to 4 hours to take the hikes mentioned as well as the geological itinerary.
- Kids **Especially for Kids:** Children will find the fossils and minerals in the Maison de la Géologie fascinating.

Massif du Ballon d'Alsace★★

1 From St-Maurice-sur-Moselle to Sentheim

38km/23.6mi – allow 2hr – local map see Parc naturel régional des BALLONS DES VOSGES.

The road leading to the Col du Ballon d'Alsace, built in the 18C, is the oldest in the area.

St-Maurice-sur-Moselle

This small industrial town (textiles and sawmills) is close to some remarkable beauty spots as well as the Rouge Gazon and Ballon d'Alsace winter resorts. It is the starting point of excursions to the Ballon de Servance and the Charbonniers Valley.

On the way up to the Col du Ballon, the road (*D 465*) offers some fine views of the Moselle Valley before going through a splendid forest of firs and beeches.

Plain du Canon

15min on foot there and back. The path leaves D 465 by an information panel tied to a tree and runs down towards a forest lodge. Go down past the lodge and follow a path on the left which meanders upwards.

The place owes its name to a small gun once used by the local gamekeeper to create an echo.

There is a charming view of the wooded Presles Valley over which tower the Ballon d'Alsace and Ballon de Servance, crowned by a fort.

Beyond **La Jumenterie**, whose name (*jument* means mare) is a reminder of a horse-breeding centre founded in 1619 by the dukes of Lorraine, there is a fine view of the Moselle Valley and Ballon de Servance to the right.

The road reaches the high-pasture area.

The **Monument aux Démineurs** by Rivière and Deschler is dedicated to bomb-disposal experts who died while performing their duty.

Col du Ballon

At the end of the parking area, there is a monument celebrating the racing cyclist René Pottier. There is a fine view of the summit of the Ballon d'Alsace, crowned with a statue of the Virgin Mary and, further right, of the Belfort depression dotted with lakes and the northern part of the Jura mountains. A path leads to Joan of Arc's statue.

Ballon d'Alsace★★★

30min on foot there and back. Preserve the environment! Walk along paths, don't cut through pastures or forests, and leave wild flowers and plants as you find them.

The path starts from D 465 in front of the Ferme-Restaurant du Ballon d'Alsace. It runs through pastures towards the statue of the Virgin Mary. Before Alsace became French once more, the statue stood exactly on the border. From the viewing platform, the **panorama**★★ extends north to Mt Donon, east across the plain of Alsace and the Black Forest and south as far as Mont Blanc.

The drive down to Lake Alfeld is very beautiful. Ahead is the Grand Ballon, the highest summit in the Vosges mountains (1 424m/4 672ft); later on there are fine views of the **Doller Valley** and of the Jura and the Alps.

As the road comes out of the forest, the lake appears inside a glacial cirque.

R. Mattès/ MICHELIN

River Doller

Lac d'Alfeld★

The artificial Lake Alfeld (covering an area of 10ha/25 acres and reaching a depth of 22m/72ft) is one of the most attractive expanses of water in the Vosges region. It ensures that the River Doller has a regular flow, particularly when the thaw comes. The lake is framed by picturesque wooded heights.

The dam, built between 1884 and 1887, is 337m/369yd long and leans against a moraine left behind by ancient glaciers.

Address Book

For coin ranges, see the Legend on the cover flap.

WHERE TO STAY

Grand Hôtel du Sommet – *On the summit of the Ballon d'Alsace – 90200 Lepuix-Gy – ☎03 84 29 30 60 hotel-dusommet@aol.com– closed Mon except school holidays – P – 25 rooms – €6.50 – restaurant.* Imagine waking up on a mountain top, surrounded by nothing but open air and fields of cows, with a view of the Belfort Valley and, on a clear day, even the Swiss Alps. A good night's sleep is guaranteed in the simple but comfortable rooms. Classic cooking.

Auberge Le Lodge de Monthury – *Monthury – 70440 Servance – 4.5km/2.8mi N of Servance on D 263 road to Beulotte-St-Laurent – ☎03 84 20 48 55. http://mouches.free.fr/monthury/index.htm– closed 20 Dec to 20 Jan – 6 rooms – €4 – meals.* Immerse yourself totally in nature in this isolated 18C farm in the forests above the Ognon Valley, facing the Ballon de Servance. Comfortable, simple rooms. The cooking uses local produce. Fishing available in 7ha/17 acres of private lakes.

SKIING

École de ski – *ESF Chalet at La Gentiane – 70440 Servance – ☎03 84 29 06 65 – Dec 15-Apr 15: 9am-6pm.* During winter Le Ballon d'Alsace offers a range of snow sports not to be sniffed at. Although essentially a domain for cross-country skiing – 8 trails, 50km/30mi – it is proud of its 19 downhill ski slopes.

Lac de Sewen

Close to Lake Alfeld, this small lake is gradually filling up with peat. Alpine and Nordic plants grow on its shores.

Farther downstream, D 466 follows the Doller which flows between high slopes covered with green pastures alternating with woods of fir and beech trees.

The valley is overlooked by the Romanesque church of **Kirchberg** perched on a moraine and, as you enter **Niederbruck**, on the left, by a monumental statue of the Virgin and Child by Antoine Bourdelle.

Masevaux

See THANN: Excursion.

Sentheim

Maison de la Géologie

Jun-Sep: daily except Sat 10am-noon, 1-6pm; Oct-May: daily except Sat 9am-noon, 1-5pm; 1 Jan, 25 Dec. Museum: €2 (children under 16: €1). 03 89 82 55v55.sentheim.geologie.free.fr. The building, located opposite the church, houses a fine collection of fossils and minerals.

Sentier géologique de Wolfloch

Drive along D 466 towards Bussang, then turn right 300m/328yd after the church and follow the arrows to the starting point of the geological trail.

The itinerary extends over a distance of 5km/3mi and includes 12 geological sites. Allow 2hr. It is essential to obtain the brochure available at the Maison de la Géologie. Guided tours possible (3hr) €5.

Start from the presentation panel and walk to the right along the fields, following the markings illustrating a fossil.

The path goes across the great Vosges fault and gives an insight into the geology of the region from the Primary Era until today. The fault separates the primary formations, uplifted when the Alps rose, from more recent sediments, often rich in fossils, which account for the presence of the sea 100 million years ago.

5 Vallée de Munster★★

See MUNSTER.

6 Vallée de la Fecht

See MUNSTER.

7 Massif du Petit Ballon★

See Massif du PETIT BALLON.

PARC NATUREL RÉGIONAL DES BALLONS DES VOSGES★★

POPULATION 240 000

MICHELIN LOCAL MAP 314: L-3 TO M-4

The nature park's main attraction is its varied landscapes – rounded summits (ballons) clad with high pastures, peat bogs, glacial cirques, lakes, rivers and hills covered with conifers – which combine to create what is called the "blue line of the Vosges", on the horizon. The park was created in 1989.

The great diversity of ecosystems creates an ideal environment for deer, roe-deer, wild boars, chamois and even lynx. Bird life is also plentiful in the forested and mountainous areas (in particular species such as the peregrine, capercaillie and blackbirds). Aquatic ecosystems also have a rich fauna (crayfish, common trout, Alpine newt etc) and specific flora.

Villages, farms and museums illustrate agricultural and industrial traditions as well as local handicrafts: silver-mine development, weaving, wood-sledging, Munster-cheese making.

Orient Yourself: This park spans four *départements*: Haut-Rhin, Vosges, Haute-Saône and Territoire de Belfort.

Val d'Argent 4

Round tour from Ste-Marie-aux-Mines

65km/40mi – Allow 1hr 30min.

The Vosges mountains are particularly rich in mineral resources, silver, copper and other metals, extracted since the Middle Ages. The mining industry had its heyday during the reign of Louis XIV; by the mid-19C, it was in decline. Great efforts have been made to restore the region's mining heritage and develop its touristic potential. Today, several protected, restructured mining sites are open to the public.

Follow N 59 west out of Ste-Marie-aux-Mines through a green valley. The road then climbs sharply past a war cemetery on the right.

Col de Ste-Marie

From the pass (alt 772m/2 533ft), one of the highest in the Vosges mountains, look back towards the Cude Valley and ahead to the Liepvrette Valley, the Plaine d'Alsace and Haut-Kœnigsbourg Castle.

Roc du Haut de Faite

From the pass, 30min on foot there and back. Walk north along a path starting on the right of a gravestone. From the top, there is a fine **panorama** of the Vosges summits and the slopes on the Alsatian and Lorraine side.

Return to N 59 and drive towards St-Dié. Turn left onto D 23, 2km/1.2mi beyond Gemaingoutte.

Circuit minier La Croix-aux-Mines

5.6km/3.5mi walk – Allow 2hr 45min.

Start from the Chapelle du Chipal and follow the mining circuit panels marked with a black circle against a yellow background and bearing the emblem of the trail (crossed hammer and pickaxe). Miners extracted galena, a mineral ore of lead sulphide mixed with silver, from this Le Chipal site and others in the area.

Continue along D 23 to Fraize and turn left onto N 415.

Col du Bonhomme

See Val d'ORBEY.

On reaching the pass, turn left onto D 148.

Le Bonhomme

This pleasant resort was caught three times in heavy fighting during the two world wars. Mountain streams rush downwards to form the River Béhine.

Le Brézouard★★

45min on foot there and back.

You will be able to get fairly close to Mt Brézouard by car if you approach it via the **Col des Bagenelles** *(4km/2.5mi)* which offers a fine view of the Liepvrette Valley.

Leave the car in the parking area, near the Amis de la Nature refuge.

Mt Brézouard and the surrounding area suffered complete upheaval during the First World War.

From the summit, there is a sweeping **panorama**★★: the Champ du Feu and Climont to the north, with Mt Donon in the background; Strasbourg to the north-east, Mt Hohneck and Grand Ballon to the south. When the weather is clear, Mont Blanc can be seen in the distance.

Return to Ste-Marie-aux-Mines along D 48.

The road winds its way through the forest then follows the Liepvrette Valley.

Vallée de la Liepvrette★

Orchards take over from high pastures along this valley; the Liepvrette is a charming stream running between two roads on its way to Ste-Croix-aux-Mines.

Sentier patrimoine de Neuenberg

This heritage trail *(from Échery short tour: 2hr 30min, long tour: 4hr)* offers views of the mineworkers' tower, the tithe-collector's house, flanked with a turret in

R. Mattès/ MICHELIN

Landscape in the Regional nature park

characteristic Renaissance style, and a research gallery for the Enigma mine.

▶ *Turn right in Échery.*

St-Pierre-sur-l'Hâte

Where there was once a Benedictine priory, an ecumenical church remains, known as the miners' church, built in the 15C-16C and restored in 1934.

Ste-Marie-aux-Mines

This small industrial town, located in the Liepvrette Valley, owes its name to its former silver mines. Today, it is the meeting place of rock and fossil collectors who gather for the exhibition and exchange market organised every year during the last weekend in June. Ste-Marie has a famous weaving industry specialising in fine woollen cloth, both factory and homemade by craftsmen who have been passing their skills on from one generation to the next since the 18C. Twice a year, in spring and autumn, a fabric fair offers buyers from various countries a choice of fabrics woven in Ste-Marie, in particular tartans and a variety of new textiles largely headed for the haute-couture trade.

Address Book

PRACTICAL INFORMATION

Maison du Parc – *Cour de l'Abbaye, 68140 Munster, ☎03 89 77 90v34. www.parc-ballons-vosges.fr – early Jun to mid-Sep, daily except Mon 10am-noon, 2-6pm; mid-Sep to late May, daily except Sat-Sun – closed Jan 1-15.*
The park headquarters offers over 600m²/656yd² of permanent and temporary exhibitions devoted to the Vosges mountains.

WHERE TO STAY

The park federation and the WWF have selected a few gîtes in splendid farmhouses and chalets, etc. Referred to as "panda gîtes", they are an ideal means of getting back to grass roots.

OUTDOOR ACTIVITIES

Hiking – One option is to follow waymarked discovery and historic trails. Some of these are detailed in a small brochure (on sale in the Maison du Parc). A calendar of winter and summer events is also published by the park, featuring outings (nature and heritage) organised by local associations, museum exhibitions and a diary of traditional and cultural events.

Skiing, sledging – Some 20 resorts offer Alpine skiing, cross-country skiing, snow-shoeing and sledging. A few are equipped for night skiing.

Other activities – The park lends itself to the practice of paragliding, rock-climbing and mountain biking, bearing in mind, of course, that nature is vulnerable.

The Birthplace of Patchwork

Every year in September, a historic and artistic exhibition on patchwork and the Amish community takes place in Ste-Marie-aux-Mines. Founded in 1693 in Ste-Marie, the Amish movement emigrated to Pennsylvania in 1740. Amish women used to make up blankets with pieces of fabric and thus initiated the art of patchwork. Lessons in patchwork-making are available and there are lectures on the history of the Amish movement and the various techniques of patchwork-making in several venues throughout the valley.

Maison de Pays

Jun-Sep: 10am-1pm, 2-6pm; Oct-May: daily, by request. Guided tour available (1hr 30min). €5 (children: €2.50). 03 89 58 56v67. http://maisondepays.site.voila.fr/ Place du Prensureux. The building houses a rich collection of rocks, along with reconstructions of a workshops, tools and models where visitors can follow the different stages of mining and the manufacturing process of fabrics.

The **Mine St-Barthélemy** *(rue St-Louis)* (*May-Sept, 10am-noon, 2-6pm; Jul-Aug, 10am-6pm; €5.50 (children: €4); 03 89 58 72 28*) organises tours of the galleries hewn out of the rock by 16C miners and the **Mine d'argent St-Louis-Eisenthur** presents the various mining sites and techniques used in the 16C. (*Guided tour (3 hr) by reservation at the ASEPAM, centre du patrimoine minier, 4 rue Weisgerber, 68160 Ste-Marie-aux-Mines, 03 89 58 62 11 or at the tourist office, 03 89v58v80v50. Wear walking shoes and warm clothes (boots, waterproof and helmet provided). €10 (Children 5-12: €5).*

A **historic trail** (*2hr 30min, booklet available at the tourist office*) enables visitors to discover miners' houses and mansions which show how flourishing the mining industry was in the 16C and early 17C.

Leave Ste-Marie-aux-Mines by D 459 towards Ste-Croix.

Sentier minier et botanique de Ste-Croix-aux-Mines

A mining and botanic trail (3.8km/2.4mi; allow 2hr 30min; on the left of the road as you leave the town, 100m/110yd before the panel marked "les halles").

The trail winds through the Bois de St-Pierremont where several silver mines were located in the 16C. All along the way, panels provide information about the various species of trees.

Massif du Ballon d'Alsace★★

From St-Maurice-sur-Moselle to Sentheim 1

See BALLON D'ALSACE.

Ballon de Servance★★

Itinerary starting from Servance 2

20km/12.4mi – allow 1hr

Situated a few miles west of the Ballon d'Alsace (crowned by a statue of the Virgin Mary), the Ballon de Servance (crowned by a military fort) reaches an altitude of 1 216m/3 990ft. The River Ognon begins here as a modest mountain stream.

Servance

The syenite quarries (producing a reddish stone used in the Paris opera pillars) are no longer in operation.

As you leave the village, a footpath starting on your right (*15min there and back*) leads to the **Saut de l'Ognon**, a picturesque waterfall gushing forth from a narrow gorge.

Col des Croix

Alt 679m/2 228ft. Overlooked by the Château-Lambert Fort, this pass is the watershed between the North Sea and the Mediterranean Sea.

PARC NATUREL RÉGIONAL DES BALLONS DES VOSGES

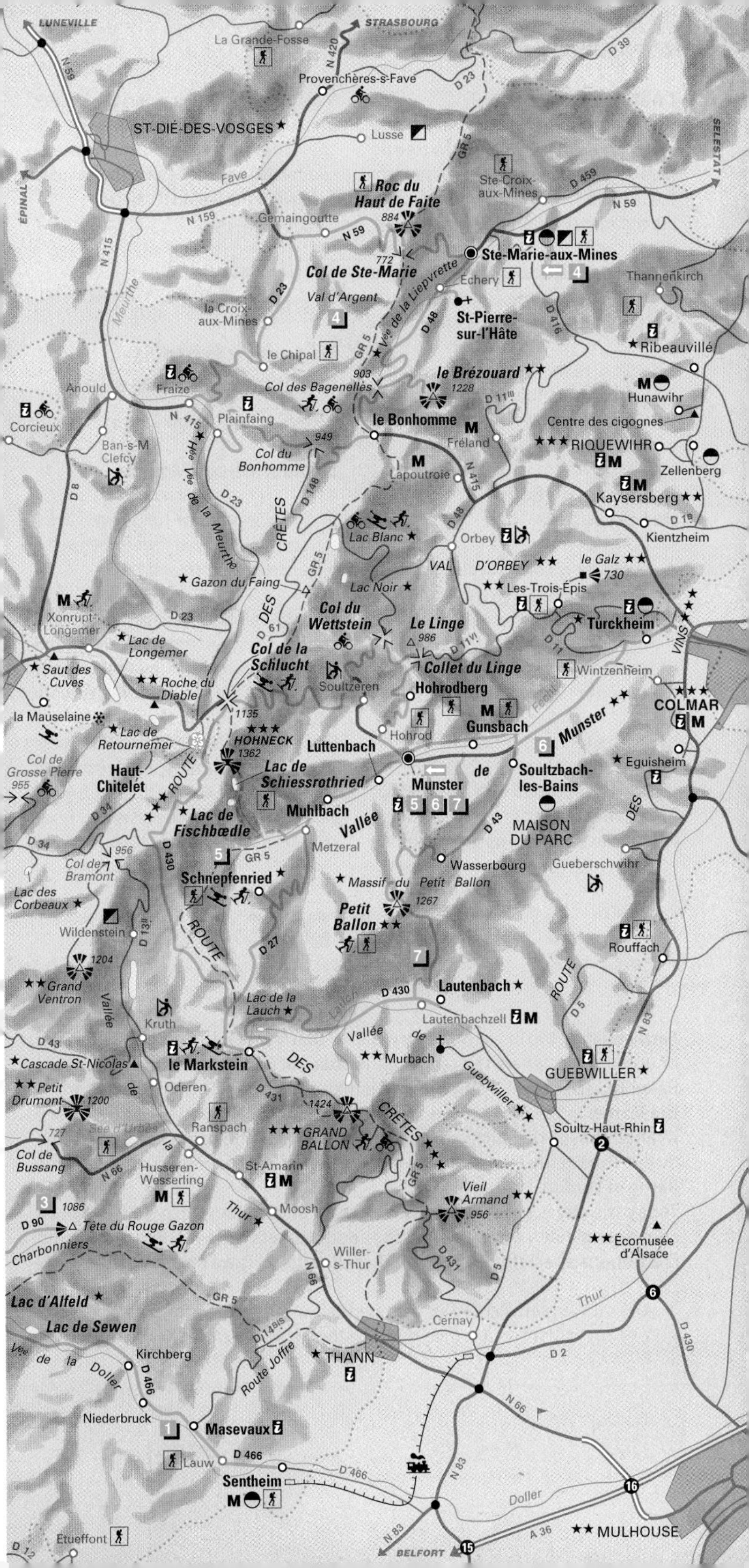

LUNEVILLE
STRASBOURG
La Grande-Fosse
N 420
D 39
N 59
Provenchères-s-Fave
D 23
ST-DIÉ-DES-VOSGES
Lusse
SELESTAT
GR 5
ÉPINAL
Fave
Roc du Haut de Faite
Ste-Croix-aux-Mines
D 459
N 59
N 159
Gemaingoutte
884
N 415
N 59
Ste-Marie-aux-Mines
772
Col de Ste-Marie
4
Echery
Thannenkirch
Meurthe
D 23
Val d'Argent
Vée de la Liepvrette
St-Pierre-sur-l'Hâte
D 416
La Croix-aux-Mines
4
D 48
Ribeauvillé
le Chipal
GR 5
903
le Brézouard
Anould
Fraize
Col des Bagenelles
1228
D 11III
M
Hunawihr
Corcieux
N 415
Plainfaing
le Bonhomme
M
Centre des cigognes
Ban-s-M Clefcy
Hée Vée de la Meurthe
949
Fréland
RIQUEWIHR
Col du Bonhomme
M
Lapoutroie
Zellenberg
D 8
D 23
CRÊTES
D 148
N 415
M
Kaysersberg
D 48
D 1B
GR 5
Lac Blanc
Orbey
Kientzheim
VAL
D'ORBEY
le Galz
730
Gazon du Faing
Lac Noir
Les-Trois-Épis
M
DES
Col du Wettstein
Le Linge
Turckheim
D 23
Xonrupt-Longemer
61
986
VINS
D 11VI
D 11
Lac de Longemer
Col de la Schlucht
Collet du Linge
Saut des Cuves
Roche du Diable
Soultzeren
Wintzenheim
Hohrodberg
COLMAR
la Mauselaine
1135
M
M
HOHNECK
Gunsbach
Lac de Retournemer
Hohrod
Munster
Col de Grosse Pierre
1362
Luttenbach
6
Haut-Chitelet
ROUTE
Lac de Schiessrothried
Munster
de
Soultzbach-les-Bains
Eguisheim
955
D 34
Lac de Fischbœdle
Muhlbach
5 6 7
Vallée
D 43
MAISON DU PARC
DES
D 34
956
Metzeral
Col de Bramont
5
GR 5
Gueberschwihr
D 430
Schnepfenried
Wasserbourg
Lac des Corbeaux
Massif du Petit Ballon
1267
Wildenstein
D 13II
ROUTE
Petit Ballon
Rouffach
1204
Grand Ventron
D 27
7
ROUTE
Vallée
Lac de la Lauch
D 430
Lautenbach
D 5
Lauch
N 83
Kruth
Lautenbachzell
M
D 43
Vallée
de
Cascade St-Nicolas
le Markstein
DES
Murbach
GUEBWILLER
de
Oderen
Guebwiller
Petit Drumont
1200
D 431
1424
CRÊTES
Ranspach
Soultz-Haut-Rhin
727
Lac d'Urbès
la
GRAND BALLON
2
Col de Bussang
N 66
Husseren-Wesserling
St-Amarin
M
GR 5
Vieil Armand
M
956
3
1086
Thur
Moosh
D 90
Tête du Rouge Gazon
Écomusée d'Alsace
Charbonniers
Willer-s-Thur
D 431
N 66
D 5
6
GR 5
Thur
Lac d'Alfeld
D 430
Lac de Sewen
D 14BIS
Cernay
Vée de la Doller
Kirchberg
THANN
D 2
D 466
Route Joffre
Niederbruck
N 66
1
Masevaux
N 83
D 466
Lauw
D 466
Sentheim
Doller
16
M
N 83
A 36
MULHOUSE
Etueffont
BELFORT
15
D 12

Château-Lambert

Just 1km/0.6mi from the pass, this charming village has an interesting **Musée de la Montagne** (*Apr-Sep: daily except Tue 9.30am-noon, 2-6pm (last entrance 30 min before closing); Oct-Mar: daily except Tue 2-5pm; Christmas holidays, 1 and 11 Nov €4; 03 84 20 43 09*), with a farmer-miner's house, a mill, a smithy, a 17C press, and a former classroom.

Return to the Col des Croix and turn left onto D 16; the road rises above the Ognon Valley, offering fine views, before meandering through the forest.

Panorama du Ballon de Servance★★

Leave the car at the beginning of the military road (no entry) for the Fort de Servance and take a marked path on the right which leads (15min on foot there and back) to the summit of the Ballon (alt 1 216m/3 990ft).

The panorama is magnificent: the Ognon Valley, the glacial Plateau d'Esmoulières dotted with lakes and the Plateau de Langres to the west; Monts Faucilles to the north-west; the Moselle Valley further to the right; the Vosges mountain range to the north-east (with their foothills stretching south and south-east) and to the east, the rounded summit of the Ballon d'Alsace.

Vallée des Charbonniers

Itinerary from St-Maurice-sur-Moselle 3

12km/7.4mi – Allow 30min

St-Maurice-sur-Moselle

From St-Maurice-sur-Moselle, drive east along the road which follows the Charbonniers stream.

The inhabitants of this valley are believed to be the descendants of a Swedish and German colony hired by the dukes of Lorraine in the 18C for forestry work and coal mining. In the village of Les Charbonniers, turn left onto the Rouge Gazon road (winter sports): from the **Tête du Rouge Gazon**, there are good views of the Ballon de Servance.

BAR-LE-DUC★

POPULATION 16 944

MICHELIN LOCAL MAP 307: B-6

Partly built on top of a promontory, Bar-le-Duc is split into two: the Ville Haute or upper town, where the castle of the dukes of Bar once stood, and the Ville Basse or lower town, lying on both banks of the River Ornain, a tributary of the Marne. In the 10C, Bar was already the capital of a county whose influence rivalled that of the duchy of Lorraine, and in 1354 the counts of Bar became dukes. During the First World War, Bar-le-Duc played an important role in the Battle of Verdun.

Today the city is the administrative centre of the Meuse *département* and a commercial town where regular fairs and markets are held. Redcurrant jam is a famous speciality (Alfred Hitchcock claimed it was his favourite).

Orient Yourself: Bar-le-Duc is located half-way between Strasbourg and Paris, exit 30 (Verdun) on A 4, then N 35. The town is 40km/24.8mi to the south.

Visit *Allow 30min*

Ville Haute★

The former aristocratic district of Bar still boasts a stellar ensemble of 16C, 17C and 18C architecture.

Place St-Pierre

This triangular area in front of the west front of the Église St-Étienne, is lined with houses from different periods.
On the right as you face the church, **No 25** is a fine medieval timber-framed house with corbelled upper floor, while **no 21** has an Alsatian Renaissance façade. And **no 29** is strictly Classical, with early-17C columns and windows.

Église St-Étienne

Jul-Aug: 10am-7pm; May-Jun and Sep: 10am-6pm; Apr-Oct: Sat-Sun 2-5pm. Guided tour of Église St Étienne and Renaissance quarter, enquire at the tourist office. ☎03 29 79 11 13.
This former collegiate church of the late 14C contains several works of art including the famous **Transi**★★ by Ligier Richier *(in the south transept)*, which depicts the Prince of Orange, René de Chalon, killed during the siege of St-Dizier in 1544 (the work was commissioned by his widow, Anne de Lorraine). A **Calvary** scene behind the high altar is also by Richier. In the north transept the **Statue of Notre-Dame-du-Guet** is revered locally: legend claims it shouted warnings during the siege of 1440.

Place de la Halle

You can glimpse the arcades of the former 13C covered market through the gateway of **no 3**, which has a beautiful though damaged Baroque façade.

Take rue Chavée and turn right.

Belvédère des Grangettes

This offers a view of the lower town,.

Return to rue Chavée, turn right onto rue de l'Armurier then left onto rue de l'Horloge.

Only the **clock tower** remains of the former ducal castle.

Rue de l'Horloge on the left leads to avenue du Château; turn left.

Collège Gilles-de-Trèves

The university college was founded in 1571 by the dean of St-Maxe, Gilles de Trèves, who wished to prevent young aristocrats from attending universities where the Reformation was gaining ground.
Access is through a long porch with vaulting with a Latin inscription: "Let this house remain standing until ants have drunk the oceans dry and tortoises have gone all the way round the world".

Continue along rue du Baile.

R. Mattès/ MICHELIN

Bar-le-Duc

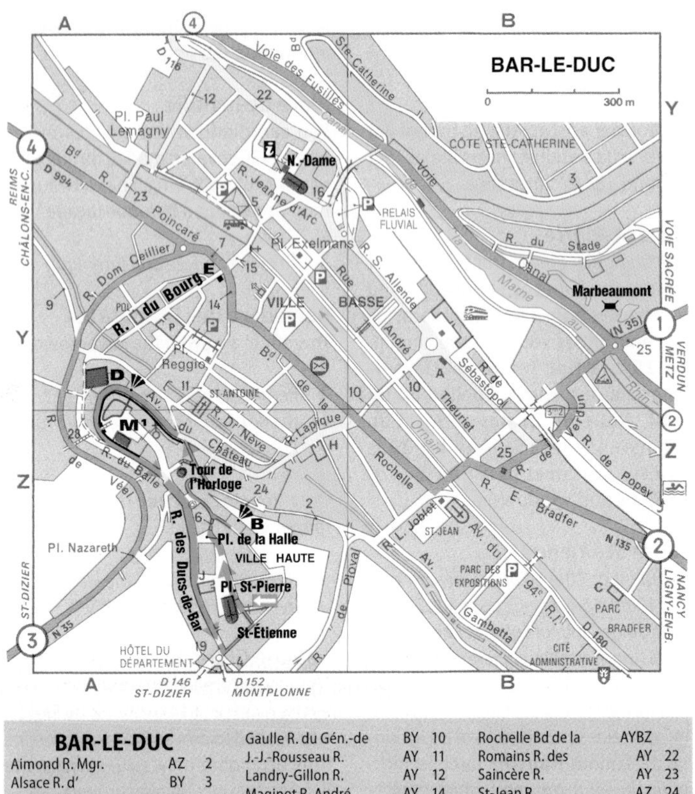

BAR-LE-DUC

Aimond R. Mgr.	AZ	2	Gaulle R. du Gén.-de	BY	10	Rochelle Bd de la	AYBZ	
Alsace R. d'	BY	3	J.-J.-Rousseau R.	AY	11	Romains R. des	AY	22
Aulnois R. d'	AZ	4	Landry-Gillon R.	AY	12	Saincère R.	AY	23
Bar-la-Ville R.	AY	5	Maginot R. André	AY	14	St-Jean R.	AZ	24
Chavée R.	AZ	6	Notre-Dame R.	AY	15	St-Mihiel R. de	BYZ	25
Cygne R. du	AY	7	Pont Triby R. du	ABY	16	Trèves R. Gilles de	AZ	28
Foulans R. des	AY	9	Reggio Pl.	AY				
			Résistance R. de la	AZ	19			

Belvédère des Grangettes	AZ	B	Monument à P.- et E. Michaux	AY	E	Musée Barrois	AZ	M1
Collège Gilles-de-Trèves	AY	D						

Rue des Ducs-de-Bar

This high street has several beautiful façades, including **No 41**, with two 16C friezes decorated with military motifs, **No 47** with gargoyles, and **no 73** adorned with musical instruments. In a building at the end of the courtyard of **no 75**, there is a 15C **winepress**.

Ville Basse

Château de Marbeaumont

This early-20C castle, once owned by bankers Varin-Bernier, was General Pétain's headquarters during the First World War. The vast surrounding park has sports facilities and a campsite.

Rue du Bourg

The lower town was essentially a shopping district; from the 16C onwards, its high street became a highly-coveted address (richly decorated façades include **nos 26, 42, 46, 49** and **51**).

Sights

Musée Barrois

Daily except Mon-Tue 2-6pm, Sat-Sun and holidays 3pm-6pm. 1 Jan, 1 May, 14 Jul, 15 Aug, 1 Nov and 25 Dec. €2. 03 29 76 14 67 www.barleduc.fr

Housed in the buildings of the former tax office (1523) and the new castle built in 1567, the museum contains a rich archaeological collection ranging from

Address Book

For coin ranges, see the Legend on the cover flap.

PRACTICAL INFORMATION

Tourist office – *7 r. Jeanne-d'Arc, 55000 Bar-le-Duc, ☎03 29 79 11v13 – www.barleduc.fr*

WHERE TO EAT

Grill Restaurant de la Tour – *15 r. du Baile – ☎03 29 76v14 08 – closed Sat lunchtime, Sun and public holidays – booking advisable.* This restaurant on the way into the upper part of town is in a former 16C watchtower. At mealtimes, the tiny restaurant (maximum 20 placesettings) with exposed stone walls and beams is lit by the glow from the fireplace where the chef prepares grilled dishes. On the menu, home-made duck terrine (with gherkins as a condiment) and other heartily rustic meals.

La Meuse Gourmande – *1 r. F. – de-Guise –Ville Haute – ☎03 29 79 28 40 – closed 19-31 Aug, Sun Eve, Wed, Feb school holidays and public holidays.* Located in a handsome 18C residence, this restaurant is built on the foundations of the castle of the dukes of Bar. Plushly decorated interior; the tables near the windows command a fine view of the lower town. Up-to-date cuisine and mouthwatering desserts.

SHOPPING

Ets Dutriez, À la Lorraine – *35 r. de l'Étoile – ☎03 29 79 06v81 – www.groseille.com – Mon 2.30-6pm, Tue-Fri 9am-noon, 2.30-6pm, Sat 10am-noon.* The Maison Dutriez, which was founded in 1879, is the only establishment still producing redcurrant jam, deseeded with the help of a goose feather. It met with great success when introduced at Court in Versailles.

the Bronze Age to Merovingian times with many Gallo-Roman exhibits.
The **Chambre du Trésor** houses medieval and Renaissance sculptures (Pierre de Milan, Gérard Richier).
The museum also contains paintings of the French and Flemish Schools (Heindrick de Clerck, David Teniers Junior and Jan Steen), a collection of 16C and 17C weapons and armour, a collection of ethnography and local-history exhibits.

Église Notre-Dame

This Romanesque church was remodelled in the 17C following a fire.

Excursion

Rembercourt-aux-Pots

18km/11mi.

- *Drive N out of Bar-le-Duc along D 116 towards Vavincourt.*

The 15C village **church** has a magnificent **west front★** in a successful blend of Flamboyant and Renaissance styles. The two towers were never completed.

BAR-SUR-AUBE

POPULATION 6 261

MICHELIN LOCAL MAP 313: I-4

In medieval times, an important fair took place in Bar-sur-Aube; today, the town thrives on the Champagne trade.

- **Orient Yourself:** Bar-sur-Aube is located on N 19, a starting point to drive the Champagne Route.
- **Don't Miss:** A tour of the Champagne cellars.
- **Especially for Kids:** Children will love Nigloland.

Bayel online

For a virtual visit of the *Cité du Cristal*, go to the web page www.bayel-cristal.com. There are photographs of the crystal works and the museum, a text on the history of the town and a local map. You can also order brochures online from the Bayel Tourism office.

Walking Tour

▶ *Start from place de l'Hôtel-de-Ville.*

Hôtel de ville

The town hall is housed in the former Ursuline convent (1634).

Rue d'Aube

The post office (**nos 16 and 18**) is a fine 18C mansion with beautiful wrought-iron balconies. **No 15** is another 18C house. **No 33** dates from the end of the 16C, whereas **no 44** boasts a Renaissance rounded arch over the door.

▶ *Turn left onto rue Jeanne-de-Navarre.*

Église St-Maclou

Not open to the public. 11C former chapel for the counts of Bar.

▶ *Walk round the right side of the church.*

A small circular window in the east end made it possible for the Blessed Sacrament to be visible even at night.

▶ *Continue along rue Mailly.*

Note the elaborate doorway of the *sous-préfecture*, a former salt storehouse.

▶ *Continue along rue Armand then rue Nationale, the town's lively shopping street.*

At **no 14**, the deconsecrated **Chapelle St-Jean**, dating from the 11C and 12C, once belonged to the Order of St John.

▶ *Follow rue St-Jean then turn left onto rue du Général-Vouillemont.*

Cellier aux Moines

Near the east end of the church, this former town house of the Clairvaux monks (*now a restaurant*) has a 13C cellar, used by local wine-growers as their headquarters during the 1912 rebellion, when the Bar region won the right to continue calling its wine Champagne.

Église St-Pierre★

The west front and south side of this 12C church are lined with a covered gallery (making it look like a *halle* or covered market, hence its name Halloy).

Médiathèque

13 rue St-Pierre. The library is housed in the early-17C Hôtel de Brienne.

Turn left onto rue Thiers, which has retained some timber-framed houses.

▶ *Cross rue Nationale again and follow the narrow rue de la Paume and rue du Poids to return to the town hall.*

Excursions

Chapelle Ste-Germaine

4km/2.5mi. Leave Bar-sur-Aube by D 4, SW of the town, 3km/1.9mi further on, turn left in a bend onto a steep path and continue on foot.

The path leads to a pilgrimage chapel dedicated to Germaine, a virgin martyred by the Vandals in 407. Walk beyond the chapel and around the house to the viewing table which offers **glimpses** of Bar-sur-Aube, the valley, Colombey-les-Deux-Églises and its cross of Lorraine, and the Dhuits and Clairvaux forests.

Hikers might prefer to walk all the way to the chapel: beyond the bridge on the River Aube, take rue Pierre-Brossolette then continue straight on alongside the *lycée* (secondary school) and follow the path climbing through the woods (*30min*) up to the chapel.

Arsonval

6km/3.7mi NW along N 19.

The **Musée Rostislas-Loukine** (*R. Nationale; Tours by request. No charge. ☎ 03 25 27 92 54*), housed in a former primary school, celebrates **Rostislas Loukine** (1904-88), a Belgian of Russian origin who spent time in the region (also has temporary exhibitions).

Nigloland★

9km/5.6mi. Leave Bar-sur-Aube NW by N 19 to Dolancourt. mid-Jul to Aug: 10am-7pm; Apr: 10.15am-5.30m; May hours vary for holiday weekends; Sep-Nov 7: Sa-Sun 10.15-17.30; €18 (children under 12: €16.50, less than 1m/3ft tall: no charge). 03 25 27 94v52. www.nigloland.fr. Kids This leisure park offers attractions such as trips in a vintage car dating from 1900 and along an enchanting river. Do not miss the cinema show on the 180° screen or the presentation of the Niglo Company (electronic automata) staged in the theatre of the Canadian Village.

The Enchanted River at Nigloland

Soulaines-Dhuys

18km/11.2mi N along D 384. Follow the white and yellow markings to explore this charming village through which flows the River Laines (brochure available at the tourist office).

The local tile factory produces tiles decorated with medieval motifs.

Bayel

7.5km/4.7mi SE along D 396.

Crystalworks

Guided tour (1hr 30min) daily except Sat-Sun 9.30 and 11am holidays, Aug and 25 Dec-1 Jan. €5.30 (combined ticket cristallerie and écomusée: €7.60). 03 25 92 42 68. Bayel is famous for its prestigious crystalworks founded in 1666 by the Venetian glass-blower Jean-Baptiste Mazzolay.

Those who are unable to tour the factory can visit the **Écomusée du Cristal** (*Centre Mazzolay, 2 rue Benne-Verrière; Early Apr to Sep: 9.15am-1pm, 2.15-6pm, Sun 2.15-6pm; Oct to Mar: daily except Sun 9.15am-1pm, 2.15-6pm; 1 May, 1 Nov, 25 Dec-1 Jan; €3.80 (combined ticket écomusée and cristallerie: €7.60); 03 25 92 42 68*), housed in three small workers' cottages (*entrance through the tourist office*).

The plain 12C **church** contains a 16C polychrome stone **Pietà**★ likely created by the Master of Chaource, who worked also in Troyes. (*see TROYES*).

BITCHE

POPULATION 5 752

MICHELIN LOCAL MAP 307: P-4

Lying at the foot of a famous citadel that used to guard one of the main routes through the Vosges, Bitche is unusual in that its main street follows the outline of the imposing citadel.

- **Orient Yourself:** Bitche, 21km/13mi from the German border and 80km/49.7mi from Strasbourg, is encircled by dense forest.

Sight

Citadel★ *1hr 30min*

Jul-Aug:10am-6pm; mid-Mar to Jun and early Sep to mid-Nov: 10am-5pm. Guided tour possible (2hr). €6/7 depending on the time of year (children: €5/4). 03 87 96 18 82 or 03 87 06 16 16 (Tourist office).

R. Mattès/ MICHELIN

The citadel stands above the town

Rebuilt by Vauban c 1680, subsequently dismantled, then rebuilt once more between 1741 and 1754.

Beyond the ramp and monumental doorway, you will reach a platform which offers a 360° view of the town with the armoured steeples of Simershof (Maginot Line) to the west. At the foot of the citadel is a **Jardin pour la Paix**.

Excursions

Reyersviller

5km/3mi W along N 62. Just beyond the village on the right stands the ancient **Swedish oak**; according to legend, the invading Swedes used it as a gallows during the Thirty Years War.

Simserhof★

See Ligne MAGINOT.

Ossuaire de Schorbach

6km/3.7mi NW along D 962 and D 162B to the left.

Near the church there is a small ossuary with Romanesque arcading.

Volmunster

11km/6.8mi NW along D 35A and D 34.

The **Église St-Pierre**, destroyed during the Second World War, was rebuilt in 1957.

Nearby (*4km/2.5mi, signposted*) is **Eschviller Mill**, now a museum; an inn offers visitors a pleasant break.

BOURBONNE-LES-BAINS

POPULATION 2 495

MICHELIN LOCAL MAP 313: O-6

Already known in Roman times, this spa resort overlooking the Apance Valley became very popular between the 16C and 18C. The three hot springs treat rheumatism, arthritis, fractures, osteoporosis and respiratory complaints.

- **Orient Yourself:** Bourbonne-les-Bains is located on the south-western most edge of the Alsace-Lorraine region, south of other well-known spa towns such as Contrexéville and Vittel.
- Kids **Especially for Kids:** Children will love the Animal Park of Bannie and the Guy-onville theme park.

Visit

Quartier thermal

The hydrotherapy establishment was entirely renovated in 1997 and now features hydromassage, hot mud baths, individual hammam cabins, a swimming pool and power showers. The former military hospital, the first of its kind to be built in France (1732) is now home to

the Borvo centre, a hotel and entertainment centre (lectures, shows, various other activities).
The **Parc des Thermes** (Gallo-Roman remains) and **Parc d'Orfeuil** offer peace and quiet, walking facilities and relaxation.

Ville haute

The gatehouse of the early-16C fortress marks the entrance to the castle park. The **museum** (♿ 🕓 *Daily except Tues and Fri, 3-6pm, Wed 1-6pm, Sat 10.30am-4pm; €2; ☎03 25 90 69 47*), housed in the outbuildings, contains 19C paintings by René-Xavier Prinet, Georges Freset and Horace Vernet (*the Fall of Constantine*) as well as temporary exhibitions in summer. The **castle**, built on the site of the former stronghold and bequeathed to the town as a gesture of gratitude for treatment received, houses the town hall. The early-13C **Église Notre-Dame-de-l'Assomption** houses a graceful 14C marble statue of the Virgin Mary.

The **Arboretum de Montmorency** is an English-style park.

Excursions

Abbaye de Morimond

16km/9.9mi NW. This Cistercian abbey is the fourth house founded by the Abbaye de Cîteaux in 1115. With its position on the border of Champagne and Lorraine, it spearheaded the expansion of the Cistercian order in Germany.
Only part of the gatehouse and the Chapelle Ste-Ursule remain; the chapel was remodelled in the 17C, and recently restored. Nearby, the Morimond Forest is the subject of mysterious legends; follow the path to the atmospheric pond.

Châtillon-sur-Saône

11.5km/7mi E along D 417. This large village, overlooking the River Saône, has retained part of its 14C fortifications.

Address Book

For coin ranges, see the Legend on the cover flap.

PRACTICAL INFORMATION

Tourist office – *34 Pl. des Bains – ☎03 25 90 01 71 – www.bourbonne.com/otsi*

WHERE TO STAY AND EAT

Chambre d'hôte Ferme Adrien – *rte du Val-de-la-Maljoie – 52400 Coiffy-le-Haut – 10km/6.3mi SW of Bourbonne-les-Bains on D 26 – ☎03 25 90 06 76 – – 5 rooms – evening meal .* It's a treat to stay on this farm that dates from 1845 and is surrounded by meadows and forests. Among its attractions are the massive fireplace in the dining room, its antique furniture and its little rural life museum.

Hôtel des Sources – *pl. des Bains – ☎03 25 87 86 00 – hotel-des-sources@wanadoo.fr – closed Dec-Mar – 23 rooms – €5.50 – restaurant .* No effort is spared to make you feel comfortable in this hotel near the baths. The dining room opens onto a pleasant terrace. Tasty dishes to tempt spa patrons.

SHOPPING

Les Côteaux de Coiffy – *r. Bourgeois – 52400 Coiffy-le-Haut – ☎03 25 84 80 12 – Mar-Nov: 2.30-6.30pm; Dec-Mar: week-ends only.* In this cellar you can sample the wines from the 18ha/45 acres of vineyards around Coiffy-le-Haut.

SPORTS & RECREATION

Établissement thermal – *☎03 25 90 07 20 – www.valvital.fr – Mar-Nov.* At this spa treatment centre, three hot springs flow constantly: the St-Antoine spring or Roman pool, the Matrelle spring (small temple on the place des Thermes) and the Patrice spring in the former military hospital. Recommended for rheumatic disorders and respiratory ailments.

Keep-fit track – At Serqueux *(4km/2.5mi from Bourbonne)*, a hilly path winds its way through the forest of leafy and fir trees. Pic-nic area and view of the Apance Valley.

Parc animalier de la Bannie

2.5km/2.2mi SW along D 26. ♿ ⊙ Early Apr to mid Oct: daily except Mon and Tue 2-6pm, Sun 11.30am-6.30pm; Mar: daily except Mon and Tue 2-5pm, Sun 11.30am-6.30pm; mid Oct to end Oct and Feb: Wed, Sat 2-5pm; Nov-Jan: Wed, Sat 2-4pm. ⊙ During rutting period (around mid-Sep to mid-Oct). No charge. ☎03 25 90 14 80.

Kids Deer, does and moufflons roam freely in this 100ha/247-acre park.

Aventure Parc Guyonvelle

13km/8mi S along D 460. ⊙ Jul-Aug: 10am-6pm; mid-Apr to Jun: Sat-Sun and holidays 10am-6pm.; Sep-Oct: Sat-Sun and holidays 10am-5pm. ⊙ 1 Nov to Easter. €17 (children: €12). ☎03 25 90 00 02.

Kids Calling all Tarzans... This park provides you with the equipment you need to swing from the trees (overalls, harness, protective gloves, pulley); listen attentively to the instructor's advice!

Return to Bourbonne-les-Bains along D 158.

BRIENNE-LE-CHÂTEAU

POPULATION 3 336

MICHELIN LOCAL MAP 313: H-3

The town is now a major supplier of cabbage for sauerkraut; one quarter of the cabbages of France are grown here. A festival celebrating *la choucroute au champagne* **(sauerkraut cooked in Champagne) takes place on the third Sunday in September.**

- **Tourist office:** 34 r. de l'Ecole Militaire ☎03 25 92 82 41 www.ville-brienne-le-chateau.fr
- **Orient Yourself:** Brienne lies across a flat area, close to the River Aube, within the Parc naturel régional de la Forêt d'Orient.

A Bit of History

Napoleon Bonaparte in Brienne

At age 9, Napoleon Bonaparte began military school here. He excelled in mathematics and military exercise and after 5 years was recommended for school in Paris. He returned briefly to Brienne in 1814, at the end of the Napoleonic Wars, when he attacked a coalition of Prussian and Russian troops. During his exile on the island of St Helena, he recalled his youthful years in Brienne and left the town a considerable sum of money.

Sights *Allow 1hr*

Musée Napoléon

34 rue de l'École-Militaire. ♿ ⊙ Apr-Sep: 10am-12.30pm, 2-6pm (last entrance 30min before closing time); enquire for the rest of the year. €4.20 (children: €2.60). ⊙ 1 May. ☎03 25 92 82 41.

Housed in the former military school, the museum contains mementoes of Napoleon and relates the various episodes of the French campaign of 1814. The chapel houses an exhibit of the **Treasuries** of nearby churches: sculptures, paintings, and gold plate.

Hôtel de ville

The sum of money bequeathed by Napoleon was partly used to build a town hall (1859). Note the building's pediment: Napoleon surmounted by an eagle.

Église St-Pierre-et-St-Paul

The nave dates from the 14C and the chancel, surrounded by an ambulatory, from the 16C (lierne and tierceron vaulting).

Covered market

A market takes place regularly beneath the fine 16C timberwork and tiled roof.

Castle★

Not open to the public. The imposing white castle crowns the hill overlooking Brienne; built between 1770 and 1778 in typical Louis XVI style, it now houses a regional centre of psychotherapy. For a glimpse, take the alleyway past the 18C almshouse to the main gate.

Excursions

Brienne-la-Vieille

1km/0.6mi S of Brienne-le-Château along D 443. This port used to be the main timber supplier of the capital by the log-floating method. Rough timber would come by cart from the nearby forests of Orient, Temple and Clairvaux. The logs would then be tied into floats which would be guided down the River Aube, then the Seine until they reached Paris. The 12C **church** boasts 15C statues.

Écomusée de la Forêt d'Orient

See Parc naturel régional de la Forêt d'Orient.

Rosnay-l'Hôpital

9km/5.6mi N along D 396. The **Église Notre-Dame** (*Jul-Aug: Sun 3-5pm, rest of the week: key available upon deposit of ID card; 03 25 92 40 67 or 03 25 92 45 20*), dating from the 12C and 16C, stands on a once-fortified mound, on the banks of the River Voire. Walk along the left side of the church to reach the stairs leading to the vast **crypt**, erected in the 12C but rebuilt in the 16C at the same time as the church above it.

CHÂLONS-EN-CHAMPAGNE★★

POPULATION 45 400

MICHELIN LOCAL MAP 306: I-9

Formerly known as Châlons-sur-Marne, the town recently resumed its original name of Châlons-en-Champagne.
A number of 17C and 18C mansions give the city a certain bourgeois character, which contrasts with the charm of its restored timber-framed houses and its old bridges spanning the Mau and the Nau canals. The banks of the Marne, lined with beautiful trees, form an attractive sight in the western part of the town.

- **Orient Yourself:** Châlons-en-Champagne lies in the heart of the Champagne-growing region on N 44, half-way between Épernay and Vitry-le-François.
- **Don't Miss:** St-Étienne Cathedral in town and farther afield, the Basilique Notre-Dame-de-l'Épine.

A Bit of History

Catalaunum (Châlons-en-Champagne) was an active Gallo-Roman city; in June 451, the Roman army under General Aetius defeated the Huns led by their powerful chief **Attila**. The exact location of the battle is uncertain, but it was in the fields around the city of Catalaunum, hence the name of **Champs Catalauniques** which later became a symbol of deliverance from the Barbarian threat.

A site known as the Camp d'Attila, lying 15km/9.3mi north-east of Châlons, is said to be the place where the Huns camped on the eve of the battle.

During the Middle Ages, the town became important for the coronation ceremonies in Reims (*see REIMS*).

During the Wars of Religion, the town remained loyal to the king.

In 1856, a vast military camp was created near the town, with a special pavilion for **Napoleon III**.

Sights

Quartier de la Préfecture

▶ *Start from place Foch overlooked by the town hall and the north side of the Église St-Alpin.*

Hôtel de ville

The town hall was designed in 1771 by Nicolas Durand; the main hall is Doric.

Bibliothèque

Jul-Aug: Tue, Wed, Sat, 10am-noon, 2-6pm, Thu, Fri 2-6pm; Sep-Jun: Tue, Wed, Sat 10am-6pm, Thu 3pm-7pm, Fri 2-6pm. Sun, Mon, holidays, 1st week Aug. 03 26 26 94 26.

The library is housed in a beautiful 17C residence, once the home of the governors of the city. It was raised by one storey in the 19C. It holds some precious manuscripts and books (*not on display*) such as the **Roman de la Rose**, a famous 13C allegory in medieval French, and Queen Marie-Antoinette's book of prayers bearing her farewell to her children, written on the day of her execution.

Walk through the **Henri-Vendel passageway**. Note the former doorway of Église St-Loup closing the courtyard.

▶ *Return to rue d'Orfeuil and continue along rue de Chastillon.*

On the corner of rue des Croix-des-Teinturiers stands a fine Art Nouveau house built in 1907.

Rue de Chastillon

The street was once lined with workshops. Even numbers were occupied by well-off people whereas odd numbers were lived in by manual workers. .

▶ *Turn left onto rue de Jessaint which crosses the Mau.*

Couvent Ste-Marie

Visits by request to tourist office. 03 26 65 17 89.

▶ *Cross rue Carnot and follow rue Vinetz.*

A steep passageway leads to **place du Forum-de-l'Europe**.

The late 17C **Couvent de Vinetz** now houses the **Hôtel du Département**, the *département* administrative headquarters. *Not open to the public.*

▶ *Return to rue Carnot.*

Préfecture

The 1759 Préfecture occupies the former residence of the royal treasurers of the Champagne region; the design by Legendre and Durand already points to Louis XVI's sober style. **Marie-Antoinette**, who stopped in on her way to marry the heir to the French throne, returned after her arrest in Varennes (*see ARGONNE: Varennes-en-Argonne*).

Behind the Préfecture, in a circus modelled in 1887 on the Cirque d'Hiver in Paris, the **Centre National des Arts du Cirque** trains all-round circus artists.

Porte Ste-Croix

This triumphal gateway, erected in 1770 to welcome **Marie-Antoinette** en route to her marriage, was known as the Porte Dauphine; it was never completed (only one side is decorated with carvings).

Le Jard

Part of the bishop's estates, this former meadow is where St Bernard probably preached in 1147 (visit his mat in the nearby Treasury); Pope Eugene III consecrated the church the same year.

The 18C park is crossed by avenue du Maréchal-Leclerc; it has three sections:

- the **Petit Jard**, a landscaped garden in the Napoleon III style, with a flower clock, laid on the site of the former ramparts;
- the **Grand Jard**, with its views from the footbridge linking it to the Jardin Anglais across the canal;
- the **Jardin anglais**, an 1817 English-style garden alongside the Marne.

Additional Sights

Cathédrale St-Étienne★★

Mid *Jun-mid Sep: daily except Mon 10am-noon, 2-6pm, Sun and holidays 2.30-*

6pm. No charge. Tours by appointment, ☎03 26 68 00 98, Mme Hubert. Two royal marriages took place here during the reign of Louis XIV.

Exterior

The north side is in Gothic style, though the transept is flanked by a partly-Romanesque tower, part of a previous cathedral destroyed by fire in 1230.

Interior

The edifice is nearly 100m/110yd long and looks quite imposing in spite of its relatively short chancel. Daylight pours generously into the 27m/89ft high nave. The Gothic west front and the two bays closest to it were erected in 1628.

The cathedral has wonderful **stained-glass windows★**, which reveal the evolution of stained-glass making between the 12C and 16C:

Address Book

PRACTICAL INFORMATION

Tourist Office – *3 Quai des Arts, 51000 Châlons-en-Champagne – ☎03 26 65 17 89.*

WHERE TO EAT

See the Legend for coin categories.

Le Chaudron Savoyard – *9 r. des Poissoniers – ☎03 26 68 00 32 – www.surf-en-ville.com/le-chaudron-savoyard – closed 1-15 Jul.* Don't go by the Champagne-style façade of the building; here the cooking is devoted to the Savoy region. It can either be enjoyed in the ground-floor dining room with its exposed beams, or in the first-floor dining room, where the atmosphere is more reminiscent of the mountains.

Le Pré St-Alpin – *2 bis r. de l'Abbé-Lambert – ☎03 26 70 20 26 – pre.saint.alpin@wanadoo.fr – closed Sun evening.* Good food to be enjoyed in the attractive setting of a 1900 bourgeois town house which has retained all its former charm. Light floods into the two dining rooms with decorated glass roofs. There's another dining room with attractive panelling.

Auberge du Cloître – *9 pl. Notre-Dame-en-Vaux – ☎03 26 65 68 08 – closed Mon evenings and Tue.* Local connoisseurs frequent this centrally located restaurant whose large bay windows look out onto a pretty little paved square. Carefully prepared traditional fare is served in the pleasant dining room with pastel hues and attractively set tables.

Ferme-auberge des Moissons – *8 rte Nationale – 51510 Matougues – 12 km/7.5mi W of Châlons on the Épernay road (D 3) – ☎03 26 70 99v17 – bjacquinet@aol.fr – closed Jan, 15-31 Aug, open Sat evening and Sun lunchtime – booking essential.* Those who enjoy good food will appreciate the home-raised chicken, duck, rabbit and turkey. After a hearty meal, don't miss the small farm museum, or a visit to the stables, the garden and the farmyard.

WHERE TO STAY

Pasteur – *46 r. Pasteur – ☎03 26 68 10 00 – contact@hotel-pasteur.com – closed 26 Dec-3 Jan – P – booking advisable – 28 rooms – €5 – meals .* A slightly antiquated bourgeois atmosphere pervades this establishment located close to the town centre. A beautiful 17C staircase leads to the spacious, comfortable rooms with high ceilings.

The ground-floor rooms have been refurbished. Pleasant inner courtyard planted with trees.

La Grosse Haie – Kids *– Chemin de St-Pierre – 51510 Matougues – 12km/7.5mi W of Châlons on D 3, Épernay direction – ☎03 26 70 97 12 – songy.chambre@wanadoo.fr – – 3 rooms – evening meal .* Little matter that this farm-inn is close to the road: the land (orchard, vegetable garden, and botanical garden), children's activities, colourful rooms and farm produce combine to ensure you have an enjoyable stay.

Hôtel Le Pot d'Étain – *18 pl. de la République – ☎03 26 68 09 09 – hotel.le.pot.detain@wanadoo.fr – 27 rooms – €10.* The hotel is located on a lively, town-centre square. The rooms are soundproofed, with sober decor, rustic or modern furniture and good quality beds. The owner, formerly a baker, makes it a point of honour to serve an impeccable breakfast.

GOING OUT

Philippe Génin – *27 pl. de la République – ☎03 26 21 46 63 – Tue-Sat 8am-7.30pm; Sun 8am-1pm, 3-7pm*. This tearoom serving pastries, ice cream, chocolate and light lunches is the ideal place for a snack. Be sure to sample the home-made chocolate, as well as the delicious Châlonnais cake, which goes marvellously with a glass of champagne. Terrace in summer.

Brasserie de La Bourse – *32 pl. de la République – ☎03 26 65 18 04 – 9.30am-2am*. Mahogany panelling, red or black velvet covered seats, gleaming copperware and numerous mirrors make this one of the most chic and pleasant places in town. Huge terrace on the busiest square in Châlons-en-Champagne.

GUIDED TOURS & BOAT TRIPS

Promenades sur l'eau – 3 *quai des Arts – ☎03 26 65 17 89 – off.tourisme.chalons-en-champagne@wanadoo.fr – Jun-Sep: tour daily from 2.30pm (some Fri evenings)*. Boat tours on the Mau and the Nau give a surprising new perspective to many of Châlon's sights.

Châlons-en-Champagne on foot – The Office de tourisme also organises (2hr) walking tours of Châlons in summertime. *Jul-Aug: from 2.30pm; rest of the year, 1 week/month at 2.30pm. €4.50. Enquiries to tourist office (above).*

- In the chancel stands an imposing 17C high altar with a baldaquin, believed to be the work of Jules Hardouin-Mansart. The windows above the high altar, dating from the 13C, depict Christ in glory, the Crucifixion and the Holy Mother.

Treasury

The lower part of the Romanesque tower adjacent to the north transept houses the treasury, including 12C stained-glass panels (representing the Crucifixion and the discovery of St Stephen's relics).

Église Notre-Dame-en-Vaux★

Early May to mid-Sep: 10am-noon, 2-6pm, Sun 2-6pm; rest of the year: daily except Sun 10am-noon, 2-6pm.

This former collegiate church is in the Romanesque style from the beginning of the 12C, but the vaulting, the chancel and the east end date from a century alter, fine examples of the Early Gothic style (go to the far side of place Monseigneur-Tissier in order to get a good overall view). There is a peal of 56 bells.

A garden *(not open to the public)*, on the north side of the church marks the site of the former cloisters.

Ph. Gajic/ MICHELIN

Inside Notre-Dame-en-Vaux

Enter the church through the south doorway.

The **interior**★★ has harmonious simple proportions; the nave features a marked contrast between the pillars topped by Romanesque capitals, supporting vast galleries, and pointed Gothic vaulting. The nave is lit by a harmonious set of **stained-glass windows**★. The finest, from the 16C, are on the north side.

Walk up the north aisle starting from the west doorway:

Second bay: the *Legend of St James* (1525) by the master glass-maker from Picardie, Mathieu Bléville, illustrates a battle which took place in 1212 between Christians and Moors (the pilgrims' route to Santiago de Compostela went through Châlons);

Third bay: the *Dormition* and *Coronation of the Blessed Virgin*, red and gold symbolising her glory; dated 1526;

Fourth and fifth bays: *Legends of St Anne and Mary; Christ's childhood;* **Sixth bay**: The *Compassion of the Virgin Mary*, against a blue background dotted with silver stars, with a *Deposition*, a *Pietà* and *Mary Magdalene* (1526).

Walk round the church to rue Nicolas-Durand where the entrance of the Musée du cloître de Notre-Dame-en-Vaux is situated.

The late-15C **Maison Clémangis**, opposite the entrance, has exhibitions.

Musée du cloître de Notre-Dame-en-Vaux★

Rue Nicolas-Durand. Apr-Sep: daily except Tue 10am-noon, 2-6pm; Oct-Mar: daily except Tue 10am-noon, 2-5pm, Sat-Sun 10am-noon, 2-6pm. 1 Jan, 1 May, 1 and 11 Nov, 25 Dec. €5, (no charge: 1st Sun of the month, Oct-May). 03 26 64 03 87.

The cloister museum contains remarkable sculptures from Romanesque cloisters, discovered in 1960. Built in the 12C next to Notre-Dame-en-Vaux, they were demolished in 1759 by the canons who replaced them with their own quarters.

A vast room contains reconstructions and several valuable exhibits such as carved or ringed columns and 55 **statue columns**★★: the finest depict prophets, famous biblical characters or saints and characters from the Middle Ages. The transition from the Romanesque to the Gothic style is emphasized by the expressive features of the characters, and the tendency for some of them to be separate from the column.

Musée municipal

Place Godart. Daily except Tue 2-6pm, Sun 2.30-6.30pm. Holidays. €2.50. 03 26 69 38 53.

The town museum offers two floors.

Ground floor: collection of Hindu deities (16C-17C), 13C recumbent figure of Blanche de Navarre, Countess of Champagne, 15C Head of Christ from the rood screen of Notre-Dame-en-Vaux, three polychrome wooden altarpieces, and a Head of St John the Baptist by Rodin.

Ph. Gajic/ MICHELIN

A turret on the Château du Marché

First floor: fine arts gallery and local archaeological finds from the Palaeolithic period to the 17C; the Gallic period is particularly interesting.

The ornithological collection includes some 3 000 birds, mostly from Europe. The last room contains furniture (16C-20C) and tapestries (15C-17C).

Église St-Alpin

Mid May-mid Sep: daily except Sun and Mon 10am-noon, 2-6pm.

Partly surrounded by houses, the church, built between the 12C and 16C, is a mixture of Flamboyant Gothic and Renaissance styles. In the south aisle chapels, there are **Renaissance windows**★ with magnificent grisaille stained glass.

Musée Jules-Garinet

13 rue Pasteur. Daily 2-6pm. Holidays. €1.65. 03 26 69 38 53.

This partly Gothic mansion houses a 19C bourgeois interior, paintings from the 14C to 19C, and a collection models of French churches and cathedrals.

Église St-Jean

Access via rue Jean-Jacques-Rousseau.

The raised area in front of the church allows access to the 14C west section. A small 15C chapel, known as the **Crossbowmen's Chapel**, sits off the south aisle (19C stained-glass windows).

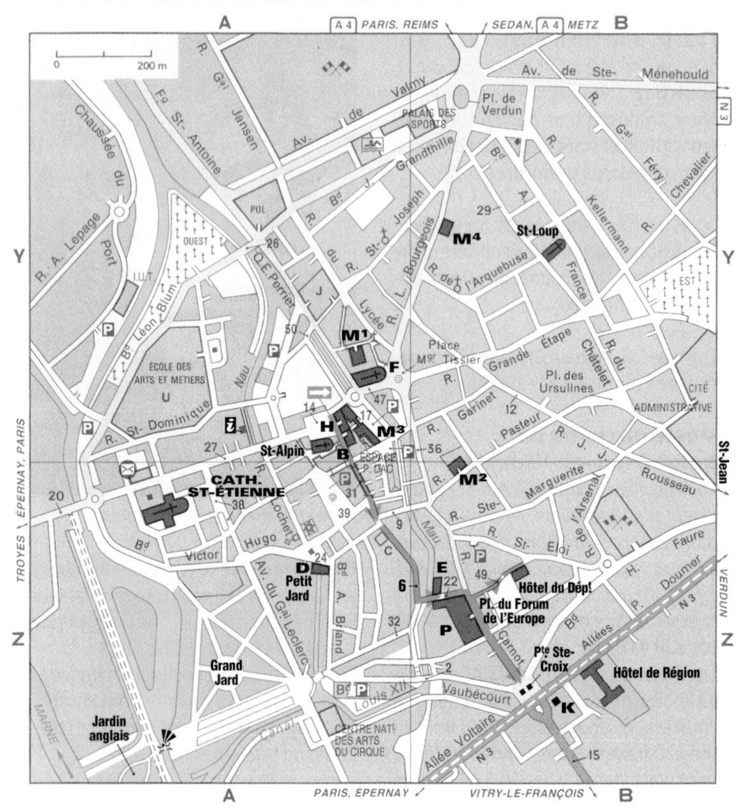

CHÂLONS-EN-CHAMPAGNE

Street	Grid	No.
Anatole-France Bd	BY	
Arche-de-Mauvillain Pt de l'	BZ	2
Arquebuse R. de l'	BY	
Arsenal R. de l'	BZ	
Blum Bd Léon	AY	
Bourgeois R. Léon	ABY	
Briand Bd A.	AZ	
Carnot R.	BZ	
Chastillon R. de	ABZ	6
Châtelet R. du	BY	
Chevalier R.	BY	
Croix-des-Teinturiers R.	AZ	9
Doumer Allées P.	BZ	
Faure Bd H.	BZ	
Féry R. Gén.	BY	
Flocmagny R. du	BY	12
Foch Pl. du Maréchal	AY	14
Forum de l'Europe Pl. du	BZ	
Garinet R.	BY	
Gaulle Av. du Gén. Charles-de	BZ	15
Godart Pl.	AY	17
Grande Étape R.	BY	
Grandthille Bd J.	ABY	
J.-J.-Rousseau R.	BYZ	
Jansen R. Gén.	AY	
Jean-Jaurès R.	AZ	20
Jessaint R. de	BZ	22
Kellermann R.	BY	
Leclerc Av. Mar.	AZ	
Lepage R. A.	AY	
Libération Pl. de la	AZ	24
Lochet R.	AZ	
Lycée R. du	AY	
Mariniers Pt des	AY	26
Marne R. de la	AY	27
Martyrs-de-la-Résistance R. des	BY	29
Orfeuil R. d'	AZ	31
Ormesson Cours d'	AZ	32
Pasteur R.	BYZ	
Perrier Quai E.	AY	
Port Chaussée du	AY	
Prieur-de-la-Marne R.	BY	36
Récamier R. Juliette	AZ	38
République Pl. de la	AZ	39
St-Antoine Fg	AY	
St-Dominique R.	AY	
St-Éloi R.	BZ	
St-Joseph R.	ABY	
Ste-Marguerite R.	BZ	
Ste-Ménehould Av. de	BY	
Tissier Pl. Monseigneur	ABY	
Ursulines Pl. des	BY	
Valmy Av. de	ABY	
Vaubécourt Bd	ABZ	
Vaux R. de	AY	47
Verdun Pl. de	BY	
Victor-Hugo Bd	AZ	
Vinetz R. de	BZ	49
Viviers Pt des	AY	50
Voltaire Allées	BZ	

Sight	Grid	Key
Bibliothèque	AY	B
Cathédrale St-Étienne	AZ	
Château du Marché	AZ	D
Couvent Ste-Marie	BZ	E
Grand Jard	AZ	
Hôtel de Région	BZ	
Hôtel de Ville	AY	H
Hôtel du Département	BZ	
Jardin Anglais	AZ	
Monument à Nicolas Appert	BZ	K
Musée Garinet	BZ	M^2
Musée Schiller-et-Goethe	BY	M^4
Musée du Cloître de N.-D.-en-Vaux	AY	M^1
Musée municipal	AY	M^3
Petit Jard	AZ	
Porte Ste-Croix	BZ	
Préfecture	BZ	P
Église Notre-Dame-en-Vaux	AY	F
Église St-Alpin	AY	
Église St-Jean	BYZ	
Église St-Loup	BY	

Musée Schiller-et-Goethe

68 rue Léon-Bourgeois. ⏲ Jul-Aug: daily except Tue 2-6pm, Sun 2.30-6.30pm; Sep-Jun: Sat 2-6pm, Sun 2.30-6pm. ⏲ Holidays. €1.70. ☎03 26 69 38 53.
The collections were donated to the museum in 1952 by Baroness von Gleichen-Russwurm, the widow of Schiller's great-grandson.

Ph. Gajic/ MICHELIN
Curious characters

Excursions

Basilique Notre-Dame de l'Épine★★

8km/5mi E along N 3. Modelled on Reims Cathedral in the early 15C, this basilica has been an important place of pilgrimage since the Middle Ages, when shepherds discovered a statue of the Virgin Mary in a burning thorn bush.

Exterior

The south spire (55m/180ft high) is ringed by a crown made up of fleurs-de-lis; the north spire, demolished in 1798 to make room for a telegraph installation, was rebuilt in 1868. Walk along the south side of the church to observe the numerous realistic **gargoyles**★.

Interior

The basilica is a pinacle of Gothic architecture. The chancel is closed off by an elegant **rood screen** from the late 15C (note the 14C statue of the Virgin Mary under the right-hand arcade) and by a stone screen which is Gothic on the right side and Renaissance on the left.
Walking round the chancel (starting from the north side) you will see a Gothic **tabernacle-reliquary** with Renaissance ornamentation. Farther on, a chapel houses a fine 16C **Entombment**.

ROUTES DU CHAMPAGNE★★★

MICHELIN LOCAL MAP 306

The Champagne vineyards, known since ancient times, produce a type of wine that is famous throughout the world. The reputation of the so-called Devil's Wine grew considerably from the 10C onwards, as a consequence of the fairs which took place during the 12C and 13C; by the time the Renaissance came, it had spread beyond the borders of France. Yet, up to the 17C, Champagne was a predominantly red wine with a slight tendency to sparkle. According to tradition, modern Champagne was "invented" by Dom Pérignon, a monk from the Benedictine abbey of Hautvillers, who mixed various local wines. Success was almost immediate: kings, princes and European aristocrats elected Champagne as their favourite drink for festive occasions.
The great Champagne firms were set up in Reims and Épernay from the 18C onwards: Ruinart in 1729, Fourneaux (which later became Taittinger) in 1734, Moët in 1743, Clicquot in 1772, Mumm in 1827. Since then, Reims and Épernay have consistently prospered as tourists continue to enjoy winding their way through the Champagne vineyards. The TGV train from Paris (inaugurated in spring 2007) enhances the region's accessiblity.

- **Orient Yourself:** The Champagne Route is signposted by an official logo and most of the drives leave from Reims, Épernay or Château-Thierry.
- **Don't Miss:** The Champagne cellars of Reims.

Organising Your Time: To do full justice to this magnificent region, allow at least 2 full days. Start with a day in Reims before setting out on a choice of 4 different itineraries.

Champagne Cellars In Reims★★

Allow half a day or a whole day – for a map of Reims, see REIMS.

The famous Champagne firms are gathered in the Champ de Mars district and along the limestone slopes of St-Nicaise hill, full of galleries known as crayères, often dating from the Gallo-Roman period. The depth and extent of the galleries (totalling 250km/155mi) makes them ideal Champagne cellars.

Pommery

5 place du Gén.-Gouraud. Easter to mid-Nov: guided tour (1hr) 9.30am-7pm, Sat and Sun 10am-7pm; mid-Nov to Easter: 9.30am-6pm, Sat and Sun 10am-6pm. Christmas school holidays. €8 (children under 12: no charge). 03 26 61 62 56. www.pommery.com.

This firm, founded in 1836 by Narcisse Gréno and Louis Alexandre Pommery, was expanded by the latter's widow who inaugurated Brut Champagne and built the present buildings in 1878. She also linked the Gallo-Roman crayères by building 18km/11mi of galleries, and acquired many vineyards so that Pommery now owns 300ha/731 acres of the finest Champagne vines.

The tour enables visitors to discover the different stages of Champagne-making through galleries decorated with 19C sculptures, and to see a 75 000l/16 500gal tun by Émile Gallé, from 1904.

Taittinger

9 place St-Niçaise. Guided tour (1hr). Mid-Mar to mid-Nov: 9.30am-Noon, 2-6.30pm; rest of the year: daily except Sat-Sun and holidays, 9.30am-noon, 2-4.30pm. 1 Jan, 25 Dec. €7. 03 26 85 84 33.

In 1734, the Fourneaux family of wine merchants launched into the production of sparkling wine made according to Dom Pérignon's methods. In 1932, Pierre Taittinger took over the management of the firm which was renamed after him. Today, the Taittinger vineyards extend over 250ha/618 acres and the firm owns 6 grape-harvesting centres on the Montagne de Reims, the Château de la Marquetterie in Pierry, the Hôtel des Comtes de Champagne in Reims (*see REIMS*) and superb cellars.

Visitors can enjoy a fascinating tour of the cellars among 15 million bottles maturing in the cool Gallo-Roman galleries and in the crypts of the former 13C Abbaye St-Nicaise, destroyed during the Revolution.

Veuve Clicquot-Ponsardin

1 place des Droits-de-l'Homme. Guided tour and tasting (1hr 30min). Apr-Oct: daily except Sun 10am-6pm; Nov-Mar: daily except Sat-Sun 10am-6pm. €7 (children under 17: no charge). 03 26 89 53 90. www.veuve-clicquot.fr.

This firm, founded in 1772 by Philippe Clicquot, was considerably expanded by his son's widow whose maiden name was Ponsardin. In 1816, she introduced *remuage* into the process of Champagne-making. Today, Veuve Clicquot-Ponsardin, which owns 265ha/655 acres of vines and exports three quarters of its production, is one of the best-known Champagne firms outside France.

Ruinart

4 rue des Crayères. Guided tour (1hr 30min) by request to the "visites et réceptions" department. Prices start at €10/person, and depend on the programme. 03 26 77 51 21. www.ruinart.com.

Founded in 1729, this Champagne firm prospered during the Restoration period (1814-30) and again after 1949, having gone through years of decline during the two world wars. Today Ruinart, which belongs to the Moët-Hennessy group, specialises in top-quality Champagne. Its three levels of Gallo-Roman galleries are particularly interesting.

Address Book

WHERE TO EAT

See the Legend for coin categories.

Auberge de la Chaussée – *La Chaussée de Damery – 51480 Vauciennes – 6km/3.75mi W of Épernay on N 3 – ☎03 26 58 40 66 – closed 1st week of Jan, Fri and Sun evening.* Fans of traditional dishes such as calf's head will love this inn, which is easily accessible by the N 3. Unpretentious setting with black and white chequered floor. Simple, clean rooms.

Au Bateau Lavoir – *3 r. Port-au-Bois – 51480 Damery – 5km/3mi W of Épernay on D 22 then N 13 – ☎03 26 58 40 88 – closed 1 week in Feb, 2 weeks in Aug and Mon.* This pretty, flower-decked little building enjoys a prime location on the banks of the Marne. The dining room is modern and bright thanks to its large bay windows. Traditional cooking.

Le Caveau – *R. de la Coopérative – 51480 Cumières – 5km/3mi NW of Épernay on D 301 – ☎03 26 54 83 23 – closed Sun evening, Tue evening and Wed.* Cross a small room decorated on a wine theme, then go down the long hallway leading to this superb restaurant in a cellar dug out of the chalk. Carefully set tables. Regional specialities.

WHERE TO STAY

Chambre d'hôte M. et Mme Tarlant – *R. de la Coopérative – 51480 Œuilly – 13km/8mi W of Épernay on N 3 (Dormans road) – ☎03 26 58 30 60 – champagne@tarlant.com – closed Dec-Mar – 4 rooms.* Staying with a wine-grower, you will be able to visit the cellars and sample the champagne. The building itself is plain but the huge, ground-level rooms overlook the vineyards and are wonderfully peaceful. Courteous service and family atmosphere.

Chambre d'hôte Ferme du Grand Clos – *R. Jonquery – 51170 Ville-en-Tardenois – 17km/10.6mi SW of Reims on D 980 – ☎03 26 61 83 78 – closed end Dec-beginning Mar – ⊭ – 4 rooms.* In this old farmhouse, built out of local stone, the spacious rooms have been completely refurbished and include their own lounge area. A warm welcome and very reasonable prices make this a good place to stay on the champagne route.

Chambre d'hôte Les Botterets – *7 r. du Fort – 51190 Oger – 13km/8 mi S of Épernay on D 10 – ☎03 26 57 94 78 – closed 20 Nov-28 Feb – ⊭ – 6 rooms.* Recently renovated bed and breakfast rooms in two traditional village houses. The rather ordinary decor is compensated for by the genuinely friendly welcome and the typical atmosphere of a wine-producing village.

CHAMPAGNE TASTING

In addition to the major wine cellars in Reims and Épernay, here we have selected a few of the many others recommended for their winemaking premises:

Breton Fils – *12 r. Courte-Pilate – 51270 Congy – 15km/9.3mi S of Épernay on N 951 and D 943 – ☎03 26 59 31 03 – contact@champagne-breton-fils.fr – daily 9am-noon, 2-5.30pm – closed 3rd Sun in May, Christmas Day and 1 Jan.* This vineyard owner and grower will let you visit his cellars, which are typical of the Champagne region.

Champagne Milan – *6 rte d'Avize – 51190 Oger – 15km/9.3mi S of Épernay – ☎03 26 57 50 09 – www.champagne-milan.com – Oct-May: 10am-noon, 2-5pm ; Jun-Sep daily 10am-7pm – closed Jan.* The convivial visit to the cellars and manufacturing premises culminates with a champagne tasting.

Corbon – *541 av. Jean-Jaurès– 51190 Avize – 10km/6.2mi S of Épernay – ☎03 26 57 55 43 – www.champagne-corbon.com – by appointment only – closed late Dec to late Jan.* This family-run champagne producer's organises tastings of two champagnes with a commentary (2hr). Among the interesting options are the process of dégorgement à la volée, when the cork is taken out and the sediment removed, and blending.

Dehu Père & Fils – *3 r. St-Georges – 02650 Fossoy – 9km/5.6mi SE of Château-Thierry on N 3 – ☎03 23 71 90 47 – varocien@aol.com – Mon-Sat by appointment only.* After visiting the museum, which exhibits a collection

of tools used in the cultivation of vines and winemaking, you will be invited to a champagne tasting.
F.P. Arnoult Coopérative vinicole – *rte de Damery – 51480 Fleury-la-Rivière – 4km/2.5mi NW of Épernay on N 3 and D 22 – ☎03 26 58 42 53 – Mon-Fri 8.30am-12.30pm, 2-5.15pm, Sat 9am-12.30pm and 2-6pm, Sun by appointment. Closed Mon afternoon and Wednesdays.* The walls of this cooperative cellar are decorated with a superb 550m²/658sq yd fresco, depicting the region's history. The tasting room, where home-made products are sold, boasts a magnificent view over the vineyard and the Marne Valley.
Launois Père & Fils – *2 av. Eugène-Guillaume – 51190 Le Mesnil-sur-Oger – 11km/6.8mi S of Épernay on D 40 – ☎03 26 57 50 15 – www.champagne-launois.fr – Mon-Fri 8am-noon, 2-6pm, Sat-Sun 10am-1pm, 3-5pm. Museum: by appointment Mon-Fri 10am-3pm, Sat-Sun 10.30am-3pm – closed Christmas Day, 1 Jan and Easter.* Founded in 1872, this owner-grower's establishment includes his own wine museum, and the visit includes a wine tasting.

Piper-Heidsieck

51 boulevard Henri-Vasnier. Open 9.30-12.30pm, 2-6pm (last admission 1hr before closing time). Closed Jan-Feb and 25 Dec. €7.50. ☎03 26 84 43 44. www.piper-heidsieck.com.
The firm was founded in 1785. The various stages of Champagne-making are explained by an audio-visual presentation; visitors can afterwards tour the cellars, extending 16km/10mi underground, in a gondola car.

Mumm

34 rue du Champ-de-Mars. Guided tour (1hr 15min). Open Mar-Oct: 9-11am, 2-5pm; Nov-Feb: 9-11am, 2-5pm, (by appointment), Sat-Sun and holidays 2-5pm. Closed 1 Jan, 25 Dec. €7.50. ☎03 26 49 59 70. www.mumm.com.
After its creation in 1827, this firm prospered throughout the 19C in Europe and in America; today, it owns 218ha/539 acres of vines and its cellars (open to the public) extend over a total distance of 25km/16mi.

Maxim's

17 rue des Créneaux. Guided tour (1hr). Open 10am-7pm (last admission 1hr before closing time) 10am-7pm. Closed 1 Jan, 25 Dec. €4.50. ☎03 26 82 70 67.
Tour of the galleries dug between the 4C and 15C: a visit to the cellars is followed by a film and ends with a Champagne tasting. The museum houses a collection of machinery and tools used during the different stages of wine-growing.

Champagne Kingdom★★

Round tour starting from Montchenot 1

See Parc naturel régional de la MONTAGNE de REIMS.

Côte des Blancs★★

From Épernay to Mont-Aimé 2

28km/17.4mi. Allow 2hr
Stretching between Épernay and Vertus, the Côte des Blancs or Côte Blanche, owes its name to its white-grape vineyards consisting almost exclusively of **Chardonnay** vines. The refined grapes grown in the area are used to produce vintage and blanc de blancs (made solely from white grapes) Champagne. The majority of the great Champagne firms own vineyards in this area; some of these are even equipped with a heating system to protect the vines from frost. Like the Montagne de Reims, the Côte des Blancs is a bank sloping down from the edge of the Île-de-France cuesta, facing due east and almost entirely covered with vines. In front of this limestone cuesta stand outliers such as Mont Saran (239m/784ft) and Mont Aimé (240m/787ft).
The twisting lanes of the villages dotted along the slopes are lined with wine-growers' houses with their characteristic high doorways.

The road described below runs half way up the slopes, offering views of the vineyards and the vast plain of Châlons.

Épernay★

See ÉPERNAY.

Leave Épernay SW along D 951.

Château de Pierry

Daily except Sun and Holidays: 9am-noon, 2-6.30pm. Guided tours and wine tasting possible (1hr 30min) by appointment. Holidays. €8. 03 26 54 02 87.

The town hall now occupies the house where Jacques Cazotte lived; the author of Le Diable amoureux (the Devil in Love) was guillotined in 1792. A tour of the 18C Château de Pierry includes reception rooms, private apartments, a wine-press and cellars dating from 1750 as well as a small museum. A glass of Champagne is offered at the end of the visit.

In Pierry, turn left onto D 10.

This road offers views of Épernay and the Marne Valley on the left.

Cuis

The Romanesque **Église St-Niçaise** (*Tour by request except Sat-Sun; Town hall (Mairie); 03 26 59 78 60*) stands on a platform overlooking the village. From D 10, there are interesting vistas of the Montagne de Reims.

Note the huge bottle (over 8m/26ft tall) marking the village of Cramant.
D 10 affords views of the Montagne de Reims.

Continue along this road.

Cramant★

This village lies in a pleasant setting, in the heart of an area producing the famous Cramant wine made from white Chardonnay vines, sometimes called Blanc de Cramant. At the village entrance stands a giant Champagne bottle over 8.6m/28ft tall and measuring nearly 8m/26ft round the base created in 1974.

Avize

Also famous for its wine, Avize runs a school for future Champagne wine-growers. The 12C church has a 15C chancel and transept. A walk above the little town to the west offers views of the whole area.

Continue along D 10.

Oger

Producing a *premier cru de la Côte des Blancs*, one of the area's top quality wines, Oger has a fine church dating from the 12C-13C with a high square tower and flat east end.

S. Sauvignier/ MICHELIN

La Côte des Blancs, near Cramant

Musée des Traditions, de l'Amour et du Champagne

Apr-Nov: 9.30-11am, 2-6pm, Sun 9.30-11am, 3pm-6pm; Dec-Mar: by request. €6. 03 26 57 50 89. www.mariage-et-champagne.com.

This charming museum examines wedding traditions between 1880 and 1920, including bouquets made of paper, leather, gilt-metal and shell flowers. Champagne is of course part of the tradition and there is a display of old labels and a tour of the 18C cellars with their collection of old tools (tasting).

Le Mesnil-sur-Oger

This wine-growing village is strangely spread out but features a grotto dedicated to the Virgin.

Musée de la Vigne et du Vin★

Guided tour (1hr 30min) by appointment. Daily *10am-3pm; Sun and holidays 10.30am.* *1 Jan, Easter, 25 Dec. €7. 03 26 57 50v15 www.champagne-launois.fr* This museum displays wine-presses and tools that illustrate wine-growing's history; the traditional production techniques of corks, bottles, and barrels are also featured.

A small road winds its way across the vineyards to Vertus.

Vertus

This charming town surrounded by vineyards had several springs and was once the property of the counts of Champagne who lived in a castle now demolished except for the Porte Baudet. During the Middle Ages, Vertus was enclosed by a defensive wall.

Église St-Martin was built on piles in the late 11C and early 12C. Damaged by fire in 1167, partly destroyed during the Hundred Years War and remodelled several times, it was finally restored after a 1940 fire. The pointed vaulting over the transept and east end dates from the 15C. Note the delicately carved 16C *Pietà* in the south transept and the 16C stone statue of St John the Baptist near the christening fonts. Stairs lead from the north transept to three 11C crypts; note the capitals of the central crypt, beautifully carved with foliage motifs.

On the way down to **Bergères-lès-Vertus** with its small Romanesque country church, the road affords pleasant views of the surrounding area.

South of Bergères-lès-Vertus, turn right onto the road leading to Mont Aimé.

Mont Aimé★

Inhabited since prehistoric times, this isolated hill (237m/778ft high) was fortified successively by the Gauls, the Romans and the counts of Champagne who built a feudal castle; its ruins are today scattered among the greenery.

On 10 September 1815, the Russian army held a great parade here; they were stationed in this area during the occupation of France by several European countries following the fall of Napoleon.

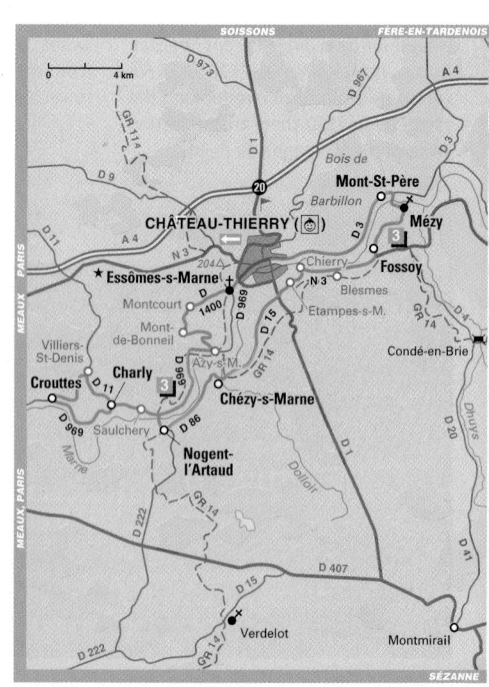

In one of the corners of the old fortifications, a viewpoint (viewing table) offers an extended **view** of the Côte des Blancs to the north and of the plain of Châlons to the east.

Vallée de la Marne★

The round tours starting from Épernay and Château-Thierry offer an opportunity of discovering wine-growing villages climbing the vine-covered hillsides on both banks of the River Marne. During the First World War, the fate of France and of the Allies was sealed on these banks during two decisive battles, which took place in 1914 and 1918.

Round tour west of Épernay 3

Allow 4hr. 63km/39mi.

Leave Épernay along N 3, turn right towards Mardeuil then cross the Marne and follow the north bank of the river to Cumières.

Cumières

Lying at the foot of vineyards shaped like an amphitheatre, this village nestles on the banks of the River Marne, with fishing boats gently swinging along the quays. There are **boat trips** (*Cruises (1hr 30min) on the Marne; Reservation at Croisi-Champagne, BP 22, 51480 Cumières; ☎03 26 54 49 51; www.champagnecroisiere.com; the pier is by place du Kiosque*) on board the Champagne Vallée through vineyard country. Locks are negotiated along the way.

Continue W on D 1.

Damery

Damery offers fine walks along the banks of the River Marne; the 12C-13C **church** once belonged to the Benedictine abbey of St-Médard de Soissons; it contains a *Virgin with Child* by Watteau (18C). Note the carved capitals of the pillars supporting the belfry: they represent an interesting bestiary against a background of intertwined stems.

Turn right towards Fleury-la-Rivière.

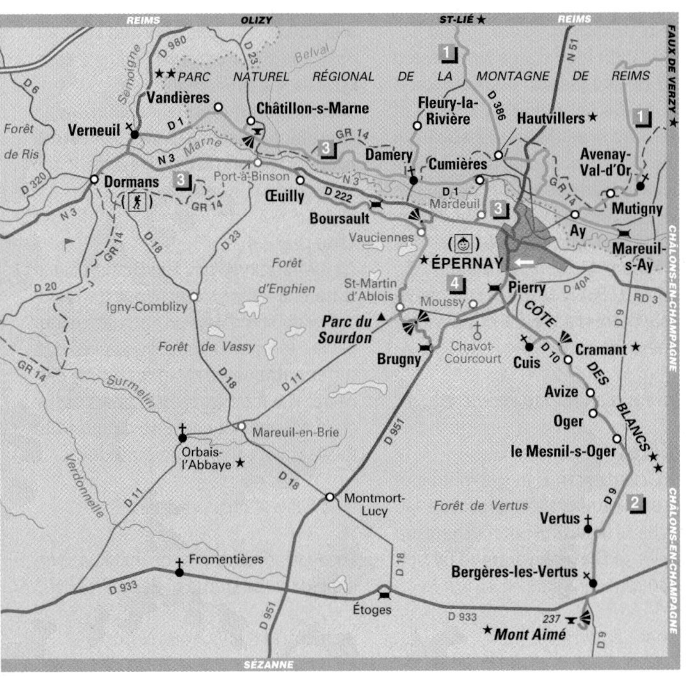

Fleury-la-Rivière

The walls of the **Coopérative vinicole** (wine-growers' cooperative society) (*Guided tour (45min) by request daily except Mon morning and Wed 8.30am-12.30pm, 2-5.15pm, Sat 9am-12.30pm, 2-6pm, Sun and holidays by request; 25 Dec, 1 Jan, 1 May; €4; 03 26 58 42 53*) are decorated with a huge **fresco** by Greg Gawra, which depicts the history of the Champagne region, work in the vineyards and the cellars.

D 324 runs through villages and across vineyards and fields.

In Cuchery, turn left to Châtillon-sur-Marne.

Châtillon-sur-Marne

Camped on a vine-covered hill overlooking the Marne, this ancient fortified town was the fief of Eudes de Châtillon who became Pope under the name of Urbain II (1088-99) and launched the first crusade.

Leave the car in the car park and follow rue de l'Église then turn right onto rue Berthe-Symonet.

Statue d'Urbain II

The 33m/108ft high statue was erected in 1887 on the mound once crowned by the castle keep. Eighty blocks of granite were brought all the way from Brittany in carts pulled by oxen. Inside, a **staircase** leads up to the arm of the statue (*May-Sep 10am-12.30pm, 2.30-6pm; Mar-Apr: Mon-Fri 11am-5pm, Sat-Sun 10am-12.30pm, 2.30-6pm; €1; 03 26 53 32 86*). From the nearby viewing table there is a **view**★ of the valley and vineyards.

Drive W along D 1 to Vandières.

Vandières

The 18C castle stands in the middle of a park, at the top of the village. The 11C church has a beautiful porch. There are fine views of the valley framed by hills to the south.

Continue along D 1.

Verneuil

The small 12C-13C **church**, carefully restored, stands beside the Sémoigne, a tributary of the Marne.

Continue to Vincelles then Dormans.

Dormans

The park of this peaceful flower-decked riverside town is the setting of the **castle** (housing the tourist office and temporary exhibitions) and of the **Mémorial des Batailles de la Marne** (*Apr-Nov 11: daily 2.30-6.30pm; Sun: 10am-noon, 2.30-6.30; no charge; 03 26 57 77 87*), a memorial chapel dedicated to the battles of the Marne, consisting of two storeys and a crypt surmounted by a chapel. On the lower level, note the marble sundial to the right of the crypt, and the viewing table illustrating the course of events during the second battle of the Marne to the left. The upper level features the chapel and an ossuary containing the remains of 1 500 unknown soldiers.

From the memorial it is possible to reach the mill across the park.

Moulin d'en Haut

Jun-Aug: 11am-6pm, Sat 2.30-6pm, Sun and holidays 3-6pm; May and Sep-Oct: daily 2.30-6pm, Sun and holidays 3-6pm. Mon. €4. 03 26 58 85 46.

This former communal mill houses an interesting collection of over 3 000 **rural tools** for working in the vineyards, in the fields and in the woods.

Church

Jul-Aug: 9am-7pm. This Gothic church features a square tower above the crossing, with paired bays on each of the four gables; the north transept is flanked by a turret surmounted by an octagonal pinnacle. The most interesting part of the church is the flat east end dating from the 13C, with High Gothic windows.

Follow N 3 to Port-à-Binson.

The road affords a view of Châtillon overlooked by the statue of Pope Urbain II.

Drive to Œuilly along N 3.

Ph. Gajic/ MICHELIN

Painted wall in the cooperative vineyard at Fleury-la-Rivière

Œuilly

This old fortified hillside village has a three-part **eco-museum**(*Apr-Oct: guided tour (1hr 15min) daily except Tue 10am-Noon,2-6pm; Nov-Mar: daily except Tue 2-5pm.* *Christmas holidays, 1 May; €5.50 (children: €2.50); 03 26 57 10 30).*

The **Maison champenoise**, dating from 1642, illustrates the life of a wine-grower and his family at the end of the 19C; the **Musée de la Goutte** (a famous wine brandy) houses the former village still and an exhibition on the traditional techniques used by coopers; the **École communale 1900** (village school) retains its desks, stove and blackboard.

Follow D 222 to Boursault.

Château de Boursault

Built in 1848 in neo-Renaissance style for the famous Veuve Clicquot, this vast castle was the venue of magnificent receptions given by Madame Clicquot and later by her great-granddaughter, the Duchess of Uzès.

Continue to Vauciennes and follow D 22 towards the River Marne, then N 3 to Épernay.

The road offers fine **views**★ of the Marne Valley, the village of Damery and the Montagne de Reims.

Round tour from Château-Thierry 2

60km/37mi Allow 4hr.

The Aisne vineyards that follow the River Marne between Crouttes and Trélou (near Dormans) belong to the Champagne wine-growing region.

The *pinot meunier* vines thrive on the Marne Valley soil and grow on half the area covered by the Champagne vineyards.

Leave Château-Thierry SE along D 969 which follows the meanders of the river.

Essômes-sur-Marne

The **Église St-Ferréol**★ (Mon-Wed 9am-Noon, 2-6pm, Thur 9am-Noon, Fri 9am-Noon, 2-5pm, *Sat 10am.* *Jul-Aug. 03 23 83 08 31*) was founded as an Augustinian abbey church in 1090 by Hugues de Pierrefonds. The **interior**★ shows Lancet-Gothic architecture. Note the elegant triforium with its narrow twin openings, the Renaissance choir stalls and, in the south transept, the 16C chapel closed off by a colonnade.

Make a detour via Montcourt then turn left onto D 1400.

The road runs through vineyards, offering, between Mont-de-Bonneil and Azy, an interesting **panorama** of a meander of the Marne with the wooded Brie region in the background.

Rejoin D 969 in Azy and continue past Saulchery to Charly.

Charly-sur Marne

This is the most important wine-growing centre of the Aisne département.

Follow D 11 to Villiers-Saint-Denis and turn left onto D 842 to Crouttes.

The road offers a wide **view** of the deep meander of the Marne to the south.

Crouttes-sur-Marne

This wine-growing village owes its name to its cellars dug out of the rock. Leave the car near the town hall and walk up to the church picturesquely perched above the village.

Return to Charly along D 969 and cross the river; turn left onto D 86 to Nogent-l'Artaud.

Nogent-l'Artaud

Very little remains of the former 13C abbey of the Poor Clares Order.
Between Nogent and Chézy, the road (*D 86*) overlooks the Marne and offers fine views of the slopes planted with vines.

Chézy-sur-Marne

There are fine walks along the banks of the Dolloir, a tributary of the Marne.

Follow D 15. The road runs under D 1 to Étampes-sur-Marne and joins N 3 in Chierry.

Between Chierry and Blesmes, the road offers a fine **panorama** of the valley. Turn left onto a minor road 1.5km/0.9mi beyond Blesmes.

Fossoy

The Déhu cellars, run by the seventh generation of a wine-growing family, welcome tourists along this Route du Champagne. Former stables have been turned into a small museum.

Le Varocien: musée de la Vigne et du Vin

Guided tours (20min) by appointment with M. Dehu, 3 rue St Georges, 02650 Fossoy. Sun and holidays. €4. 03 23 71 90 47. There are explanations about the vines and tools used in the area by wine-growers. Note the refractometer dating from 1863, used for measuring alcoholic concentration.

Continue along the minor road to Mézy.

Église de Mézy

The triforium of this 13C Gothic church conceals a circular gallery.

Cross the River Marne and turn left onto D 3 which runs along the north bank.

Mont-St-Père

Paintings by Léon Lhermitte (1844-1925), a native of this village, were inspired by rural life and landscapes (*Harvesters' Payday* can be seen in the Musée d'Orsay in Paris).
On its way to Château-Thierry, the road (*D 3*) skirts the Bois de Barbillon.

Coteaux Sud d'Épernay★

Round tour south of Épernay 4

See ÉPERNAY: Excursion.

CHARLEVILLE-MÉZIÈRES★

POPULATION 53 000

MICHELIN LOCAL MAP 306: K-4

LOCAL MAP SEE MÉANDRES DE LA MEUSE

The commercial city of Charleville stretches along the north bank of the river overlooked by Mount Olympus, whereas Mézières, an administrative and military centre, nestles inside a meander of the Meu se. The town were united in 1969.

- **Orient Yourself:** Charleville-Mézières is located right in the north of Champagne, on A 34 and 87km/54mi from Reims on N 19 and A 34.
- **Don't Miss:** Place Ducale is one of the finest Louis XIII-style squares in France.
- **Especially for Kids:** The clock embedded in the wall of the Institute of Puppetry is the scene of puppet shows every day *(see Horloge du Grand Marionnettiste below)* and the Institute can also be visited. At Christmastime the tiny village of Poix-Terron *(18km/11.2mi SW from Charleville-Mézières on A 34)* transforms an old mill into Father Christmas' house (Christmas decorations, elves, etc.). Also farther afield is the Animal Park of St-Laurent.

A Bit of History

A Gallo-Roman city destroyed in the 5C by Barbarian invaders stood on the site of Montcy-St-Pierre; the market town of **Arches** developed on the site of Charleville from the 9C onwards, acquring a royal palace while Mézières, founded around the year 1000, was just a village; in the 13C, both towns belonged to the Count of Rethel and Nevers.

In 1565, Louis de Gonzague of the House of the dukes of Mantua, acquired the duchy of Nevers and the earldom of Rethel. **Charles de Gonzague** (1580-1637) succeeded his father and in 1606, he decided to turn Arches into the main city of a principality named for himself. By 1627 the building of the town was completed, under the supervision of architect Clément Métezeau.

In 1590, a citadel was built to reinforce the strategic position of Mézières; the Prussian advance was stopped here for 45 days in 1815. During the First World War, Mézières was the headquarters of the German forces.

Visit of Charleville

Place Ducale★★

Designed by **Clément Métezeau** (1581-1652), the square is characteristic of the Louis XIII architectural style and shows numerous similarities with place des Vosges in Paris, which is attributed to Louis Métezeau, Clément's brother.

In Rimbaud's footsteps

A native of Charleville, **Arthur Rimbaud** (1854-91) was a brilliant student at the local college and one of his most famous poems, *Le Bateau ivre* (The Drunken Boat) dates from his student days. Unhappy at home, he became a rebel and often ran away to Charleroi and Paris where he met Verlaine. He followed the older poet to Belgium and London and, in 1873, he wrote another of his famous poems, *Une Saison en Enfer* (A Season in Hell). He later abandoned literature to travel to the Red Sea and the Far East. Repatriated for health reasons at the age of 37, he died in hospital in Marseille and was buried in the old cemetery of his home town.

The poet's childhood house (7 quai Rimbaud) and his college, now the local library (4 place de l'Agriculture) is near the museum; his birthplace (12 rue Bérégovoy) is situated south of place Ducale; his grave is near the entrance of the old cemetery (avenue Charles-Boutet); a bust of Rimbaud was erected on square de la Gare in 1901.

Address Book

PRACTICAL INFORMATION

Tourist Office – *4 Pl. Ducale, 08102 Charleville-Mézières – ☎03 24 55 69v90.*

WHERE TO EAT

See the Legend for coin categories.

La Côte à l'Os – *11 cours Aristide-Briand – ☎03 24 59 20 16 – closed Sun evening.* You can be sure of a warm welcome in this town-centre restaurant, situated in an avenue lined with horse chestnut trees. With a pleasant terrace, a traditional winstub-style "La Taverne", and a traditional regional menu.

Le Val Fleuri – *25 quai Arthur-Rimbaud – ☎03 24 59 94 11 – closed Sat lunchtime and Sun evening.* This first floor restaurant on the Meuse is run by a pleasant couple. Among the local specialities, don't miss the t'chu nous, a white blood sausage from Haybes.

Armorini – *46. pl.Ducale – ☎03 24 37 48 80 – closed 1-22 Aug, Sun and Mon – €15/26.* This trattoria offers Italian dishes and wines to eat in or take away.

TEA AND CAKES

Sutter Côté Salon – *Passage République – ☎03 24 58 33 62 – Mon 2-7pm, Tue-Wed 9am-7pm, Thu 2-7pm, Fri-Sat 9am-7pm; closed 2 weeks in summer and holidays.* One of this tearoom's delicious specialities are Carolos, meringues made with praline and macaroons. At lunchtime, simple meals are served, including mixed salads and snacks.

WHERE TO STAY

Hôtel de Paris – *24 av. Georgres-Corneau – ☎03 24 33 34 38 – www.hoteldeparis08.fr – closed 9-22 Aug and 20 Dec-6 Jan – 27 rooms – ☕ €6.30.* This early 20C hotel is situated on a busy avenue near the station. The light, simple rooms are well soundproofed. Pleasant, helpful staff.

ON THE TOWN

La Petite Brasserie Ardennaise – *25 quai Arthur-Rimbaud – ☎03 24 37 53 53 – Mon-Sat 5pm-1am – closed 1 Jan and 1 May.* The micro-brewery offers a wide selection of beers. In the back room seven varieties of beer are brewed, including one called oubliette – which you are not likely to forget, despite its name – available in blonde (pale), ambrée (dark) or stout.

Le Mawhot – *Quai Charcot – ☎03 24 33 54 35 – summer: daily 4pm-1am – closed Oct, Mon and Tue in winter.* The Mawhot is a legendary reptile from the Ardennes region. The barman, Philippe, pays homage to this beast by telling wonderful tales of the legendary Aymon brothers and and their black steed Bayard. Drink in the stories while sipping a home-made brew.

PUPPETRY

Institut International de la Marionnette – Kids – *7 pl. Winston-Churchill – ☎03 24 33 72 50 – www.marionnette.com – Mon-Fri 9am-1pm, 2-6pm – closed holidays – €10 (children: €5).* Run by the pupils of the National College of Puppetry, the institute's theatre offers a high-quality programme that will appeal to young and old alike. Courses, workshops and meetings are also organised. Note the giant automaton that recites the local legend of the four Aymon brothers in twelve short plays.

SHOPPING

Pâtisserie du Mont Olympe – *7 r. du Moulin – ☎03 24 33 25 11 – Tue-Sun 8am-12.30pm and 2-7pm – closed Feb holidays and public holidays.* – This pastry shop is renown for what may be the finest Carolos (a succulent mixture of praline chocolate and macaroons) in town and the Rimbaud, made out dark chocolate, praline and nougat.

The square (126m/138yd long and 90m/98yd wide) is lined with **arcades** surmounted by pink brick and ochre-coloured stone **pavilions** topped by slate-covered pitched roofs, forming a harmonious and colourful ensemble.

A public passageway (*same opening times as the museum*), which crosses the museum courtyard, links place Ducale and place Winston-Churchill.

Horloge du Grand Marionnettiste

Place Winston-Churchill. Incorporated into the façade of the Institut international de la Marionnette, this 10m/33ft high brass automaton is by Jacques Monestier; its head and eyes are moved by clockwork on the hour between 10am and 9pm. A short puppet show depicts an episode of the legend of the Four Aymon Brothers, the 12 scenes being enacted every Saturday at 9.15pm.

Rue de la Paix

Each pavilion contains shops on the ground floor and two homes under a large slate-covered roof. There are other similar houses in **rue du Moulin**.

Vieux Moulin

The former ducal mill looks more like a monumental gate with its imposing Henri IV-Louis XIII façade; it was designed to match the Porte de France in the south. It houses the **Musée Rimbaud** (*see entry heading*).

Visit of Mézières

Basilique Notre-Dame-d'Espérance

Jul-Aug: Guided tours possible (stained glass windows) by appointment. 03 24 57 50 62.

Although it was remodelled over several centuries, this basilica is essentially in Flamboyant-Gothic style, except for the belfry-porch erected in the 17C. The interior is grandiose; light pours in through beautiful abstract **stained-glass windows**★, made between 1955 and 1979 by René Dürrbach.

In the 19C, the basilica was dedicated to the black Notre-Dame-d'Espérance; the statue stands on top of an altar situated to the right of the chancel.

Ramparts

Part of the medieval ramparts remain: Tour du Roy, Tour de l'École, Tour Milart, Porte Neuve, and Porte de Bourgogne.

Préfecture

House in the former Royal Engineers School (17C-18C).

Sights

Musée de l'Ardenne★

31 place Ducale. Daily except Mon 10am-noon, 2-6pm. 1 Jan, 1 May and 25 Dec. €4 (children under 18: no charge), no charge 1st Sun of the month. 03 24 32 44v60 NOTE: one ticket gives access to all.

This modern museum contains a large **archaeology** department illustrating the first human settlements in the Ardennes, while the first-floor rooms display **weapons** made in the royal weapon manufacture, documents about the founding of Charleville (17C relief maps) and 3 000 **coins** and **medals**.

The **pharmacy** (1756) was originally in the former Hôtel-Dieu hospital; it was still in use 25 years ago!

The top floor houses collections devoted to **folk art and traditions**.

Musée Rimbaud

Quai Rimbaud. Same conditions as Musée de l'Ardenne. 03 24 32 44 65.

Housed inside the old mill, the museum contains mementoes of the poet Arthur Rimbaud. *For a brief biography of the poet, see In Rimbaud's footsteps above.*

A footbridge, behind the museum, gives access to Mount Olympus.

Excursions

Mohon

Opposite Mézières, on the south bank of the Meuse.

This town has a 16C church, **Église St-Lié** (*Daily except Mon 8.30am-noon; In case of absence, enquire at the presbytery; 03 24 57 13v15*), where pilgrims once flocked to see St. Lié's relics.

Parc animalier de St-Laurent

Route de St-Laurent. 6km/3.7mi E along D 979. Mon-Fri 1-6pm, Sat-Sun 1.30-7pm. Thu. No charge. 03 24 57 39 84-www.mairiecharlevillemezieres.fr.

Kids Stroll through this zoological park covering 45ha/111 acres.

Forêt d'Élan★

8.5km/5.3mi S.

Place Ducale

- *Drive out of Mézières along D 764 to Flize and continue S along D 33 to Élan.*

Although close to the River Meuse, the Vallon d'Élan, with its steep pasture-covered slopes framed by the forest of the same name, looks like a mountain valley. The Cistercian abbey, founded in 1148, was wealthy during the Middle Ages. The Gothic **abbey church**, with its 17C Classical west front, forms a harmonious architectural ensemble with the **abbey manor** flanked with elegant turrets (beautiful chestnut timberwork).

At the end of the valley, the 17C **Chapelle St-Roger** stands on the spot where the first abbot, St Roger, liked to meditate. There is a spring nearby.

The **Forêt d'Élan**, covering 872ha/2 006 acres, has beautiful oaks and beeches.

CHÂTEAU-THIERRY

POPULATION 14 967

MICHELIN LOCAL MAP 306: C-8

Château-Thierry is mainly renowned as the birthplace of the French poet and world-famous fable-writer, Jean de la Fontaine.

- **Orient Yourself:** Château-Thierry is located on the A 4 between Paris and Reims.
- **Organising Your Time:** Start by touring the town on foot before heading farther afield.
- **Especially for Kids:** La Fontaine's birthplace is generally a hit with younger children, while teenagers might find a tour of the battle sites and war cemeteries interesting.

Visit

- *Start from place de l'Hôtel-de-Ville and walk up rue du Château to Porte St-Pierre.*

Porte St-Pierre

This is the only one of the four town gates still standing.

Château

Go in through **Porte St-Jean**; note the embossed decoration, characteristic of the late-14C. The former garrison (now razed) offers fine **views** of the town, the Marne Valley and the monument on top of Cote 204 (*see Excursions*).

The **Maison Gondobald** (*Guided tours 1hr 30min; Jul-Aug: Tues-Fri 10.30am-12.30pm, 2-6.30pm, Sat-Sun*

La Fontaine

While living as a lawyer in Château-Thierry, 1621 born La Fontaine remained a daydreamer and neglected both his work and his wife. Then he heard an officer recite a poem and had a revelation: he had to become a poet himself. .

10.30am-12.30pm, 2-7pm; Jun and Sep: Wed-Fri 3-6.30pm;€1.65;☎03 23 83 00 07 or 03 23 83 03 46 – www.virgesarmes.com), within the fortifications, illustrates the living quarters of a castle around the year AD 1000.

▶ *Walk back along Grande Rue.*

Sights

Maison natale de La Fontaine

Apr-Sep: daily except Tue 9am-noon, 2-6pm; Oct-Mar: daily except Tue 10am-noon, 2-5pm. 1 Jan, 1 May, 1 Nov and 25 Dec. €3.30, no charge Wed. ☎03 23 69 05 60.

This 16C mansion now houses the museum devoted to La Fontaine.

Kids It contains magnificent editions of the *Fables* and *Tales*, including those illustrated by Oudry in 1755 and Gustave Doré in 1868, along with objects decorated with scenes from the *Fables*.

Caves de champagne Pannier

23 r. Roger-Catillon, W of town. Tour (1hr) by request, daily except Sun and holidays 9am-12.30pm, 2-6.30pm. €5. ☎ 03 23 69 51 33. www.champagnepannier.com

An audio-visual presentation and a tour of the cellars located in 13C stone quarries enable visitors to follow the process of Champagne-making.

Excursions

Vallée de la Marne★

This Route du Champagne meanders through woods or across vineyards along the hillsides overlooking the River Marne (*see Routes du CHAMPAGNE*).

Condé-en-Brie

▶ *16 km/10mi E along N3.*

This small town has retained an interesting covered market with Doric columns and a castle (*mid-Apr to mid Oct 2.30-5.30pm, last admission 30min before closing time Monday;€8;☎03 23 82 42 25; www.chateaudeconde.com*)

The Battle of the Marne

16km/10mi NW; allow 2hr.

▶ *Drive west out of Château-Thierry along N 3 and turn left at the top of*

Ph. Gajic/ MICHELIN

Condé-en-Brie

Address Book

PRACTICAL INFORMATION

Tourist office – *11 r. Vallée, 02400 Château-Thierry – ☎03 23 83 10 14 – www.otischateau-thierry.com.*

WHERE TO STAY

Chambre d'hôte La Grange du Moulin – *15 r. du Moulin – 02810 Bussiares – 13km/8mi W of Château-Thierry on N 3 and D 9 – ☎03 23 70 92 60 -lagrangedumoulin@hotmail.fr – closed 15 Dec – 15 Jan – – 4 rooms – evening meal* . This ancient ivy-covered building houses beautifully refurbished and comfortable rooms and a pleasant dining room with exposed beams and old-fashioned furniture. The small garden is very popular in summer.

Chambre d'hôte M. et Mme Leclère – *1 r. de Launay – 02330 Connigis – 12km/7.5mi E of Château-Thierry on N 3 and D 4 – ☎03 23 71 90 51 – closed 24 Dec-1 Jan – 5 rooms – evening meal* . The owners are champagne producers and will make you welcome in their 16C home, set in a park and surrounded by vineyards. This old farm has retained its simple country style

the hill along the avenue leading to Cote 204.

Monument de la Cote 204

Cote 204 (today with an American monument) was held by the Germans in June 1918. It took both a French and an American division over five weeks to dislodge them.

Enjoy the fine **view** of Château-Thierry, the castle and the Marne Valley.

Return to N 3 and, at the crossroads, continue straight on along D 9 to Belleau.

Bois-Belleau

These woods were taken by the Marines in June 1918. The vast **American cemetery** contains 2 280 graves. An American aircraft carrier was named USS Bois Belleau in commemoration; the ship was sold to France in 1953.

The **German cemetery** is situated 500m/547yd farther on.

Return to the crossroads where the American cemetery is located and turn right onto a narrow road marked Belleau Wood.

The Marines **monument** is inside the wood, the scene of fierce fighting.

CHAUMONT

POPULATION 25 996

MICHELIN LOCAL MAP 313: K-5

Chaumont-en-Bassigny has retained part of its medieval character, boasts a collection of old and contemporary posters and stages several annual events.

- **Orient yourself:** Chaumont occupies the edge of a steep plateau separating the River Suize and the River Marne. It is 100km/62mi SE of Troyes.
- **Don't miss:** the **International Poster Festival** in June ; **Grand Pardon** street procession (midsummer) or the **Hunting and Country** fair at Chateauvillain in August. (*see Address Book).*
- Kids **Especially for kids:** Children will love romping around the **Zoo de bois** (*see Excursions).*

Old Town

Start from square Philippe-Lebon.

The town organises guided tours of the town with an audio-guide system *(enquire at the tourist office).*

From the square there is a **view** of the keep, the ramparts, the towers of the Basilique St-Jean, the steeple of the Jesuits' chapel and the town hall.

Walk down rue de la Tour-Chartron on the right which runs along the former ramparts.

Look out for the **Tour d'Arse**, a hexagonal 13C tower below.

Walk up rue Monseigneur-Desprez to place St-Jean.

Note the mansion dating from 1723.

Follow rue du Palais leading to place du Palais and walk up the steps to the esplanade surrounding the keep (view of the Suize Valley). The former tanners' district lies below.

Donjon

Early Jul-mid-Sep; Guided tours (30min) daily (except Tue) 2pm, book the day before. €1.60. ☎03 25 03 80 80.

Follow rue Hautefeuille on the left.

Rue Guyard and **rue Gouthière** have retained historic mansions and towers.

Continue along rue Hautefeuille then take rue Decrès.

Note at no 17, the Louis XIV doorway.

Basilique St-Jean-Baptiste★

The west front, surmounted by two towers, dates from the 13C. (Later parts are from the 16C).
In the chapel at the west end of the nave, on the left-hand side, there is a highly realistic **Entombment**★★ (1471).
The basilica also contains various paintings and sculptures from the School of Jean-Baptiste Bouchardon.

Turn left onto rue Girardon.

Two mansions with splendid doorways stand on a small square: Hôtel de Grand on the left is in Louis XIII style and Hôtel de Beine on the right (Louis XIV style).

Walk along rue Damrémont then to scenic rue Bouchardon. Rue St-Jean leads to place de la Concorde overlooked by the town hall.Then return to square Philippe-Lebon via rue Laloy, rue Toupot-de-Beveaux and rue de Verdun.

Sights

Musée d'Art et d'Histoire

Pl. du Palais. Early Jul to mid-Sep: daily except Tue 2.30-6.30pm; mid-Sep to Jun: daily except Tue 2-6pm. 1 Jan, 1 May and 25 Dec. €1.50, no charge 1st Sun of the month. ☎03 25 03 01 99.

Address Book

PRACTICAL INFORMATION

Tourist office – *Pl. du Gén.de-Gaulle – ☎03 25 03 80 80.*

DIARY

Festival International de l'Affiche – *May-June in various locations around town. Information: ☎03 25 03 86 80. www.ville-chaumont.fr.*

"Grand Pardon de peine et de coulpe", has been celebrated since the 15C to ward off plague, famine and war, whenever midsummer's day falls on a Sunday, with processions in the streets, floral decorations in the town centre, and theatre performances.

Plaisirs de la Chasse et de la Nature fair – *last Sat-Sun of Aug, at Chateauvillain.* Equipment, displays and fireworks.

See the Legend at the back of the guide for coin categories.

WHERE TO STAY

⊜⊜ **Grand Hôtel Terminus-Reine** – *Pl. du Gén.-de-Gaulle – ☎03 25 03 66 66 – www.relais-sud-champagne.com – 61 rooms – €8.50 – restaurant ⊜⊜.* Most of the rooms of this hotel opposite the station have been renovated and are bright and welcoming. The restaurant serves pizzas and traditional cuisine.

Ph. Gajic/ MICHELIN

Tour d'Arse

Housed in the vaulted rooms of the former palace of the counts of Champagne, the museum displays **archaeological collections, paintings and sculptures** from the 16C to the 20C (works by Paul de Vos, Nicolas Poussin, François Alexandre Pernot).

Musée de la Crèche

Rue des Frères-Mistarlet. Early Jul to mid-Sep: daily except Tue 2.30-6.30pm; mid-Sep to Jun: daily except Tue 2-6pm. Guided tour by request. €1.50. Combined ticket with Musée d'Art et d'Histoire. 03 25 03 01 99.

This museum exhibits a collection of **crèches★** (nativity scenes with figurines) from the 17C to the 20C.

Les silos, Maison du livre et de l'affiche

Jul-Aug: daily 2-6.30pm, Sat 9am-1pm; Sep-Jun: Tue-Fri 2-7pm, Wed and Sat 10am-6pm. Sun, Mon and holidays. No charge. 03 25 03 86 86.

The former grain silos are now a cultural centre housing a library, reference room with multimedia facilities, and a poster museum with themed **exhibitions**.

Excursions

Viaduc★

1km/0.6mi west.

Approaching Chaumont from the west along D 65, one immediately spots the magnificent 654m/715yd long **viaduct★**, towering 52m/171ft above the valley.

Driving Tour

Plateau de Langres

94km/58mi from Chaumont to Langres. Allow half a day.

The watershed between the Paris Basin, the Rhine Valley and the Rhône Valley is situated on this plateau and the Seine, the Aube, the Marne and the Meuse all have their source in the area.

Leave Chaumont along D 65 and follow it to Châteauvillain.

Châteauvillain

Parts of the town's fortifications (14C to 16C) survive. The west front of the **Église Notre-Dame de l'Assomption** is believed to have been designed by architect Soufflot (the Paris Panthéon).

Continue along D 65 then turn left onto D6 towards Arc-en-Barrois.

Arc-en-Barrois

This town is a lovely place to stay.

Follow D 159 towards Aubepierre-sur-Aube and turn left onto D 20 to Auberive.

Auberive

A Cistercian abbey founded in 1133 (*not open to the public*).

On the way out of Auberive, take the Acquenove forest road. The source of the River Aube is signposted.

Source de l'Aube

A pastoral setting with picnic facilities.

Follow D 293 to Baissey.

Moulin de Baissey

Jun-Aug: Sat-Sun and holidays, 2.30pm-5.30pm, last admission 1hr before closing time. €2.30. 03 25 87 67 67. Tour this functioning medieval mill to see paddle wheel, millstones, gears.

Drive to Sts-Geosmes along D 141 then N 74.

Sts-Geosmes

The 13C **church**, dedicated to three saints martyred on this site, is built over a 10C crypt with three naves.

N 74 leads to Langres.

ABBAYE DE CLAIRVAUX

MICHELIN LOCAL MAP 313: I-5

On 25 June 1115, St Bernard settled with 11 monks in the remote Val d'Absinthe, to found one of the four major houses of the new Cistercian Order. The Abbaye de Clairvaux (the name means "clear valley") soon acquired considerable influence. However, post-Revolution, the abbey became a prison in 1808. It still belongs to the Ministry of Justice.

A Bit of History

St Bernard and Cistercian architecture

Simplicity and voluntary deprivation led to a plain and austere architectural style. St Bernard strove to fight against the sumptuosity of so many abbey churches (excessive size, a wealth of ornamentation and interior decoration).

Clairvaux and the art of illumination

The abbey workshop produced over 1 400 illuminated manuscripts – almost all preserved in Troyes' municipal library.

Visit

Allow 2hr. Jul-Sep. Guided tour (1hr 30min) daily 2, 3.30 and 5pm, Sat 2, 3, 4 and 5pm; Mid Mar-Mid Apr: daily 2 and 3.30pm, Sat 2, 3.30 and 5pm, Sun 3pm; Oct-mid-Nov; Wed-Sat 2 and 3.30pm, Sun 3pm; rest of the year Sun 2.30pm by request. Mon, Tues, 1 Jan, 25 Dec. €6.50. 03 25 27 52 55.

A high wall, 2.7km/1.6mi long, which encloses an area of 30ha/75 acres, has replaced the fortified wall built by the monks in the 14C.

Enter through the Porte du Midi. Immediately to the left is the former Hostellerie des Dames and, Petit Clairvaux; opposite stand the austere monastic buildings of Haut Clairvaux.

Hostellerie des Dames

When Clairvaux was a monastery, women were not allowed to enter; wives of the abbey's visitors stayed here.

Petit Clairvaux

The site where Bernard de Clairvaux built his *monasterium vetus* in 1115 is now by the living quarters of the personnel of a nearby penal establishment.

Haut Clairvaux

It is possible to go into the courtyard and admire the beautiful 18C façades. A small doorway leads to the lay brothers' courtyard and into Haut Clairvaux.

Bâtiment des convers★

The lay brothers' 12C building is all that remains of Clairvaux II.

Clairvaux as a prison

When the abbey became state property in 1808, considerable work was undertaken to turn it into a prison. The socialist and revolutionary Louis-Auguste Blanqui (1872), members of the Paris Commune, Philippe d'Orléans (1890), deserters from Verdun (1917), many Resistance members (1940-44) of whom 21 were shot, several ministers of the Vichy government (after the Liberation of France) and insubordinate generals during the Algerian War of Independence were all held in Clairvaux.

COLMAR★★★

POPULATION 65 136
MICHELIN LOCAL MAP 315: I-J 8
ALSO SEE ROUTE DES VINS

The great appeal of Colmar lies in the typical Alsatian character of its streets lined with picturesque flower-decked houses and its Little Venice district unaltered by time and wars. Situated in the heart of the Alsatian vineyards, Colmar is the starting point of numerous excursions along the Route des Vins. The town proudly hosts the international festival of gastronomy (Festiga), which gathers many culinary talents and presents food products from all over the world.

- **Orient Yourself:** Colmar lies half-way between Strasbourg and Basle, on the A 35.
- **Don't Miss:** The Unterlinden Museum with its Issenheim altarpiece.
- **Parking:** The majority of the town centre is pedestrian with car parks located on the main avenues into town.
- **Organising Your Time:** Start by heading for Unterlinden Museum, before embarking on a tour of the old town on foot, by train or by boat (Little Venice). If you have more time, treat yourself to a drive along the Wine Route.
- Kids **Especially for Kids:** The Toy and Train Museum delights younger children.

A Bit of History

Idyllic beginnings

A Frankish town developed in the Rhine Valley, on the banks of the River Lauch, a tributary of the Ill. Emperor Charlemagne, and later his son, often visited. Labourers and craftsmen lived round the royal villa. In its centre stood a tower with a dovecote which is said to have given its name to the town: Villa Columbaria (*colombe* means dove in French), then Columbra and eventually Colmar.

A heroic mayor

Despite its peaceful doves, Colmar often had to fight for its freedom. In 1261 the son of a tanner, **Roesselmann**, bravely led the town militia against the bishop of Strasbourg's soldiers, paying for the city's freedom with his life.

A ruthless tyrant

Two centuries later, Colmar temporarily came under the rule of the Duke of Burgundy, Charles le Téméraire, and his cruel bailiff, Pierre de Hagenbach. When the latter was at last defeated and condemned to death, the executioner of Colmar was chosen to carry out the sentence. The sword he used is still kept in the Musée d'Unterlinden.

Natives of Colmar

Colmar is the birthplace of several famous artists, including **Martin Schongauer** (1445-91) whose altarpieces and engravings were admired by Dürer and Venetian artists of the Renaissance, and

St Bernard (1090-1153)

Bernard de Fontaine (later known as Bernard de Clairvaux), a young aristocrat from the Bourgogne region, should have become a soldier to comply with his family's wishes. Yet, at the age of 21, he entered the Abbaye de Cîteaux together with his brothers and several uncles and cousins whom he had persuaded to follow him. He was only 25 when Étienne Harding, the abbot of Cîteaux, sent him away with the mission of founding Clairvaux. Being both a mystic and a fine administrator, Bernard soon embodied the Cistercian ideal: the strict observance of the rule of St Benedict (prayer and work) which had, according to him, been relaxed by the Benedictine Order.

Deprived of everything, the young abbot encountered immense difficulties: the harshness of the climate, diseases, physical hardship. For his monks and himself, he set the hardest tasks; "they ate boiled vegetables and drank water, slept on pallets, had no heating in winter and wore the same clothes day and night". Yet this new form of spirituality and Bernard's reputation attracted many enthusiasts and the success of the new abbey was immediate.

The young mystic wanted to reform the whole religious life of his time and he played a part in many of its concerns: the election of bishops, various councils, the papal schism, and the second crusade which he preached in Vezelay in 1146. His moral ascendancy gave him a considerable influence in European courts as well as in Rome where he pushed for the election of Pope Innocent II (1130-43) and then Eugene III, a former monk at Clairvaux who was elected Pope in 1145.

Shocked by the failure of the crusade (1148) and by the rise of heretic beliefs, which he fought without success, he died in 1153 and was canonised in 1174.

St Bernard was one of the strongest personalities of medieval times; his authoritarian behaviour was inspired by his passionate faith ("the way to love God is to love him without limit or measure", he said) combined with his taste for simplicity and voluntary deprivation.

Auguste Bartholdi (1834-1904), best remembered for the Statue of Liberty. Between 1870 and 1914, when Alsace was occupied by Germany, a talented caricaturist and watercolour artist, Jean-Jacques Waltz, better known as **Hansi**, stimulated the town's passive resistance to German influence and kept alive the traditional image of Alsace with his humoristic drawings of grotesque-looking German soldiers and good-natured, likeable villagers in regional costume.

Musée d'Unterlinden★★★

May-Oct: 9am-6pm; Nov-Apr: daily except Tue 9am-noon, 2-5pm. 1 Jan, 1 May, 1 Nov and 25 Dec. €7 (with recorded tour). 03 89 20 15 50. www.musee-unterlinden.com.

This museum (opened in 1849 on place d'Unterlinden near the Logelbach canal) was formerly a 13C convent whose name means "Under the lime trees". TFor 500 years, its nuns were famous for their mysticism and austere way of life.

Ground floor

The 13C **cloisters**★ are built of pink sandstone from the Vosges mountains. Note the larger arch half way down the western gallery, which stands over the old *lavabo*; the basin is still visible. In a corner is a Renaissance well.

The rooms surrounding the cloisters are devoted to **art** from the **Rhine Valley**. There are rich collections of late-medieval and Renaissance painting and sculpture, as well as stained glass, ivories and tapestries.Primitive art from the Rhine region is represented by Holbein the Elder, Cranach the Elder, Caspar Isenmann and Martin Schongauer (copper engravings).

It is advisable to visit rooms 1, 3 and 4 as a preliminary step to the discovery of the Retable d'Issenheim, which remains the prize exhibit.

Retable d'Issenheim ★★★ (Issenheim Altarpiece)

This is displayed in the chapel together with works by Martin Schongauer and members of his school (24-panel altarpiece depicting the **Passion**★★). The gallery of the former Dominican chapel (early-16C sculpture) makes a good viewpoint, enabling visitors to have an overall view of the different panels and fully appreciate the composition of the famous polyptych.

Painted by **Matthias Grünewald** at the beginning of the 16C for the high altar of the monastery at Issenheim, which was founded in 1298 and devoted to curing ergotism (also known as St Anthony's fire). The altarpiece was moved to Comar in 1793. Very little is known about the artist's life, but he is admired for his expressionist style, his daring colours and light effects, and the poetry and humour that pervade his paintings.

Taken apart during the Revolution, the polyptych was only put together again in 1930. It is made up of a carved central part, two fixed panels, two pairs of opening panels and a lower part which also opens. In order to preserve this unique work of art, the different parts were dismantled and are now displayed separately in the chancel. Several models with opening panels have been fixed to the chapel's walls, allowing visitors to see how the altarpiece opened out.

First floor

The collections here focus on regional history, Alsatian art, furniture, weapons, pewter, gold plate, wrought iron, 18C porcelain and earthenware (Strasbourg), including reconstructed interiors.

Basement

The Gallo-Roman room contains fragments of the 3C Bergheim mosaic. Farther on, the two barrel-vaulted naves of the former **cellar** of the convent (house the archaeological collections, from prehistory to the Merovingian period. Two rooms are devoted to 20C paintings by Renoir, Rouault, Picasso, Vieira da Silva, Nicolas de Staël and Poliakoff.

Old Town★★

Round tour starting from place d'Unterlinden 1

▸ *Walk along rue des Clefs.*

The Hôtel de Ville is on the left; this 18C building belonged to the Abbaye de Pairis.

▸ *When you reach place Jeanne-d'Arc, turn right onto Grand'Rue.*

Temple protestant St-Matthieu

Mid May-Jun: Daily 10am-Noon, 3-7pm; End Jul-mid Oct: Daily 10am-Noon, 3-7pm.

This former Franciscan church, now Protestant, is decorated with fine 14C and 15C **stained-glass windows**. At the top of the south aisle is the remarkable **Vitrail de la Crucifixion**★ (15C), believed to be the work of Pierre d'Andlau.

▸ *Turn left along the side of the church to reach place du 2-Février and look at the old hospital.*

The roof of the 18C **Ancien Hôpital** features Alsatian dormer windows.

▸ *Return to Grand'Rue and turn left.*

The world's longest walk

The **Paris-Colmar** walk through 171 municipalities and eight *départements* has, since 1981, been a hard test for some 50 of the best hikers in the world. They cover the 540km/234mi in about 70hr (an average of 7.5kph/4.6mph) to arrive on the picturesque place de l'Ancienne-Douane in Colmar where great festivities take place in their honour.

The women's event is a walk from Châlons-en-Champagne to Colmar (360km/220mi). Rendez-vous late May, or follow the race on *www.csf-paris-colmar.org*

Address Book

PRACTICAL INFORMATION

Tourist office – *4 r. des Unterlinden, ☎03 89 20 68 92, www.ot-colmar.fr*
Guided tours – Tours of the old town are organised from Jul-Sep. €4. Enquire at the tourist office.
Colmar by night – The town's most beautiful buildings are lit up at night. *May-Sep, Sat evenings.* Christmas show: *late Nov-late Dec, Tue, Thu, Fri and Sat. Departures from tourist office, 7pm (1hr 15min). €4.*
Tourist train – *Easter-Nov 1: commentary, departures every 30min Quai de la Sinn (opposite Unterlinden Museum), 9am-noon and 1.30-6pm, €5.50 (2-12 year olds: €3). ☎03 89 24 19 82.*
Boat trips – *See Little Venice.*

WHERE TO EAT

See the Legend for coin categories.
Winstub La Krutenau – *1 r. de la Poissonnerie – ☎03 89 41 18 80 – closed Christmas to end Jan, Sun and Mon out of season* . At this winstub beside the River Lauch you can go boating in Little Venice and eat a flammekueche on the flower-decked terrace beside the canal in summer.
Le Caveau St-Pierre – *24 r. de la Herse (Little Venice) – ☎03 89 41 99 33 – michel.francois@caveaustpierre.com – closed Jan – booking advisable.* A pretty wooden footbridge across the Lauch leads to this 17C house, which offers a little slice of paradise with its rustic, local-style decor, cuisine, and a terrace stretching out over the water.
Schwendi Bier-U-Wistub – *23-25 Grand'Rue – ☎03 89 23 66 26 – closed evenings on Christmas and New Year's Day.* You will instantly warm to this charming winstub with its ideal location in the heart of old Colmar. The principally wooden decor and the cooking, which is good quality and served in generous portions, are a tribute to Alsace. The terrace is a treat in summer.
La Maison Rouge – *9 rue des Écoles – ☎03 89 23 53 22 – closed Sun.* The somewhat ordinary façade hides a delightful rustic interior with excellent regional and home-made cooking.
Chez Bacchus – *2 Grand'Rue – 68230 Katzenthal – 5km/3mi NW of Colmar, Kaysersberg direction, then D 10 – ☎03 89 27 32 25 – closed 1-27 Jan, 1 week in Jul and in Nov, open Thu-Sat evening from 1 Oct-14 Jul, Sun and 15 Jul-30 Sep every evening except Tue – booking advisable at weekends.* There's a lovely friendly atmosphere in this wine bar dating from 1789 in a winemaking village. Massive exposed beams and helpings of Alsatian cuisine to match – guaranteed to satisfy the healthiest of appetites. Automated puppets will entertain the children with a lively show.
Winstub Brenner – *1 r. de Turenne – ☎03 89 41 42 33 – closed 6-23 Feb, 20-29 Jun, 15-24 Nov, 24 Dec-2 Jan, Tue and Wed.* The terrace by the Lauch in Little Venice is very popular on fine days and the whole of Colmar meets here with obvious enjoyment.

WHERE TO STAY

Colbert – *2 r. des Trois-Épis – ☎03 89 41 31 05 -www.villes-et-vignoble.com – 50 rooms – €6.* This functional hotel near the station provides a comfortable place to stay for those travelling by train. Bar and disco for those in search of nightlife.
Chambre d'hôte Les Framboises – *128 r. des Trois-Épis – 68230 Katzenthal – 5km/3mi NW of Colmar, Kaysersberg direction then D 10 – ☎03 89 27 48 85 – sarl.amrein@wanadoo.fr – 4 rooms.* Leave Colmar behind and head for this village out in the vines. The proprietor distils his own marc (grape brandy) from Gewürztraminer, with accommodation in wood-panelled attic rooms. Don't miss the morning puppet show!
Hôtel Au Moulin – *Rte d'Herrlisheim – 68127 Ste-Croix-en-Plaine – 10km/6.2mi S of Colmar on A 35 and D 1 – ☎03 89 49 31 20 – closed 5 Nov-31 Mar – P – 17 rooms – €8.* This old mill deep in the country is perfect for those seeking peace and quiet. A small museum of old local objects has been created in a neighbouring building.
Hôtel Turenne – *10 rte de Bâle – ☎03 89 21 58 58 – helmlinger@turenne.com – 82 rooms – €7.50.* On the edge of the old town, this hotel occupies a large, pleasing building with

a pink and yellow façade. Its rooms have been nicely renovated and are well soundproofed.
A few small but neat and reasonably priced single rooms are available.
Hôtel Le Colombier – *7 r. de Turenne –6km/3.5miles south of Colmar on D 14, then D 45 ☎03 89 23 96 00 – info@hotel-le-colombier.com – closed Christmas holidays – 24 rooms – €10.* This lovely 15C house in old Colmar combines old stone and contemporary decor by retaining elements from its past, such as the superb Renaissance staircase. Contemporary furniture and modern paintings in the rooms.

ON THE TOWN

La Manufacture – *6 rte d'Ingersheim – ☎03 89 24 31 78.* Programme of contemporary theatre, as well as music and dance.
Folk nights – *Pl. de l'Ancienne Douane – May-Sep: Tue at 8.30pm.*
Théâtre municipal – *Pl. du 18-Novembre – ☎03 89 20 29 01. culture@ville-colmar.com.* Classic plays, comedy and opera.

SHOPPING

Domaine viticole de la Ville de Colmar – *2 r. Stauffen – ☎03 89 79 11 87 – www.domaineviticolecolmar.com – Mon-Fri 8am-12pm, 2-6pm, Sat 9am-noon.* Closed Sun. Founded in 1895, this estate grows seven *cépages* and boasts a host of *grands crus* in addition to sparkling wines.
Caveau Robert-Karcher – *11 r. de l'Ours – ☎03 89 41 14 42 – www.vins-karcher.com – daily 8am-noon, 1.30-7pm – closed Sun afternoon, Good Friday, Easter, Christmas Day and Boxing Day.* The vineyards of this family business are north-west of Colmar, but the cellar, dating from 1602, is in a pedestrian street in the town centre.
You can taste the whole range of Alsace wines and be shown around the cellar.
Fortwenger – *32 r. des Marchands – ☎03 89 41 06 93 – www.fortwenger.fr – Mon-Fri 9.30am-12.30pm, 1.30-7pm, Sat 9.30am-12.30pm, 1.30-6.30pm, Sun 10am-12.30pm, 1.30-6pm.* Closed 25-26 Dec and 1 Jan. Charles Fortwenger founded his gingerbread factory in Gertwiller in 1768, but this Colmar shop sells a wide range of delicious products, made with chocolate, honey, icing sugar, aniseed and cinnamon.
Also local souvenirs.
Maison des Vins d'Alsace – *Civa – 12 av. de la Foire-aux-Vins – BP1217 – 03 89 20 16 20 – www.vinsalsace.com – Mon-Fri 9am-noon, 2-5pm – closed 25 Dec-1 Jan.* Five important local organisations concerned with Alsace wines are based in this centre. The visitor can study a map six metres (nearly 20 feet) long, showing all the winemaking villages and grands crus, as well as learn about the process of winemaking from hands-on models and a film.

Admire along the way the Renaissance **Maison des Arcades**★, framed by two octagonal turrets and the **Schwendi Fountain**.
Walk past the **Maison du Pèlerin** (1571) to reach place de l'Ancienne-Douane.

Place de l'Ancienne-Douane

This picturesque square features timber-framed houses such as the **Maison au Fer Rouge**.

Ancienne Douane or "Koifhus"★

This former customs house is the most important civilian edifice in Colmar. The main building is from 1480; its ground floor was used as a warehouse to stock goods subject to municipal tax. The great hall on the first floor, known as the Salle de la Décapole (the union formed by 10 Alsatian cities), was the meeting place for representatives of those cities. In the late 16C, a second building was added.
This is attractively decorated with a wooden gallery and flanked by a stair turret with canted corners; on the ground floor, three arches underline the opening and form a passage. Walk through to the other side and admire the fine outside staircase.

Take rue des Marchands opposite the customs house.

Maison Pfister★★

A hatter from Besançon had this lovely house built in 1537 and decorated with frescoes and medallions.
The arcaded ground floor is surmounted by an elegant wooden gallery.
Next to the Maison Pfister, at no 9, stands a fine house (1609) adorned with a wooden gallery and a corner sculpted figure representing a merchant.
On the left of rue des Marchands, the 15C **Maison Schongauer**, also known as **Maison de la Viole**, belonged to the painter's family.
The small house opposite is known as the **Maison au Cygne**, where Schongauer reputedly lived from 1477 to 1490.

Walk through the arcades opposite the Musée Bartholdi (see below), to place de la Cathédrale.

R. Mattès/ MICHELIN

Schwendi Fountain

On the square stand the oldest house in Colmar, **Maison Adolphe** (1350), and the **Ancien Corps de garde**★ (1575). The town's magistrate was sworn in on this lovely Renaissance loggia; infamous sentences were also proclaimed here.
Opposite the former guardhouse stands the collegiate church of St-Martin, known as the cathedral.

Collégiale St-Martin★

This imposing edifice decorated with glazed tiles and red-sandstone projections was built in the 13C and 14C on the site of a Romanesque church.
The west doorway is flanked by two towers. The south tower is decorated with a sundial bearing the inscription *Memento Mori* (think of death). **St Nicholas' doorway**, which gives access to the south transept, is decorated with 13 small statues; the fourth one on the left represents the builder who signed in French, Maistre Humbert.
Inside, note a 14C **Crucifixion**★ in the axial chapel and a magnificent 18C organ loft by Silbermann.

R. Mattès/ MICHELIN

A quiet canal in old Colmar

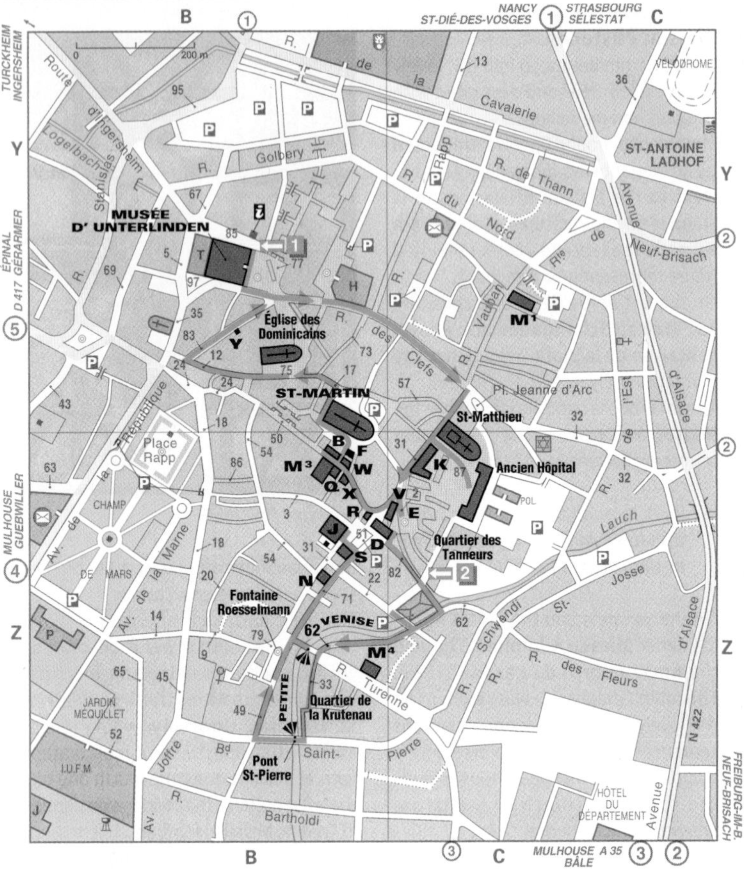

▶ *Leave place de la Cathédrale along rue des Serruriers.*

Église des Dominicains

🕓 *Apr-Dec: 10am-1pm and 3-6pm. €1.50 (children: €0.50).*

Work began on the chancel in 1283, but the main part of the edifice was only completed in the 14C and 15C. Inside, altars and stalls date from the 18C; but the magnificent **stained-glass windows**★ are contemporary with the construction of the church.

The famous 1473 painting by Martin Schongauer, the **Virgin of the Rose Bower**★★, can be seen at the entrance of the chancel; Virgin and Child form a charming picture against a golden background with rose bushes full of birds.

▶ *Walk along rue des Boulangers then turn right onto rue des Têtes.*

The fine Renaissance **Maison des Têtes**★ (*no 19*) owes its name to the numerous carved heads decorating the façade. The graceful gable is underlined by rows of scrolls; oriel windows complete the elaborate ornamentation.

▶ *Return to place d'Unterlinden.*

R. Mattès/MICHELIN

"House of the Heads"

COLMAR		
18 Novembre Pl. du	BY	97
2 Février Pl. du	CY	87
5e Division-Blindée R. de la	BY	95
Alsace Av. d'	CYZ	
Ancienne Douane Pl. de l'	CZ	2
Augustins R. des	BZ	3
Bains R. des	BY	5
Bartholdi R.	BCZ	
Blés R. des	BZ	9
Boulangers R. des	BY	12
Brasseries R. des	CY	13
Bruat R.	BZ	14
Cathédrale Pl. de la	BY	17
Cavalerie R. de la	BCY	
Champ-de-Mars Bd du	BYZ	18
Chauffour R.	BZ	20
Clefs R. des	BCY	
Écoles R. des	BZ	22
Est R. de l'	CYZ	
Fleurent R. J.-B.	BY	24
Fleurs R. des	CZ	
Fribourg Av. de	CZ	
Golbéry R.	BY	
Grand'Rue	BCZ	31
Grenouillère R. de la	CYZ	32
Herse R. de la	BZ	33
Ingersheim Rte d'	BY	
Jeanne d'Arc Pl.	CY	
Joffre Av.	BZ	
Kléber R.	BY	35
Ladhof R. du	CY	36
Lattre-de-Tassigny Av. J. de	BY	43
Leclerc Bd du Gén.	BZ	45
Manège R. du	BZ	49
Marchands R. des	BYZ	50
Marché-aux-Fruits Pl. du	BZ	51
Marne Av. de la	BZ	
Messimy R.	BZ	52
Molly R. Berthe	BYZ	54
Mouton R. du	CY	57
Neuf-Brisach Rte de	CY	
Nord R. du	BCY	
Poissonnerie R. et Q. de la	BCZ	62
Preiss R. Jacques	BZ	63
Rapp Pl.	BZ	
Rapp R.	BCY	
Reims R. de	BZ	65
République Av. de la	BZ	
Ribeauvillé R. de	BY	67
Roesselman R.	BY	69
St-Jean R.	BZ	71
St-Josse R.	CZ	
St-Nicolas R.	BY	73
St-Pierre Bd et Pont	BCZ	
Schwendi R.	CZ	
Serruriers R. des	BY	75
Sinn Quai de la	BY	77
Six-Montagnes-Noires Pl. des	BZ	79
Stanislas R.	BY	
Tanneurs R. des	CZ	82
Têtes R. des	BY	83
Thann R. de	CY	
Turenne R.	BCZ	
Unterlinden Pl. d'	BY	85
Vauban R.	CY	
Weinemer R.	BZ	86

Ancien Hôpital	CZ	
Ancien corps de garde	BZ	B
Ancienne Douane	BZ	D
Collégiale St-Martin	BY	
Fontaine Roesselmann	BZ	
Fontaine Schwendi	CZ	E
Maison Adolphe	BZ	F
Maison Kern	BZ	S
Maison Pfister	BZ	W
Maison Schongauer	BZ	X
Maison au Fer Rouge	BZ	R
Maison au cygne	BZ	Q
Maison des Arcades	CZ	K
Maison des Chevaliers de St-Jean	BZ	N
Maison des Têtes	BY	Y
Maison du Pèlerin	CZ	V
Musée Bartholdi	BZ	M3
Musée animé du Jouet et des Petits Trains	BZ	M1
Musée d'Histoire Naturelle et d'Ethnographie	BZ	M4
Musée d'Unterlinden	BY	
Petite Venise	BZ	
Quartier de la Krutenau	BZ	
Quartier des Tanneurs	CZ	
Temple protestant St-Matthieu	CYZ	
Tribunal civil	BZ	J
Église des dominicains	BY	

Petite Venise★
(Little Venice)

Round tour starting from place de l'Ancienne-Douane 2

From the square, follow rue des Tanneurs which runs along the canal.

Quartiers des tanneurs

The tanners' district (renovated in 1974) is named for the inhabitants who used the river to tan and wash hides (a practise discontinued in the 19C). Timber-framed houses were narrow but high, creating lofts to dry the skins.

Cross the River Lauch to enter the **Krutenau district**★, once a fortified outlying area; this district's market gardeners once used flat-bottomed boats, similar to Venetian gondolas.

Turn right along quai de la Poissonnerie.

Cross the next bridge to the corner of rue des Écoles and rue du Vigneron, to see Batholdi's **Fontaine du Vigneron,** a celebration of Alsatian wines.

Continue along quai de la Poissonnerie then **rue de la Poissonnerie**★ lined with picturesque fishermen's cottages. It runs into rue de Turenne, formerly rue de Krutenau, the old vegetable market.

Take rue de la Herse then turn right onto a narrow street leading to the river.

Pleasant stroll along the bank to **Pont St-Pierre**. From the bridge, there is a lovely **view**★ of Petite Venise.

Below the bridge, **boat trips** (*Apr-Sep: 30min trips 10am-7pm; Oct and Mar: Sat-Sun 10am-noon, 1-6pm; €5.50 (children under 10: no charge); 03 89 41 01 94*) are available to explore the district further.

Turn right onto rue du Manège leading to place des Six-Montagnes-Noires.

Batholdi's **Fontaine Roesselmann**, stands on the square; it is dedicated to the town's hero (*see A Bit of History*). Walk towards the bridge on the right: the river, lined with willow trees, flows between two rows of old houses.

Continue along rue St-Jean.

On the left is the rather Venetian **Maison des Chevaliers de St-Jean** (1608). A little farther is the lovely place du Marché-aux-Fruits with its Renaissance style **Maison Kern,** the pink sandstone **Tribunal civil**★ and the Ancienne Douane.

Return to place de l'Ancienne-Douane.

Sights

Musée Bartholdi

Mar-Dec: daily except Tue 10am-noon, 2-6pm (last entrance 30min before closing). 1 May, 1 Nov and 25 Dec. €4.20 (children under 12: no charge). ☎ 03 89 41 90 60, www.musee-bartholdi.com.

The house in the heart of town where **Frédéric-Auguste Bartholdi** (1834-1904) was born is now a museum dedicated to the sculptor whose Statue of Liberty stands at the entrance of New York harbour. The second floor is entirely devoted to the statue's history.

The downstairs rooms have been turned into a museum of local history.

On the first floor, Bartholdi's private quarters, furnished exactly as they were when he lived here, celebrate the artist's life and works, while the last room displays a collection of Jewish art.

Bartholdi's works in Colmar:

- Statue of General Rapp, place Rapp
- Monument to Admiral Bruat, place du Champ-de-Mars
- Schwendi Fountain, place de l'Ancienne-Douane
- Wine-grower's Fountain, corner of rue des Écoles and rue du Vigneron.

WHERE TO EAT

La Petite Palette – *☎ 03 89 72 73 50 – closed 1-12 Aug, Sun evening, Tue evening and Mon.* For those who appreciate good meat, this is the place to go. Located along a main shopping streets in the town centre, this restaurant belongs to a butcher who serves meat from his shop. The meat is raised by his parents in the Savoie. Various menus are available.

Musée animé du Jouet et des Petits Trains

Jul-Aug: 10am-7pm (last entrance 30min before closing); Sep-Jun: 10am-noon, 2-6pm; Dec: 10am-6pm. Tue (except Jul-Sep and Dec),10 days in Jan (enquire), 1 Jan, 1 May, 1 Nov and 25 Dec. €4, (children under 8: Free). ☎ 03 89 41 93 10. www.museejouet.com.

Kids This collection, housed in a former cinema, includes railway engines (the Britannia, British model Pacific 213), trains on landscaped tracks, dolls, circus rides, and automated figures – guaranteed to appeal to the child in us all.

Muséum d'Histoire naturelle et d'Ethnographie

Daily except Tue 10am-noon, 2-5pm, Sun 2-6pm (last entrance 30min before closing). Jan, 1 May, 1 Nov and 25 Dec. €5. ☎ 03 89 23 84 15. www.ac-strasbourg.fr/microsites/MHN_COLMAR

The region's fauna and geological diversity, along with an Egyptian room and ethnographical collection (particularly from the Marquesas Islands) are housed in a 17C building.

Excursion

Neuf-Brisach

16km/10mi E of Colmar.

Leave by S on the town plan and drive along N 415.

This octagonal stronghold built by Vauban, Louis XIV's military engineer and architect has retained its austere 17C character in spite of the damage incurred during the 1870 siege and the Second World War.

The area within the 2.4km/1.5mi long walls is divided by a network of streets intersecting at right angles. In the centre stands the Église St-Louis and the vast place d'Armes (parade ground) with

a well in each of its four corners. It is possible to walk along the ditch from the Porte de Belfort (south-west) to the Porte de Colmar (north-west). This pleasant stroll (about 30min) reveals the main elements of the fortifications: bartizaned bastions, ravelins etc.
The **Porte de Belfort**, no longer used as a gate, houses the **Musée Vauban** (*May-Oct: daily except Tue 10am-noon, 2-5pm.€2.50. 03 89 72 03 93.*) which contains a relief map of the stronghold with a *son et lumière* show.
Slightly farther east (*5km/3mi*), at **Vogelgrün**, the border-bridge over the Rhine offers a **view**★ of the river, the hydro-electric power station (*see Vallée du RHIN*) and Vieux-Brisach (Breisach) across the border.

COLOMBEY-LES-DEUX-ÉGLISES

POPULATION 650

MICHELIN LOCAL MAP 313: J-4

Colombey rose to fame through its most illustrious citizen, Charles de Gaulle, who had his home at La Boisserie from 1934 until his death in 1970. He is buried in the village cemetery, near the church. In his *Memoirs*, De Gaulle lovingly described this Champagne region: "steeped in sadness and melancholy... former mountains drastically eroded and resigned... quiet, modest villages whose soul and location has not changed for thousands of years...."

- **Orient Yourself:** On the edge of the Champagne region and on the borders of Burgundy and Lorraine, Colombey has, since time immemorial, been a stopover on the road from Paris to Basle.
- **Don't Miss:** Look out for eight informative panels dotted round the village, bearing quotes from General de Gaulle.

La Boisserie

Mid-Apr to mid-Oct, 10am-12.30pm, 2-6.15pm, Sun 10am-6.15pm; rest of the year, 10am-12.30pm and 2-5.15pm. Guided tours possible (1hr). Dec. €4 (children under 12: no charge). 03 25 01 52 52.

During the Second World War, La Boisserie was severely damaged by the Germans; General de Gaulle only returned with his family in May 1946 after repairs. It has not changed since that time and the public is encouraged to visit this home, where the great (and flawed) French leader spent so much relaxing and thoughtful time.
German Chancellor Konrad Adenauer was the only politician ever to be invited to La Boisserie. In order to secure Franco-German reconciliation, De Gaulle invited him to his home in September 1958 during the German Chancellor's state visit to France.
The public is allowed into the downstairs drawing room, full of mementoes, books, family portraits and photographs of contemporary personalities, into the vast library and the adjacent study where General de Gaulle spent many hours, and into the dining room.

> Silence fills my house. From the corner room where I spend most of the day, I embrace the horizon towards the setting sun. No house can be seen over a distance of 15 kilometres. Beyond the plain and the woods, I can see the long curves sloping down towards the Aube Valley and the heights rising on the other side. From a high point in the garden, I behold the wild forested depths. I watch the night enveloping the landscape and then, looking at the stars, I clearly realise the insignificance of things.
>
> Charles de Gaulle,
> *Mémoires de guerre*

Address Book

PRACTICAL INFORMATION

Tourist office – *72 r. du Gén.-de-Gaulle, 52330 Colombey-les-Eglises – ☏03 25 01 52 33.*

WHERE TO STAY AND EAT

See the Legend for coin categories.

Auberge de la Montagne – *17 r. Argentolles – ☏03 25 01 51 69 – closed 17 Jan-2 Feb, 8-16 Mar, 13-21 Sep, 20-29 Dec, Mon and Tue.* A peaceful inn just outside this famous village. Traditional cooking and a decor of stone walls and exposed beams. The rooms overlook the Champagne countryside.

LOCAL BUBBLY

Local champagne can be enjoyed at **Cellier de la confrérie St-Vincent**, *r. de la Mairie. Apr-Nov: Sat-Sun and public holidays 11am-noon, 2-6pm (8pm in summer). €2.60 ☏03 25 02 58 05.*

Mémorial

Mid-Apr to mid-Oct: Daily 10am-12.30pm, 2-6.15pm, Sun 10-6.15pm; rest of the year: 10-12.30pm, 2-4.45pm. Mid-Dec, Jan and Tue. €4. ☏03 25 01 50v50.
Inaugurated on 18 June 1972, the memorial stands on the "mountain". This overlooks the village and surrounding forests (including the Clairvaux Forest where St Bernard founded his famous abbey in the 12C) from a great height of 397m/1 302ft.

Excursion

Argentolles

4km/2.5mi NW along D 104.
This village on the "Route touristique du Champagne" itinerary (*see Planning Your Trip*) offers visitors an **exhibition on vines and wine** (*Apr-Nov: Sat-Sun and holidays 11am-noon and 2-6pm (summer 8pm); €2.60; ☏03 25 02 58v05*) housed in a former wash house: video presentation, wine-grower's tools, Champagne production process etc. Champagne-tasting in the **Confrérie St-Vincent cellars** (*same conditions as above*).

ROUTE DES CRÊTES★★★

MICHELIN LOCAL MAP 315: G-8 TO 10

This strategic road was built during the First World War at the request of the French High Command, in order to ensure adequate north-south communications between the various valleys along the front line of the Vosges.
The magnificent (80km/49.7mi) itinerary enables motorists to admire the most characteristic landscapes of the Vosges mountains, its passes, its *ballons* (rounded summits), its lakes, its *chaumes* (high pastures where cattle graze in summer) and offers wide panoramas and extended views.
Between the Hohneck and the Grand Ballon, the road is lined with *fermes-auberges* (farmhouses turned into inns during the season) where snacks and regional dishes are served from June to October. In winter the snowfields offer miles of cross-country tracks.

- **Orient Yourself:** This route starts 30km/18.6mi west of Comar and heads south to Thann.
- **Don't Miss:** The stunning panoramas from Le Hohneck and the Grand Ballon.
- The Route des Crêtes is generally closed between the Hohneck and the Grand Ballon from mid-November to mid-March. (*Enquire at the Tourist Office: see Address Book*).

Driving Tour

From Col du Bonhomme to Thann

83km/52mi – allow half a day

Col du Bonhomme

Alt 949m/3 114ft. The pass links the two neighbouring regions of Alsace and Lorraine (See Val d'ORBEY).

Beyond the pass, the road offers fine vistas of the Béhine Valley to the left, with the Tête des Faux and Brézouard towering above. Farther on, the Col du Louchbach affords a beautiful view of the valley of the River Meurthe to the south.

Turn right at Col du Calvaire.

Gazon du Faing★

45min on foot there and back.

As you reach the summit *(1 303m/4 275ft)*, climb up to a large rock from where an extended panoramic **view** is to be had. In the foreground, the small Étang des Truites, changed into a reservoir by a dam, lies inside the Lenzwasen glacial cirque. Farther afield, one can see, from left to right, the Linge, the Schratzmaennele and the Barrenkopf heights; more to the right, beyond the Fecht Valley and the town of Munster, a long ridge slopes down from the Petit Ballon; to the right of this summit, the silhouette of the Grand Ballon *(alt 1 424m/4 672ft)* rises in the distance; the twin summits of the Petit Hohneck *(alt 1 288m/4 226ft)* and Hohneck *(alt 1 362m/4 469ft)* can be seen farther to the right.

Lac Vert

A path starting near the 5km/3mi mark from the Col de la Schlucht leads to the Lac Vert, also known as the Lac de Soultzeren (coloured by lichens).

Col de la Schlucht

Alt 1 135m/3 360ft. The pass links the upper valley of the River Meurthe (which takes its source 1km/0.6mi away from the pass) with that of the River Fecht. It is a popular ski resort with a chair-lift to the summit of Montabey *(Enquire at the Maison du Parc, ☎03 89 77 90 34).*

Jardin d'Altitude du Haut-Chitelet

Jul-Aug: 10am-6pm; Jun: 10am-noon, 2-6pm; Sep: 10am-noon, 2-5.30pm. €2.30. ☎03 29 63 31 46.

Alt 1 228m/4 029. 2km/1.2mi from the Col de la Schlucht towards Le Markstein, on the right-hand side of D 430.

These botanical gardens cover an area of 11ha/27 acres; rockeries spreading over more than 1ha/2.5 acres shelter 2 700 species of plants from the main mountain ranges of the world.

Farther on, the road offers a fine **view**★ of the Valogne Valley, Lake Longemer and Lake Retournemer. Note the village

R. Mattès/ MICHELIN

Summer pastures

of Xonrupt and the suburbs of Gérardmer in the distance *(viewpoint)*.

Le Hohneck★★★

The steep access path starts from the Route des Crêtes, 4km/2.5mi S of the Col de la Schlucht; do not follow the private path which starts closer to the pass (3km/1.9mi) as it is in bad condition. Beware of freezing winds near the summit.

This is one of the most famous and one of the highest summits in the Vosges mountains (alt 1 362m/4 469ft).

A splendid **panorama**★★★ *(viewing table)* unfolds, encompassing the Vosges from Donon to the Grand Ballon, the Plaine d'Alsace and the Black Forest. In clear weather, the summits of the Alps are visible.

The road runs through high pastures, known as **chaumes**. The Lac de Blanchemer can be seen on the right. Farther on there is a magnificent view of the Grande Vallée de la Fecht, followed by the lake and valley of the Lauch with the Plaine d'Alsace in the distance.

Le Markstein

This winter-sports resort is situated at the intersection of the Route des Crêtes and the upper Lauch Valley. Some of the Alpine World Championship events took place here in 1983 and 1987. Hikes and pony rides through forested areas are popular activities in summer.

As you drive along the cliff road, there are alternate views of the Thur Valley and Ballon d'Alsace massif on one side and the Lauch Valley and Petit Ballon on the other. The small **Lac du Ballon** lies inside a funnel-shaped basin.

Grand Ballon★★★

Leave the car by the hotel and follow the path on the left (30min on foot there and back).

There is a radar station at the summit. Grand Ballon, also known as Ballon de Guebwiller, is the highest summit (alt 1 424m/4 672ft) in the Vosges mountains. Just below the summit, the Monument des Diables Bleus was erected to commemorate various regiments of *chasseurs* (mountain troops). From the top of Grand Ballon, the **panorama**★★★ embraces the southern Vosges, the Black Forest and, when the weather is clear, the Jura mountains and the Alps.

Vieil-Armand★★

The name was given by the soldiers of the First World War to the foothills of the Vosges (Hartmannswillerkopf) which slope steeply down to the Plaine d'Alsace. This strategic position was one of the most bloody battlefields along the Alsatian front (30 000 French and German soldiers killed). In 1915, attacks and counter attacks were repeatedly launched on its slopes.

The **Monument national du Vieil-Armand** (*Apr-Oct: 8.30am-noon, 2.30-6.30pm; €2; 03 89 75 50 35*) was built over a crypt containing the remains of 12 000 unknown soldiers.

The **summit** can be reached on foot (*1hr there and back*). Walk through the cemetery situated behind the national monument, which contains 1 260 graves and several ossuaries. Follow the central alleyway and the path beyond it. Walk towards the summit of Vieil-Armand *(alt 956m/3 136ft)* surmounted by a 22m/72ft high luminous cross which marks the limit of the French front. Turn right towards the iron cross erected on a rocky promontory to commemorate the volunteers from Alsace-Lorraine. A wide **panorama**★★ can be had of the Plaine d'Alsace, the Vosges mountains, the Black Forest and, in clear weather, the Alps. Several commemorative monuments are located here.

On the way down to Uffholtz, the road affords views of the Plaine d'Alsace and the Black Forest.

Cernay

This small industrial town lies at the foot of Vieil-Armand and including the Porte de Thann, with its small **museum** (*Closed for renovation*) illustrating the wars of 1870, 1914-18 and 1939-45.

Kids From St-André, south of Cernay, it is possible to go on a **tour** (*Jun-Sep: Sun and holidays 11am and 3.30pm – departing Cernay St André. €9.50 there and back – children: €7.50; Jul-Aug: daily except Mon and Tue 3pm – departing Cernay St André. €7.50 there and back – children:*

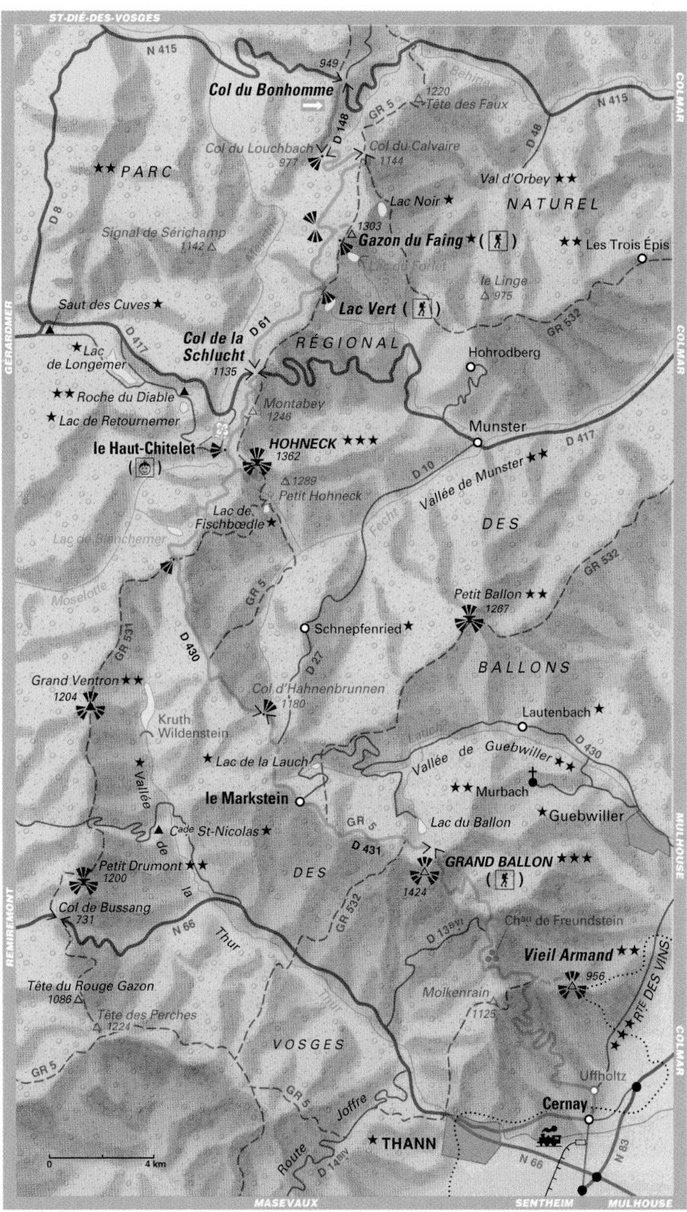

€6. ☎03 89 82 88 48) of the Doller Valley aboard a **steam train**, covering a distance of 14km/8.7mi to Sentheim.

▶ *Drive W along D 35.*

Thann★ – *See THANN.*

LAC DU DER-CHANTECOQ★★

MICHELIN LOCAL MAP 306: K/L-11

Created in 1974, this artificial lake, the largest in France (4 800ha/11 861 acres, 1.5 times the area of the Lac d'Annecy), was intended to regulate the flow of the River Marne; a feeder canal, 12km/7.5mi long, diverts two-thirds of the flow when the river is in spate and another canal supplies the Paris region.
This low-lying area was chosen because of the waterproof qualities of its clay soil. Part of the Der Forest (whose name means oak in Celtic) disappeared beneath the surface of the lake together with the three villages of Chantecoq, Champaubert-aux-Bois and Nuisement. However, the churches of the last two villages were spared.

- **Orient Yourself:** Der-Chantecoq Lake is located roughly half-way between Châlons-en-Champagne and Bar-sur-Aube. It is a 40km/25.5mi drive from the Parc Naturel Régional de la Forêt d'Orient.
- Kids **Especially for Kids:** Giffaumont watersports centre will give children ample opportunity to work off surplus energy, after which you can take them to the nature museum and/or to the Regional Der Museum*(see below)*.

Driving Tour

83km/52mi – allow 3hr

- *Start from Giffaumont where the Maison du Lac (tourist office of Lake Der-Chantecoq) is located. A cycle track runs right round the lake.*

Giffaumont-Champaubert

Kids The **watersports centre** offers activities for children, fountains, roller-skating and mountain-biking tracks. There are **beaches** on Champaubert and Larzicourt peninsulas as well as at Nuisement and Cornée du Der.

A **marina**, which can accommodate up to 500 boats, is the place to buy your **fishing permit** (*for a day, a month or a year*). Boat trips on the lake are organised in summer. Opposite (*access on foot along the dike*), Champaubert Church stands alone on a piece of land jutting out into the lake.

Grange aux abeilles

Jul-Aug: daily and Sat-Sun morning and afternoon; Apr-Jun and Sep: daily except Mon and Tue afternoon; Mar and Oct-Nov: Sat-Sun and holiday afternoons. No charge. ☎*03 26 72 61 97.*
An exhibition, an audio-visual show and glass beehives enable visitors to

Cranes' Migratory Habits

Every year in autumn, cranes leave Scandinavia and travel to milder climates in Spain or Africa. They fly over Champagne in successive waves, usually by night, and give out an impressive loud cry. Some of these cranes remain in the region throughout the winter and show a particular liking for meadows situated near a lake. They fly back north in the spring. Thousands of them stop by the Ferme aux Grues, near the Lac du Der-Chantecoq, where grain is purposely spread over a large area to attract them.

This large grey bird, with its long neck and long legs, has a wing span of 2m/6.5ft and weighs 4-7kg/9-15lb. It feeds on grain, grass and young shoots as well as insects, molluscs and worms.

R. Corbel/ MICHELIN

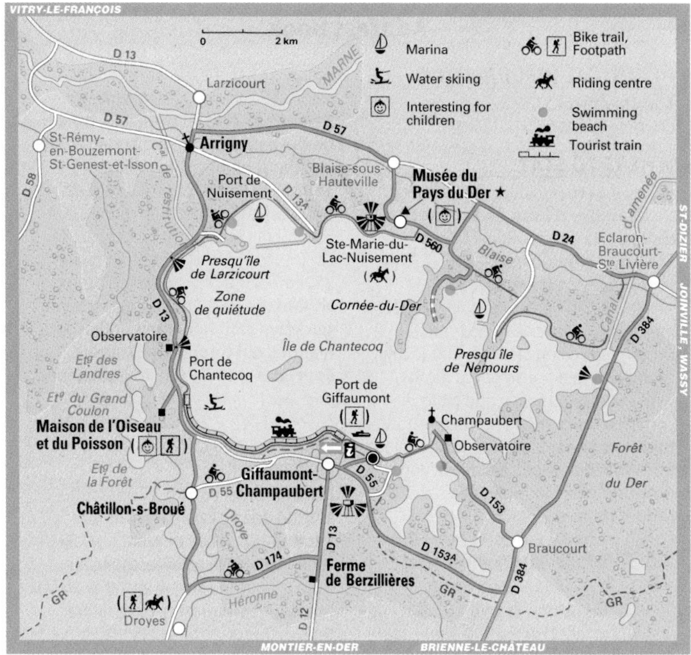

appreciate the work accomplished by bees and bee-keepers.

Follow D 13, then D 12 towards Montier-en-Der.

Ferme de Berzillières

Jul-Aug: afternoon; May-Jun and Sep: Sat-Sun and holiday afternoons. €3.05. 03 25 04 22 52.

This entirely restored farmhouse contains a museum of agricultural tools.

Go back along D 12 and, 500m/547yd farther on, turn left towards Troyes then right towards Châtillon-sur-Broué.

Châtillon-sur-Broué

This village is characteristic of the Der area, with its square **church** steeple and its timber-and-cob houses.

Continue towards the lake.

The road skirts the dike and runs past the small harbour of Chantecoq. Opposite the harbour, a path (P *at the entrance*) leads to the Maison de l'Oiseau et du Poisson.

Maison de l'Oiseau et du Poisson

Between Giffaumont and Arrigny. Jul-Aug and Oct-Nov: 10am-6.30pm (last entrance 45min before closing); rest of the year: daily except Sat, 1.30-6pm. Week of Christmas to last week in Jan. €6 (children under 16: €3.50). Discovery field trips: by request. 7€. 03 26 74 00 00.

Kids This nature museum is housed in the very characteristic timber-framed Ferme des Grands Parts.

Several **aquariums** present the main local species of fish: carp, perch, pike etc. The **panoramic tower** offers superb views of the Champagne countryside.

Nature-discovery trails lasting half a day or a day are organised around various themes: the lake's bird population, aquatic life, ponds around the lake, the forest, and interpreting landscapes.

Birdwatching: Two **roads** run along dikes; several peaceful areas have been set aside as bird sanctuaries (Chantecocq, Champaubert, Étangs d'Outines and d'Arrigny) and there are **nature trails** and **observatories** nearby.

Continue along D 13.

Address Book

PRACTICAL INFORMATION

Tourist office: *51290 Lac-du-Der-Chantecoq – ☎03 26 72 62 80.*

WHERE TO STAY

See the Legend for coin categories.

Chambre d'hôte Au Brochet du Lac – *15 Grande-Rue – 51290 St-Remy-en-Bouzemont – 6km/3.75mi W of Arrigny on D 57 and D 58 – ☎03 26 72 51 06 – www.au-brochet-du-lac.com– closed 24 Dec-3 Jan – 5 rooms – evening meal.* This lovely timber-framed house offers rooms with country furniture and a big common room with a fireplace and traditional floor tiles. The perfect place from which to explore the lake and surroundings. Mountain bikes and canoes for hire.

Le Cheval Blanc – *21 r. du Lac – 51290 Giffaumont-Champaubert – ☎03 26 72 62 65 – www.lecheval-blanc.net– closed 2-24 Jan, 6-23 Sep, Tue lunchtime, Sun evening and Mon – – 14 rooms – €8 – restaurant.* Simple, bright rooms in this peaceful lakeside resort. Varied, attractive menus. Summer terrace.

SPORTS & RECREATION

Boat trips – *51290 Giffaumont-Champaubert – Jul-Aug: daily from 2pm; May-Jun: daily except Mon from 2pm; Apr and 1st two weeks of Sep: Sat from 3pm, Sun and holidays at 11am and from 3pm; €5.60 (children: €3).* Tours on the lake starting at the Giffaumont water sports centre.

Water sports – There are two marinas, one in Nemours, the other in Nuisement, a waters ports centre in Giffaumont, six beaches with lifeguards, a 650-hectare/1,600-acre zone for motorboats and water-skiing, fishing on the banks or in a small boat, as well as various night-fishing routes.

Tours – Walking: 225km/140mi of waymarked footpaths in circuits of 5 to 15km (3 to 9.4mi). By bicycle: 4 circuits to explore. Mountain biking: 250km/155mi of waymarked paths around the lake. *Calèche*: ride in a horse-drawn cart. Horse and pony: route mapped out through the trees.

Tourist train – *All year round except mid-Dec to mid-Feb. ☎06 07 96 57 15 or Tourist Office. €6 (children: €3.50). Station Nautique, 51260 Giffaumont-Champaubert.*

Nature observation – Contact the Maison du Lac in Giffaumont for information. All year round the lake sees a wealth of wildlife, especially from autumn to spring with the arrival of the great migratory birds. More than 270 species have been observed, including cranes, white-tailed eagles, herons, tundra swans etc, which makes the lake the third richest migratory stopover area in France. **Observatories** and a footpath have been set up near Chantecoq, Champaubert and the lakes of Outines and Arrigny, to promote understanding and respect of this natural environment. **Oct-Apr**: cranes, greylag geese, wigeons, common teals, white-tailed eagles etc. **Apr-May** and **mid-Aug-Oct**: ospreys, (godwits, sandpipers) various types of tern etc. **Mar-Aug:** nesting of great-crested grebes, grey herons, mallards, gadwall etc.

Arrigny

There is a fine timber-framed church.

Drive east out of Arrigny and follow D 57 to Blaise-sous-Hauteville then turn right onto D 60.

Musée du Pays du Der★

Jul-Aug: 10am-7pm; May-Jun, Sep-Oct: 10am-6pm; 21 Jan to 30 Apr: 10am-5pm, Sat-Sun and holidays 10am-6pm. Christmas to 3rd week of Jan. €4 (children: €2.80). ☎03 26 41 01 02.

Kids This place is a village and a museum (**Village-musée**) at the same time, made up of several timber-framed buildings saved from flooding when the lake was created, illustrating regional **crafts and traditions**, the school-town hall housing the **Maison de la Nature**, the **smithy's house**, a dovecote, etc.

Château d'eau panoramique

In Ste-Marie-du-Lac-Nuisement as in Giffaumont-Champaubert, the water towers stand 20m/66ft high and afford views of the lake (*viewing table, telescope and audio-guide; no admission charge;* *☎03 26 72 62 80*).

Road D 560 leads to the Cornée du Der, a wooded peninsula jutting out into the lake.

Return to D 24 and turn right to Éclaron, then right again onto D 384.

The road offers a fine view of the lake before entering the Der Forest.

In Braucourt, it is possible to turn right onto D 153 leading to **Champaubert Church** at the tip of the peninsula of the same name.

Turn right 1.5km/0.9mi beyond Braucourt onto D 153A. Continue along D 55 to return to Giffaumont-Champaubert.

MASSIF DU DONON★★

MICHELIN LOCAL MAP 315: G-5

The Donon massif is recognisable from afar with its two-tier summit marking the boundary between Alsace and Lorraine. Numerous streams taking their source near the summit radiate across the splendid forests that cover the area. A road runs alongside each valley and there are cross-country skiing tracks and ski lifts.

Orient Yourself: The Donon massif forms the southern part of the sandstone Vosges mountains, reaching their highest point at the Donon summit *(alt 1 009m/3 311ft).*

Don't Miss: The panoramic view from the summit of the Donon.

Especially for Kids: The Lac de la Plaine recreation and sports centre is ideal for children.

A Bit of History

Celts, Romans, Franks and all the Germanic tribes travelling west came through the Donon pass and there is evidence that an ancient god, probably Mercury, was worshipped here.

Driving Tours

Sarre Rouge and Sarre Blanche Valleys – Round tour from the Col du Donon

55km/34mi – allow 2hr

Col du Donon

Alt 718m/2 356ft.

Donon

Alt 1 009m/3 311ft. About 1hr 30min on foot there and back.

It is possible to leave the car at the Donon pass and follow the footpath starting on the right of Hôtel Velléda; alternatively, one can drive for 1.3km/0.8mi along the road branching off D 993 on the right, 1km/0.6mi from the pass; P leave the car in the parking area (barrier) and walk the last 2km.

There are two viewing tables on the summit. The **panorama**★★ includes the Vosges mountain range, the Lorraine plateau, the Plaine d'Alsace and the Black Forest.

From the Col du Donon, the itinerary follows the **Vallée de la Sarre Rouge** or Vallée de St-Quirin then goes across the Lorraine plateau.

Continue straight on along D 145 and then D 44, ignoring the Cirey-sur-Vezouze road on your left. The itinerary enters the Lorraine region.

Grand Soldat

This hamlet is the birthplace of Alexandre Chatrian (1826-90), who collaborated with Emile Erckmann (1822-99) to write a series of novels inspired by Alsatian traditions and legends.

R. Mattès/ MICHELIN

Atop Donon

Abreschviller

A small **forest train** (*Jul-Aug: 3 and 4.30pm, Sun and holidays 10.30am, 2, 3, 4 and 5pm; May-Jun: Sat 3pm, Sun and holidays 2, 3 and 4pm; Sep: Sat 3pm, Sun and holidays 3 and 4.30pm; Apr and Oct: Sun and holidays 3pm. € 7.70(children: €5.40). 03 87 03 79 12*), steam or diesel-powered, leads to Grand Soldat (*6km/3.7mi*).

3km/1.9mi farther on, turn left onto D 96F towards St-Quirin.

Vasperviller

Camped on the lower foothills of Donon, this village offers amateurs of modern sacred art a remarkable little church designed in 1968 by the architect Litzenburger, the **Église Ste-Thérèse**.

St-Quirin

The 18C priory **church** is surmounted by two towers and a pinnacle crowned by onion-shaped domes. It houses a restored organ made in 1746 by Silbermann.

Drive W out of St-Quirin along D 96 and, 2km/1.2mi farther on, turn left onto D 993.

The road follows the **Vallée de la Sarre Blanche** through lovely forests.
At the end of the tour, you are back in Alsace as you leave the Abreschviller road on your left to return to the Donon pass.

Plaine Valley—from the Col du Donon to Badonviller

60km/37mi – Allow 2hr 30min

Col du Donon

Alt 718m/2 356ft. On the way down from the pass, the picturesque road offers views of the twin villages of Raon-sur-Plaine and Raon-lès-Leau (note the memorial to escaped prisoners of war and their guides inside the bend to the right).

Raon-sur-Plaine

A small road leads up the mountain (4km/2.5mi) to a well-preserved **Roman way** running through woods over a distance of approximately 500m/547yd.

Lac de la Maix

1hr on foot there and back, starting from Vexaincourt; follow a narrow forest road on the left.

A path runs round this dark green lake overlooked by a chapel.
Between Allarmont and Celles-sur-Plaine, the former **Scierie de la Hallière** (*closed for renovation*) houses a folklore museum displaying tools and equipment once used for sawing (*demonstrations in summer*) and for woodwork; interesting waterwheel.
Celles-sur-Plaine is close to the two lakes of Pierre Percée.

Kids The **Lac de la Plaine** (36ha/89 acres) is now a leisure and water sports centre (swimming, sailing, rowing, canoeing).

After the Plaine dam, turn right onto the scenic road to Badonviller (D 182A).

The **road**★ leads to the tiny village of **Pierre-Percée**.
The road then climbs up to the foot of a ruined castle (P) perched on top of a knoll, which has retained a 12C keep. From there, extended **views**★ of the lake in its romantic setting of hills.

Lac de Pierre-Percée

Park near the Vieux-Pré dam. Walk towards the viewpoint where the construction of the dam is explained on several panels.

Kids A boat trip aboard the **Vedette Cristal** (*Mid-Jun to Aug: 2, 3, 4 and 5pm; early Apr to mid-Jun and Sep: Sun and holidays 2, 3, 4 and 5pm; €7 – children between 6 and 12: €4; ☎03 83 73 15 25 or 06 87 86 77 15*) offers varied views of the surrounding mountains.
The nature trail of the Roche aux Corbeaux and a **birdwatching post** offer the opportunity of discovering the forest environment (*access by the scenic road*).

Return to D 182 and continue to Badonviller.

Badonviller

This industrial town, partly destroyed in August 1914, was, 30 years later, one of the first towns to be liberated by the French second armoured division.

Return to the Col du Donon along D 992 then D 183 via the Col de la Chapelotte, Vexaincourt and Raon-sur-Plaine.

ÉCOMUSÉE D'ALSACE★★

MICHELIN LOCAL MAP 315: H-9

9KM/5.6MI SOUTH-WEST OF ENSISHEIM, IN UNGERSHEIM

Some 50 traditional old houses scattered over an area of almost 25ha/50 acres give an insight into housing in the different rural areas of Alsace.

The wish to preserve the regional heritage was at the origin of this open-air museum: old houses from the 15C to 19C, doomed to be demolished, were patiently located all over Alsace, then carefully taken apart and rebuilt in the new village. The museum, inaugurated in 1980 and continually expanding, has now turned to the region's industrial heritage with the renovation of the various buildings of the potash mine Rodolphe (1911-1930) adjacent to the museum.

- **Orient Yourself:** The Écomusée d'Alsace is 9km/5.6mi south-west of Ensisheim along A 35 in the heart of the Alsatian countryside in Ungersheim.
- **Organising Your Time:** Allow at least half a day and be aware that most of the events take place in the evenings in summertime.
- Kids **Especially for Kids:** The entire complex will appeal to children of all ages.

Visit

Museum

Jul-Aug: 9.30am-7pm; Mar-Jun and Sep: 10am-6pm; early Oct-mid-Nov: 10am-5pm; mid-Nov-mid-Dec Sun only; Christmas holidays: daily. Early Jan to mid-Feb. €15.50 (children over 4: €9.50). Combined village + mine ticket valid 2 days: €17.50 (children over 4: €10); mine only: €7.50 (children over 4: €4). ☎03 89 74 44 74. www.ecomusee-alsace.com.
Visitors can walk through the museum's vast area and take as much or as little time as they wish, although half a day

R. Mattès/ MICHELIN

Traditional architecture of the Écomusée d'Alsace

seems to be the minimum; activities centred on Alsatian life are organised in the evening, particularly in summer. Kids Some 70 **timber-framed Alsatian houses** with their courtyards and gardens, grouped according to their original area, Sungdau, Ried, Kochersberg, or Bas-Rhin, illustrate the evolution of building techniques and give an insight into social life in traditional Alsatian villages. These fine buildings have one thing in common, the *stube* or living room, the focus of family and social life (meals, Sunday receptions, evening gatherings, sometimes even serving as master bedroom). But, most important, it contained an imposing earthenware stove! You will see several such stoves during your tour of the museum.

Other buildings house exhibitions or shows on such themes as the Alsatian headdress, fishing, and recurring feasts. Several workshops are operating: a blacksmith's, a potter's with an impressive wood oven, a cartwright's, a distillery, and an oil-mill.

Address Book

For coin ranges, see the Legend on the cover flap.

VISIT

Purchases – You may purchase souvenirs, crafts and local delicacies on site; there are also telephone booths, letter boxes, a hotel, bakery, and restaurants.

Events – Wide range of activities depending on the season (boat trips, funfair, theme days, International Festival of the Home and guided tour of the potash mines by train). *www. ecomusee-alsace.com.*

WHERE TO EAT

La Taverne – *At the Écomusée – ☎03 89 74 44 49 – closed evenings from 3 Jan-5 Feb.* The decor is that of an old Alsatian inn, with beams and roof timbers, while the hearty cooking includes pork, sauerkraut and other typical regional dishes. A nice way of discovering more about the traditions mentioned in the museum, with a good atmosphere as well.

WHERE TO STAY

Hôtel Les Loges de l'Écomusée – *At the Écomusée – ☎03 89 74 44v95 – closed 3 Jan-20 Feb – hotel.loges@ecoparcs.com* P *– 30 rooms – €7.* Right next to the museum, this attractive hotel consists of small, locally inspired buildings. It has been designed as a village, and offers simple, modern rooms with mezzanines, split-level and studio apartments.

Natural environment
Ancient plant species can be seen growing in their recreated natural environment and there are demonstrations of traditional farming methods. There are beehives, an apple orchard, as well as cowsheds and stables sheltering domestic animals. Storks return regularly to nest on the weathered roofs.

Merry-go-rounds
A section of the museum is devoted to funfairs; note in particular the **Eden-Palladium** merry-go-round, the last of the great Belle Epoque merry-go-rounds in France (1909).

EGUISHEIM★

POPULATION 1 548

MICHELIN LOCAL MAP 315: H-8

ALSO SEE ROUTE DES VINS

This ancient village developed round an octagonal 13C castle. Surrounded by 300ha/741 acres of vines and lying at the foot of three ruined towers, used as sundials by workers in the plain below, the village has hardly changed since the 16C. Two famous wines are produced locally. The wine-growers festival takes place during the fourth weekend in August. Visitors can follow the wine trail (*1hr on foot; guided tours of cellars with wine-tasting included*).

- **Orient Yourself:** Eguisheim is 7km/4.3mi from Colmar, 41km/25.5mi north of Mulhouse via N 83 or E 225-A 35 Colmar-Mulhouse road.
- **Organising Your Time:** Allow at least half a day and be aware that most of the events take place in the evenings in summertime.

Visit

Grand'Rue
The doorways of the picturesque houses lining this street are adorned with coats of arms, with dates; also note the two Renaissance fountains.

Tour of the ramparts
The signposted itinerary follows the former watch path; the houses here offer a wealth of architectural features (balconies, oriels, and timber frames).

R. Mattès/ MICHELIN

Cobblestone streets of the old town

Church

Inside the modern church, to the right of the entrance, there is a chapel beneath the steeple. It contains the old doorway with its 12C tympanum illustrating Christ between St Peter and St Paul; the procession of Wise Virgins and Foolish Virgins forms the lintel. 19C Callinet organ.

Driving Tour

Route des Cinq Châteaux★

20km/12.4mi round tour including five castles, plus about 1hr 45min on foot.

Drive to Husseren (see Routes des VIN) along D 14. As you come out of the village, turn right onto the forest road, known as the Route des cinq Châteaux; 1km/0.6mi farther on, leave the car in the parking area and walk to Eguisheim's three castles (5min uphill).

Donjons d'Eguisheim

Three massive square keeps built of red sandstone and known as Weckmund, Wahlenbourg and Dagsbourg stand at the top of the hill. They belonged to the powerful Eguisheim family (*see MULHOUSE*). Pope Léon IX was most probably born here (*see WANGENBOURG: Excursions*).

From here, the Château de Hohlandsbourg can be reached on foot *(1hr)*.

Alternatively, return to the car and drive on for about 6km/3.7mi.

The road offers many fine viewpoints.

Château de Hohlandsbourg

Jul-Aug: guided tour (45min) 10am-7pm; Jun and early Sep to mid-Oct: 2-6pm, Sun and holidays 11am-6pm; mid-Apr to late May and mid-Oct to late Nov: Sat 2-6pm, Sun and holidays 11am-6pm. €4 (children 8-16: €1.50). 03 89 30 10 20.

The imposing granite castle stands on the left; built c 1279, it first belonged to the powerful House of Habsburg and was destroyed during the Thirty Years War. Restored in the 16C, it was adapted to the use of artillery.

From the watch path, there is a magnificent view of the Pflixbourg keep and Hohneck summit to the west, the Haut-

Address Book

PRACTICAL INFORMATION

Tourist office – *22a Grand'Rue, 03 89 23 40 33, www.ot-eguisheim.fr*

WHERE TO EAT

See the Legend for coin categories.

La Grangelière – *59 r. du Rempart-Sud – 03 89 23 00 30 – closed mid-Feb-mid-Mar, Sun evenings from Nov-Apr and Thu.* This Alsatian house near the ramparts is slightly off the tourist trail. But you won't regret making the detour: the chef, who has worked in some major establishments, offers cooking that is both contemporary and very tempting.

Le Caveau d'Eguisheim – *3 pl. du Château-St-Léon – 03 89 41 08v89 – closed end Jan-end Feb, Mon and Tue.* Only regional wines are on offer in this pretty local-style restaurant, situated in the village square. Fortunately they go very well with the young chef's inventive cooking, which combines regional dishes and contemporary flavours, making eating here a pleasure.

WHERE TO STAY

Hostellerie du Château – *2 r. du Château – 03 89 23 72 00 – info@hostellerieduchateau.com – closed 2 Jan-10 Feb – 11 rooms – €10.* This old building on the village square has been completely renovated by the architect owner. Its stylish modern decor offers charming, light, pleasant rooms with old-fashioned bathrooms.

SHOPPING

Charles Baur – *29 Grand'Rue – 03 89 41 32v49 – cave@vinscharles-baur.fr – Mon-Sat 8am-noon, 1-7pm, Sun 9am-noon (Sun afternoons by appointment) – closed Christmas.* Tour of the cellar, tasting and sale of Alsace wines.

Kœnigsbourg to the north, and Colmar and the Plaine d'Alsace to the east. Medieval shows are held in summer.

Donjon de Pflixbourg

A path, branching off to the left 2km/1.2mi further on, leads to the keep.

The fortress was the former Alsatian residence of the representative of the Holy Roman Emperor. Fine viewpoint.

As you rejoin D 417, turn right towards Colmar. On leaving Wintzenheim (see Route des VINS: From Châtenois to Colmar), turn right onto N 83 then right again onto D 1bis to return to Eguisheim.

ENSISHEIM

POPULATION 6 164

MICHELIN LOCAL MAP 315: I-9 – ALSO SEE ROUTE DES VINS

Excavations undertaken south of the town have revealed that the site was inhabited as far back as the fifth millennium BC, but the name of Ensisheim was mentioned for the first time in 765. The city became the capital of the Habsburgs' territories in Alsace and remained the capital of western Austria until 1648. The town has fine Gothic and Renaissance mansions.

Orient Yourself: Ensisheim (just 9km/5.6mi from the Écomusée d'Alsace) is also a mere 27km/16.8mi from Colmar.

Visit

Palais de la Régence

This fine Gothic edifice erected in 1535 was decorated in Renaissance style. Note the ground floor vaulting of the arcade, decorated with emblems bearing the coats of arms of Alsatian towns.

Musée de la Régence

Daily except Tue 2-6pm. Holidays and every other Sat-Sun from Oct to Apr. €2. 03 89 26 49 54.

In the first room of the museum is a meteorite which fell on Ensisheim on 7 November 1492. It is believed to be the first fall of a meteorite ever recorded.

Hôtel de la Couronne

Turenne, Louis XIV's great general, stayed here in 1675 before his victory at the battle of Turckheim, which led to the Peace of Nijmegen and the final union of France and Alsace

ÉPERNAY★

POPULATION 25 844

MICHELIN LOCAL MAP 306: F-8

Épernay is with Reims, the main wine-growing centre of the Champagne region and the meeting point of three major wine-growing areas: the Montagne de Reims, the Côte des Blancs and the Marne Valley. There are many opulent 19C buildings, particularly around the avenue de Champagne where you will see the great names of the famous sparkling wine such as Moët et Chandon and Mercier.

- **Orient Yourself:** Épernay is more or less half-way between Reims and Châlons-en-Champagne and 145km/90mi from Paris on A 4.
- **Don't Miss:** It would be a crime not to visit at least one of Épernay's prestigious Champagne cellars.

Visit

Champagne Cellars★★

The main Champagne firms line both sides of the avenue de Champagne (*east of the town centre*), above the limestone cliff riddled with miles of galleries which remain at a constant temperature of 9-12°C/48-54°F.
Many firms organise tours.

Moët et Chandon

20 avenue de Champagne. Early Mar to mid-Nov: guided tour (1hr) 9.30-11.30am, 2-4.30pm; mid-Nov to late Feb: daily except Sat-Sun and holidays. €8 (children: €4.70). 03 26 51 20 20. www.moet.com.
Moët et Chandon was the first Champagne firm; its story is linked to that of Hautvillers Abbey (*see MONTAGNE DE REIMS: Hautvillers*) which it owns, and to Dom Pérignon whom it honoured by naming its prestigious Champagne after him.
The founder of the firm, Claude Moët, began producing Champagne in 1743; in 1962, the firm became a limited company (the Moët-Hennessy-Louis Vuitton group).
During the very thorough tour visitors can observe the complete Champagne process, including *remuage* (moving the bottles) and *dégorgement* (releasing the deposit).

Mercier

73 avenue de Champagne; and opposite the main building. Mid-Mar to late Nov: guided tour (45min) 9.30-11.30am, 2-4.30pm; early Dec to mid-Mar: daily except Tue and Wed 9.30-11.30am, 2-4.30pm. Enquire beforehand. €7 (children: €3.50). 03 26 51 22 22.
In 1858, Eugène Mercier merged several Champagne firms under his own nameand had 18km/11.2mi of galleries dug. Mercier is the second Champagne producer after Moët et Chandon and it belongs to the same group.
Vistors descend in a panoramic lift for a cellar tour in a small automatic train.

De Castellane

57 rue de Verdun. Apr-Dec: guided tour (45min) 10am-noon, 2-6pm (last entrance 45min before closing). €7 (children: €4). 03 26 51 19 11.
The 10km/6mi long cellars, the **tower** and the museum can be visited. A climb of 237 steps leads to the top of the tower, which is 60m/197ft high, which affords a view of Épernay and its vineyards.
The **museum** is devoted to the evolution of the Champagne-making process.

Sights

Take a break in the **Jardin de l'Hôtel de ville**, designed in the 19C by the Bülher brothers; these famous landscape gardeners also designed the Parc de la Tête d'Or in Lyon.

Address Book

PRACTICAL INFORMATION

Tourist Office – *7 av. de Champagne, ☎03 26 53 33 00, www.ot-epernay.fr*

WHERE TO EAT

See the Legend for coin categories.

Les Cépages – *16 r. de la Fauvette – ☎03 26 55 16 93 – lescepages@wanadoo.fr – closed 26 Feb-11 Mar, 12-30 Jul, 25-30 Dec, Wed and Sun evenings and Thu.* The restaurant refers to grape varieties. With an excellent choice of champagnes, the meny is decidely contemporary and well prepared.

La Table de Kobus – *3 r. du Dr-Rousseau – ☎03 26 51 53v53 – closed 19-29 Apr, 1-19 Aug, 24 Dec-31 Dec, Sun evening, Thur evening and Mon.* The attractive, contemporary yet unpretentious dishes are served in a large, high-ceilinged room, decorated in bistro style. This modern restaurant is popular with groups – you are welcome to bring your own wine, at no extra charge.

Auberge Saint-Vincent – 1 r. St-Vincent, *51150 Ambonnay – 20km E of Épernay on D 201, D 1 and D 37 – ☎03 26 57 01 98 – www.aubergest-vincent.com – closed Feb holidays, 18 Aug-1 Sep, Sun evenings and Mon.* A pretty, regional-style inn with a happy combination of traditional and modern decor. Traditional cuisine.

WHERE TO STAY

Les Berceaux – *13 r. des Berceaux – ☎03 26 55 28 84 – www.lesberceaux.com – 28 rooms – €11 – restaurant* . A warm welcome and high-quality service in this hundred-year-old hotel. The façade is pleasing and the modern rooms are soundproof. Indulge your taste buds with the restaurant's classic, refined cuisine, or eat lightly in the wine bar.

Chambre d'hôte Manoir de Montflambert – *51160 Mutigny – 7km/4mi NE of Épernay on D 201 – ☎03 26 52 33 21 – manoir-de-montflambert@wanadoo.fr – 6 rooms – €4.* This old hunting lodge dates from the 17C. Overlooking the Marne plain and the vineyards, it stands proudly on the edge of the forest. The prices in this peaceful bed and breakfast are justified by the open fireplaces, the lovely wood panelling and the imposing staircase leading to the bedrooms.

ON THE TOWN

La Marmite Swing – *160 av. Foch – ☎03 26 54 17 72 – lamarmiteswing@infonie.fr – bar and restaurant: Tue-Thu 11am-midnight, Fri 11am-1.30am, Sat 5pm-3am – cabaret and nightclub: Fri, Sat and day before public holidays midnight-5am – closed Aug.* Three ingredients add up to an original mix: a brightly coloured bistro with hanging tables and swing chairs; a dining room/cabaret which offers paella with flamenco, or couscous with Arabic/Andalusian music; a concert room (jazz, blues, rock, world music) which turns into a nightclub after midnight. Rum and Afro-West Indian evenings are a speciality.

SHOPPING

Dallet – *26 r. du Gén.-Leclerc – ☎03 26 55 31 08 – www.chocolat-vincentdallet.com – Tue-Sun 7.15am-7.45pm – closed fortnight in Feb and in Jul.* Something different for a sweet tooth: chocolates flavoured with aromatic herbs from the garden! The house speciality le pavé d'Epernay is prepared using marzipan and marc de champagne.

Beaumont des Crayères *– 64 r. de la Liberté – 51530 Mardeuil – ☎03 26 55 29 40 – www.champagne-beaumont.com – Mon-Fri 9am-noon, 1.30-6pm, Sat 10am-noon, 2-6pm – closed Easter and 25 Dec.* This Champagne museum includes among its exhibits the biggest champagne bottle in the world. You can also taste and buy.

Chocolat Thibaut – *ZA de Pierry – Pôle d'activités St-Julien – 51530 Pierry – 2km/1.2mi S of Épernay on D 11 – ☎03 26 51 58 04 – Mon-Sat 9am-noon, 2-7pm – Guided tours 9-11.30am and 2-6.30pm – No visits fortnight before Christmas and Easter and last week of Jan and public holidays.* This chocolate craftsman will make his specialities while you watch. You can taste and buy the produce in the shop next door.

Driving Tour

Round trip south of Epernay★

28km/17.4mi – Allow 1hr – Local map *see Routes du CHAMPAGNE*
The Épernay hills form the edge of the Île-de-France cuesta.

Leave Épernay along D 51.

The road follows the Cubry Valley with vineyards on both sides of the river.

Château de Pierry

See Routes du CHAMPAGNE.
As you come to Moussy, look left towards the church of Chavot (13C), on a peak.

Turn right 1km/0.6mi beyond Vaudancourt onto D 951.

Château de Brugny

The castle overlooks the Cubry Valley. Built in the 16C, remodelled in the 18C, the square stone keep and round brick bartizans, are particularly attractive.

In Brugny, take D 36 leading to St-Martin-d'Ablois.

There are interesting **views**★ of the glacial Sourdon cirque, with the church of Chavot on the right, Moussy in the centre and Épernay Forest on the left.

Turn left onto D 11 towards Mareuil-en-Brie.

Parc du Sourdon

Apr-Oct: 9am-7pm. No charge.
The Sourdon takes its source under a pile of rocks then flows through the park.

Drive back to D 22 and turn left. The road runs through Épernay Forest (private property) and the village of Vauciennes then reaches N 3. Turn right towards Épernay.

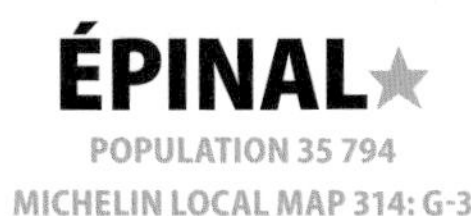

ÉPINAL★

POPULATION 35 794

MICHELIN LOCAL MAP 314: G-3

Flower-bedecked Épinal spreads along both banks of the River Moselle. It has a historic prints and cotton industry, now declining; the splendid surrounding forested area covers 3 600ha/8 896 acres.

- **Orient Yourself:** In the south of the Alsace Lorraine region, Épinal is 110km/68.4mi from Mulhouse and 71km/44.1mi from Nancy.

A Bit of History

Épinal prints

The enormous success of the Épinal prints lasted for almost two centuries. Most popular prints used to depict religious subjects until Jean Charles **Pellerin** began to illustrate secular subjects such as traditional songs, riddles, La Fontaine's fables and scenes of traditional French life.

Once it had been carved on wood (generally pear tree wood), the picture was printed on a Gutenberg type press. The different colours were hand-applied using stencil-plates; Pellerin is the only printing works of its kind still operating in Europe. The two world wars and new printing techniques have impacted but not destroyed this fascinating industry.

Sight

Cité de l'Image

Entrance via no 42 quai de Dogneville. ♿ ◷ Jul-Aug: 9am-12.30pm, 2-7pm; Sep-Jun: 9am-noon, 2-6.30pm, Sun and holidays 2-6.30pm. Guided tour (1hr) 9.30, 10.30am, 3 and 4.30pm. ◷ Sun and public holiday mornings, 1 Jan, Easter Mon and Tue and 25 Dec. €4.70 (children 6-16: €1). ☎ 03 29 31 28 88. www.imagerieepinal.com.

The **Imagerie d'Épinal workshops** offer an insight into the techniques used by the 200-hundred-year-old firm, with demonstrations of equipment.

Opposite, the **Musée de l'Image** is devoted to old Épinal prints and temporary exhibitions.

R. Mattès/ MICHELIN

A pleasant park and garden for an outdoor break

Visit

Old Town★

Parc du Château★

May-Aug: 7.30am-8pm; Sep: 7.30am-7pm; Mar, Apr and Oct: 7.30am-6pm; Nov-Feb: 8am-5pm. No charge. 03 29 68 50 61. www.epinal.fr.*

This huge wooded park covers an area of 26ha/64 acres.

Kids In the park there is a mini zoo, a playground and a plane to climb on – a perfect place for kids to let off steam!

Basilique St-Maurice★

8am-noon, 1.30-7pm. 03 29 82 53 32.

The basilica was consecrated in 1051 by Pope Léon IX.

The west front has a belfry-porch characteristic of the Meuse region.

The 15C main doorway on the north side, known as the Portail des Bourgeois, is preceded by a deep porch, characteristic of the Champagne region.

The 13C nave has three storeys, arcades, triforium and high windows separated by moulded string-courses and is prolonged by a 14C chancel (*choeur des chanoinesses*).

Walk to the right of the basilica.

Rue du chapitre

This street features a group of 17C and 18C houses built for the canonesses.

Walk back past St-Maurice Basilica.

Place des Vosges

On this former market square, note the 1604 so-called former bailiff's house – in fact built for a paper manufacturer.

Walk to the river and turn left along quai Jules-Ferry towards place Foch.

Sights

Musée départemental d'Art ancien et contemporain★

1 pl. Lagarde Apr-Sep: daily except Tue 10am-6pm; Oct-Mar: daily except Tue 10am-12.30pm, 1.30-6pm. 1 Jan, 1 May, 1 Nov and 25 Dec. €4.60 (children under 16: no charge). 03 29 82 20 33.

Located at the tip of an island in the River Moselle, the museum houses regional Gallo-Roman finds; and a paintings department devoted mainly to the French School of the 17C and 18C and to the Northern School (Gellée, La Hyre, Vignon, **La Tour** and his *Job mocked by his Wife*, Brueghel, Van Goyen, Van Cleeve and, of course, **Rembrandt** and his *Mater Dolorosa*). The superb contemporary art section includes Minimal Art (Donald Judd), Arte Povera (Mario Merz) and Pop Art (Andy Warhol).

Église Notre-Dame

Rebuilt between 1956 and 1958, the church has *cloisonné* enamel doors.

Excursions

Fort d'Uxegney

6km/3.7mi NW by ⑥ on the town plan (D 166 to Dompaire).

Jul-Aug: guided tour (2hr) 2 and 4pm; mid to end Jun and early Sep to mid-Sep: Sat-Sun 2 and 4pm. €5. 03 29 38 32 09.

Uxegney was one of the last forts built near Épinal.

Cimetière et Mémorial américains

7km/4.3mi S along D 157.

The path leading to the cemetery (0.5km/0.3mi) starts on the right 1.8km/1.1mi beyond Donizé.

The cemetery, which occupies a vast area (20ha/49 acres) on top of a wooded plateau overlooking the River Moselle, contains the graves of 5 255 American soldiers killed during the Second World War marked by white-marble crosses and Jewish steles.

PELLERIN & Cie, imp.-édit. **L'ILLUSTRE FAMILLE DES JEAN,** IMAGERIE D'ÉPINAL, No 1337

Jeanfesse!	J'enseigne.	J'embrasse.	J'embrouille.	Jean pèche.
Jean jean.	Jean rage!!	Ô J'empeste !	Jean chante.	J'emmaillotte.
J'embroche .	J'enfonce.	J'embellis.	Ô J'enlaidis !	J'empoche .
J'empiffre.	J'engraisse.	J'embaume.	J'embête.	J' enfourne.

L'ARBRE D'AMOUR

Image D'epinal

L'illustre Famille des Jean

Address Book

PRACTICAL INFORMATION

Tourist Office – *6 Pl. St Goëry – ☎03 29 82 53v32-www.epinal.fr*
Guided tours – The town of Épinal organises guided tours of the town (1hr 30min to 2hr) in the summer. *Mid Jun-mid Aug, Thu and Tues 3pm. Enquire at tourist office.*

WHERE TO EAT

See the Legend for coin categories.
Le Bagatelle – *12 r. des Petites-Boucheries – ☎03 29 35 05 22 – le-bagatelle@wanadoo.fr – closed 2nd half of Jul and Sun (except by reservation).* On a little island between two branches of the River Moselle, this spruce 1940s restaurant is the best place for watching the canoeing/kayak competitions, as well as for enjoying inspired cooking.
Ferme-auberge des 7 Pêcheurs – *28-32 r. de la Division-Leclerc – 88220 Méloménil-Uzemain – 15km/9.3mi SW of Épinal on D 51 (via Chantraine) – ☎ 03 29 30 70 79 – closed Jan and Wed out of season –* . The dining room here is an 18C forge, which feels solidly authentic with its old beams, exposed stone walls and open fireplace. There are bedrooms to let and a large, simply furnished holiday cottage for those who want to enjoy the peace and quiet of this old farm. A lovely area for walks.
Le Calmosien – *88390 Chaumousey – 10km/6.2mi W of Épinal on D 36 and D 460 – ☎03 29 66 80 77 – lecalmosien@wanadoo.fr – closed 17 Jul-2 Aug, Sun evening and Mon.* In the village centre, this 1900s building is reminiscent of a school, with its white façade, brick-edged windows and steeply sloping roof. The old-fashioned decor and garden terrace are the setting for contemporary cooking, served either on fixed menus or à la carte.

WHERE TO STAY

Hôtel Kyriad – *12 av. du Gén.-de-Gaulle – ☎03 29 82 10 74 – hotel-kyriad-epinal@wanadoo.fr – closed 23 Dec-1 Jan – 45 rooms – €6.50.* This hotel opposite the station is a good place to stay: the rooms are well kept and welcoming, as well as being soundproofed. Friendly staff and good value for money.

SIT BACK AND RELAX

Daval – *44 r. Léopold-Bourg – ☎03 29 35 60 60 – www.chocolats-daval@tiscali.fr – Mon 2-7pm, Tue-Sat 7.30am-7pm, Sun 9am-12.30pm – closed 1 May, Easter Monday and Pentecost.* This town centre cake shop and tearoom is an ideal place to stop for a quiet break.
Pâtisserie du Musée – *2 quai du Musée – ☎03 29 82 10 73 – Tue-Fri 7.30am-7pm, Sat-Sun 7.30am-12.30pm, 2-7pm – closed Mon.* This cake shop and tearoom must be one of the nicest in town, near the museum. Try the chocolate-praline charbonettes des Vosges.

ON THE TOWN

Le Wellington – *11 r. Chipotte – ☎03 29 64 03 78 – Mon-Sat from 11.30am – closed fortnight in Jul, Sun and holidays.* A pleasant, British-style pub with a lively spacious terrace.

SPORTS & RECREATION

Parks – Épinal boasts many parks: Parc entrances in rue d'Ambrail and rue St-Michel; Parc du plateau de la Justice, rue Henri-Sellier; Espace du Port, quai de Dogneville. Fitness trails available less than 2km/1.2mi from city centre(Parc du Mont-Carmel and Fontaine Guéry).
Club Vosgien – *5 rue François-Blaudez – ☎03 29 35 45 44 – www.clubvosgiene-pinal.com – Tue 3-6pm, Wed 10am-noon, Sat 10am-noon and 3-7pm – closed holidays.* The oldest hiking club in France conducts guided hikes through the forested area surrounding Épinal.
Golf d'Épinal – *R. du Merle-Blanc – ☎03 29 34 65 97 – www.epinal.fr – Mid-Feb-Oct.*

CALENDAR

Feast of St-Nicolas – *1st Sat of Dec from 5pm.* Saint Nicolas and the Père Fouettard (Bogeyman) go to infant schools distributing gingerbread and oranges. Decorated floats tour the streets and an immense firework display ends the day.
Fête des champs golot – *Sat before Palm Sunday.* This festival marks the thaw of the fields and streams. An artificial pond is placed in rue du Gén.-Leclerc and children pull home-made illuminated boats through the water.

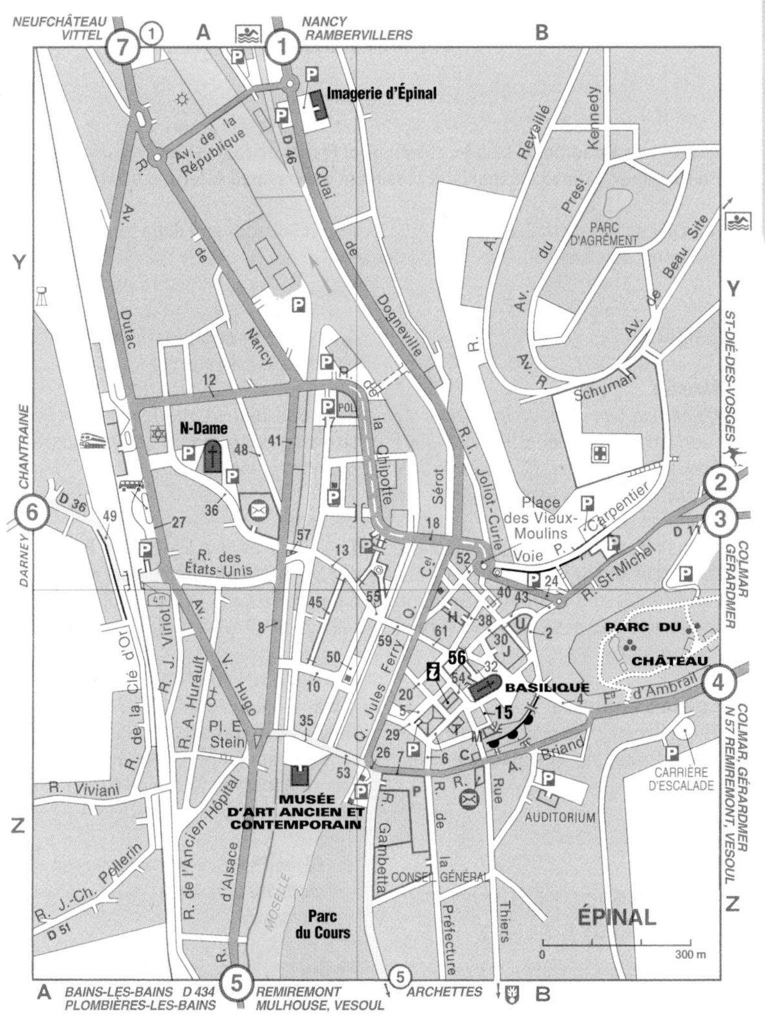

ÉPINAL

170e Régt-d'Inf. Pont du	BZ	59
170e-Régt-d'Inf. R. du	BZ	61
4-Nations Pl. des	AY	57
Abbé-Friesenhauser R.	BZ	2
Ambrail R. d'	BZ	4
Bassot Pl. Cl.	BZ	5
Blaudez R. F.	BZ	6
Boegner R. du Pasteur	BZ	7
Bons-Enfants Quai des	AZ	8
Boudiou Pt et R. du	AZ	10
Boulay-de-la-Meurthe R.	AY	12
Bourg R. L.	AY	13
Chapitre R. du	BZ	15
Clemenceau Pl.	AY	17
Clemenceau Pont	BY	18
Comédie R. de la	BZ	20
Entre-les-Deux-Portes R.	BYZ	24
États-Unis R. des	AY	
Foch Pl.	BZ	26
Gaulle Av. du Gén.-de	AY	27
Georgin R.	BZ	29
Halles R. des	BZ	30
Henri Pl. E.	BZ	32
Lattre Av. Mar.-de	AY	36
Leclerc R. Gén.	BZ	38
Lormont R.	BZ	40
Lyautey R. Mar.	AY	41
Maix R. de la	BZ	43
Minimes R. des	AZ	45
N.-D.-de-Lorette R.	AY	49
Neufchâteau R. F. de	AY	48
Pinau Pl.	AZ	50
Poincaré R. Raymond	BY	52
Sadi-Carnot Pont	AZ	53
St-Goery R.	BZ	54
Schwabisch Hall Pl. de	BZ	55
La Tour R. G. de la	AZ	35
Vosges Pl. des	BZ	56

FISMES

POPULATION 5 313

MICHELIN LOCAL MAP 306: E-7

Fismes was a traditional stop for the kings of France en route to being crowned in Reims. Albert Uderzo, cartoonist for the team who created Asterix, is from Fismes.

- **Orient Yourself:** Fismes is on N 31 between Soissons and Reims and not far from Laon, Château-Thierry and Épernay.

Sights

Musée

Jul-Aug: 9am-noon, 2-5pm; rest of the year: daily except Mon and Sun, enquire about opening times. 10 days in Sep, public holidays (except Jul-Aug). No charge. 03 26 48 81 28.
A small local museum, housed on the first floor of the tourist office, contains fossils and sharks' teeth found in the area, old postcards and Vernon 19C porcelain.

Église Ste-Macre

The 11C church was over an ancient oratory to house the remains of the saint.

Driving Tour

Romanesque Churches in the Ardre Valley

Round tour of 52km/32mi – allow half a day The Romanesque churches in this area are shaped like a basilica.

PRACTICAL INFORMATION

Tourist Office – *28 r. René-Letilly, 03 26 48 81 28.*

WHERE TO EAT

See the Legend for coin categories.

La Boule d'Or – *11 r. Lefèvre – 03 26 48 11v24 – boule.or@wanadoo.fr – closed 20 Jan-11 Feb, Sun evening, Tue lunchtime and Mon – – 8 rooms – €8 – restaurant* . This cheerful little roadside house has newly refurbished rooms and traditional food.

- *Leave Fismes S along D 386 towards Épernay.*

The road follows the River Ardre, a favourite haunt of anglers. Quarries once provided stone for Reims.

Crugny

The nave of the **Église St-Pierre** (*Sat-Sun: 9am-6pm. Collect the keys from M. Pichon, 10 rue Clémenceau, 03 26 97 47 49*) dates from the 11C.

Savigny-sur-Ardres

It was from Savigny that General de Gaulle (who was only a colonel at the time) broadcast his first appeal to the French people on 28 May 1940 (plaque on the house opposite the church).

- *Beyond Faverolles and Tramery, the road runs beneath the A4 motorway.*

Poilly

11C and 12C **church** dedicated to St Rémy.

- *Turn right onto D 980 to Verneuil.*

Ville-en-Tardenois

The 12C **church** is surmounted by an elegant tower and saddleback roof.

Romigny

Romanesque doorway on this **church**.

- *Turn right onto D 23 to Lhéry.*

Lhéry

The late 12C **church** marks the transition from the Romanesque to the Gothic.

Lagery
On the village square stands a fine 18C covered market next to a picturesque wash house.

Drive W along D 27 towards Coulonges-Cohan.

Abbaye Notre-Dame d'Igny
This Cistercian monastery was founded by St Bernard in 1128.

Return to the intersection with D 25 and turn left.

Arcis-le-Ponsart
A picturesque fortified wall encloses this 12C **church** and a ruined 17C castle.

Continue N along D 25 to Courville.

Courville
In medieval times, the archbishop of Reims had a castle here.

Turn left onto D 386.

St-Gilles
The present church is all that remains of the former priory.

D 386 leads back to Fismes.

PARC NATUREL RÉGIONAL DE LA FORÊT D'ORIENT★★

MICHELIN LOCAL MAP 313: F-3 TO H-4

Created in 1970 round the artificial Lac d'Orient, the nature park extends over 70 000ha/172 977 acres and comprises vast forests and three large artificial lakes. It lies on the border of two contrasting areas known as *Champagne crayeuse* and *Champagne humide*. The park aims to preserve the natural environment as well as cultural and architectural heritage while offering a wide choice of outdoor activities, including hiking, boat trips, water sports, fishing, swimming and diving.

Orient Yourself: In the south of the Champagne region, the Forêt d'Orient can be reached from Troyes east on N 19 or D 960 or from Bar-sur-Aube west on N 19.

Kids **Especially for Kids:** At Mesnil-St-Père are an animal reserve (especially interesting at dusk) and a bird sanctuary – don't forget your binonculars! The automata museum at Lusigny might also be an alternative on wet days.

A Bit of History

Forêt d'Orient
Once part of the vast Der Forest stretching from the Pays d'Othe in the south-west to St-Dizier in the north-east, the Forêt d'Orient today covers 10 000ha/24 711 acres of wetlands dotted with lakes. It is named for the Knights Hospitallers and Knights Templars, the Chevaliers d'Orient (Knights from the East) who once owned the area. (*See the educational trail running through the forest*).

Two long-distance and several short-distance footpaths run through the forest, popular with hikers and cyclists alike: itineraries totalling 140km/87mi are detailed in a topographical guide available from the Maison du Parc.

Lakes
The park includes three lakes used to regulate the flow of the River Seine and the River Aube. The oldest (1966) and largest of the lakes, **Lac d'Orient** covers 2 500ha/6 178 acres and offers many leisure activities such as sailing and scuba diving. There are two marinas and three sand beaches in Géraudot, Lusigny-sur-Barse and Mesnil-St-Père. A scenic road runs round the lake, affording fine views, particularly between Mesnil-St-Père and the Maison du Parc.

The **Lac du Temple**, created in 1991 and covering an area of 1 830ha/4 522 acres, is enjoyed by anglers and canoeists. **Lac Amance**, the smallest lake with an area of only 490ha/1 211 acres, is reserved for motorised water sports. The last two lakes are linked by a canal 1.6km/1mi long.

Angling is allowed in all three lakes except in the southern creek of the Lac du Temple and the north-east creek of the Lac d'Orient, a bird sanctuary.

Driving Tour

Tour of the Lakes

64km/40mi – allow half a day – Start from the Maison du Parc

Maison du Parc

10220 Piney (between Lac d'Orient and Lac du Temple, on D 79), ☏03 25 43 81 90. www.pnr-foret-orient.fr. Jul-Aug: 10am-6pm; Apr-Jun and Sep-Oct: 10am-noon, 2-6pm.; Sat-Sun and holidays 10am-1pm, 2-6pm.; Nov-Dec and Jan-Mar: 1-5pm. Christmas to 1 Jan. No charge.

This traditional timber-framed house was taken apart and rebuilt in the Forêt de Piney. It is both an information centre about the park and an exhibition area.

Drive along D 79 for 4km/2.5mi towards Vendeuvre-sur-Barse then turn left onto the Route forestière du Temple (closed at some periods of the year).

This road running through the Forêt du Temple guides visitors among the species of trees using informative panels.

A forest trail (*2.5km/1.5mi*), the **Sentier des Salamandres**, starting oppo-

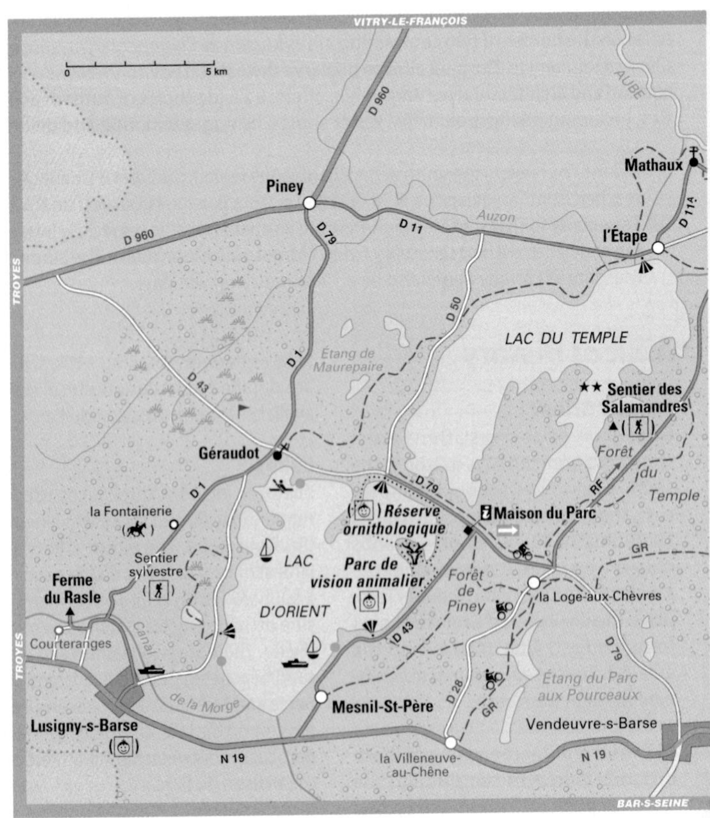

site Lusigny beach, introduces visitors to a dozen characteristic species.
In Lusigny, you can enjoy a **boat trip** (*See Address book*).

Continue along the forest road to Radonvilliers then turn right onto D 11 towards Dienville.

Dienville

This small town, lying on the banks of the River Aube, has an impressive stone-built **covered market** and an unusual 16C-18C pentagonal **church**.

Port Dienville

Jul-Aug: 9.30am-6.30pm; Apr-Jun and Sep: daily except Thu 10am-noon and 2-5pm, Sat-Sun and holidays 9.30am-12.30pm and 1.30-6pm; Oct and last Sat-Sun of Mar: daily except Wed and Thu 10am-noon, 2-5pm. 03 25 92 27 69. www.pnr-foret-orient.fr.

Situated on the outskirts of the town, this leisure and water-sports centre on the edge of Lake Amance attracts speed-boat and motorboat racing enthusiasts. (*boats for hire on Lake Amance*).

Continue northwards to Brienne-la-Vieille (D 443).

Brienne-la-Vieille

See BRIENNE-LE-CHÂTEAU: Excursions.

Return to Radonvilliers along D 11B then turn right onto D 61 towards Mathaux.

Écomusée de la Forêt d'Orient

1 chemin Milbert. Mar-Sep: daily except Mon 10am-6pm, Sat, Sun and holidays 2-6pm; Oct-Nov: 2-6pm, Sat, Sun and holidays by appointment. 4€. 03 25 92 95 84 or 03 25 92 88v83.
Administered by the Parc naturel régional de la Forêt d'Orient, this

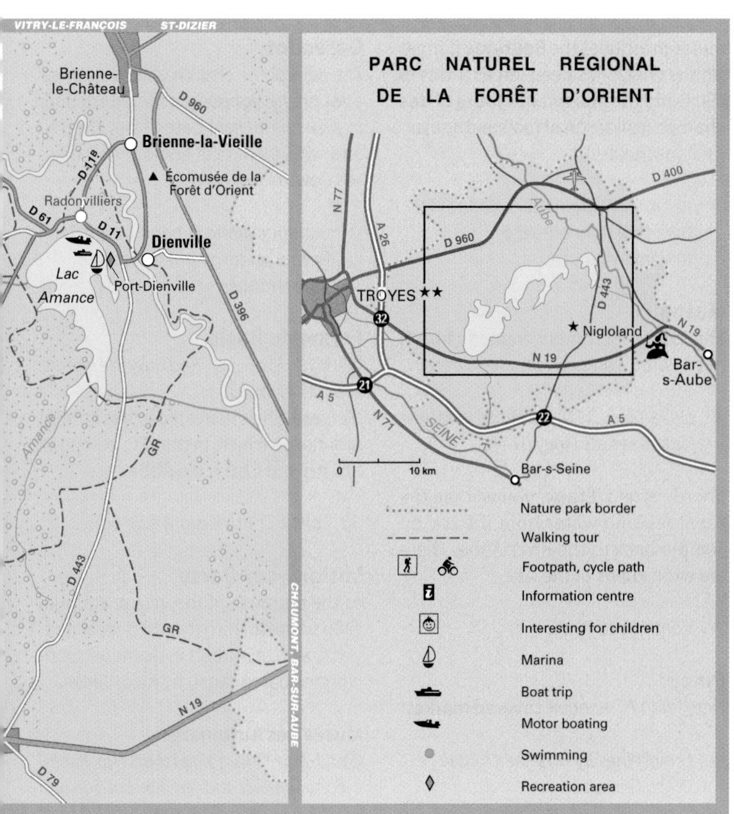

Address Book

PRACTICAL INFORMATION

Maison du Parc – *10220 Piney, ☎03 25 43 81 90, www.pnr.foret-orient.fr*

WHERE TO EAT

See the Legend for coin categories.

Auberge du Lac Au Vieux Pressoir – *5 r. du 28-août-1944 – 10140 Mesnil-St-Père – ☎03 25 41 27 16 – closed 7-23 Nov, Sun evenings Oct-Mar and Mon lunchtime.* In this attractive half-timbered house on the outskirts of a village on the edge of the Forêt d'Orient, you can sample regional cooking. Terrace, pleasant bar-patio with a glass roof, and comfortable rooms.

WHERE TO STAY

Chambre d'hôte Mme Jeanne – *Les Colombages Champenois – 33 r. du Haut – 10270 Laubressel – 7km/4.3mi NW of Lusigny-sur-Barse on N 19 and D 186 – ☎03 25 80 27 37 – – 6 rooms.* Two lovely local-style half-timbered guest houses offering comfortable rooms with exposed beams and local farm produce at the dinner table. Holiday cottage nearby.

La Bergeotte – *6 r. de Dienville – 10220 Brevonnes – ☎03 25 46 31 44 – – 3 rooms – evening meal .* A faultlessly warm welcome awaits you on this little farm, which was entirely rebuilt in 1940. The rooms are plain but extremely well-kept. Kitchen facilities available and pleasant garden.

SPORTS & RECREATION

Boating – *Mid-Apr-mid-Sep: 1hr trips 9am-7pm; Boat trip €8. Reservations cruise+meal: ☎03 25 41 20 72 – www.la-mangeoire.fr*

You can also rent your own boat at Port-Dienville (even if you don't have a boating license). *Mid-Apr-mid-Sep: 9am-noon, 1:30-6pm; daily except Thur. ☎03 25 92 27 69.*

museum includes the **Boutique** (former smithy which has been left as it was in 1903) and the **Maison des jours et des champs** (collection of tools and agricultural machinery).

Return to Radonvilliers along D 11B then turn right onto D 61 towards Mathaux.

Mathaux

The lovely 18C timber-framed **church** has a wood-shingled square tower.

Drive along D 11A to L'Étape, then bear right towards Piney (D 11).

Shortly after **L'Étape**, you will see the canal feeding water from the Lac du Temple back to the River Aube. There are wide **views** of the lake.

Continue to Piney.

Piney

Note fine 17C wooden **covered market**.

Leave Piney by D 79 then follow D 1 to Géraudot.

Géraudot

The nave of the **church** (*follow the directions on the signpost on the church door to pick up the key*) dates from the 12C and with a chancel and stained glass windows from the 16C.

Continue along D 1 and 1km/0.6mi farther on turn right towards Courteranges.

Ferme du Rasle

Mid-May to Sep: By request. ☎03 25 41 26 53.

Medieval life is recreated in this ancient farmhouse which, in the 12C, belonged to Larrivour Cistercian Abbey.

Follow D 1 to Lusigny-sur-Barse.

Lusigny-sur-Barse

At the entrance of the village stands a 1986 **sculpture** (a galvanised-steel-and-wood arch, 25m/82ft in diameter spanning the Barse canal) by Klaus Rinke.

Musée des Automates

Jul-Aug: guided tours (1hr 45min) 3-6pm; Sep-Oct and Apr-Jun: Sat-Sun and holidays 3pm-6pm. 7€ (children: 5.50€). ☎03 25 41 55 51.

Kids Fascinating automata come to life in front of you, such as a monkey with his top hat and Mozart at the harpsichord.

Nature trail

Opposite Lusigny beach.

Drive along N 19 then turn left to Mesnil-St-Père.

Mesnil-St-Père

This village, with its timber-and-brick houses, is the largest **water sports centre** on the shores of Lac d'Orient.

Boat trips on the lake are organised aboard panoramic motorboats.

Follow D 43 back to the Maison du Parc.

Parc de vision animalier

Jul-Aug: daily except Thu and Fri from 5pm to nightfall; Apr-Jun and Sep: Sat-Sun and holidays, 5pm to nightfall; Oct-Mar: Sun and holidays (1st and 3rd Sun of the month), 2pm to nightfall. No charge. ☎03 25 43 38 88.

Kids Located on a peninsula (89ha/220 acres), this **wildlife observation** is a chance to discover the local fauna.

Nature lovers know:

- *not to pick flowers, fruit or plants, or gather fossils;*
- *to take all rubbish and empty cans out of the protected zone;*
- *to leave pets, particularly dogs, at home because they might frighten young wild animals;*
- *to stay on the paths, because hillside shortcuts cause erosion.*

Two observation points on the edge of the forest offer good views of wild boars, deer and roe-deer roaming around freely. The former eat acorns, roots, rodents and insects; they remain active day and night, which makes it easier to see them. Deer and roe-deer on the other hand are plant eaters and are mainly active at night, which means waiting patiently and silently if you wish to catch a glimpse of them.

Go past the Maison du Parc and turn left onto D 79 towards Géraudot.

Réserve ornithologique

Kids The north-east bank of Lake Orient, is a **bird sanctuary** for waterfowl with an **observation point**.

GÉRARDMER★

POPULATION 8 845

MICHELIN LOCAL MAP 314: J-4

Gérardmer was destroyed by fire in November 1944, a few days liberation, but the town has been completely rebuilt as a popular winter and summer resort. Every two years, there is a glorious daffodil festival in mid-April. The tourist office, created in 1865, is the oldest in France.

- **Orient Yourself:** In the heart of the Parc Naturel Régional du Ballon des Vosges, Gérardmer is 80km/50mi from Mulhouse and 53km/33mi from Colmar.
- **Don't Miss:** The entire region is a treasure trove of beautiful countryside; the highlight is undoubtedly the panorama from Le Hohneck.

Visit

Lakes

Lac de Gérardmer★

This is the largest lake in the Vosges region (2.2km/1.3mi long, 0.75km/0.45mi wide and 38m/125ft deep). A walking or driving **tour**★ round the lake (6.5km/4mi) offers varied views of the lake framed by mountains. A **boat trip** (*lake cruise+commentary (20min): 4€; boat hire: electric motorboat: 14€ for 30min; pedal boat 2 or 4 passengers:*

6.50/9.50€ for 30min) is a fun excursion; various boats are available for hire.

Lac de Longemer★

5km.3mi E along D 417 and D 67A.

This lake (2km/1.2mi long, 550m/0.3mi wide and 30m/98ft deep) is surrounded by meadows.

Lac de Retournemer★

12km/7.5mi E along D 417 and D 67.

This small lake, fed by the waterfalls of the Vologne, is set inside a green basin.

Ski Resorts

Gérardmer-la Mauselaine❄

Free shuttle service in winter (weekends and school holidays) from Gérardmer to La Mauselaine.

The ski resort enjoys good snow cover which enhances the appeal of its 40km/25mi of ski runs (including the longest run in the Vosges massif: 4km/2.5mi) accessible to beginners as well as experienced skiers; snow-cannon equipment is used on some of the runs and there is also a special run for night skiing. The first Nordic ski area in the Vosges massif, the Domaine des Bas-Rupts is only 2.5km/1.5mi out of Gérardmer. Cross-country tracks totalling 100km/62mi run through the forest forming loops of various levels of difficulty located within the municipalities of Gérardmer, La Bresse and Xonrupt, accompanied by snowshoe trails.

La Bresse-Hohneck

The largest ski area in the Vosges region is equipped with 200 snow cannon and includes 36 ski runs spread over three main areas, between Hohneck and La Bresse, around Lac de Retournemer and near the Col de la Schlucht. La Bresse has produced several ski champions.

Excursions

The Gérardmer region was deeply marked by glaciers that once covered the Vosges massif.

Valleys of the Meurthe and Petite Meurthe★—Round tour north-east of Gérardmer 1

55km/34mi – allow 2hr.

▶ *Leave Gérardmer NE along D 417.*

Saut des Cuves★

▶ *Leave the car near the Saut des Cuves Hotel. Take the path starting upstream of the bridge and leading to the River Vologne spanned by two footbridges.*

The mountain stream cascades down over granite in a succession of waterfalls; the largest is the Saut des Cuves.

▶ *Turn left onto D 23 and drive for 2km/1.2mi then turn right.*

Expo Faune Lorraine

2-6pm, school holidays: 10am-noon, 2-6.30pm.

Kids This exhibition offers attractive dioramas and four aquariums illustrating aquatic life of the area.

▶ *Continue driving and, 1km/0.6mi farther on, turn right onto D 23.*

The road runs through the forest to the River Meurthe at Le Valtin. The slopes of the **upper valley of the Meurthe** are covered with pastures and forests.

▶ *In Plainfaing, turn left onto N 415 then left again onto D 73.*

On the way back to Gérardmer, the road follows the **valley of the Petite Meurthe**, which gradually narrows to go through the steep Straiture gorge.

Glacière de Straiture

▶ *A small road branches off to the right; 0.7km/0.4mi beyond this intersection, a path to the south-east allows one to cross the river and reach the Glacière.*

A pile of rocks that holds traces of ice even at the height of summer.

At the end of the gorge, the road crosses the Petite Meurthe, leads to the Col du Surceneux and back to Gérardmer.

La Bresse – Hohneck – Col de la Schlucht★★★— Round tour south-east of Gérardmer 2

54km/34mi – allow 2hr 30min

Leave Gérardmer S along D 486.

The road rises through the woods then runs down towards the green valley of the River Bouchot to rise again towards the Col de Grosse Pierre. There are lovely views of the upper valley of the Moselotte and of its tributary, the Chajoux.

La Bresse

Founded in 7C, this picturesque town has strong cheesemaking traditions and a textile industry; as a result, it remained independent until 1790. Ruined in 1944, La Bresse had to be entirely rebuilt.

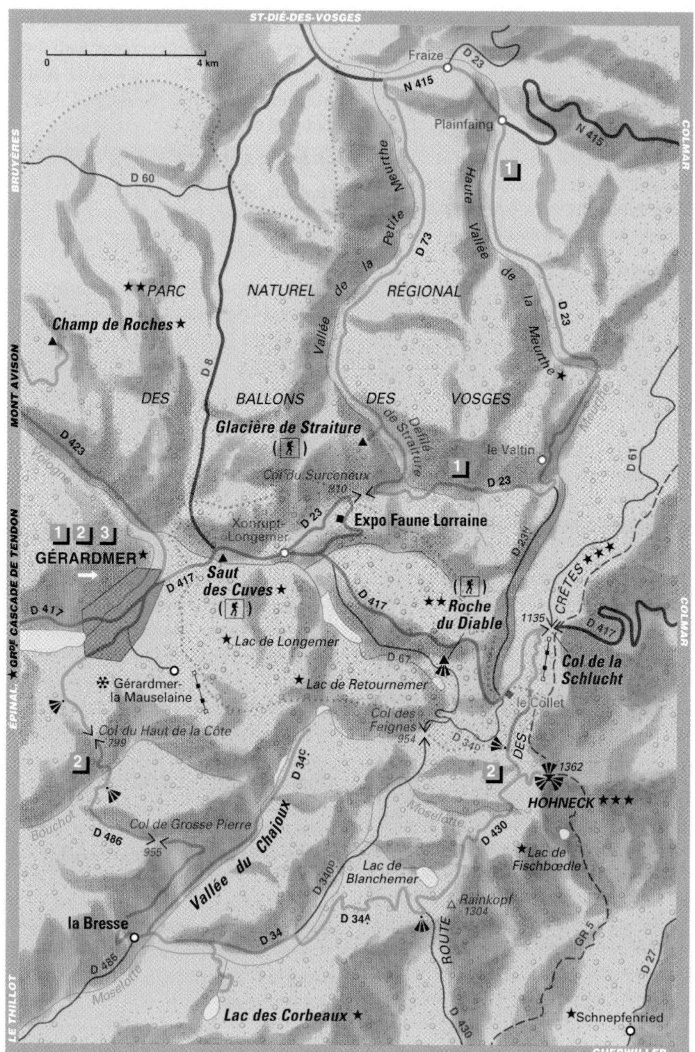

Address Book

PRACTICAL INFORMATION

– 88400 Gérardmer – ☎03 29 27 27 27 – www.gerardmer.net

WHERE TO EAT

See the Legend for coin categories.

Auberge Liézey – *9 rte de Saucefaing – 88400 Liézey – 9.5km/6mi W of Gérardmer on D 417 and D 50 – ☎03 29 63 09 51 – open Fri eve-Sun from 2 Nov-15 Dec – closed Mon and Tue except in school holidays.* In the snow or among the pine forests, depending on the season, this spacious chalet-farm, dating from 1799, offers hearty meals using produce from neighbouring farms. Horse-riding in summer. Seven simple, well-kept rooms.

Cap Sud – *88400 Bas-Rupts – 4km/2.5mi S of Gérardmer on D 486 – ☎03 29 63 06 83.* To get away from it all and for a taste of the sea, head for this boat-like wooden terrace with views onto the mountains.

WHERE TO STAY

Hôtel Le Chalet du Lac – *1km/0.5mi W of Gérardmer on D 417 (Épinal road) – ☎03 29 63 38 76 – closed Oct – P – 11 rooms – €7.50 – restaurant.* This large chalet overlooks the lake. Run by two couples, it has a pleasant small family hotel feel to it, with simple but well-kept rooms, and a wood-panelled dining room with unpretentious regional cooking – and a lovely view.

Viry – *Pl. des Déportés – ☎03 29 63 02 41 – www.gerardmer.net/hotel-viry – 17 rooms – €9.* The façade and the plain but well-kept rooms of this family-run hotel are adorned with Tyrol-style frescos. Balconies on the first floor. Lovely little lounge with hearth. The restaurant and its warm rustic atmosphere are reminiscent of Austria. Traditional recipes and local foods.

Hôtel Les Vallées – *31 r. P.-Claudel – 88520 La Bresse – 14km/8.75mi S of Gérardmer on D 486 – ☎03 29 25 41 39 – hotel.lesvallees@remy-loisirs.com – P – 54 rooms – €9.50 – restaurant.* In this central hotel, you can relax in the pleasant modern rooms and enjoy the indoor swimming pool. Studio apartments to let. Explore the mountain paths in summer or ski in winter, either way there's plenty to do at La Bresse.

ON THE TOWN

Casino du Lac – *3 av. de la Ville-de-Vichy – ☎03 29 60 05 05 – Mon-Fri 1pm-2am, Sat-Sun 1pm-3am.* This leisure centre includes fruit machines and traditional gambling activities (boule, roulette, blackjack), a cinema-theatre and a seasonal restaurant with a lakeside terrace.

Les Rives du Lac – *1 av. de la Ville-de-Vichy – ☎03 29 63 04 29 – daily from 9am – closed 4-30 Jan and Nov-20 Dec.* As you will quickly be able to tell, this is one of the nicest cafés in town, with the sound of water and the view of the blue lake and surrounding mountains. Music nights in summer.

SPORTS & RECREATION

Fantasticable-Aérofunparc – *La Mauselaine – Chalet ESF, at the foot of the ski slopes, around 1km/0.5mi from Gérardmer on chemin de Rayée – ☎03 29 60 09 10 – www.fantasticable.com – mid-May-mid-Sep and mid-Sep-mid-Oct, Sat-Sun and holidays 9am-noon, 1.30-6.30pm – Jun-mid-Sep, daily – closed winter – €23.* This leisure centre offers a "hair-raising" experience you're not likely to forget in a hurry. Accessible to children over 35kg/77lbs/5.5st. The Aérofunparc also features four attractions.

SHOPPING

Craft market – *Pl. du Vieux-Gérardmé – Jul-Aug: Sat 8am-7pm.* This weekly market of local craftsmen and producers is one of the most popular in the region.

Le Jacquard Français – *35 r. Charles-de-Gaulle – ☎03 29 60 82 50 – www.le-jacquard-francais.com – 10am-noon, 2-7pm, closed 1 Jan, 1 May and 25 Dec.* Table linen, bath and beach towels.

Linvosges – *6 pl. de la Gare – ☎03 29 60 11 00 – www.linvosges.com – daily 9am-noon, 2-6pm – closed Sun except school holidays.* This company, founded in 1922, continues the Vosges tradition of high-quality household linen, including bedding and table linen as well as products for the kitchen and bathroom. Tour of the production site and boutique.

La Saboterie des Lacs – *25 bd de la Jamagne – ☎03 29 60 09 06 – www.atoutvosges.com – Mon-Fri 10am-noon, 2-5pm.* This is a clog maker's workshop where you can watch clogs being manufactured from start to finish, complete with explanations. You can also buy all types of clogs, from utility to decorative, made out of ash or maple wood.

Les Petits Crus Vosgiens – *10 chemin de la Scierie – Le Beillard – Coming from Gérardmer on D 417, take the 1st left after passing the D 50 – ☎03 29 63 11 70 – daily 10.30am-12.30pm 2-7pm – closed Mon and Sep.* Daniel Villaume, proprietor of this former sawmill, will let you sample the fruit and flower wines that he makes from red and blackcurrants, rhubarb, cherries, apples, dandelion and elder flowers. These specialities of the Vosges can be drunk as aperitifs or dessert wines.

Association des Artisans du Village de Liézey – *17 rte de Saucéfaing – 88400 Liézey – 7km/4.3mi NE of Gérardmer on D 50 – ☎03 29 63 16 50 – Apr-Nov: Sun 2.30-6.30pm, daily 2.30-6.30pm in school holidays – closed Nov-Easter.* More than 50 local craftsmen and producers exhibit their wares in this old farm: wooden toys, enamels, embroidery, lace, honey, jam, sweets, brandies, regional liqueurs, stone and leatherwork.

The **Église St-Laurent**, rebuilt in the 18C, has retained its Gothic chancel.

Musée du textile

Via D 43, 1.5km/0.9mi from Ventron on the way to Col d'Oderen.

Jun-Sep: 10am-noon, 2-7pm; Apr-May and Oct: daily except Tue 2-6pm; Dec-Mar: weekend 2-6pm (school holidays: daily). 1 Jan, 1 Nov, 25 Dec. €4 (children under 10: no charge, children under 16: €2). ☎03 29 24 23 06.

This museum is devoted to the textile industry (one of the main branches of industry in the Vosges region).

Vallée du Chajoux

D 34C runs north-east from La Bresse along a fish-abounding stream.

Lac des Corbeaux★

A road, branching off to the right near the Hôtel du Lac, leads to this remote lake (23m/75ft deep).

The lake occupies the centre of a glacial cirque with densely forested slopes. A footpath runs all the way round it (*30min on foot*).

Return to D 34 and turn right along the Moselotte Valley. Cross the river, ignoring D 34D on the left, and 2km/1.2mi farther on, after a bend to the right, leave the Col de Bramont road and follow the twisting D 34A, known as the Route des Américains.

As you reach the high pastures, the view extends to the right over the upper valley of the Thur, Wildenstein village and the Kruth-Wildenstein dam.

Turn left onto the Route des Crêtes (D 430) which goes round the Rainkopf summit.

Down on the left in a wooded basin, you can see **Lac de Blanchemer**.

The road then reaches the chaumes (high pastures) of Hohneck.

Le Hohneck★★★

See Route des CRÊTES. Beyond the Hohneck heights, there are glimpses of Lake Longemer in the distance to the left and later on there are splendid **views**★ of the Valogne Valley, Lake Retournemer and Lake Longemer.

Col de la Schlucht

See Route des CRÊTES.

Roche du Diable★★

15min on foot there and back.

Leave the car near the tunnel and follow a steep path leading to the viewpoint.

R. Mattès/ MICHELIN

Vologne Valley from the Roche du Diable

The **view**★★ extends to the Valogne Valley between Lake Retournemer and Lake Longemer.

Saut des Cuves★

See 1 above.

Valleys of the Tendon and the Valogne—Round tour northwest of Gérardmer 3

61km/38mi – allow 2hr

- *Leave Gérardmer W along D 417. At the entrance of Le Tholy, turn right onto D 11 towards Épinal and drive for 5km/3mi. Turn left 200m/219yd before the Grande Cascade Hotel and follow the road down to the waterfall (800m/875yd).*

Grande cascade de Tendon★

This double waterfall drops 32m/105ft.

- *Farther on, as you reach Faucompierre, turn right towards Bruyères along D 30 and D 44. In Bruyères, take the street to the left of the cemetery (towards Belmont), which leads to the foot of Mt Avison. Leave the car.*

Tour-belvédère du mont Avison

45min on foot there and back.

This 15m/49ft high tower stands on the top (alt 601m/1 972ft) of one of the hills surrounding Bruyères; from the platform (82 steps, viewing table), the **panorama**★ extends to the Tête des Cuveaux, Hohneck and Donon.

Champ-le-Duc

The village was burnt down by the Germans in 1944, and a large proportion of its male population was deported.

Champ de roches de Granges-sur-Vologne★

- *In Granges-sur-Vologne, an industrial town with textile factories, turn left onto D 31 then right in Barbey-Seroux onto the forest road (second crossroads) which runs through the Vologne Forest. 2.4km/1.5mi farther on, you come to another crossroads with a house standing nearby; turn left and leave the car 150m/164yd farther on.*

This horizontal moraine, 500m/547yd long, cuts through the forest.

- *Return to Barbey-Seroux and Granges, then follow D 423 back to Gérardmer.*

GIVET

POPULATION 7 372

MICHELIN LOCAL MAP 306: K/L-2

This border town, guarded by the Charlemont fortress, is made for wandering. From the bridge over the River Meuse, there is a fine overall view of the old town, the Tour Victoire and the Fort de Charlemont.

- **Orient Yourself:** In the northernmost tip of Champagne, Givet is closer to Brussels (109km/68mi) than to Reims (133km/83mi).
- Kids **Especially for Kids:** Children will appreciate the chance to let off steam at the water sports centre of Givet.

A Bit of History

Givet Notre-Dame, on the east bank, is a former industrial district whereas **Givet St-Hilaire**, on the west bank, is the old town nestling round a church built by Vauban and described by Victor Hugo in derisive terms: "the architect took a priest's or a barrister's hat, on this hat he placed an upturned salad bowl, on the base of the salad bowl he stood a sugar basin, on the sugar basin a bottle, on the bottle a sun partly inserted into the neck and finally on the sun he fixed a cock on a spit".

Sights

Givet was fortified by Charles V of Spain in 1555; the town retains three of its old gates with drawbridges, Porte Charbonnière, Port de Rancennes and **Porte de France** (to the south).

Centre européen des métiers d'art

10am-noon, 2.30-6pm, Sun and Mon 2.30-6pm. Feb, 1 Jan, 25 Dec. No charge. 03 24 42 73 36.
Located in a former 17C toll-house. You can watch craftsmen at work and buy local products in the vaulted cellar.

Fort de Charlemont★

Jul-Aug: daily except Mon 2-6pm; guided tours possible (1hr); last admission 1hr before closing time. €3. 03 24 42 03 54.

- *The fort is accessible via a narrow road on the left, which rises through the woods before the first entrance to the military camp.*

This small citadel was fortified by Emperor Charles V and named after him, then was redesigned by Vauban. Since 1962, the fort has been used as a commando training centre.

Pointe Est du Fort

From the east end of the fort, there are fine views of Givet, the Meuse Valley, the Mont d'Haurs and the Belgian hills with the Château d'Agimont, which once belonged to the Comte de Paris.

Excursions

Grottes de Nichet

4km/2.5mi E along D 46. Jun-Sep: guided tour (1hr) 10am-noon, 1.30-7pm; Apr-May and Sep: 2-6pm (last tour begins 1hr before closing). €5. 03 24 42 00 14 or 03 24 42 06 54.
Near the village of Fromelennes, these impressive caves are on two levels, with numerous concretions (sound effects).

For coin ranges, see the Legend on the cover flap.

WHERE TO STAY AND EAT

Val St-Hilaire – *7 quai des Fours – 0324 42 38 50 – www.hotel-val-saint-hilarie.com – closed 20 Dec-15 Jan – P – 20 rooms – €7.70.* This large building on the Meuse quayside has comfortable contemporary. Pleasant terrace in an inner courtyard in the summer.

Vallée de la Meuse – South of Givet

23km/14.3mi

Leave Givet by N 51 which runs along black-marble quarries.

Hierges★

The villagesits below the ruins of a castle built between the 11C and 15C, once the seat of a barony. *(illuminated at night).*

Some 2km/1.2mi farther on, turn right onto D 47 to Molhain.

Ancienne collégiale St-Hermel

Guided tours by appointment, contact the Tourist office in Viroquois, 10am-noon, 2-6pm. 03 24 40 06 59.

This former collegiate church, built over a 9C-10C crypt, was remodelled in the 18C.

Return to N 51 then cross the river 2km/1.2mi beyond Fépin.

Haybes

This resort offers several walks, in particular to the viewpoint at **La Platale** (*2km/1.2mi from Haybes along the scenic Morhon road: picnic area*), which affords a close-up view of Fumay, and to the viewpoint of **Roc de Fépin** (*8km/5mi E along D 7; access signposted*).

Return to N 51 which follows a deep meander of the Meuse to Fumay.

Fumay

Pretty Fumay is known for blue slate. The **Musée de l'Ardoise** (*Apr-Sep: 10am-noon, 2-6pm; Oct-Mar: daily except Sat-Sun 1-5.30pm; €2.50; 03 24 41 10 25*) Housed in the former Carmelite convent, this museum illustrates the hard work of miners extracting schist during the past 800 years.

GUEBWILLER★

POPULATION 11 525

MICHELIN LOCAL MAP 315: H-9

ALSO SEE ROUTE DES CRÊTES AND ROUTE DES VINS

This small yet lively town, situated along the Route des Vins, has retained a wealth of architectural features.

- **Orient Yourself:** Guebwiller is located 25km from Colmar and Mulhouse on N 63.
- **Don't Miss:** A drive through the enchanting Guebwiller Valley.
- **Especially for Kids:** The Vivarium of Lautenbach provides a fascinating insight into the world of creepy-crawlies.

A Bit of History

Guebwiller developed from the 8C onwards under the control of the abbots; in 1275, the city was granted its own charter and allowed to build its own fortifications. Throughout the Middle Ages, vineyards were the main source of wealth; today the surrounding area produces four great wines, Kitterlé, Kessler, Saering and Spiegel.

St Valentine's Day

These fortifications turned out to be very useful in 1445, on St Valentine's day, when the Armagnacs (opposed to the Burgundians and the English during the Hundred Years War) tried to take the town by surprise by crossing the frozen moat. A townswoman named Brigitte Schick gave the alarm; her shrieks were so loud that the attackers thought the whole population had been warned and they ran away, leaving their ladders behind. These are still kept in the Église St-Léger.

SHOPPING

Pâtisserie Christmann – *Pl. de l'Hôtel-de-Ville – ☎03 89 74 27 44 – www.Patisserie-Christmann.fr – 7.30am-7pm – closed mid June-end June, end Jan and 1 May.* Cakes, chocolates and delicious fruit tarts to be enjoyed in this tearoom.

Foire aux vins – This wine fair takes place every Ascension Thu, offering the opportunity to taste and purchase sylvaner, pinot blanc, muscat d'Alsace, riesling, tokay d'Alsace, gewurztraminer, pinot noir, pinot rosé and crémant d'Alsace.

Sights

Église Notre-Dame★

Built between 1760 and 1785 by the last prince-abbot of Murbach, the lofty **interior**★★ of this church contains the striking high altar by Sporrer, representing the **Assumption**★★ (1783).

Walk along rue de la République.

Place de la Liberté with its fountain (1536) is on the right.

Hôtel de ville★

Built in 1514 for a wealthy draper; note the 16C statue of the Virgin in a corner recess on the right.

Continue to the Église St-Léger.

Église St-Léger★

The **west front**★★ of this church dates from the 12C and 13C.

Walk round the church.

The former bailiff's court of justice is located in a fine house dating from 1583 (no 2 rue des Blés). Next comes a lovely **tithe cellar** and last is the **former 16C town hall.**

Visit

Musée du Florival★

Daily except Tue 2-6pm, Sat-Sun and holidays 10am-noon, 2-6pm. 1 Jan, 1 May and 25 Dec. €4. ☎03 89 74 22 89.

The museum, housed in the former 18C residence of aristocratic canons from the chapter of Murbach Abbey, focues on the geology and history of the Florival Valley, but it is most interesting for its display of the **works**★ of **Théodore Deck**, such as a glazed tile veranda and vases coloured in a special blue named after the artist (1823-1891).

Ancien couvent des Dominicains

Aug: daily except Mon 10am-6pm. Guided tours available at 3pm and 4.30pm; May-Jul and Sep-Oct: Tue-Fri 10am-1pm, 2-5pm. €4. ☎03 89 62 21 81. www.les-dominicains.com

This convent, founded in 1294, is now the **Centre polymusical des Dominicains de Haute-Alsace** (music centre). The Jazz Cellar organises jazz sessions on Fridays and Saturdays (Sept-June).

Église St-Pierre-et-St-Paul

Erected between 1312 and 1340, the nave of this Gothic church is the venue of prestigious concerts of classical music.

A. de Valroger/ MICHELIN

Guebwiller – Église St-Léger

Théodore Deck (1823-91)

This native of Guebwiller was a potter and ceramist of genius. His research led him to discover in 1874 the lost formula of the turquoise blue characteristic of Persian ceramics; this blue was henceforth known as the *Bleu Deck*. Deck also found the secret of the famous Chinese celadon, reproduced oriental *cloisonné* and succeeded in decorating his ceramics with a gilt background. In his book, *Ceramics*, published in 1887, he disclosed his formulae and offered anyone interested in the subject the benefit of his experience. He was put in charge of the Manufacture nationale de Sèvres and spent the last years of his life perfecting his art and creating new types of porcelain. His funeral monument in Montparnasse cemetery in Paris, where he is buried, was carved by his friend Frédéric Auguste Bartholdi who sculpted the famous Statue of Liberty.

Excursions

Guebwiller Valley★★— From Guebwiller to Le Markstein

30km/17mi – allow 2hr *Local map see Parc naturel régional des BALLONS DES VOSGES*

The **Lauch Valley** or Guebwiller Valley is known as Florival (literally flower valley); hikers will appreciate the *zone de tranquillité* or car-free quiet area at the end of the valley, on either side of D 430.

Drive out of Guebwiller along D 430 towards the Route des Crêtes and Le Markstein.

The road follows the River Lauch.

Église de Murbach★★

See MURBACH.

Lautenbach★

The village, which goes back to the 8C, developed round a Benedictine abbey. Today, only the **church**★ remains.

Kids The **vivarium** of the Moulin de Lautenback-Zell houses some fascinating insects. *Jul-Aug daily except Mon, 10am-7pm; rest of the year daily except Mon 2-6pm.* *3 weeks early Dec, 25 Dec and 1 Jan. €5.60 (children: €2.80).* *03 89 74 02 48 www.vivariumdumoulin.org.*

Just beyond Linthal, the Lauch Valley becomes narrow and wild.

Lac de la Lauch★

This artificial lake allows angling.

HAGUENAU★

POPULATION 32 242

MICHELIN LOCAL MAP 315: K-4

Haguenau lies on the banks of the River Moder, on the edge of the vast Haguenau Forest with its excellent footpaths and cycle tracks.

- **Orient Yourself:** Haguenau is located 25km/15.5mi north of Strasbourg on A 4 and easily in reach of many of the region's famous pottery villages (Betschdorf and Soufflenheim). It is 20km/12.4mi from the German border.
- Kids **Especially for Kids: Fantasialand** in Morsbronn-les-Bains and **Nautiland** in Haguenau are theme parks popular with younger tourists.

A Bit of History

According to legend, **St Arbogast**, entrusted by the king of the Franks with the christianisation of northern Alsace, stayed in this forest, which was thereafter known as the **holy forest** until the end of the Middle Ages.

The town prospered in the shadow of the massive castle, a favourite residence of

Frederick I Barbarossa (Redbeard) of the House of Hohenstaufen, who ruled the Holy Roman Empire from 1152 to 1190. The verses by Longfellow quoted here are part of a poem set in Haguenau; it tells the story of a local cobbler.

Sights

Musée historique★

Early Jul to mid-Sep: 10am-noon, 2-6pm, Tue, Sat-Sun and holidays 2-6pm; mid-Sep to Dec and Jan-Jun: daily except Tue 10am-noon, 2-6pm, Sat-Sun and holidays 3pm-5.30pm. 1 Jan, Easter, 1 May, 1 Nov and 25 Dec. €3.10 (children 14-18: €1.55) ☎03 88 93 79 22.

The history museum is housed in an imposing edifice built at the beginning of the 20C, partly in neo-Gothic and partly in neo-Renaissance style. It contains an important collection of Bronze and Iron-Age objects found in the region (Haguenau Forest, Seltz) along with a collection of Alsatian coins, medals, and written works printed in Haguenau during the 15C and 16C.

On the first floor are the collections of ceramics, in particular those produced by the Hannong factory (*See STRASBOURG*).

Église St-Georges

This octagonal steeple of this 12C and 13C church houses the two oldest bells in France (1268).

Inside, note the superb **altarpiece**★ representing the Last Judgement.

Église St-Nicolas

This Gothic church was founded by Emperor Frederick Barbarossa in 1189. The remarkable 18C **woodwork**★ (*switch on the light to the left of the chancel*) decorating the pulpit, the organ loft and the choir stalls, was brought to St-Nicolas from the former Abbaye de Neubourg after the Revolution.

Musée alsacien

9am-noon, 1.30-5.30pm, Tue 1.30-5.30pm, Sat-Sun and holidays 2-5pm. 1 Jan, Easter, 1 May, 1 Nov and 25 Dec. €2.40 (14-18 year olds: €1.20). ☎03 88 73 30 41.

The museum inside the restored 15C chancellery displays various local collections along with reconstructions (a potter's workshop, a peasant's living room or stube).

Excursions

Gros Chêne

6km/3.7mi E of Haguenau.

Leave by ② on the town plan.

This barely-standing ancient oak is the starting point of a botanic trail, a fitness itinerary and walks through the forest (*marked paths*). *Playground for children.*

Soufflenheim

14km/8.7mi E.

Leave Haguenau by ② on the town plan.

Famous for its **ceramic workshops** (*Tours Mon-Fri: 9am-noon, 2-5pm; enquire at the Tourist office, ☎03 88 86 74 90 or contact M. Streissel – Confrérie des potiers, ☎03 88 86 64 69*).

Betschdorf

16.5km/10mi NE by ① on the town plan.

This village is famous for its grey sandstone pottery with blue decoration.

A **museum** (*Easter to 1 Nov, 10am-noon, 1.30-6pm, Sat-Sun 2-5.30pm; €3.50. Museum, ☎03 88 54 48 07 – www.betschdorf.org*), displays pottery from the Middle Ages to the present time.

R. Mattès/ MICHELIN

Painted façade, Musée alsacien

Address Book

For coin ranges, see the Legend on the cover flap.

PRACTICAL INFORMATION

Tourist Office – *Pl. de la Gare, ☎03 88 93 70 00, www.ville-hagenau.fr* Guided tours of the town mid-Jun to mid-Sep: Wed at 10am.

WHERE TO EAT

Au Bœuf – *48 Grand'Rue – 67620 Soufflenheim – 15km/9.3mi E of Haguenau on N 63 – ☎03 88 86 72 79 -resto@boeuf-soufflenheim.com.* Good beef features prominently on the menu, along with Alsatian dishes and flammekueches.

WHERE TO STAY

Chambre d'hôte Krumeich – *23 r. des Potiers – 67660 Betschdorf – 15km/9.3mi NE of Haguenau, Wissembourg direction on D 263 and D 243 – ☎03 88 54 40 56 – – 3 rooms.* You can learn how to make salt-glazed stoneware from the owner of this house, who is descended from an old family of Betschdorf potters. Or you can simply stay in one of the pretty rooms, furnished in old-fashioned style, and enjoy the garden.

SPORTS & RECREATION

Établissement thermal de Morsbronn – *12 rte d'Haguenau – 67360 Morsbronn-les-Bains – ☎03 88 09 83 93 – info@curethermale.com – Mar-Nov: 8am-noon, 1.30am-5pm – closed Dec-Feb and Sun.*The thermal springs are recommended for treating rheumatic disorders and post-traumatic injuries. You can choose between the classic spa treatment (72 treatments) and shorter pick-me-ups.

Kids **Nautiland** – *8 r. des Dominicains – ☎03 88 90 56 56 – www.nautiland.net – Daily 12am-9pm, Wed 9.30am-21pm, Sat 10am-10pm, Sun and holidays 9am-7pm; closed 25 Dec, 1 Jan.* A water leisure centre offering cascades, springs, slides, sauna and Turkish bath.

Kids **Didi'Land** – *1 r. de Gunstett – 67360 Morsbronn-les-Bains – ☎03 88 09 46 46 – www.didiland.fr – from early Apr-early Sep 10am-6pm – €12.50 (children: €11.50).* Theme park with carousels, rafts, dodgems, pirate ship and live shows in summer.

SHOPPING

Markets – Weekly market Tue and Fri mornings in the Halle du Houblon. Organic market Fri afternoons, Rue du Rempart.

Atelier de poterie Michel-Dupuy – *13 r. du Moulin Neuf – Parc des sports direction – 67620 Soufflenheim – ☎03 88 93 28 18 – www.michel-dupuy.com – guided tours of the workshop by prior arrangement: Mon-Sat 10am-12.30pm, 2-7pm – closed mid Jan-mid Feb.* Miniature terracotta Alsace houses.

Potiers de Soufflenheim (Tourist Office) – *20B Grand'Rue – 67620 Soufflenheim.fr – ☎03 88 86 74 90 – www.ot-soufflenheim – Mon-Fri 9am- noon, 2-5pm; shop Mon-Sat 9am-noon and 2-6.30pm, Sun 2-6.30pm.* Around ten workshops (exhibitions/sales) which produce ovenproof earthenware pots in glazed colours, with floral motifs.

Céramiques Vincent-Pirard – *10 rte de Bischwiller – 67620 Soufflenheim – ☎03 88 86 60 07 – Mon-Sat 9am-7pm, Sun 2-6pm – closed Jan.* You can look around the pottery workshop and learn all the secrets of these "craftsmen-creators", before purchasing some earthenware and other fruits of their labours.

Hatten

22km/13.7mi NE.

▶ *Leave Haguenau by ① on the town plan. Drive to Hatten via Betschdorf.*

The **Musée de l'Abri and Casemate d'infanterie Esch** is in the village; the **casemate** is situated on the left, 1km/0.6mi beyond Hatten on the way to Seltz (*see Ligne MAGINOT*).

Walbourg

10km/6.2mi N of Haguenau by ① on the town plan. The village name comes from a Benedictine abbey dedicated to St Walburga, an English nun who helped to convert Germany to Christianity.

Morsbronn-les-Bains

11km/6.8mi north by ① on the town plan (D 27). These hot-water (41.5°C/106.7°F) springs contain sodium chloride.

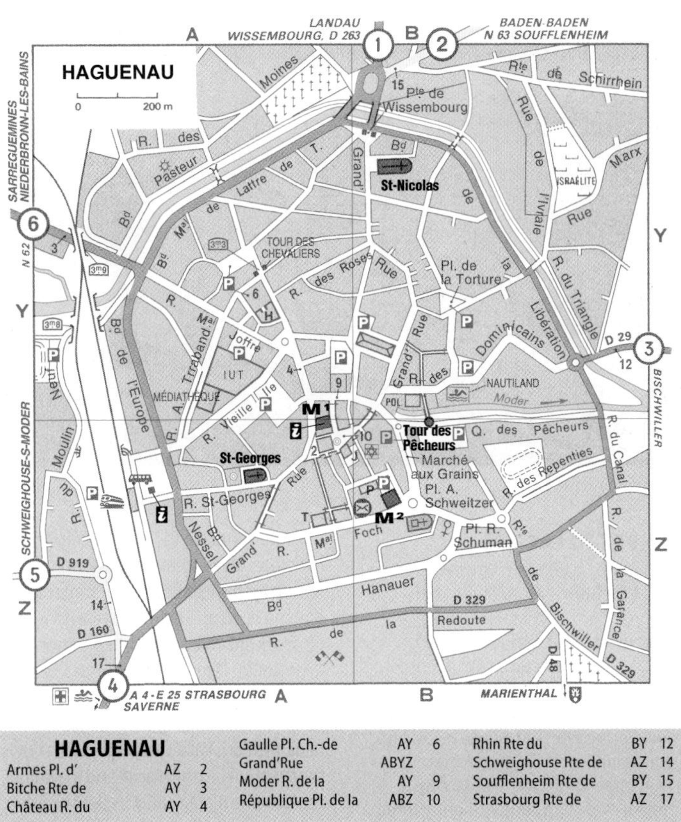

HAGUENAU								
Armes Pl. d'	AZ	2	Gaulle Pl. Ch.-de	AY	6	Rhin Rte du	BY	12
Bitche Rte de	AY	3	Grand'Rue	ABYZ		Schweighouse Rte de	AZ	14
Château R. du	AY	4	Moder R. de la	AY	9	Soufflenheim Rte de	BY	15
			République Pl. de la	ABZ	10	Strasbourg Rte de	AZ	17

Musée alsacien	AY	M1	Musée historique	BZ	M2

Sessenheim

21km/13mi E. This charming village was immortalized by **Goethe** as the setting of his romance with the pastor's daughter **Friederike Brion**.

Inside the **Église protestante**, note the pastor's stall (Pfarrstuhl) where Goethe and Friederike used to sit side by side to listen to her father preaching. On the left of the church stands the **Auberge Au bœuf** (*Daily except Mon and Tue; call for closing times ☎03 88 86 97 14; post card: €1*), an Alsatian inn, displaying Goethe prints, letters and portraits.

The **Mémorial Goethe**, next to the presbytery, was inaugurated in 1962.

CHÂTEAU DU HAUT-BARR★

MICHELIN LOCAL MAP 315: I-4

ALSO SEE PARC NATUREL RÉGIONAL DES VOSGES DU NORD

Solidly camped on three huge sandstone rocks overlooking the valley of the River Zorn and the Plaine d'Alsace, the 12C castle was completely remodelled by Bishop Manderscheidt of Strasbourg who, legend claims, founded the Brotherhood of the Horn dedicated to drinking Alsace wine out of the horn of an aurochs!

- **Orient Yourself**: 5km/3mi. From Saverne, follow D 102 which offers views of the Black Forest. Turn onto D 171 winding through the forest. Park the car near the entrance of the castle.

R. Mattès/ MICHELIN

Château du Haut-Barr

WHERE TO EAT

See the Legend for coin categories.

Au Bain – *7 r. du Mar.-Leclerc – 67700 Haegen – 6km/3.75mi S of Château du Haut-Barr on D 10 and D 102 – ☎03 88 71 02 29 – closed 3 weeks in Feb and 3 weeks in Aug.* The younger generation of proprietors has transformed this old village bistro into a restaurant. It is simply decorated, with paper tablecloths and a classic menu, except on Sunday nights, when it's tarte flambée for everyone.

Visit *about 30min*

A paved ramp leads from the main gate to a second gateway. Past the chapel, there is a terrace (*viewing table*), from which the **view★** extends towards Saverne, the Kochersberg hills and the Black Forest in the distance.

A metal staircase (*64 steps*), fixed to the rock face, gives access to the first rock. Return to the restaurant and, immediately beyond it, go up 81 steps to reach the second rock linked by a footbridge, known as the Pont du Diable, to the third rock. This **view★★** is even better as it offers a 360° panorama including the Vosges mountains, the Zorn Valley (through which flows the canal linking the Marne and the Rhine), the Lorraine plateau and, in clear weather, the Strasbourg Cathedral's spire.

A reconstruction of **Claude Chappe's telegraph tower** stands on its original site; as a relay tower of the famous optical telegraph invented in 1794 by the engineer Chappe, it was used between Paris and Strasbourg from 1798 to 1852. The small **museum** includes an audio-visual presentation (*Early Jun to mid-Sep daily except Mon 1-6pm; Guided tours possible – 30min. €1.50. ☎03 88 52 98 99*).

CHÂTEAU DU HAUT-KŒNIGSBOURG★★

MICHELIN LOCAL MAP 315: I-7 – ALSO SEE ROUTE DES VINS

First mentioned in 1147, the castlestands at an altitude of more than 700m/2 297ft, overlooking the Plaine d'Alsace.

- **Orient Yourself:** The castle is about 21km/13mi north of Colmar. The road leading to it (2km/1.2mi) branches off D 159 at the intersection of the latter with D 1B1, near the Haut-Kœnigsbourg Hotel; 1km/0.6mi farther on, follow the one-way road on the right that goes round the castle (leave your car on the left).

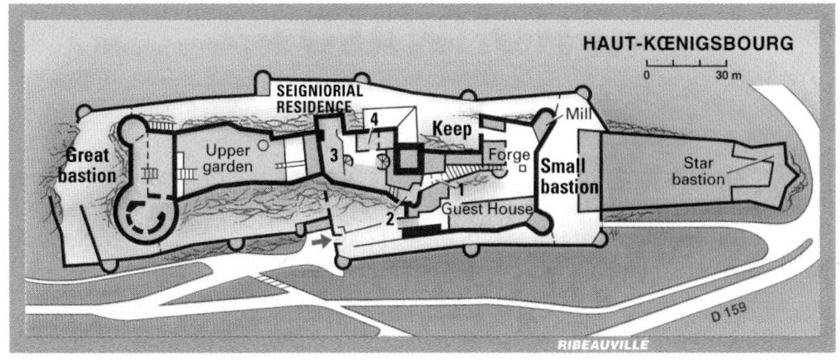

A Bit of History

In 1479 the castle became the property of the Habsburgs; in the 17C, it was destroyed by the Swedish artillery.
In 1899 the ruined castle was offered by the town of Sélestat to Kaiser William II who had Bodo Ebhardt, an architect from Berlin, restore it. The castle was returned to France 10 years later.

Visit

Allow about 1hr. Jun-Aug 9.30am-6.30pm (last admission 30min before closing time); Apr-May and Sep 9.30am-5.30pm; Mar and Oct, 9.45am-5pm; Nov-Feb 9.45am-noon, 1-5pm. 1 Jan, 1 May, 25 Dec. €7.50 (18-25 year olds: €4.80). 03 88 82 50 60.
Beyond the gate and the portcullis lies the lower courtyard surrounded by the buildings. A ramp leads to the lions' doorway (**1**) and to the moat separating the seigneurial residence from the rest of the castle. A fortified well (**2**), 62m/203ft deep, is located on the edge of the rocky promontory, near the residence. On the ground floor, there is a cellar (**3**) on the west side and kitchens (**4**).

Panorama★★

Walk across the upper garden to the great bastion for panoramic views including; to the north, the ruins of Franckenbourg, Ramstein and Ortenbourg castles; to the east, across the Rhine, the heights of Kaiserstuhl with the Black Forest behind; to the south, Hohneck and, on the horizon, Grand Ballon and Route des Vins; about 200m/218yd to the west, you can see the ruins of Œdenbourg or Petit-Kœnigsbourg.

Address Book

WHERE TO STAY

See the Legend for coin categories.

Relais du Haut-Kœnigsbourg *– Rte du Haut-Kœnigsbourg – 67600 Orschwiller – 03 88 82 46 56 – lerelais@calixo.net – closed 2-31 Jan, Sun evenings, Mon evenings and Tue from Oct to Apr – – 26 rooms – €7 – restaurant* . This hotel-restaurant is worth a visit for its setting: just five minutes from the castle, it commands superb views over the forest. The 1960s decor is in need of sprucing up, and only a few rooms have been redecorated; choose one of these if you are staying. Folk evenings.

Auberge La Meunière *– 68590 Thannenkirch – 5km/3mi SW of castle on D 159 and D 42 – 03 89 73 10 47 – info@aubergelameuniere.com – closed 23 Dec-24 Mar – – 25 rooms – €7 – restaurant* . Although situated in the village centre, some of the best rooms in this brick and wood-built inn have views over the countryside with a distant glimpse of the castle.
The restaurant's terrace enjoys the same view.

LE HOHWALD★★

POPULATION 386

MICHELIN LOCAL MAP 315: H-6

This prosperous and secluded resort is the starting point of a variety of drives through a picturesque region of forests, vineyards and charming villages. There are many traces of the area's ancient past, such as the pagan wall round Mont Ste-Odile, believed to have been built by the Celts.

Don't Miss: The hikes and panoramic views in this region are breathtaking, notably from Mont Ste-Odile, Rocher de Neuenstein and the Champ du Feu.

Kids **Especially for Kids:** Les Naïades aquarium is home to 3000 species of fish including sharks, piranhas and electric eels!

Driving Tours

North Hohwald★★—Round tour starting from Le Hohwald 1

91km/56.5mi – allow one day.

Leave Le Hohwald along D 425, which follows the wooded Andlau Valley dotted with sawmills.

The ruins of Spesbourg and Haut-Andlau castles can be seen high up on the left.

Andlau★ – *See ANDLAU.*

Between Andlau and Obernai, the road runs through vineyard-covered hills.

Mittelbergheim

Place de l'Hôtel-de-Ville is lined with lovely Renaissance houses with porches and window frames of typical sandstone from the Vosges region. Wine-growing here goes back to Roman times.

Barr – *See Route des VINS.*

Beyond **Gertwiller**, famous for wine and glacé gingerbread, Landsberg Castle can be seen in the Vosges foothills with, on the right, the convent of Ste-Odile and, lower down, Ottrott's ruined castles.

Obernai★★ – *See OBERNAI.*

Ottrott

Famous for its red wine and its two castles, the 12C Lutzelbourg Castle and the larger 13C Rathsamhausen Castle.

Kids Coming out of Ottrott towards Klingenthal, you will see, on the site of a former spinning mill, a large aquarium known as **Les Naïades** (*10am-6.30pm (ticket window closes 1hr before); 24 and 31 Dec 10am-4pm; 25 Dec and 1 Jan: 1.30-6.30pm. €10 – 3-10 year olds: €7.50; ☎03 88 95 90 32; www.parc-les-naiades.com*), containing more than 3 000 fish from all over the world.

Klingenthal

This small village was once famous for its sword and bayonet **weapons factory** (*Work in progress; telephone ☎03 88 95 93 23*) founded in 1776.

Drive through the forest along D 204 as far as the Fischhütte inn and leave the car; 150m/164yd farther on, a path to the right leads (6km/3.7mi there and back) to the ruins of Guirbaden Castle.

Despite being ruined in the 17C, the 11C **Château fort de Guirbaden** has retained the outer shell of its seigneurial residence and its keep, offering an extended view over the forests, the Plaine d'Alsace and the Bruche Valley.

Signal de Grendelbruch★

15min on foot there and back. The wide **panorama**★ encompasses the Plaine d'Alsace to the east and, to the west, the Bruche Valley and the Vosges mountain range with Donon in the foreground, crowned by a small temple.

Mittelbergheim village and vineyard

R. Mattès/ MICHELIN

The road continues towards the Bruche Valley (see SCHIRMECK).

Schirmeck – *See SCHIRMECK.*

In Rothau, turn left onto D 130 which follows the Rothaine Valley for 3km/1.9mi then veers suddenly left before reaching Le Struthof, which is now a memorial dedicated to victims of the Second World War.

Le Struthof

During the Second World War, the Nazis built a death camp on this site.

Centre européen du résistant déporté

May-Sep: 9am-6pm (last entrance 1hr before closing); Mar-Apr & mid-Sep to mid-Dec: 10am-5pm. €5 (children: €2.50). 03 88 76 78 94.

Opened in autumn 2005, the centre includes sections of the former concentration camp which still stand. The **necropolis** above the camp contains the remains of 1 120 prisoners. In front stands the **memorial**; the base is the tomb of an unknown French prisoner.

The road crosses a plateau, enters the forest and descends to La Rothlach.

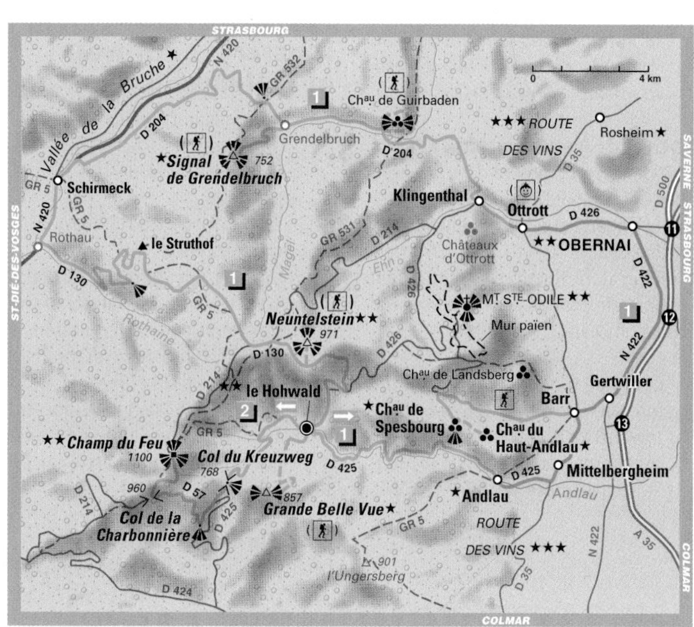

Address Book

PRACTICAL INFORMATION

Tourist Office – *Sq. Kuntz, 67140 Le Hohwald, ☎03 88 08 33 92, www.leholward.fr.*

WHERE TO EAT

See the Legend for coin categories.

Ferme-auberge Lindenhof – *11 rte du Kreuzweg – 2km/1mi W of Hohwald on D 425 – ☎03 88 08 31 98 – closed 16 Dec-6 Jan, Wed evening from 1 Oct-30 Jun and Thu – – booking advisable.* Farm cooking (fromage blanc, Munster, gruyère as well as poultry and rabbit) is served on the large veranda of this ordinary-looking building, situated on the edge of the forest.

WHERE TO STAY

Chambre d'hôte Tilly's Inn – *28 r. Principale – ☎03 88 08 30 17 – – 3 rooms – €8 – by reservation only – restaurant* . The building has an appealing red façade decorated with naïve drawings. Two apartments.

SHOPPING

Lips – Musée du pain d'épices et de l'Art Populaire Alsacien – *Pl. de la Mairie – 67140 Gertwiller – ☎03 88 08 93 52 – Shop: Mon-Sat 8am-noon, 1.30-7pm, Sun 10-noon, 2-6pm. Museum: early Jul-mid Sep: Mon, Wed and Fri 2-6pm, Tue and Thu 9am-noon, 2-6pm; rest of year: Sun 2-6pm – closed 1st fortnight Jan (shop), Jan-Feb (museum).* A celebration of the historic gingerbread makers in the small wine-making village of Gertwiller, near Barr. Tasting. Daily tours in summer.

SPORT

École de parapente Grand Vol – *Ferme Niedermatten – 67220 Breitenbach – Villé direction on D 425 – ☎03 88 57 11 42 – www.grandvol.com – weekends from Apr-Nov.* Qualified instructors teach paragliding and monitor your progress. Special rates for beginners. Minimum age: 14.

Stade de neige du Champ du Feu – *☎03 88 97 35 05.* In the heart of the area known as the Vosges moyennes, and situated at an altitude ranging between 900m/984yd and 1 100m/1 200yd, this vast plateau is not only ideal for cross-country skiing and walks with snows-hoes, but also has 17 ski lifts. École de ski français (Frenh Ski School).

Leave the car 1.5km/0.9mi beyond La Rothlach and follow a path on the left leading to the Neuntelstein viewpoint.

Rocher de Neuntelstein★★

30min on foot there and back.

There is a splendid **view**★★ of Mont Ste-Odile, Ungersberg, Haut-Kœnigsbourg and the Champ du Feu. You can try rock-climbing at the Rocher de Neuntelstein School (information available from the tourist office in Le Hohwald).

Continue along D 130 and, at the intersection with D 426, turn right towards Le Hohwald. A left turn at that point would lead you to Mont Ste-Odile (see Mont STE-ODILE).

Champ du Feu—Itinerary south-west of Le Hohwald 2

11km/6.8mi – about 30min

Drive W out of Le Hohwald along D 425.

Col du Kreuzweg

From the pass (alt 768m/2 520ft), the view extends over the valleys of the River Breitenbach and River Giessen.

The road (D 57) climbs towards the Charbonnière pass, offering superb views of the Villé Valley, the Plaine d'Alsace and the Black Forest. Frankenbourg Castle and Haut-Kœnigsbourg Castle can be seen from afar.

Col de la Charbonnière

Beyond the heights overlooking the Villé Valley, one can see the Plaine d'Alsace with the Black Forest in the distance.

On reaching the pass, turn right onto D 214 which goes round the Champ du Feu.

Champ du Feu★★

The vast **panorama**★★ unfolding from the top of the now-closed observation tower includes the Vosges mountains, the Plaine d'Alsace, the Black Forest and, when the weather is clear, the Swiss Alps. The slopes all around are a popular ski area.

North of the tower, 1km/0.6mi to the left, D 414 leads to the Chalet Refuge and ski slopes of La Serva open in winter.

Hiking Tours

Haut-Andlau and Spesbourg castles★

1hr 30min on foot there and back.

Drive W along D 854 then, 1.5km/0.9mi beyond Holzplatz, continue on a surfaced path to the left which leads to Hungerplatz forest lodge. Leave the car there and follow the path running along the mountain ridge to the ruins.

The ruined 14C **Château du Haut-Andlau**★ was lived in until 1806.
The **Château de Spesbourg**★ had an unusually short life for a castle: built in the 13C, it was destroyed in the 14C.

Grande Bellevue★ (Viewpoint)

1hr 30min on foot there and back. After a few minutes, you will get a clear view of Le Hohwald and the surrounding area.

As you reach the former Belle-Vue inn (1km/0.6mi), take a path on the left and climb for 3km/1.9mi through the forest before reaching high pasture. From the summit (100m/110yd to the left), the viewa extends to Le Climont on the right, the Villé Valley in the foreground and Haut-Kœnigsbourg farther ahead.

Col d'Urbeis★

This mountain pass is a favourite of local hiking clubs. The view is splendid, encompassing the valleys of the Fave and Giessen rivers. The **observation tower**★ at Le Climont provides an exceptional panorama.
1hr 30min on foot there and back. North of Climont, near the church, there is a sign pointing the way to the trail (marked in yellow). It is a steep climb.

You can continue the itinerary southward on D23 to Provenchères-sur-Fave.

Provenchères sur-Fave

This town on the northern edge of the Parc Naturel Régional des Ballons de Vosges straddles de River Fave. It is a good place to set out on a bike excursion into the nature park.

R. Mattès/ MICHELIN

Champ du Feu

JOINVILLE

POPULATION 4 380

MICHELIN LOCAL MAP 313: K-3

This small town nestles between the River Marne, dotted with mills, and a hill crowned by a ruined feudal castle once owned by the dukes of Guise.

Orient Yourself: Joinville lies off the N 67 which skirts the town, 32km/20mi south of St Dizier and 45km/28mi north of Chaumont.

A Bit of History

One of the most prominent lords of this barony was the famous 13C chronicler, **Jean de Joinville** (1224-1317), a loyal companion of King Louis IX, better known as St Louis, whom he followed to Egypt in 1248 to take part in the seventh crusade. A 3m/10ft high statue of Joinville, with a book and quill pen, was erected in 1861 in rue Aristide-Briand.

Sights

Château du Grand Jardin★

Early Jun to mid-Sep: 9.30am-7pm; mid-Sep to late Oct and mid-Mar to late May: 10am-noon, 2-7pm; early Nov to mid-Mar: 10am-noon, 2-5.30pm. Dec to early Jan. €4. 03 25 94 17 54. www.legrandjardin.com

The 16C castle is named for its large well-maintained garden. Exhibitions, performances and concerts are organised in the castle throughout the year.

Auditoire

Mid-May to late Oct: Guided tour (1hr 30min) 3-6pm; late Oct to mid-May: tours by request at the Tourist office at least 7 days in advance, daily except Mon, 2-6pm. €4 (children under 16: no charge). 03 25 94 17 90.

This seigneurial tribunal erected in the 16C also served as a prison.

Chapelle Ste-Anne

Daily except Sun by request at the Tourist office, €2.50 03 25 94 17 90.

The chapel (1504) stands in the centre of the cemetery; light pours in through lovely stained-glass windows by artists

Ph. Gajic/ MICHELIN

Château du Grand Jardin

Address Book

PRACTICAL INFORMATION

Tourist Office – *Pl. Saunoise, 52300 Joinville, ☎03 25 94 17 90.*

WHERE TO EAT

See the Legend for coin categories.

La Poste – *Pl. de la Grève – ☎03 25 94 12 63 – closed 10-27 Jan and Sun evenings.* This family-run establishment in the town centre offers traditional cooking and small, functional rooms for a simple stay.

WHERE TO STAY

Le Soleil d'Or – *9 r. des Capucins – ☎03 25 94 15 66-www.hotellesoleildor.com – closed 1-15 Feb – 22 rooms – €9.50 – restaurant.* You will be utterly charmed by this late-17C house with a traditional decor of stone and exposed beams, artfully combined with contemporary materials, especially glass. Comfortable rooms. Classic menu or more elaborate cooking.

Camping La Forge de Ste-Marie – *52230 Thonnance-les-Moulins – 13km/8mi E of Joinville on D 427 – ☎03 25 94 42v00 – la.forge.de.sainte.marie@wanadoo.fr – open 1 Mai-10 Sep – booking advisable – 133 sites – restaurant.* Located in the countryside near a forest and a lake, the buildings of this former 18C forge have been turned into holiday accommodation. The forge itself contains a heated indoor pool with a terrace. Shady camping areas. Indoor tennis court, golf course, fishing, boating, jacuzzi, cabaret and kids's club.

Chambre d'hôte Le Moulin aux Écrevisses – *Rte de Nancy – 52300 Thonnance-lès-Joinville – 5km/3mi E of Joinville on D 60 – ☎03 25 94 13 76 –http://ecrevisses.fr – – 3 rooms – restaurant.* This former mill by a small river on the edge of a forest is the ideal place to relax and enjoy yourself, thanks to its garden, fishing lake and the numerous walks possible in the region. The rooms are plain but comfortable. This is also the site of a crayfish-farming scheme – the only one in Europe – so prepare your palate!

from the Troyes School. Note the 15C **Christ in bonds** in polychrome wood.

Excursions

Blécourt

9km/5.6mi S along N 67 to Rupt then right onto D 117.

This 12C Gothic **church** (*Daily 10am-6pm. Information from M. Bertrand; ☎03 25 94 14 44*) contains a 13C *Virgin and Child* (Champagne School).

Lacets de Mélaire

19km/11.8mi SE via D 960; 4km/2.5mi beyond Thonnance-lès-Joinville, take the small road on the right which runs through the woods.

These hairpin bends with steep slopes offer good **views** of the wide valley below and the village of Poissons.

Return to Joinville along D 427.

KAYSERSBERG★★

POPULATION 2 676

MICHELIN LOCAL MAP 315: H-8 – ALSO SEE ROUTE DES VINS

Kaysersberg is a small city with a quaint medieval character, built on the banks of the Weiss, where the river runs into the Plaine d'Alsace.
From the ruins of the medieval castle (*30min on foot there and back*), there is a lovely general view of the town and its famous vineyards.

A Bit of History

In Roman times, it was already called *Caesaris Mons* (the emperor's mountain) because of its strategic position along one of the most important routes linking ancient Gaul and the Rhine Valley.

Town Walk

This walk is centred on the high street, rue du Gén.-de-Gaulle.

Hôtel de ville★

Built in the Renaissance style characteristic of the Rhine region.

Église Ste-Croix★

Kaysersberg parish church stands beside a small square adorned with a 16C fountain, restored in the 18C and surmounted by a statue of Emperor Constantine.

The chancel contains, above the high altar, a wooden **altarpiece**★★ in the shape of a triptych, a magnificent work by Jean Bongartz, the master from Colmar (1518).
The north aisle shelters a damaged 1514 Holy Sepulchre; note the group representing the holy women, by Jacques Wirt. According to an Alsatian tradition, a slit in Christ's chest is intended for the host during Holy Week.

Chapelle St-Michel

The two-storey chapel was built in 1463; the lower level is an ossuary and contains a stoup decorated with a skull.

Cimetière

A 16C wooden gallery provides a shelter for the unusual cross, known as the plague cross, dating from 1511.

▸ *Go back to rue du Gén.-de-Gaulle, also known as Grand'Rue.*

R. Mattès/ MICHELIN

Kaysersberg is attractive and inviting

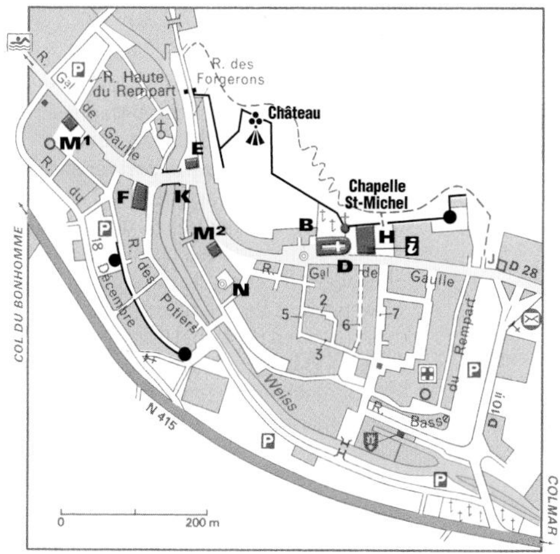

KAYSERSBERG	
Ancien Hôpital R. de l'	2
Ancienne Gendarmerie R. de l'	3
Commanderie R. de la	5
Église R. de l'	6
Rieder R. du Gén.	7

Cimetière	B
Hostellerie du Pont	E
Hôtel de ville	H
Maison Brief	F
Musée Albert-Schweitzer	M[1]
Musée communal	M[2]
Pont fortifié	K
Puits Renaissance	N
Église Ste-Croix	D

Vieilles maisons★

There are many old houses along rue de l'Église, rue de l'Ancien-Hôpital, rue de l'Ancienne-Gendarmerie and rue du Général-de-Gaulle (also called Grand-Rue). Note the humorous **Renaissance well** dating from 1618, situated in the courtyard of no 54 Grand-Rue.

▸ *Continue towards the River Weiss.*

Hostellerie du Pont

On the corner of rue des Forgerons, this hostel was the former baths.

Address Book

PRACTICAL INFORMATION

Tourist Office – *39 rue du Gén. - de-Gaulle, 68240 Kayserberg, ☎03 89 78 22 78, www.kayserberg.com*

WHERE TO EAT

See the Legend for coin categories.

Le Couvent – *1 r. Couvent – ☎03 89 78 23 29 – closed Thu out of season.* Another unassuming restaurant that is worth finding. You won't be disappointed: run by a young couple, it has a good local reputation and is much frequented by winemakers. Alsace dishes and traditional cuisine.

WHERE TO STAY

Hôtel Les Remparts – *☎03 89 47 12 12 – hotel@lesremparts.com – closed 2 to 28 Feb – 40 rooms – €7.* This hotel is situated in a quiet residential area not far from the market of the old town. Some of the rooms have lovely terraces; those in the annex are more modern.

Hostellerie Schwendi – *68240 Kientzheim – ☎03 89 47 30 50 – hostellerie.schwendi@wanadoo.fr – closed 20 Dec-15 Mar – P – 17 rooms – €8 – restaurant.* With its pretty pale yellow, half-timbered façade, the hotel is located in the centre of a wine-making village. Charming and personalised rooms. Terrace near the fountain in nice weather. Sample the family estate wines, available in the dining room.

SHOPPING

Caveau des Vignerons de Kientzeim-Kaysersberg – *20 r. du Gén.-de-Gaulle – ☎03 89 47 18 43 – Easter-mid-Nov and Christmas holidays: Wed-Mon 10am-noon, 2-6pm.* Alsace crémant (sparkling wine) and wines to taste and buy.

Pâtisserie Lœcken – *46 r. du Gén.-de-Gaulle – ☎03 89 47 34 35 – Tue-Sun 8am-6.30pm (7pm in summer) – closed 25 Dec and 1 Jan.* Cake shop in a superb 16C wood-shingled house. The chocolates are home-made, while the teas come from all over the world. Alsace foie gras and coffee roasting.

Pont fortifié★

A fortified bridge built in the 15C and 16C.

The **Maison Brief**★ is an elaborately carved 16C timber-framed house.

Museum

Musée Albert-Schweitzer

♿ *Easter to Nov: 9am-noon, 2-6pm; during Advent: Fri and Sat-Sun 9am -noon, 2-6pm. 2€. ☎03 89 47 36 55.*

Standing next to Albert Schweitzer's birthplace, the museum retraces the life of the great humanist.

Albert Schweitzer

Born in Kaysersberg on 14 January 1875, Albert Schweitzer became a clergyman, a theologian, a famous organist, a musicologist, a writer and a missionary doctor. After the First World War, he spent most of his life in West Africa where he founded a hospital, occasionally returning to Europe to give organ concerts. He was awarded the Nobel Peace Prize in 1952 and died in 1965 in Lambaréné (Gabon) where his work lives on. He had a house built in Gunsbach, where he spent his childhood during the time his father was the village pastor.

LANGRES

POPULATION 9 586

MICHELIN LOCAL MAP 313: L-M 6

A promontory of the Langres plateau forms the remarkable setting★★ of this ancient city, one of the three capitals of Burgundy under the Gauls.

- **Orient Yourself**: Langres is one of the gateways of Burgundy and a tourist stopoff on the north-south European route (A5, A31).

A Bit of History

Gallo-Roman city

The Lingons, a Gaulish tribe who gave their name to Langres, became Caesar's allies; the town prospered under Roman occupation. However, when Nero died in AD 70, one of their chiefs, by the name of **Sabinus**, tried to usurp the supreme power but failed and, according to legend, found temporary refuge in a cave close to the source of the Marne..

St Didier

According to legend, St Didier, who was the third bishop of Langres was made a martyr for having defended the town: after he was beheaded, he picked up his head, left on horseback and died on the spot where a chapel was later built.

Royal stronghold

During the Middle Ages, the bishops of Langres became dukes and peers of the realm, and often advisors to the king. When Champagne was united with France in 1284, Langres became a royal fortress.

Langres is the birthplace of **Denis Diderot**, the 18C philosopher, **Jeanne Mance,** the missionary who founded Canada's first hospital in Montreal in the mid 17C, and painter **Claude Gillot** (1674-1722), one of Watteau's masters.

Visit

Walk Along the Ramparts★★

4km/2.5mi – about 1hr 30min.

The ramparts evolved from the Hundred Years War to the 19C and offer a magnificent panorama, including: to the east the Marne Valley, the Lac de la Liez and the Vosges mountains when the weather is clear; to the north the Colline des Fourches crowned by a chapel; to the west the slopes of the Bonnelle

Valley and farther afield the Plateau de Langres and its wooded slopes.
Start from place des États-Unis south of the old town.

Porte des Moulins
This is the monumental entrance (1647) to the city; its style is characteristic of Louis XIII's military architecture.

Tour St-Ferjeux
This tower, built around 1469-72, was specially adapted to artillery warfare. A polished-steel sculpture by the Dutch artist Eugene Van Lamsweerde, *Air,* dedicated to the philosopher Gaston Bachelard, stands on the tower.

Tour Virot
This semicircular tower used to defend the Sous-Murs district, an area below the walls of the city.

Porte Henri IV
This gate (1604) has retained traces of its defence system.

Viewing table
From this point, the view encompasses the Sous-Murs district below, surrounded by its own wall, and the ramparts on either side; the Lac de la Liez and the Vosges mountains can be seen in the distance.

Tour St-Jean
This former gun tower was fitted as a military dovecote in 1883.

Tour du Petit-Sault
This elongated gun tower (c 1517-21) contains two vaulted rooms linked by a large staircase. From the terrace *(viewing table)*, there is a view of the Bonnelle Valley and of the Plateau de Langres.

Porte gallo-romaine
Set within the walls, this gate (1C AD) was used as a tower in medieval times.

Porte Neuve or Porte des Terreaux
This is the most recent of the gates (1855).

Tours de Navarre et d'Orval
Jul-Aug, 10am-12.30pm, 4.30-8pm, May-Jun and Sep Sat-Sun and public holidays, 4.30-8pm. Admission charge. 03 25 87 67 67.
This defensive complex, inaugurated by François I in 1521, was designed to guard the southern access to the town; the walls are 7m/23ft thick in places.

Old Town

A slanting elevator links the Sous-Bie parking area, situated outside the walls, to the town centre, offering a panoramic view of the town, the Lac de la Liez and the Vosges mountains.

Rue Diderot
Lined with shops, the town's high street runs past the **theatre** housed since 1838 inside the former Chapelle des Oratoriens (1676).

Denis Diderot (1713-84)

The son of a cutler, Denis Diderot was a brilliant pupil of the local Jesuit college and he seemed destined for a religious career, but he went on to study in Paris instead and only came back to Langres five times during his life. However, he spoke about his native town in his *letters* to Sophie Volland and in his *Journey to Langres.*

Interested in many subjects, he wrote numerous works, including essays such as *Letters about the blind for the attention of those who can see,* for which he was imprisoned in Vincennes, novels *(The Nun)*, satires *(Jacques the Fatalist)*, and philosophical dialogues *(Rameau's Nephew)*. He was also an art critic *(Salons)*. Yet his name is first and foremost linked with that of the *Encyclopaedia,* a monumental work which he undertook to write with D'Alembert in 1747 and to which he devoted 25 years of his life. Completed in 1772, the 35-volume *Encyclopaedia* represents the sum total of scientific knowledge and philosophical ideas during the Age of Enlightenment.

Address Book

PRACTICAL INFORMATION

Tourist Office – *Pl. Bel Air, 52200 Langres – ☏03 25 87 67 67, www.tourisme-langres.com*

WHERE TO EAT

See the Legend for coin categories.

Aux Délices – Pâtisserie Henry – *6 Rue Diderot – ☏03 25 87 02 48.* This lovely building dating from 1580 is situated in the old town of Langres. Inside, recent frescoes depict some of the interesting features of the town. The quiches, meat pies and pastries make this a tempting option for a light meal or afternoon tea.

Auberge des Voiliers – *Au Lac de la Liez – 4km/2.5mi E of Langres on N 19 and D 284 – ☏03 25 87 05 74 – auberge.voiliers@wanadoo.fr – closed 1 Dec-2 Mar and Mon.* The Lac de la Liez is well known by sailors and windsurfers, and this lakeside inn is ideal for weekend breaks or short holidays. The rooms are simple and the cooking varied and appetising.

Auberge des Trois Provinces – *52190 Vaux-sous-Aubigny – 25km/15.5mi S of Langres on N 74 – ☏03 25 88 31 98 – closed 12 Jan-2 Feb, Sun evening from 15 Sep-22 Jun and Mon.* The decor in this little inn is decidedly modern, with beams and painted ceilings and brightly coloured frescoes. Only the stone walls give it a country feel. The helpings are generous enough to satisfy the biggest appetites.

Le Parc – *1 pl. Moreau – 52210 Arc-en-Barrois – ☏03 25 02 53 07 – closed 15 Feb-30 Mar, Sun evening and Mon from 30 Mar-15 Jun, Tue evening and Wed from 1 Sep-15 Feb.* After visiting the attractions of the Haut-Marne area, you can enjoy regional specialities in this peaceful restaurant. Large, light dining room, enclosed terrace with flowers. Functional rooms.

WHERE TO STAY

Chambre d'hôte Japiot – *52250 Flagey – 15km/9.4mi S of Langres on D 428 et D 6 – ☏03 25 84 45 23 – ⊭ – 4 rooms – evening meal.* Hospitality and spontaneity are the name of the game in this B&B that has been run by the same family for four generations. The rooms are modernly furnished and the one with a terrace is especially nice. Hiding in the dining room are two 245-year-old box beds. The food served is made with produce from the farm, which is also open to visitors.

Chambre d'hôte L'Orangerie – *Pl. Adrien-Guillaume (formerly pl. de l'Église) – 52190 Prangey – 16km/10mi S of Langres on N 74 and D 26 – ☏03 25 87 54 85 – ⊭ – 3 rooms.* This charming ivy-clad B&B stands in a rural setting, between the castle and the village church. Its comfortable rooms have a romantic atmosphere.

Le Cheval Blanc – *4 r. Estres – ☏03 25 87 07 00 – info@hotel-langres.com – closed 15-30 Nov – 22 rooms – €9 – restaurant.* This 9C abbey church was converted into a hotel in 1793 and some of the bedrooms have retained the typical vaulted ceilings. Behind the house, opposite the town ramparts, the remains of the old buildings enhance the pretty summer terrace. Traditional menu and nicely presented tables.

SHOPPING

Fromagerie Schertenleib – *R. de la Laiterie – 52140 Saulxures – ☏03 25 90 33 20.* Langres, which has been awarded AOC quality status, is a soft cheese with a washed rind. It is made throughout the year using milk from the cows that graze on the pastures of Bassigny and the Langres plateau.

Jean-Michel-Rousselle – *Chemin départemental 54 – 52210 Bugnières – ☏03 25 31 00 95 – 8am-8pm by appointment only – closed end Dec. Rubis de groseilles* is a red currant drink that is fermented and made using traditional methods. It is best drunk cold, either as an aperitif or at the end of a meal.

Caves de la Vingeanne – *78 r. Diderot – ☏03 25 87 18 83.* Montsaugeonnais (a local wine) on sale.

SPORTS & RECREATION

Lac de la Liez – *☏03 25 87 09 03.* Rent electric and pedal boats for your own excursions.

Lac de la Liez – *☏03 25 87 09 03 .* Electric-powered boats and pedalos for rent.

Collège
This vast Baroque edifice is the former 18C Jesuit college.

Place Diderot
This is the town's main square, adorned with a statue of Diderot by Bartholdi famed for the Statue of Liberty.
As you walk down rue du Grand-Cloître, admire the view of the Lac de la Liez. Note the 15C timber-framed house at the beginning of rue Lhuillier.

Walk along the south side of the cathedral.

Cloître de la cathédrale
Tue, Thu and Fri, 1.30-6.30pm, Wed and Sat, 8.45-11.45am, 1.30-6pm and by appointment. 03 25 87 63 00.
The cloisters date from the early 13C.

Walk across place Jeanne-Mance.

Note the bronze statue of **Jeanne Mance** (1606-73) by Jean Cardot.

Maison Renaissance
Jul-Aug, 2:30-6pm. 2€ 03 25 87 67 67.
This 16C Renaissance house has a splendid façade overlooking the garden. Follow the side passage *(spiral staircase)* to in rue Cardinal-Morlot; turn left.

Continue along rue Lambert-Payen and rue Gambetta leading to the charming place Jenson.

Église St-Martin
Daily except Sun and Mon, 2-6pm.
Note the elegant campanile.

Sights

Cathédrale St-Mammès★
The cathedral (94m/308ft long and 23m/75ft high) was built during the second half of the 12C but it was subsequently remodelled many times.
The vast **interior** is in Burgundian Romanesque style.

Trésor
Jul-Aug, daily except Mon 2.30-6pm, May-Jun and Sep, Sun and public holidays, 2.30-5.30pm. 03 25 87 67 67. www.paysdelangres.com
The treasury houses objects such as a reliquary from Clairvaux Abbey.

Tour sud
Jul-Aug, daily 4-6pm, May-Jun and Sep, Sun and public holidays, 4.30-5.30pm. closed during services 03 25 87 67 67.
From the top of the South tower (45m/148ft), there is a panoramic view.

Musée d'Art et d'Histoire
Place du Centenaire. Apr-Oct, 10am-noon, 2-6pm, Nov-Mar, daily except Tue, 10am-noon, 2-5pm. Guided tours possible first Sun of the month. 03 25 87 08 05.
The department of **prehistory and ancient history** includes items discovered during excavations made in the region (Farincourt, Cohons).
The **Gallo-Roman department**★ displays stone fragments.
Painting from the 17C, 18C and 19C is represented by Gustave Courbet and Camille Corot as well as by local artists Jean Tassel and Edmé Bouchardon.

Excursions

Land of the four lakes
Four reservoirs were created in the late 19C and the early 20C in order to supply the Marne-Saône canal.
During the summer, the surface of these reservoirs may shrink; the extremities are then turned into reedy marshland sheltering interesting fauna and flora.

Lac de la Liez
5km/3mi E of Langres.
This is the largest of the four lakes (270ha/667 acres).
It is possible to walk along the earth dike (460m/503yd long and 16m/53ft high) with views of fortified Langres.
A footpath runs round the lake. There is a **boat hire** (*See Address Book*) service.

Lac de la Mouche
6km/3.7mi W of Langres.
This is the smallest of the four lakes (94ha/232 acres).

Lac de Charmes

8km/5mi N of Langres.

Trips on the lake aboard electricity-powered boats.

Lac de la Vingeanne

12km/7.5mi S along N 74.

A footpath (8km/5mi) runs all the way round this lake (190ha/250 acres) which has the longest dike (1 254m/1 371yd).

Gorges de la Vingeanne

From the Lac de Vingeanne, drive along D 141C towards Bayssey then Aprey (8km/5mi) and leave the car in the parking area.

A botanical trail leads from the village of Aprey to the source of the Vingeanne.

Northwest of Langres

Tuffière de Rolampont

14km/8.7mi along N 19 to 1km/0.6mi beyond Rolampont then left onto D 254; follow the arrows.

The cascade on this site has been formed over time as mineral spring water, rich in calcium, has made the rock porous through the deposit of microscopic algae and moss.

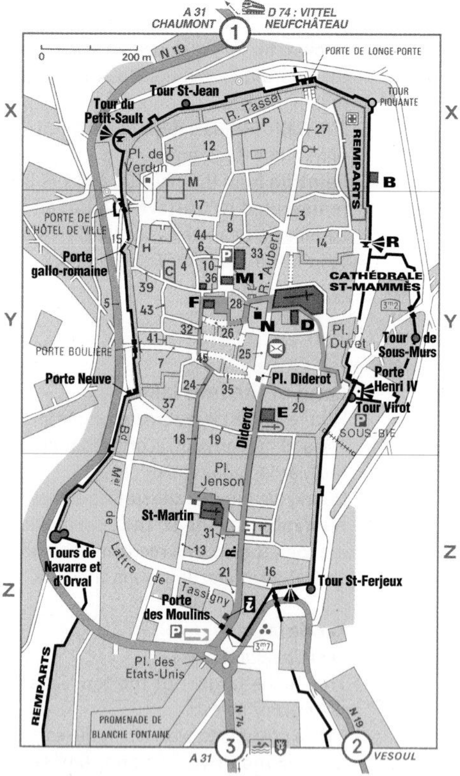

Ancienne Automotrice	X	B	Porte des Moulins	Z	
Cathédrale St-Mammès	Y		Porte gallo-romaine	Y	
Cloître de la Cathédrale	Y	D	Statue de Jeanne Mance	Y	N
Collège	Y	E	Table d'Orientation	Y	R
Église St-Martin	Z		Tour St-Ferjeux	Z	
Maison Renaissance	Y	F	Tour St-Jean	X	
Musée d'Art et d'Histoire	Y	M[1]	Tour Virot	Y	
Porte Henri-IV	Y		Tour de sous Murs	Y	
Porte Neuve	Y		Tour du Petit Sault	X	
			Tours de Navarre et d'Orval	Z	

LANGRES

Aubert R.	Y	
Barbier-d'Aucourt R.	Y	3
Beligné R. Ch.	Y	4
Belle-Allée La	Y	5
Boillot R.	Y	6
Boulière Porte	Y	
Boulière R.	Y	7
Canon R.	Y	8
Centenaire Pl. du	Y	10
Chambrûlard R.	X	12
Chavannes R. des	Z	13
Crémaillière R. de la	Y	14
Croc R. du	Y	15
Denfert-Rochereau R.	Z	16
Diderot Pl.	Y	
Diderot R.	YZ	
Durand R. Pierre	Y	17
Duvet Pl. J.	Y	
États-Unis Pl. des	Z	
Gambetta R.	Y	18
Grand-Bie R. du	Y	19
Grand-Cloître R. du	Y	20
Grouchy Pl. Col.-de	Z	21
Hôtel-de-Ville Porte de l'	Y	
Jenson Pl.	Z	
Lambert-Payen R.	Y	24
Lattre-de-Tassigny Bd Mar.-de	YZ	
Leclerc R. Général	Y	25
Lescornel R.	Y	26
Longe-Porte Porte de	X	
Longe-Porte R. de	X	27
Mance Square J.	Y	28
Minot R.	Z	31
Morlot R. Card.	Y	32
Roger R.	Y	33
Roussat R. Jean	Y	35
St-Didier R.	Y	36
Tassel R.	X	
Terreaux R. des	Y	37
Tournelle R. de la	Y	39
Turenne R. de	Y	41
Ursulines R. des	Y	43
Verdun Pl. de	X	
Walferdin R.	Y	44
Ziegler Pl.	Y	45

S. Sauvignier/MICHELIN

Tuffière de Rolampont

Mausolée gallo-romain de Faverolles

10km/6mi along N 19 to Rolampont, then left along D 155 and D 256.

The ruins of this mausoleum were discovered in 1980 in the forest, 3.5km/2.2mi outside the village (it is possible to visit the excavation site during the course of a walk through the forest).
Fragments of the mausoleum are displayed in an **Atelier archéologique** (*Jul-Aug, Wed-Sun, 2-8pm, May-Jun and Sep, Sat-Sun and public holidays, 2-8pm; €3; 03 25 87 67v67).*

From the Marne to the Saône

80km/50mi round tour – allow half a day.

Leave Langres SE along N 74.

Source de la Marne

Drive along N 74 then follow D 122 on the left towards Noidant-Chatenoy; 2.5km/1.5mi farther on, turn left onto D 290 towards Balesmes-sur-Marne; drive for another 1km/0.6mi and turn right towards the parking area; a path on the left leads down to the source of the River Marne (400m/437yd).

45min on foot there and back.
The Marne springs from a kind of vault closed by an iron door. Footpaths meander through the rocks. Picnic area.

Return to Noidan-Chatenoy and turn left onto D 51.

Fort du Cognelot

Jul-Aug – Guided 1hr 30min tours Sun and public holidays, 3pm and 5pm. €3.50. 03 25 87 67 67.
This is one of eight forts built round Langres after the 1870 war to defend France's eastern border.

Continue along D 51 to Chalindrey and turn right onto D 17.

Château de Pailly

May-Sep *by appointment. Admission charge (except children under 16). 03 25 87 67 67.*
An elegant Renaissance residence was built in 1560 round a feudal castle by Marshal de Saulx-Tavannes.

Return to Chalindrey and follow D 26 to Chaudenay then N 19 to Fayl-Billot.

Fayl-Billot

Famous for cane furniture and wickerwork, the tourist office is located inside the **basket-maker's house**.
The **National School of Basket-making and Wickerwork** houses three exhibition rooms (*Daily except Tue, 10am-noon, 2-6pm. Jan-Feb, 1 May, 25 Dec; €2.40; 03 25 88 63 02).*

Follow D 17 to Bussières-lès-Belmont.

Bussières-les-Belmont

Daily except Sun, 9am-noon, 2-6pm, Sat 2-6pm. Basket-making dem-

The Marne-Saône Canal

Inaugurated in 1907, the canal makes it possible to travel across France along various waterways from Dunkerque to Marseille. A **tunnel** (4.8km/2.5mi long) had to be built to negotiate the watershed between north and south. You can watch the canal disappear into the tunnel, which is so narrow that an alternating traffic system has been installed.

onstrations in Jul-Aug. Public holidays. No admission charge. 03 25 88 62 75. The local association presents a video and display of finished willow articles.

Take D 125 to Chaudenay then follow N19 back to Langres.

PARC NATUREL RÉGIONAL DE LORRAINE

POPULATION 60 000

MICHELIN LOCAL MAP 307: K TO L-6

Straddling the three *départements* of the Meurthe-et-Moselle, Meuse and Moselle, close to the towns of Nancy and Metz, this nature park offers visitors the wonderful variety of its natural environment from the Ste-Croix Safari Park to the numerous lakes home to thousands of migrating birds.

A Bit of History

Created in 1976, the park surrounds the River Moselle.

Sights

Nature trails

The area is crisscrossed with marked footpaths with explanatory panels: forest trails in the Forêt de la Reine, Forêt de Bride-et-Kœking and Forêt de Fénétrange, salt-marsh trail in Marsal, limestone-meadow trail in Génicourt-sur-Meuse, trails of the Étang de Lindre and Étang des Essarts, a vineyard trail in Lucey, and an educational hemp-growing trail around Toul.

Lac de Madine

W of Pont-à-Mousson, western part of the nature park (map 242 fold 13). Nonsard, on the north-east shore of the lake lies 25km/15mi W of Pont-à Mousson along D 958 to Flirey (15km/9.3mi) then right onto D 904 to Pannes (7km/4.3mi) and left onto D 133 (3km/1.9mi).

This large lake (1 100ha/2 718 acres) forms a vast outdoor leisure park offering many water sports and other activities (tennis, golf and riding) as well as the opportunity to relax (catering, accommodation and camping).

It is also possible to take a 20km/12.4mi walk, or bike ride, round the lake.

Parc animalier de Ste-Croix

Rhodes, 12km/7.5mi NW of Sarrebourg along D 27, eastern part of the nature park.

Jul-Aug, 10am-7pm (8pm Sat-Sun and public holidays); Apr-Jun and early Sep-mid-Nov, 10am-6pm (7pm Sat-Sun and public holidays); Guided tours possible (by train), allow a whole day. €11 (3-11 year olds: €8). 03 87 03 92 05. www.parcsaintecroix.com.

Kids This safari park shelters 1 200 animals from 80 different European species including wolves, lynxes, foxes, storks, deer, aurochs and capercaillies.

R. Mattès/MICHELIN

American monument at the Butte de Monsec

Excursion

Côtes de Meuse★ – Itinerary from Verdun to St-Mihiel

83km/52mi – allow 2hr 30min.

Leave Verdun by D 903 towards Metz and Nancy.

Soon after leaving Verdun, look to the right for a fine view of the Meuse Valley and its wooded rolling countryside.

7km/4.3mi beyond the intersection of D 903 and D 964, turn right onto DST 31, signposted Les Éparges, Hattonchâtel, then right again onto D 154.

Site des Éparges

Marked footpaths running through a dense forest (scarred by mines) lead from the Le Trottoir national cemetery to the site of the fighting.

Turn back and drive to D 908 via St-Rémy-la-Calonne and Combres-sous-les-Côtes. In St-Maurice-sous-les-Côtes, turn right onto D 101 then left onto the narrow DST 31 to Hattonchâtel.

Hattonchâtel★

This once fortified village, built on a promontory, owes its name to a 9C castle belonging to a bishop of Verdun named Hatton. The neo-Romanesque town hall houses the **Musée Louise-Cottin** containing about 100 paintings by this artist (1907-74).

Situated at the end of a promontory, the former **castle**, dismantled in 1634 by order of Richelieu, was restored between 1924 and 1928. The view extends as far as Nancy.

Follow D 908 S to Woinville then turn left onto D 119 to Montsec.

Butte de Montsec★★

The **monument**★ at the top of an isolated hill (alt 275m/902ft) commemorates the American offensive of September 1918. From the memorial, the **view**★★ embraces the Woëvre Valley and Côtes de Meuse to the west and Lake Madine to the north.

Turn round and drive back along D 119 to Woinville then on to St Mihiel.

St-Mihiel★ – *See ST-MIHIEL.*

Address Book

PRACTICAL INFORMATION

Maison du Parc – *Logis Abbatiale, r. du Quai, BP35, 54702 Pont-à-Mousson – ☎03 83 81 67v67, Mon-Fri, 9am-6pm.*

Nature walks – *☎03 83 81 12v77.* From Apr-Sep, the Parc naturel régional de Lorraine (Lorraine regional nature reserve) organises countryside outings. In additon to rental cottages listed with **gîtes de France**, some WWF-appro ved **Panda gîtes** are to be found in Lorraine. An information pack including guides to local wildlife, observation equipment (binoculars and compass) and maps are provided. Rental via individual owners, or through the **Loisirs-Accueil de Moselle** reservation service, *☎03 87 37 57 69.*

Observatoire des Côtes de Meuse – *8 pl. de Verdun – 55210 Vieville-sous-les-Côtes – ☎03 29 89 58v64 – www.assoc.wanadoo.fr/observatoire.t.83/.* The Observatory is home to one of the most powerful telescopes in Europe. (Newton telescope with 83cm/33inch diameter).

Golf de Madine – *55210 Nonsard – ☎03 29 89 56 00.*

Lac de Madine – Madine Accueil – *55210 Nonsard – ☎03 29 89 32 50.* Tourist facilities and accommodation mainly on the lake's north-east bank.

Madine 1 – *Camping de Nonsard – 55210 Nonsard – ☎03 29 89 56 76.* Sailing harbour, restaurant, beach, bicycles for hire, and golf.

Madine 2 – *Camping d'Heudicourt – 55210 Nonsard – ☎03 29 89 36 08.* Beach, playground and horse-riding centre.

Madine 2-3 – *55210 Nonsard.* Village of gîtes, sailing school, indoor tennis courts, bird park and communal hall (events organised in evenings).

LUNÉVILLE

POPULATION 20 200

MICHELIN LOCAL MAP 307: J-7

Bedecked with wide streets, vast park and beautiful monuments, Lunéville sits between the River Meurthe and its tributary, the Vezouze.

▶ **Orient Yourself**: Lunéville is located 30km/18.6mi E of Nancy.

B. Kaufmann/MICHELIN

Lunéville ceramic "Bébé", King Stanislas' dwarf

A Bit of History

At the beginning of the 18C, the duke of Lorraine, **Leopold**, often stayed in the town. Later on, Lunéville was the favourite residence of King Stanislas (*see NANCY*); writers and artists, among them Voltaire, Montesquieu, Saint-Lambert and Helvetius flocked to his court. Stanislas died in the castle in 1766.

Sights

Château★

A fire in January 2003 destroyed most of the castle's collections. The South wing remains but the rest is in ruins. Reconstruc-

Address Book

PRACTICAL INFORMATION

Tourist Office – *South wing of the castle, 54300 Lunéville* – ☎*03 83 74 06 55 – www.ville-luneville.fr*

WHERE TO EAT

See the Legend for coin categories.

Les Bosquets – *2 r. des Bosquets – ☎03 83 74 00 14 – closed 15-30 Aug, Wed evening, Thu evening and Sun evening.* This small family restaurant is frequented by the locals and proposes several fixed menus, including one for children. The fixed-price lunch is particularly good value and the three simple dining rooms are often full.

WHERE TO STAY

Hôtel des Pages – *5 quai des Petits-Bosquets – ☎03 83 74 11 42* – – *36 rooms* – €6. A good place to stay if you are visiting the castle. Most of the rooms have been renovated in contemporary style, and these are the ones to choose. Bistro cooking is available at the Petit Comptoir restaurant.

SHOPPING

Manufacture de faïences de Lunéville-St-Clément – *1 r. Keller-et-Guérin – ☎03 83 74 07 58 – open Tue-Sat 10am-noon, 2-6.30pm.* Factory outlet and exhibtion of old earthenware.

Établissements Ciepielewski – *74 r. de Viller – ☎03 83 73 26 61.* Crystal engraving, demonstration, film and items for sale.

tion has begun and is expected to last ten years, beginning with the chapel which should be as "good as new" during 2006. This imposing castle surrounds a vast courtyard (*see Introduction: Art and Culture*). The **museum** (*located on the first floor of the château*) houses an important collection of ceramics.

Parc des Bosquets★

Laid out at the beginning of the 18C by Yves des Hours, the park was successively embellished by Leopold and Stanislas.

Synagogue

Rue Girardet. 1785.

LUXEUIL-LES-BAINS

POPULATION 8 414

MICHELIN LOCAL MAP 314: G-6

Luxeuil is a well-known spa resort offering visitors a wide choice of activities (concerts, casino, tennis, golf and swimming).
The town is proud of its lace-making tradition, an internationally successful activity in the 19C.

- **Orient Yourself**: Despite its eccentric position at the foot of the Vosges, Luxeuil-les-Bain lies on the N57 which skirts the town.
- **Don't miss**: A 4km/2.5mi long footpath, known as the "path of the Gauls," starts from the baths.

Sights

Hôtel du cardinal Jouffroy★

Abbot of Luxeuil, then archbishop of Albi and finally cardinal, Jouffroy was King Louis XI's favourite until the end of his life.

Maison François I★

This Renaissance edifice is not named after the king of France but after one of the abbots of Luxeuil Abbey.

G. Magnin/MICHELIN

Unique lacework

Ancienne abbaye St-Colomban★

Guided tours on request. ☎03 84 40 13 38.

The present basilica was built in the 13C and 14C on the site of an 11C church. Note the impressive **organ case**★.

Musée de la Tour des Échevins★

May-Sep: daily except Mon and Tue 2-6pm, Closed Nov and Jan, 25 Dec. 2€. ☎03 84 40 06v41.

The museum is housed in an imposing 15C crenellated building and displays splendid Gallo-Roman funeral monuments as well as votive **steles**★. From the top of the tower *(146 steps)*, there is an overall **view** of the town and the Vosges, Jura and Alps in the distance.

Address Book

PRACTICAL INFORMATION

Tourist Office – *R. Victor-Genoux, 70303 Luxeuil-les-Bains – ☎03 84 40 06v41.*

WHERE TO STAY

See the Legend for coin categories.

Hôtel Beau Site – *18 r. Georges-Moulimard – ☎03 84 40 14 67 – – 33 rooms – €7.50 – restaurant .* This imposing building is set in a flower garden a little way from the town centre, near the baths. Spacious rooms. Have breakfast on the terrace in fine weather, after a morning dip in the swimming pool.

WHERE TO PLAY

Casino Paradise – *16 av. des Thermes – ☎03 84 93 90 90 – open from 11am.* To finish off your evening, roulette, blackjack, traditional fruit machines and even a piano bar await you just a few minutes away from the baths.

SPA

Chaîne Thermale du Soleil – *3 r. des Thermes – ☎03 84 40 44 22 – Mar-Oct.* The spa treatment centre, rebuilt in red sandstone in the 18C, is surrounded by a beautiful shady park. In addition to the usual facilities, there is a highly modern aquatherapy centre open to all. Treatments available for phlebology and gynaecology. Revitalising treatments.

SHOPPING

The local speciality is jambon de Luxeuil. The proximity of Fougerolles explains the plethora of products made with cherries, including kirsch and Morello cherries.

Conservatoire de la dentelle – *Pl. de l'Abbaye, B.P 77 – ☎03 84 93 61 11 – dentelledeluxe@free.fr – 2-5.30pm Tue and Fri.* Dentelle de Luxeuil (lace) knew its finest hour in the 19C. Courses for beginners and experts all year round.

LIGNE MAGINOT★

MICHELIN LOCAL MAP 307: A-1 TO R-5, 315: G-1 TO M-3

Between the two world wars French people put all their pride and trust in this north-eastern shield, created by war minister Paul Painlevé and his successor André Maginot (1877-1932). The name is now synonymous with disaster.

A Bit of History

The lessons of the First World War led France's politicians to design a new defensive perimeter, skirting the new 1919 borders. Modern warfare with tanks, aircraft and the use of gas ruled out a defence system based on isolated strongholds or forts and a network of open trenches. Instead, plans were drawn to divide the length of the border into fortified areas consisting of a continuous frontline, 20-60km/12-37mi long, and underground fortifications adapted to modern warfare. The project was launched on 14 January 1930 as France's economy was gaining strength. Once completed, the Maginot Line consisted of mixed large works, infantry or artillery small works, shelters, strings of casemates and, behind a flood zone, simple pillboxes linked by barbed wire, minefields or anti-tank ditches and supporting one another by crossfire. Troops were meant to fill gaps in these fortified areas.

France's eastern wall

The number of works built in less than 10 years is amazing: 58 works along the north-east border, along with about 410 casemates and shelters for the infantry; 152 revolving turrets; 1 536 fixed cupolas with special armour-plating crowning the superstructures in reinforced concrete, the only parts of the fortifications that could be seen. Beneath, there were 100km/62mi of underground galleries. Yet from the very beginning, the project was cut back owing to lack of funds. From 1935 onwards, it was clear that the original purpose was being thwarted: several large works were replaced by pillboxes and casemates, artillery from the First World War was substituted for ultra-modern technology, and there were too few anti-tank guns. Large works were linked to an ammunition dump by electrified railway lines, today used to visit the galleries.

Defeat

By 1939 the Maginot Line, which did not extend along the northern border of France for political as well as economic reasons, was sadly under-equipped; moreover, it was not used as an offensive base during the Phoney War and was even deprived of part of its troops at the crucial moment when the German onslaught came in May-June 1940. It is hardly surprising that it did not fulfil the task assigned to it by its promoters.

Sights

The various works are described from the north-west to the south-east, from the Ardennes to the Rhine.

Visits often last 2hr. Wear warm clothing and walking shoes.

During the cold war, some of the structures formed part of NATO's defence system. In 1965 the French army decided to stop maintaining the Maginot Line, leaving several of the works to be restored voluntarily by former soldiers.

Works not described in this guide include Ouvrage du Galgenberg and Abri du bois de Cattenom, both located near Cattenom. *For more informa-*

WHERE TO STAY

See the Legend for coin categories.

Auberge de la Tour – *3 r. de la Gare – 57230 Bitche – 4km/2.5mi E of Simserhof on D 35 – ☎03 87 96 29 25 – closed 16-25 Feb, 14-30 Jul and Mon.* The Belle Époque-style dining rooms lend an undeniable charm to this traditional restaurant, which is housed in a turreted building. .

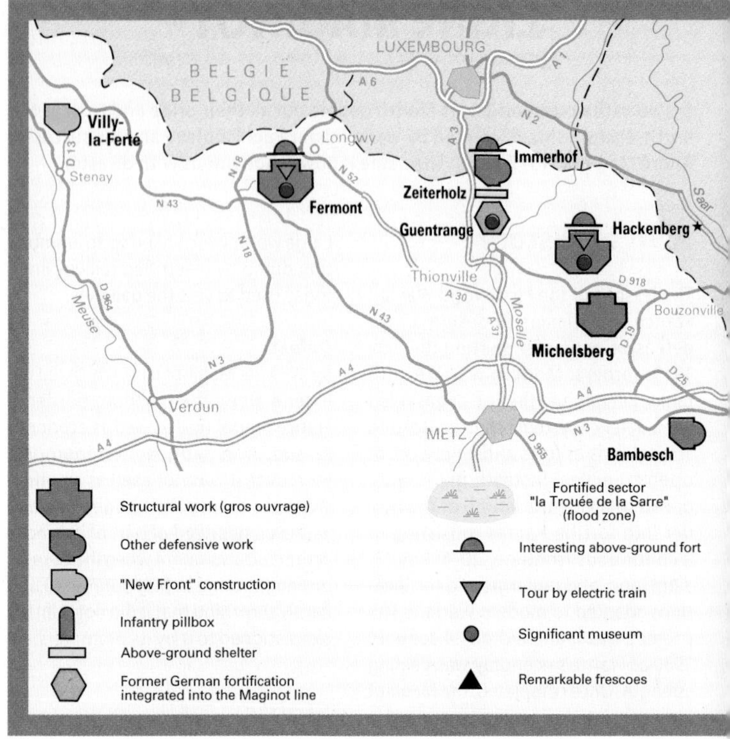

tion, contact the Association A15, allée des Platanes Sentzich, 57570 Cattenom, ☎03 82 55 34 69, www.forticat.com

Petit ouvrage de Villy-la-Ferté

18km/11mi NW of Montmédy along N 43 and D 44. Jul-Aug, guided tours (1hr 30min) daily except Mon, 2-5pm; week before Easter to late Jun and Sept-Oct, Sun and public holidays 2-5pm. €3.50. ☎03 24 22 06 72.

This is one of the new front constructions built from 1935 onwards with zig-zag entrances, revolving firing positions offering more protection, mixed-gun cupolas equipped and extremely precise anti-tank guns. Villy was meant to be the main western work of the Maginot Line, defending the Chiers Valley, but it was eventually reduced to a couple of infantry blocks flanked by two artillery casemates (one remains beside the road opposite the access path).

On 18 May 1940, the fort, no longer defended from the outside was encircled by German sappers; the more than 100 crew took refuge in the badly ventilated underground gallery and suffocated.

Outside, close to the field of anti-tank obstacles, a monument recalls this sacrifice. The overground constructions bear the mark of the attack: damaged cupolas, turret overturned by an explosion.

Gros ouvrage de Fermont

13km/8mi SW of Longwy along N 18 and D 172 to Ugny, then right onto D 17A and left onto D 174. Jul-mid-Sep, guided tours (2hr) daily, 2-4.30pm; Apr and mid-Sep-end-Oct, 2pm and 3.30pm; May-Jun, 3pm, Sat-Sun and public holidays 2 and 3.30pm; Apr-May, Sat-Sun and public holidays 2 and 3.30pm. Wear warm clothing and walking shoes. €5. ☎03 82 39 35v34.

This most western position on the Line consisted of two entrance blocks and seven combat blocks, including three equipped with artillery. In front, there is a monument dedicated to the troops.

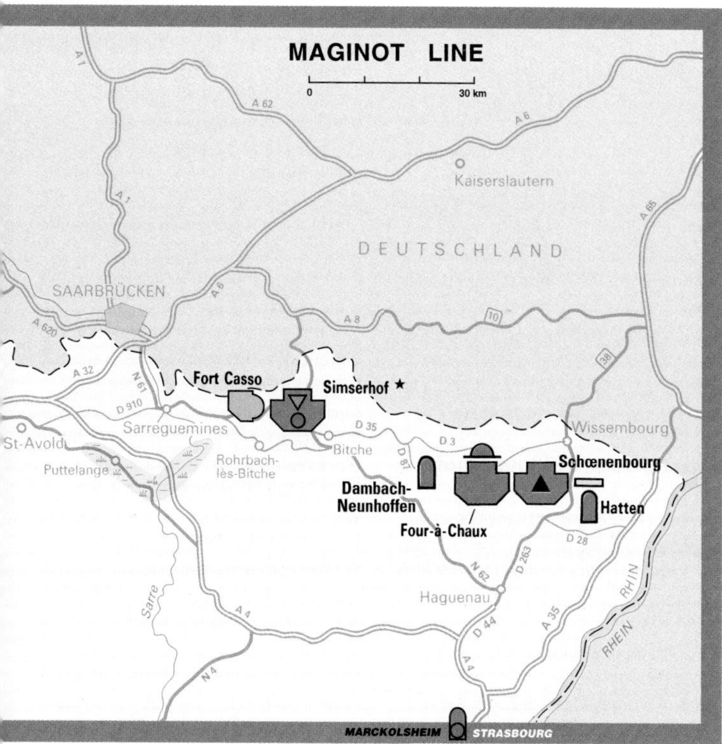

Ammunition elevators and small electric trains convey visitors to Block 4, an imposing artillery casemate covered with a concrete slab (3.5m/11.5ft thick, the maximum protection along the Maginot Line) and fitted with 75mm/3in guns. The barracks have been left as they were in 1940, with kitchens, a bakery, a cold room, a sick bay, dormitories, NCOs' and officers' quarters, showers, soldiers' quarters etc. The tour of the overground installations includes revolving turrets, cupolas with periscopes and automatic rifles, cupolas equipped with grenade-launchers and casemates. Damage caused by 1940 fighting is clearly visible: submitted to heavy shelling, then attacked by assault troops from 21 June onwards, Fermont did not suffer defeat but was compelled to surrender six days later by the French high command.

Fort de Guentrange

2km/1.2mi NW of Thionville.

Leave town along allée de la Libération then turn right towards Guentrange.

May-Sep, guided tours (1hr 30min) 1st and 3rd Sun of the month, 3pm. €2.50. ☎03 82 88 12 15. www.fort-guentrange.com

This former German stronghold, built from 1899 to 1906 and occupied by French troops in 1918, was integrated into the Maginot Line in 1939-40 to support the Thionville area. Some of its technical advantages were adopted throughout the Maginot Line: electrical machinery, telephone transmissions etc. Besides the power station and its still-functional eight diesel engines, the most spectacular feature of the fort is the 140m/153yd long barracks on four levels, suitable for 1 100 men.

Abri du Zeiterholz

14km/8.7mi N of Thionville.

Drive towards Longwy then turn right onto D 57. Go through Entrange and follow the signposts from the chapel.

May-Sep, guided tours (1hr 30min) 1st and 3rd Sun of the month, 3-5pm. €2 (no charge 1 May). ☎03 82 55 10 15.

The Zeiterholz is the only shelter along the Maginot Line that can be visited; it was built of reinforced concrete on two levels as an overground shelter, quite different from cave shelters in which men were accommodated in underground areas. Its occupants were entrusted with the defence of pillboxes scattered between the larger works and casemates.

Petit ouvrage de l'Immerhof

From the Zeiterholz shelter, go to Hettange-Grande via Entrange-Cité then turn left onto D 15 (signpost) which leads to the Immerhof.

Apr-Sep, guided tours only (1hr 30min) 2nd and 4th Sun of the month and public holidays 2-5pm. €3.50 (no charge 1 May). ☎03 82 53 09 61.

This is one of only two works along the Maginot Line (and the only one open to the public) which were built overground owing to the lie of the land and completely covered with concrete. Bedrooms, sick bay, washrooms etc are in excellent condition because the fort was, for a long time, used by NATO as one of its headquarters. Note the false cupolas intended to deceive the enemy.

Gros ouvrage du Hackenberg★

20km/12.4mi E of Thionville. Leave the town by D 918. The route is signposted from Metzervisse.

Mid-Jun-mid-Sep, guided tours only (2hr), at 3pm, Sat-Sun and public holidays 2-3.30pm (leaves every 15min); early Apr-mid-Jun and mid-Sep- late Oct, Sat-Sun and public holidays 2-3.30pm (leaves every 15min). €6 (children: €3). Wear warm clothing. ☎03 82 82 30v08.

The largest fort of the Maginot Line lies hidden in the heart of a forest covering 160ha/395 acres, near the village of Veckring. It illustrates the definition of fan-shaped forts given by André Maginot, "forts split into several parts placed at strategic points." The fort could accommodate 1 200 men and its power station could supply a town of 10 000 inhabitants.

On 4 July 1940, the crew here was forced to surrender by order of the liaison officer of the French government, whose members had retreated to Bordeaux.

Everything here is monumental: the massive blastproof door, the high-vaulted central station, miles of empty galleries and the huge power station all suggest an abandoned metropolis.

In order to understand the strategic importance of the fort, whose defence works overlooked both the Nied Valley and the Moselle Valley, drive up (or walk up if the weather is fine) to the fort chapel surrounded by ancient graves (*2.5km/1.5mi along the road starting from the end of the parking area; in front of the men's entrance, take the surfaced path on the left*). One can see the two observation towers emerging from the Sierck Forest. Behind the chapel, a path leads to a unique defence line (700m/765yd long) reinforced by five blockhouses.

Gros ouvrage du Michelsberg

22km/13.7mi E of Thionville along D 918 (access from the village of Dalstein). From Hackenberg, drive E along D 60, turn right onto D 60B then left onto D 118N to Dalstein.

Apr-Sep, guided tours (1hr 30min), Sun and public holidays 2-6pm. 1 Jan, 25 Dec. €3. ☎03 82 34 66 67.

The fort successfully withstood the attack launched against it on 22 June 1940 thanks to its own fire-power and crossfire from nearby forts. The crew only left Michelsberg on 4 July by order of the French high command and was granted military honours.

The medium-size fort includes an entrance block, two infantry and three artillery blocks. Artillery block no 6 has the famous turret fitted with a 135mm/5.3in gun which smashed the German attack on 22 June 1940; the gun, still in good condition, weighs 19t and was the largest gun along the Line.

Petit ouvrage du Bambesch

9km/5.6mi W of St-Avold along N 3. *Apr-Sep, guided tours only (1hr 30min), 2nd and 4th Sun of the month, 2.30, 3.30 and 4.30pm. Wear warm clothing. €4. ☎03 87 90 31 95.*

This is a good example of a work that was gradually modified owing to the shortage of funds: the number of blocks was reduced as was the artillery and the flanking support. The fort, limited to three infantry blocks, was attacked from the rear with heavy guns on 20 June 1940 and the cupolas were burst open. The crew, having heard of the tragedy of Villy-la-Ferté, chose to surrender.

The tour includes the barracks and combat blocks. The machine-gun turret is particularly narrow. Block no 2 bears the marks of the 1940 German assault.

Zone inondable de la Trouée de la Sarre

This section, situated between two large fortified sectors of the Maginot Line, that of Metz and that of the Lauter, was not defended by fortified works but by a flood zone controlled by a system of diked reservoirs. When the Saarland became German once more in 1935, this system was reinforced by a network of pillboxes and anti-tank obstacles.

Drive from St-Avold along N 56 to Barst (8km/5mi), turn right past the church then twice left onto rue de la Croix and the first path.

The path is lined with about a dozen pillboxes of the types built after 1935.

Leave the path and take the next one on the right; park the car.

Some 50m/164ft underwater, the concreted railway carriage is the last anti-tank obstacle of the Trouée de la Sarre.

Drive E out of Barst.

Between Cappel and Puttelange-aux-Lacs, the road overlooks some reservoirs that were used to flood the area.

Gros ouvrage du Simserhof★

4km/2.5mi W of Bitche along D 35 then the military road starting opposite the former barracks of Légeret. Park the car and take the shuttle or walk to the site (10min).

Guided tours (1hr), Jul-Aug, 10am-6pm; mid-Mar-late Jun and early Sep-mid-Nov, daily except monday10am-5pm. Wear warm clothing. €8. ☎03 87 96v39v40 or 03 87 06 16 16, www.simershof.fr.

The only parts visible from the outside are the south-facing entrance block, with its 7t armoured door and its flankers, and the firing cupolas surmounting the combat blocks scattered over several miles so as to overlook the plain below (a few can be seen from D 35A, Hottwiller road, 1km/0.6mi from D 35).

The underground part of the work is in two sections, both on the same level and linked by a 5km/3mi gallery fitted with a 1.7km/1mi long railway line.

A documentary film retracing the history of the Maginot Line begins the tour, then a fully automatic vehicle takes visitors on a journey 30m/98ft below the surface, punctuated by moving accounts of what the troops defending the Maginot Line went through during the Phoney War, their heroic and mostly useless resist-

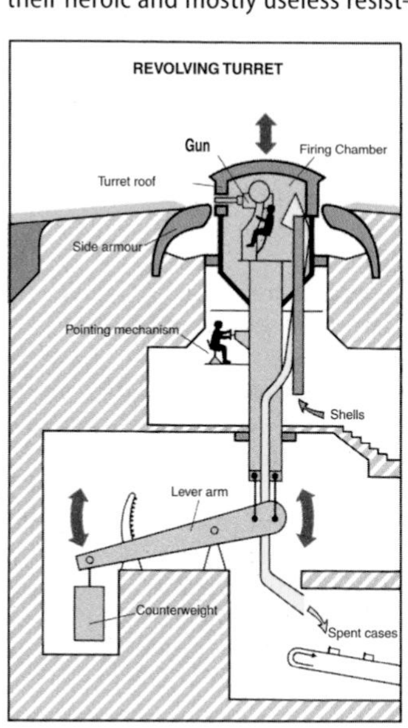

R. Mattès/MICHELIN

Lembach

ance to the German onslaught that followed and eventually led to defeat.

Fort Casso

Rohrbach-lès-Bitche, 18km/11mi E of Sarreguemines along N 62. Turn left onto D 84 1km/0.6mi before Rohrbach.

Mid-Jun-mid-Sep, guided tours (2hr) 10am and 2, 3 and 4pm, Sat 3pm, Sun and public holidays 3 and 4pm; mid-Mar-mid-Jun and mid-Sep-mid-Nov, 3pm; mid-Nov-late Nov, Sat-Sun, 3pm; Dec-Mar: 1st Sat-Sun of the month, 3pm. Wear warm clothing. €5. ☎03 87 02 70 41- www.casso.shorturl.com

There is a marked contrast between the Simserhof and this smaller front work, which features hammocks in the dormitories, a mixed-weapon turret (the structure dates from the First World War) and machine-gun turret in working order. Attacked on 20 June 1940, Fort Casso was able to resist with the support of the guns of Simserhof and to avoid the fate of Villy-la-Ferté but the crew was eventually ordered to surrender.

Casemate de Dambach-Neunhoffen

Between Neunhoffen and Dambach, 20km/12.4mi E of Bitche along D 35, then right onto D 87 and D 853.

May-Sep, Sun 2-5pm. Guided tours possible (20min) by prior appointment. €2. ☎03 88 09 21 46.

This very basic model, consisting of a small concrete block on one level defended one of the 12 dikes of the flooding system of the Schwarzbach Valley. It was not equipped with electricity; the ventilation system was operated by hand and foot pedal.

Four à Chaux de Lembach

15km/9.3mi W of Wissembourg along D 3 then D 27 on the way out of Lembach.

Jul-Sep, guided tours (1hr and 30min – 2hr) 10 and 11am and 2, 3, 4 and 5pm; May-Jun, 10am, 2, 3, and 4pm; late Mar-late Apr and early Oct-early Nov, 10am, 4 and 3pm; early Nov-late Mar, Sat-Sun, 10.30am and 2.30pm (daily from 27-30 Dec). €4.50. ☎03 88 94 43 16.

This medium-size artillery work (6 combat blocks, 2 entrances, crew: 580 men) has a unique inclined plane fitted with a rack, for the transport of small trucks between the fort and the entrance of the ammunition dump below. The museum includes a video room.

Ouvrage d'artillerie de Schœnenbourg

12km/7.5mi S of Wissembourg along D 264. Follow the signposts.

May-Sep, 2-4pm, Sun 9.30-11.30am and 2-4pm; Apr and Oct, Sat 2-4pm, Sun, 9.30-11.30am, 2-4pm (enquire during Easter school holidays). €5. ☎03 88 80 96 19.

This fort was one of the main components of the Haguenau fortified sector; its design took into consideration the experience gained at Verdun from 1916 to 1918; on completion in 1935, it was considered impenetrable.

On 20 June 1940, Schœnenbourg, having withstood the assault of a German division, was attacked by bombers and heavy mortars, the only fort to submit to such fire power. The fort managed to hold on until the armistice of 1 July.

Hatten

- *22km/13.7mi NE of Haguenau along D 263 then right onto D 28. From Schœnenbourg (14km/8.7mi), drive to Soultz-sous-Forêts along D 264 then turn left onto D 28.*

Abri de Hatten

Mid-Jun-mid-Sep, 10am-6pm; early Mar-mid-Jun and mid-Sep-11 Nov, Thu-Fri, 10am-noon and 2-6pm, Sat-Sun and public holidays, 10am-6pm. €4. ☎03 88 80 14 90 www.musee-abri-hatten.com
The half-buried casemate provided shelter for the troops defending areas situated between fortified works of the Maginot Line. There is also an open-air display of vehicles including a T34 Russian tank, a US Sherman tank, some jeeps, and lorries.

Casemate d'infanterie Esch

May-Sep, Sun, 10am-noon, 1.30-6pm. €2. ☎03 88 80 05 07. This casemate was situated in the heart of the battle that took place in January 1945 between American and German tanks, devastating Hatten and the nearby villages.

Mémorial musée de la Ligne Maginot du Rhin

- *Marckolsheim, 15km/9.3mi SE of Sélestat along D 424. Leave Marckolsheim by D 10.*

Mid-Jun-mid-Sep, 9am-noon and 2-6pm; mid-Mar-mid-Jun and mid-Sep-mid-Nov, Sun and public holidays, 9am-noon and 2-6pm. €2. ☎03 88 92 57 03. On the esplanade, note the Soviet gun, Sherman tank, machine-gun truck etc. Inside the eight compartments (beware of the metal steps) of the casemate, which were bravely defended by 30 men during the battle of 15-17 June 1940; Hitler visited it after the battle.

MARMOUTIER★

POPULATION 2 436
MICHELIN LOCAL MAP 315: I-4
6KM/3.7MI SOUTH OF SAVERNE

Marmoutier's former abbey church is one of the most remarkable examples of Romanesque architecture in Alsace.

- **Orient Yourself**: Marmoutier is 6km/3.7mi south of Saverne on N4 and accessible off the A4-E25 Paris-Metz-Strasbourg motorway, Saverne exit.

R. Mattès/MICHELIN

Part of the façade of the abbey church

A Bit of History

The abbey was founded in 590 by St Leobard, a disciple of St Columba (*see Luxeuil-les-Bains*). In the 8C it was named Maurmunster after one of its abbots, Maur. By the 14C, craftsmen and farmers lived in the shadow of the abbey and one of the oldest Jewish communities in Alsace was most probably invited by the abbots to deal with the abbey's trading activities. In 1792, during the Revolution, the abbey was abolished and the monks dispersed.

From **Sindelsberg** (*1.5km/0.9mi NW along the old Saverne road and a small surfaced road on the left)*, there is a lovely bird's-eye view of Marmoutier.

Sights

Abbey church★★

8.30-11.30am, 1.30-6pm. Guided tours possible: enquire at tourist office. 03 88 71 46 84.

The **west front**★★ (*See Introduction: Art and Culture*) is the most interesting part of the edifice. Built in local red sandstone, it consists of a heavy square belfry and two octagonal corner towers.

The narthex, with several domes, is the only Romanesque part of the interior. The transept houses some funeral monuments built in 1621 and the chancel contains beautiful carved wooden furniture. The 1710 organ by Silbermann is one of the finest in the whole of Alsace.

MARSAL

POPULATION 284

MICHELIN LOCAL MAP 307: K-6

Situated in the western part of the Parc naturel régional de Lorraine, an area once liable to flooding, this village has retained numerous Gallo-Roman ruins and a section of its defensive wall fortified by Vauban in the 17C, including an elegant gate, the Porte de France, which has been restored.

- **Orient Yourself**: Marsal lies 11km/6.8mi south-east of Château-Salins on the D38.; 60km/37mi south-east of Metz on the D955; 33km/20.5mi north-east of Nancy on the N74.

Visit

Maison du Sel

Apr-Sep, daily except monday 9.30am-noon, 2-7pm: Oct-Mar, daily except monday 9.30am-noon, 2-6pm 24 Dec-7 Jan and 1 May. €3. 03 87 01 16 75.

Housed in the Porte de France, part of Vauban's fortifications, the salt museum relates the history of this precious commodity, gathered since Antiquity in the salt mines of the Seille Valley.

A marked footpath leads to the nearby salt ponds.

Ancienne collégiale

This 12C collegiate church, built without a transept, like a basilica, has a Romanesque nave and a Gothic chancel.

Excursions

Vic-sur-Seille

7km/4.3mi W along D 38.

The administration of the diocese of Metz and the residence of the bishop were established here from the 13C to 17C. Visitors can still see the ruins of the bishop's castle. Vic is well known by art lovers as the birthplace of **Georges de La Tour** (1593-1652). A few of the artist's works are displayed in the town hall.

Kids The Base de loisirs de la Tuilière (leisure park), situated close to Vic-sur-Seille, offers fishing, swimming and other activities.

METZ★★★

POPULATION 123 776

MICHELIN LOCAL MAP 307: I-4

In the past, Metz played an important role as a religious centre (with nearly 50 churches) and a military stronghold; the wealthy medieval city has become an administrative and intellectual centre, with its university founded in 1972 and its European Ecological Institute.
Metz is also an attractive tourist centre with a choice of pleasant walks in the pedestrianised historic district, and interesting monuments, including one of the finest Gothic cathedrals in France, enhanced at night by special light effects. A tourist train takes visitors on a 45min ride through the town centre *(departure from place d'Armes).*
The poet Paul Verlaine (1844-96) paid homage to his native town in the *Ode to Metz* **written in 1892, shortly before his death.**

- **Orient Yourself**: Situated between the Côtes de Moselle and the Plateau Lorrain, Metz occupies a strategic position at the confluence of the Seille and the Moselle, which temporarily divides into several arms as it flows through the town. Metz is a major junction at the heart of Lorraine (with railway lines, roads and motorways, waterways and air traffic), only 50km/31mi from the border with Germany. Metz-Nancy-Lorraine airport lies 25km/15.5mi south of the town.
- **Don't Miss**: It would be a pity to leave town without admiring the Cathedral and its stained-glass windows.
- **Especially for Kids**: Those travelling with children might want to save time for a trip to the Walibi-Lorraine theme park *(15min drive from Metz).*

A Bit of History

In the 2C AD, Metz was already an important Gallo-Roman trading centre with 40 000 inhabitants and a 25 000-seat amphitheatre. It soon became a bishopric and, in 275, fortifications were built round the city to ward off Germanic invasions.
According to legend, **St Livier**, a local nobleman, fought the Huns then tried to christianise them but Attila had him beheaded; the saint picked up his head and climbed a mountain where he was

R. Mattès/MICHELIN

The Protestant church and the Cathedral on either side of the Moselle

Address Book

For coin ranges, see the Legend on the cover flap.

PRACTICAL INFORMATION

Tourist Office – *Pl. d'Armes – ☎03 87 55 53 76 – http://tourisme.mairie-metz.fr.*

Public transport: **Espace-bus** – *Pl. de la République – ☎03 87 76 31 11.* The Metz bus service operates all over Metz and the vicinity. **Visi'Pass**: one-day ticket (€3).

Guided tours – *Daily except Sun and public holidays 3 and 4pm, €4 (1hr), €7 (2hr), enquire at the tourist office or www.vpah.culture.fr* Metz organises guided tours-conferences by approved government guides to discover the town and its culture.

Tours for disabled visitors – The tourist office has designed a number of visits for disabled visitors so that they can discover the town, its monuments and museum. Wheelchairs loaned.

Illuminations – Metz was awarded the "Illuminated City" prize for its night-time street, square and monument illuminations (*brochure from the tourist office*).

Tourist train – *Early Apr to early Oct: leaves at 10.30am, 11.30am, 1, 2, 3, 4 and 5pm and sometimes at 6pm in summer, €5.50 (children: €3.50, lasts 45min, ☎03 87 73 03 08.*

WHERE TO EAT

La Migaine – *1-3 pl. St-Louis – ☎03 87 75 56 67 – closed 1-15 Aug.* You can eat at any time here, from morning to late afternoon. The tearoom in a pretty square surrounded by arcades serves copious breakfasts, meat pies, quiche Lorraine, cakes and tea – the choice is yours. Terrace in summer.

La Robe des Champs – *14 en Nouvelle rue – ☎03 87 36 32 19 – metz@larobedeschamps.com*. You can't miss the yellow façade and Provençal-style terrace of this pleasant bistro in a pedestrian town centre street. Potatoes, as the name infers ("In its jacket"), take pride of place in this friendly unpretentious establishment.

Restaurant du Pont-St-Marcel – *1 r. du Pont-St-Marcel – ☎03 87 30 12 29 – info@port-saint-marcel.com. A 17C* restaurant not far from St Étienne's cathedral, standing on piles beside a branch of the Moselle. Inside, an amusing contemporary fresco depicts a 17C fairground scene, complete with acrobats and theatre. The staff wear costumes to serve the local cuisine.

La Gargouille – *29 pl. de Chambre – ☎03 87 36 65 77 – closed Mon lunchtime, Tue evening and Wed.* Don't be fooled by the ordinary façade of this restaurant located down from the cathedral: behind it lies a sumptuous interior with velvet-covered seats, cosy little booths and 1900-style decor typical of the Nancy School, all making for a warm ambiance. The food is exceedingly refined: *carpaccio de fois gras au sel de Guérande*, or *joue de bœuf sauce vigneronne*. Highly professional service.

Restaurant du Fort – *Allée du Fort – 57070 St-Julien-lès-Metz – 8km/5mi NE of Metz, Bouzonville direction on D 3, then a minor road – ☎03 87 75 71 16 – closed 1-10 Jan, 24 Jul-9 Aug, Sun evening and Wed – booking advisable at weekends.* At the end of a forest track you will be amazed to discover this 1870 fort, evidence of the Moselle's turbulent history. Part of it has been restored to create a restaurant offering Lorraine cuisine.

L'Écluse – *45 pl. de la Chambre – ☎03 87 75 42 38 – closed 5-20 Aug, Sun and Mon.* A taste of Brittany, near the cathedral. The chef's enthusiasm for the region is evident in the decor, inspired by the Breton coast, with blue chairs and a menu that includes seafood served in an attractive, bright dining room.

Maire – *1 r. du Pont-des-Morts – ☎03 87 32 43 12 – restaurant.maire@wanadoo.fr – closed Wed lunchtimes and Tue.* There is a superb view of the Moselle from this town-centre restaurant. You will enjoy the young chef's carefully prepared dishes, whether in the salmon-pink dining room with its pale wood furniture or on the attractive terrace.

WHERE TO STAY

Chambre d'hôte Bigare – *23 r. Principale – 57530 Ars-Laquenexy – 9km/5.6mi E of Metz, Château-Salins direction then D 999 – ☎03 87 38 13 88 –* *– 2 rooms.* If the bustle of city life doesn't suit you, a short journey will bring you to this friendly local village house. Simple rooms and reasonable prices.

Hôtel de la Cathédrale – *25 pl. de la Chambre – ☎03 87 75 00 02 – hotelcathedrale-metz@wanadoo.fr – closed 1-15 Aug – 20 rooms – €11. A charming hotel situated in a lovely 17C* house that was completely restored in 1997. The attractive rooms have cast iron or cane beds, old parquet flooring and furniture, some of which is oriental. Most rooms face the cathedral, just opposite.

Hôtel Bleu Marine – *23 av. Foch – ☎03 87 66 81 11 – bleumarine-metz@bplorraine.fr – 62 rooms – €9.50 – restaurant* . In an old building (1906) in the station area, this hotel has been completely renovated. Its rooms are modern, spacious and well soundproofed. Buffet meals served. Gym and sauna.

ON THE TOWN

Café Jehanne-d'Arc – *Pl. Jeanne-d'Arc – ☎03 87 37 39 94 – Mon-Thu 11-2am, Fri 11-3am, Sat 3pm-3am – closed Sun.* One of the most famous cafés in Metz, for its decor, which still includes Gallo-Roman stones, 13C frescoes and 17C stencils. Terrace in the attractive square, where jazz concerts are organised in summer. Relaxed clientele, including students and intellectuals.

SHOWTIME

L'Arsenal – *Av. Ney – ☎03 87 39 92 00 or 03 87 74 16v16 – www.mairie-metz.fr/arsenal – Ticket sales: box office Tue-Sat 1-6pm, by phone Tue-Fri 9am-noon, 1-6pm, Sat 1-6pm – closed 31 Jul to 6 Aug, 29 Dec-1 Jan, 3-4 Jan, Mon and public holidays.* Built to a 1989 design by Ricardo Bofill within the walls of a former 19C arsenal, this concert hall is said to be the finest in Europe, with "fantastic acoustics," according to Rostropovitch. Apart from the main hall, which can seat 1 354, there is another hall seating 352, an exhibition gallery, and a museum/shop. With nearly 200 events each year, the programme is far-ranging, from contemporary dance to classical music, and from jazz to world music.

SPORTS & RECREATION

Golf *– R. de la Grange-aux-Ormes – Exit Metz-Centre, towards Montigny and Marly – 57155 Marly – ☎03 87 63 10 62 – www.grange-aux-ormes.com – summer 8am-11pm, winter 8am-7pm.*

Golf du Château de Chérisey *– 38 r. Principale – 57420 Chérisey – ☎03 87 52 70 18 – www.golfcherisey.com – 9am-6.30pm.* A lovely 18-hole golf course in a hilly, partially wooded site, dotted with ponds. Restaurant inside the château, putting-green and practice.

SHOPPING

Boucherie-charcuterie-traiteur Éric Humbert – *8 r. du Grand-Cerf – Quartier St-Louis – ☎03 87 75 09 38 – humbert.eric@wanadoo.fr – Mon-Thu 8.15am-12.40pm, 2.45-7pm, Fri-Sat 7.30am-12.40pm, 2.30-7pm – closed 2 weeks in Feb, July, Sun and public holidays.* Eric Humbert has been honoured by an award from a major design magazine, which is explained by the fact that this butcher/delicatessen/caterer is just as talented a designer as he is a cook. He himself designed the avant-garde counters in his otherwise traditional shop, adding a visual treat to that in store for the taste buds. Try the chicken and pistachio sausage, or the foie gras in aspic with Riesling.

CALENDAR

Fontaines Dansantes – *Jul-Sep: Fri, Sat, Sun and public holidays until dusk. Lac aux cynes, beneath the Esplanade (Bd Poincaré).* Dancing fountains...

Grandes Fêtes de la mirabelle – *Late August.* Election of festival ambassadress, folklore and fireworks.

Christmas Market – *December: parade of St Nicholas and the "bogey man." Christmas market: daily from late Nov to Christmas eve, on Place St-Louis, l'Esplanade, Place du Gén.-de-Gaulle and Place du Forum.*

buried. Later, the city became a favourite residences of Emperor Charlemagne.
In the 12C, Metz became a free city and the capital of a republic whose citizens were so wealthy that they often lent money to the dukes of Lorraine, the kings of France and even the Holy Roman emperors.
In 1552, the French king, Henri II, annexed the three bishoprics of Metz, Toul and Verdun. The Holy Roman Emperor, Charles V, then besieged Metz but all his attempts to take the city were thwarted by the young intrepid François de Guise.
During the 1870 war with Prussia, part of the French army was encircled in Metz and eventually surrendered, its general being booed by the population.
On 19 November 1918, French troops entered the town after 47 years of German occupation.
In 1944, Metz was at the heart of heavy fighting once more as it lay on the path of the advancing American Third Army. It was bitterly defended for two and a half months by the German forces stationed in the town; the surrounding forts were pounded by heavy allied artillery but the town was spared in memory of La Fayette who commanded the garrison in 1777. American troops eventually entered Metz on 19 November 1944, 26 years to the day after French troops had entered the town at the end of the First World War.

Sights

Cathédrale St-Étienne★★★

Allow 1hr 30min. Guided tours possible on request to the Association de l'Oeuvre de la cathédrale, 2 pl. de Chambre or to the office inside the cathedral. ☎03 87 75 54 61.

The entrance of the cathedral is on **place d'Armes**. From the square, there is a fine view of the south side of the cathedral. One is impressed by the harmonious proportions of the cathedral, built of yellow stone from Jaumont like several other edifices in Metz. The north and south sides are most remarkable.
In order to appreciate the south side, it is better to stand on the pavement running along the town hall on the opposite side of the square.
The church is flanked by two symmetrical towers, the chapter tower on the north side and the **Tour de Mutte** on the south side; both built from the 13C onwards. The Tour de Mutte owes its name to the famous bell known as Dame Mutte, dating from 1605 and weighing 11t; the name is derived from the verb *ameuter* which originally meant "to call for a meeting." The bell used to ring for all major events and even today, it sounds the 12 strokes of midday and every quarter hour on election days.

Enter through the Virgin's doorway, located to the left of the Tour de Mutte.

The sides of the Notre-Dame-la-Ronde portal (second bay on the north side) are decorated with carved draperies and small 13C low-relief sculptures: note the supernatural animals on the left, and, on the right, the scenes from the Life of King David, St Margaret and St Stephen.
Inside the cathedral, the most striking feature is the height of the nave (41.77m/137ft), dating from the 13C and 14C. The impression of loftiness is enhanced by the fact that the aisles are rather low. This nave is, with that of Amiens Cathedral and after the chancel of Beauvais Cathedral, the highest of any church in France.
A frieze decorated with draperies and foliage runs all the way round the edifice, between the triforium and the impressively large high windows.
Note the overhanging 16C choir organ (**1**) situated at the end of the nave, on the right-hand side. Its unusual position enhances its outstanding acoustic features.

Stained-Glass Windows★★★

These form a splendid ensemble covering more than 6 500m²/7 774sq yd. They are the work of famous as well as unknown artists, completed or renewed through the centuries: 13C (**2**) and 14C (Hermann from Munster), 16C (Theobald from Lyxheim **3**, followed by Valentin

Bousch **4**), 19C and 20C (Pierre Gaudin, Jacques Villon, Roger Bissière **5**, Marc Chagall **6** and **7**).

The west front is adorned with a magnificent 14C rose-window by Hermann from Munster, which unfortunately lost its base part when the large doorway was built in 1766.

The openwork design of the edifice is even more apparent in the **transept** built in the late 15C and early 16C. The stained-glass window in the north part of the transept (**3**) is decorated with three roses; that in the south part of the transept (**4**) is by Valentin Bousch, an artist from Strasbourg. These two windows light up the cathedral in a remarkable way.

The eastern wall of the south part of the transept has the oldest stained-glass windows (**9**) which illustrate six scenes from the Life of St Paul (13C).

Note the starlike vaulting of the middle part of the transept.

The stained-glass window in the western wall of the north part of the transept, designed by Chagall in 1963, depicts scenes from the Garden of Eden (**6**).

In the ambulatory, two more stained-glass windows by Chagall can be seen above the sacristy door and the door leading to the Tour de la Boule d'Or on the left. Designed in 1960, they illustrate scenes from the Old Testament (Jacob's Dream, Abraham's Sacrifice, and Moses and David).

Crypt

Tue-Sat, 10am-noon, 2-5pm; Sun 2-5pm. 15 Aug and mornings of Jan 1, Good Friday, Ascension and Whit Monday. €2. ☎03 87 75 54 61.

This was adapted in the 15C to preserve some elements from the 10C Romanesque crypt, the damaged tympanum of the 13C Virgin's doorway as well as various objects, carvings and reliquaries from the treasury.

Note in particular a 16C **Entombment,** originally in the church of Xivry-Circourt, and, hanging from the vaulting, the famous Graoully, the legendary dragon slain by St Clement, which used to be carried in procession round the town until 1785. In the chancel, St Clement's episcopal throne (**8**), carved out of a cipolin-marble column, dates back to Merovingian times.

Treasury

access as for Crypt.

This is housed in the 18C sacristy. The most remarkable items include St Arnoult's gold ring (primitive Christian art), a 12C enamel reliquary, 12C and 13C ivory crosiers, Pope Pius VI's mule, and precious religious objects.

The Gueulard, a 15C carved-wood head, originally decorating the organ, used to open its mouth (hence its name) when the lowest note was sounded.

During the storm in December 1999, a pinnacle weighing several tonnes was torn off, fell through the roof and lodged itself in the ceiling of the sacristy.

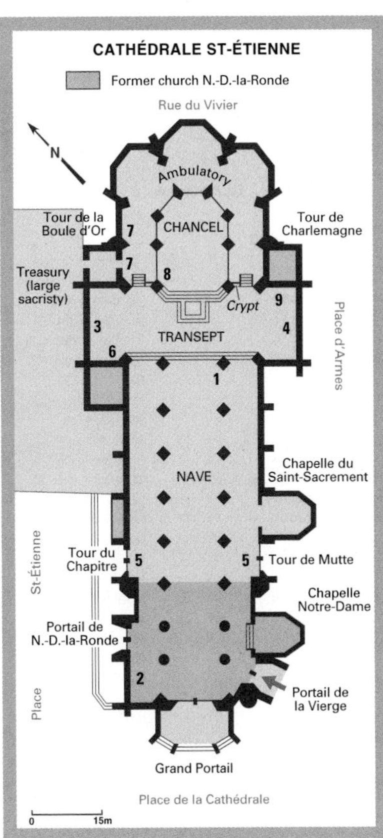

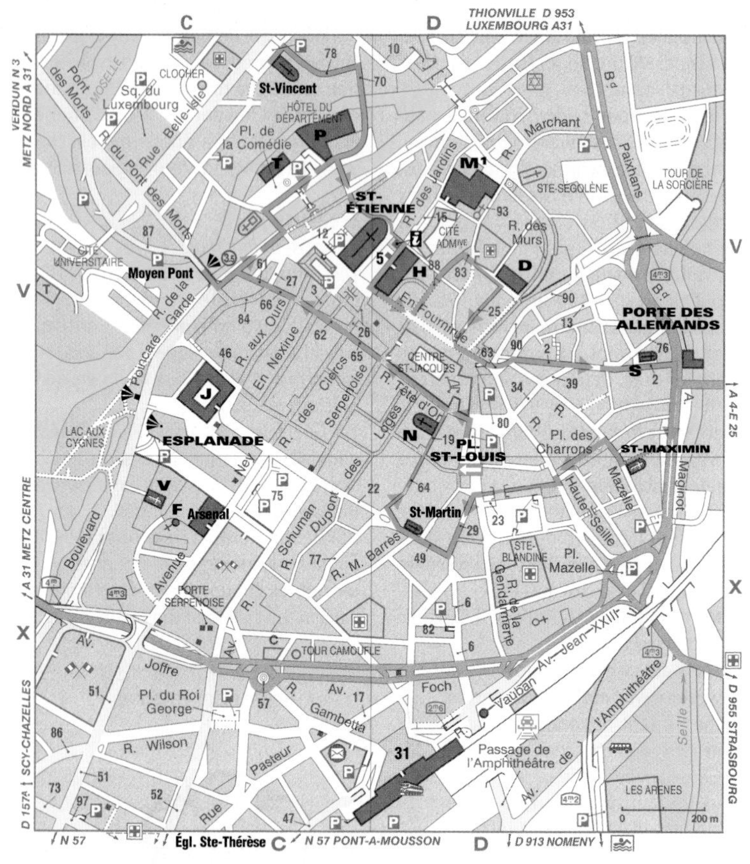

METZ

Street	Grid	No.
Allemands R. des	DV	2
Ambroise-Thomas R.	CV	3
Amphithéâtre Av. et Passage de l'	DX	
Armes Pl. d'	DV	5
Augustins R. des	DX	6
Barrès R. M.	CDX	
Belle-Isle R.	CV	
Chambière R.	DV	10
Chambre Pl. de	CV	12
Champé R. du	DV	13
Chanoine-Collin R.	DV	15
Charlemagne R.	CX	17
Charrons Pl. des	DV	
Chèvre R. de la	DX	19
Clercs R. des	CV	
Coëtlosquet R. du	CX	22
Coislin R.	DX	23
Comédie Pl. de la	CV	
Dupont des Loges R.	DX	
En Fournirue	DV	
En Nexirue	CV	
Enfer R. d'	DV	25
Fabert R.	CV	26
Faisan R. du	CV	27
La-Fayette R.	CX	47
Foch Av.	CDX	
Fontaine R. de la	DX	29
Gambetta R.	CX	
Garde R. de la	CV	
Gaulle Pl. du Gén.-de	DX	31
Gendarmerie R. de la	DX	
Georges Pl. du Roi	CX	
Grande-Armée R. de la	DV	34
Hache R. de la	DV	39
Haute Seille R.	DVX	
Jardins R. des	DV	
Jean XXIII Av.	DX	
Joffre Av.	CX	
Juge-Pierre-Michel R. du	CV	46
Lasalle R.	DX	49
Lattre-de-T. Av. de	CX	51
Leclerc-de-H. Av.	CX	52
Luxembourg Square du	CV	
Maginot Bd A.	DVX	
Marchant R.	DV	
Mazelle Pl.	DX	
Mazelle R.	DVX	
Mondon Pl. R.	CX	57
Morts Pont des	CV	
Moyen-Pont	CV	
Murs R. des	DV	
Ney Av.	CX	
Ours R. aux	CV	
Paix R. de la	CV	61
Paixhans Bd	DV	
Palais R. du	CV	62
Paraiges Pl. des	DV	63
Parmentiers R. des	DX	64
Pasteur R.	CDX	
Petit-Paris R. du	CV	65
Pierre-Hardie R. de la	CV	66
Poincaré Bd	CVX	
Pont-Moreau R. du	CDV	70
Prés.-Kennedy Av.	CX	73
République Pl. de la	CX	75
St-Eucaire R.	DV	76
St-Gengoulf R.	CX	77
St-Georges R.	CV	78
St-Louis Pl.	DVX	
St-Simplice Pl.	DV	80
St-Thiébault Pl.	DX	82
Ste-Croix Pl.	DV	83
Ste-Marie R.	CV	84
Salis R. de	CX	86
Schuman Av. R.	CX	
Sérot Bd Robert	CV	87
Serpenoise R.	CV	
Taison R.	DV	88
Tanneurs R. des	DV	90
Tête d'Or R. de la	DV	
Trinitaires R. des	DV	93
Vauban R.	DX	
Verlaine R.	CX	97
Wilson R.	CX	

Ancien couvent des Récollets	DV	D	Église St-Eucaire	DV	S	Esplanade	CV	
Arsenal	CX		Église St-Martin	DX		Hôtel de ville	DV	H
Cathédrale St-Étienne	CDV		Église St-Maximin	DVX		La Cour d'Or, musées	DV	M[1]
Chapelle des Templiers	CX	F	Église St-Pierre-aux-Nonnains	CX	V	Palais de Justice	CV	J
Église Notre-Dame-de-l'Assomption	DV	N	Église St-Vincent	CV		Porte des Allemands	DV	
			Église Ste-Thérèse	CX		Préfecture	CV	P
						Théâtre	CV	T

Musée de la Cour d'Or★★

Allow around 2hr. Daily except Tue, 9am-5pm, Sat-Sun, 10am-5pm. Some public holidays. €4.60 (under 18-yr-olds: no charge), no charge 1st Sun of month. ☎03 87 68 25 00.

The museum is housed in the buildings of the former Couvent des Petits Carmes (17C), the Grenier de Chèvremont (15C) and in several rooms that link or prolong this monumental ensemble. Elements of the antique baths are displayed in situ in the basement.

Extended in 1980, the museums were organised along the most modern lines and offer a unique journey into the past.

Section archéologique★★★

The exhibits, which were mostly found during excavations in Metz and the surrounding region, testify to the importance of the city, a major road junction in Gallo-Roman times and a thriving cultural centre during the Carolingian period.

Social life during the **Gallo-Roman period** is illustrated by remains of the large baths, the town wall and the drainage system as well as by everyday items (relating to meals, garments, jewellery and trade).

Various glass-cases are devoted to the methods of producing ironwork, bronze-work, ceramics and glasswork.

Metz was the capital of Austrasia during the **Merovingian period** illustrated by graves, sarcophagi and tombstones bearing Christian emblems, jewels and objects of daily life (crockery), and damascened metal objects.

In the rooms devoted to **palaeo-Christian archaeology**, there is an important ensemble dating from the early Middle Ages, surrounding the chancel of St-Pierre-aux-Nonnains. This stone screen comprises 34 carved panels admirably decorated and extremely varied.

Architecture et cadre de vie

Exhibits in this section illustrate daily life, building techniques and decorative styles in the past, up to the Renaissance period. There are reconstructed façades including the front of a house decorated with four busts. Several mansions and ordinary houses have been reconstructed round the museum courtyard.

Grenier de Chèvremont★

This well-preserved edifice dating from 1457 was once used to store the tithe taken on cereal crops.

Note in particular the beautiful collection of regional religious art: *Pietà*, a recumbent Virgin Mary, and 15C statues of St Roch and St Blaise.

Beaux-Arts

First and second floors. Interesting paintings from the French School (Delacroix, Corot, Moreau), and the German, Flemish and Italian Schools. The School of Metz (1834-70) is mainly represented by its leading exponent, the painter, pastellist and stained-glass artist Laurent-Charles Maréchal.

The modern-art gallery contains works by artists including Bazaine, Alechinsky, Dufy, and Soulages.

Grenier de Chèvremont

R. Mattès/MICHELIN

View of the Moyen Pont, quai Vautrin and St-Étienne

Collection militaire

Gathered by Jacques Onfroy de Bréville (JOB), who specialised in the illustration of school manuals and history books, this collection consists of weapons, uniforms and accessories from the late 18C and the 19C.

Walking Tour

Esplanade★

This is a splendid walk laid out at the beginning of the 19C on the site of one of the citadel's moats: from the terrace, there is a fine view of Mount St-Quentin crowned by a fort and of one of the arms of the River Moselle.

Palais de Justice

Built in the 18C, during the reign of Louis XVI, this edifice was intended to be the military governor's palace but the Revolution changed all that. Sentry boxes on either side of the entrance remind visitors of the military origins of the building. In the courtyard, there are two interesting low-relief sculptures: one shows the Duc de Guise during the 1552 siege of the town, the other celebrates the 1783 peace treaty between England, France, the USA and Holland.

Walk across the gardens to the arsenal.

Arsenal

The walls of the 19C arsenal were partially used to build this ultra-modern centre dedicated to music and dance. Designed by Ricardo Bofill, the large hall fitted with a central stage was intended for a variety of shows. Its special shape and elaborate acoustics were inspired by the Musikverein in Vienna. Surrounded by warm wood panelling, the 1 500 spectators get the impression that they are at the centre of a huge musical instrument.

Old Town

Place St-Louis★

Situated in the heart of the old town, the rectangular place St-Louis is lined on one side with buttressed arcaded buildings dating from the 14C, 15C and 16C that once housed the money-changers' shops. At the end, on the corner of rue de la Tête-d'Or, note the three golden Roman heads protruding from the wall, which gave the street its name.

Follow rue de la Tête-d'Or to the River Moselle.

Moyen Pont★

Pleasant **view**★ of the arms of the River Moselle, the islands, the neo-Romanesque Protestant church (1901) and the two small bridges reflected in the water.

Walk to place de la Comédie.

The 18C **theatre** overlooking place de la Comédie is the oldest in France; opposite stands the **Hôtel du Département**, also dating from the 18C.
Walk round to the back of the Hôtel du Département and along rue du Pont Moreau then rue St-Georges and finally rue St-Vincent.

Église St-Vincent

The Gothic chancel of the church, flanked by two elegant steeples, is in striking contrast with the west front, rebuilt in the 18C and reminiscent of that of St-Gervais-St-Protais in Paris *(outside only)*.

Walk back to the Hôtel du Département and cross the river.

Place d'Armes

The square was designed in the 18C by Jacques François Blondel on the site of the former cloisters. The **town hall**, facing the south side of the cathedral has an elegant Louis XVI façade with two pediments. The two remaining sides of the square are lined with the district hall, a former guard-house whose pediment is decorated with trophies, and with the regional parliament, now a residential building.

Follow rue En-Fournirue to the right of the town hall then turn left onto rue Taison. Turn right when you get to place Ste-Croix.

The **Ancien couvent des Récollets** (former convent) now houses the European Ecological Institute. The 15C cloisters have been restored.

Follow rue d'Enfer opposite and turn left onto rue En-Fournirue to place des Paraiges then continue along rue des Allemands.

Église St-Eucaire

The fine square belfry dates from the 12C and the west front from the 13C. The small 14C nave with its huge pillars looks out of proportion. The aisles, lined with low arcades, lead to unusual 15C chapels, surmounted by pointed vaulting converging on carved corbels.

Porte des Allemands★

This massive fortress, which formed part of the town walls running along the Moselle and the dual-carriageway ring road south and east of Metz, straddles the River Seille. It gets its name from a 13C order of German hospitallers.
There are in fact two gates: the first one, dating from the 13C and standing on the town side, is flanked by two round towers topped with slate pepper-pot roofs; the other tower, facing the opposite way, dates from the 15C. The edifice was remodelled in the 19C.
North of the Porte des Allemands, the fortified wall continues for another 1.5km/0.9mi, with numerous towers at regular intervals: Tour des Sorcières (Witches' Tower), Tour du Diable (Devil's Tower), Tour des Corporations (Guilds' Tower). A path follows the ramparts, first along the Seille then along the Moselle.

Walk along boulevard Maginot and turn onto the fourth street on your right.

Église St-Maximin★

A fine carved head of Christ decorates the central pillar at the entrance. The beautiful chancel is decorated with stained-glass windows by Jean Cocteau. Note also the 14C-15C Chapelle des Gournay, named after a prominent local family, which opens onto the south transept through two basket-handled arches.

Follow rue Mazelle to place des Charrons. Cross rue Haute-Seille and walk along a street that runs under a bridge, then turn left onto rue de la Fontaine and right onto rue Lasalle.

Église St-Martin-aux-Champs

A Gallo-Roman wall, once part of the town's fortifications, forms the base of the church; it is visible on both sides of the entrance. The most attractive feature of this 13C church is its very low **narthex**★ whose three sections, covered with pointed vaulting resting on four Romanesque pillars surrounded by colonnettes, open onto the lofty nave. The 15C transept and chancel have stained-glass windows dating from the 15C, 16C and 19C, an organ case in Louis XV style, various tombstones and a fine sculpture representing the Nativity (in the north transept).

▶ *Walk past the church and turn right onto rue des Parmentiers which runs onto rue de la Chèvre.*

Église Notre-Dame-de-l'Assomption

This Jesuit church was erected in 1665 but the west front was completed in the 18C. The interior, decorated in the 19C, is lined with rich wood panelling. The Rococo confessionals come from the German city of Trier, as does the Baroque organ built by Jean Nollet.

▶ *Continue along rue de la Chèvre then turn right onto rue de la Tête-d'Or to return to place St-Louis.*

Modern Town

After 1870, William II wanted to turn Metz into a prestigious German city. He entrusted his plan to Kröger, an architect from Berlin, who used pink and grey sandstone, granite and even basalt. The new district includes the wide avenue Foch, the chamber of commerce, the old station (1878), and the post office.

Place du Général-de-Gaulle★

The **station** (1908) a huge neo-Romanesque edifice (300m/328yd long), profusely decorated (capitals, low-relief sculptures), is one of several buildings erected by the Germans at the beginning of the 20C to assert the power of their empire. The vast pedestrianised semicircular area in front of the station is lit by lamp posts designed by Philippe Stark.

Église Ste-Thérèse-de-l'Enfant-Jésus

Entrance along avenue Leclerc-de-Hauteclocque. 🕓 9am-noon, 3-7pm.
Consecrated in 1954, this large church, topped by a 70m/230ft mast known as the pilgrim's staff, has an imposing nave and fine stained-glass windows by Nicolas Untersteller.

Additional Sights

Église St-Pierre-aux-Nonnains★

🕓 Jun-Sep, daily except Mon, 2-6pm. ☎03 87 39 92 00. By Esplanade.
Around 390, during the reign of Emperor Constantine, a **palæstra** or gymnasium was built on this site. When Attila plundered the town in 451, the edifice was partially destroyed, but the walls built of rubble stones reinforced at regular intervals by ties of red bricks were spared and used again in the building of a chapel c 615. The nuns settled here.
Excavations undertaken in the 20C enabled archaeologists to reconstruct the history of this ancient building, which is believed to be the oldest church in France. Important repair work has made it possible to restore the volume of the original building.

Chapelle des Templiers

♿ 🕓 Jun-Sep, daily except Mon and holidays, 2-6pm; Oct-May, Sat-Sun, 2-6pm. No admission charge. ☎03 87 39 92 00.
This chapel, built at the beginning of the 13C by the Knight Templars established in Metz since 1133, marks the transition between the Romanesque and Gothic styles. The building is shaped like an octagon, each side except one having a small rounded window; the last side opens onto a square chancel prolonged by an apse. Buildings of this type are rare and this chapel is, in fact, the only one of its kind in Lorraine. The paintings are all modern except one which decorates a recess on the right (14C).

Excursions

Scy-Chazelles

4km/2.5mi W along D 157A then turn right.

Robert Schuman's house is located in the village, near the 12C fortified church where the "father of Europe" (1886-1963) is buried. This austere building, characteristic of Lorraine, conveys an impression of calm and serenity which this generous and modest man found conducive to meditation. His library, diplomas and decorations are among Schuman's personal mementoes.
In the park, beyond the terrace, there is a sculpture by Le Chevallier entitled *The European Flame.*

Vallée de la Canner

Departure from Vigy, 15km/9mi NE along D 2 then D 52.

From Vigy to Hombourg *(12km/7.5mi)*, a small tourist train, pulled by a real steam engine, follows the remote Canner Valley through a densely forested part of the Lorraine plateau.

Château de Pange

10km/6mi E along D 999, D 70 and D 6.

Built between 1720 and 1756 on the site of an ancient fortress, along the banks of the Nied, a small tributary of the Moselle, the castle has retained its plain Classical façade.
The dining room in Louis XV style is still decorated with green wood panelling and a primitive regional stove.

Groupe fortifié de l'Aisne

14km/8.7mi S along D 913.

The former Wagner Fortress, built by the Germans between 1904 and 1910, formed part of the outer defences of Metz. Renamed Aisne after 1918, it was not, unlike Guentrange, incorporated into the Maginot Line (*see Ligne MAGINOT*); during the Second World War, it was only used to store torpedo heads. This type of fortified complex replaced massive fortresses at the end of the 19C; it consisted of several works linked by underground galleries. The Aisne for instance comprises four infantry blocks with up to three levels of underground barracks, three artillery blocks fitted with revolving turrets suitable for heavy guns and about 15 armour-plated observatories.

Sillegny

20km/12.5mi S along D 5.

This village in the Seille Valley has a small 15C **church**, which looks unassuming but is entirely covered with **murals★** dating from 1540. Note the warmth of the colours and the great number of naive details in these murals representing the Apostles, the Evangelists, the Tree of Jesse (in the chancel on the right), the Last Judgement above the entrance and the huge St Christopher, 5m/16ft high.

Gorze

18km/11mi SW along D 57, then right onto D 6B.

This village, which developed round a Benedictine abbey founded in the 8C, has retained a number of old Renaissance residences dating from the 17C and 18C. The surrounding forest offers a choice of fine walks along a network of marked paths.
The **Maison de l'Histoire de la Terre de Gorze** (*Jun-Sep, 2-6pm; Apr and Oct, Sat-Sun, 2-6pm. €2, under 12-yr-olds: €1.50. ☎03 87 52 04 57*) relates episodes of Gorze's prosperous past.
The **Église St-Étienne** is Romanesque on the outside and Early Gothic (late 12C and early 13C).
The former **abbatial palace**, built in 1696, is a Baroque edifice designed by Philippe-Eberhard of Lowenstein and Bavaria; note the staircase.

Aqueduc romain de Gorze à Metz

12km/7.5mi SW. Drive along N 3 to Moulins then continue along D 6 to Ars-sur-Moselle.

Seven arches of this 1C AD Roman aqueduct, which spanned the Moselle, are still standing alongside D 6, south of **Ars-sur-Moselle** (west bank). Excavations have revealed pipes and sections of masonry. In **Jouy-aux-Arches** (east bank), another 16 arches, in a better state of preservation, span N 57.

Kids **Parc d'attractions Walibi-Schtroumpf** – See *AMNÉVILLE: Excursions*.

MÉANDRES DE LA MEUSE★★

MICHELIN LOCAL MAP 306: K-3/4

The River Meuse takes its source in the foothills of the Plateau de Langres, not far from Bourbonne-les-Bains, at an altitude of only 409m/1 342ft; it flows into the North Sea 950km/590mi farther on, forming with the Rhine a common delta along the coast of The Netherlands where it is known as the Maas.

Geographical Notes

The course of this peaceful river often changes, for instance when it flows along the bottom of the ridge known as the Hauts de Meuse, or crosses a large alluvial plain (beyond Dun-sur-Meuse), or meanders through the Ardennes. The section from Charleville-Mézières to Givet is the most picturesque part of the river's journey through France: the Meuse has dug its deep and sinuous course through hard schist, which is sometimes barren and sometimes forested (hunting for wild boar and roe-deer is a favourite pastime in the area. The railway line linking Charleville and Givet follows the river, which is linked to the Aisne by the Canal des Ardennes dug in the mid-19C. River traffic is reduced to barges not exceeding 300t because the rate of flow is insufficient and the river bed not deep enough in places, whereas downriver from Givet, the river has been adapted to allow barges of up to 1 350 tonnes through.

Driving Tours

The Four Aymon Brothers—

1 Round tour from Charleville-Mézières

57km/35mi – allow 4hr

Leave Charleville along D 1 which soon follows the Meuse.

Nouzonville

This industrial centre (metalworks and mechanical industries), situated at the confluence of the Meuse and the Goutelle, follows a long-standing nail-making tradition introduced in the 15C by people from Liège running away from the duke of Burgundy, Charles the Bold.

Bogny-sur-Meuse

Bogny-sur-Meuse, which stretches for 7km/4.3mi on both sides of the river, evolved in 1967 from the merging of three villages, Braux, Levrézy and Château-Regnault. There are several marked footpaths starting from the tourist office.

The **Sentier Nature et Patrimoine du Pierroy** (the Pierroy Nature and Heritage Trail) leads past typical geological features (conglomerate and schist) and the remains of quartzite quarries, offering fine views of the Meuse Valley.

Continue along D 1 to Braux.

Braux

The former collegiate **church** has retained its Romanesque apse, chancel and transept but the nave and the aisles date from the 17C and 18C. Note the rich 17C marble altars with low-relief sculptures and above all the fine 12C christening font, carved out of blue stone from Givet and decorated with grotesques.

Cross the River Meuse.

From the bridge, there is an interesting vista on the left of the Rocher des Quatre Fils Aymon (alt 260m/853ft).

Levrézy

A former factory houses the **Musée de la Métallurgie** (*Jul-Aug, 10am-noon, 2-6pm; May-Jun and early Sep-mid-Sep, 2-6pm; €3; 03 24 35 06 71*) which illustrates the making of nuts and bolts with tools and machines still in working order (forge, and planing and milling machines).

Château-Regnault

Once the main centre of a principality, Château-Regnault had its castle razed to the ground by Louis XIV. The village lies at the foot of the **Rocher des Quatre Fils Aymon**★ whose outline formed by four sharp points suggests the legend of the Four Aymon Brothers escaping from Charlemagne's men on their famous horse Bayard.

The **Centre d'exposition des Minéraux et Fossiles des Ardennes** (*Mid-Jun-late Sep, daily except Mon, 2-6pm; €2; 03 24 32 05 02*) displays rocks from the Ardennes region together with fossils from various parts of the world.

In order to reach the **Monument des Quatre Fils Aymon**, drive up rue Léon-Bosquet then rue du Château to the parking area.

A footpath *(300m/328yd)* leads to an artificial ledge on the site of the former Château Regnault (12C) of which nothing remains. Steps lead up to the monument: from there, the **view** extends over the meanders of the Meuse, the factories lining its course, workers' housing estates and private mansions.

Continue along D 1 which runs beneath the railway line before crossing the Semoy that flows into the Meuse at Laval-Dieu.

Laval-Dieu

See MONTHERMÉ.

Turn right onto D 31 to Thilay.

The road follows the Semoy Valley (*see Vallée de la SEMOY*).

Address Book

For coin ranges, see the Legend on the cover flap.

WHERE TO STAY AND EAT

Debette – *Pl. de la Mairie – 08320 Aubrives – 03 24 41 64 72 – contact@hotel-debette.com – closed 18 Dec-3 Jan, Sun evening and Mon lunchtime.* This restaurant opposite the town hall has a large, bright dining room and classic, unpretentious cooking. Attic rooms under the sloping ceiling on the second floor.

Le Moulin Labotte – *52 r. Edmond-Dromard – 08170 Haybes – 03 24 41 13 44 – closed Sun evening and Mon.* From your table you can admire the fine restored machinery of this old water mill, which stands on the edge of a river surrounded by woods. Game features prominently on the menu. A few rooms are available.

MINI CRUISES

Boat trips on the Meuse are organised with boarding points at Charleville, Monthermé and Revin. *Between 1hr 30min and 2hr 30min. 03 24 33 77 70.*

JULY FESTIVALS

Story-tellers relate local legends during the Festival des Trois Vallées. *Enquire at Bogny-sur-Meuse tourist office, 03 24 33 94 78.*

Street festival, concerts and theatre are staged for 3 days and nights on one of the last weekends of the month of July. *03 24 41 22 51.*

Return to Charleville along D 13 which runs through the Bois de Hazelles.

Mont Malgré Tout – 2 Round tour from Revin

40km/25mi – allow 2hr 30min including 1hr 15min on foot

Revin

Revin occupies an exceptional position within two deep meanders of the Meuse. There are a few 16C timber-framed houses along quai Edgar-Quinet; note in particular the **Maison espagnole** (*May-Sep: Sat-Sun and holidays 10am-noon, 2-6.30pm. 1.60€. 03 24 40 19 59*) on the corner of rue Victor-Hugo, which has been turned into a museum holding a yearly exhibition about traditions and customs of the Ardennes.

A building situated on the edge of the **Parc Maurice-Rocheteau** (*Apr-Oct: daily 10am-noon, 1-8pm; Nov-Mar: daily 1.30-5.30pm. No charge. 03 24 40 10 72.*) houses a **Galerie d'art contemporain** (contemporary art gallery – *Wed, Sat-Sun 2-6pm, last entrance 30min before closing. Closed 1 Jan, 25 Dec. No charge. 03 24 56 20v52.*) including works by Georges Cesari (1923-82).

On the outskirts of Revin, the winding Route des Hauts-Buttés branches off D 1 and rises 300m/984ft in a series of hairpin bends to the Monument des Manises standing on the roadside.

Monument des Manises

The monument is dedicated to the 106 members of the Maquis des Manises resistance group, killed by the Germans in June 1944. Bird's-eye **view** of Revin and the surrounding area.

Point de vue de la Faligeotte★

The viewing-platform of La Faligeotte also offers an interesting **view** of Revin and the meanders of the Meuse.

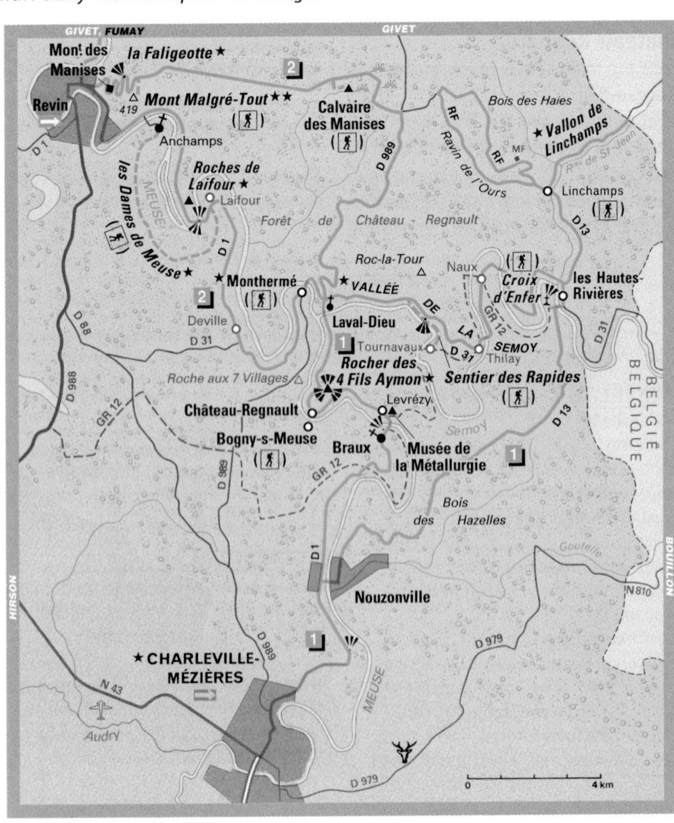

S. Sauvignier/MICHELIN

Meander of the Meuse at Monthermé

The road reaches the edge of the plateau.

Mont Malgré Tout★★

Park the car 400m/437yd from a signpost bearing the inscription "Point de vue à 100m." The footpath begins here (1hr on foot there and back).

The steep path leads to a television relay. From there it is possible to walk through a thicket of birch and oak trees and reach a higher viewpoint (alt 400m/1 312ft) offering a wide **view** of Revin, the

Four Brothers and Their Legendary Steed

The deep and impenetrable Ardennes Forest is the favourite haunt of wild animals, pagan spirits and fantastic creatures. Among the many legends that flourish in the thick woods, the most famous is undoubtedly the legend of *The Four Aymon Brothers,* sometimes called *The Renaud de Montauban Tale,* which relates the feats of four brave knights astride their mighty horse, **Bayard**.

Aymon was the Duke of Dordogne and an ardent supporter of Charlemagne. In a complicated dispute, the duke's brother killed a son of Charlemagne, and was then killed himself by supporters of the king. Aymon's four sons, handsome and valiant (as legend must have it), could not suffer their uncle's murder and finally had to flee; their mother thoughtfully provided them with the family treasury. They established themselves in the thick forest of the Ardennes in a castle, Montfort, built into the rocky cliff above the Meuse.

S. Sauvignier/MICHELIN

This epic can be compared to the *Chanson de Roland,* the earliest masterpiece of the French *chansons de gestes* (songs of deeds), which formed the core of the Charlemagne legends.

Numerous episodes were gradually added to the simple story which, in the 13C, became a poem intended to be read. The 15C prose version is a precursor of the novel form.

Precious manuscripts, incunabula and old editions of this work are kept with the archives of the *département,* and many place names recall the brothers' heroic exploits.

meanders of the Meuse, the Dames de Meuse across the river to the south and the Vallée de Misère to the west.

Drive 6km/3.7mi along Route des Hauts-Buttés to the signpost marked Calvaire des Manises, and park the car.

Calvaire des Manises

15min on foot. A path leads to the clearing where the members of the Resistance were massacred: calvary, monuments and common grave.

Continue along the same road to the intersection with D 989 and turn right. The road runs through the Château-Regnault Forest.

Monthermé

See MONTHERMÉ.

The road (D 1) crosses back to the west bank, running close to the hill topped by the **Roche aux Sept Villages** (see *MONTHERMÉ*).

Continue along D 1 which goes through Deville before reaching Laifour.

From the bridge, there is an impressive **view**★★ of the Roches de Laifour and Dames de Meuse.

Roches de Laifour★

(Not accessible to cars.)

This promontory rises 270m/886ft above the river bed; its schist slopes dropping steeply towards the river are a striking feature of this wild landscape.

Dames de Meuse★

(Not accessible to cars.)

This steep ridge line forms a black gullied mass whose curve follows the course of the Meuse; it reaches an altitude of 393m/1 289ft at its highest point and rises 250m/820ft above the river bed. According to legend, it owes its name to three unfaithful wives turned to stone by God's wrath.

Leave the car at the entrance to Laifour village.

A **path** branches off D 1 south of Laifour, climbs to the Dames de Meuse refuge and reaches the edge of the ridge *(2hr on foot there and back)*; the walk affords a fine **view**★★ of the valley and the village. From there, another path follows the top of the ridge and leads to **Anchamps** *(about 2hr 30min on foot)*.

Drive along D 1 which crosses the Meuse and offers impressive views of the Dames de Meuse before reaching Revin.

MOLSHEIM★

POPULATION 9 335

MICHELIN LOCAL MAP 315: I-5

ALSO SEE ROUTE DES VINS

This quiet old town lies in the Bruche Valley, in the heart of a wine-growing area which produces the famous Bruderthal wine. The Messier-Bugatti factory, specialising in landing gear *(not open to the public)* **is located on the outskirts of town, along the Sélestat road.**

Of its past as religious capital of Alsace, Molsheim has retained the imposing Jesuit church, which once belonged to the university transferred to Strasbourg, and part of the Carthusian monastery, the only one ever to be built in a town. Musical evenings take place every Friday in July and August.

Town Walk

Église des Jésuites★

The church belonged to the famous Jesuit university founded in 1618 by Archduke Leopold of Austria. The Cardinal de Rohan transferred it to Strasbourg in 1702 in order to counteract the influence of the town's Protestant university. Although it was built between 1615 and 1617, the

edifice was designed in the Gothic style. The two **transept chapels** are adorned with 17C-18C paintings depicting the Lives of St Ignatius and the Virgin Mary. St Ignatius' chapel contains white-sandstone fonts dating from 1624 as well as several early-15C tombstones.
The pulpit (1631) and the doorways (1618) show interesting carvings. The Silbermann organ dates from 1781.
The north entrance houses the Carthusian Cross, a beautiful stone cross dating from the late Middle Ages.

Follow rue Notre-Dame on the left of the building.

Tour des Forgerons

This 14C fortified gate, located in rue de Strasbourg, houses one of the oldest bells in Alsace, dating from 1412. The tower was flanked c 1650 by a toll-house and a guardhouse.

Rue de Strasbourg on the right leads to place de l'Hôtel-de-Ville.

La Metzig★

This graceful Renaissance building was built in 1525 by the butchers' guild whose meetings were held on the first floor, the ground floor being occupied by butchers' shops. On either side of the jack clock (1537), two angels strike the hours. An elegant carved-stone balcony runs along the façade. The centre of the square is decorated with a fountain consisting of two superposed basins and an impressive lion bearing the arms of the city.

Take rue Jenner starting on the left of the square.

Note the two Renaissance canon's houses at nos 18 and 20, dating from 1628.

Follow rue des Étudiants on the right which runs past the Musée de la Chartreuse (see description below) then turn right onto rue de Saverne.

Maison ancienne

A beautiful timber-framed Alsatian house with wooden oriel (1607) and finely decorated windows can be seen along rue de Saverne.

Continue along rue de Saverne and rue des Serruriers across rue du Mar.-Foch. Turn left onto rue de la Boucherie then right onto rue St-Joseph. Rue du Mar.-Kellermann on the right leads back to the Église des Jésuites.

Museum

Musée de la Chartreuse

Mid-Jun to mid-Sep: daily except Tue 10am-noon, 2-6pm, Sat-Sun and holidays 2-5pm; early May to mid-Oct: daily except Tue 2-5pm. 2.60€. ☎03 88 38 25 10.
The priory of the former Carthusian monastery (1598-1792) houses a museum devoted to the history of Molsheim and its region, from prehistoric times to today. Objects discovered on the archaeological sites of Dachstein, Achenheim and Heiligenberg-Dinsheim (sigillate ceramics) testify to the presence of man from the Palaeolithic period to Merovingian times. A general map dating from 1744 shows the importance of the Carthusian monastery that spread over 3ha/7.4 acres within the town. Part of the cloisters has been restored and two monks' cells have been reconstructed.
In another building, the **Bugatti Foundation** displays mementoes of the family and a few models of cars built here between the two world wars.

R. Mattès/MICHELIN

La Metzig

PARC NATUREL RÉGIONAL DE LA
MONTAGNE DE REIMS★★

MICHELIN LOCAL MAP 306: F-7/8 TO G-7/8

The Montagne de Reims is a picturesque massif covered with vineyards and woods and offering a wide choice of pleasant drives. Created in 1976, the nature park extends over an area of 50 000ha/123 555 acres between the towns of Reims, Épernay and Châlons-en-Champagne and includes 68 villages and hamlets of the Marne département. The largely-deciduous forest covers more than a third of the park's area; part of it, south of Verzy, is a biological reserve.

Geographical Notes

Forest and vines

The Montagne de Reims is a section of the Ile-de-France cuesta jutting out between the Vesle and the Marne towards the plain of Champagne. The Grande Montagne (high mountain) extends east of N 51 whereas the Petite Montagne (small mountain) spreads to the west of N 51. The highest point of the massif (287m/942ft) is located south of Vezy but, apart from Mont Sinaï (alt 283m/928ft) and Mont Joli (alt 274m/899ft), there are no distinct summits.

Wild boars and roe-deer roam freely through the vast forest. The north, east and south slopes are covered with 7 000ha/17 298 acres of vineyards producing some of the best Champagnes.

Visit

There are numerous possibilities for exploring the park: footpaths starting from Villers-Allerand, Rilly-la-Montagne, Villers-Marmery, Trépail, Courtagnon and Damery; walks along the canal picnic areas, and viewpoints in Ville-Dommange, Hautvillers, Dizy, Verzy and Châtillon-sur-Marne.

In addition to the sights listed in the itinerary, **Olizy** has a small **Musée de l'Escargot de Champagne** (snail museum) and offers a farm tour.

The Maison du Parc in **Pourcy** organises numerous cultural and outdoor activities every year. There are other information centres about the park in **Hautvillers** and **Châtillon-sur-Marne**.

Driving Tour

Champagne Kingdom—Round Tour Starting from Montchenot

100km/62mi – allow one day

Drive out of Reims along N 51 to Montchenot then turn left onto D 26 towards Villers-Allerand.

The road follows the northern ridge of the Montagne de Reims through the prosperous Champagne countryside.

Rilly-la-Montagne

The **Ferme des Bermonts** houses a collection of agricultural tools illustrating daily life in Champagne at the turn of the 20C.

From Rilly there are fine walking possibilities on the slopes of **Mont Joli** through which goes the railway tunnel (3.5km/2.2mi long) of the Paris-Reims line.

Mailly-Champagne

1km/0.6mi beyond Mailly-Champagne, there is an interesting **Carrière géologique** (geological quarry) showing a complete cross section of the Tertiary formations of the eastern Paris Basin. The geological trail *(Free access to the trail, allow 2hr 30min; we recommend purchasing a Guide €7 from the Maison du Parc if you're planning on visiting*

Address Book

PRACTICAL INFORMATION

Tourist information – *Maison du Parc, 51480 Pourcy, ☎03 26 59 44 44, www.parc-montagnedereims.fr – Apr-Oct, 2.30-6.30pm, Nov-Mar, daily except Sat-Sun and public holidays 8.30am-noon, 1.30-6pm – closed Jan 1, Dec 25.*

WHERE TO EAT

See the Legend for coin categories.

La Maison du Vigneron – *51160 St-Imoges – 8km/5mi N of Épernay on N 51 – ☎03 26 52 88v00 – closed Sun evening and Wed.* This large traditional house is set back from the road behind a verdant park. You can sample classic dishes, local wines and champagnes in the dining room, which has exposed beams and an open fireplace in winter. The terrace is very pleasant in summer.

WHERE TO STAY

Chambre d'hôte Delong – *24 r. des Tilleuls – 51390 St-Euphraise-et-Clairizet – 16km/10mi SW of Reims on D 980 and D 206 – ☎03 26 49 74 90 – jdscom@wanadoo.fr – 4 rooms.* This former cowshed in a vineyard has been renovated to provide rooms with lovely stone walls, exposed timberwork and pleasant bathrooms. You can visit the cellars and press-house and taste the champagne produced on the estate.

La Famille Guy Charbaut – *12 r. du Pont – 51160 Mareuil-sur-Aÿ – ☎03 26 52 60 59 – www.champagne-guy-charbaut.com – 6 rooms – evening meal.* As father and son wine growers since 1930, the Charbaut family accommodate you in their delightful house (1837) and show you the cellars dug out of the chalk. Spacious, nicely fixed-up rooms. Meals served in a magnificent storeroom.

Hôtel du Cheval Blanc – *51400 Sept-Saulx – 20km/12.5mi SE of Reims on N 44 and D 37 – ☎03 26 03 90 27 – cheval.blanc-sept-saulx@wanadoo.fr – closed Feb and Tue and Wed from Oct to Mar – – 26 rooms – €11 – restaurant.* This peaceful former coaching inn is well off the beaten track. The spruce, flowery courtyard has been converted into a terrace. A branch of the River Vesle winds through the attractive park, where you can play tennis, volley-ball and golf, or simply stroll around in fine weather.

CHAMPAGNE CELLARS

Institut International des Vins de Champagne – *Villa Bassinger – 15 r. Jeanson – 51160 Ay – ☎03 26 55 78 78 – www.villabassinger.com – Apr-Oct, 1st Sat of the month, 2.30pm, tasting and commentary of 4 champagnes.* The institute organises several beginners' sessions throughout the year, lasting from a few hours to a two-day-course.

Serge Pierlot – *10 r. St-Vincent – 51150 Ambonnay – 6.5km/4mi SE of Louvois on D 34 and D 19 – ☎03 26 57 01 11 – champagne-serge-pierlot@wanadoo.fr – Mon-Fri 9am-noon, 2.30-6.30pm, Sat 9am-noon, 2.30-6pm, Sun 9am-noon – closed early-end Jan, end Aug-early Sep.* In his shop at the end of an alley, Serge Pierlot exhibits an 18C winepress and other vine-growing and winemaking implements used by his ancestors. Tasting, and produce on sale, including extra dry, the house speciality.

Soutiran-Pelletier – *12 r. St-Vincent – 51150 Ambonnay – 6.5km/4mi SE of Louvois on D 34 and D 19 – ☎03 26 57 07 87 – www.soutiran.com – tasting Mon-Sat 8am-noon, 2-6pm, visit by appointment only – closed Sat from end Dec-Easter.* In this typical village, the Soutiran Pelletier establishment will take you to see its presses, vats and cellars, as well as giving explanations of the techniques used in winemaking. Tasting and sales.

the site alone; guided tours €5.50 organised by the Regional Park authorities; ☎03 26 59 44 44) takes visitors some 70 million years back in time.

From the road *(D 26)*, one can spot to the right, a contemporary **sculpture** by Bernard Pages celebrating the Earth.

Verzenay

This wine-growing village is overlooked by a **windmill** to the west and a 1909 **lighthouse**, now a wine museum.

Musée de la Vigne★

Daily except Mon, 10am-6pm, Sat-Sun and holidays, 10am-6.30pm (last admission 1hr before closing time). *Early Jan-late Feb.* €6. 03 26 07 87 87 – *www.lapharedeverzenay.com*. A wooden footbridge leads to the restored lighthouse towering above a modern wooden building.

Verzy

This village developed under the protection of the Benedictine abbey of St-Basle, founded in the 7C and destroyed in 1792.

Faux de Verzy★

In Verzy, take D 34 towards Louvois. On reaching the plateau, turn left onto the Route des Faux. From the

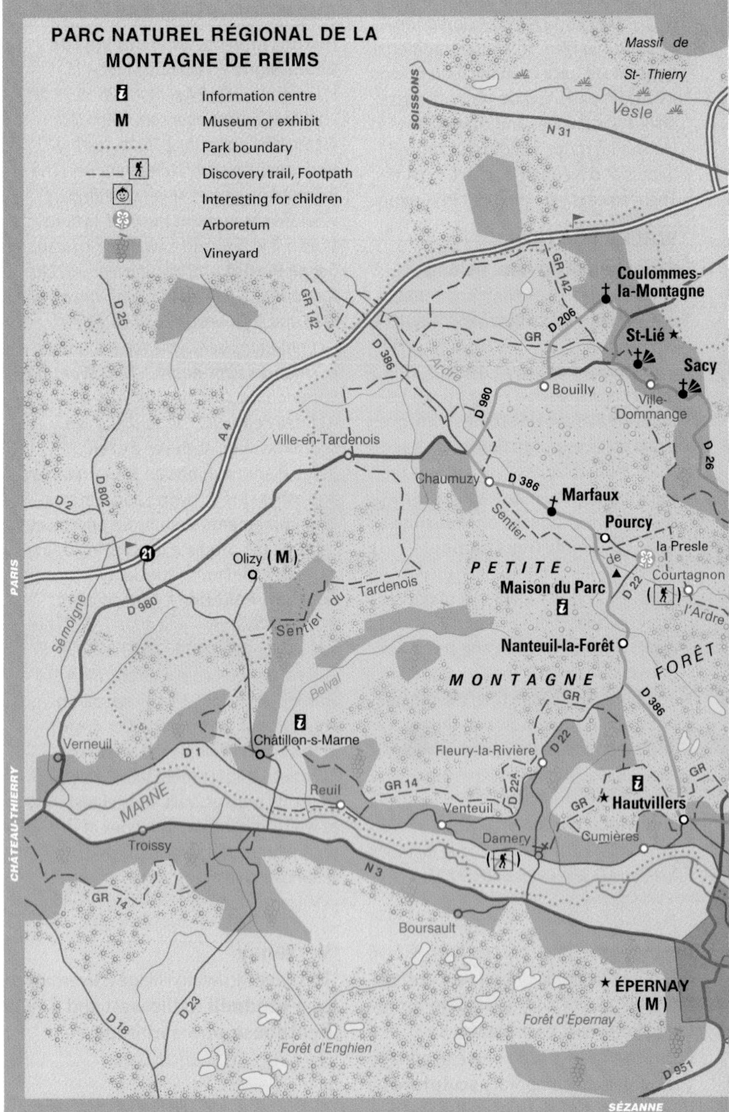

parking area, follow the path over a distance of about 1km/0.6mi.

Guided tours organised by the Regional Park authorities, €5.50. Enquire at the Maison du Parc ☎03 26 59 44 44.

The Faux (from the Latin *fagus* meaning beech) are twisted and stunted beech trees. This is the result of a genetic phenomenon, probably reinforced by natural layering. The site features footpaths, a playground and a picnic area.

Observatoire du Mont Sinaï

Parking area on the other side of D 34. Walk along the forest road and, 200m/219yd farther on, turn right onto a very wide path (30min there and back).

A casemate on the edge of the ridge marks the observation post from which General Gouraud studied the positions and the terrain during the battle of Cham-

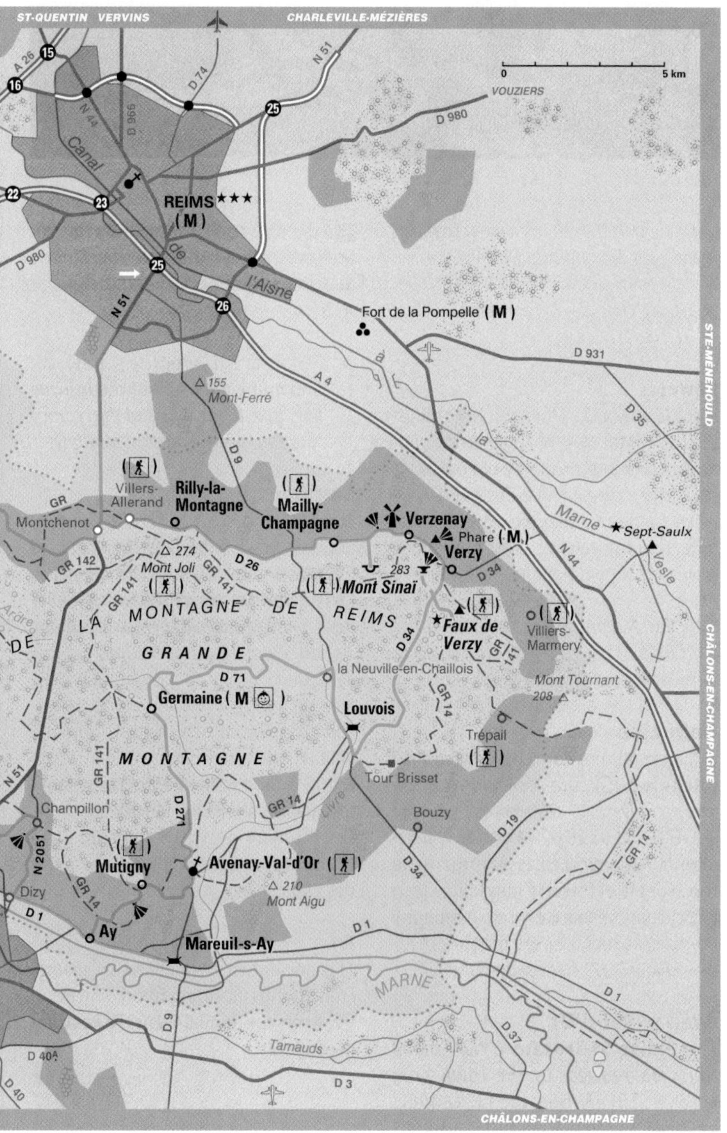

S. Chirol

Faux de Verzy

pagne in 1918. There is a view towards Reims and the Champagne hills.

▸ *Return to D 34 and continue towards Louvois.*

Louvois

Erected by Mansart for Louis XIV's minister, the **castle** (*not open to the public*) became the property of Louis XV's daughters; the park was designed by Le Nôtre but little remains today. From the gate, one can see the present castle (a pavilion partly rebuilt in the 19C).

▸ *Drive N along D 9 to Neuville-en-Chaillois then turn left onto D 71, which goes through the forest.*

Germaine

Kids A small museum, the **Maison du bûcheron** (*Late-Mar-mid-Nov, Sun and holidays, 2.30-6.30pm; €2 (children -12: €.50) ☎03 26 59 44 44; www.parc-montagnedereims.fr*), is devoted to all the aspects of forestry (marking, clearing, cutting, felling, carrying). Temporary thematic exhibitions are organised.

▸ *Follow D 271 to Avenay-Val-d'Or.*

Avenay-Val-d'Or

The **Église St-Trésain** (*Guided tours on request to the town hall; ☎03 26 52 31 33*), from the 13C and 16C, has a 16C organ in the south transept.

A discovery trail starting from the station (*brochure available from the Maison du Parc*), enables visitors to discover a rural community.

▸ *Follow D 201 opposite the station and immediately after the railway line, take the small road that climbs through the vineyards to Mutigny.*

Mutigny

Stand near the church for a **view** of Ay and the Côte des Blancs on the right, and Châlons and the plain straight ahead.

The **Sentier du Vigneron** (*Mid-Apr-early Nov, daily except Mon at 9.30am, 2 and 4.30pm, Tue 2 and 4.30pm, Sat-Sun by request; €7.50 – no charge under 12-yr-olds; ☎03 26 52 31 37; www.mutigny-en-champagne.com*), which starts from the village, offers ramblers a 2.2km/1.3mi round tour; it is lined with 12 explanatory panels about the vineyards.

On the way down to Ay, there are glimpses of Épernay and the Côte des Blancs.

Ay

This ancient city, well liked by several French kings including Good King Henri (IV),hosts the annual **Henri IV Festival** in early July.

Institut International des vins de Champagne

Located in a former 19C private mansion, the institute is devoted to research concerning Champagne, its history, artistic representations, brand image etc, and undertakes the training of students (law, economics) with the cooperation of Reims University. *See Address Book.*
Gosset, the Champagne firm whose founder is listed as a wine-grower in the city's records of 1584, prides itself in being the oldest firm in Champagne.

In Ay, turn left onto D 1 to Mareuil-sur-Ay.

Mareuil-sur-Ay

The castle was erected in the 18C and the estate was bought in 1830 by the duke of Montebello who created his own make of Champagne.

Return to Ay and continue to Dizy then turn onto N 2051 to Champillon.

Between Dizy and Champillon, the road rises through endless vineyards. There is a good **view**★ of the vineyards, the Marne Valley and Épernay from a terrace on the side of the road.

Hautvillers★

According to tradition, **Dom Pérignon** (1638-1715), who was in charge of the cellars of the Benedictine abbey, was the first to blend various wines to produce a vintage and initiated the use of corks.
Dom Pérignon is buried in **St-Sindulphe abbey church:** his black-marble tombstone is located to the left of the high altar over which hangs a vast chandelier (1950) made up of four wheels from winepresses.

Ancienne abbaye Saint-Pierre

by appointment; summer 9am-6pm, winter 9am-5pm ☎03 26 57 06 35. Founded in 650 by St Nivard, a nephew of King Dagobert, the abbey followed Saint-Maur's rule (similar to Benedictine). The most beautiful manuscripts of the **École de Reims** were produced here. Today it is owned by Moët et Chandon.
Look through the railing into the park for a glimpse of the **Pavillon des Dames de France**, used by Louis XV's daughters when on pilgrimage.

Nanteuil-la-Forêt

There was a Templars' priory here.

Centre botanique de la Presle

Carrefour de la Presle. Daily except Sun, 2-6pm, Sat 9am-noon, 2-6pm. Public holidays and some Sun afternoons, enquire). €4. ☎03 26 59 43 39. Exhibitions are organised in this garden, which features lovely spiraeas, willows and roses, including the Rose de la Marne.

Continue northwards along D 386.

Pourcy

The **Maison du Parc**, designed by Hervé Bagot, houses the offices of the nature park as well as an information centre.

Verger conservatoire

Access from the Maison du Parc. This conservatory is designed to safeguard some 25 endangered fruit tree species.

Marfaux

The **church** here boasts fine capitals.

Beyond Chaumuzy, turn right onto RD 980 then, as you reach Bouilly, turn left onto D 206 to Coulommes-la-Montagne.

Coulommes-la-Montagne

There is a fine Romanesque **church**.

Turn right to rejoin D 980 vial Pargny-les-Reims; 1.5km/0.9mi farther on, turn left towards St-Lié.

Chapelle St-Lié★

This chapel, dating from the 12C, 13C and 16C, stands on a mound near Ville-Dommange that was probably a holy grove in Gallo-Roman times.
There is an extended **view**★ of Ville-Dommange, the ridge, Reims and its cathedral and the plain as far as the St-Thierry massif.

Sacy

The Église St-Rémi has an 11C east end and a 12C square belfry. From the cemetery there is a fine view of Reims.

MONTHERMÉ★

POPULATION 2 791

MICHELIN LOCAL MAP 306: K-3

Situated just beyond the confluence of the Semoy and the Meuse, this is the ideal centre for exploring the Ardennes region on foot or by bike (*see below*).

Also See: Méandres de la MEUSE.

Visit

Vieille ville

A long street lined with old houses runs through the old town to the fortified **Église St-Léger** (12C-16C), built of fine stone from the Meuse region.

Laval-Dieu

This industrial suburb of Monthermé grew round an **abbey of Premonstratensians** established here in the 12C. The former **abbey church** (*Jul-Aug, 4-6pm, ☎03 24 54 46v73*) stands on a peaceful wooded site.

Hiking Tours

Roche à Sept Heures★

2km/1.2mi along D 989 to Hargnies then left at the top of the hill onto the tarmacked path.

From this rocky spur, there is a bird's-eye **view★** of Monthermé and the meander of the Meuse with Laval-Dieu upstream and, farther away, Château-Regnault and the Rocher des Quatre Fils Aymon.

Longue Roche★

The tarmacked path continues beyond the Roche à Sept Heures for a farther 400m/437yd to a parking area. From there, you can walk to the viewpoint (30min there and back).

This is another rocky spur (alt 375m/1 230ft) overlooking the Meuse. A path running along the ridge (12km/7.5mi) offers bird's-eye views of the valley. The **panorama★★** is wilder and sharper than that of the Roche à Sept Heures.

Roc de la Tour★★

3.5km/2.2mi E then 20min on foot there and back. The forest road (Route forestière de la Lyre) branches off D 31 on the left as you leave Laval-Dieu; it rises through the wooded vale of a stream (the Lyre). Parking 3km/1.9mi farther on; leave the car and follow the footpath.

This ruin-like quartzite spur surrounded by birches stands in a dramatic setting overlooking the Semoy and affords a panoramic **view★★** of the wooded heights of the Ardennes massif. Paths for climbers have been marked out on rocks by the Club alpin français.

From Roc-la-Tour, there are various possibilities of hikes (35km/22mi) through the Semoy and Meuse valleys (*information panels located in the parking area*).

PRACTICAL INFORMATION

Tourist office – *Pl. Jean-Baptiste Clément, 08800 Monthermé, ☎03 24 54 46 73.*

WHERE TO STAY AND EAT

See the Legend for coin categories.

Le Franco-Belge – *2 r. Pasteur – ☎03 24 53 01 20 – le.franco.belge@wanadoo.fr – 15 rooms – €6 – restaurant* If you have worked up an appetite rock-climbing, you can refuel at this unpretentious family inn, which serves simple dishes, to be enjoyed in the old-fashioned interior or, better still, on the terrace, in the shade of the trellis. Spotless rooms.

Roche aux Sept Villages★★

3km/1.9mi S. Follow the Charleville road (D 989).

As the road rises, the **view**★★ gradually extends over the valley.

Steps climb this rocky peak rising above the forest. From the top there is a view of the meandering River Meuse lined with seven villages from Braux in the south to Deville in the north. Next to Château-Regnault stands the jagged Rocher des Quatre Fils Aymon.

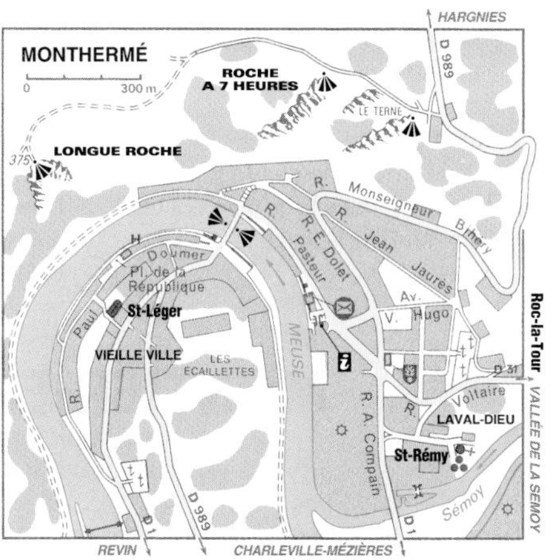

The road continues to climb beyond the Roche aux Sept Villages; at the top, a path leads to the viewpoint of the Roche de Roma.

Roche de Roma★

Alt 333m/1 093ft. **View**★ of the Meuse between Monthermé and Deville.

Mountain-biking

Monthermé is the starting point of four marked mountain-bike itineraries of varying length (*from 15 to 50km/9 to 31mi*) and difficulty; a brochure is available from the tourist office.

Excursion

Vallée de la Semoy★

27km/17mi from Monthermé to Linchamps – 1hr 30min – *local map see Méandres de la MEUSE*

From the Meuse to the Belgian border, the River Semoy (called Semois in Belgium) meanders across pastureland between steep slopes covered with forests of oak, fir and birch trees and inhabited by roe-deer and wild boar. The green secluded valley is a paradise for anglers fishing for trout and for anyone yearning for solitude.

The **Sentier du Fer, du Schiste et de la Forêt** (*75km/47mi*) runs the whole length of the Semoy Valley, offering ramblers the choice of seven round tours; a topographical guide is available from the tourist office in Monthermé. Sculptures by Jean Morette have been insatlled at the entrance to some villages by the landscape artist Marc Soucat.

Leave Monthermé along D 31.

The road runs below the Roc de la Tour.

Follow the forest road for 4km/2.5mi.

Sentier des Rapides

1hr on foot there and back. The path starts at the end of the parking area and follows river flowing to Tournavaux.

Return to D 31.

The road rises to the top of the cliff offering bird's-eye **views**★ of Tournavaux nestling in a slightly widened part of the valley. The road runs down to Thilay then crosses the Semoy. Beyond Naux, lying inside a deep meander of the river, the itinerary crosses the Semoy once more.

Les Hautes-Rivières

This is the largest village along the French section of the River Semoy. It extends over 2km/1.2mi to Sorendal.

Drive S along D 13 towards Nouzonville, climbing 1.5km/0.9mi to the beginning of the path leading to the Croix d'Enfer.

Croix d'Enfer

30min on foot there and back. **View★** of the valley, the village of Les Hautes-Rivières and the Vallon de Linchamps.

Linchamps★

N of Hautes-Rivières along D 13. The area is beautiful and remote.

The isolated village is the starting point of walks through the **Ravin de l'Ours** and **Bois des Haies**, across a hilly area reaching altitudes in excess of *500m/1 640ft.*

MONTIER-EN-DER

POPULATION 2 019

MICHELIN LOCAL MAP 313: I-3

Destroyed by intensive shelling in June 1940, Montier-en-Der was completely rebuilt. The town developed round a Benedictine monastery established on the banks of the River Voire. It is the capital of the Der (*Der* means oak copse in Celtic).

Sights

Église Notre-Dame

This is the former church of the monastery founded in Montier in 672, which followed the rule of St Columba (an Irish monk who founded Luxeuil Abbey, *see LUXEUIL-LES-BAINS*). The present edifice was built between the 10C and 13C. Damaged by fire in June 1940, it was remarkably well restored.

The **nave** (*36.50m/120ft long*) is the oldest part of the building: eight rounded arches rest on low rectangular piers.

The **chancel★** (*12C-13C*) is a splendid four-storey example of Early Gothic in the Champagne region:

Ph. Gajic/MICHELIN

The soaring chancel of Notre-Dame church

- main arches resting on twinned columns decorated with grotesques;
- upper gallery with twinned arches surmounted by an oculus;
- triforium with trefoil arches;
- clerestory windows separated by colonnettes.

A row of columns separates the radiating chapels from the ambulatory.

Haras national

2.30-5pm. Jan 1 and Dec 25. No admission charge. 03 26 04 69 17.

This stud farm, situated on the site of the former abbey, on the left of the church, looks after some 40 stallions and 15 horses for various riding clubs.

Excursion

Round tour from Montier-en-Der

60km/37mi – allow 4hr

The Lac du Der-Chantecoq (*see Lac du DER-CHANTECOQ*) and the **timber-framed churches★** are the two main attractions of the Der region. Most of these churches are decorated with stained glass from the Troyes School.

Churches are floodlit every night from May to September and at weekends only during the rest of the year. Other churches and some edifices situated round the Lac du Der-Chantecoq are also floodlit: Éclaron, Giffaumont, St-Rémy-en-Bouzemont, Larzicourt, Arrigny and the museum-village of Ste-Marie-du-Lac-Nuisement.

▸ *Drive out of Montier-en-Der along the Brienne road (D 400).*

Ceffonds

The **Église St-Rémi**, rebuilt round its Romanesque belfry at the beginning of the 16C, stands in the disused cemetery which has retained a 16C stone cross. . The transept and the chancel are decorated with fine 16C **stained-glass windows**★ made in the famous workshops of the city of Troyes.

▸ *Turn back towards Montier-en-Der then left onto D 173.*

Puellemontier

Timber-framed houses stand scattered in the fields. The **church** is surmounted by a slender pointed steeple; the nave dates from the 12C but the chancel is more recent (16C).

▸ *Continue along D 173 then D 62 to Lentilles.*

The road runs close to the peaceful **Étang de la Horre** (250ha/618 acres), lined with tall grass.

Lentilles★

This is a typical Der village with a well-ordered street plan, low timber-framed and a fine 16C timber **church**.

▸ *Follow D 2 to Chavanges.*

Chavanges

The **church**, dating from the 15C and 16C, has a 12C doorway; it contains several 16C stained-glass windows (some made after drawings by Dürer).

▸ *Drive E along D 56 to Bailly-le-Franc.*

Bailly-le-Franc

Hardly restored during the past centuries, the late 17C **church** has remained the simplest and most authentic of all the churches in the Der region.

Ph. Gajic/MICHELIN

Village church in Lentilles

▸ *Follow D 121 west to Joncreuil.*

Joncreuil

The church has a a 13C chancel.

▸ *Follow D 127 then D 128 to A rrembécourt.*

Arrembécourt

Note the **church**'scarved doorway.

▸ *Continue along D 6 then D 58.*

Drosnay

This village has retained a few timber-framed buildings and church.

Horse Sense

The Ardennes horse is one of most sought-after breeds of draught horses in France. This small, tough, calm and docile horse is essentially bred in north-east France, that is Champagne, Ardennes, Lorraine and Alsace. It is extremely useful on farms, in the fields and in forests but is also used for leisure activities (riding, barouche trips, horse-drawn caravanning, touring along bridle paths).

A competition, which takes place in Sedan every September, brings together the best representatives of the Ardennes breed.

Drive along D 55 to Outines.

Outines

This is a typical Der village.

The **Maison de l'Oiseau et du Poisson** presents the changing aspects of the Lac du Der-Chantecoq and its varied bird population through the seasons (*see Lac du DER-CHANTECOQ*).

Continue east along D 55.

Châtillon-sur-Broué

See Lac du DER-CHANTECOQ.

Droyes

The brick-built church comprises a Romanesque nave and a 16C chancel.

Take D 13 to return to Montier-en-Der.

MONTMÉDY

POPULATION 2 260

MICHELIN LOCAL MAP 307: D-1

There are two towns in one: Montmédy-Bas (lower town), on the banks of the River Chiers, and Montmédy-Haut (upper town), fortified during the Renaissance and remodelled by Vauban, which has retained its ramparts.

The town organises two lively festivals: the Fête des Remparts involving jugglers, clowns and tightrope walkers, which takes place on the first Sunday in May, and the Fête des Pommes centred on a busy market, exhibitions and tasting sessions, which takes place on the first Sunday in October.

Sights

Montmédy-Haut

The upper town is perched on an isolated peak.

Citadelle★

A walk along the ramparts (*Jul-Aug, 10am-7pm; May-Jun and Sep, 10am-6pm; Feb 10am-4pm; Mar, 10am-noon, 1-5pm; Apr and Oct, 10am-noon, 1-6pm (Oct 2-6pm), Sat-Sun and public holidays 10am-6pm; Nov, Sat-Sun holidays and Nov 11, 10am-4pm; Dec Sat-Sun 10am-4pm; Jan; €4 – combined ticket with museums; ☎03 29 80 15 90)* past glacis, curtain walls, bastions and underground passages, gives a good idea of the complexity and ingenious design of the citadel's defence system, modernised after 1870. From the top of the ramparts, the **view** extends over the lower town, the Chiers Valley and numerous surrounding villages.

R. Mattès/MICHELIN

Montmédy citadel

Musées de la Fortification et Jules Bastien-Lepage

Jul-Aug, 10am-7pm; May-Jun and Sep, 10am-6pm; Feb 10am-4pm; Mar, 10am-noon, 1-5pm; Apr and Oct, 10am-noon, 1-6pm (Oct 2-6pm), Sat-Sun and public holidays 10am-6pm; Nov, Sat-Sun holidays and Nov 11, 10am-4pm; Dec Sat-Sun 10am-4pm. Jan. €4 – combined ticket with ramparts. 03 29 80 15 90.
Situated at the entrance of the citadel, these museums are devoted respectively to the history of fortifications (models, historic documents, audio-visual presentation) and to the life and work of a native of the region, the painter Jules Bastien-Lepage (1848-84).

Église St-Martin

This vast church dating from the mid-18C has retained its stalls and woodwork.

Excursions

Louppy-sur-Loison

14km/8.7mi S. Leave Montmédy by N 43 towards Longuyon then turn right in Iré-le-Sec.

The 17C **castle** (*Guided tour available (1hr), Enquire at the Pays de Montmédy Tourist office, Citadelle, BP 28, 55600 Montmédy. 03 29 80 15 90 or 03 29 88 11 16)* built by Simon de Pouilly, governor of Stenay (*see Vallée de la MEUSE*), is still owned by his descendants.
Ruins of the original fortress can be seen near the church.

Marville

12km/7.5mi SE along N 43. Founded in Gallo-Roman times under the name of Major villa, Marville has severl 16C and 17C houses along the **Grand'Rue**.
In the **Église St-Nicolas** *(In case of closure, enquire at the town hall 03 29 88 15 15 or Auberge de Marville 03 29 88 10 10)*, note the early-16C balustrade of the organ loft.

Cimetière de la chapelle St-Hilaire

The tarmacked path leading to the cemetery branches off N 43. Situated at the top of the hill, the cemetery of the former Église St-Hilaire contains a walled ossuary said to house 40 000 skulls.

Avioth★★

8.5km/5.3mi N along D 110. See *Basilique d'AVIOTH.*

MONTMIRAIL

POPULATION 3 783

MICHELIN LOCAL MAP 306: D-9

The low roughcast houses of this once fortified town cling to the slopes of a promontory overlooking the rural valley of the Petit Morin.
Paul de Gondi, who later became the famous Cardinal de Retz, was born in Montmirail Castle in 1613. After the death of Cardinal Richelieu and Louis XIII, this dangerous schemer used his ecclesiastical influence to destabilise the regency of Anne of Austria during Louis XIV's childhood.

Château

guided tours Jul-Aug, Mon-Thu: 2.30, 3.30. 03 26 81 70 02.
The 17C brick-and-stone castle was acquired in 1685 by one of Louis XIV's ministers, the **Marquis de Louvois**; his great-granddaughter married the Duc de La Rochefoucauld whose descendants still own the castle.

Excursions

Colonne commémorative de la bataille de Montmirail

4km/2.5mi NW along RD 933.
A column surmounted by a gilt eagle (1867) commemorates one of the last battles won by **Napoleon** in 1814.
A century later, in September 1914, the German army commanded by Von

Bülow was attacked here by French troops who managed to stop the German advance.

Jardins de Vieils-Maisons

12km/7.5mi W along D 933. Early-Jun-late Sep, daily except Wed-Thu, 2-6pm. €6. 03 23 82 62 53.

The park covers 5ha/12.5 acres with 2 000 different plant species.

Verdelot

15km/9.3mi W along D 31.

The imposing **church** (*Enquire at the presbytery, 01 64 04 81 81*), dating from the 15C-16C, stands on the hillside. Note the intricate vaulting and the height of the aisles almost level with the chancel vaulting. On either side of the chancel, there are small statues of St Crépin and St Crépinien, patron saints of cobblers, to whom the church is dedicated. A seated Virgin Mary in carved walnut (Notre-Dame-de-Pitié de Verdelot), forming part of a 19C altarpiece, is reminiscent of 12C or 13C representations of the Virgin carved in the Auvergne and Languedoc regions.

Vallé du Petit Morin

24km/15mi – allow 1hr.

Leave Montmirail along D 43 heading south-east.

This 90km/56mi long tributary of the Marne, which takes its source east of Montmirail (see *Marais de ST-GOND*), flows through meadows, marshy in places, dotted with groves of poplars. The road follows the Petit Morin upriver, through charming villages.

Abbaye du Reclus

A holy hermit called Hugues-le-Reclus, retired to this remote vale (c 1123) and gave it his name. In 1142, St Bernard founded a Cistercian abbey.

Beyond Talus-St-Prix, turn left onto D 951 towards Baye.

Baye

St Alpin, a native of Baye who became bishop of Châlons, was buried in the 13C church. Baye is the birthplace of Marion de Lorme (1611-50) who, like Ninon de Lenclos, was famous for her numerous love affairs; her legend inspired Victor Hugo to write a play.

MOUZON★

POPULATION 2 616

MICHELIN LOCAL MAP 306: M-5

This small town, lying on an island formed by the River Meuse and the Canal de l'Est, was originally a Gaulish trading centre (Mosomagos) then a Roman military post. The Frankish king Clovis offered it to St Remi (who had christened the king c 498), and it later became a favourite residence of the archbishops of Reims. United with France in 1379, Mouzon was besieged by the Holy Roman Emperor Charles V in the 16C, and by Turenne and troops from Luxemburg in the mid-17C. The last factory to produce industrial felt is based in Mouzon.

Town Walk

A marked itinerary, starting from the Porte de France site in the south, follows the town's fortifications *(brochure available from the tourist office)*.

Porte de Bourgogne

This fortified gate, dating from the 12C to the 17C is all that remains of the town's fortifications.

Sights

Abbatiale Notre-Dame★

Guided tours by appointment, contact Mr. Paul Motte, 13 R. Royale, Mouzon. ☎03 24 26 10 44.

The construction of this ancient abbey church started at the end of the 12C and was completed in just over 30 years. The 13C nave and 12C **chancel** rest on massive round piers, as in Laon Cathedral on which Mouzon is modelled.

The 18C furniture is noteworthy, in particular the organ and the carved-wood organ case (1725), the only remaining example of the work of Christophe Moucherel in northern France.

Musée du Feutre

Place du Colombier. May-Sep, 2-6pm (Jun-Aug, 2-7pm last admission 1hr before closing time); Apr and Oct, Sat-Sun and public holidays, 2-6pm. €3.90 (children: €1.50). ☎03 24 26 91 12.

Kids The Felt Museum, housed in one of the abbey's former farmhouses, is devoted to the **history** and manufacture of felt (one of the world's oldest textiles). There is an **exhibition of contemporary designs** as well as workshops.

Excursions

Site gallo-romain du Flavier

4km/2.5mi SE on D 964 to Stenay.

The remains of a Gallo-Roman sanctuary, discovered on this site in 1966, include the foundations of three small temples dating from 50 BC to AD 350 *(information panels).*

Pavillon d'accueil du territoire du sanglier

- *12km/7.5mi along D 19 to Carignan then follow D 981 and turn right towards Mogues.*

Wild boars have been popular in the region from the Gallo-Roman period until today: the Sedan football club even chose a wild boar as their mascot! The exhibition offers visitors an interactive journey in the footsteps of this symbolic animal living in the Ardennes forests.

River Meuse and Canal de l'Est

36km/22mi drive S of Mouzon.

- *Leave Mouzon SE along the scenic D 964 to Stenay.*

Stenay

This former stronghold, situated on the east bank of the river and the canal, lies in the heart of beer country.

The vast **Musée européen de la Bière** (European Beer Museum – *Apr-Oct, daily except Tue 10-6pm; €5 – children €2.50; ☎03 29 80 68v78)* is housed in the former supply stores of the 16C citadel turned into a malt factory in the 19C. The uninitiated discover how brewers make beer from simple ingredients such as spring water, barley turned into malt, and hops which give beer its characteristic bitter flavour.

The 16C residence of the former governor of the citadel, situated on the edge of town, houses the **Musée du pays de Stenay** (*Mar-Nov: daily except Sat-Sun and holidays 9-11am, 2-5pm. 1€. ☎03 29 80 68 78.)* which contains collections of archaeology as well as arts and crafts.

- *Drive S along D 964 and cross the canal and the river 10km/6.2mi from Stenay. In Sassey-sur-Meuse turn left to Mont-devant-Sassey.*

Mont-devant-Sassey

The village lies at the foot of a hill on the west bank of the river. An interesting 11C **church** *(Enquire at the town hall, 23 rue d'Andenne for opening times, ☎ 03 29 80 90 92; guided tours possible, enquire at Les Amis de l'Eglise de Mont, 19 rue de Moranville, ☎03 29 74 84 93)*, remodelled later, stands on the hillside. During the 17C wars, it was turned into a fortress. The building, characteristic of the Rhine region, has square towers over the transept and a raised east end built over a crypt. Preceded by a Gothic porch decorated with statues in naive style, the monumental 13C doorway, dedicated to the Virgin Mary, is similar in design to those of the great Gothic cathedrals.

▶ *Return to Sassey-sur-Meuse, cross the river and the canal and turn right onto D 964 to Dun-sur-Meuse.*

Dun-sur-Meuse

From this **picturesque hilltop**★ (stand in the open space in front of the 16C church), there is an extended view of the Meuse Valley.

MULHOUSE★★

POPULATION 110 359
MICHELIN LOCAL MAP 315: H-I 10

Situated in the northern foothills of the Sungdau area, Mulhouse has several attractive features including its rich past as an independent republic, its strong industrial tradition and its prestigious museums.
Since 1975 this modern and dynamic town has been the seat of the Université de Haute-Alsace, which specialises in high technology.

- **Orient Yourself:** Mulhouse is on the A35 to Strasbourg (100km/62mi north) and Basles (32km/20mi south) and on the A36 which crosses through the town from east to west before heading out to Belfort and Montbéliard-Sochaux *(both less than 50km/31mi away).*
- **Don't Miss:** From the top of the Tour de l'Europe *(tearoom, revolving restaurant)*, there is a good overall **view** of the town and the surrounding area.
- Kids **Especially For Kids:** Young (and old alike) adore Mulhouse and its wealth of Industrial museums (automobiles, trains, fire engines, electricity, etc.).

A Bit of History

A passion for independence

From the 12C onwards, Mulhouse strove to liberate itself from its feudal bonds and in 1308 it acquired the status of an imperial city, thus becoming a virtually independent republic, acknowledging the Holy Roman Emperor as its sole suzerain. Encouraged by the latter, Mulhouse formed, with nine other imperial cities, a league of defence against the power of the nobility, known as **Decapolis**.
In 1515, under threat from the Habsburgs' territories which completely surrounded it, Mulhouse left Decapolis and entered into an alliance with the **Swiss cantons,** an inspired decision that placed the town under the protection of the kingdom of France: the intervention of Henri IV in favour of his allies and the cession to France of the Habsburgs' possessions in Alsace under the treaty of Westphalia (1648) enabled the Republic to retain its independence. Even the revocation of the Edict of Nantes in 1685 did not really threaten this bastion of Calvinism, which remained the only Alsatian territory not under French control after the Sun King had annexed Strasbourg in 1681.

Calvinist citadel

In 1524 the Republic's government adopted the principles of the Reformation and a little later on adhered to Calvinism. As a consequence, theatrical performances were banned, inns had to close at 10pm and the citizens' clothing had to be discreet in style and colour. However, the new religion also spurred industrial development and prompted original social and cultural initiatives.

Union with France

In 1792 the new French Republic imposed a commercial blockade on Mulhouse and the town opted for union with France. During the union festivities, which took place in 1798 on place de la Réunion, the flag of the city was rolled inside a case bearing the colours of the French flag and the following inscription was written on the case: *La République de Mulhouse repose dans le sein de la République française* (the Republic of

Address Book

For coin ranges, see the Legend on the cover flap.

PRACTICAL INFORMATION

Tourist Office – *9 av. Foch, 68100 Mulhouse – ☎03 89 35 48 48 – www.tourisme-mulhouse.com*

Guided tours – The tourist office organises 1hr 30min tours of the town. *Jul-Aug: Sat 10.30am – €4 (under 12-yr-olds: no charge).*

WHERE TO EAT

Auberge des Franciscains – *46 r. des Franciscains – ☎03 89 45 32 77 – closed Tue and Sun evenings.* Exposed timber beams, handsome copper pots and pans above the bar and shelves adorned with old beer mugs: a warm welcome awaits visitors to this beer tavern. Wide choice of local dishes: baeckehofe, choucroute, cassolette au munster, etc.

Wistuwa zum Saüwadala – *13 r. de l'Arsenal – ☎03 89 45 18v19 – closed Mon lunchtime and Sun.* You can't miss this restaurant with its typical façade in the centre of old Mulhouse. Beer mugs hang from the ceiling, the tablecloths are gingham, and the cuisine is genuine Alsace. Several menus, including one for children.

Auberge de Frœningen – *68720 Frœningen – 9km/5.6mi SW of Mulhouse on D 8BIII – ☎03 89 25 48 48 – closed 11 Jan-1 Feb, 17-30 Aug, Tue Nov-Apr, Sun evening and Mon.* Warm red colours and shining copperware set the tone: this flower-decked village inn serves rich rustic local cuisine in a comfortable setting. One of the dining rooms is decorated in Alsatian style, and is the most welcoming. Lovely terrace in summer and small individualised rooms.

Closerie – *6 r. H.- de- Crousaz – 68110 Illzach – ☎03 89 61 88 00 – hubert.beyrath@wanadoo.fr – closed 14-31 Aug, 22 Dec-5 Jan, Sat lunchtimes, Mon evenings and Sun.* An unexpected pleasure to unearth this treasure of a restaurant in the middle of the industrial area. Two dining rooms and a small lounge in a smart setting, where classic dishes are served with a smile.

WHERE TO STAY

Hôtel St-Bernard – *3 r. des Fleurs – ☎03 89 45 82 32 – www.hotel-saint-bernard.com – 21 rooms – €7.* This small, functional hotel is well situated, near the attractive Place de la Réunion and the town hall. Two of the rooms have waterbeds and another has a painted ceiling. Free Internet access available at reception, and bikes can be hired by the energetic.

Chambre d'hôte Le Clos du Mûrier – *42 Grand-Rue – 68170 Rixheim – 6km/3.75mi E of Mulhouse, Bâle direction – ☎03 89 54 14 81 – 5 rooms – €7.50.* This 16C Alsatian house in the centre of Rixheim has been attractively restored. Spacious rooms with exposed beams and stylish modern decor. All have kitchenettes. Suite for 4 people. Pretty garden.

Hôtel Bristol – *18 av. de Colmar – ☎03 89 42 12v31 – hbristol@club-internet.fr – P – 82 rooms – €8.50.* This early 20C hotel near the old town has been completely renovated. Spacious hall and lounge decorated with Art Deco-inspired furniture. The many rooms are large, well equipped and air-conditioned. Some bathrooms have corner baths. A good place to stay in Mulhouse.

ON THE TOWN

Charlie's Bar – *26 r. de Sinne – ☎03 89 66 12 22 – www.hotelduparc-mulhouse.com – daily 10-1.30am (Fri-Sat 3am) – closed 1 Jan and 1 May.* The Hotel du Parc's piano bar is a classy spot, much frequented by businessmen and the Mulhouse bourgeoisie. In this lovely setting you can hear music worthy of the best jazz clubs: nightly piano concerts (from 7pm), with duets on weekends (from 10pm). The cocktails are irresistible!

SHOPPING & BROWSING

Au Moulin Poulaillon – *176 r. de Belfort – ☎03 89 42 24 04 – Mon-Sat 6am-8pm (Sat 9am) – closed holidays.* In addition to thirty differents sorts of bread, this bakerery run by an enthusiastic young woman has a tea-room well worth a look: old wooden floorboards, beams, restored mill and oven.

Maison de la Céramique – *25 r. Josue-Hofer* – *☎03 89 43 32 55* – *open Tue-Sun 2-6pm.* International arts centre, temporary exhibitions.
Alsaticarta – *31 av. Clemenceau* – *☎03 89 46 13 57* – *coral@evhr.net* – *daily except Sun 2-6.30pm, Sat 9am-noon, 2-6pm.* Items of regional interest, books, paintings, and postcards.
Christmas market – Mid-Nov to end Dec.

SPORTS & RECREATION

Mulhouse has five municipal swimming pools, four of which are equipped for disabled persons.
Piscine Pierre-et-Marie-Curie – *7 r. Pierre-et-Marie-Curie* – *☎83 89 32 69 00.* Former municiapl baths with indoor pools (mid Sep-end May), sauna and Turkish baths, or relaxation baths and Roman baths, in a stunning marble and glass decor dating from the last century.
Stade nautique – *53 bd Charles-Stœssel* – *☎03 89 43 47 88.* Outdoor site in a shaded 7-hectare/17-acre area.

Mulhouse rests in the bosom of the French Republic).
Together with the rest of Alsace, Mulhouse was German from 1870 to 1918 and from 1940 to 1944. It took the French first armoured-car division two months to completely liberate the town.

A Famous Resident

Born in Mulhouse in 1859, **Alfred Dreyfus**, a captain in the intelligence service, was wrongly accused and convicted in 1894 of having passed on military secrets to the Germans. He spent years imprisoned in Cayenne before his case was reviewed following pressure from the press, particularly from the famous open letter by Émile Zola entitled *J'accuse* which earned its author one year's imprisonment and a heavy fine.

Industrial Museums

Musée national de l'Automobile: Collection Schlumpf★★★

Entrance along avenue de Colmar. P *Guarded paying carpark.*

R. Mattès/MICHELIN

Vintage cars in the car museum

Apr-Oct, 10am-6pm; Feb-Mar and Nov-Dec, 10am-5pm; Jan: Mon-Fri, 1-5pm, Sat-Sun 10am-5pm. Dec 25. €10.50 (7-12 yr-olds: €5.50); combined ticket with Cite du Train €14. ☎ 03 89 33 23 21, www.collection-schlumpf.com
Kids This fabulous collection of 500 vintage cars (not all of them are on permanent display) was set up with passionate enthusiasm over a period of 30 years by the Schlumpf brothers, who owned a wool-spinning mill in the Thur Valley upstream of Thann. Many of these cars can be regarded as authentic works of art such is the refinement of their bodywork, the smoothness of their aerodynamic lines, the finish of their wheels and hubs, and the design of their radiator grill.

Musée français du Chemin de fer★★★

Situated in the western part of the town, near Lutterbach. Apr-Sep, 9am-7pm; Oct-Mar, 9am-5pm. 25-26 Dec and Jan 1.€10 (7-12 yr-olds: €5); combined ticket with Musee national de l'Automobile: €14. ☎03 89 42 83v33.
Kids The French Railways (SNCF) collection, splendidly displayed, illustrates the evolution of railways from their origin until today. The main hall includes footbridges offering a view inside carriages, pits making it possible to walk beneath engines, and driver's cabins.
The panorama of steam engines that spans more than 100 years includes famous engines such as the Saint-Pierre, built of teak, which ran between Paris and Rouen from 1844 onwards, the very fast Crampton (1852) which already reached speeds of around 120kph/75mph and

the 232 U1 (1949), the last operating steam engine. The museum also boasts the drawing-room carriage of Napoleon III's aides-de-camp (1856) decorated by Viollet-le-Duc, and the French President's carriage (1925) decorated by Lalique and fitted with a solid-silver washbasin. In striking contrast, the bottom of the range includes one of the fourth-class carriages of the Alsace-Lorraine line.

Musée du Sapeur Pompier

Kids Housed under the same roof, the Fire Brigade Museum, devoted to the history of this dangerous and prestigious profession, displays some 20 hand pumps, the oldest dating from 1740, steam-powered fire engines, others dating from the early 20C, uniforms, weapons and a big collection of helmets.

Musée EDF Electropolis★

Situated in the western part of the town, Électropolis shares a vast parking area with the Musée du Chemin de Fer

Daily except Mon, 10am-6pm. Jan 1, Good Friday, May 1, Nov 1 and 11, Dec 25-26. €8 (children: €4). 03 89 32 48v50. www.electropolis.tm.fr.

Kids A large masonry cube and an elliptical gallery surrounding it are the unusual setting of the exhibition showing the different stages of the production of electricity and its various uses.

Musée de l'Impression sur étoffes★

Daily except Mon, 10am- noon, 2-6pm. Jan 1, May 1, Dec 25. €6 (12-15 yr-olds: €2). 03 89 46 83 00.

The Museum of Printed Fabric is housed in a former industrial building, which once belonged to the Société Industrielle de Mulhouse.

The Museum of Printed Fabric (created in 1857) illustrates the birth and development of the industry from 1746 onwards: engraving and printing techniques are explained, and impressive machines used throughout the ages are employed for regular demonstrations. There are displays of original 18C shawls with oriental motifs.

This museum and its lovely shop are a must for anyone interested in fashion, interior design and the decorative arts.

Musée du Papier peint★

In Rixheim, 6km/3.7mi E towards Basle; see town map.

Jun-Sep, 9am-noon (10am Sat-Sun), 2-6pm (last admission 30min before closing time); Oct-May, daily except Tue, 10am-noon, 2-6pm. Jan 1, Good Friday, May 1, Dec 25. €6 (+ 12 yr olds: €4.50). 03 89 64 24 56, www.museepapier-peint.org.

The Wallpaper Museum is housed in the right wing of the former headquarters of an order of Teutonic knights where, c 1797, Jean Zuber set up a wallpaper factory, which brought fame to his family. The superb **collection**★★ of panoramic wallpaper was exported throughout the world (mainly to North America) during the 19C.

Walking Tour

Place de la Réunion— Historic Centre of Mulhouse

Ancien hôtel de ville★★

Erected in 1552 by an architect from Basle in a kind of Renaissance style characteristic of the Rhine region and decorated on the outside by artists from the Constance area, this edifice is unique in France. The shields bearing the arms of the Swiss cantons.

On the right side of the building, you can see a grinning stone mask similar to the Klapperstein or gossips' stone weighing 12-13kg/26-28lb, which was tied to the neck of slanderers condemned to go round the town riding backwards on a donkey. This punishment was used for the last time in 1781.

Musée français du Chemin de fer, Mulhouse

Mulhouse – French Railway Museum

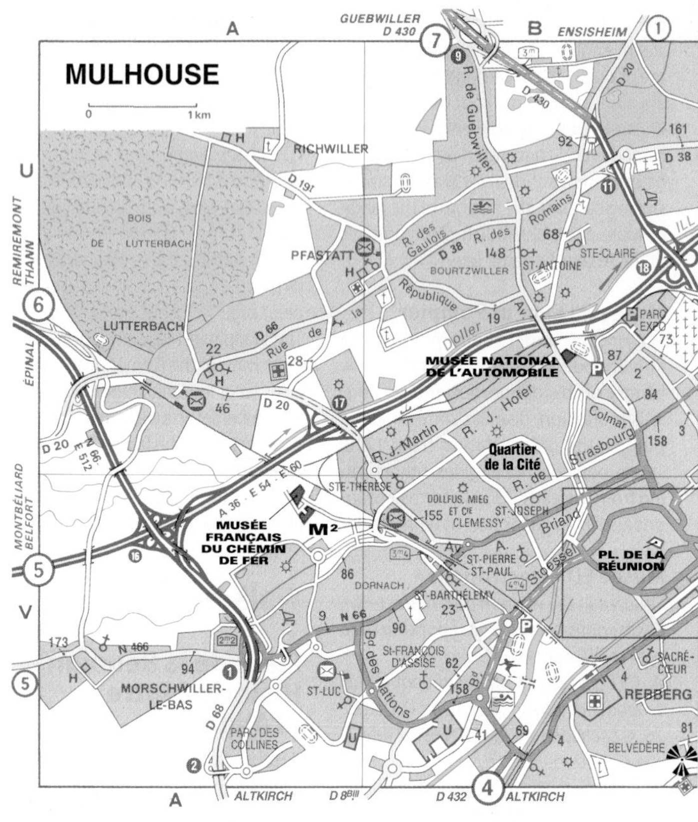

MULHOUSE

Street	Grid	No.
Agen R. d'	BU	2
Alliés Bd des	BCU	3
Alsace R. d'	CV	
Altkirch Pont d'	FZ	
Altkrich Av. d'	BV,FZ	4
Arsenal R. de l'	EY	
Augustins Passage des	EY	5
Bâle Porte de	FY	
Bâle R. de	CV,FY	
Bâle Rte de	CU	7
Bartholdi R.	CV	8
Belfort R. de	AV	9
Belgique Av. de	CU	12
Bonbonnière R.	EY	13
Bonnes-Gens R. des	FY	14
Bons-Enfants R. des	FY	17
Boulangers R. des	FY	18
Bourtz R. Sébastien	BU	19
Briand Av. Aristide	BV,EY	20
Briand R. Aristide	AU	22
Brunstatt R. de	BV	23
Clemenceau Av.	FZ	
Cloche Quai de la	EY	24
Colmar Av. de	BU,FY	
Descartes R.	EY	
Dollfus Av. Gustave	CV	27
Dornach R. de	AU	28
Ehrmann R. J.	FZ	
Engelmann R.	FY	30
Étang R. de l'	DV	
Europe Bd de l'	FY	
Europe Pl. de l'	FY	
Fabrique R. de la	CU	36
Fleurs R. des	FYZ	37
Foch Av. du Mar.	FZ	38
Fonderie R. de la	EZ	39
Franciscains R. des	EY	40
Franklin R.	EY	
Frères-Lumière R. des	BV	41
Fribourg Av. de	CU	
Gambetta Bd Léon	CV	42
Gaulle Pl. du Gén.-de	FZ	43
Gaulle R. du Gén.-de	AU	46
Gaulois R. des	BU	
Gay-Lussac R.	EZ	
Gounod R.	CUV	
Grand'Rue	EY	
Grand'Rue RIXHEIM	DV	
Guebwiller R. de	BU	
Guillaume-Tell Pl. et R.	FY	48
Habsheim R. de	DV	
Halles R. des	FZ	50
Hardt R. de la	CV	51
Henner R. J.-J.	FZ	53
Henriette R.	FY	56
Hofer R. J.	BU	
Hollande Av. de	CU	57
Ile Napoléon R. de l'	CU	58
Ile Napoléon R. de l' RIXHEIM	DU	
Illberg R. de l'	BV	62
Ilot R. de l'	DU	63
Isly Quai d'	FZ	
Jardin-Zoologique R. du	CV	64
Jeune Porte	FY	
Joffre Av. du Mar.	FYZ	65
Juin R. A.	CU	66
Katz Allée Nathan	CU	67
Kingersheim R. de	BU	68
Lagrange R. Léo	BV	69
Lattre-de-Tassigny Av. Mar.-de	FY	71
Leclerc Av. du Gén.	FZ	
Lefèbvre R.	BU	73
Loi R. de la	EY	
Lorraine R. de la	EY	78
Lustig R. Auguste	BV	81
Manège R. du	EZ	
Maréchaux R. des	FY	82
Marseillaise Bd de la	BU	84
Martin R.J.	BU	
Mer-Rouge R. de la	AV	86
Mertzau R. de la	BU	87
Metz R. de	FY	
Miroir Porte	EFZ	
Mitterrand Av. F.	BV	90
Moselle R. de la	FY	91
Mulhouse Fg de	BU	92
Mulhouse R. de	DUV	
Mulhouse (ILLZACH) R. de	CU	93
Mulhouse (MORSCHWILLER -LE-BAS) R. de	AV	94
Nations Bd des	ABV	

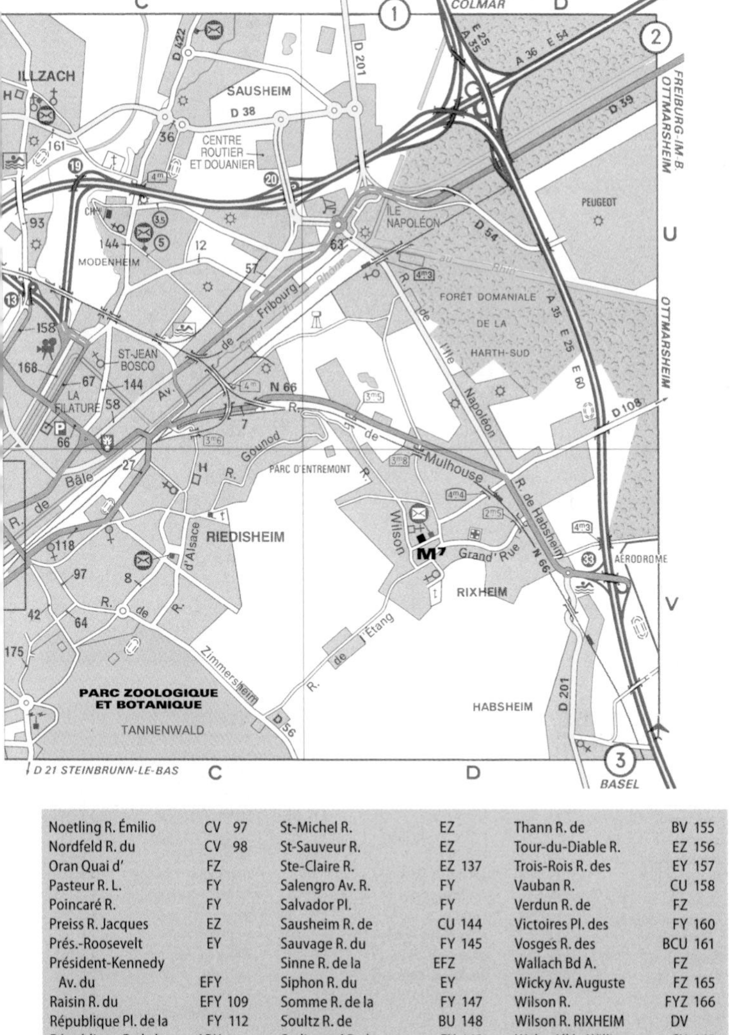

Noetling R. Émilio	CV	97	St-Michel R.	EZ		Thann R. de	BV	155
Nordfeld R. du	CV	98	St-Sauveur R.	EZ		Tour-du-Diable R.	EZ	156
Oran Quai d'	FZ		Ste-Claire R.	EZ	137	Trois-Rois R. des	EY	157
Pasteur R. L.	FY		Salengro Av. R.	FY		Vauban R.	CU	158
Poincaré R.	FY		Salvador Pl.	FY		Verdun R. de	FZ	
Preiss R. Jacques	EZ		Sausheim R. de	CU	144	Victoires Pl. des	FY	160
Prés.-Roosevelt	EY		Sauvage R. du	FY	145	Vosges R. des	BCU	161
Président-Kennedy Av. du	EFY		Sinne R. de la	EFZ		Wallach Bd A.	FZ	
Raisin R. du	EFY	109	Siphon R. du	EY		Wicky Av. Auguste	FZ	165
République Pl. de la	FY	112	Somme R. de la	FY	147	Wilson R.	FYZ	166
République R. de la	ABU		Soultz R. de	BU	148	Wilson R. RIXHEIM	DV	
Réunion Pl. de la	FY		Stalingrad R. de	FY	149	Wyler Allée William	CU	168
Riedisheim Av. de	CV	118	Stoessel Bd Ch.	BV,EYZ	152	Zillisheim R. de	EZ	
Riedisheim Pont de	FZ	119	Strasbourg R. de	BUV		Zimmersheim R. de	CV	
Romains R. des	BU		Tanneurs R. des	EFY	153	Zuber R.	FY	172
			Teutonique Passage	FY	154			

Ancien hôtel de ville	FY	H1	Musée de l'impression sur étoffes	FZ	M6	Parc zoologique et botanique	CV	
Belvédère	BV		Musée des Beaux -Arts	FY	M4	Quartier de la Cité (cités-jardins ouvrières)	BU	
Musée EDF Électropolis	AV	M2	Musée du chemin de fer	AV		Société industrielle	FZ	N
Musée Nationalde l'Automobile-Collection Schlumpf	BU		Musée du papier peint	DV	M7	Temple St-Étienne	FY	
			Musée hist orique	FY				
			Nouveau quartier	FZ				

On the left side of the square, note the Poêle des Tailleurs, once used by the tailors' guild, and, a bit farther along rue Henriette, the 16C Poêle des Vignerons, used by the wine-growers' guild.

Temple St-Étienne

daily except Tue, May-Sep, 10am-noon, 2-6pm, Sun 2-6pm; May 1; no admission charge.

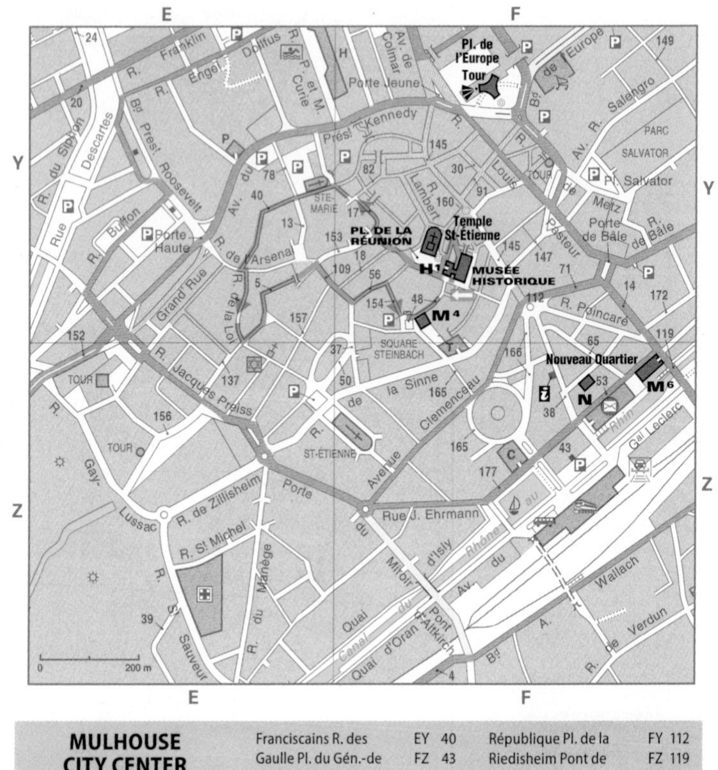

MULHOUSE CITY CENTER

Street	Grid	No.
Altkirch Av. d'	FZ	4
Augustins Passage des	EY	5
Bonbonnière R.	EY	13
Bonnes-Gens R. des	FY	14
Bons-Enfants R. des	FY	17
Boulangers R. des	FY	18
Briand Av. Aristide	EY	20
Cloche Quai de la	EY	24
Colmar Av. de	FY	
Engelmann R.	FY	30
Fleurs R. des	FYZ	37
Foch Av. du Mar.	FZ	38
Fonderie R. de la	EZ	39
Franciscains R. des	EY	40
Gaulle Pl. du Gén.-de	FZ	43
Guillaume-Tell Pl. et R.	FY	48
Halles R. des	FZ	50
Henner R. J.-J.	FZ	53
Henriette R.	FY	56
Joffre Av. du Mar.	FYZ	65
Lambert R.	FY	
Lattre-de-Tassigny Av. Mar.-de	FY	71
Lorraine R. de la	EY	78
Maréchaux R. des	FY	82
Moselle R. de la	FY	91
Président-Kennedy Av. du	EFY	
Raisin R. du	EFY	109
République Pl. de la	FY	112
Riedisheim Pont de	FZ	119
Ste-Claire R.	EZ	137
Sauvage R. du	FY	145
Somme R. de la	FY	147
Stalingrad R. de	FY	149
Stoessel Bd Charles	EYZ	152
Tanneurs R. des	EFY	153
Teutonique Passage	FY	154
Tour-du-Diable R.	EZ	156
Trois-Rois R. des	EY	157
Victoires Pl. des	FY	160
Wicky Av. Auguste	FZ	165
Wilson R.	FYZ	166
Zuber R.	FY	172
17-Novembre R. du	FZ	177

Sight	Grid	Ref.
Ancien hôtel de ville	FY	H1
Musée de l'impression sur étoffes	FZ	M6
Musée des Beaux-Arts	FY	M4
Société industrielle	FZ	N

This neo-Gothic building has retained several 14C **stained-glass windows★** from the previous church demolished in 1858, said to be the finest in all Alsace.

▶ *Walk diagonally across the square.*

On the corner of rue des Boulangers stands the oldest **pharmacy** in Mulhouse (1649).

▶ *Leave place de la Réunion and follow rue des Bouchers; turn right onto rue des Bons-Enfants then take the first turning on the left, rue des Franciscains.*

On your left you will see the mansion built by the Feer family (1765-70). Halfway along the street are the manufactures of printed calico, the most famous being the Cour des Chaînes inaugurated in 1763 in a 16C building.

▶ *Continue along rue de la Loi.*

Note to your right and on the corner of rue Ste-Claire, a manufacturing complex dating from the 18C.

Take passage des Augustins then the first street on the right followed by rue Henriette on the left; go through passage Teutonique on the right and turn left onto rue Guillaume-Tell where the Musée des Beaux-Arts is situated. The street leads back to place de la Réunion.

The Industrial Town

The Nouveau Quartier

SE of the historic centre, beyond place de la République.

A new residential complex intended for young industrialists was built from 1827 onwards on the edge of the old town centre. Known as the **Nouveau Quartier**, it consists of arcaded buildings modelled on those of rue de Rivoli in Paris, surrounding a central triangular garden, the square de la Bourse.

Working-class garden-cities

On both sides of the Ill diversion canal.

Social urban planning launched by the Société Industrielle was a novelty in Europe. From 1855 onwards, the Cité de Mulhouse and the Nouvelle Cité were built on both sides of the Ill diversion canal. Each family had lodgings with a separate entrance and a small garden. A leasing system enabled workers to become property owners.

Sights

Musée historique★★

Daily except Tue, 10am-noon, 2-6pm (Jul-Aug: 6.30pm). Jan 1, Good Friday, Easter Mon, May 1, Whit Monday, Jul 14, Nov 1 and 11, Dec 25-26. No admission charge. ☎03 89 33 78 17.

Housed in the former town hall, the collections of this museum illustrate the history of the town and daily life in the region over the past 6 000 years. The collection includes reconstructed rooms, the original Klapperstein and the **silver-gilt cup** offered by the town to the representative of the French government in 1798 when Mulhouse was united with France.

Kids The former **corn loft** (access from the second floor across a footbridge built in the 18C) contains a collection of toys: dolls' houses, outfits, crockery and games. The folk-art gallery houses reconstructions of regional interiors (kitchen and bedroom from the Sungdau area), pottery, woodcarvings etc.

Musée des Beaux-Arts

Just off place de la Réunion. Jul-Aug, daily except Tue, 10am-noon, 2-7pm; Sep-Jun, 10am-noon, 2-6pm. Jan 1, Good Friday, Easter Mon, May 1, Whit Monday, Jul 14, Nov 1 and 11, Dec 25-26. No admission charge. ☎03 89 33 78 11.

The Fine Arts Museum contains works by Brueghel the Younger, Teniers, Ruysdael, Boucher and other 17C and 18C painters; 19C landscapes and mythological scenes.

Parc zoologique et botanique★★

S of the town centre, on the edge of the Rebberg district. May-Aug, daily except Tue, 9am-7pm (last admission 30min before closing time); Apr and Sep, 9am-6pm; Oct-Mar, 9am-5pm; Dec-Feb, 10am-4pm. €9 (out of season and children: €4.50). ☎03 89 31 85 10.

Kids This zoological and botanical garden, covering an area of 25ha/62 acres and sheltering more than 1 000 animals, aims at preserving, breeding and studying rare and endangered species by collaborating with other zoos and various agencies.

R. Mattès/MICHELIN

Painted façade of the Town hall in Mulhouse

MUNSTER

POPULATION 4 884

MICHELIN LOCAL MAP 315: G-8

Irish monks arrived in the area in the 7C to complete the christianisation of Alsace and founded an abbey which gave its name to the village growing in its shadow (Munster comes from the Latin word for monastery). Today, the region lives on its traditional cheese industry and on the textile industry.
Farther up the Fecht Valley, to the south of Munster, is the rounded summit of the Petit Ballon, also known as Kahler Wasen, an area of high pastures where herds spend the summer and the famed Munster cheese is made.

Visit

The Grand'Rue is a lively shopping street with attractive boutiques. The neo-Romaneque Protestant church was built in the 1920s.
The only remaining wing of the former abbots' palace, situated south of the market square, is now the headquarters of the **Parc naturel régional des Ballons des Vosges**. The **Maison du Parc** (*Early May to mid-Sep: daily except Mon 9am-noon, 2-6pm; mid-Sep to Apr: daily except Sat-Sun (outside school holiday periods) 2-6pm. No charge. 03 89 77 90v34. www.parc-ballons-vosges.fr)* suggests various activities and presents a permanent exhibition covering 600m²/718sq yd illustrating the main features of the park.

Driving Tour

Vallée de Munster★★—Round tour from Munster 5

55km/34mi – allow 3hr – local map *see Parc naturel régional des BALLONS DES VOSGES*

- *From Munster drive NW along D 417 then turn right onto D 5bis which winds its way up to Hohrodberg.*

Hohrodberg

This summer resort spreads along sunny slopes that afford an extended **view**★★ to the south-west of Munster, its valley and, from left to right, the summits rising in the background from the Petit Ballon to Hohneck.
During the climb, stop by the picnic area and walk along the road as far as the bend to admire the countryside. A brochure available from the tourist

R. Mattès/MICHELIN

A Munster valley

office suggests three marked footpaths: **Sentier de Rosskopf** (fauna and flora), **Sentier de Katzenstein** (landscapes and economic life) and **Sentier du Barrenkopf** (the First World War).

Le Collet du Linge

On the right-hand side of the road lies a German military cemetery.

Le Linge

In 1915, following fierce fighting, French troops secured the western slopes of the Linge and Schratzmaennele. Walk to the right to reach the top of Linge, quite close, through what is left of the German sandstone trenches.

Continue along D 11 which soon overlooks the Orbey Valley.

Col du Wettstein

The cemetery contains the graves of 3 000 French soldiers.

D 48 then runs down into the valley of the Petite Fecht and joins up with D 417 near Soultzeren.

The road winds up towards the Col de la Schlucht offering views first of the Fecht Valley and then of the Petite Fecht Valley. Hohneck can be seen to the south. The road leading to Lac Vert (*see Route des CRÊTES*) branches off on the right just before a bend. The road runs through the forest, affording glimpses of the Plaine d'Alsace and of the Black Forest, finally overlooking the splendid glacial cirque, source of the Petite Fecht.

Col de la Schlucht

At the pass, D 417 joins up with the Route des Crêtes (see *Route des CRÊTES*).

Jardin d'altitude du Haut-Chitelet – *see Route des CRÊTES.*

Le Hohneck★★★

see *Route des CRÊTES.*

Le Markstein

see Route des CRÊTES.

Turn left onto the Route des Crêtes.

As you pass beneath a ski lift, you will glimpse of the Lac de la Lauch below, the Guebwiller Valley and the Plaine d'Alsace in the distance.

Turn back and follow D 27.

Address Book

For coin ranges, see the Legend on the cover flap.

PRACTICAL INFORMATION

Tourist office – *1 r. du Couvent, – 68140 Munster – ☎03 89 77 31 80, www.la-vallee-de-munster.com.*

WHERE TO EAT

Auberge de Bichstein *– 6 chemin Pflafflitt – 68140 Soultzeren – ☎03 89 77 59 64 – closed Fri –* . This farm-inn overlooking the Munster Valley enjoys a magnificent view of the surrounding mountains.

Restaurant des Cascades *– 6 chemin de Saegmatt – 68140 Stosswihr – 6km/3.75mi W of Munster on D 417 and minor road – ☎03 89 77 44 74 – closed 10-30 Jan, Mon and Tue.* Tucked away by a stream on the route des Crêtes, this popular restaurant is renowned for its flammekueches cooked on a wood fire.

Gilg – *11 Grand'Rue – ☎03 89 77 37 56-info@patisserie-gilg.fr – Daily 7.30am-6.30pm, Sat 7am-6pm, Sun 7.30am-12.30pm – closed 3rd week of Jan, two last weeks of Sep, 26 Dec, 1 Jan and Mon.* The present owner, grandson of Paul Gilg, famous for his ice-cream cakes, continues his ancestor's traditions in this pleasant tea-room.

SPORTS & RECREATION

Skiing – Munster's skiing domain is comprised of 4 main regions: Schnefenried (downhill and cross-country skiing), Gaschney (downhill skiing with ski-lift, open in summer for walking), Tanet (downhill and cross-country skiing) and Trois-Fours (cross-country skiing only).

Hiking – The Valley of Munster boasts some 350km/217.5mi of sign-posted walks and 250km/155mi of mountain-bike tracks.

After a short climb, the road leaves the high pastures and offers a fine view on the left of the Hohneck massif.

Schnepfenried★

This popular winter sports resort is equipped with several ski lifts and has a beautiful **panorama**★ of the Hohneck massif to the north with the Schiessrothried dam and lake lower down the slopes of the mountain; Munster can also be seen to the right.

From the summit of Schnepfenried (alt 1258m/4 127ft), just south of the resort, 1hr by foot there and back), there is a panoramic view★ from the Grand Ballon to Brézouard, the Fecht Valley, the Black Forest and, when the weather is perfectly clear, the Bern Oberland.

In Metzeral, take D 10VI; turn right 1km/0.6mi farther on, cross the river and leave the car.

The footpath (3km/1.9mi, about 1hr) rises through the glacial valley of the Wormsa to reach Lac de Fischbœdle.

Lac de Fischbœdle★

Alt 790m/2 592ft. This almost circular lake, barely 100m/328ft in diameter, is an artificial gem of the Vosges region, created c 1850 by Munster industrialist Jacques Hartmann. The Wasserfelsen stream supplying the lake forms a lovely waterfall at the time of the thaw.

Lac de Schiessrothried

1hr on foot there and back along the winding path starting on the right as you reach Lake Fischbœdle. It is directly accessible by car from Muhlbach along D 310. The lake, which covers 5ha/12 acres, now a reservoir, lies at an altitude of 920m/3 018ft, at the foot of Hohneck.

Return to Metzeral and turn left onto D 10.

Muhlbach-sur-Munster

The **Musée de la Schlitte** (*Jul-Aug, guided tours 45min 10am-noon, 3-6pm; €2.50, ☎ 03 89 77 61 08*), opposite the railway station, focuses on the former timber trade from the Vosges forests.

Luttenbach-près-Munster

Voltaire visited several times in 1754.

Return to Munster along the D 10 which follows the River Fecht.

Vallée De La Fecht—From Munster to Colmar 6

20km/12.4mi – local map see Parc naturel régional des BALLONS DES VOSGES

From Munster drive E along D 10.

Gunsbach

Albert Schweitzer spent part of his childhood here, where his father was vicar until his death in 1925. Schweitzer

R. Mattès/MICHELIN

Schiessrothried Lake

The Vosges Summits

Donon	1 009m/3 310ft
Champ du Feu	1 100m/3 609ft
Ballon de Servance	1 216m/3 990ft
Ballon d'Alsace	1 250m/4 101ft
Petit Ballon or Kahler Wasen	1 267m/4 157ft
Hohneck	1 362m/4 469ft
Grand Ballon or Ballon de Guebwiller	1 424m/4 672ft, highest summit

returned regularly and had a house built after he won the Goethe prize in 1928; this is now a **museum** (*Jul-Aug, daily except Mon, 9-11.30am, 2-4.30pm, rest of the year: daily except Sun-Mon; Jan 1, Easter Sun and Mon, 24-25 Dec; €3.30; 03 89 77 31 42-www.schweitzer.org)*.

There is a water-themed **walking itinerary** (*4km/2.5mi, about 2hr 30min*) along the banks of the Flecht lined with explanatory panels.

In Wihr-au-Val, cross the Fecht and D 417.

Soultzbach-les-Bains

The 17C **Chapelle Ste-Catherine** (*Jul-mid Sep, 3-7pm, guided tours possible except Sat-Sun; in case of closure ask at town hall 03 89 71 17 58)* contains two interesting paintings (1738) by Franz-Georg Hermann, *Our Lady of Solace* and *St Nicholas of Tolentino.* The isolated parish **church** houses three remarkable gilt **altars**★★ in carved wood made between 1720 and 1740. The Callinet organ dates from 1833.

Drive back to D 417 and turn right towards Colmar.

After the Fecht Valley vineyards, the ruin of Plixbourg castle keep can be seen.

Turn left onto D 10 towards Turckheim.

Turckheim★ – *See Turckheim.*

Colmar★★★ – *See COLMAR.*

Massif Du Petit Ballon★—From Munster to Le Markstein 7

40km/25mi – about 4hr 30min – local map see Parc naturel régional des BALLONS DES VOSGES

Drive out of Munster along D 417 towards Colmar then turn right 5km/3mi farther on and follow D 40.

Beyond Soultzbach, a road (D 43) on the right follows the Krebsbach Valley.
In **Wasserbourg**, turn onto a forest road leading to an inn (Auberge Ried) where there is a fine view of Hohneck. After going through a wood, the road comes out into the open again. The Kahler Wasen farm-restaurant stands on pastureland and the **view**★ extends down the Fecht Valley towards Turckheim and, beyond, across the Plaine d'Alsace.

Petit Ballon★★

Alt 1 267m/4 157ft. 1hr 15min on foot there and back from the Kahler Wasen farm-restaurant.

The **panorama** is superb: the Plaine d'Alsace, the Kaiserstuhl hills and the Black Forest to the east; the Grand Ballon massif to the south; the valleys of the two Fecht rivers to the north and west.

Drive down via the Boenlesgrab pass and forest road.

The road offers a fine view of the Lauch Valley on the right. Beware of the two hairpin bends just before Lautenbach.

Lautenbach★

See GUEBWILLER: Guebwiller Valley.

Follow D 430 on the right.

The road winds its way upwards then runs onto the next slope.

Le Markstein

See Route des CRÊTES.

ÉGLISE DE MURBACH★★

MICHELIN LOCAL MAP 315: G-9

The village of Murbach nestles round the former abbey church of the famous Romanesque-style Murbach Abbey. Founded in 727 the abbey was already rich and famous in the 9C. "As proud as the Murbach hound" became a popular saying, referring to the black hound on the abbey's coat of arms.

Visit *Allow 15min.*

The 12C church has a richly-decorated flat wall on the **east end**★★ which projects slightly. A gallery with 17 different colonnettes can be seen above two tiers of windows.

On leaving the abbey church, follow the Stations of the Cross to the Chapelle Notre-Dame-de-Lorette (1693) for enjoyable views of the surroundings.

For coin ranges, see the Legend on the cover flap.

WHERE TO EAT

Auberge de l'Abbaye – *20 r. de Guebwiler – 68530 Murbach – ☎03 89 74 13 77 – closed 3 weeks in Feb, 25 Dec-1 Jan, Tue and Wed.* The menu is classic rather than regional, but *flammekueches* are served on Friday and Sunday evenings. Terrace and garden.

Excursion

Buhl

3km/1.9mi E along D 40. The large neo-Romanesque **church** of this lively village (metalworks and plastics) houses a rare Alsatian painted triptych (7m/23ft wide) not inside a museum. The **Buhl altarpiece**★★ was probably made c 1500 by artists from the Schongauer School (*see COLMAR: Musée d'Unterlinden*).

B. Kaufmann/MICHELIN

The church in Murbach

NANCY★★★

POPULATION 331 363

MICHELIN LOCAL MAP 307: H-I 6

The former capital of the dukes of Lorraine offers visitors elegant 18C town planning, aristocratic architecture and beautiful vistas, including the most famous place Stanislas, a World Heritage site since 1983. The town has retained a remarkable ensemble of buildings from the turn of the 20C, fine examples of the decorative style of the École de Nancy.
Nancy is also an important intellectual centre with several scientific and technical institutes, a higher school of mining engineering, national centres of forestry research and study, and a cultural centre and theatre housed in a former tobacco manufacture.

- **Orient Yourself**: Nancy stands on the banks of the Meurthe, not far from the junction with the Moselle, and on the Marne Canal to the Rhine. It is 56 km/34.8mi south of Metz.
- **Don't Miss:** Place Stanislas or the Historic Museum of Lorraine.
- **Especially for Kids**: La Pépinière zoo is good for younger children, while La Haye Leisure Park, outside Nancy, is ideal for older kids to let off steam.

A Bit of History

Medieval beginnings

The foundation of Nancy occurred only in the 11C. Gérard d'Alsace, the first hereditary duke of Lorraine, chose to build his capital between two marshes; Nancy's only real advantage was its location in the middle of the Duke's land. At first the new capital consisted of the ducal castle and a few monasteries.
In 1228 Nancy was destroyed by fire and rebuilt almost immediately. In the 14C, what is now the old town was surrounded by a wall of which only the Porte de la Craffe has survived.
In 1476 Charles the Bold, Duke of Burgundy, occupied Lorraine as it was between Burgundy and Flanders (both belonging to him) but the following year, Duke **René II** returned to Nancy and stirred up a rebellion. Charles then lay siege in front of the town; he was killed at St-Nicolas-de-Port (*see ST-NICOLAS-DE-PORT*); his body was found in a frozen lake, half eaten by wolves.

Croix de Lorraine

The distinctive Croix de Lorraine, with two crosspieces, was a reminder of Duke René's illustrious ancestors, his grandfather good King René, Duke of Anjou and Count of Provence, and a the more remote founder of the dynasty, the brother of Godefroy de Bouillon who led the first crusade and became king of Jerusalem. Used as a distinguishing mark by René II's troops on the battlefield of Nancy, the cross later became a patriotic symbol; (*see Colline de SION-VAUDÉMONT*) in July 1940 it was adopted as the emblem of the Free French Forces.

The dukes and their city

As they became more powerful, the dukes of Lorraine set out to develop their capital city. A new palace was erected and, at the end of the 16C, Duke Charles III built a new town south of the old one. At the same time, Nancy became an important religious centre; in the space of 40 years, 13 monasteries were founded. However, the **Thirty Years War** stunted Nancy's economic growth as illustrated by **Jacques Callot**'s engravings entitled *Misfortunes of War*. When peace returned, Duke Leopold began the present cathedral designed by **Germain Boffrand** (1667-1754), who also built several mansions north of place Stanislas.

Stanislas the Magnificent

In the 18C, François III exchanged the duchy of Lorraine for the duchy of Tuscany. Louis XV, King of France, seized the opportunity and gave Lorraine to

Address Book

For coin ranges, see the Legend on the cover flap.

PRACTICAL INFORMATION

Tourist Office – *14 pl. Stanislas, 54000 Nancy – ☎03 83 35 22 41, www.ot-nancy.com.*

Guided tours – Nancy, City of Art, organises 1hr30min guided tours by approved guides. Audioguides with a recorded commentary also available on the Art nouveau theme. *Enquire at tourist office.*

Tourist train – *May-Sep: 45min tour of the historic town by miniature train. Departs from Porte d'Héré (near Place Stanislas) from 10am-6pm, reservations possible. €5.50 (6-14 year olds: €4). ☎03 89 73 74v24, www.petit-train.com*

City pass – This pass from the Office de tourisme offers 3 services with 13 different possibilities. *€13.*

WHERE TO EAT

Les Nouveaux Abattoirs – *4 bd Austrasie – ☎03 83 35 46 25 – closed end Jul-mid Aug, Sat, Sun and public holi days.* This sombre-looking restaurant in a dull area away from the city centre has dark, old-fashioned dining rooms – but don't let all this put you off! The meat is of excellent quality, which gives this authentic restaurant its good name.

Les Pissenlits – *25 bis r. des Ponts – ☎03 83 37 43 97 – pissenlits@wanadoo.fr – closed 1-16 Aug, Sun and Mon.* There's always a crowd in this bistro near the market, and with good reason: the atmosphere is relaxed, the cuisine innovative and diverse.

Le Foy – *1 pl. Stanislas – ☎03 83 32 21 44 – closed 29 Jul-21 Aug, Sun evening, Tue evening and Wed.* Climb the lovely stone staircase to reach this first-floor restaurant above the café-brasserie of the same name.

Le V Four – *10 r. St-Michel – ☎03 83 32 49 48 – closed 1-7 Feb, 30 Aug-9 Sep, Sat lunchtime, Sun evening and Mon.* It may be small, but this restaurant in the heart of the old city is popular among the locals, who enjoy its simple modern decor and its trendy cuisine. Terrace.

Le Gastrolâtre – *1 pl. Vaudémont – ☎03 83 35 51 94 – closed 1-6 May, 15-30 Aug, Christmas holidays, Mon lunchtimes, Thu evenings and Sun.* This popular bistro just behind place Stanislas is run with a master's hand by a media boss. Its menu and characterful cuisine combine local flavours with those from the south of France.

Grenier à Sel – *28 r. Gustave-Simon – ☎03 83 32 31 98 – patrick.frechin@free.fr – closed 23 Jul-15 Aug, Sun and Mon.* This restaurant is in a little-frequented street on the first floor of one of the oldest houses in town. In the large country-style dining room you can enjoy food with a modern flair.

WHERE TO STAY

Weekends in Nancy – Hotel stays of two nights and more are rewarded by a welcome gift and reductions on visits to the town. Ask at the tourist office for the list of hotels and conditions.

Chambre d'hôte Ferme de Montheu – *54770 Dommartin-sous-Amance – 10 km/6.25mi NE of Nancy, Sarreguemines and Agincourt direction – ☎03 83 31 17 37 –mgranddidier@wanadoo.fr – – 5 rooms – evening meal.* This working farm in the middle of the country has lovely uninterrupted views, apart from a nearby high-tension power line. But that's soon forgotten in the peace of the simple rooms with their old furniture. Evening meal by arrangement.

Portes d'Or – *21 r. Stanislas – ☎03 83 35 42 34 – contact@hotel-lesportesdor.com – 20 rooms – €6.*
The main advantage of this hotel is its proximity to the Place Stanislas. The pastel-coloured rooms are not very large, but have modern furniture and are reasonably well equipped.

Hôtel Crystal – *5 r. Chanzy – ☎ 03 83 17 54 00 – hotelcrystal.nancy@wanadoo.fr – closed 24 Dec-2 Jan – 58 rooms – €9.* This entirely renovated hotel near the station is a good place to stay in Nancy. Its modern, spacious rooms have been nicely arranged and decorated and feel welcoming. Cosy bar-lounge.

ON THE TOWN

L'Arquebuse – *13 r. Héré – ☎03 83 32 11 99 – Tue-Sun 6.30pm-4am, until 5am Fri and Sat.* This high-class bar with a refined decor has a good view of the place Stanislas. A wide choice of cocktails with atmospheric music and disco, attracting a mixed clientele of smart students and businessmen. The place to go after 2am.

L'Échanson – *9 r. de la Primatiale – ☎03 83 35 51 58 – Tue-Sat noon-2.30pm, 5.30-9.30pm – closed public holidays.* A pleasant little wine bar that also serves as the local bistro. A dozen or so wines are available by the glass, which can be accompanied by a savoury snack, and the cellar comprises 500 different wines for sale.

Nouveau Vertigo – *29 r. de la Visitation – ☎03 83 32 71 97 – www.nouveau-vertigo.com – Tue-Thu 11am-2am, Fri 11am-4am, Sat 4pm-5am – closed Mon-Sun.* The centre-piece of Nancy cultural life, this bar doubles up as a restaurant and venue for café-theatre evenings and concerts (jazz, Afro-jazz, rock and French music). It is often packed, and the drink flows freely, mainly beer and cocktails.

SHOWTIME

Get hold of a programme – The magazine *Spectacles à Nancy* will keep you informed. *Information from: www.spectacles-nancy.presse.fr.*

Shows – The Opéra de Nancy et de Lorraine, Ballet de Nancy, Théâtre de la Manufacture, Centre dramatique national Nancy-Lorraine, Association de musique ancienne de Nancy, Ensemble Poirel, Orchestre symphonique et lyrique de Nancy, Association lorraine de musique de chambre, Gradus Ad Musicam, La Psalette de Lorraine put on numerous concerts and shows each year in various venues around the city.

Opéra de Nancy et de Lorraine – *Pl. Stanislas – ☎03 83 85 33 20 – daily except Mon and Sun.*

CCN Ballet de Lorraine – *3 r. Henri-Bazin – ☎03 83 85 69 01 – www.ballet-de-lorraine.com– 10am-1pm and 2-6pm.*

Zénith – *R. Zénith – 54320 Maxéville – ☎03 83 93 27 27 – info@zenith-de-nancy.com*

Ensemble Poirel – *R. Victor-Poirel – ☎03 83 32 31 25 – www.nancy.fr* Stages an eclectic selection of theatre, opera, ballet, concerts and readings throughout the year, with shows by well-known and as well as lesser known names.

Théâtre de la Manufacture – *10 R. Baron-Louis – ☎03 83 37 42 42 – manu@theatre-manufacutre.fr – 1.30-7pm – closed Jul-Aug.* National drama centre of Nancy-Lorraine.

MJC Lillebonne – *14 r. du Cheval-Blanc – ☎03 83 36 82 82 – www.mjclillebonne.org – Mon-Fri 9am-11pm, Sat 9am-7pm – closed 2-22 Aug, Sun and public holidays.* Wide choice of socio-educational and cultural concerts, theatre and dance.

Gastronomie en musique – *Jul-Aug:* evening musical performances on Thu, Fri and weekends near terraces in different areas of the city.

Patrimoine en musique – Classical concerts in city-centre churches in the afternoons.

RECREATION AND SPORT

Golf – *10 r. du Golf – 54425 Pulnoy – ☎03 83 18 10 18 – www.golfnancypulnoy.com – 8.30am-7pm – closed 25 Dec-1 Jan.* 18-hole golf course in woodlands.

L'Est républicain – *R. Théophraste-Renaudot – 54180 Houdemont – ☎03 83 59 80 26 – 9.40pm-12.30am by reservation at Tourist Office, no charge -closed Aug.* Guided tour of one of Lorraine's best-known daily newspapers.

SHOPPING

Adam – *3 pl. St-Epvre – ☎03 83 32 04 69 – Tue-Sat 7.30am-7.30pm, Sun 7.30am-6pm, public holidays and Sun (summer 7.30am-1pm) – closed Mon.* This confectioner sells St-Epure, a registered trade name, made of almond meringue, vanilla cream and crushed nougatine, together with a host of other delights for those with a sweet tooth.

Confiserie Chocolaterie Alain Batt – *30 imp. du Tapis-Vert – ☎03 83 35 70 00 – Daily except Sat, Sun 9am-5.30pm, tour by appointment – closed public holidays.* Before your very eyes, this confectioner will create macaroons and bergamotes de Nancy, plums in marzipan, and chocolates. Products to taste and buy.

Maison des Sœurs Macarons – *21 r. Gambetta – ☎03 83 32 24 25 –*

www.macaron-de-nancy.com – Mon 2-7.30pm; Tue-Sat 9.30am-12.30pm, 2-7pm – closed Sun. The secret recipe for macaroons has been handed down within the family since the 18C. Other Lorraine specialities are available here: bergamots (hard sweets flavoured with citrus rind), Berg'amours (crystallized fruits), perles de Lorraine (crystallized fruits with plum liqueur centres), Florentines des sœurs, Babas du Roi, gingerbread, etc.

his father-in-law, **Stanislas Leszczynski**, the deposed king of Poland, on the understanding that the duchy would naturally become part of the kingdom of France after Stanislas' death. Stanislas was a peaceful man who devoted himself to his adopted land, embellished his new capital and made it into a symbol of 18C elegance with the magnificent square which bears his name in its centre. He encouraged artists of genius such as Jean Lamour, who made Nancy's superb wrought-iron railings.

Modern times

Between 1871 and 1918, Nancy welcomed refugees from the nearby regions occupied by the Germans and a modern town developed next to the three already existing ones – the old town, the dukes' town and Stanislas' town. The population of the new industrial town doubled in the space of 50 years.
In 1914 Nancy was barely saved from occupation but was bombed.
Occupied in 1940, Nancy was liberated in September 1944 by General Patton's army, with the help of the Résistance.

Lorraine's Capital City

Place Stanislas★★★

The collaboration between architect **Emmanuel Héré** and craftsman **Jean Lamour** resulted in a superb architectural ensemble (1751-60) characterised by the perfect harmony of its proportions, layout and detail. Place Stanislas forms a rectangle with canted corners, measuring 124m/136yd by 106m/116yd. Louis XV's statue in its centre was destroyed during the Revolution; in 1831 a statue of Stanislas replaced it and the square was renamed after him.
The square is surrounded by five tall **pavilions** and two one-storey pavilions; this emphasises the impression of space and harmony. The façades designed by Emmanuel Héré are elegant, graceful and symmetrical without being monotonous. The wrought-iron balconies by Lamour enhance the richness and elegance of the ensemble.

Arc de Triomphe★

This deep triumphal arch, built between 1754 and 1756 to honour Louis XV, is modelled on Septimus Severus' arch in Rome.
On the right-hand park side, there is a monument dedicated to Héré, on the left a monument dedicated to Callot.

Place d'Alliance

Designed by Héré, the square is lined with 18C mansions and adorned with a fountain by Cyfflé, commemorating the alliance signed by Louis XV and Maria-Theresa of Austria in 1756.

Hôtel de ville

The town hall was erected between 1752 and 1755. The pediment is decorated with the coat of arms of Stanislas Leszczynski: Polish eagle, Lithuanian knight, Leszczynski buffalo.
The interior rooms offer a splendid vista of place Stanislas, place de la Carrière and the Palais du Gouvernement.

Place de la Carrière★

This elongated square dates from the time of the dukes of Lorraine; originally used for cavalry drills, it was remodelled by Héré and is now lined with beautiful 18C mansions. Fountains decorate the corners and at each end there are railings and lanterns by Lamour.

Palais du Gouverneur★

Facing the Arc de Triomphe across place du Général-de-Gaulle and place de la Carrière, this edifice is the former residence of the governors of Lorraine. The peristyle is linked to the other buildings in the square by an Ionic **colonnade**★.

Palais ducal★★

Dating from the second half of the 13C, the palace was in ruins when René II had it rebuilt after his victory over Charles the Bold of Burgundy.

In the 16C, Duke Antoine had the Porterie (gateway) completed together with the Galerie des Cerfs (Deer Gallery). In 1792 the palace was ransacked and skilfully restored in 1850. The northern part was entirely rebuilt.

The plain façade overlooking Grande-Rue enhances the elegant and rich decoration of the **Porterie**★★.

The former Ducal palace houses the Historical Museum of Lorraine.

Église Notre-Dame-de-Bon-Secours★

Avenue de Strasbourg. Built in 1738 for Stanislas by Emmanuel Héré, on the site of René II's chapel commemorating his victory over Charles the Bold (1476), this church is a well-known place of pilgrimage. Note the Baroque west front.

The richly decorated interior includes carved confessionals in Louis XV style, railings by Jean Lamour and a splendid Rocaille pulpit. The chancel contains **Stanislas' tomb**★ and the monument carved by Vassé for the heart of Marie Leszczynska, Louis XV's wife, on the right-hand side and, on the left, the **mausoleum of Catherine Opalinsk**★★, Stanislas' wife.

École De Nancy

Musée de l'École de Nancy★★

Daily except Mon and Tue 10.30am-6pm. €6(children under 18: no charge), no charge 1st Sun of the month 10.30am-1.30pm-closed public holidays. ☎03 83 40 14 86-http://edn.fitech.fr.

Housed in an opulent residence dating from the turn of the 20C, this museum offers a remarkable insight into the renewal movement in the field of decorative arts that took place in Nancy between 1885 and 1914 and became known as the **École de Nancy**. Taking

R. Mattès/MICHELIN

Wrought-iron craftsmanship on Place Stanislas

inspiration in nature, this movement blossomed under **Émile Gallé**.

The museum contains exhibits characteristic of this movement: carved and inlaid furniture by Émile Gallé, Louis Majorelle, Eugène Vallin, Jacques Gruber and Émile André; book bindings, posters and drawings by Prouvé, Martin, Collin and Lurçat; glassware by Gallé, the Daum brothers and Muller; ceramics; and stained glass.

Several furnished rooms, including a splendid **dining room** by Vallin (painted ceiling and leather wallcovering with delicate floral motifs by Prouvé) show the changing styles of middle-class interiors at the turn of the 20C. On the first floor, there is an interesting bathroom decorated with ceramics by Chaplet, a businessman's office comprising leatherwork with floral motifs, seats, a bookcase and a monumental filing cabinet.

Art Nouveau Architecture in Nancy

Much of Nancy's architecture (commercial buildings, villas, houses) was influenced by the Art Nouveau movement. Interesting examples include:

- **Brasserie Excelsior** (*70 rue Henri-Poincaré*), built in 1910 and decorated by Majorelle.
- **Chamber of commerce** (*40 rue Henri-Poincaré*), designed by members of the École de Nancy in 1908,

NANCY

Street	Grid	No.
Adam R. Sigisbert	BX	2
Albert-1er Bd	DV	3
Alliance Pl. d'	CY	
Anatole-France Av.	DV	6
Armée-Patton R.	DV	7
Austrasie Bd d'	EV	
Auxonne R. d'	DV	8
Barrès R. Maurice	CY	10
Bazin R. H.	CY	13
Benit R.	BY	14
Blandan R. du Sergent	DX	15
Boufflers Av. de	DV	
Braconnot R.	BX	19
Carmes R. des	BY	20
Carnot Pl.	AY	
Carrière Pl. de la	BY	
Chanoine-Jacob R.	AX	23
Chanzy R.	AY	24
Charles III R.	CYZ	
Charles V Bd	AX	
Cheval-Blanc R. du	BY	25
Claude-le-Lorrain Quai	AY	
Clemenceau Bd G.	EX	26
Craffe R. de la	AX	27
Croix de Bourgogne Espl.	AZ	28
Déglin R. H.	BX	
Désilles R.	AX	
Dominicains R. des	BY	29
Erignac R. C.	BY	31
La-Fayette Pl. de	BY	47
Foch Av.	DV	34
Foucauld R. Ch.-de	BX	
Gambetta R.	BY	36
Gaulle Pl. Gén.-de	BX	37
Grande-Rue	BXY	
Grandville R.	BX	
Haussonville Bd d'	DX	38
Haut-Bourgeois R.	AX	39
Héré R.	BY	40
Ile de Corse R. de l'	CY	41
Jardiniers R. des	CYZ	
Jean-Jaurès Bd	EX	43
Jeanne-d'Arc R.	AZ	44
Joffre Bd	ABZ	
Keller R. Ch.	AX	46
Lamour R. J.	AX	
Lebrun R. A.	CZ	
Leclerc Av. du Gén.	DEX	
Léopold Cours	AXY	
Libération Av. de la	DV	
Linnois R.	EX	49
Lobau Bd	CY	
Louis R. Baron	AXY	50
Loups R. des	AX	51
Majorelle R. Louis	DX	52
Malzeville R. de	BX	
Mazagran R.	AY	54
Mengin Pl. Henri	BY	55

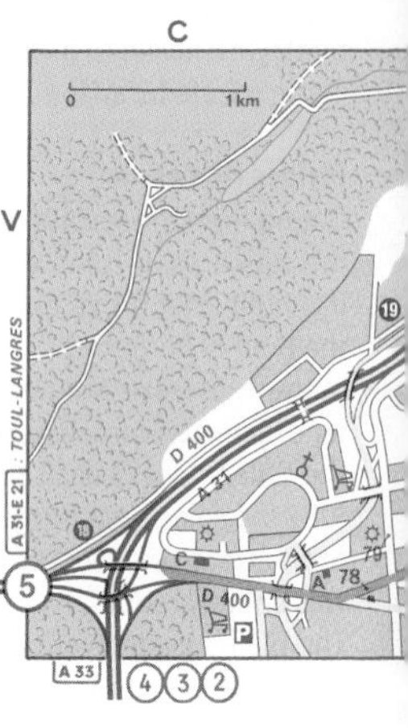

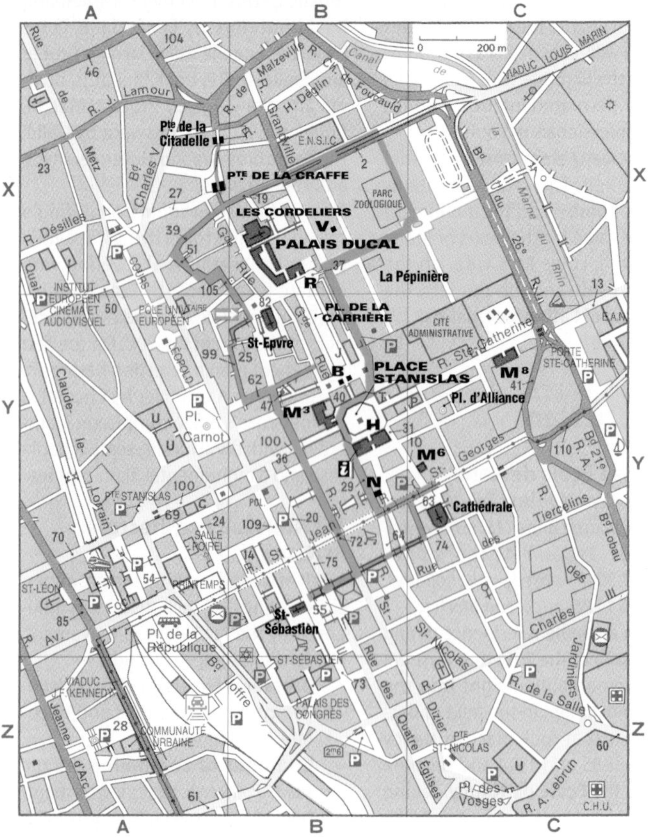

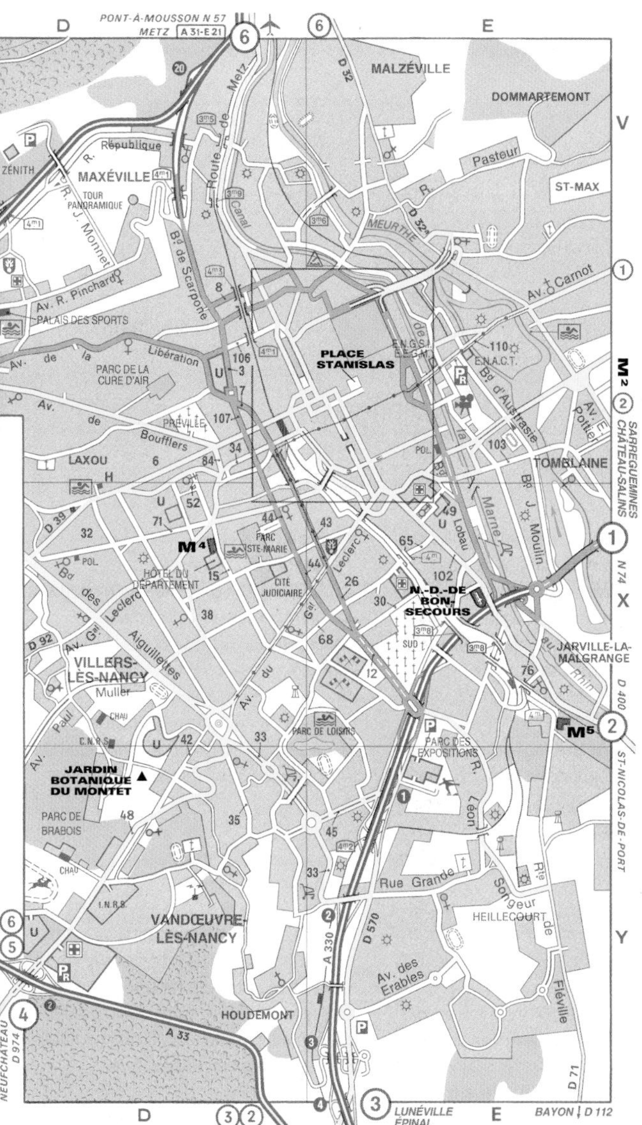

Metz R. de	AX		Pottier R. Eugène	EV		Stanislas Pl.	BY	
Mgr-Ruch Pl.	CY	63	Primatiale R. de la	CY	74	Stanislas R.	BY	100
Molitor R.	CZ	60	Quatre-Églises R. des	BCZ		Strasbourg Av. de	EX	102
Mon-Désert R. de	ABZ	61	Raugraff R.	BY	75	Tiercelins R. des	CY	
Monnaie R. de la	BY	62	St-Dizier R.	BCYZ		Tomblaine R. de	EV	103
Mouja R. du Pont	BY	64	St-Épvre Pl.	BY	82	Trois-Maisons R. du Fg des	AX	104
Moulin Bd J.	EVX		St-Georges R.	CY		Trouillet R.	AXY	105
Muller Av. Paul	DX		St-Jean R.	BY		Verdun R. de	DV	106
Nabécor R. de	EX	65	St-Lambert R.	DV	84	Victor-Hugo R.	DV	107
Oudinot R. Maréchal	EX	68	St-Léon R.	AY	85	Visitation R. de la	BY	109
Pinchard Av. R.	DV		St-Nicolas R.	BCY		Vosges Pl. des	CZ	
Poincaré R. H.	AY	69	Ste-Catherine R.	CY		XXe-Corps Av. du	EV	110
Poincaré R. R.	AY	70	Salle R. de	CZ		21e-R.-A. Bd	CY	
Point-Central	BY	72	Scarpone Bd de	DV		26e-R.-I. Bd du	CX	
Ponts R. des	BYZ	73	Source R. de la	AY	99			

Arc de Triomphe	BY	B	Jardin botanique du Montet	DY		Musée des Beaux-Arts	BY	M[3]
Basilique St-Epvre	BY		La Pépinière	BCX		Musée-aquarium de Nancy	CY	M[8]
Cathédrale	CY		Maison des Adam	BY	N	Palais du Gouverneur	BX	R
Église N.-D.-de-Bonsecours	EX		Musée "Maison de la Communication"	CY	M[6]	Palais ducal et musée historique lorrain	BX	
Église St-Sébastien	BY		Musée de l'Aéronautique	EV	M[2]	Porte de la Citadelle	AX	
Église et couvent des Cordeliers	BX		Musée de l'Histoire du Fer	EX	M[5]	Porte de la Craffe	ABX	
Hôtel de ville	BY	H	Musée de l'école de Nancy	DX	M[4]	Statue Rodin	BX	V

HEILLECOURT			Rhin Av. du	CV	79	Frère R. Gén.	DY	35
Érables R. des	EY		**MAXÉVILLE**			Jean-Jaurès Av.	DXY	42
Fléville Rte de	EY		Metz Rte de	DV		Jeanne-d'Arc Av.	DEY	45
Grande R.	EY		Monnet R. J.	DV		Leclerc Av. Gén.	DY	48
JARVILLE			République R.	DV		**VILLIERS**		
République R. de la	EX	76	**ST-MAX**			Aiguillettes Bd des	DX	
Songeur R. Léon	EY		Carnot Av.	EV		Leclerc Av. Gén.	DX	
LAXOU			**VANDOEUVRE**			Muller Av. Paul	DX	
Europe Av. de l'	DX	32	Barthou Bd L.	EX	12			
Poincarré R. R.	DX	71	Doumer Av. P.	EX	30			
Résistance Av. de la	CV	78	Europe Bd de l'	DEY	33			

with wrought-iron work by Majorelle and stained glass by Gruber.

- **Maison Weissenburger** (1 boulevard Charles V), the architect's own 1904 house, with decorations and wrought-iron work by Majorelle.
- **House** (*86 rue Stanislas*) built in 1906 by Eugène Vallin.
- **Building of the regional newspaper** *L'Est Républicain* (*5 avenue Foch*), dating from 1912.
- **BNP bank** (*9 rue Chanzy*), built in 1910, wrought-iron work by Majorelle.
- **Shop** (*2 rue Bénit*), dating from 1900-01, the first metal-framed building to be erected; the stained glass is the work of Gruber.
- **Block of flats** (*42-44 rue St-Dizier*) built in 1902 by Georges Biet and Eugène Vallin.
- **Crédit Lyonnais building** (*7 bis rue St-Georges*) with stained glass by Gruber (1901).
- **Semi-detached houses** (*92-92 bis quai Claude-le-Lorrain*) built by Émile André in 1903.
- **Villa Majorelle** (*1 rue Louis-Majorelle, ⊶ Not open to the public*).
This house, originally named Villa Jika, was designed in 1899 by the Parisian architect Henri Sauvage (1873-1932) and built in 1901 for Louis Majorelle. Originally, it stood in a large park on the edge of town. It is possible to walk through the garden surrounding the villa.
- **House of the printer Jules Bergeret** (*24 rue Lionnois*), built in 1903-04 and decorated with stained glass by Gruber and Janin.

A brochure entitled *"École de Nancy, itinéraire Art Nouveau"* suggests five itineraries which will help you discover the town's architectural heritage (*available from the tourist office; audio-guided tours are also available here*).

Old Town and New Town

The Old Town is the historic heart of the city, centred on place St-Epvre. When it extended outside its original gates, the New Town was born. *Brochures are available from the tourist office to help you make the most of your tour.*

Basilique St-Epvre

Built in the 19C, in neo-Gothic style, this imposing church is dedicated to a 6C bishop of Toul. Its elegant west front is preceded by a monumental staircase (a present from the emperor of Austria). The roof was blown off during the severe storm in December 1999.

▶ *Turn right onto rue de la Charité then right again onto rue du Cheval-Blanc.*

The **Hôtel de Lillebonne** (*no 12 rue de la Source*), with its fine Renaissance staircase, houses the American library. Next door at no 10, note the unusual doorway of the Hôtel du Marquis de Ville, decorated with a bearded head. Rue de la Monnaie on the left (the Hôtel de la Monnaie at no 1 was built by Boffrand) leads to place de La-Fayette adorned with a statue of Joan of Arc by Frémiet, (a replica of the statue is in Paris).

Follow rue Callot to Grande-Rue: on the corner note the 17C turret. Retrace your steps and turn left onto rue d'Amerval which runs into rue St-Dizier, then turn right on place Henri-Mengin.

Église St-Sébastien

This masterpiece by architect Jenesson was consecrated in 1732; it has a striking concave Baroque **façade**★. Inside, the three naves are surmounted by unusual flattened vaulting resting on massive Ionic columns. The chancel has retained some elegant woodwork. The side altars are the work of Vallin (École de Nancy).

Walk back and take rue de la Faïencerie which becomes rue de la Primatiale; this leads to place Mgr-Ruch via rue Montesquieu on the left.

Cathédrale

This imposing 18C edifice features superb railings inside the chapels, from Jean Lamour and François Jeanmaire. The graceful Virgin and Child in the apse was carved by Bagard in the 17C. The sacristy houses the **treasury** (♿ *Daily 8.45am-6.45, Sun and Holidays 9.45am-7.45; no charge: donations welcome;* ☎ *03 83 35 26 03*) containing the ring, the chalice, the paten, the comb and the evangelistary of St Gauzelin, who was bishop of Toul during the first half of the 10C.

Follow rue St-Georges on the left and turn right onto rue des Dominicains.

Maison des Adam

57 rue des Dominicains. This is the elegant home of the Adam family, who were renowned sculptors in the 18C and decorated the house themselves.

Walk to place Stanislas then along the Pépinière on the right.

La Pépinière

Kids This fine 23ha/57 acre open space includes a terrace, an English garden, a rose garden and a zoo. Note the statue of the artist, Claude Gellée, known as Le Lorrain, by Rodin.

On leaving the park, turn left onto rue Sigisbert-Adam then continue along rue Braconnot and turn right towards the Porte de la Craffe.

R. Mattès/MICHELIN

Brasserie Excelsior Flo, Art Nouveau and traditional cooking

Porte de la Craffe★

This gate, which formed part of the 14C fortifications, is decorated with the thistle of Nancy and the cross of Lorraine (19C). The gate was used as a prison until the Revolution.
To the north stands the **Porte de la Citadelle** which used to secure the old town. This Renaissance gate is decorated with low-relief sculptures and trophies by Florent Drouin.

▸ *Retrace your steps then turn right onto rue Haut-Bourgeois.*

Private mansions

Admire the Hôtel de Fontenoy (*no 6*) designed by Boffrand at the beginning of the 18C, the **Hôtel Ferrari** (*no 29*) also by Boffrand with emblazoned balcony, monumental staircase and a Neptune fountain in the courtyard, the Hôtel des Loups (*no 1 rue des Loups*) again by Boffrand and the Renaissance doorway of Hôtel de Gellenoncourt (*no 4*).

▸ *Walk across place de l'Arsenal* (16C arsenal at no 9, decorated with trophies) *towards rue Mgr-Trouillet.*

Admire the Renaissance **Hôtel d'Haussonville** *(no 9)* with its outside galleries and Neptune fountain.

R. Mattès/MICHELIN

Porte de la Craffe, the oldest of the city gates still standing

▸ *Continue to place St-Epvre adorned with the equestrian statue of Duke René II by Schiff.*

Additional Sights

Musée des Beaux-Arts★★

♿ 🕓 *Daily except Tue 10am-6pm.* 🕓 *1 Jan, 1 May, 14 Jul, 1 Nov, 25 Dec. €6 (under 18 year-olds: no charge), no charge 1st Sun of the month.* ☎ *03 83 85 30 72.*
The impressively refurbished Museum of Fine Arts, housed in one of the pavilions on place Stanislas, contains rich collections of European art from the 14C to the present day which are not arranged chronologically – to their great advantage. For instance, the display of works illustrating the transition between the 18C and 19C takes us on a journey to the early 1940s then goes back to the Italian Renaissance and concludes in the 18C. The most remarkable paintings of the 17C French School include *Love taking its revenge* by Vouet, *Pastoral Landscape* by Claude Lorrain and *Charity* by Philippe de Champaigne.
The Modern Art collection, housed in the contemporary extension, is essentially represented by Manet, Monet, Henri Edmond Cross, Modigliani, Juan Gris, Georg Grosz, Picasso, and a few early-20C artists from Lorraine. Sculptures include works by Rodin, Duchamp-Villon, Lipchitz, and César.
Italian painting is well represented; also noteworthy are the landscapes and still-life paintings by Joos de Momper, Jan II Bruegel and Hemessen as well as The **Transfiguration** by Ruben.
18C painting, housed in the Emmanuel Héré pavilion, includes works by Jean-Baptiste Claudot, Desportes, François Boucher and Carle Van Loo.
The department of **graphic art** holds remarkable collections of prints by Jacques Callot (787 engravings) and 1 438 drawings by Grandville.
The Daum collection (300 pieces of glassware and crystal) is housed in what remains of the 15C-17C fortifications found while building the extension.

Musée historique lorrain★★★

Housed in the former Palais Ducal; entrance: no 64 Grande-Rue.

Daily except Tue 10am-12.30pm, 2-6pm. 1 Jan, 1 May, 14 Jul, 1 Nov and 25 Dec. €4,60(children under 12: no charge). ☎03 83 32 18 74.

The museum contains a wealth of exceptional documents illustrating the history of Lorraine, its artistic production and its folklore, displayed on three floors.

On the first floor, the Galerie des Cerfs, 55m/180ft long, contains mementoes of the House of Lorraine, as well as tapestries from the early 16C, paintings by Jacques Bellange, **Georges de La Tour** (*Woman with a Flea, Discovery of St Alexis' Body, Young Smoker, St Jerome reading*), Charles Mellin and Claude Deruet.

The pavilion at the bottom of the garden houses an **archaeological gallery** concerned with prehistory, the Celtic period, and Gallo-Roman and Frankish times.

Walk across the garden.

The collections, displayed in the vaulted vestibule and gallery, illustrate the history of Lorraine from the Middle Ages to the 16C (sculptures).

A large area is devoted to Lorraine and Nancy during the lifetime of Stanislas: his creations including the square which bears his name, as well as to political, military and literary history from the Revolution to the Empire.

Église and Couvent des Cordeliers★

Daily except Mon 10am-12.30pm, 2-6pm. 1 Jan, 1 May, 14 Jul, 1 Nov, 25 Dec. €4.60 (children under 12: no charge). ☎03 83 32 18 74.

The now-restored 15C Franciscan convent and adjacent church were erected on the initiative of Duke René II.

Église★

The church has only one nave as is usual for the church of a mendicant order. All the dukes are buried in the crypt. Most of the funeral monuments are the works of three great Renaissance artists, natives of Lorraine: Mansuy Gauvain, Ligier Richier and Florent Drouin.

A chapel on the left-hand side contains the **recumbent figure of Philippa of Gelderland**★★, René II's second wife, carved in fine limestone, one of the finest works of Ligier Richier. Against the south wall (near the high altar), note the funeral recess of **René II's funeral monument**★, carved by Mansuy Gauvain in 1509. The effigy of Cardinal de Vaudémont (d 1587) is the work of Florent Drouin. The latter is also the author of a remarkable Last Supper, a low-relief sculpture after the famous painting by Leonardo da Vinci.

Chapelle ducale★

On the left of the chancel. Built from 1607 onwards over the tomb of the dukes of Lorraine, the octagonal chapel was modelled on the Medici Chapel in Florence at the request of Charles III.

Couvent

The cloisters and some rooms of the former monastery are restored and now house a rich **Musée d'Arts et Traditions populaires** (Museum of Folk Art and Traditions).

Jardin botanique du Montet★

Gardens: 10am-noon, 2-5pm, Sat 2-5pm, Sat, 2-5pm, Sun and holidays 2-6pm (5pm Oct-Mar); greenhouses: 2-5pm, Sun and holidays 2-6pm (5pm Oct-Mar). 1 Jan, 25 Dec and 1st Tue of the month (greenhouses). €3.80 greenhouses (gardens: no charge). ☎ 03 83 41 47 47. www.cjbn.uhp-nancy.fr/montet.html.

The botanical gardens cover an area of 25ha/62 acres including hot houses extending over 2 000m²/2 392sq yd. The gardens contain some 15 thematic collections (Alpine, ornamental, medicinal plants, an arboretum etc) and 6 500 species grow in the hot houses: orchids, and insect-eating and succulent plants.

Musée du Téléphone

Daily except Sun, Mon 10am-7pm, Sat 2-7pm, 1st Sun of the month 2-6pm. €3. ☎03 83 86 50 00. www.maison-communication.asso.fr.

The museum illustrates the history of telecommunications over the past 200 years with the help of objects, documents, reconstructions of historic scenes, and technical demonstrations..

Musée-aquarium de Nancy

Apr-Aug: 10am-noon, 2-6pm; Sep-Mar: 2-6pm, Sun and holidays 10am-noon, 2-6pm. 1 Jan, 25 Dec and 1 May 03 83 32 99 97 or www.man.uhp-nancy.fr

Kids On the ground floor is the **tropical aquarium**★ which comprises 70 ponds full of numerous species of fish; the first floor has over 10 000 stuffed animals.

Excursions

Musée de l'Histoire du fer

Jul-Sep: daily except Tue 2-6pm; Oct-Jun: daily except Tue 2-6pm, Sat-Sun and holidays 10am-noon, 2-6pm. 1 Jan, Easter Sun, 1 Nov, 25 Dec. €2.30 (€3.80 during exhibitions). 03 83 15 27 70.

Located in **Jarville-la-Malgrange**, this museum is housed in a building that illustrates the role of metallic architecture in contemporary design and illustrates the evolution of iron-working from prehistoric times to the present.

Chartreuse de Bosserville

5km/3mi. Leave Nancy by S on the town plan. In Laneuville, immediately after the bridge on the Marne-Rhine canal, turn left onto D 126. The road veers to the right, offering a fine overall view of the Chartreuse de Bosserville before crossing the Meurthe. Turn left onto D 2; 1km/0.6mi farther on, an alleyway lined with plane trees leads to the Chartreuse de Bosserville.

Not open to the public. Founded in 1666 by Duke Charles IV, this former Carthusian monastery is now occupied by a technical college. Bosserville was used as a military hospital from 1793 to 1813; hundred of French and foreign soldiers died there, their bodies deposited in the former lakes of Bois Robin.

Château de Fléville

9km/5.6mi SE. Leave Nancy by ③ on the town plan along A 330 and continue to the Fléville exit (8km/5mi).

Jul-Aug: guided tour (45min) daily 2-7pm; Apr-Jun and early Sep to mid-Nov: Sat-Sun and holidays 2-7pm. €7.50. 03 83 25 64 71-www.fleville.com.

The present edifice, erected in the 16C, replaced a 14C fortress of which only the square keep remains.

Once across the former moat, you are in the main courtyard. The tour of the interior includes the dukes of Lorraine's hall, Stanislas' bedroom, the 18C chapel, as well as several bedrooms.

After the visit, take a walk round the outside of the castle through the park.

Parc de loisirs de la forêt de Haye

9km/5.6mi W. Leave Nancy by ⑤ on the town plan and continue along D 400. There is an information centre near the entrance on the right.

Kids This leisure park lies in the heart of the Haye Forest, a vast area of rolling hills covering 9 000ha/22 240 acres, used as hunting grounds by the dukes of Lorraine. The park includes several sports grounds, tennis courts, playgrounds, picnic areas, and marked itineraries for walking or running. It is also the starting point of long hikes, as well as riding and mountain-bike tours (*130km/81mi of paths and trails*) through the forest.

Musée de l'Automobile

Jul-Aug: 2-6pm; Sep-Jun: Wed, Sat-Sun and holidays 2-6pm. €5 (children under 12: €2.50). 03 83 23 28 38. www.en-lorraine.com/alaacl

The museum houses about 100 vehicles of different makes, dating from 1898 (such as the Aster of 1900) to 1989; note the collection of GT saloon cars from the 1960s, radiator stoppers and posters.

NEUFCHÂTEAU

VOSGES. POPULATION 7 533

MICHELIN LOCAL MAP 314: C-2

Although there's no longer a castle, Neufchâteau owes its name to the former castle of the dukes of Lorraine destroyed together with the 18C fortifications. A prosperous medieval market town and the first free city of the duchy of Lorraine, it later became a busy industrial city specialising in furniture and food-processing. Its annual fair in mid-August is one of the oldest in the Vosges region.

- **Tourist office**: 3 parking des Grandes-Ecuries, 88300 Neufchâteauf. 03 29 94 10 95, www.neufchatel-tourisme.com
- **Orient Yourself**: The heart of town is the place Jeanne d'Arc, which is surrounded by old houses, mainly from the 17C and 18C.
- **Also See**: Domrémy-la-Pucelle, *see VAUCOULEURS: Excursions.*

Sights

Hôtel de Ville

Place Jeanne-d'Arc.

The late-16C town hall has a fine Renaissance doorway. inside, there is a richly decorated **staircase**★ dating from 1594 and 14C cellars with Gothic vaulting.

Église St-Nicolas

Jul–Aug guided tour 10am-noon, 2-6pm. Rest of the year, by appointment at the Tourist office, 03 29 94 10 95.

The church stands on the mound where the dukes of Lorraine's castle once stood and, due to the sloping site, consists of two superposed churches. The doorway and tower of the upper church are modern, but the nave dates from the 12C and 13C. The side chapels contain funeral monuments of wealthy 15C and 16C burghers; note the late-15C polychrome **stone group**★ representing the deposition of Christ.

Église St-Christophe

Jul-Aug guided tour 10am-noon, 2-6pm. Rest of the year, by appointment at the Tourist office, 03 29 94 10 95.

The church is mostly 13C, but parts date back to 1100. On the west front, arcading supported by slender colonnettes denotes a Burgundian influence. On the south side, the 16C christening-font chapel has remarkable vaulting with 12 keystone pendentives.

Excursions

Pompierre

12km/7.5mi S along D 74 then left on D 1.

The **Église St-Martin**, rebuilt in the 19C, has guarded its 12C Romanesque **doorway**★. Superbly carved recessed arches frame the three historiated bands of the tympanum depicting Biblical scenes.

Grand

22km/13.7mi W along D 53, then left onto D 3 to Midrevaux and by D 71E.

In Roman times, Grand, which was then called Andesina, was a water sanctuary dedicated to Apollo Grannus; the healing and oracular powers of this god attracted crowds of pilgrims including the emperors Caracalla in AD 213 and Constantine in AD 309.

A 1 760m/1 925yd long **rampart** surrounding a sacred area reserved for the deities was fortified with 22 round towers, three of which have been uncovered, and with gates every 80m/88yd. Excavations have revealed some 60 kinds of marble from all over the Empire, testament to the town's splendour.

Amphitheatre

Open Apr-Sep daily 9am-noon, 1.30-6.30pm. Oct–Mar Wed–Mon 9am-noon, 2-5pm. Closed Mid-Dec to mid-Jan. €2.50 (€3 combined ticket with mosaic). 03 29 06 77 37.

Built c AD 80 on a semi-oval plan, it could hold 17 000 spectators for gladiators fights. Abandoned at the end of the

R. Mattès/MICHELIN

Roman amphitheatre in Grand

4C, part of the walls and some arcades remain. Some tiers of wooden seating have recently been rebuilt so that the amphitheatre can be used for shows.

Mosaic★

same hours and conditions as Amphitheatre.

Dating from the first half of the 3C AD, this is the biggest and one of the best-preserved Roman mosaics ever found in France; it used to pave the floor of an administrative basilica. In the centre are two characters thought to represent a pilgrim and a priest of Apollo Grannus.

NEUWILLER-LÈS-SAVERNE★

BAS-RHIN. POPULATION 1 146

MICHELIN LOCAL MAP 315: I-4

ALSO SEE PARC NATUREL RÉGIONAL DES VOSGES DU NORD

Situated in the forested foothills of the northern Vosges mountains, this pleasant village has several fine balconied houses and two interesting churches.

- **Tourist office**: 68 rue du Général-Goureau, 67340 Ingwiller – ☎03 88 89 23 45.
- **Orient yourself**: On the D 219, 13km/8.1mi. N of Saverne.

Sights

Église St-Pierre-et-St-Paul★

Allow 30min. The former abbey church of one of the wealthiest abbeys in Alsace, the original church was remodelled in the 9C to receive the relics of the bishop of Metz, St Adelphus. The chancel, transept and first bay of the nave were built in the 12C. Two doorways on the north side face a vast square surrounded by canons' houses: on the right, a 13C doorway, framed by the statues of St Peter and St Paul, and on the left a 12C doorway with a fine tympanum depicting Christ giving his blessing.

Interior

Guided tours available (2hr) of the crypt and the upper basilica (with tapestries of St-Adelphes). Contact the parish priest, 5 cour du Chapitre. ☎03 88 70 00 51 or the Tourist office.

The gallery and the organ situated at the end of the nave date from 1773-77. At the west end of the south aisle, the 13C tomb of St Adelphus rests on top of eight tall columns, which enabled the congregation to pass beneath the saint's tomb. The south transept contains a 15C seated Virgin Mary★.

The north transept houses a polychrome Holy Sepulchre dating from 1478. Above the group formed by the three Marys carrying perfume vases and surrounding Christ's body, a niche contains a 14C statue of the **Virgin Mary**★.

The **superposed chapels★** were both built in the 11C on identical plans. Round piers support the vaulting. The capitals of the lower chapel are plain whereas of the upper chapel, dedicated to St Sebastian, are carved with beautiful motifs. In addition, this chapel houses four remarkable 15C **tapestries**★★., which depict St Adelphus' life and the miracles he accomplished.

Église St-Adelphe

This church is characteristic of the transition between the Romanesque and Gothic styles (12C-13C). During the Reformation, in 1562, St-Adelphe was the first church to adopt the simultaneum, which consisted in sharing the premises between Catholics and Protestants. Today it is used solely by the Lutheran church.

NIEDERBRONN-LES-BAINS

BAS-RHIN. POPULATION 4 319

MICHELIN LOCAL MAP 315: J-3

ALSO SEE PARC NATUREL RÉGIONAL DES VOSGES DU NORD

Lying in the heart of a hilly area, this ancient spa town isa pleasant holiday resort and the ideal starting point for hikes and excursions in the Northern Vosges Regional Park.

- **Tourist Office**: 6 pl. de l'Hôtel-de-Ville, 67110 Niederbronn-les-Bains, ☎03 88 80 89 70, www.niederbronn.com
- **Orient yourself**: In the Northern Vosges Regional Park, 50km/31.1mi. N of Strasbourg.
- **See also**: Parc Naturel régional des Vosges du Nord.

A Bit of history

Founded by the Romans c 48 BC and destroyed in the 5C AD, when barbarian tribes swept across Western Europe, the town grew up around its mineral springs. it was restored in the 16C by Count Philip of Hanau; his work was continued in the 18C by the Dietrich family. In the second half of the 19C, the resort became popular and 3 000 people took the waters in 1869. The Dietrich metalworks prospered during the same period and today is the city's main employer.

Visit

There are two springs:

- the **Source Romaine** (Roman spring) which gushes forth in the town centre, in front of the municipal casino, recommended for various forms of rheumatism;
- the **Source Celtic** (Celtic spring) relatively low in mineral content, bottled since 1989.

Sights

Maison de l'Archéologie des Vosges du Nord

44 av. Foch ♿. Mar-Oct: daily except Tue and Sat 2-6pm; Nov-Feb: Sun 2-5pm. 1 Jan, 25 Dec. €2.50. ☎03 88 80 36 37.

Modern display of local archaeological finds. One room is devoted to cast-iron stoves, which have been the speciality of Niederbronn for over 300 years.

Address Book

For coin ranges, see the Legend on the cover flap.

WHERE TO EAT

⊖⊖ **Anthon** – *40 rue Principale, 67510 Obersteinbach, 14km/8.75mi N of Niederbronn on D 653 and D 53. ☎03 88 09 55 01. www.restaurant-anthon.fr. Closed Tue–Wed & Jan.* This pretty red-painted house is a lovely place in a small picturesque village in the Vosges. The fine rotunda dining room has large French windows leading into the garden, where you can eat in summer. Two of the bedrooms have interesting Alsatian box-beds.

WHERE TO STAY

⊖⊖ **Hôtel Cully** – *R. de la République. ☎03 88 09 01 42. hotel-cully@wanadoo.fr. Closed 7-28 Feb, 20 Dec-3 Jan. 37 rooms. ☕ €8.50 – restaurant ⊖⊖.* In a busy street not far from the town centre, this hotel consists of two buildings separated by a lovely flower-decked terrace. The spacious, well-kept rooms in the main building are the best. Alsace and Italian cuisine served outdoors in summer.

ON THE TOWN

Casino de Niederbronn-les-Bains – *10 pl. des Thermes. ☎03 88 80 84 88. www.Alsace-casino.com. Open Sun-Thu 11-2am, Fri-Sat 11-4am.* The only casino in Alsace, comprising 135 slot machines and a room for traditional gambling. Three restaurants, including an Alsace brasserie.

Villa Le Parc (au Casino de Niederbronn) – *Pl. des Thermes. ☎03 88 80 84 84. www.casinodeniederbronn.com. Open daily Jul–Aug noon–midnight; rest of the year Tue–Sat. Closed in Feb and 24 Dec.* In summer the casino orchestra plays daily on the terrace of this restaurant where dinner with dancing also takes place. Enjoy the music while relaxing in the brasserie. Concerts every night in Jul-Aug. Colonial-style interior.

Ferme Charles-Dangler – *Lieu-dit Haul , 6km SE of Niederbronn in Haguenau direction on D 662, 67110 Gundershoffen. ☎03 88 72 85 73. Open daily 10am-noon, 2-8pm.* Accompanied treks (one to eight hours) for all levels on one of the farm's ten horses, to enjoy some of the 360km/225mi of waymarked paths around the town.

Établissement thermal – *Pl. des Thermes. ☎03 88 80 30 70. niederbronn@ugecam-alsace.com – Mar-Nov: daily 7am-5pm, Dec-Feb – closed Sun.* The spa proposes balneotherapy and fitness cures.

Château de Wasenbourg

W of the town. 15min on foot there and back.

From the station, follow the alleyway lined with lime trees. Walk under the bypass and turn left onto the sentier promenade et découvertes (discovery trail), which leads to the ruins of the 13C castle. Nearby there are traces of a Roman temple.

NOGENT-SUR-SEINE

AUBE. POPULATION 5 963

MICHELIN LOCAL MAP 313: B-3

This small town lying on both banks of the Seine and on an island linked to the river bank by a watermill, is overlooked by mills, silos and the cooling towers of the nuclear power station.

- **Tourist office**: 53 rue des Fossés, 10401 Nogent-sur-Seine. www.tourisme-nogentais.fr.
- **Orient yourself**: on the Seine, 19 km/11.8mi. SE of Provins.

B. Kaufmann/MICHELIN

Château de la Motte-Tilly

Sights

Old town

The old town has several timber-framed houses including the **Pavillon Henri IV** and the **Maison de la Turque**, mentioned by Flaubert in his novel *L'Éducation sentimentale.*

Église St-Laurent

Built in the 16C, the church is a pleasant blend of Flamboyant Gothic and Renaissance styles. An imposing tower on the left of the main doorway is decorated in the Renaissance style and surmounted by a lantern which supports the statue of St Laurence holding the grid on which he was roasted alive. The Renaissance aisles have large windows and the buttresses are adorned with carved capitals and gargoyles. Note the fine pediment on the south doorway.

Musée Paul-Dubois-Alfred-Boucher

Rue Alfred-Boucher. Open May–Oct Wed–Mon 2.30-6.30pm. Feb–Apr & Nov weekends and holidays 2-6pm. Closed Dec–Jan, 1 & 8 May. €3. 03 25 39 71 79. www.ville-nogent-sur-seine.fr

The **archaeological** collection featurs Gallo-Roman pottery found in Villeneuve-au-Châtelot, and coins. On the first floor, there are **paintings** (17C-19C), **sculptures** and plaster casts by regional artists including the two sculptors after whom the museum is named.

Note in particular a landscape of Nogent painted in 1764 by Joseph Vernet, entitled *Le Livon*. The painting was believed lost until it was found in Great Britain and bought in London in 1996. It forms a pair with another painting owned by the Fine Arts Museum in Berlin.

Address Book

For coin ranges, see the Legend on the cover flap.

PRACTICAL INFORMATION

Tourist Office – *27 Grand'Rue St-Laurent, 10401 Nogent-sur-Seine– 03 25 39 42 07.*

WHERE TO EAT

Le Beau Rivage – *R. Villiers-aux-Choux – 03 25 39 84 22 – aubergerivage@wanadoo.fr – closed 18 Feb-4 Mar, 16-31 Aug, Sun evening and Mon.* Near the Château de La Motte-Tilly, the white-washed façade of this modern house hides a terrace on the banks of the Seine. Simple cooking and functional rooms.

WHERE TO STAY

Chambre d'hôte Rondeau – *12 r. Chêne, 10400 La Motte-Tilly – 6km/3.75mi SW of Nogent-sur-Seine on D 951 towards Fontainebleau – 03 25 39 83 85 – – 5 rooms €28/42 – €3.* Time passes peacefully on this property located in the heart of a tiny village in the Seine Valley. The rooms, which are in a modern building looking onto a courtyard, are simply decorated. Impeccable service.

Excursions

Jardin botanique de Marnay-sur-Seine

10km/6mi W along N 19 then left on D 68. Open mid-Apr–mid-Oct Mon–Fri 9am-noon, 2-6pm, weekends and holidays 3-7pm. €3.50. 03 25 21 94 18.

Created in 1999, these botanical gardens house some 3 000 species of plants, including many endangered ones. The gardens offer a pleasant stroll along the Evolution path or among medicinal plants and herbs. There are regular lectures, exhibitions and botanical trails.

Château de la Motte-Tilly★

6km/3.7mi SW along D 951. Guided tour (1hr) mid-May–Sep Wed–Sun 10am-noon, 2-6pm. Oct–mid-May Wed–Sun 2-5pm. €6.10. Closed 1 Jan, 25 Dec. 03 25 39 99 67. www.chateau-mottetilly.com

The château was designed by François Nicolas Lancret, a nephew of the artist Nicolas Lancret. It was built in 1754 on a natural terrace overlooking the Seine for Abbé de Terray (1715-78), one of Louis XV's finance ministers. Simple yet elegant, its main features are the unusually high roofs and the arcades linking the main building to the pavilions.

The château was opened to the public following the bequest of the Marquise de Maillé (1895-1972), an archaeologist and art historian. The family furniture was restored and has been added to, with a preference for the 18C.

The ground-floor **reception rooms**★★ are beautifully furnished and decorated with painted panelling, which adds to the refined atmosphere. Two rooms on the first floor recall the benefactress: her bedroom with its green decoration and the Empire-style bedroom of her father, the Count of Rohan-Chabot.

Dangerous Liaisons by Milos Forman was filmed in the château in 1989.

After visiting the interior, admire the **park** with its beautiful ornamental lake and canal.

Ancienne abbaye du Paraclet

6km/3.7mi SE along N 19 and D 442. Guided tour (15min) mid-Jul–Aug Mon–Sat 10am-noon, 2-6pm. €2. 01 42 27 88 24.

Little remains of this once important abbey associated with celebrated medieval lovers **Abélard** (1079-1142) and **Héloïse** (1101-1164). A theologian and philosopher, Abélard retired to this remote place with one of his companions after the Church had condemned his teaching in 1121. He built a modest oratory with reeds and straw and was soon joined by a group of students who camped round the oratory and helped rebuild it in stone. Héloïse became the abbess of Le Paraclet in 1129. There is nothing left of the abbey except a cellar located beneath some farm buildings. Behind the chapel, an obelisk marks the site of the crypt where Abélard and Héloïse were buried. Transferred in the 15C to the main church of Le Paraclet, their remains were taken away during the Revolution and now rest together in a grave in the Père-Lachaise cemetery in Paris.

Villenauxe-la-Grande

15km/9.3mi N along D 951.

This small town sits amid the rolling hills of the Île-de-France cuesta. The 13C **Eglise St-Pierre-et-St-Paul** has a striking Gothic chancel and 13C **ambulatory**★, lit by twin windows with five-foiled oculi. The south aisle has fine pendentives. The **modern stained glass windows**★, inaugurated in 2005, are the work of artist David Tremlett and glassmakers Benoît and Stéphanie Marq (Ateliers Simon-Marq, Reims).

OBERNAI★★

BAS-RHIN. POPULATION 10 471
MICHELIN LOCAL MAP 315: I-6

In the heart of wine-growing country, Obernai is a pleasant holiday resort. The picturesque old town, with its gabled houses, old shop signs and its well, is still partly surrounded by ramparts.

- **Information**: Place du Beffroi, 67213 Obernai. ☎03 88 95 64 13. www.obernai.fr
- **Orient Yourself**: Obernai nestles beneath Mont Ste-Odile amid vineyards, 27 km/16.8 mi. SW of Strasbourg.
- **Don't Miss**: the Hans em Schnokeloch folk festival in July and the harvest festival in October.
- **Also See:** Le HOWALD and Route des VINS.

Town Walk

Place du Marché★★

The golden hues of the surrounding buildings add to the charm of the picturesque market square; in its centre is a fountain with a statue of St Odile. The **Ancienne Halle aux blés**★ (old grain market) at one end dates from 1554.

Tour de la Chapelle★

This 13C belfry with a 16C Gothic spire was the tower of a chapel of which only the choir remains.

Hôtel de ville★

Despite being remodelled in 1848, the town hall has kept some of its 14C-17C features. The oriel window and balcony on the facade date from 1604.

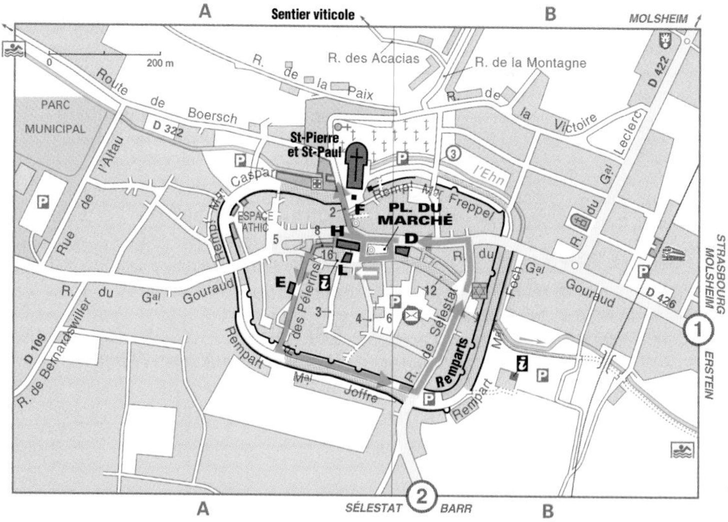

OBERNAI								
Chanoine Gyss R. du	A	2	Dietrich R.	A	4	Juifs Ruelle des	A	8
Chapelle R. de la	A	3	Étoile Pl. de l'	A	5	Marché R. du	B	12
			Fines Herbes Pl. des	AB	6	Sainte-Odile R.	A	16

Ancienne halle aux blés	B	D	Maison de pierre du 13e s.	A	E	Tour de la Chapelle	A	L
Hôtel de ville	A	H	Puits aux six-seaux	A	F			

Address Book

For coin ranges, see the Legend on the cover flap.

WHERE TO EAT

La Cour des Tanneurs – *Ruelle du Canal-de-l'Ehn. ☎03 88 95 15 70. Closed 1-14 Jul, 21 Dec-3 Jan, Tue & Wed.* In a tiny narrow street in the town centre, this neat restaurant serves updated regional cooking along with well-chosen wines in a family atmosphere. A satisfying halt after a walk around the old town.

Winstub O'Baerenheim – *46 r. du Gén.-Gouraud. ☎03 88 95 53 77. Closed Jan & 14-30 Nov.* This restaurant in Obernai's main street is good for an inexpensive lunch on typical Alsace cuisine and wines. Notice the barrel-making tools over the d oorway. Eat in the dining room with a big chimney or outdoors in the courtyard.

WHERE TO STAY

Hostellerie Duc d'Alsace – *6 r. de la Gare. ☎03 88 95 55 34. 19 rooms. €7.50.* This constantly updated hotel occupies two 17C houses. Bedrooms are spacious and well equipped.

A la Cour d'Alsace – *3 r. Gail. ☎03 88 95 07 00. www.cour-alsace.com. Closed 24 Dec–1 Feb. 42 rooms. 2 restaurants and .* This typical Alsatian building is just next to the ramparts in the charming medieval old town. Comfortable, carefully decorated rooms and two restaurants, one gastronomic, the other a homelier winstub.

ON THE TOWN

L'Athic – 6 *pl. de l'Étoile. ☎03 88 95 50 57. Jul-Aug daily 11am-3pm; rest of the year 3pm-3am . Cosed 21 Feb-16 Mar,22 Nov-2 Dec and 24 and 31 Dec.* This elegant cocktail bar, furnished with velvet armchairs and a piano for customers' use, also has a billiard room and another bar with a pewter counter.

SHOPPING

Cave d'Obernai-Divinal – *30 r. du Gén.-Leclerc. ☎03 88 47 60 21 – www.cdhv.fr . Open Mon-Sat 10am-noon, 2-6pm. Closed public holidays.* Tasting and wine for sale. Guided tour by appointment.

Aux Caves d'Obernai – *14 r. du Marché. ☎03 88 95 36 94. Ope, Mon 2-6.30pm, Tue-Sat 9.30am-noon, 2-6.30pm, 6pm Sat. Closed mid Jan-early Feb.* The wines of Clos Ste-Odile, whose vines surround the town, are on sale in this shop: Riesling, Tokay, Gewürztraminer, pinot noir, sparkling *blanc de blanc*, liqueurs, and raspberry and plum brandies. Also a selection of regional products.

Domaine Seilly – *1 r. de la Paille. ☎03 88 95 46 82 – www.seilly.com. Open Mon 9.30am-noon, Tue-Sat 9.30am-noon, 2-7pm.* Situated in an old draper's shop dating from 1628, this is now the shop of the wine-grower Seilly. Among other treats, you can try the *vin de pistolet*, which gets its name from an amusing local story, which is explained to you in the shop.

HIKING

Sentier viticole du Schenkenberg – *This 3.6km/2.2mi circuit (1hr 30min on foot) runs across 250ha/618 acres of vineyards.* Park by the ADEIF Memorial, with its 12m/40ft high cross. In summer, there is a weekly guided tour (Wed mornings) followed by a visit to a cellar. *Apply to the Tourist office.*

CALENDAR

Hans em Schnokeloch Festival – *Mid-July – summer festival.*

Vendanges festival – *3rd Sun of Oct.*

Puits aux six seaux

This elegant Renaissance well has a baldaquin with a weather cock on the top dated 1579. Six pails hang from the three pulleys.

Église St-Pierre-et-St-Paul

Open daily 2-6pm. This imposing 19C neo-Gothic church houses a Holy Sepulchre altar (1504) and a reliquary containing the heart of the bishop of Angers, Charles Freppel, a native of Obernai, who died in 1891 and asked in his will that his heart be returned to the church of his native town once Alsace became French again. His wish was fulfilled in 1921. The four 15C stained-glass windows are believed to be the work

R. Mattès/MICHELIN

Market square in Obernai

of Pierre d'Andlau or his pupil Thibault de Lyxheim.

Old houses★
There are many old houses in the streets around place du Marché, notably ruelle des Juifs, and towards place de l'Étoile.

In rue des Pèlerins, note the three-storey stone house dating from the 13C.

Ramparts
The double ring of ramparts, built in the 12C, make a pleasant promenade.

ORBAIS-L'ABBAYE

MARNE. POPULATION 567

MICHELIN LOCAL MAP 306: E-9

This pretty village has one the finest Gothic churches in Champagne, remnant of an important Benedictine abbey founded in the 7C. The village is a starting point for excursions through the Surmelin Valley and Vassy Forest.

- **Orient yourself:** Orbais is situated on the D 11 between Epernay and Montmirail.

Sights

Church★
The building of the church (end of the 12C and 13C) was probably supervised by Jean d'Orbais, one of the master builders of Reims Cathedral. It incorporates the chancel and transept of the former abbey church as well as two bays from the original nave. Note the unusual flying buttresses of the transept and the apse which meet on the same abutment; the slender spire dates from the 14C. Inside, the **chancel**★, with its ambulatory and radiating chapels, is considered to be the prototype of that of Reims Cathedral. The entrance to the transept is furnished with early-16C choir stalls carved with Biblical scenes and amusing figures on the misericords.

Driving Tour

Churches and Castles

- *From Orbais, take the D 242 to Fromentières (6km/3.7mi).*

Ph. Gajic/MICHELIN

Scene on the magnificent 16C altarpiece in Fromentières

Église de Fromentières

Behind the high altar, the church contains a monumental early 16C Flemish **altarpiece**★★, which was bought by the vicar in 1715 for a modest sum. The signature, a severed hand, is the emblem of Antwerp. The paintings on the side panels depict episodes from the New Testament; the central panel comprises three tiers of delicately carved scenes, illustrating Christ's Life and Passion.

▶ *Drive along D 933 to Étoges (11km/6.8mi).*

Étoges

This wine-growing village is close to the Côte des Blancs. There is a fine view of the elegant 17C **château**, now a hotel, from the bridge across the moat.

The 12C **church** (*open Jun-Sep 9am-6pm)*, remodelled in the 15C and 16C, has a Gothic rose window and a Renaissance doorway; it contains several 16C recumbent tomb figures.

▶ *Drive 8km/5mi along D 18.*

Château de Montmort-Lucy

Guided tour (1hr) Mid-Jul to mid-Sep Tue–Sat 2.30pm, 4.30pm, Sun & 15 Aug 2.30pm, 3.30pm, 5pm, 5.30pm, Whit Sun & Whit Mon 2-6pm. €6.50. 03 26 59 10 04.

The brick and stone château occupies a commanding position above the Surmelin Valley. It was here that General von Bülow ordered the retreat from the Marne in 1914 (*see MONTMIRAIL*).

Begun in the 12C but rebuilt in the late 16C, still has a rather feudal appearance with its 14m/46ft deep moat. The lower part of the castle is reached by a ramp designed for horses, similar to that in the château at Amboise.

For coin ranges, see the Legend on the cover flap.

WHERE TO STAY

Le Château d'Étoges

– 4 r. Richebourg, 51270 Étoges. 03 26 59 30 08. www.etoges.com. Closed mid-Jan–mid-Feb. 20 rooms. €12. Restaurant . For an evening of refinement, why not stay at this 17C château with its ceremonial reception rooms, grand dining room and old-fashioned bedrooms, which is set in spacious grounds just outside the village.

VAL D'ORBEY★★

HAUT-RHIN. MICHELIN LOCAL MAP 315: G-8

The austere landscapes of Lac Noir and Lac Blanc contrast with the picturesque valleys of the River Béhine and the River Weiss. The circular tour also leads to Le Linge, one of the most dramatic battlefields of the First World War. This is Welche country, a kind of French enclave (linguistically speaking) in Alsace. Welche is a Romance dialect, derived from vulgar Latin.

Information: 2 impasse Président-Poincaré, 68410 Les Trois-Épis. ☎03 89 49 80 56.

Orient yourself: Located at the northern end of the Route des Crêtes, W of Colmar, between Kayserberg, Munster and the Col du Bonhomme pass.

Driving tour

Les Trois-Êpis

57km/35mi – allow 4hr

Les Trois-Épis★★

This resort, which is a starting point for numerous hikes and interesting drives, gets its name from an apparition by the Virgin Mary in 1491, to a blacksmith on his way to market. In her left hand she held a piece of ice as a symbol of a hardened heart and in her right hand she had three ears of corn (*épis de maïs*) as a symbol of divine mercy and blessing.

Le Galz★★

1hr on foot there and back.

At the top a monument by Valentin Jæg commemorates the return of Alsace to France in 1918. The view extends as far as the Plaine d'Alsace, the Black Forest, the Sundgau and the Jura mountains.

Sentier de la forêt de St-Wendelin

1hr 30min on foot from the car park on place des Antonins (brochure available from the tourist office). Follow the green squirrel markings.

This forest trail explores the flora covering the Val d'Orbey slopes.

From Les Trois-Épis drive W along D 11 for 3km/1.9mi then left onto D 11VI.

The road follows the ridge separating the Val d'Orbey and the Munster Valley, offering fine views of both. It then runs through the forest right round the Grand Hohneck.

Le Linge

See MUNSTER: Vallée de Munster.

Turn right at Collet du Linge then, leaving the Glasborn path on your left, continue to the Col du Wettstein (war cemetery) and turn right again.

Lac Noir★

Park by the lake.

Lac Noir (alt 954m/3 130ft) sits inside a glacial cirque. A moraine reinforced by a dam retains the water on the east side; the lake is otherwise surrounded by high granite cliffs which contribute to the austerity of the landscape. Fishing is allowed but swimming is strictly forbidden.

Lac Blanc★

The road skirts Lac Blanc (alt 1 054m/3 458ft), offering beautiful views of the glacial cirque that surrounds the lake (area: 29ha/72 acres, depth: 72m/236ft). A strange rock, shaped like a fortress known as **Château Hans**, overlooks the lake.

The road joins the Route des Crêtes at the Col du Calvaire. Turn right through the forest.

The road gives glimpses of the Béhine Valley and the Tête des Faux, before reaching the Col du Bonhomme.

Col du Bonhomme

Alt 949m/3 114ft. This pass links Alsace and Lorraine via the Col de Ste-Marie in the north and the Col de la Schlucht in the south (*see also Route des CRÊTES*).

R. Mattès/MICHELIN

Lac Blanc

The road twists down from the pass into the Béhine Valley offering fine views of the valley with the Brézouard summit in the distance and the Tête des Faux quite close by to the right, then passes beneath a rocky spur topped by the ruins of Gutenburg Castle.

Le Bonhomme

This is the beginning of Welche country. Streams rush down the slopes to form the River Béhine.

Lapoutroie

In this village a small **Musée des Eaux-de-Vie** (liqueurs and traditional distillery) is housed in an 18C coaching inn (*open daily 9am-noon, 2-6pm. 25 Dec. No charge. 03 89 47 50 26, www.musee-eaux-de-vie.com*).

Continue along N 415 towards Kaysersberg, past the intersection with D 48 (roundabout), then immediately left onto D 11IV leading to Fréland.

Fréland

The name means free land; miners from Ste-Marie-aux-Mines (*see Parc naturel régional des BALLONS DES VOSGES: Val d'Argent*) enjoyed various privileges such as the right to cut timber.

Maison du Pays Welche

2 rue de la Rochette. Guided tour (1–2hr) Jun-Sep Thur-Tue 10am-4.30pm; Mar-May and Oct-Dec by appointment. Jan-Feb. €3. 03 89 71 90 52.

Local people have gathered objects illustrating the region's traditions and displayed them in an 18C presbytery.

Musées de la Vieille Forge, Musée de la Traversée des siècles, Musée des Automates

Guided tour (2hr30–3hr) by appointment. €3. 03 89 47 58 30.

Here you can see an old water-powered smithy with its water-wheel and two adjacent museums, devoted to unusual tools and a collection of automatons.

Return to N 415, at the roundabout take the D 48 towards Orbey.

Orbey

This village, made up of several hamlets, stretches along the verdant valley of the River Weiss; the heights overlooking the valley, crisscrossed by paths, are ideal hiking country.

Beyond Orbey, the *D 11* climbs up a narrow valley past Tannach then, after a deep bend, continues to climb offering fine views of the Weiss Valley overlooked by Grand Faudé. Further on it changes direction revealing the Walbach Valley ahead with Le Galz and its monument beyond and the Plaine d'Alsace in the distance. Leaving **Labaroche** on your left, you will soon notice Grand Hohneck straight ahead and, nearby on your right, the conical summit of Petit Hohneck.

Return to Les Trois-Épis, 3km/1.9mi beyond the intersection of D 11 and D 11VI.

OTTMARSHEIM

HAUT-RHIN. POPULATION 1 926

MICHELIN LOCAL MAP 315: J-10

This village, situated on the edge of the vast Harth Forest, acquired fame through its church, a unique example of Carolingian architecture in Alsace. Nowadays, Ottmarsheim is also known for its hydroelectric power station, the second of eight such power stations along the Grand Canal d'Alsace (*see VALLÉE DU RHIN*).

- **Orient yourself**: Just off the A 36 Mulhouse- Bâle-Fribourg-en-Brisgau motorway.

Sights

Église★

The church, consecrated by Pope Leo IX c 1040, is a rare example of Carolingian architecture. With its unusual octagonal floor plan, topped by a cupola, it is a reduced-scale replica of the Palatine chapel in Aachen Cathedral. All the measurements are divisible by three, the figure symbolising the Holy Trinity. The upper part of the belfry is 15C as is the rectangular chapel on the south-east side, whereas the Gothic chapel left of the apse was built in 1582. The church was badly damaged by a fire in 1991 but some 15C murals depicting St Peter's Life and Christ in Glory presiding over the Last Judgement have been skilfully restored.

Centrale hydro-électrique★

The power station is open subject to Vigipirate security plan, enquire at ☎03 89 83 51 23.

The Ottmarsheim hydroelectric power station, the reach and the locks, built between 1948 and 1952, form the second section of the Grand Canal d'Alsace, which was the first stage of the harnessing-of-the-Rhine project between Basle and Lauterbourg.

Locks are of equal length (185m/202yd) but different widths (23m/75ft and 12m/40ft). They are closed by angled gates upstream and by lifting gates downstream. The whole operation takes less than half an hour: 11min in the small lock and 18min in the large lock. The control room overlooks the two locks.

Power station – The engine room is vast and light. The four units have a total output of 156 million watts and produce an average of 980 million kWh every year.

LA PETITE-PIERRE★

BAS-RHIN. POPULATION 612

MICHELIN LOCAL MAP 315: H-3

A properous medieval town, later fortified by Vauban, Louis XIV's military engineer, La Petite-Pierre, also known as Lützelstein or Parva Petra, is a popular summer resort in the heart of the forested massif of the low Vosges and the starting point of more than 100km/62mi of marked footpaths.

- **Information**: 2 rue du Château, 67290 La Petite-Pierre. ☎03 88 70 42 30. www.ot-paysdelapetitepierre.com
- **Orient Yourself:** Situated in the Parc Naturel Régional des Vosges du Nord, 55km/34.2mi. NW of Strasbourg.
- **Also See:** Parc naturel régional des VOSGES DU NORD.

Address Book

For coin ranges, see the Legend on the cover flap.

WHERE TO EAT AND STAY

Auberge d'Imsthal – *At Imsthal lake, 3.5km/2mi SE of La Petite-Pierre on D 178. 03 88 01 49 00. www.petite-pierre.com. 23 rooms. €9. Restaurant* . This half-timbered inn set on the edge of a lake just outside the village is a lovely place for a weekend stay, in a peaceful country setting. The newer rooms are more spacious. Pleasant rustic dining room. Sauna, Turkish baths and solarium.

Aux Trois Roses – *19 r. Principale. 03 88 89 89 00. Closed 7-18 Jan. 40 rooms. € 11. Restaurant* . Comfortable hotel behind an 18C facade in the centre of the village. Typical Vosges specialities are served in the restaurant.

Old Town

The old town is reached up a steep path; then follow rue du Château.

Église

The belfry and the nave were rebuilt in the 19C, but the Gothic chancel dates back to the 15C. Since 1737, the church has been used for Catholic and Protestant services.

Maison des Païens

This Renaissance house in the gardens of the town hall was built in 1530 on the site of a Roman watchtower.

Chapelle St-Louis

Built in 1684 and once reserved for the garrison (funeral monuments of former governors and military chiefs), the chapel now houses the unusual **Musée du Sceau alsacien** (Museum of Alsatian Heraldry) (*open Jul–Sep & 26-31 Dec, depending on weather Tue-Sun 10am-noon, 2-6pm; Oct-Jun weekends and holidays 10am-noon, 2-6pm; closed Jan, 25 Dec; no charge; 03 88 70 48 65*). It illustrates the history of Alsace through reproductions of the seals that used to be the distinguishing marks of cities, stately homes, important families, crafts or guilds, religious orders or chapters.

R. Mattès/MICHELIN

Medieval piece, Museum of Alsatian Heraldry

Château and Maison du Parc

Built in the 12C, the castle was remodelled several times, at the instigation of Georg Hans von Veldenz, the Count Palatine of the Rhine region. Today it houses the **Maison du parc** (*open daily 10am-noon, 2-6pm (last entrance 45min before closing); closed Jan, 24-25 and 31 Dec; €2.50 ; 03 88 01 49 59; www.parc-vosges-nord.fr*). Skilfully displayed (reconstructions, games, slide shows) in six thematic multimedia rooms, the permanent exhibition helps visitors to discover the historic, cultural and technical heritage of the Parc naturel régional des Vosges du Nord as well as its fauna and flora.

Follow rue des Remparts which offers views of the surrounding countryside.

Musée des Arts et Traditions populaires

Jul-Sep and 26-31 Dec: guided tour (1hr) Tue-Sun 10am-noon, 2-6pm; Oct-Jun: weekends and holidays only 10am-noon, 2-6pm. . Closed Jan, 25 Dec. No charge. 03 88 70 48 65.
The small museum of folk art and customs, housed in a 16C Magasin or warehouse, displays an interesting collection of cake tins, such as *springerle* (aniseed cake) and *lebkuche* (gingerbread).

Continue along rue des Remparts back to rue du Château.

PFAFFENHOFFEN

BAS-RHIN. POPULATION 2 468

MICHELIN LOCAL MAP 315: J-3

Once the main centre of the bailiwick of Hanau-Lichtenberg, the small industrial town of Pfaffenhoffen was fortified in the 15C to guard the south bank of the River Moder. In the 16C, it became one of the rallying points of rebellious peasants (*see SAVERNE*). Today, the remaining fortifications enclose lovely timber-framed houses as well as an interesting museum of folk imagery, which testifies to one of the oldest artistic traditions in Alsace.

- **Orient yourself**: Located 15km/9.3 mi. W of Haguenau, 37km/23mi. NW of Strasbourg.

Sights

Musée de l'Imagerie populaire★

24 rue du Dr-Albert-Schweitzer. Open May-Sep Tue-Sun 2-6pm, Wed 10am-noon, 2-6pm; Oct-Apr: Tue-Sun 2-5pm, Wed 10am-noon, 2-5pm, Sat-Sun 2-6pm. Closed 24 Dec–1 Jan, Good Friday, 1 May, 1 Nov €3.50. 03 88 07 80 05.

Housed in an old brewery, the museum illustrates the long-standing Alsatian tradition of popular pictures painted on request by itinerant or local painters. Whether painted on paper or vellum, behind glass or on objects, the rich collection includes religious pictures intended to encourage prayers, and protect houses, cattle and crops, and memento pictures illustrating important events in peoples' lives.

Among the exhibits are pictures under glass, which are very brightly coloured despite being very old. There is also a collection of *églomisés*, pictures with black backgrounds and gilt decoration and texts, which were intended to adorn oil-lamp or candle-lit rooms and date from the Second Empire (1852-70).

Other rooms house a collection of *Goettelbriefe* or christening wishes, one of the oldest traditions in Alsace, which lasted for nearly 400 years.

Hôtel de ville

The façade is adorned with a medallion of Dr Schweitzer, who was made a freeman of the city. The hall contains sculptures and Impressionist-style figurative paintings by Strasbourg artist, Alfred Pauli (1898-1988).

Musée de l'Imagerie peinte et populaire alsacienne, Pfaffehoffen

Regimental memento

Old houses

There are many half-timbered houses dating from the 16C to 19C, particularly in rue du Docteur-Schweitzer and rue du Marché.

Synagogue

Dating from 1791, this is the oldest intact Alsatian synagogue. The imposing yet discreet building testifies to the importance of the Jewish community in the late 18C. Note the Kahlstub (communal room) and the room reserved for occasional guests.

Driving Tour

6km/3.7mi SW.

- *From Pfaffenhoffen take the D 419A, then right along the D 25 to Ettendorf.*

At the end of the village, a small road parallel to the railway line leads to the cemetery (500m/547yd).

Cimetière juif d'Ettendorf

This is the oldest Jewish cemetery in Alsace; its stele spread over the hillside, blending into the landscape.

- *Continue NW along D 735 to Buswiller (2km/1.2mi).*

Buswiller

The village has some fine timber-framed houses. In the high street, note the carved gable of no 17, painted in cobalt blue; the house, dated 1599, escaped destruction in the Thirty Years War.

PLOMBIÈRES-LES-BAINS

VOSGES. POPULATION 1 906

MICHELIN LOCAL MAP 314: G-5

A tranquil spa and holiday resort, Plombières has preserved the 19th-century charm of the days when it was frequented by Napoléon III.

- **Tourist Office**: Place Maurice-Janot, BP 1, 88370 Plombières-les-Bains, ☎03 29 66 01 30. www.vosgesmeridionales.com.
- **Orient yourself**: In the picturesque Augronne valley, on the N 57 between Êpinal and Vesoul.
- **Parking**: Streets are very narrow, so use the free car parks on Promenades Mesdames, pl. Beaumarchais, parterre de l'ex-Hôtel du Parc, pl. Napoléon III.
- **Don't miss**: the Thermes Napoléon.

A Bit of History

The Romans built imposing baths in Plombières. Revived in the Middle Ages, the spa developed steadily and welcomed many a famous person.

The dukes of Lorraine were regular visitors. Montaigne took the waters in 1580 and Voltaire spent several summers here. Louis XV's daughters stayed in Plombières for two consecutive seasons accompanied by a great many followers. Napoleon's wife Josephine and her daughter Queen Hortense also spent some time in Plombières. In 1802, American engineer Robert Fulton gave a demonstration of the first steamship on the River Augronne, in front of the Empress. Napoleon III stayed in Plombières several times and decided to embellish the town. In 1858, he met the Italian minister, Cavour, here, and together they planned Italy's future and agreed on Nice and the Savoie being united with France.

Spa Town Walk

The historic baths and thermal establishments lie along the lively high street, rue Stanislas and rue Liétard.

Bain Stanislas

The former house of the Ladies of the Chapter of Remiremont. Built 1733-1736. A gallery carries the water to the Thermes Napoléon 600 m further on.

Étuve romaine

Guided tour (2hr) Apr–Oct and school holidays: Thu by reservation, departs 3pm from the Tourist office. €4.50. 03 29 66 01 30.

The Roman steam room was discovered during excavations in 1856. In a nearby basement, the **Bain romain** can also be visited *(staircase on the square).*

Maison des Arcades

This fine 18C house (note the wrought-iron balconies) was built in 1762 for Stanislas Leszczynski whose coat of arms is carved on the façade. Under the arcade, the Crucifix spring was, for a long time, a public drinking fountain.

Bain national

Rebuilt in 1935, the baths have retained their First Empire (1800-14) façade. In the hall, the pump room is still in use.

Pavillon des Princes

This surprisingly modest pavilion was built during the Restoration (1814-30) for members of the royal family, and is now used for temporary exhibitions. It is here that Napoleon III secretly met Cavour in 1858.

Musée Louis-Français

Open end Apr–mid-Oct Thur Sat 3–6pm. Closed 1 May. €1. 03 29 30 06 74.

The museum contains paintings by Louis Français, a native of Plombières, and his friends from the Barbizon School: Corot, Courbet, Diaz, Harpignies, Monticelli and Troyon.

Thermes Napoléon

See opening times of Étuve Romain.

These were erected by Napoleon III, whose statue adorns the entrance. The vast hall (55m/180ft long) is reminiscent of the Caracalla Baths in Rome.

Address Book

For coin ranges, see the Legend on the cover flap.

PRACTICAL INFORMATION

Tourist train – *Tour with commentary (1hr) leaves from the Tourist office. 03 29 66 01 30.*

WHERE TO STAY

Hôtel de la Fontaine Stanislas *– 4km/2.5mi W of Plombières on D 20 – 03 29 66 01 53. hotel.fontaine.stanislas@wanadoo.fr. Closed 16 Oct-31 Mar. 16 rooms. €6.40. Restaurant* A good night's sleep is guaranteed in this hotel in a lovely setting overlooking the Plombières valley. The decor is slightly outdated, but nevertheless well kept. Veranda dining room.

Le Prestige Impérial – *av. des Etats-Unis. 03 29 30 07 07. prestige-imperial@wanadoo.fr. 80 rooms. €12.50. Restaurant* . This Second Empire hotel attached to the municipal spa has been totally renovated in a contemporary style. The restaurant, which has preserved its grandiose period, setting serves modern cuisine.

RECREATION & SPORTS

Spa – *av. des Etats-Unis. 03 29 30 07 00. thermes-pbl@wanadoo.fr. Spa treatment centre: Mon-Sat 5.30am-noon; Calodae health and fitness centre: Mon, Tue, Wed, Sat 1.30-8pm, Fri 1.30-9pm, Sun 10am-8pm. Closed 1 Jan, 25 Dec.* Plombières waters are recommended for treating digestive ailments, nutritional problems, rheumatic disorders and post-traumatic osteo-articular therapy. Revitalising cures and weekend deals available for a "quick fix".

Plombières Ice Cream

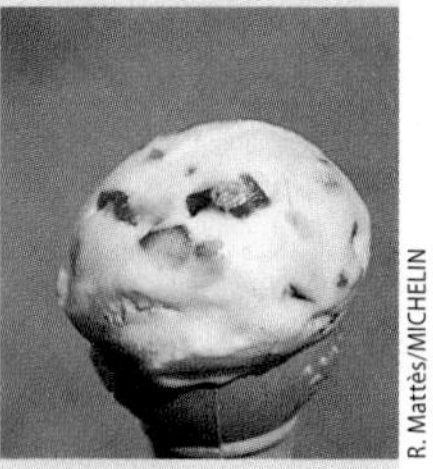
R. Mattès/MICHELIN

This ice cream, flavoured with kirsch and glacé fruit, was supposed to have been invented accidentally in 1858 by a chef preparing a dessert ordered by Napoleon III for his guests during his famous visit to Plombières. The cream having turned out wrong, the chef added the kirsch and fruit to save the day and the guests were delighted. It so happened that, in 1798, an Italian confectioner was already serving a similar kind of ice cream in the Paris region; it was called Plombières because it was left to set in lead *(plomb)* moulds. The name was originally spelled without an "s," but it was eventually confused with the name of the town where it became a speciality.

The tradition lives on at Fontaine Stanislas where the ice cream is still handmade.

Parc impérial

The park on the south of town was laid out by Baron Haussmann. It contains beautiful trees and some rare species.

Excursion

Fontaine Stanislas

4 km/2.5 mi. SW by D20.

In the middle of beechwoods, the spring surges out of a rock covered in 18C inscriptions.

Driving tour

Augronne and Semouse Valleys★

33km/21mi round tour – allow 1hr

Leave Plombières along D 157bis.

Vallée de l'Augronne

The road follows the river through pastureland and forested areas.

In Aillevillers-et-Lyaumont, drive N along D 19 to la Chaudeau then turn right onto D 20 which follows the Semouse Valley upstream.

Vallée de la Semouse★

This peaceful green valley with densely forested slopes is barely wide enough for the river, although there are a few narrow strips of pasture here and there. Wireworks, rolling mills and sawmills once lined the banks, making use of its rapid flow (only one mill remains at Blanc Murger).

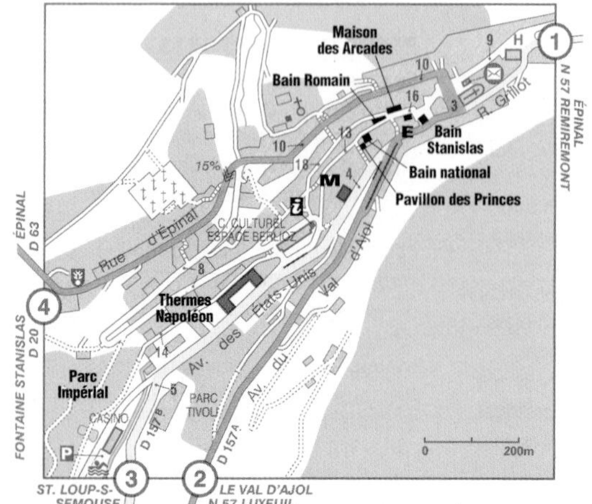

PLOMBIÈRES-LES-BAINS

Église Pl. de l'	3
Français Av. Louis	4
Franche-Comté Av. de	5
Gaulle Av. du Gén.-de	8
Hôtel-de-Ville R. de l'	9
Léopold Av. du Duc	10
Liétard R.	13
Parc Av. du	14
Stanislas R.	16
Sybilles R. des	18

Musée Louis-Français	M
Éture romaine	E

Turn right onto D 63 which leads back to Plombières with fine views of the town.

Vallée des Roches

47km/29mi round tour – allow 2hr.

Leave Plombières along N 57 towards Luxeuil.

The road soon climbs onto the plateau that marks the watershed between the Mediterranean and the North Sea, and then descends towards Remiremont.

Remiremont

See REMIREMONT.

Drive S out of Remiremont along D 23. 3.5km/2.2mi further on, turn left onto D 57. Just after La Croisette d'Hérival, turn right onto a surfaced forest road through the Hérival Forest. Shortly after passing a turning to Girmont and an inn on your left, you will reach the Cascade du Géhard.

Cascade de Géhard★

The waterfall is on the left below the level of the road. Foaming water cascades down into a series of potholes.

Continue past the forest lodge on your left and the path to Hérival on your right and turn left along the Combeauté Valley, also known as the Vallée des Roches. In the village of Faymont, turn right near a sawmill and leave the car 50m/55yd farther on; continue on foot to the Cascade de Faymont (300m/328yd).

Cascade de Faymont

The waterfall makes a remarkable setting amid coniferous trees and rocks.

Le Val-d'Ajol

Le Val-d'Ajol includes more than 60 hamlets scattered along the Combeauté and Combalotte valleys which have retained their traditional industrial activities (metalworks, weaving, sawmills).

Turn right towards Plombières.

PONT-À-MOUSSON★

MEURTHE-ET-MOSELLE. POPULATION 14 647

MICHELIN LOCAL MAP 307: H-5

Pont-à Mousson developed from the 9C onwards around a bridge over the Moselle, beneath a knoll crowned with a fortress. This strategic position accounts for the heavy shelling that the town was subjected to between 1914 and 1918 and in 1944. Pont-à-Mousson's industrial activity centres on a foundry of the St-Gobain group.The town is the headquarters of the Parc naturel régional de Lorraine and a convenient starting point of hikes and excursions.

- **Tourist office:** 52 pl. Duroc, 54700 Pont-à-Mousson. ☎03 83 31 06 90. www.ville-pont-a-mousson.fr.
- **Orient yourself**: At a bridging point on the River Moselle; equidistant between Metz (31km/19.3mi.) and Nancy (30km/18.6mi.) by A31 motorway.
- **Don't miss**: The Ancienne Abbaye des Prémontrés and place Duroc.

Sights

Ancienne abbaye des Prémontrés★

9 rue St-Martin. ♿ daily 10am–6pm. Closed 1 Jan and 25 Dec. €5. ☎03 83 81 10 32. www.abbaye-premontes.com. Allow 1hr.

The former Premonstratensian abbey is a rare example of 18C monastic architecture and is now a cultural centre.Around the cloisters are the warming-room, refectory, chapter house, sacristy, former chapel etc. Three lovely **staircases**★ lead to the conference rooms, bedrooms and library: the small spiral-shaped staircase, situated in a corner of the cloisters near the warming-room, is very elegant; on the other side of the chapel *(used as a concert hall)*, the oval Samson staircase is one of abbey's finest features; as for the great square staircase, located on the right of the sacristy, it is concealed by a beautiful wrought-iron handrail and matching banisters.

Ste-Marie-Majeure

The Baroque interior of the former abbey church has been preserved. Note the slightly curved piers supporting the vaulting.

Musée Au fil du papier

13 rue Magot-de-Rogeville. ♿ ⏲ May–Oct Wed–Mon 2–6pm, Sun 10am–noon, 2–6pm. Nov–Apr Wed–Mon 2–5pm. ⏲ Closed major holidays. €4. ☎03 83 87 80 14.

The University of Lorraine, based in Pont-à-Mousson from 1572 to 1768, attracted printers, engravers and booksellers to the town. The museum shows their work and displays a remarkable collection of objects made of papier mâché.

Place Duroc★

The square is surrounded by 16C arcaded houses. In its centre is a monumental fountain dating from 1931, offered to the town by the American ambulance service. Several fine buildings include the 18C **Hôtel de Ville**, which has a monumental clock over the pediment, and the **Maison des Sept Péchés Capitaux**, adorned with caryatids representing the seven deadly sins and flanked by a Renaissance turret.

Église St-Laurent

The chancel and the transept date from the 15C and 16C. The central doorway and first two storeys of the tower date from the 18C, the rest of the west front being completed in 1895. Inside, note the polychrome triptych of a 16C altarpiece from Antwerp and a statue of Christ carrying his Cross by Ligier Richier; the chancel is decorated with fine 18C woodwork.

Église St-Martin

The church, located on the east bank of the Moselle, was built in the 14C and 15C and extended with side chapels in the 17C and 18C. The 15C west front is flanked by two dissimilar towers. Inside, note a Flamboyant Gothic funerary recess containing two medieval recumbent figures. In the north aisle, is an Entombment comprising 13 characters by early-15C artists from Champagne and Germany; Ligier Richier was probably influenced by this work when he carved the St-Mihiel Entombment half a century later.

Excursions

Butte de Mousson★

7km/4.3mi by N57, then along D910 and D34 to Mousson, then 15 min. by foot.

A modern chapel stands at the top of the knoll alongside the ruins of the feu-

G. Magnin/MICHELIN

The old abbey is a now a cultural centre

Address Book

For coin ranges, see the Legend on the cover flap.

WHERE TO EAT

Ferme-auberge Les Verts Pâturages – *14 rue St-Christophe, 54610 Éply. 14km/8.75mi E of Pont-à-Mousson on D 910, D 110L and D 70. ☎03 83 31 30 85. Booking essential.* Why not stop for lunch in this peaceful village and enjoy a meal based on home produce, or stay a night in one of the rooms in a separate house, with a small garden. The attic room is the largest.

Le Fourneau d'Alain – *64 pl. Duroc. ☎03 83 82 95 09. Closed Mon, dinner Wed, dinner Sun, 3-14 Jan, 1-15 Aug.* Appetising cooking by chef Alain Fournara in a pleasant dining room on the first floor of one of the fine arcaded houses on the main square.

SHOPPING

Brasseurs de Lorraine – *3 rue du Bois-le-Prêtre. ☎03 83 80 02 64. www.brasseurs-lorraine.com. Tue-Sat 10am-noon, 2-6pm. Guided tour of brewery (1hr) Fri 5pm.* Traditionally made beers.

dal castle of the counts of Bar. From the viewpoint, there is a fine **panorama**★ of Lorraine and Moselle.

Prény

13km/8mi N along D 958 then right onto D 952, and left onto D 82 at Pagny-sur-Moselle.

On a hill overlooking the village are the substantial ruins of the 13C castle of the dukes of Lorraine, which was dismantled by order of Richelieu in the 17C and finally abandoned in the early 18C.

PROVINS★★

SEINE-ET-MARNE. POPULATION 11 667

MICHELIN LOCAL MAP 312: I-4

Whichever way one approaches the medieval town of Provins, the outline of the Tour César and the dome of the Église St-Quiriace can be seen from afar. The lower town lies on the banks of the Voulzie and the Durteint, beneath the promontory on which stand the romantic ruins celebrated by Balzac and painted by Turner. The formidable ramparts are the backdrop for medieval festivals and displays in summer. The town, which boasts no fewer than 58 historic monuments, is on UNESCO's World Heritage list.

Clay from the Provins Basin, extracted from open quarries since time immemorial, supplies potters as well as brick and tile manufacturers with a complete range of raw materials.

- **Tourist office**: Chemin de Villecran, 77160 Provins. ☎01 64 60 26 26, www.provins.net
- **Orient yourself**: 80km/50mi. SE of Paris by A4 motorway.
- **Don't miss**: The rampart walk and the Tour de César.
- **Especially for kids**: The medieval jousting and falconry displays: La Bataille des Remparts, Les Aigles des Remparts and La Légende des Chevaliers, see Address Book.

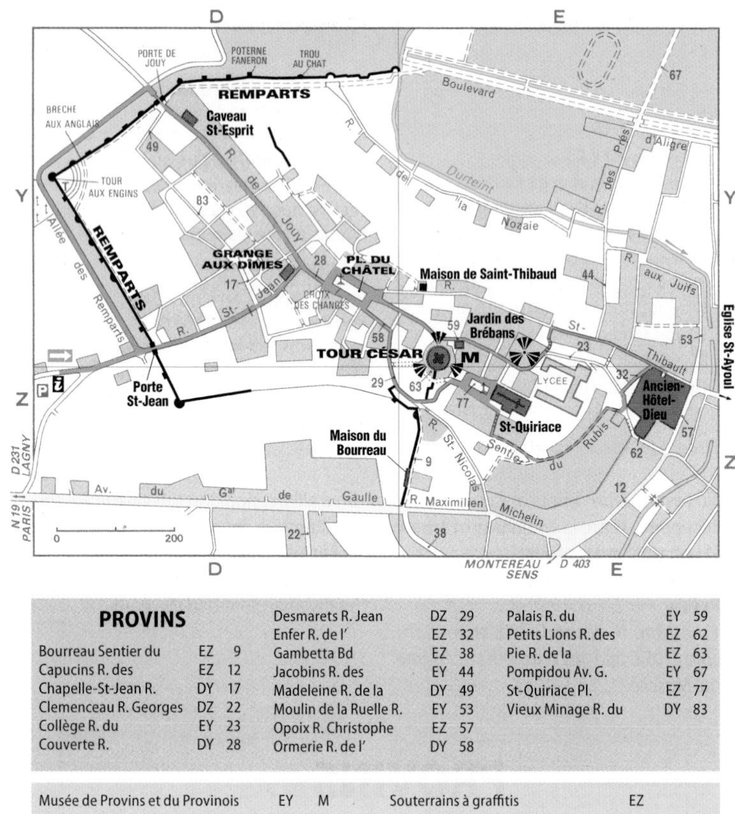

PROVINS

Street			Street			Street		
Bourreau Sentier du	EZ	9	Desmarets R. Jean	DZ	29	Palais R. du	EY	59
Capucins R. des	EZ	12	Enfer R. de l'	EZ	32	Petits Lions R. des	EZ	62
Chapelle-St-Jean R.	DY	17	Gambetta Bd	EZ	38	Pie R. de la	EZ	63
Clemenceau R. Georges	DZ	22	Jacobins R. des	EY	44	Pompidou Av. G.	EY	67
Collège R. du	EY	23	Madeleine R. de la	DY	49	St-Quiriace Pl.	EZ	77
Couverte R.	DY	28	Moulin de la Ruelle R.	EY	53	Vieux Minage R. du	DY	83
			Opoix R. Christophe	EZ	57			
			Ormerie R. de l'	DY	58			

Musée de Provins et du Provinois	EY	M	Souterrains à graffitis	EZ

A Bit of History

The lower town developed from the 11C on around a Benedictine priory built on the spot where the relics of St Ayoul (or Aygulf) had been miraculously found. Under the leadership of Henri I (1152-81), Count of Champagne, known as the Liberal, Provins became a prosperous trading town and one of the two capital cities of the Champagne region.

The Provins fairs

The two fairs, held in Provins from May to June and from September to October, were, with those of Troyes, the most important of the Champagne fairs. There were three stages to each fair: first of all there was the display during which traders showed their merchandise, comparing prices and quality; next came the sale during which goods changed hands; the payment of the goods came last and, for this operation, sellers and buyers needed the help of money changers, notaries and fair keepers. The latter were initially police officers responsible for the prevention of theft and fraud, but by the 13C they had acquired real judicial power.

During the fair, the city looked like a huge market hall full of a colourful crowd of people from northern regions as well as from the Mediterranean. Transactions were made in local currency, hence the growing importance of Italian bankers who could calculate complex exchange rates; by the end of the 13C, they had taken control of the fairs and money changing took precedence over the sale of goods. The first annual fair, which was the most important, took place on the hilltop, near the castle, the second near the Église St-Ayoul.

Medieval town

Two separate towns developed simultaneously: the Châtel or upper town and the Val or lower town. They were later included within the same fortifications. In the 13C the city already had a population of more than 10 000 inhabitants. Apart from numerous merchants, there were weavers, fullers, dyers, cloth-makers, shearers, without forgetting money changers, guards entrusted with police duties, and other judicial representatives of the counts of Champagne. Numerous inns, shops and a thriving Jewish community added to the town's cosmopolitan atmosphere.

The counts of Champagne stayed in Provins for long periods and were surrounded by a lively court. Thibaud IV (1201-53), known as the Chansonnier, encouraged the arts and wrote songs that rate among the best 13C literature. In the 14C, the town's activities declined and the fairs were supplanted by those of Paris and Lyon. The Hundred Years War confirmed the end of economic prosperity for Provins.

Roses

According to tradition it was **Thibaud IV the Troubadour** who brought roses back from Syria and grew them successfully in Provins. Edmund Lancaster (1245-96), brother of the King of England, married Blanche of Artois and was for a while suzerain of Provins, at which time he introduced the red rose into his coat of arms.

Walking Tour

Upper Town★★

Allow 2hr. It is advisable to park in the car park near Porte St-Jean. This is also the location of the tourist office and the departure point for the small tourist train.

Porte St-Jean

St John's Gateway was built in the 13C. This stocky construction is flanked by two towers that are partially hidden by the buttresses that were added in the 14C to support the drawbridge.

Follow allée des Remparts which overlooks the old moat.

Remparts★★

The town walls were built in the 12C and 13C along an existing line of defence. They constitute a very fine example of medieval military architecture. A house straddling the curtain wall was the home of the Provins executioners. The last one to live here was Charles-Henri Sanson who executed Louis XVI. The most interesting part of the ramparts runs between Porte St-Jean and Porte de Jouy. The Tour aux Engins, on the corner, links the two curtain walls; it derives its name from a barn nearby in which engines of war were housed.

In summer, shows are organised within the ramparts: **Les Aigles des remparts**; **A l'assaut des remparts** and **La Légende des Chevaliers** (see Address Book).

Beyond the 12C Porte de Jouy, take rue de Jouy which is lined by picturesque low houses with long tiled roofs or an overhanging upper storey.

Place du Châtel

This vast rectangular square is bordered by attractive old houses: the 15C Maison des Quatre Pignons (south-west corner), the 13C Maison des Petits-Plaids (north-west corner), and the Hôtel de la Coquille to the north. The remains of Église St-Thibault (12C) stand on the north-east corner. In the centre, next to an old well stands the Croix des Changes, where the edicts of the Counts of Champagne were posted.

Walk past the **Musée de Provins et du Provinois**, housed in the "Maison Romane" (Romanesque house).

Jardin des Brébans

From the public garden, there is a striking view of the nearby Église St-Quiriace and, next to it, of the Lycée (high school) built on the site of the former palace of the counts of Champagne.

Follow rue St-Thibaud.

Ancien Hôtel-Dieu

This former hospital was originally a palace founded in the 11C by Count Thibaud I for the countesses of Blois and Champagne. Remodelled several times, the building has retained its 13C Gothic

Address Book

For coin categories, see the Legend on cover flap.

PRACTICAL INFORMATION

Pass Provins – *Valid 1 yr. €9.20 (children €6.10).* Gives one entry to the Tour César, Souterrains, Grange-aux-Dîmes and the museum, plus discounts on the spectacles and the tourist train.

Guided tours of the town – The town organises 2hr tours by approved guides. *Late Mar to late Sep: Sat-Sun and public holidays (except 11-12 Jun, 28 Aug), dep. tourist ofice at 3pm. €6.10. No charge on National Heritage Day. ☎01 64 60 26v26, www.provins.net.*

WHERE TO EAT

⊖ **La Patache** – *6 pl. Honoré-de-Balzac. ☎01 64 00 01 19. Closed Mon, Sun dinner, Thur dinner, two weeks in Oct.* The friendly service and delicious cooking combining traditional and Provence styles will make you want to come back to this restaurant decorated in blue, white and yellow hues. In summer you can enjoy the terrace which looks on to a quiet square.

⊖⊖ **Le Petit Écu** – *9 pl. du Châtel (upper town). Closed end Dec–mid-Jan. ☎01 64 08 95 00.* In the lovely Place du Châtel in the heart of old Provins, this pretty half-timbered restaurant offers an original rustic buffet menu at weekends during the season. On weekdays the menu is more traditional.

⊖⊖ **La Table de St-Jean** – *1 r. St-Jean. ☎01 64 08 96 77. www.latablesaintjean.com. Closed Feb and Nov school holidays, Sun evenings in winter, Tue evenings and Wed.* In the upper town, opposite the tithe barn, this restaurant is in a half-timbered house that probably dates back to the 11C. Depending on the season, you can enjoy your meal in the rustic dining room or on the terrace in a pretty little flower-decked courtyard.

WHERE TO STAY

⊖ **Chambre d'hôte Christine et Jean Claude-Dormion** – *2 r. des Glycines, 77650 Lizines. 15km/9.4mi SW of Provins on N 19 and D 209. ☎01 60 67 32 56. 5 rooms.* This farm dating back three centuries and still in operation offers wonderful rustic rooms, each with basic kitchen facilities. Lovely breakfast room with large bay window. The garden and orchard are very inviting.

⊖ **La Ferme de Toussacq** – *In the hamlet of Toussacq, alongside the Seine – 77480 Grisy-sur-Seine – 20km/12.5mi S of Provins on N 19, Nogent-sur-Seine road on D 78 and D 411 – ☎01 64 01 82 90 – toussacq@terre-net.fr – 5 rooms – meal ⊖.* In a rural setting on the banks of the Seine lies this hamlet with 17C, 18C and 19C buildings. The simple rooms are located in what were formerly the outhouses of the château. In the restaurant, traditional recipes made with produce from the farm; vegetarian dishes sometimes available.

⊖⊖ **Chambre d'hôte Ferme du Chatel** – *5 r. de la Chapelle-St-Jean. ☎01 64 00 10 73. fermeduchatel@wanadoo.fr. 5 rooms.* The main attraction of this farmhouse, built from the 12C to the 18C, is its location in the heart of the medieval city. The rooms are quiet, well maintained and have exposed timberwork. Huge garden with fruit trees.

SHOWTIME

Les Aigles des Remparts – Kids *Théâtre des Remparts, Porte de Jouy. ☎01 60 58 80 32 or 01 64 60 17 90. Apr–early Nov. – €7.70 (children €5.40).* One of the nobility's favourite pastimes in the Middle Ages was to watch a display of falconry. This show of equestrian falconry includes birds of prey in free flight, cavaliers and wolves. Don't miss a visit to the breeding cages, accompanied by the falconers, after the display.

La Bataille des Remparts – *☎01 64 60 26 26. www.provins.net. Apr–Jun. Opening times and ticket sales at the tourist office. €6.10 (children €4.50).* Near the porte St-Jean and in the moat you can watch an impeccably produced medieval show. You will discover how the old war machines and arms were used.

La Légende des Chevaliers – *☎01 64 60 26 26 – www.provins.net. Apr–early Nov. Opening times and ticket sales at the tourist office – €10 (children €7).* Within the defensive ditches, go back to the 13C and watch knights battle it out on horseback, in from the epoch of Thibault de Champagne battle it out in lance and sword combats, as well as hand-to-hand fighting, with weapons of the time including axes and iron balls on chains.

SHOPPING

La Chèvrerie – *1 r. de Jouy (upper town). ☎01 64 01 04 62. Open Fri–Sun and public holidays 11am–7pm.* The Favreau brothers never tire of talking about their beloved goats' cheeses, made in their goat farm (which can also be visited). Substantial snacks also available.

Gaufillier – *2 av. Victor-Garnier. ☎01 64 00 03 71. Open Tue–Sat 8am–12.30pm, 2.30–7.15pm; Sun 8am–12.30pm.* This chocolate maker-baker-confectioner has been wowing his customers for more than ten years with rose-flavoured treats: jam, ice cream, caramels, fruit jellies, nougats, tea, lemonade.

La Ronde des Abeilles – *3 r. des Beaux-Arts (upper town). ☎01 60 67 65 97 – la-ronde-des-abeilles@provins.org Open Wed-Mon 2-7pm.* The speciality of this pretty sweetshop is Provins rose-flavoured honey, but it also sells other products originating in the beehive (royal jelly, pollen and wax) as well as numerous treats such as fruit and vegetables cooked or preserved in honey, gingerbread and mead.

doorway, a Romanesque doorway supported by two colonnettes and a 12C vestibule surmounted by groined vaulting. Note the carved-stone Renaissance **altarpiece** depicting the Virgin and Child implored by a kneeling donor.

▸ *Follow the Sentier du Rubis and turn right to reach the collegiate church.*

Collégiale St-Quiriace

The church was begun in the 11C. The transept and nave date from the 13C, the dome from the 17C. In front of the church a Cross stands on the site of the old bell-tower which collapsed in 1689. The **chancel**★ and square ambulatory are the oldest parts (second half of the 12C). Note early-Gothic features such as the rounded arcading of the blind triforium. The south bay of the chancel was covered in 1238 by an octopartite vault (formed by assembling four diagonal arches), characteristic of the region. Flying buttresses were then built on the outside to strengthen the vaulting.

Tour César★★

Apr–Oct daily 10am–6pm. Nov–Mar: daily 2–5pm. Closed 1 Jan, 25 Dec. €3.40. ☎01 64 60 26 26.

This superb 12C keep, 44m/144ft high and flanked by four turrets, is the emblem of the town. It was once part of the walls of the upper town. The pyramidal roof was built in the 16C.

The revetment wall which encloses the base of the keep was added by the English during the Hundred Years War, in order to house the artillery.

The guardroom on the first floor is octagonal and 11m/36ft high; it is topped by vaulting formed of four arcades of pointed arches ending in a dome and pierced by an orifice through which the soldiers on the floor above were passed supplies. The gallery encircling the keep at the height of the turrets was originally roofed over. The **view**★ extends over the town and the countryside.

A very narrow stairway leads to the top level. Under the fine 16C wooden roof, the bells of St-Quiriace have hung here since the church lost its bell-tower.

S. Sauvignier/MICHELIN

Tour César

Ph. Gajic/MICHELIN

Doorway of église St-Ayoul.

Return to Porte St-Jean via place du Châtel then rue St-Jean on the left.

Sights

Grange aux Dîmes★

Rue St-Jean. Apr–Oct Mon-Fri 2-6pm, weekends 10am-6pm; Nov-Mar weekends and school holidays 2-5pm. Closed 1 Jan, 25 Dec. €3.40. 01 64 60 26 26. www.provins.net.

This massive 13C building belonged to the canons of St-Quiriace, who hired out the space to merchants during the fairs. Later the barn became a store for the tithes (dîmes) levied on the harvests of the peasants. The ground floor consists of a vast hall. The atmosphere of the town's famous fairs is realistically recreated in a permanent exhibition.

Musée de Provins et du Provinois

7 rue du Palais. mid-Jun–mid-Sep daily 11am–6.30pm. Apr–mid-Jun, mid-Sep–Oct daily noon–5.30pm. Nov-Mar weekends and school holidays 2-5pm. Closed 24 Dec-5 Jan. €3. 01 64 01 40 19.

The museum is housed in one of the oldest buildings in the town, "The Romanesque House". A low door leads to the cellar containing capitals and Merovingian sarcophagi displayed round an 11C pier.

On the ground floor are displayed **the sculpture and ceramic collections**★. Stone and polychrome carved-wood statues, most of them from demolished churches, are valuable examples of medieval and Renaissance art in the Provins region. The collection of ceramics illustrates the great quantity and diversity of the local production since prehistoric times: Neolithic pottery, Gallo-Roman tiles, fragments of sigillate bowls and goblets (stamped with seals and hallmarks), funeral vases, floor tiles with inlaid decoration (12C-13C), glazed jugs, and finials. Iron-Age and Bronze-Age jewellery, Merovingian iron buckles and sarcophagi decorated with fishbone patterns are also exhibited.

Église St-Ayoul

In 1048 Thibaud I, Count of Troyes and Meaux (and Count Thibaud III of Blois), grand protector of the abbeys, installed the monks from Montier-la-Celle in the St-Ayoul district in the Lower Town.

The three doorways project far beyond the line of the gable on the west front. Missing parts of the **central doorway**★ were replaced with new pieces by the sculptor Georges Jeanclos, who was responsible for the bronze **statues**★ with antique patina which harmonise well with the medieval reliefs.

Note the beautiful woodwork by Pierre Blasset (1610-63): the high altar and altarpiece as well as panelling and carved coffers in the aisles. In the north aisle are three 16C **statues**★★: a graceful if rather affected Virgin Mary and two musician angels with wonderfully draped clothes.

Tour Notre-Dame-du-Val

This belfry, standing within the ruins of the former Porte Bailly, is all that remains of the collegiate church founded in the 13C by Countess Marie de Champagne and rebuilt in the 15C-16C. The tower, surmounted by a lantern, houses the bells of St-Ayoul.

Église Ste-Croix

According to local legend, the church gets its name from a fragment of the True Cross brought back by Thibaud IV from the seventh crusade. A second aisle in Flamboyant style was added in the 16C. The Romanesque belfry, topped by a modern spire, towers above the crossing. Note the Burgundy-style modillioned cornice round the east end. The left doorway of the three-gabled west front is richly decorated in the Flamboyant and Renaissance styles.

Souterrains à graffiti

Entrance in rue St-Thibault, left of the Ancien Hôtel-Dieu. Guided tour (45min). Jul–Aug, Nov–Dec daily 1.45-6pm. Apr–Jun, Sep–Oct Mon–Fri 3pm, 4pm, weekends and holidays 10.30am-6pm;. Jan–Mar weekends and school holidays 2pm, 3pm, 4pm. Closed 1 Jan, 25 Dec. €3.70. 01 64 60 26 26. www.provins.net

Provins has a substantial network of underground passages, some marked with ancient graffiti. The section that is open to the public, entred through a vaulted chamber in the old hospice, runs through a layer of tufa which lies parallel to the base of the spur on which the Upper Town stands.

Excursions

St-Loup-de-Naud★

9km/5.6mi SW. This once fortified village is built on a rocky spur. The early 11C **church**★ belonged to a Benedictine priory. Under the 12C **doorway**★★, reminiscent of the royal doorway of Chartres cathedral: the tympanum is decorated with a Christ in Glory surrounded by the emblems of the Evangelists, the apostles framed by arcading adorn the lintel, statue-columns line the embrasures and various characters decorate the recessed arches of the archivolt. The St-Loup sculptures mark a transition in architectural style that eventually led to Gothic realism. The evolution is even more obvious inside: the early Romanesque style of the chancel switches to early Gothic in the nave which includes two 12C bays with ribbed vaulting next to the porch, followed by two older bays, one withbarrel vaulting, the other with groined vaulting.

Beton-Bazoches

18km/11mi N. This village boasts a huge **cider press** (*Guided tour (30min) 10am-7pm by appointment. €2.20. 01 64 01 06 96*), built in 1850, which was worked by a horse.

REIMS★★★

MARNE. POPULATION 215 581

MICHELIN LOCAL MAP 306: G-7

Reims is famous for its magnificent cathedral, where French kings were traditionally crowned. Despite heavy damage in the First World War, the city also has a wealth of other architectural masterpieces, including the UNESCO World Heritage listed Basilique St-Remi and Palais du Tau. Reims is also, together with Épernay, the capital of Champagne and most cellars are open to the public.

- **Tourist office**: 2 rue Guillaume-de-Machault, 51000 Reims. 03 26 77 45 25, www.reims-tourisme.fr
- **Orient Yourself:** Reims is 112km/69.6mi NE of Provins and 143km/89mi from Paris on the A26 motorway.
- **Don't Miss:** The magnificent Cathedral Notre-Dame and the interior of the Basilica of St Rémi.
- **Organising Your Time:** Allow at least one day to see the city's main sights.
- Kids **Especially for kids**: Motor enthusiasts love the Musée de l'Automobile, while the Parc nature des Sept-Saulx has activities for all ages.
- **Also See**: Many of the leading Champagne houses are located in Reims, see Routes du Champagne.

Address Book

For coin ranges, see the Legend on cover flap.

PRACTICAL INFORMATION

Pass' citadine – *comprises a museum pass (Musée des Beaux-Arts, Musée-abbaye St-Remi, Musée de l'Ancien Collège des Jésuites, Musée de la Reddition, Planetarium and Chapelle Foujita), a Champagne cellar tour and a one-day bus pass. €12. Enquire at tourist office.*

Guided tours – Reims, City of Art, organises tours by approved guides. *Enquire at tourist office.*

WHERE TO EAT

Au Congrès – *41 bd. Foch. 03 26 88 68 08. www.hotel-univers-reims.com.* The dining room of this hotel provides an elegant setting for the classical dishes. Excellent value-for-money. Cosy sitting room-bar.

Brasserie Le Boulingrin – *48 r. de Mars. 03 26 40 96 22. boulingrin@wanadoo.fr. Closed Sun.* This Art Deco restaurant dating from 1925 is an institution in Reims. The owner is much in evidence, overseeing operations and ensuring a convivial mood. The menu is inventive and the prices reasonable.

La Table Anna – *6 r. Gambetta. 03 26 89 12 12. www.latableanna.com.* Champagne takes pride of place in the window of this establishment next door to the music conservatory. Some of the paintings adorning the walls are the work of the owner, an artist at heart. Traditional dishes are renewed with the seasons.

La Vigneraie – *14 r. de Thillois. 03 26 88 67 27. www.vigneraie.com.* La Vigneraie, situated just off pl. Drouet-d'Erlon, boasts a fantastic collection of carafes. Tasty classical menu and fine wine list. Excellent value-for-money.

Le Continental – *95 pl. Drouet-d'Erlon. 03 26 47 01 47.* A giant gilded vine sits in the dining room at this classic brasserie and champagne bar. Specialities include lobster and foie gras.

Le Jamin – *18 bd. Jamin. 03 26 07 37 30. Closed Mon, Sun dinner, end Jan, end Aug.* In this little local bistro, perfectly mastered traditional cooking is served in a rustic dining room. Look for the good-value daily specials on the blackboard.

Café du Palais – *14 pl. Myron-Herrick. 03 26 47 52 54. Closed Sun and public holidays.* This lively café near the cathedral was founded in 1930, and still has its original glass roof. Popular with locals for its generous salads, daily dishes and home-made patisseries. You can also enjoy a reasonably priced glass of champagne.

Au Petit Comptoir – *17 r. de Mars. 03 26 40 58 58. au.petit.comptoir@wanadoo.fr . Closed Sat lunch, Mon lunch and Sun and 24-31 Dec–2 Jan.* This trendy restaurant behind the town hall has a striking modern interior to match the updated dishes of Patrice Maillot.

Da Nello – *39 r. Cérès. 03 26 47 33 25. Closed Aug.* A Mediterranean welcome awaits you at this Italian restaurant where the tables all have a view of the kitchen and the pizza oven is right in the centre of the room. Fresh pasta, grills and daily specials according to what the market has to offer… all served with an authentic Italian accent.

Le Millénaire – *4 r. Bertin. 03 26 08 26 62. www.lemillenaire.com.* A spacious dining room near place Royale is hung with modern paintings. Appetising modern cooking.

Château Les Crayères – *64 bd. Vasnier. 03 26 82 80 80. www.relaischateaux.com/crayeres. Closed late Dec–late Jan.* A gorgeous château sitting in lovely parkland is the setting for sumptuous updated grand cuisine by chef Didier Elena, including a special Autour de Champagne menu.

WHERE TO STAY

Ardenn Hôtel – *6 r. Caqué. 03 26 47 42 38. 14 rooms. €5.50.* This hotel with an attractive brick façade has many points in its favour. You will certainly be won over by its location in a quiet little town-centre street, the unfailing cleanliness of the tastefully decorated rooms and the smiling service.

Chambre d'hôte Lapie – *1 r. Jeanne-d'Arc. 51360 Val-de-Vesle. 21km/12.5mi SE of Reims on N 44 and left on D 326. 03 26 03 92 88. joyhello@*

free.fr. Closed 15 Dec-15 Jan. 5 rooms. Five lovely pastel-toned rooms are available on this farm in the heart of a village. The ttractive decor mixes old and modern styles and there's an immaculate downstairs breakfast room.

Grand Hôtel du Nord – *75 pl. Drouet-d'Erlon. 03 26 47 39 03. www. grandhoteldunord.com. Closed Christmas holidays. 50 rooms.* *€6.* Mostly refurbished rooms in a 1920s building set on Reims' pedestrianised main square. The rooms at the rear are quieter. Many restaurants and lots going on nearby.

Hôtel de la Cathédrale – *20 r. Libergier. 03 26 47 28 46 . hoteldelacathedrale@wanadoo.fr. 17 rooms* – *€7.* This smart but welcoming hotel stands in one of the streets that lead to the cathedral. The small rooms have comfortable beds and are bright and cheerful, while the breakfast room is decorated with old engravings.

Hôtel Crystal – *86 pl. Drouet-d'Erlon. 03 26 88 44 44. www.hotelcrystal.fr. 31 rooms* – *€9.* An astonishing haven of greenery right in the centre of town is an attractive feature of this 1920s house. The renovated bedrooms all have excellent bedding. Breakfast is served in a delightful flowered courtyard-garden in summer.

Hôtel Continental – *93 pl. Drouet-d'Erlon. 03 26 40 39 35. www. grand-hotel-continental.com. Closed 21 Dec-7 Jan. 50 rooms.* *€11.50.* The attractive façade of this central hotel adorns the city's liveliest square. The rooms, renovated in varying styles, are reached by a splendid staircase (if you're after calm avoid the rooms overlooking bd du Général-Leclerc). Elegant Belle Epoque sitting rooms.

Hôtel Porte Mars – *2 pl. de la République. 03 26 40 28 35. www. hotelportemars.com. 24 rooms.* *€10.* It's a pleasure to drink tea near the fire in the cosy sitting room, or enjoy a drink in the sophisticated bar. A delicious breakfast is also served in the attractive glass-roofed dining room decorated with photographs and old mirrors. The comfortable, well sound-proofed rooms all have a personal touch.

ON THE TOWN

Place Drouet-d'Erlon – This square is the prime starting point for anyone wanting to go out on the town, whether you are looking for a bar, pub, restaurant, tearoom or brasserie.

La Chaise au Plafond – *190 av. d'Épernay. 03 26 06 09 61 – Mon-Sat 7am-8pm, public holidays: open mornings . Closed last week of Feb, 1st week of Mar and 3 weeks in Aug.* Founded in 1910, this bar and tobacconist is famous for the chair that has remained stuck to the ceiling ever since a shell hit the establishment on 12 September 1914. Terrace in summer. Huge cigar selection.

SPORTS AND RECREATION

Le César's Club – *17 r. Lesage. 03 26 88 24 80. Mon-Fri noon-3am, Sat-Sun 2pm-3am.* Two former national billiards champions run this attractive club, which offers 21 tables in all (snooker, pool, French billiards). Tournaments on Monday evenings, 8pm. Occasional regional competitions and exhibitions.

Kids **Parc de Champagne** – *03 26 77 45 00. Mon-Fri 9.30am-6.30pm, Sat 2-7.30pm, Sun 9.30am-6.30pm.* This park has over 22 hectares of children's play areas and sports facilities and is also used for cultural events.

SHOPPING

Deleans – *20 r. Cérés. 03 26 47 56 35. Tue-Sat 9am-noon, 2-7pm (Fri-Sat 7.30pm); mid-Oct-Apr Mon-Sat 9am-noon, 2-7pm; Sun 10am-noon. Closed 8 May, 14 Jul & Aug.* Cocoa-based specialities have been made here in the old-fashioned way since 1874. Those to try include Néluskos (chocolate-coated cherries in cognac) and petits bouchons de champagne.

Fossier – *25 cours Jean-Baptiste Langlet – 03 26 47 59 84 – Mon 2-7pm, Tue-Sat 9am-7pm.* Founded in 1756, the biscuit and chocolate maker Fossier creates the ultimate in Reims confectionary (biscuits roses and croquignoles). Pay a visit to the shop and factory and learn how to "piouler" (stir) your glass of champagne correctly!

La Petite Friande – *15 cours Jean-Baptiste Langlet – 03 26 47 50 44. summer: Tue-Sat: 10am-noon, 2-7pm; winter: Mon-Sat 10am-noon, 2-7pm.* For more than 170 years, the establishment has prided itself on being the specialist in authentic bouchons de champagne, made with *marc de champagne*. Another of its delicious creations are *bulles à la vieille fine de la Marne*.

CALENDAR

Fêtes johanniques – *2nd weekend in June*. 2 000 walk-ons in period costume accompany Joan of Arc and Charles VII during a massive street festival.

Flâneries musicales d'été – *Jul and Aug*. Over 150 free concerts all over the town, including shows by major classical musicians in some of the town's most prestigious and unlikely venues.

A Bit of History

Ancient times

The origins of Reims go back to pre-Roman times when it was the fortified capital of a Gaulish tribe, the Remes. After the Roman conquest, it became a thriving administrative and commercial city with many public buildings. The **Porte de Mars** and the **Cryptoportique** are the only two to have survived to this day. In the 3C, the town's strategic position increased its military importance as the Romans desperately tried to stop invading hordes from the east. At the same time, Reims became a Christian city and the first cathedral was built.

Clovis' christening

Then came the conversion of **Clovis**, king of the Franks, who was baptised by the bishop of Reims, **Remi** (440-533), on Christmas Day shortly before the year 500. The whole population rejoiced and led a procession from the former imperial palace to the baptistery situated near the cathedral. According to legend, a dove brought a phial containing holy oil used by Remi to anoint Clovis. This phial was carefully preserved and used for the coronation of every king of France from the 11C to 1825, the most famous being that of Charles VII in 1429, at the height of the Hundred Years War, in the presence of Joan of Arc.

Medieval Reims

From the end of the 5C and during the whole medieval period, Reims was an important religious, political and artistic centre (**École de Reims**). The powerful archbishops of Reims played the role of arbiters between kings and princes who came to stay at the Abbaye de St-Remi. One of the archbishops, **Gerbert,** became Pope in 999.

During the 11C, 12C and 13C, the town expanded and acquired some splendid edifices such as the abbey church of St-Remi and the cathedral. **Guillaume aux**

Jean-Baptiste de la Salle and Schooling for the Poor

Small schools intended for children of poor families began to open in Reims from 1674 onwards, at the instigation of Canon Roland. His work was continued by Jean-Baptiste de la Salle.

Born in Reims in 1651, Jean-Baptiste de la Salle belonged to a rich aristocratic family who intended him to pursue a brilliant career within the Church. However, the young canon decided instead to devote his energies and his wealth to educating the poor. He began by founding the Communauté des Sœurs du Saint Enfant Jésus, which spread throughout the countryside. The nuns ran schools and catechism classes but they also taught adults. A few years later, Jean-Baptiste de la Salle founded the Communauté des Frères des Écoles Chrétiennes, which expanded considerably.

In 1695 he published a work entitled *The Running of Schools,* in which he explained his theories about teaching: he was in favour of collective teaching and wanted French to replace Latin. However, his ideas, which were revolutionary at the time, only triumphed long after his death (Rouen 1719).

Blanches Mains, who was archbishop from 1176 to 1202, contributed to the prosperity of the town by granting it a charter and, by the beginning of the 13C, Reims had doubled in size.

Modern times

Badly damaged during the First World War when 80% of the town's buildings were destroyed, Reims was spared during the Second World War. The capitulation of the German forces on 7 May 1945 was signed in Reims where General Eisenhower had his headquarters.

Today the textile industry, which brought prosperity to the town as early as the 12C, has practically disappeared but the production of Champagne remains one of the town's main activities. The city's artistic tradition is also maintained by the famous stained-glass workshops which once employed the talents of Villon, Chagall, Braque and Da Silva.

Cathédrale Notre-Dame★★★

Its homogenous architectural style and superb sculptures make Cathédrale Notre-Dame one of the finest cathedrals in Christendom.

In 1210, Archbishop Aubry de Humbert decided to build a Gothic cathedral (the third to be erected on this site) modelled on those being built at the time in Paris (1163), Soissons (1180) and Chartres (1194). The edifice was designed by Jean d'Orbais and five successive architects followed the original plans, which accounts for the extraordinary homogeneity of the cathedral. Their names were inscribed on the original paving stones which unfortunately disappeared in the 18C. Jean d'Orbais built the chancel, Jean le Loup the nave and the west front which Gaucher de Reims decorated with statues and three portals, Bernard de Soissons designed the rose-window and the gables and finished the nave vaulting. By 1285, the interior had been completed. The towers were erected in the 15C; others were planned but a severe fire, which damaged the roof structure in 1481, halted the project.

Ph. Gajic/MICHELIN

Stained-glass window, Reims Cathedral

The cathedral was regrettably altered in the 18C (suppression of the rood screen, some stained glass and the labyrinth), but it was not damaged during the Revolution. Unfortunately, a long restoration programme had just been completed when, in September 1914, heavy shelling set fire to the timber roof structure causing the bells and the lead of the stained glass to melt and the stone to split. More shell damage occurred throughout the First World War and a new restoration programme was launched, partly financed by the Rockefeller Foundation. The damaged timber vault was replaced by a concrete roof structure. The cathedral was finally reconsecrated in 1937.

Exterior

More than 2 300 statues decorate the exterior. Some of them, which were badly damaged by war and bad weather, are now exhibited in the Palais du Tau and have been replaced by copies.

West front

Best seen in the setting sun, the west front of Reims Cathedral is reminiscent of Notre-Dame in Paris but here the vertical lines are emphasized by the pointed gables and pinnacles, the slender colonnettes and the tall statues decorating the kings' gallery.

The **three doorways**, lined up with the three naves, are surmounted by elaborately carved gables contrasting with the openwork tympanums. The 13C statues adorning the doorways are from four workshops employed successively.

Central doorway (the Virgin's portal)

This is composed of several elements starting with, against the upright post, the smiling Virgin Mary; on the right, the Visitation and the Annunciation; on the left, Jesus at the Temple; on the gable, the Coronation of the Virgin (copy).
Situated above the rose-window and the scene depicting David slaying Goliath, the **kings' gallery** includes 56 statues (4.5m/15ft high and weighing 6-7t); in the centre, Clovis' christening.

North side

On the north side of the cathedral the **flying buttresses** are surmounted by recesses, each containing a large angel with open wings, among them the famous "smiling angel".

North transept

The façade has three **doorways** decorated with statues which are older than those of the west front. The right doorway comes from the Romanesque cathedral: the tympanum is adorned with a Virgin in glory framed by foliage. The upright post of the middle portal is decorated with a statue of Pope Calixtus. The embrasures of the left doorway have six fine statues representing the Apostles and the **tympanum** is carved with scenes of the Last Judgement.

East end

From cours Anatole-France, there is a fine **view**★ of the east end of the cathedral with its radiating chapels surmounted by arcaded galleries and its superposed flying buttresses.

Interior

Inside, the cathedral is well lit and its proportions are remarkable (138m/151yd long and 38m/42yd high); the impression of loftiness is enhanced by the narrowness of the nave in relation to its length and by the succession of very pointed transverse arches.

The three-storey elevations of the **nave** consist of the main **arcading** supported by round piers, a blind **triforium** (level with the roofing of the aisles) and tall **clerestory windows**, divided into lancets by mullions. **Capitals** are decorated with floral motifs.
The chancel has only two bays but the space used for services extends into the nave as there was always a large number of canons and a lot of space was needed for coronations. The chancel used to be closed off by a rood screen on which the royal throne was placed. **Pillars** get gradually narrower and closer together, thus increasing the impression of height. The **radiating chapels** are linked by a passage typical of the region's architectural style.
The inside of the **west front**★★ was the work of Gaucher from Reims. The large rose-window (12m/40ft in diameter) is located above the triforium arcading backed by stained-glass windows of similar shape. A smaller rose decorates the doorway. On either side, a number of recesses contain statues. Floral motifs, similar to those of the nave capitals, complete the decoration. The very well preserved **inside of the central doorway** has scenes of the life of the Virgin and the life of john the Baptist.

Stained glass★★

The 13C stained-glass windows suffered considerable damage: some were replaced by clear glass in the 18C, others were destroyed during the First World War. Those of the **apse** are still intact: in the centre is the donor with suffragan bishops on either side. The great 13C **rose-window**, dedicated to the Virgin Mary, looks its best in the setting sun.
Jacques Simon, a member of the family of stained-glass makers who have been restoring the cathedral for generations, has reconstructed some of the missing windows, notably the wine-growers' window (**a**). His daughter Brigitte Simon-Marcq made a series of abstract windows including one entitled the River Jordan to the right of the christening font (**b**) in the south transept.
In 1974, **Marc Chagall** decorated the apsidal chapel (**c**) with luminous blue-dominated stained-glass made in the

Simon workshop: in the centre, Abraham's Sacrifice and the Crucifixion; on the left, a Tree of Jesse and on the right, great events which took place in the cathedral such as Clovis' christening.
The cathedral has a 15C **astronomical clock**. Each hour struck starts two processions: the Adoration of the Magi and the Flight into Egypt.

Walking Tour

Town Centre

Allow 2hr.

- *From the square in front of the cathedral, walk along rue Rockefeller and turn right onto rue Chanzy, passing the Musée des Beaux-Arts (see Sights). Turn left on pedestrian rue de Vesle. Turn right onto rue Max-Dormoy.*

Église St-Jacques

Open Mon-Sat 9am–noon, 2–6pm, Sun 8.30am–noon, 5.30-7pm. ☎ 03 26 47 55 34.
The 13C-14C Gothic nave with a traditional triforium is prolonged by a Flamboyant Gothic chancel (early 16C) framed by two Renaissance chapels (mid-16C) with Corinthian columns. The modern abstract stained-glass was designed by Vieira da Silva (side chapels) and Sima (chancel).

Place Drouet-d'Erlon

Named after one of Napoleon's generals, this lively pedestrianised space lined with cafés, restaurants, hotels and cinemas is the heart of the city.

- *At the Fontaine Subé, turn right onto rue de l'Étape and continue as far as rue de l'Arbalète.*

Hôtel Saint-Jean-Baptiste de la Salle★

This Renaissance house, built in 1545-56, is the birthplace of **Jean-Baptiste de la Salle** (*see below*). The harmonious façade, adorned with Doric pilasters on the ground floor and Ionic ones on the first floor, is flanked by a pavilion whose carriage entrance is decorated by statues of Adam and Eve on either side.

- *Turn left onto rue du Dr-Jacquin.*

Hôtel de ville

The imposing 17C façade survived the fire that destroyed the building in 1917. The pediment is decorated with an equestrian bas-relief of Louis XIII.

- *Turn left on rue du Général-Sarail.*

Basses et Hautes Promenades

These vast shady squares were laid out in the 18C to replace the moat and glacis of the old fortifications. They provide a useful parking area close to the town centre. A fun fair invades the Hautes Promenades at Christmas and Easter. A remarkable wrought-iron railing, made in 1774 for the coronation of Louis XVI, stands at the end of the Basses Promenades.
Nearby on boulevard du Général-Leclerc, stand two 19C buildings, the **Cirque** (1 100 seats) and the **Manège** (600 seats) where various events are held.

Porte Mars★

This triumphal arch (height: 13.5m/44ft) of the Corinthian order was erected in honour of the Roman Emperor Augustus some time after the 3C AD. During the Middle Ages, it was incorporated into the ramparts and used as a town gate. It consists of three arches decorated inside with bas-reliefs depicting Jupiter and Leda, as well as the founders of Rome, Romulus and Remus.

- *Walk along rue de Mars.*

Rue de Mars

The façade of no 6 is decorated with mosaic panels illustrating the Champagne-making process.

Hôtel des Comtes de Champagne

This Gothic mansion belongs to the Taittinger Champagne house.

- *The street leads to place du Forum.*

REIMS

Alsace-Lorraine R. d'	CX	2
Anatole-France Cours	BY	3
Arbalète R. de l'	BY	4
Barbâtre R. du	BCYZ	
Barbusse R. H.	CY	
Bétheny R. de	CX	
Bocquaine Chaussée	ABZ	
Boulard R.	BY	6
Boulingrin Pl. du	BX	7
Brébant Av.	AY	8
Briand Pl. A.	BX	
Buirette R.	AY	12
Cadran St-Pierre R.	BY	13
Capucins R. des	BYZ	
Carmes R. des	BZ	16
Carnégie Pl.	BY	17
Carnot R.	BY	19
Carteret Bd	CX	
Cérès R.	BY	
Cernay R. de	CX	
Champ-de-Mars R. du	BCX	
Champagne Av. de	CZ	22

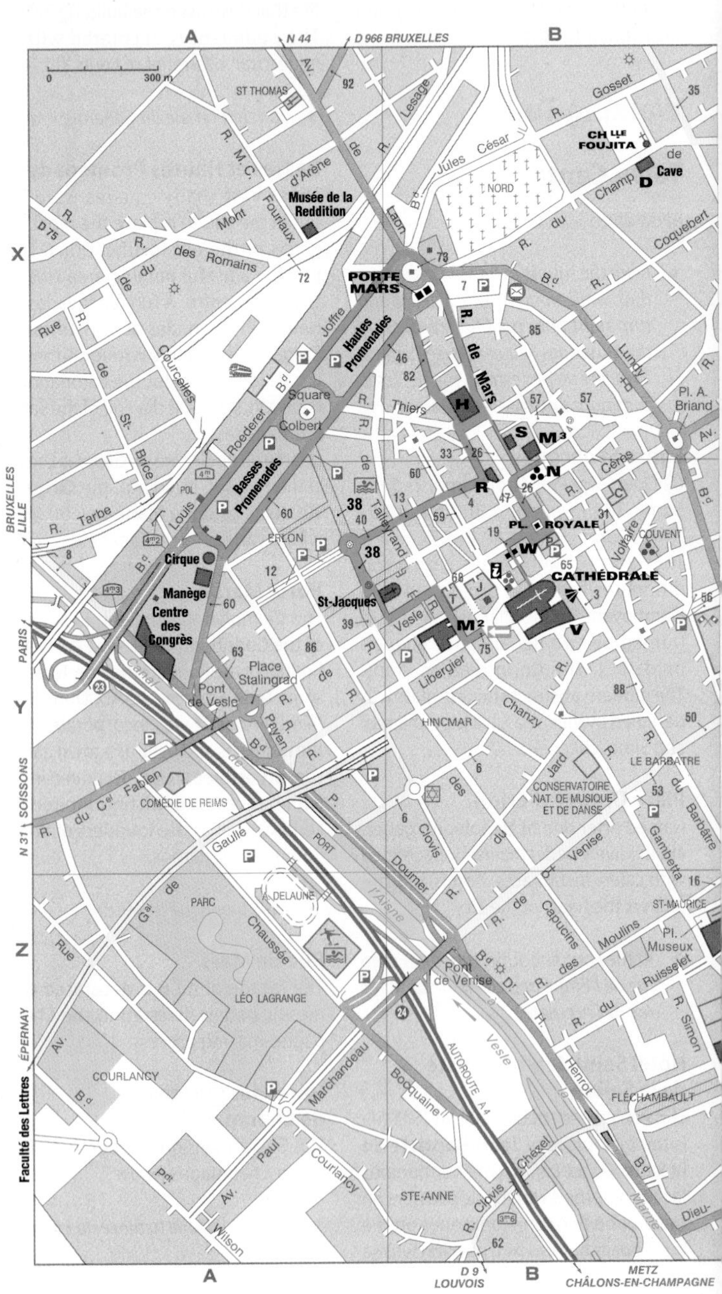

Street	Grid	No.
Chanzy R.	BY	
Chemin Vert R. du	CZ	23
Chézel R. C.	BZ	
Clemenceau Av. Georges	CY	
Clovis R.	ABY	
Colbert R.	BXY	26
Colbert Square	AX	
Coquebert R.	BX	
Courcelles R. de	AX	
Courlancy R. de	AZ	
Coutures R. des	CY	
Crayères R. des	CZ	
Dauphinot Bd	CX	
Desteuque R. E.	BY	31
Dieu-Lumière Bd	BCZ	
Dieu-Lumière R.	CZ	32
Dr-H.-Henrot Bd	BZ	
Dr-Jacquin R.	BXY	33
Dr-Knoéri Pl. du	CX	34
Dr-Lemoine R.	BX	35
Doumer Bd Paul	ABYZ	
Droits-de-l'Homme Pl. des	CZ	37
Drouet d'Erlon Pl.	AY	38
Dubois R. Th.	AY	39
Étape R. de l'	AY	40
Fabien R. du Colonel	AY	
Farman Av. H.	CZ	43
Foch Bd	ABX	46
Forum Pl.	BY	47
Fouriaux R. M.-C.	AX	
Gambetta R.	BYZ	
Gaulle Av. Gén.-de	AYZ	
Gerbert R.	BCY	50
Giraud Av. Gén.	CZ	
Gobelins R. des	CX	
Gosset R.	BX	
Gouraud Pl. Gén.	CZ	51
Grand-Cerf R. du	CZ	52
Herduin R. Lt	BY	53
Houzeau-Muiron R.	CY	54
J.-J.-Rousseau R.	BX	57
Jamin Bd	CX	
Jamot R. Paul	BY	56
Jean-Jaurès Av.	BCX	
Joffre Bd	AX	
Jules-César Bd	BX	
Lambert Bd Victor	CZ	58
Langlet Crs J.-B.	BY	59
Laon Av. de	ABX	
Laurent R. Gustave	CY	
Leclerc Bd Général	AX	60
Lefèbvre R. E.	CX	61
Lenoir R. C.	CX	
Lesage R.	BX	
Libergier R.	ABY	
Louvois R. de	BZ	62
Lundy Bd	BX	
Magdeleine R.	AY	63
Marchandeau Av. Paul	AZ	
Mars R. de	BX	
Martyrs-de-la-Résistance Pl. des	BY	65
Moissons R. des	CY	
Mont d'Arène R. du	AX	
Montlaurent R.	CY	67
Moulins R. des	BZ	
Museux Pl.	BZ	
Myron-Herrick Pl.	BY	68
Paix Bd de la	BCY	
Pasteur Bd	CY	
Payen R.	AY	
Philipe R. Gérard	CZ	70
Pommery Bd	CYZ	
Prés.-F.-Roosevelt R.	AX	72
Prés.-Wilson Bd	AZ	
République Pl. de la	BX	73
Rockefeller R.	BY	75
Roederer Bd Louis	AXY	
Romains R. des	AX	
Royale Pl.	BY	
Ruisselet R. du	BZ	
St-Brice R. de	AXY	
St-Marceaux Bd	CY	
St-Nicaise Pl.	CZ	78
Salines R. des	CZ	80
Sarrail R. Gén.	BX	82
Sébastopol R. de	CX	

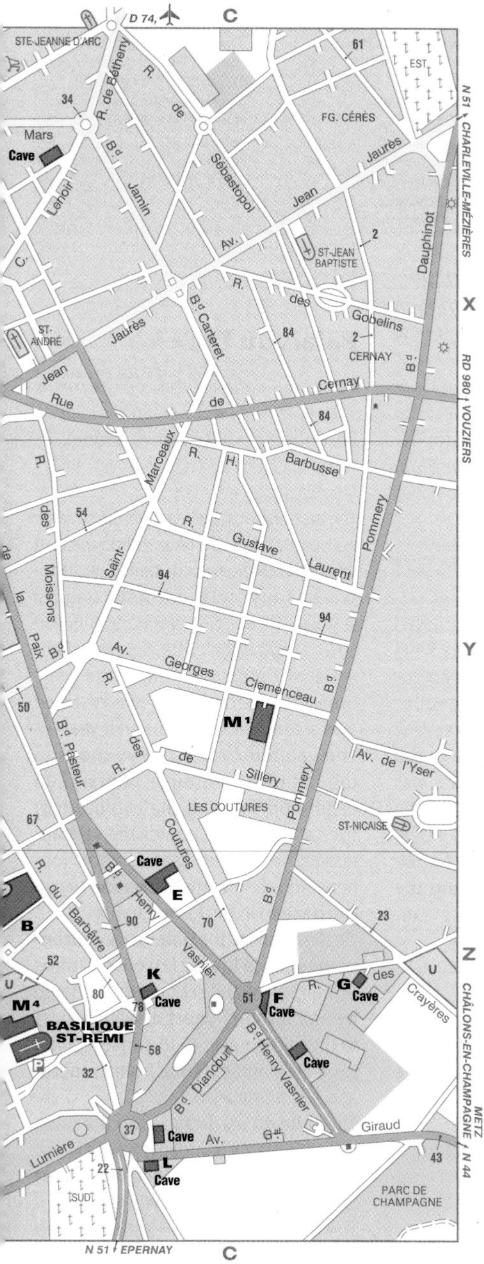

Sillery R. de	CY		Thillois R. de	AY	86	Voltaire R.	BY	
Simon R.	BZ		Université R. de l'	BY	88	Yser Av. de l'	CY	
Stalingrad Pl.	AY		Vasnier Bd Henri	CZ		Zola R. Émile	AX	92
Strasbourg R. de	CX	84	Venise Pont de	BZ		16e-et-22e-Dragons R. des	CY	94
Talleyrand R. de	ABY		Venise R. de	BYZ				
Tarbe R.	AY		Vesle Pont de	AY				
Temple R. du	BX	85	Vesle R. de	ABY				
Thiers R.	ABX		Victor-Hugo Bd	CZ	90			

Ancien Collège des Jésuites	CZ	B	Cave Veuve Clicquot-Ponsardin	CZ	L	Manège	AY	
Basilique St-Rémi	CZ		Centre des Congrès	AY		Musée Automobile de Reims-Champagne	CY	M1
Basses et Hautes Promenades	ABY		Chapelle Foujita	BX		Musée St-Rémi	CZ	M4
Cathédrale Notre-Dame	BY		Cirque	AY		Musée de la Reddition	AX	
Cave Mumm	BX	D	Cryptoportique gallo-romain	BY	N	Musée des Beaux-Arts	BY	M2
Cave Piper-Heidsieck	CZ	E	Église St-Jacques	AY		Musée-Hôtel le Vergeur	BX	M3
Cave Pommery	CZ	F	Hôtel de la Salle	BY	R	Palais du Tau	BY	V
Cave Ruinart	CZ	G	Hôtel de ville	BX	H	Porte Mars	BX	
Cave Taittinger	CZ	K	Hôtel des Comtes de Champagne	BX	S	Porte du Chapitre	BY	W

Cryptoportique gallo-romain

Early Jun to mid-Sep Tue-Sun 2-5pm. No charge. 03 26 35 34 70. www.ville-reims.fr.

This large half-buried Gallo-Roman monument, dating from the 3C AD, stands on the site of the ancient city's forum. The lower level was used as a grain store and the upper level for promenades.

Take rue Colbert to place Royale.

Place Royale★

This arcaded square with balustraded roofs, designed by Legendre in 1760, is characteristic of the Louis XVI style. The Hôtel des Fermes, on the south side, houses administrative offices. The statue of Louis XV by Pigalle, which used to stand in the centre of the square, was destroyed during the Revolution and the holy coronation phial was smashed on the pedestal; another statue by Cartellier replaced the original during the Restoration (1814-30).

Turn right along rue Carnot.

Porte du Chapitre

This 16C gate, flanked by two corbelled turrets, formed the main entrance to the chapter house.

Go through the gateway to return to the cathedral.

Sights

Palais du Tau★★

2 place du Cardinal-Luçon. Open early May –early Sep daily 9.30am–6.30pm. Rest of the year 9.30am–12.30pm, 2–5.30pm. Closed 1 Jan, 1 May, 1 and 11 Nov, 25 Dec. €6.50. 03 26 47 81 79.

The archbishops' palace owes its strange name to its T shape, resembling ancient episcopal croziers; it contains the cathedral treasury and some of the original statues. The building was remodelled in 1670 by Robert de Cotte. Severely damaged in September 1914, at the same time as the cathedral, it was restored over a considerable number of years.

The vaulted Gothic **lower room** to the left of the entrance contains an exhibition showing the evolution of the cathedral site and of the canons' district, which has disappeared. From here, stone fragments of the rood screen can be seen in the lower chapel.

On the first floor, the **Galerie du couronnement de la Vierge** (**1**) contains some of the 17 wool-and-silk tapestries offered by Archbishop Robert de Lenoncourt to the Cathedral in 1530, together with large 13C statues of kings from the north and south transepts.

The **Salle du roi de Juda** (**2**) contains a huge 14C statue of Judah from the kings' gallery), tapestries and the upper part of an angel with spread wings.

The **Salon carré** (**3**) is adorned with 17C tapestries, depicting scenes from

Christ's childhood, woven in Reims. The two large statues of the Magdalene and St Peter came from the west front.

Note, in the **Salle du Cantique des Cantiques** (**4**), four precious 17C hand-embroidered hangings.

The **Salle des petites sculptures** (**5**) houses masks and gargoyles, as well as the statues of Abraham and Aaron from the south doorway.

The **Salle du Goliath** (**6**) contains monumental statues of St Paul, St James, Goliath (5.4m/18ft) wearing a coat of mail, as well as allegorical representations of the Synagogue (blindfolded) and the Church, damaged by shelling. Fragments of the rood-screen, demolished in 1744, can also be seen.

The **Salle du Tau** (**7**) was used for the festivities that followed coronations. Lined with cloth bearing fleurs-de-lys, the symbol of French royalty, and decorated with two huge 15C Arras tapestries illustrating the story of Clovis, it is has an elegant vaulted ceiling, shaped like a ship's hull.

The **Salle Charles X** (**8**) is devoted to the coronation of 1825. It contains the royal cloak as well as garments used by heralds and a painting of *Charles X in regal dress* by Gérard.

The **treasury** (**9**) is exhibited in two rooms: the left one houses royal gift, such as Charlemagne's 9C talisman, which contains a piece of the True Cross, the coronation chalice, the reliquary of the Holy Thorn, carved out of crystal, the 15C reliquary of the Resurrection and the reliquary of St Ursula, a delicate cornelian vase decorated with enamelled statuettes dating from 1505.

The right-hand room contains ornaments used for the coronation of Charles X: the reliquary of the Holy Phial, a large offering vase and two gold and silver hosts, the necklace of the Order of the Holy Spirit worn by Louis-Philippe and a copy of Louis XV's crown.

The 13C doorway of the **palatine chapel** (**10**) is surmounted by the Adoration of the Magi. On the altar are the cross and six gilded candelabra made for the wedding of Napoleon and Marie-Louise.

Basilique St-Remi★★

Remi was buried in 533 in a small chapel dedicated to St Christopher. Shortly afterwards, a basilica was constructed. In the 8C, the Abbaye de St-Remi was founded here by a group of Benedictine monks. Work on the present basilica began c 1007 and was consecrated by Pope Leo IX in 1049. The chancel was built over the grave of St Remi.

The building was remodelled in the late 12C and the Gothic basilica we see today dates from that period. A few minor changes occurred in the 16C and 17C. Used as a barn during the Revolution, the church was restored in the 19C and again after the First World War. Many archbishops of Reims and the first kings of France were buried inside; the Holy Phial was kept in the church.

Interior★★★

The basilica is very narrow (26m/85ft) in relation to its length (122m/400ft) and dimly lit, which makes it look even longer. The 11C nave consists of 11 bays with rounded main arches resting on piers whose capitals are decorated with animals and foliage. Note the crown of light symbolising the life of St Remi, a copy of the original destroyed during the Revolution.

The four-storey Gothic **chancel** is closed off by a 17C Renaissance screen and lit by 12C stained-glass windows depicting

B. Kaufmann/MICHELIN

Reliquary of St Ursula

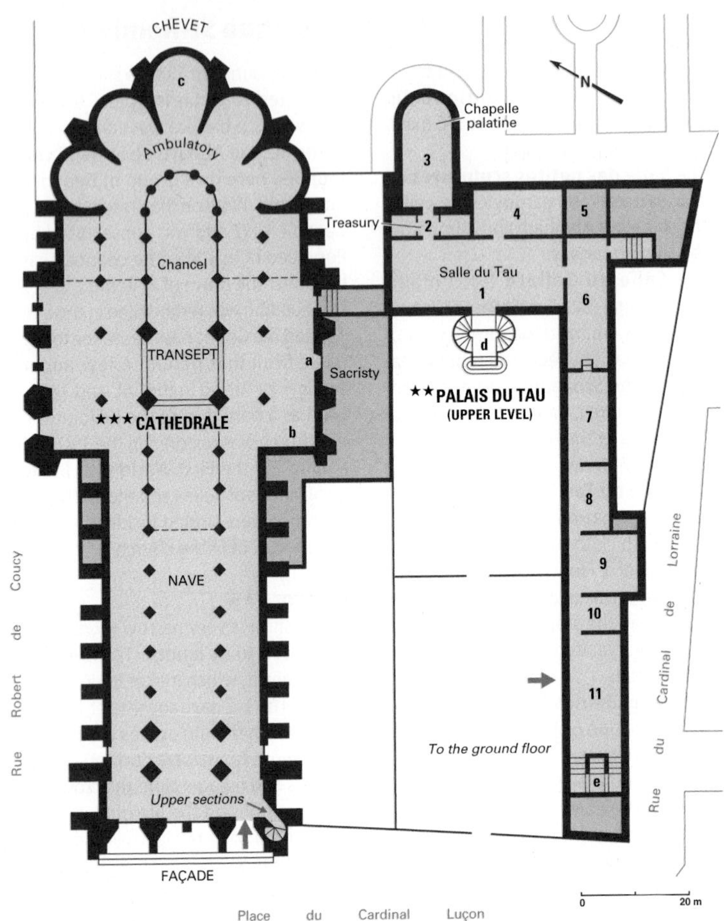

the Crucifixion, the Apostles, Prophets and archbishops of Reims.

Behind the altar, St Remi's grave, rebuilt in 1847, has retained its 17C statues located in the recesses and representing **St Remi**, Clovis and the 12 peers who took part in the coronation.

Colonnades surrounding the chancel separate the ambulatory from the **radiating chapels** whose entrance is marked by two isolated columns. The polychrome motifs decorating the capitals are the original ones and the statues date from the 13C and 18C.

The 45 stone slabs, inlaid with lead (biblical scenes), which can be seen in the first bay of the north aisle, come from the former Abbaye St-Nicaise.

The south transept houses an Entombment dating from 1530 and the altarpiece of the Three Christenings (1610) showing Christ between Constantine and Clovis.

Musée-abbaye St-Remi★★

53 rue Simon. Open Mon-Fri 2-6.30pm, weekends 2-7pm. Closed 1 Jan, 1 May, 14 Jul, 1 and 11 Nov, 25 Dec. €3; no charge pass découverte and 1st Sun of the month. 03 26 85 23 36.

The former royal abbey comprises a group of well-restored 17C and 18C buildings and some remnants of the medieval abbey.

Ground floor

The main courtyard leads to a building with an imposing façade in the Louis XVI style. The cloisters, designed by Jean Bonhomme, date from 1709; they adjoin

the basilica whose flying buttresses overlap into one of the galleries.
The **chapter house** has some magnificent Romanesque capitals. The former 17C refectory and kitchen contain the **Gallo-Roman collections** illustrating the ancient city of Durocortorum which later became Reims. Note the fine mosaics, the large relief map (1:2 000) and **Jovin's tomb**★, a splendid 3C and 4C Roman sarcophagus.

First floor
A superb staircase (1778) leads to the gallery where the **St-Remi tapestries**★★ are exhibited; commissioned by Archbishop Robert de Lenoncourt for the basilica, they were made between 1523 and 1531. Each one consists of several scenes depicting various episodes of St Remi's life and the miracles he accomplished.
On the left of the staircase, four rooms (10-13 and 25) are devoted to the **history of the site** on which the abbey was built: 12C stone and bronze sculptures, and 17C enamel work from the Limoges area illustrating the lives of St Timothy, Apollinarius and Maurus.
Follow the **regional archaeological trail** (rooms 20-27) from the **Palaeolithic** and **Neolithic** periods (tools and funeral objects) via the **Protohistoric** period (Bronze Age to the Roman conquest, including objects discovered in chariot graves and Gaulish necropolises) and up to **Gallo-Roman times** (handicraft, agriculture, clothing, jewellery, medicine, games, household items). The **Merovingian** period is represented by jewellery, pottery, glassware and weapons found in nearby necropolises. The exhibits displayed in the flying-buttress gallery were seized during the Revolution: St Gibrien's crozier, and the 14C Virgin's triptych, carved out of ivory.
The next gallery shows the evolution of **medieval sculpture** from the 11C to the 16C; note the delicately carved tympanum and the carved-wood console representing Samson and the Lion.
The **Gothic room** contains fragments of destroyed lay and religious buildings: carvings from the Église St-Nicaise, and the reconstructed façade of the 13C Maison des Musiciens (House of Musicians), formerly on rue de Mars.
A large room contains uniforms, military gear, weapons, documents etc illustrating the main events of the city's **military history;** note in particular the glass cabinets devoted to the Champagne regiments, the famous battles of the Revolutionary period, and the military parade which took place on the occasion of Charles X's coronation in 1825.

Additional Sights

Musée des Beaux-Arts★

8 rue Chanzy. Open Wed–Mon 10am-noon, 2-6pm. Closed 1 Jan, 1 May, 14 Jul, 1 and 11 Nov, 25 Dec. 3€; no charge pass découverte and 1st Sun of the month. 03 26 47 28 44, www.reims.fr.
The art museum, housed in the 18C former Abbaye St-Denis, covers the period from the Renaissance to the present.

Ground floor
The highlight is 13 portraits (16C) of German princes by **Cranach the Elder** and **Cranach the Younger;** these are extremely realistic drawings enhanced by gouache and oil paint. Admire also 27 landscapes by **Corot** (1796-1875) and the portrait of a seated Italian youth, painted by Corot during his stay in Rome in 1826. The Flemish, Dutch and French schools are also represented. There are also ceramics from the principal French and foreign manufacturers and some sculptures by Reims artist, René de Saint-Marceaux (1845-1915).

First floor
The first room contains some strange 15C and 16C grisaille paintings heightened by colours, which include four series of picturesque scenes (the *Apostles*, *Christ's Vengeance* and *Christ's Passion*). They may have been used as sets for mystery plays or lined along the way from St-Remi Basilica to the cathedral on coronation days.
The following rooms are devoted to French painting from the 17C on.

Musée-hôtel le Vergeur★

36 place du Forum. Guided tour (1hr20) Tue–Sun 2-6pm. Closed 1 Jan, 1 May, 14 Jul, 1 Nov, 25 Dec. €4. 03 26 47 20 75, www.museelevergeur.com.

This 13C-16C mansion, which belonged to **Nicolas Le Vergeur**, a wealthy grain merchant, has a picturesque gabled façade with a timber-framed upper part over a stone base. A Renaissance wing, overlooking the garden, has an interesting frieze carved with battle scenes. The 13C great hall and the floor above it contain paintings, engravings and plans concerning the history of Reims and the splendour of coronation ceremonies. The living quarters, decorated with panelling and antique furniture, recall the life of Baron **Hugues Krafft**, a patron of the arts who lived in the mansion until his death in 1935 and bequeathed it together with its contents to the Friends of Old Reims. One of the drawing rooms contains an exceptional collection of **engravings by Dürer**★ including the Apocalypse and the Great Passion.

Ancien collège des Jésuites

1 place Museux. Closed for renovation until 2008. 03 26 85 51 50. www.ville-reims.com.

In 1606, the Jesuits were allowed by King Henri IV to found a college in Reims; they then erected the chapel (1617-78) . Clinging to one of the walls and still giving grapes is a 300-year-old vine, brought back from Palestine by the Jesuits. The college prospered until the Jesuits were expelled from France in 1762; it was then turned into a general hospital.

The tour includes the **refectory**, decorated with 17C woodwork and paintings by Jean Helart depicting the Life of St Ignatius Loyola and St Francis-Xavier. Note the magnificent table top carved out of a single piece of oak; a branch of the same tree was used for the table of the public prosecutor's office upstairs. A Renaissance staircase leads to the **library**★, elaborately adorned with Baroque woodwork and a coffered ceiling supported by garlands, scrolls and cherubs. It was the setting chosen by Patrice Chéreau for his film *La Reine Margot* with Isabelle Adjani and Daniel Auteuil. Note the small reading cubicles and the table with hoof-shaped feet. The tour of the underground galleries (refreshing in summer) includes a 17C cellar, a 12C gallery and a Gallo-Roman gallery. One wing of the former college houses the Planetarium, the other is a temporary exhibition space for the **Fonds régional d'art contemporain**.

Planétarium et Horloge astronomique

1 place Museux. Horloge Astronomique 2-6pm, Planetarium tour (50min) weekends and zone b school holidays 2.45, 3.30 and 4.45pm. Closed 1 Jan, 1 May, 14 Jul, 1 and 11 Nov, 25 Dec. €3, no charge pass découverte and 1st Sun of the month. 03 26 35 34 70.

A wing of the former Jesuit college houses a planetarium and an astronomical clock made between 1930 and 1952 by Jean Legros, a native of Reims.

Chapelle Foujita★

33 rue du Champ-de-Mars. Open May-Oct Thur–Tue 2–6pm. Closed 1 Jan, 1 May, 14 Jul, 1 and 11 Nov, 25 Dec. €3, no charge pass découverte and 1st Sun of the month. 03 26 40 06 96, www.reims.fr

Designed and decorated by **Léonard Foujita** (1886-1968) and donated by the Champagne firm Mumm, the chapel was inaugurated in 1966. Stained glass and frescoes depicting Biblical scenes celebrate the mystical inspiration felt by the Japanese painter in the Basilique St-Remi. Foujita, who belonged to the early-20C school of art known as the École de Paris, converted to Christianity and was baptised in Reims Cathedral.

Musée de la Reddition

12 rue Franklin-Roosevelt. Open Wed-Mon 10am-noon, 2-6pm. Closed 1 Jan, 1 May, 14 Jul, 1 and 11 Nov, 25 Dec. €3, no charge pass découverte and 1st Sun of the month. 03 26 85 23 36. www.reims.fr.

General Eisenhower established his headquarters in this technical college towards the end of the Second World War and this is where the German capitulation act was signed on 7 May 1945.

The Salle de la Signature (Signing Room) has remained as it was at the time.

Musée automobile de Reims-Champagne

Kids 84 avenue Georges-Clemenceau. Open mid-Mar–Oct Wed–Mon 10am-noon, 2-6pm; rest of the year Wed–Mon 10am-noon, 2-5pm. Closed 25 Dec-15 Jan. €5.50 (children €2.50). 03 26 82 83 84.

Created in 1985, this car museum houses a collection of 100 vintage cars and prototypes in excellent condition including famous makes such as Delahaye, Salmson, Porsche, Jaguar, a Sizaire-Berwick limousine dating from 1919 and a Messier coupé from 1929. Models, pedal cars, posters, early-20C advertisements and enamelled plates are also displayed.

Excursions

Fort de la Pompelle

9km/5.6mi SE by N 44 towards Chalons-en-Champagne. Open Apr–Oct 11am–6pm, weekends and holidays 11am–7pm. Nov–Mar Wed–Mon 10am-5pm. Closed late Dec–early Jan. €3.50. 03 26 49 11 85.

The fort sits on top of a 120m/394ft-high hill. It was built between 1880 and 1883 for the defence of Reims. At the beginning of the First World War, it was under constant German attack but its resistance contributed to the victory of the Battle of the Marne.

A path leads from the lower car park to the fort, which has remained in the state it was in at the end of the war. Guns are displayed in front of the fort and trenches and casemates are visible on the south side. The **museum** houses mementoes of the war: medals, uniforms, weapons and a collection of 560 **German helmets**★.

Parc nature de Sept-Saulx★

22km/13.7mi SE by N 44 towards Châlons-en-Champagne. Open Jul–Aug Mon–Sat 11am–6.30pm, Sun and holidays 10am–10pm. May–Jun Wed, Fri & weekends 11am–6.30pm. Apr & Sep–Oct Wed & weekends 11am–6.30pm. . €7 (children: €3.50). 03 26 03 24 91. www.parcnature.fr

Kids This nature park, situated in the east of the Parc naturel regional de la Montagne de Reims, has a water theme. Visitors can cross a **peat bog** via a succession of wooden footpaths winding their way just above the water. These unusual paths are lined with willows and reeds as well as explanatory panels and games. The park is dotted with thematic islets, including bamboo island, flower island and duck island.

Canoes are available for a trip along the canals (1km/0.6mi); picnic areas equipped with tables and play areas are also at the disposal of visitors (open-air dancing at weekends in summer).

Driving Tour

Massif de St-Thierry

50km/31mi round tour – Allow 1hr 30min.

- *Leave Reims along avenue de Laon, N 44 and take the first left (D 26) after La Neuvillette.*

The road climbs up the Massif de St-Thierry, a section of the Île-de-France cuesta jutting into the plain of Champagne. The area has a wealth of Romanesque porch churches.

St-Thierry

This village overlooking the plain of Reims has a 12C church with a porch

Musée automobile de Reims-Champagne

Citroën Type A, 1919

characteristic of Champagne Romanesque architecture. In the 18C Archbishop Talleyrand, uncle of the famous 19C minister, built a château on the site of an abbey founded in the 6C by St Thierry. It was demolished on the eve of the Revolution except for the five Romanesque pillars of the chapter house, turned into a **chapel** by the Benedictine nuns who settled here in 1968.

Continue to Trigny along D 26 via Chenay with fine views of Reims.

Trigny

This picturesque village was the starting point of the route taken by kings on their way to be crowned in Reims. A viewpoint offers a fine panorama.

In Trigny, turn right onto D 530 leading to Hermonville.

Hermonville

An imposing arcaded porch extends across the west front of the **church** (late 12C). The doorway recess shelters an 18C statue of the Virgin Mary. The Early Gothic interior offers a striking contrast with the 18C baldaquined altar.

Detour via D 530 N to Cauroy-lès-Hermonville.

Cauroy-lès-Hermonville

The early 12C **church** is worth seeing for its wood-panelled Romanesque nave and Champagne-style porch, said to be the oldest in the region.

Return to Hermonville and drive W along D 30 across the highest point of the Massif de St-Thierry. In Bouvancourt, turn left onto D 375.

Just before reaching Pévy, enjoy the charming bird's-eye **view** of the village nestling in the valley.

Pévy

This village has an interesting **church** whose Romanesque nave contrasts with the Gothic chancel. The interior contains a Romanesque font and a 15C stone altarpiece.

Follow D 75 down to the River Vesle and cross over at Jonchery; N 31 leads back to Reims.

REMIREMONT

VOSGES. POPULATION 8 538

MICHELIN LOCAL MAP 314: H-4

The small town of Remiremont, situated in the deep and densely forested upper valley of the River Moselle, was once the seat of a famous abbey.

- **Tourist office**: 2 r. Charles-de-Gaulle, 88200 Remiremont. ☎03 29 62 23 70. www.ot-remiremont.fr
- **Orient yourself**: on the River Moselle on the N 57 S of Êpinal.
- **Don't Miss:** The **Promenade du Calvaire** offers an overall view of the town and the Moselle Valley to the north.

A Bit of History

The Ladies of Remiremont

In 620, two disciples of St Columban, Amé and Romaric, founded two monasteries, one for men and one for women, on a summit overlooking the confluence of the Moselle and the Moselotte. The convent, which later moved down to the valley, became the Chapter of the Ladies of Remiremont under the direct control of the Pope and the Holy Roman Emperor. The canonesses were all aristocrats of ancient lineage. The mother superior, who had the title of Princess of the Holy Empire, and her two assistants were the only ones to take their vows; the other nuns had only to attend services, thus making the convent a sort of finishing school for noble maidens.

Sight

Abbatiale St-Pierre

Allow 15min. The former abbey church, topped by an onion-shaped belfry, is mostly Gothic but the west front and the belfry were rebuilt in the 18C. Note the beautiful 17C marble ornamentation of the chancel and the 11C statue of Notre-Dame-du-Trésor in the chapel on the right. Beneath the chancel, there is an 11C **crypt**★ with rib vaulting.

Next door, the 18C former **abbatial palace** has a beautiful façade. A few of the 17C and 18C mansions inhabited by the canonesses still surround the church and the palace.

Rue Charles-de-Gaulle★

This picturesque arcaded street is a fine example of 18C town planning.

Musée municipal Charles-de-Bruyère

70 rue Charles-de-Gaulle. Open Apr–Sep Wed-Mon 10am-noon, 2-6pm; rest of the year Wed-Mon Tue 2-6pm (5pm Nov-Dec). Closed Oct, 1 Jan, 1 May, 1 Nov, 25 Dec. €1.60, no charge Sun. ☎03 29 62 59 14.

The collections are devoted to local history and handicraft from Lorraine; precious manuscripts and tapestries from the former abbey are displayed together with Gothic sculpture from the Lorraine region, 18C ceramics and 17C northern paintings by followers of Rembrandt.

Maison-musée Charles-Friry

12 rue du Général-Humbert. Same hours as the municipal museum.

This former canonesses' mansion (18C and 19C) contains documents, statues and *objets d'art* connected with the Ladies from Remiremont and regional history. 17C-18C paintings include *Le Vielleur à la sacoche* (the Hurdy-gurdy Player) by Georges de La Tour.

The garden, which partly recreates the Grand Jardin of the abbey, is decorated with two ornamental fountains and a few other features from the abbey.

Driving Tour

Upper Moselle Valley Downriver from Remiremont★

27km/16.8mi – allow 30min

Leave Remiremont N along D 42 which follows the east bank of the Moselle.

Forêt de Fossard

The road runs between the river and the forest which bears traces of ancient religious settlements. It is crisscrossed by marked footpaths ideal for hiking.

3hr. Start opposite the Gendarmerie in St-Étienne-lès-Remiremont. St-Mont offers a fine view as well as the ruins of the abbey (private property) founded by Amé and Romaric. A path leads to the mysterious Pont des Fées (Fairies' bridge).

Tête des Cuveaux★

30min on foot there and back. Follow the road leading to the ridge line marked by a spruce forest and leave the car in the parking area (picnic area).

Turn right along the ridge to reach a viewing table, where there is a **panoramic view**★ of the Moselle Valley, the Lorrain plateau and the Vosges.

Arches

Arches is known for its traditional paper industry; a paper mill was already operating here in 1469. The playwright **Beaumarchais**, author of *The Barber of Seville* and *The Marriage of Figaro*, bought the mill in 1779 in order to produce the necessary paper for the complete edition of Voltaire's works. As most of the great philosopher's writings had been banned in France, he printed what are now known as the Kehl editions in Kehl (across the Rhine from Strasbourg).

Address Book

For coin ranges, see the Legend on cover flap.

WHERE TO EAT

Le Clos Heurtebise – *13 chemin des Capucins, off r. Capit.-Flayelle. ☎03 29 62 08 04.Cosed 14-27 Jan, 5-14 May, Sun evening, Mon and Tue.* In a former textile manufacturer's residence in the upper part of the town, this restaurant's terrace overlooks the valley and the forest in fine weather. Fish is a house speciality, and the menus combine regional and traditional flavours.

Le Chalet Blanc – *34 r. des Pêcheurs (opposite the shopping centre), 88200 St-Étienne-lès-Remiremont, 2km/1.2mi E of Remiremont on D 417, Gérardmer road. ☎03 29 26 11 80. Closed Feb school holidays and 1-20 Aug, Sat lunch, Sun evening and Mon.* A large white modern building reminiscent of a chalet. Much frequented by the locals, who enjoy the good cooking. Dining room decorated with light-coloured wood, and pretty, reasonably priced bedrooms.

WHERE TO STAY

Hôtel du Cheval de Bronze – *59 r. Charles-de-Gaulle. ☎03 29 62 52 24. hotel-du-cheval-de-bronze@wanadoo.fr. Closed Nov. 35 rooms. €6.50.* The façade of this former coaching inn in the town centre is decorated with arches. The atmosphere and standard of comfort are slightly outdated, but it's a good place to stay for a night.

SHOPPING

Distillerie Lecomte-Blaise – *10 r. Gare Nol, 88120 Le Syndicat. By the D 43 (La Bresse direction) for 4km/2.5mi, turn right towards Nol. ☎03 29 24 71 04. www.lecomte-blaise.com. Mon-Sat 10am-noon, 2-6pm.* This traditional distillery founded in 1820 produces brandy made from fruit (pear, plum, raspberry, quetsche plums) and wild berries (wild rose, bilberry, elderberry, sorb) picked in the surrounding orchards and forests. Tour of the manufacturing premises, tasting and produce for sale.

Moulin à huile – *68470 Storckensohn. ☎ 03 89 82 75 50. May-Jun and Sep-Oct, Sat-Sun 2-5.30pm, Jul-Aug, Wed-Sun 2-5.30pm.* A restored 1732 mill with apple and walnut presses: watch the pressing process before trying it yourself, and making your own oil.

Épinal★ – See ÉPINAL.

To the source of the Moselle★

50km/31mi – allow 2hr

La Beuille

Drive 6km/3.7mi along D 57 then turn left onto a tarmacked path leading to the parking area overlooking the Chalet de la Beuille. From the terrace-viewpoint at the chalet, there is a fine **view**★ of the Moselle Valley and the Ballon d'Alsace in the distance.

At Col des Croix, turn NE onto D 486 to Le Thillot, ignoring D 16 which winds past the Ballon de Servance (see Parc naturel regional des BALLONS DES VOSGES) to Plancher-les-Mines.

Le Thillot

Many tourists go through this busy industrial centre (textiles, tanning, industrial woodwork) on their way to the Vosges mountains.

Les mines de cuivre des ducs de Lorraine

Guided tours (1hr 30min to 2hr 30min depending on the circuit). Apr-Sep 10am-7pm (last departure 5pm); Oct-Mar: daily during school holidays (Wed, Sat, Sun outside school holiday periods) 1-7pm (last departure 4pm). Closed 1 Jan, 25 Dec. Wear good shoes. €5 or €7 depending on circuit. ☎ 03 29 25 03 33.

A tour of these copper mines offers a journey back in time to the 16C to the 18C. The Musée des Hautes-Mines further satisfies the visitors' curiosity.

St-Maurice-sur-Moselle – See BALLON D'ALSACE.

Between St-Maurice and Bussang, morainic deposits at the bottom of the valley have created a landscape of rolling hills dotted with gabled farmhouses.

Bussang

Bussang is a summer and winter resort. The **Théâtre du Peuple** (folk theatre) founded in 1895, consists of a mobile stage using nature as its background and can seat 1 100 spectators. The actors, many of them local inhabitants, give performances of folk plays as well as plays by Shakespeare, Molière etc.

Petit Drumont★★

15min on foot there and back. Turn onto the forest road branching off D 89 just before the Col de Bussang. Leave the car near the inn and follow the path which rises through high pastures.

At the top of Petit Drumont (alt 1 200m/3 846ft), admire the **panorama**★★ from the viewing table.

Col de Bussang

At the pass (alt 727m/2 388ft) a monument by Gilodi (1965) marks the source of the Moselle, which at this point is no more than a small stream.

RETHEL

ARDENNES. POPULATION 7 923

MICHELIN LOCAL MAP 306: I-5

The town has been almost entirely rebuilt after destruction in the First and Second World Wars. French poet, Paul Verlaine, spent several quiet years in the town in the 1870s teaching literature, history, geography and English.

Tourist office: 3 quai d'Orfeuil, 08300 Rethel. ☎ 03 24 38 54 56.

Orient yourself: Rethel lies on the banks of the River Aisne and the Canal des Ardennes halfway between Reims and Charleville-Mézières.

WHERE TO STAY AND EAT

Le Moderne – *2 pl. Victor Hugo. 03 24 38 44 54. 21 rooms. €6.50. Restaurant.* Many of the rooms have been pleasantly renovated, living up to the establishment's name.

SHOPPING

Charcuterie Yves Duhem – *9 r. Colbert. 03 24 38 46 19. Tue-Sat 8.30am-12.30pm, 2.30-7pm; Sun 9am-noon.* Since 1798, this shop has been making boudin blanc and other high-quality pork meat specialities.

CALENDAR

Festival de viole de gambe – *Held every two years (next in June 2008) in Asfeld: concerts, musical walk, exhibition by stringed-instument makers. 03 24 72 96 99.*

Sight

Église St-Nicolas

Jul-Aug daily 2.30-5.30pm. 03 24 38 41 50.

This unusual Gothic edifice consists of two churches built side by side. The left-hand church (12C-13C) was used by monks from a Benedictine monastery. The right-hand church (15C-16C) was the parish church. Characteristic features include a wide aisle lit by Flamboyant Gothic windows and a richly decorated doorway completed in 1512: note the statue of St Nicholas, and the Assumption decorating the gable, reminiscent of the Coronation of the Virgin on the central doorway of Reims Cathedral.

Excursions

Asfeld

22km/13.7mi SW along D 18 then D 926.

This village on the south bank of the River Aisne, which once belonged to the counts of Avaux, has an unusual Baroque church, **Église St-Didier**★ built in brick in the shape of a viol, which was designed in 1683 by the Dominican priest, François Romain, who built the Pont-Royal in Paris. Consisting entirely of curves, it has a central rotunda flanked by four semi-oval cupollas and a brick colonnade round the outside.

Wasigny

16km/10mi N along D 10.

On the way, the road goes through **Séry** where a 1.7km/1mi **botanic trail** allows nature lovers to discover the local flora: orchids as well as other flowers, plants and bushes characteristic of sheep pasture.

A 16C-17C **manor house** by the river guards the entrance to the village. A fine 15C covered market stands in the village centre.

Boudin Blanc

This white sausage made from fresh pork meat without any preservatives is the gastronomic speciality of Rethel and carries the *Ardennes de France* seal as a guarantee of quality. The original recipe is said to have been invented by a chef of Cardinal Mazarin to whom the Comté of Rethel once belonged. Today *boudin blanc*, which is celebrated in Rethel in an annual fair on the last weekend in April, comes in different sizes and can be prepared in various ways: in a pastry case, barbecued or as a tasty stuffing for *crêpes* (pancakes).

VALLÉE DU RHIN★★

HAUT-RHIN. BAS-RHIN. MICHELIN LOCAL MAP 315 : N 3 TO J 11

Marking the border between France and Germany, the River Rhine is flanked on the French side by the foothills of the Vosges, along which runs the Route des Vins, and on the German side by the dense Black Forest. From time immemorial men have attempted to harness its fast impetuous flow and its fearsome spates by building dikes, cutting its arms off and gradually forcing it to follow an artificial course. In spite of this, the "Vater Rhein" is still there, ready to welcome you along part of its fabulous journey to the North Sea.

A Bit of History

With a total length of 1 298km/807mi, including 190km/118mi along the Franco-German border, the Rhine is the seventh longest river in Europe. The spates of the Rhine were fearsome; this is the reason why no town, not even Strasbourg, settled on its banks. When the water level rose, local people took turns to watch the dikes day and night. In spite of this, catastrophes were frequent and many an Alsatian village was destroyed by flooding.

In the 8C and 9C, boatmen from Strasbourg sailed downriver to the North Sea in order to sell wine to the English, the Danes and the Swedes. At the end of the Middle Ages, these boatmen controlled the Rhine between Basle and Mainz and theirs was the most powerful guild in Strasbourg. Some 5 000 wagoners, with 20 000 horses at their disposal, carried inland goods unloaded in Strasbourg.

Harnessing of the Rhine

Water transport was at its height under Napoleon I and in 1826, the first steamships, operating regular sailings along the Rhine, called at Strasbourg. Unfortunately, dikes built along the Rhine during the 19C to control the river flow caused the river bed to become deeper by 6-7cm/2-3in per year. This, in turn, uncovered rock lying at the bottom of the river and rendered navigation impossible when the water level was low. Water transport consequently declined. In order to bring boats and barges back to the Alsatian section of the Rhine, the French decided in 1920 to divert part of the river between Basle and Strasbourg to a low-gradient canal. Begun in 1928 and completed in the 1960s, the Grand Canal d'Alsace also offers the possibility of tapping the river's considerable potential of hydroelectric power.

R. Mattès/MICHELIN

Barges on the Rhine

River Traffic

Rhine barges are between 60m/197ft and 125m/410ft long, and between 8m/26ft and 13m/43ft wide. Among these, there are many self-propelled barges with a capacity of 3 000t for carrying gas. Navigable between Basle and Rotterdam, the Rhine carries more than 10 000 boats every year and these in turn transport 190 million tonnes of freight. It is interesting to note that water transport on the Canal d'Alsace uses only a fourth of the energy required on the Rhine. Strasbourg is France's second largest river port after Paris.

Driving Tour

Grand Canal d'Alsace and the Harnessing of the Rhine★★

From Kembs to Strasbourg

Barrage de Kembs

9km/5.6mi S of Kembs. The dam was the only one built along the first four reaches; it diverts the major part of the river flow towards the Grand Canal d'Alsace. A hydroelectric power station uses the remaining flow.

Hydroelectric power station★

Built between 1928 and 1932, the power station was damaged during the Second World War but repaired in 1945. Today, it produces 938 million kWh every year.

Bief de Kembs★

Situated downriver from the dam, the reach includes the canal and a recently modernised double lock.

Petite Camargue alsacienne

9km S of Kembs along D 468. Parking area near the stadium in St-Louis-la-Chaussée. Three marked footpaths, one all the way round the large marsh *(3km/1.9mi)*, offer the opportunity of observing many species of fauna and flora through copses, ponds, marshland and heaths.

The Canal de Huningue branches off near Niffer towards Mulhouse. The canal and its access lock form the first section of the Rhine-Rhône link.

Address Book

For coin ranges, see the Legend on cover flap.

THE PRACTICAL RHINE

Locks and dams on the Rhine have information panels relating the history of the Rhine, explaining how power stations work and describing the role of locks and dams. Visits of hydro-electric power stations are restricted by the Vigipirate security plan.

Dams at Kembs, Rhinau and Strasbourg can be used by cyclists and pedestrians to cross between France and Germany.

Boat trips – Themed cruises starting from Huningue or Rheinfelden, Augst, Basel, lasting half a day or a day. Various sections of the Rhine are explored.

WHERE TO EAT

Les Écluses – *8 r. Rosenau, 68680 Kembs-Loéchlé. ☎03 89 48 37 77. restaurant.les.ecluses@freesbee.fr. Closed Feb and Nov school holidays, Wed evenings Oct-Apr, Sun evening and Mon.* This small family restaurant has a good local reputation. The building has been entirely renovated, and the dining room is small but pleasantly decorated, with modern furniture. Regional specialities and fish feature on the menu. Pretty terrace in summer.

SPORTS AND RECREATION

Canoës du Ried – *68970 Illhauesern. ☎03 89 73 84 82. www.canoes-du-ried.com.* With its vast network of rivers, the Ried area is ideal for discovering by canoe. Canoes can be hired for between 2hr and 3 days, with or without accompaniment.

Each of the following reaches along the Grand Canal d'Alsace comprises a hydro-electric power station and a double lock, which attracts many curious observers when in operation.

Bief d'Ottmarsheim★

See OTTMARSHEIM.

Bief de Fessenheim★

Situated less than 1km/0.6mi from the Fessenheim lock, it is the first French **nuclear power station** to have used a high-water-pressure reactor.

The reach is about 17km/11mi long and has two locks of the same length (185m/202yd) but different widths (23m/75ft and 12m/39ft).

Bief de Vogelgrün★

The power station is similar to those at Ottmarsheim and Fessenheim.Downstream from Vogelgrün are four more reaches; each one comprises a dam on the river, a feeder canal supplying water to the power station and navigation locks and another canal returning the diverted flow to the Rhine.

The power station is decorated with a huge fresco (1 500m^2/1 794sq yd) by Daniel Dyminski from Mulhouse, entitled *Nix from Vogelgrün*, and a large bronze allegorical sculpture by Raymond Couvègnes, entitled *Electricity*.

Bief de Gerstheim

The power station produces 818 million kWh per year.

Bief de Strasbourg

1970. A regulating reservoir forms a lake with a water sports centre at Plobsheim. The Pont de l'Europe is a must for anyone visiting Strasbourg (*see STRASBOURG*), but you can also approach the Rhine between Lauterbourg and Strasbourg, by side roads branching off D 468.

The harnessing of the Rhine was prolonged beyond Strasbourg in the 1970s by a Franco-German project, the two countries sharing the power produced by the **Gambsheim** power station, on the French side, and the **Iffezheim** power station, on the German side.

RIBEAUVILLÉ★

HAIT-RHIN. POPULATION 4 929

MICHELIN LOCAL MAP 315: H-7 – ALSO SEE ROUTE DES VINS

Ribeauvillé occupies a picturesque site at the foot of the Vosges mountains crowned with old castles. The small town is renowned for its Riesling and Gewürztraminer, Alsatian white wines, and is home to a wine festival in July.

Pfifferdaj

The "day of the fifes" is one of the oldest festivals in Alsace. It takes place on the first Sunday in September. Travelling musicians used to gather in the town to pay homage to their suzerain. The statutes of their powerful corporation were recorded by Colmar's Council. Today, the Pfifferdaj or **Fête des Ménétriers** is a folk festival with a historic procession and free wine tasting at the Fontaine du Vin, place de l'Hôtel-de-Ville.

Grand'Rue Walking Tour★★

- *Start at the tourist office housed in the former guardroom at no 1.*

This semi-pedestrianised street lined with half-timbered houses runs through the whole town. At the southern and eastern entrances,two old towers are crowned by storks' nests.

Pfifferhüs (Restaurant des Ménétriers).

No 14. Note the two statues standing on a loggia above the door, which illustrate the Annunciation.

Halle au Blé

Place de la 1re-Armée.
The old covered corn exchange sits atop a secret passageway.

Fontaine Renaissance

The red-and-yellow-sandstone fountain (1536) is crowned by a heraldic lion.

Tour des Bouchers★

This old belfry used to mark the separation between the upper and the middle town. The base dates from the 13C. Beautiful 17C timber-framed house at no 78 Grand'Rue.

Place de la Sinne

This is a charming little square, lined with timber-framed houses, with a fountain (1860) in its centre.

Église St-Grégoire-le-Grand

The church dates from the 13C-15C. Note the tympanum of the west doorway and the fine ironwork on the door. In the south aisle, there is a 15C carved-wood Virgin and Child, gilt and painted, wearing the local headdress; the Baroque organ was made by Rinck.

Return along Grand'Rue then take rue Klobb and rue des Juifs.

Maisons anciennes

16C and 17C houses can be seen on rue des Juifs, rue Klobb, rue Flesch and rue des Tanneurs (note the openings in the roof of no 12 for drying skins).

Hôtel de ville

guided tour (1hr) May–Sep Tue–Fri & Sun 10am, 11am and 2pm. holidays. No charge. 03 89 73 67 79.
The town hall houses a small **museum** with 17C gold plate and vermeil goblets that belonged to the local lords.

Walk back along rue Flesch and rue des Tanneurs.

Hiking Tour

Leave Ribeauvillé by ⑤ on the town plan. Leave the car in the parking area situated on the roadside (D 416), about 800m/875yd out of town.

Walk up the Chemin des Stations (20min) or the Chemin Sarassin (40min).

Notre-Dame-de-Dusenbach

The three chapels of this popular place of pilgrimage were destroyed on three occasions: by the English

B. Kaufmann/MICHELIN

Ribeauvillé

in 1365, by the Swedes in 1632 and by the Republicans in 1794. The **Virgin's Chapel**, a convent, a neo-Gothic church (1903) and a pilgrims' shelter (1913) were built over the ruins. The chapel stands on the edge of a promontory towering above the Dusenbach Valley. Inside, above the altar, there is a 15C polychrome wood **Pietà**, said to perform miracles.

▶ *Follow the Chemin Sarassin then the path leading to the castles.*

Stop by the **Rocher Kahl**, at the halfway mark. From this granite scree, there is a fine bird's-eye view of the Strengbach Valley and its forested slopes.

▶ *At the intersection of forest lanes go straight on along the path signposted Ribeauvillé par les châteaux.*

Château du Haut-Ribeaupierre

It is possible to walk through the ruins of this 12C castle (⊶ *the keep is closed to the public*).

▶ *Retrace your steps (avoiding the direct path linking Haut-Ribeaupierre and St-Ulrich) back to the intersection and follow the marked path to St-Ulrich.*

Château de St-Ulrich★

The stairs leading to the castle start from the foot of the keep, on the left. The **castle** was not only a fortress, like most castles in the Vosges region, but also the luxury residence of the Comtes de Ribeaupierre. The stairs lead through the castle gate to a small courtyard. A door at the end of the courtyard gives access to the Romanesque Great Hall, lit by nine twinned rounded windows, which was once covered by a timber ceiling.

▶ *Return to the small courtyard and go up the stairs to the chapel.*

Retrace your steps to visit the oldest part of the castle including Romanesque living quarters, whose windows are decorated with fleurs-de-lys, another courtyard and the keep. The red-sandstone keep, built on a granite base, towers

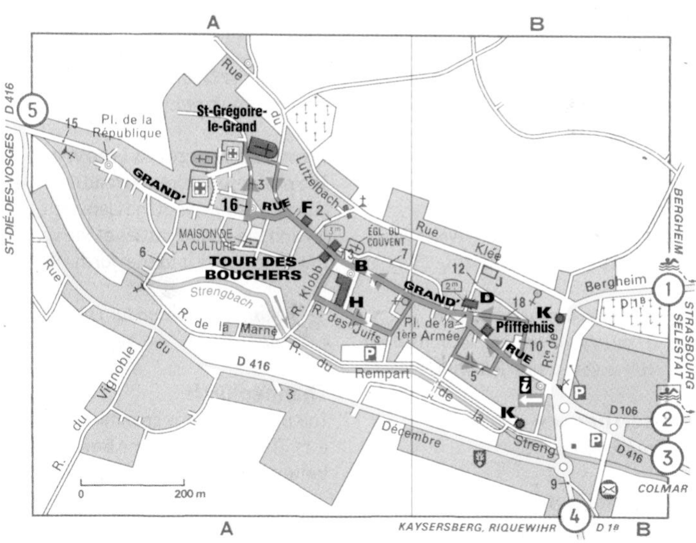

RIBEAUVILLÉ								
Abbé-Kemp R. de l'	A	2	Fontaine R. de la	A	6	Halles-aux-Blés R.	B	12
Château R. du	A	3	Frères-Mertian R. des	A	7	Mairie Pl. de la	A	13
Flesch R.	B	5	Gaulle Av. du Gén.-de	B	9	Ste-Marie-aux-Mines Rte	A	15
			Gouraud Pl.	B	10	Sinne Pl. de la	A	16
			Grand'Rue	AB		Tanneurs R. des	B	18

Fontaine Renaissance	A	B	Hôtel de ville	A	H	Nids de cigognes	B	K
Halle au Blés	B	D	Maison ancienne	A	F			

over the rest of the castle. From the top, the **panorama★★** extends over the Strengbach Valley, the ruins of the **Château de Girsberg** (dating from the 12C and abandoned in the 17C), Ribeauvillé and the Plaine d'Alsace.

Driving tour

Col de Fréland

47km/29mi round tour – allow 5hr

- *Leave Ribeauvillé by ⑤ on the town plan. The D 416 follows the River Strengbach which flows through the beautiful Ribeauvillé Forest. After 7km/4.3mi, turn left towards Aubure along a picturesque cliff road.*

Aubure

The resort is situated on a sunny plateau and surrounded by pine and fir forests.

- *Turn left onto D 11III. On the descent from the Col de Fréland, 1.5km/0.9mi from the pass, turn left onto a narrow road.*

The road runs through one of the finest **pine forests★** in France.

- *After leaving the forest, drive on for 1km/0.6mi to return to D 11III.*

There is a good view of the Weiss Valley and part of the Val d'Orbey.

- *Continue past Fréland and, 1.5km/0.9mi beyond the intersection with D 11IV to Orbey, turn left onto N 415.*

Kaysersberg★★

See KAYSERSBERG.

- *The road joins the Route des Vins back to Ribeauvillé (see Route des VINS).*

Beblenheim

The village, which boasts a 15C Gothic fountain, lies close to Sonnenglantz (Sunshine), a famous hillside producing high-quality wines (Alsatian Tokay, Muscatel and Gewürztraminer).

Riquewihr★★★– *See RIQUEWIHR.*

Hunawihr – *See Route des VINS.*

- *Drive back to Ribeauvillé.*

Castles Overlooking the Plaine d'Alsace★★

46km/29mi round tour – allow 2hr

- *Leave Ribeauvillé W along D 1B.*

Bergheim – *See Route des VINS.*

St-Hippolyte

An attractive village with flower-decked fountains and Gothic church.

- *As you enter the village, turn left towards Haut-Kœnigsbourg then right 4km/2.5mi beyond St-Hippolyte and left 1km/0.6mi further on to take the one-way road round the castle.*

Château du Haut-Kœnigsbourg★★

See Château du HAUT-KŒNIGSBOURG.

- *Return to D 1B1 and turn right then right again onto D 481.*

From Schaentzel to Lièpvre★

The picturesque forested road descends amid superb views of the Liepvrette Valley and the ruined castles of the Vosges towering above it to the north.

- *Return to D 1B1 and turn right onto D 42.*

Thannenkirch

This peaceful village lies amid dense forests. The road follows the **Bergenbach Valley** down to the Plaine d'Alsace.

- *At Bergheim, turn right towards Ribeauvillé.*

RIQUEWIHR★★★

HAUT-RHIN. POPULATION 1 212

MICHELIN LOCAL MAP 315: H-8 – ALSO SEE ROUTE DES VINS

The attractive little town of Riquewihr was for several centuries the property of the Dukes of Wurtemberg. Spared by the many wars that ravaged the region, the town looks today just as it did in the 16C. It lies in the heart of a wine-growing area, and is especially lively during the grape harvest.

- **Tourist office:** 2 rue de la Première Armée, 68340 Riquewihr. ☎03 20 36 09 22 /0820 360 922. www.ribeauville-riquewihr.com
- **Orient Yourself:** Riquewihr lies 13km/8mi north of Colmar, just off the N63 within the Parc Régional des Ballons des Vosges.
- **Organising Your Time:** Don't try to find a parking space in town; use one of the many outside car parks. Allow 2hr to fully admire the town's old medieval houses.

Town Walk

Go through the archway of the town hall and follow rue du Général-de-Gaulle straight ahead. On the left the Cour du Château leads to the Château.

Château des Ducs de Wurtemberg

Completed in 1540, the castle has kept its mullioned windows, its gable decorated with antlers and its stair turret. It houses the **Musée de la Communi-**

Address Book

For coin ranges, see Legend on the cover flap.

WHERE TO EAT

Auberge St-Alexis – *68240 St-Alexis 6km W of Riquewihr on minor road and forest track. ☎03 89 73 90 38. www.saint-alexis.com. Closed Fri.* It's definitely worth venturing into the forest to this old 17C hermitage. You will be rewarded with simple authentic dishes, such as vegetable soup, choucroute and fruit tarts, made from local farm produce.

Le Sarment d'Or – *4 r. du Cerf. ☎03 89 86 02 86. info@riquewihr-sarment-dor.com. Closed 5 Jan-11 Feb, 28 Jun-6 Jul, Sun evening, Tue lunch and Mon.* Pale wood panelling, a pretty fireplace and huge beams create a lovely warm atmosphere in this restaurant in one of Riquewihr's fine 17C houses. The cooking is traditional with some modern touches. Plush, comfortable rooms.

WHERE TO STAY

Chambre d'hôte Schmitt Gérard – *3 chemin des Vignes. ☎03 89 47 89 72. Closed Jan-Mar. 2 rooms.* A house with a garden at the top of the village, on the edge of a vineyard. Impeccably clean panelled rooms under the roof.

Hôtel L'Oriel – *3 r. des Écuries-Seigneuriales. ☎03 89 49 03 13. www.hotel-oriel.com. 19 rooms. €9.50.* This 16C hotel is easily recognised by its wrought-iron sign. The sloping walls, maze of staircases, exposed beams and bedrooms with Alsatian furniture create a romantic atmosphere. Also three more modern rooms in the annexe.

SHOPPING

Domaine Dopff Au Moulin – *2 av. Jacques-Preiss. b03 89 49 09 69. www.dopff-au-moulin.fr. Open Jan-Mar daily 10am-noon, 2-6pm. Closed 1 Jan, 25-26 Dec.* The Dopff family has been making wines in Alsace since 1550. Reputed for its sparkling wines, Rieslings and Gewurztraminers.

Féerie de Noël – *1 r. du Cerf. ☎03 89 47 94 02 – feerie.de.noel@wanadoo.fr. Open daily 15 Feb-Jun 10am-12.30pm, 1.45-6pm, Jul-Aug 9.30am-7pm, Sep-Dec 10am-12.30pm, 1.45-6.30pm. Closed early Jan-mid-Feb, 25-26 Dec.* Over 2,000 Christmas decorations and ideas for the home and tree.

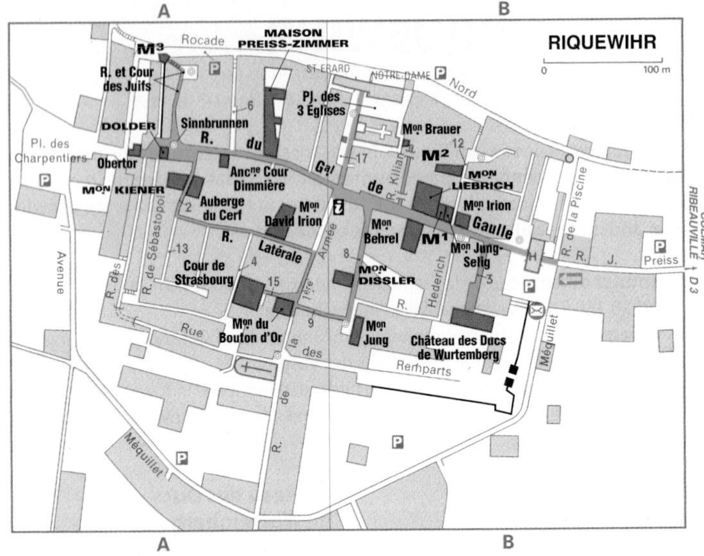

RIQUEWIHR

Street			Street			Street		
Cerf R. du	A	2	Cheval R. du	A	4	Écuries R. des	B	12
Château Cour du	B	3	Cordiers R. des	A	6	St-Nicolas R.	A	13
			Couronne R. de la	B	8	Strasbourg Cour de	A	15
			Dinzheim R. de	A	9	3-Églises R. des	B	17

Maison Hansi	B	M1	Musée de la Tour des Voleurs	A	M3
Musée de la Diligence	B	M2			

cation en Alsace (see Museums). A small open-air museum of architectural remains and the 1790 Altar of Freedom can be seen in front of the east side.

Continue along rue du Général-de-Gaulle.

No 12, known as the **Maison Irion** (1606) has a corner oriel; opposite, there is a 16C well. Next door, the **Maison Jung-Selig** (1561) has a carved timber frame.

Maison Liebrich★ (cour des cigognes)

A well dating from 1603 and a huge winepress from 1817 stand in the picturesque courtyard of this 16C house, surrounded by balustraded wooden galleries (added in the 17C).
Opposite stands the **Maison Behrel** adorned with a lovely oriel (1514) surmounted by openwork added in 1709.

Take the first turn on the right and follow rue Kilian.

Maison Brauer

This house, at the end of the street, has a fine doorway dating from 1618.

Continue along rue des Trois-Églises.

Place des Trois-Églises

The square is framed by two former churches, St-Érard and Notre-Dame, converted into dwellings, and a 19C Protestant church.

Return to rue du Général-de-Gaulle.

Maison Preiss-Zimmer★

The house that belonged to the winegrowers' guild stands in the last but one of a succession of picturesque courtyards.
Further on, on the right, stands the former **tithe court** of the lords of Ribeaupierre.
On place de la Sinn, which marks the end of rue du Général-de-Gaulle, is the pretty 1580 **Fontaine Sinnbrunnen**.

Rue et cour des Juifs

Narrow rue des Juifs leads to the picturesque Cour des Juifs, the old ghetto, from which a narrow passageway and wooden stairs lead to the ramparts and the **Musée de la Tour des Voleurs** (see Museums).

Dolder★

Built in 1291, this gate was reinforced during the 15C and 16C.

Go through the gate to the Obertor.

Obertor (upper gate)

Note the portcullis and the place where the former drawbridge was fixed. On the left, you can see a section of the ramparts and a defence tower.

Return through Dolder and along rue du Général-de-Gaulle then turn right onto rue du Cerf.

Maison Kiener★

No 2. The house built in 1574 has a pediment with an inscription and a bas-relief depicting Death getting hold of the founder of the house. Opposite, the **Auberge du Cerf** dates from 1566.

Continue along rue du Cerf then turn left onto rue Latérale.

Rue Latérale

Lovely houses on this street include the **Maison du marchand Tobie Berger** at no 6, which has a 16C oriel and a Renaissance doorway in the courtyard.

Turn right onto rue de la 1re-Armée.

Maison du Bouton d'Or

No 16. The house goes back to 1566. An alleyway, just round the corner, leads to another tithe court known as the Cour de Strasbourg dating from 1597.

Retrace your steps then continue past the Maison du Bouton d'Or along rue Dinzheim to rue de la Couronne.

Maison Dissler★

No 6. With its scrolled gables and loggia, this stone house (1610) is an interesting example of Renaissance style.

Continue along rue de la Couronne back to rue du Général-de-Gaulle.

Museums

Musée de la Communication en Alsace

Château des Ducs de Wurtemberg. Open Easter-Oct and during Christmas market Wed–Mon 10am–5.30pm. Closed Tue. €4. 03 89 47 93 80. www.shpta.com.

An 1835 stagecoach with three compartments is parked at the entrance. Housed inside the castle, the museum follows the evolution of means of communication in Alsace from Gallo-Roman times to the 20C, including the history of foot messengers, the postal service, airmail, the telegraph and the telephone. Housed in the stables (16C) are stagecoaches from the 18C to early 20C, postilions' uniforms and boots, mail record-books and signs.

R. Mattès/MICHELIN

Riquewihr and its vineyards

Maison Hansi

Open Aug daily 10.30am–6pm. May–Jul and Sep–Dec Tue-Sun 10.30am-6pm. Jan weekends 2-6pm. Feb-Apr Tue-Sun 2-6pm. Closed 1 Jan, 25 Dec. €2. 03 89 47 97 00.

This museum contains watercolours, prints and decorated ceramics by the Colmar artist and cartoonist, JJ Waltz, known as Hansi (*see COLMAR*), whose brother was a chemist in Riquewihr.

Musée de la Tour des Voleurs

Open Easter–Oct daily 10am-12.30pm, 2-6.30pm. Closed Nov to Easter. €2 (combined ticket with Musée du Dolder €3).

The tour includes the torture chamber, the dungeon, guardroom and the caretaker's lodgings of this former prison.

Musée du Dolder

Access by staircase to left of the Porte du Dolder. Open Jul-Aug daily 10.15am-12.30pm, 2-6.30pm. Apr-Jun and Sep-Oct Sat-Sun and holidays 10am-12.30pm, 2-6.30pm. 1 Nov to Easter. €2 (combined ticket with the Tour des Voleurs: €3).

The museum houses mementoes, prints, weapons, tools and furniture, associated with local history.

ROCROI★

ARDENNES. POPULATION 2 420

MICHELIN LOCAL MAP 306: J-3

Sitting in the middle of a star-shaped Citadelle, the small 16C town of Rocroi was the site of one of the most famous battles of the Thirty Years War . Later, Vauban, Louis XIV's military engineer, redesigned the stronghold around a vast parade ground. Rocroi, whose name means King's Rock, changed its name to Roc Libre (free rock) during the Révolution.

- **Tourist office:** Place d'Armes, 08230 Rocroi. 03 24 54 20 06, www.otrocroi.com
- **Orient yourself:** On the Ardennes plateau 6 km /3.7 mi from the Belgian frontier, 28 km /17.4 mi. NW of Charleville-Mézières.

Sights

La Citadelle

Built by Henri II in 1555 to counter the threat of Charlemont fort in Givet, occupied by the Spaniards, the stronghold was further fortified in 1675 by Vauban, who was appointed *Commissaire général des fortifications* in 1678. Starting from the Porte de France to the south-west, follow the tourist trail running along the east front, which gives a good idea of the complexity of the defence system.

Musée de la Bataille de Rocroi

Pl. du Luxembourg. Open May–Oct daily 1.30-6.30pm. €4. 03 24 54 20 06.

Housed in the former guardhouse, the museum presents an audio-visual show illustrating the sequence of manoeuvres which led the young duke of Enghien, the future Grand Condé, to victory over the Spanish army at the battle of Rocroi (1643). There is also a reconstruction of the battle with tiny lead soldiers.

Circuit de la Bataille

A waymarked footpath *(13.5km/8.5mi)* leads from the museum to the site of Rocroi battle through moorland dotted with a wide variety of interesting plants, including wild orchids and gentians.

WHERE TO EAT

Le Vauban – *2 pl. d'Armes. 03 24 54 18 69 . Closed Wed, holidays and evenings except at weekends.* This venerable building and its lovely terrace are situated on the huge parade ground. Inside is cheerful with pink walls and flowery tablecloths. The cooking is traditional with some regional dishes.

ROSHEIM★

BAS-RHIN. POPULATION 4 548

MICHELIN LOCAL MAP 315: I-6 – ALSO SEE ROUTE DES VINS

Hiding amid the vineyards and ruined ramparts of the small wine-producing town of Rosheim are some of the oldest buildings in Alsace, including an interesting Romanesque church.

- **Tourist office:** 94 rue du Général-de-Gaulle, 67560 Rosheim. ☎03 88 50 75 38. www.rosheim.com
- **Orient yourself**: 27 m/16.8 mi. W of Strasbourg.
- **See also**: the Route des Vins.

Sights

Église St-Pierre-et-St-Paul★

Built in yellow sandstone in the 12C, although substantially restored in the 19C, the church has a massive 14C octagonal belfry over the transept crossing. Note the Lombardy banding decorating the west front and the walls, which is linked by aracading along the top of the nave and aisles. Lions devouring humans adorn the gable on the west front are another Lombard feature. Inside, strong piers alternate with weak piers surmounted by carved capitals (note in particular the ring of small heads, all different). The restored organ by Silbermann dates from 1733.

Porte du Lion, Porte Basse and Porte de l'École

These gates are remnants of the town's fortifications.

Puits à chaîne and Zittglœckel

A well dating from 1605 and a clock tower stand on the town hall square.

Maison romane

Amid numerous old houses on rue du Général-de-Gaulle, this house, situated between no 21 and no 23, is the oldest construction in Alsatian stone (second half of the 12C). It has two storeys pierced by small openings. The building, restored in 2002, is intended to house a museum devoted to Romanesque art.

For coin ranges, see the Legend on the cover flap.

WHERE TO EAT

Auberge du Cerf – *120 r. du Gal-de-Gaulle. ☎03 88 50 40 14. Closed 5-12 Jan, mid-June, Sun evening and Mon.* This inn on the high street serves regional dishes in a family atmosphere.

Hostellerie du Rosenmeer – *45 av. de la Gare, 2km N by D 35. ☎03 88 50 43 29. Closed end Jul-early Aug, mid-Feb–mid-Mar, Sun evening, Mon and Wed. 20 rooms.* Tasty inventive gourmet cuisine inspired by regional ingredients, served in a comfortable dining room.

WINE TASTING

Ten wine-makers open their cellars for tastings; ask at the Tourist office.

Ten wine growers welcome visitor for tastings and sales; *apply to the Tourist office.*

R Mattès/MICHELIN

Sculpted capital

ROUFFACH★

HAUT-RHIN. POPULATION 4 187

MICHELIN LOCAL MAP 315: H-9 – ALSO SEE ROUTE DES VINS

Nestling at the foot of vine-covered hills, Rouffach is a prosperous agricultural centre, which has preserved many traces of its medieval past.

- **Tourist office**: Place de la République, 68250 Rouffach. ☎ 03 89 78 53 15, www.ot-rouffach.com
- **Orient yourself**: 15 km/9.3 mi. S of Colmar and 28 km/17.4 mi.N of Mulhouse.

Sights

Église Notre-Dame-de-l'Assomption

This church is mostly 12C-13C although the transept is older (11C-12C). The north and south towers were added in the 19C; the latter was never completed owing to the Franco-Prussian War of 1870. Inside, strong piers alternate with weak ones as is the custom in 12C architecture from the Rhine region. Note the octagonal christening font (1492) in the south transept. An elegant staircase, leaning against the piers of the crossing, is all that remains of the 14C rood screen. On the left of the high altar, there is a lovely 15C tabernacle. A Virgin and Child under a canopy, carved c 1500, adjoins a pillar on the north side of the nave.

Tour des Sorcières

The machicolated tower covered with a four-sided roof crowned by a stork's nest dates from the 13C and 15C and was used as a prison until the 18C.

Old houses

On place de la République are the old grain market (late 15C-early 16C), the Gothic Maison de l'Œuvre Notre-Dame and the former town hall, which has a fine twin-gabled Renaissance façade.

Excursion

Pfaffenheim

3km/1.9mi N along N 83.

This ancient wine-growing village has a church with a 13C apse, adorned with floral friezes. The notches visible on the lower part of the apse were perhaps made by wine-growers sharpening their pruning knives.

R. Mattès/MICHELIN

Church tower and spire and Tour des Sorcières

Address Book

For coin rangs, see the Legend on the cover flap.

WHERE TO EAT

Brasserie Chez Julien – *R. Raymond-Poincaré. ☎03 89 49 69 80. Closed mid-Mar, 24-26 Dec, Wed & Fri lunch and Mon.* A convivial restaurant located in a converted cinema.

Auberge au Vieux Pressoir – *68250 Bollenberg, 6km/3.75mi SW of Rouffach on N 83 and minor road. ☎03 89 49 60 04. info@bollenberg.com. Closed mid-Jan-mid-Feb, 23-26 Dec, Sun evening from Nov-Mar and Mon.* A large wine-maker's house sitting in vineyards, with typical Alsatian decor and a collection of old weapons. Carefully prepared local cuisine and tastings of the Auberge's own wines.

WHERE TO STAY

Hôtel Relais du Vignoble – *68420 Gueberschwihr, 6km/3.75mi N of Rouffach on N 83 and minor road. ☎03 89 49 22 22. hotelrelaisduvignoble@wanadoo.fr. Closed 26 Jan-6 Mar. 30 rooms.* €8.50. A hotel run by a family of wine-growers. The large modern building faces the plain, with spacious, rather fussily decorated rooms on the second floor.

12C Heroes

In 1106, Emperor Henry V kidnapped a young girl and settled her in Rouffach Castle. In defense of the young girl, the village women took up arms. Their husbands followed and together they attacked the castle. Panic-stricken, Henry V fled from Rouffac leaving behind his crown, his sceptre and his imperial cloak, which were placed as offerings on the Virgin's altar.

ST-DIÉ-DES-VOSGES★

VOSGES. POPULATION 22 569

MICHELIN LOCAL MAP 314: J-3

Situated in a fertile basin overlooked by pine-covered red-sandstone ridges, St-Dié owes its name to a monastery founded in the 7C by St Déodat. The town was partly destroyed by fire on four occasions, most recently in November 1944, towards the end of the Second World War. Textile and wood industries are the town's main economic activities.

Tourist office: 8 quaidu Maréchal de Lattre de Tassigny, 88100 St-Dié-des-Vosges. ☎03 29 42 22 22. www.ville-saintdie.fr

Orient yourself: St-Dié is 30 km/ 18.6 mi. N of Gerardmer on the N 59.

A Bit of History

The continent discovered by Christopher Columbus was first named America, in honour of the explorer Amerigo Vespucci, in a work entitled *Cosmographiæ Introductio*, published in St-Dié in 1507 by a team of scientists who called themselves the Gymnase Vosgien. In October, the town hosts an international event devoted to geography.

Sights

Cathédrale St-Dié★

Open *Jul-Aug 10am-12.15pm, 2-6.15pm, Sun and holidays 2-6.15pm; Sep-Jun 10am-noon, 2-4.30pm, Sun*

B. Kaufmann/MICHELIN

Cathedral cloisters

ask at the Musée Pierre-Noël. No charge. ☎03 29 56 12 88 (presbytery) or 03 29 51 60 35 (Musée Pierre-Noël).
The former collegiate church became a cathedral in 1777. Its imposing Classical west front dating from the early 18C is flanked by two square towers. The vaulting and the east end have been rebuilt after being blown up in 1944. Inside, the Romanesque nave, strong piers alternate with weak ones, topped by carved **capitals★** miraculously spared by the explosion. There is a 14C Virgin and Child against the column situated on the right of the crossing. Some 13C windows in the second chapel on the north side illustrate episodes from the Life of St Déodat. In 1987, the cathedral acquired some fine abstract **stained-glass windows★** made by a team of 10 artists headed by Jean Bazaine.

Cloître gothique★

The 15C and 16C canons' cloisters, linking the cathedral and the Église Notre-Dame-de-Galilée are remarkable, although they were never completed. Note the Flamboyant openings on the side of the courtyard, the ribbed vaulting and the 15C outdoor pulpit.

Église Notre-Dame-de-Galilée★

Same hours and conditions as the cathedral.

The church is typical of Romanesque architecture in southern Lorraine: a plain west front preceded by a belfry-porch with simple capitals. The originality of the nave lies in its groined vaulting, an unusual feature in such a large nave.

Musée Pierre-Noël – musée de la vie dans les Hautes-Vosges

Place Georges Trimouille. ♿ Open May-Sep Tue-Sat 10am-noon, 2-7pm, Sun 2-7pm. Oct-Apr Tue-Sat 2-6pm, Wed 10am-noon, 2-6pm. Closed Mon and holidays. €1.50. ☎03 29 51 60 35.
The museum built on the site of the former bishop's palace includes an archaeological finds from La Bure, stuffed birds and sections devoted to the Vosges Forest, wood and textile crafts, agriculture and stock farming, ceramics and glassware. A room is devoted to Jules Ferry, a native of St-Dié. A Franco-German military exhibition has a display about pilot René Fonck, an ace of the First World War, born near St-Dié. In addition, the museum houses the Goll collection of modern art.

Bibliothèque

11 rue St-Charles. Open Tue-Fri 10am-noon, 2-6.30pm, Thur 2-6.3pm, Sat 10am-noon, 2-5pm. Closed holidays. No charge. ☎03 29 51 60 40. www.ville-saintdie.fr.

The library contains 230 000 works including 600 manuscripts and 140 incunabula (early printed books). Two treasures are the extremely rare *Cosmographiæ Introductio* and an illuminated gradual from the early 16C, with miniatures illustrating work in the mines during the Middle Ages.

Tour de la Liberté

Open Apr-Oct daily 2-6pm. Nov-Mar during school holidays 2-6pm. €3. 03 29 42 22 22. www.ville-saintdie.fr.

The 36m/118ft Tower of Liberty, made of steel, canvas and cables, was erected in Paris for the Bicentenary of the Revolution in 1989 and moved to its present location a year later. It contains an unusual display of **jewellery** created by Heger de Lœwenfeld after paintings by Georges Braque, one of the initiators of Cubism.A spiral staircase leads up to a viewpoint, from where there is a stunning view of the town and the blue line of the Vosges mountains.

Address Book

For coin ranges, see the Legend on the cover flap.

WHERE TO EAT

Voyageurs – *22 r. Hellieule. 03 29 56 21 56. Closed Feb school holidays, 21 Jul-4 Aug, Christmas holidays, Sun evening and Mon.* Some of the tables in this bright restaurant have a view of the extraordinary Tour de la Liberté. The decor is pastel-toned and contemporary. Traditional cooking and good choice of wines by the glass.

WHERE TO STAY

Chambre d'hôte Le Bout du Chemin – *6 rte d'Hadremont, 88580 Saulcy-sur-Meurthe, 4.5km/2.7mi S of St-Dié on N 415 towards Colmar. 03 29 50 90 13. bourg.jean-claude@wanadoo.fr. Closed Nov. 5 rooms. Reservation essential. Meals.* The rooms in this B&B just outside St-Dié all have private terraces, ideal for looking at the wildlife that includes deer and squirrels. An attractive lounge has a fireplace and piano.

Hôtel Le Haut Fer – *Rougiville, 88100 Taintrux. 6km/3.75 W of St-Dié on N 420 and minor road. 03 29 55 03 48. www.lehautfer.fr. Closed 1-8 Jan, Sun except Jul-Aug and public holidays. 16 rooms. €8. Restaurant.* This 1960s hotel is built outside the village on the site of a sawmill. The rooms are old-fashioned but well kept. There are a swimming pool, two tennis courts and a restaurant serving regional cuisine.

ON THE TOWN

Le FBI – *82 r. d'Alsace. 03 29 55 09 81. www.ca-saintdie.com/fbi . Open Tue-Thu 6pm-3am, Fri-Sat 6pm-4am. Closed Mon.* This popular intimate bar is decorated with gleaming copperware, mahogany panelling and red velvet seats.

CALENDAR

Crayfish festival – *Mid-June in Etival-Clairefontaine.*

Relieving of the Guard of the Princes of Salm – *Some Sun mornings in Jul and Aug. 03 29 57 91 03. www.paysdesabbayes.com*

OUT AND ABOUT

Pisciculture Ste-Odile – *27 r. Ste-Odile, 88480 Étival-Clairefontaine. 10km/6.25mi NE of St-Dié, towards St-Rémy on D 424. 03 29 41 40v83. Opn Tue-Sun 7am-8pm. Closed 2nd fortnight Jan.* A fish farm that raises trout, char, pike and other fish and which creates all kinds of wonderful dishes with them: trout pâté with plums, trout mousse with herbs, aniseed-flavoured carp sausage, and trout in aspic. Rods can be hired for catching your own fish.

Papeteries de Clairefontaine – *19 r. de l'Abbaye, 88480 Étival-Clairefontaine. 03 29 42 42 42 – clarisse.cherrier@clairefontaine.com. Mon afternoon, Tue and Thu, Fri morning. Closed 15 Jul-1 Sep, Wed and weekends.* Learn about paper-making on a guided tour at this papermill belonging to the famous stationers. The smell of exercise books will take you back to your school days.

Excursions

Camp celtique de la Bure

7.5km/4.6mi then 45 min there and back on foot. Take N 59 and turn right 4km/2.5mi further on towards La Pêcherie then right onto the forest road to La Bure and left to La Crenée.

Leave the car at the Col de la Crenée and take the path running along the ridge (starting behind a forest shelter) to the main entrance of the camp.

This archaeological site has revealed traces of constant human occupation beginning roughly in 2000 BC and ending in the 4C AD.

Occupying the western end (alt 582m/1 909ft) of a ridge known as the Crête de la Bure, the camp is elliptical and measures 340m/372yd by 110m/120yd diagonally. The outer wall consisted of an earth base (2.25m/7.5ft thick) and a wooden palisade interrupted by two gates and two posterns. The eastern approach of the camp was barred as early as the 1C BC by a wall (murus gallicus, 7m/23ft thick) preceded by a ditch and from AD 300 onwards by a second Roman-type rampart. There were several pools in the camp (two of them dedicated to Gaulish goddesses) and important ironworks. The archaeological finds are exhibited in the St-Dié Museum. From the camp, there are fine **views**★ *(viewing table)* of the Meurthe Valley and St-Dié Basin.

For coin ranges, see the Legend on the cover flap.

WHERE TO STAY

Hôtel Picardy – *15 av. de Verdun. 03 25 05 09 12. 12 rooms. €5.30.* This hotel near the town centre and the station has 12 simply decorated rooms. Dinner can be served on request. Friendly welcome. Reservation necessary.

WHERE TO EAT

La Gentilhommière – *29 r. Jean-Jaurès. 03 25 56 32 97. Closed late Feb–early Mar, three weeks in Aug, Sat lunch, Sun dinner, Mon.* You'll easily spot the building with its two mannequins in costume in a little balcony vitrine. Traditional cooking.

Jardins de Callunes

In Ban-de-Sapt, 10km/6.2mi NE. Take D 49 from St-Die and then D 32 at St-Jean d'Ormont. Open Jul-Aug daily 10am-7pm. May-Jun daily 10am-noon, 2-7pm (10am-7pm Sun and holidays. Apr and Sep-Oct Wed-Mon 2-5.30pm. €6. 03 29 58 94v94.

These landscaped botanical gardens present 230 species of heather, as well as rhododendrons, azaleas, perennials and maple trees.

Driving Tour

From St-Dié to the Donon pass

43km/27mi – allow 2hr 30min.

Drive out of St-Dié along N 59.

Étival-Clairefontaine

This small town known for its paper mills lies on the banks of the Valdange, a tributary of the River Meurthe. The ruins of a paper mill dating from 1512 can still be seen on the riverside. The **church**★ (*Jul-Aug, 9am-1pm, 2-6pm (Sun 10am-1pm), Sep-Oct, 10am-noon, 2-5pm, Sun 10am-1pm)* built in local Vosges sandstone has a transitional style (Romanesque to Gothic) nave and aisles.

Moyenmoutier

The vast abbey **church** (*guided tours possible, ask at the Tourist office in Senones; 03 29 57 91 03; www.paysdesabbayes.com)* is one of the finest Baroque religious buildings in the Vosges.

Senones

This small town grew up near a Benedictine abbey. From 1751 to 1793, it was the capital of the principality of Salm, a sovereign state. Senones has guarded a few princely residences and 18C mansions. The **former abbey** has a fine 18C stone staircase with wrought-iron banisters, which used to lead to the apartments where Voltaire stayed in 1754.

From Senones, drive N along D 424 to La Petite-Raon (2km/1.2mi) then turn left onto D 49.

The forest road, which prolongs D 49, runs along the valley of the River Rabodeau. The **Col de Prayé** marked the old border between France and Germany. The road reaches the **Col du Donon** (*alt 727m/2 385ft;* *see Massif du DONON*).

ST-DIZIER

HAUTE-MARNE. POPULATION 38 086

MICHELIN LOCAL MAP 313: J-2

This iron and steel town was once a mighty stronghold with a garrison of 2 500 soldiers. In 1544 it withstood an attack by the Holy Roman Emperor, Charles V, and his army of 100 000 men. It was here that, in 1814, Napoleon won his last victory before being exiled to the island of Elba. in 1900, Hector Guimard, one of the initiators of Art Nouveau in France, used the St-Dizier ironworks for his ornamental creations, leaving the town with a heritage of fine balconies and banisters.

- **Tourist office**: 4 avenue de Belle-Forêt-sur-Marne, 52100 St-Dizier. ☎03 25 05 31 84.
- **Orient yourself**: The biggest town in the Haute-Marne département, roughly equidistant between Troyes and Nancy.
- **See also**: the Lac du DER-CHANTECOQ artificial lake and bird reserve.

Town Walk

In Search of Guimard's Cast-Iron Ornaments

Many houses were decorated by Guimard, outside and inside, in Art Nouveau style: balconies, window sills, palmettes, door panels and banisters.

Start from place de la Liberté (tourist office).

At the beginning of rue de la Commune-de-Paris, **no 29** has a door panel decorated with tulips dating from 1900.

Follow rue de l'Arquebuse.

Rue de l'Arquebuse

No 1: railing, banisters and window sills dating from 1900; **nos 1bis** and **1ter**: window sills by Guimard; **no 31**: window sills, door panels, basement window by Guimard; **no 33**: window sills from 1900.

Turn left onto rue du Colonel-Raynal.

Rue du Colonel-Raynal

No 4: window sills; **no 6**: window sills and door panel by Guimard; **no 8**: window sills.

Before turning left onto rue du Général-Maistre, note the window sills of **no 39**.

Rue du Général-Maistre

No 24 on the street corner: window sills; **no 15** and **no 13**: door panels by Guimard.

Return to the square via rue Robert-Dehault.

Quartier de la Noue

This suburb west of the town centre was inhabited by boatmen who floated convoys of logs down the River Marne to Paris and returned on foot. They lived in low houses built in cob, with a yard backing onto gardens and fields. 80 tiny alleyways, known as *voyottes* and accessible to pedestrians, run at right angles off avenue de la République. A footpath has been laid out along the Marne.

Additional Sights

Musée municipal

17 rue d e la Victoire. Open Tue-Sat 2-6pm, Wed 10am-noon, 2-6pm. Closed public holidays. No charge. ☎03 25 07 31 50. www.saint-dizier.fr.

The museum contains interesting palaeontological collections (including an 11m/36ft long iguanodon, the largest ever found in France) as well as ornithological collections, local history collections, paintings and cast-iron ornaments by Guimard.

MARAIS DE ST-GOND

MARNE. MICHELIN LOCAL MAP 306: F-9/10

This marshland, situated below the Île-de-France cuesta and covering more than 3 000ha/7 413 acres, owes its name to a 7C coenobite.

In September 1914, the area and the surrounding heights were the scene of fierce fighting between Von Bülow's second German army and General Foch's 9th French army. Foch eventually succeeded in driving the Germans back to the River Marne.

A botanic trail starting from Reuves allows you to discover the diversity of marshland fauna and flora.

Driving tour

36km/22mi round tour starting from Mondement – allow 1hr 30min

This drive goes through lonely expanses of marshland, which has been partly drained and turned into pastures or arable land. The south-facing slopes of the limestone hills around the marsh produce a fine white wine.

Mondement

Mondement hill (alt 223m/732ft) was at the heart of the fighting in September 1914. The German troops eventually withdrew after suffering heavy losses. A monument commemorates events.

Allemant

This tiny village clinging to the hillside has a surprisingly large Flamboyant Gothic **church** with a double transept and a high tower over the crossing.

Follow D 39 to Le Mesnil then D 45.

Coizard

Charming Romanesque village church.

Drive east along D 43.

Villevenard

Wine-growing village. The tastefully-restored 12C church has a Romanesque nave and a fine octagonal tower.

ST-MIHIEL★

MEUSE. POPULATION 5 260

MICHELIN LOCAL MAP 307: E-5

Situated on the western edge of the Parc naturel régional de Lorraine, St-Mihiel has an important religious heritage as birthplace of the sculptor Ligier Richier. It is also a good base for river trips on the Meuse and exploring the First World War battlefields.

Tourist office: Rue du Palais du Justice, 55300 St-Mihiel. ☎03 29 89 06 47.

Orient yourself: S of Verdun at the junction of the D 901 and D 964.
Don't miss: The Sepulchre by Ligier richier in the Eglise St-Etienne.

A Bit of History

St-Mihiel's history was long intertwined with an important Benedictine abbey founded in 709 near the present town and relocated in 815 on the banks of the Meuse.

In 1301, St-Mihiel became the main town of the Barrois region east of the River Meuse. The city prospered both economically and culturally, notably in the 16C when renowned drapers and goldsmiths settled in St-Mihiel and the fame of **Ligier Richier** and his school of sculpture spread throughout eastern France. Born in St-Mihiel in 1500, Richier surrounded himself with talented sculptors and apprentices. In 1559 he was asked to decorate the town for the arrival of Duke Charles III and his wife. In later life, he converted to the Protestant faith and moved to Geneva where he died in 1567. Fine examples of his considerable output can be seen in Bar-le-Duc, Hattonchâtel, Étain and Briey.

In September 1914, the German army launched a thrust in the area in order to skirt round the powerful stronghold of Verdun. They succeeded in establishing a bridgehead on the west bank of the Meuse, known as the St-Mihiel Bulge, which prevented supplies and reinforcements from reaching Verdun via the Meuse Valley.

Sights

Église St-Michel

The abbey church was almost entirely rebuilt in the 17C, though kept its 12C square belfry and Romanesque porch. The first chapel on the south side contains a masterpiece by Ligier Richier: the **Fainting Virgin supported by St John**★. This walnut sculpture (1531) formed part of a calvary representing Christ (his head is now in the Louvre), St Longin, Mary Magdalene and four angels. The baptismal chapel on the same side contains a funeral monument, carved in 1608 by Jean Richier, Ligier Richier's grandson. The magnificent organ case dates from 1679 to 1681.

Former Abbaye

Rue du Palais-de-Justice. Open Jun-Sep Wed-Mon 2–6pm. Apr–May, Oct–Nov weekends 2-6pm. Closed Nov-Mar and public holidays. €2.30, €4 (library and museum). 03 29 89 06 47.

The conventual buildings, next to the Église St-Michel, were rebuilt in the 17C and are almost intact. A large hall decorated with woodwork and ceilings in the Louis XIV style houses the **Bibliothèque bénédictine**, a rich collection including 74 manuscripts and 86 incunabula. In the south wing, the **Musée départemental d'Art sacré** contains religious paintings, sculptures, gold plate and liturgical ornaments from the Meuse.

Maison du Roi

2 rue Notre-Dame.

This 14C Gothic house belonged in the 15C to King René of Anjou, who also had the title of Duc de Bar.

Église St-Étienne

The nave of this original hall-church was built between 1500 and 1545. Note the modern stained-glass windows and the Renaissance altarpiece in the apse. But the church is above all famous for the **Sepulchre**★★ or Entombment sculpted by Ligier Richier from 1554 to 1564. Extensive restoration, in progress since 2000, has made it necessary to cut the work into several blocks; 13 life-size figures depict the preparations for Christ's Entombment: Salomé prepares the funeral bed, Joseph and Nicodemus hold the body of Christ, Mary Magdalene kisses Christ's feet. In the background, St John supports the Virgin Mary, an angel holds the instruments of the Passion, and two guards are seen throwing the dice for Christ's tunic.

The cliffs

Seven limestone cliffs, over 20m/66ft high, overlook the east bank of the river. In 1772, Mangeot, a native of St-

Mihiel. carved a representation of the Holy Sepulchre in the first rock. From the top of the cliffs, there is a fine view of the town and the Meuse Valley.

Excursions

Bois d'Ailly

7km/4.3mi SE along D 907 and a sign-posted forest road.

There are several reminders of the heavy fighting which took place here in September 1914: from the memorial a row of trenches (complete with shelters and communication trenches) leads to the Tranchée de la Soif (thirst trench) where a few soldiers held on for three days against the German Imperial Guard.

Commercy

18km/11.2mi S along the River Meuse.

Commercy occupied a strategic position on the west bank of the River Meuse and the number of fortified houses and churches are a reminder of the constant threat of invasion the whole area lived under in the past. The town is famous for its madeleine cakes.

An imposing horseshoe esplanade precedes the **Château Stanislas** (*open only during exhibitions Jul–Aug Wed–Mon 3-6pm, no charge; 03 29 91 02 18*). Designed in 1708 by Boffrand and d'Orbay for the Prince de Vaudémont, it was used as a hunting lodge by the dukes of Lorraine before becoming the property of Stanislas Leszczynski, King Louis XV's father-in-law.

The former municipal baths, dating from the 1930s, have been turned into the **Musée de la Céramique et de l'Ivoire,** (*Jul-Aug Wed–Mon 2-6pm; May-Jun and Sep Sat, Sun and holidays 2-6pm; €3; 03 29 92 04 77*) .

ST-NICOLAS-DE-PORT★★

MEURTHE-ET-MOSELLE. POPULATION 7 702

MICHELIN LOCAL MAP 307: I-7

The impressive Flamboyant basilica of St-Nicolas-de-Port dominates the centre of this small industrial town. It has been a popular place of pilgrimage since the 11C, when the city became the most prosperous economic centre in Lorraine and the venue of international fairs. In 1635, during the Thirty Years War, the town was ransacked by the Swedes and only the church was spared.

- **Tourist office**: Place Camille-Croué-Friedmann, 54210 St-Nicolas-de-Port. 03 83 48 58 75.
- **Orient yourself**: 12km/7.5mi. SE of Nancy.

Sights

Basilique St-Nicolas★★

The splendid Flamboyant Gothic basilica was built as a shrine for one of St Nicholas' fingers, which had been brought here from Bari in Italy by knights from Lorraine and placed in a chapel dedicated to Our Lady. There followed a series of miracles and a church had to be built to accommodate the growing number of pilgrims, among them Joan of Arc in 1429. The huge late 15C and early 16C church suffered fire and war damage and the roof was only repaired in 1735. After bomb damage in 1940, the church was again in need of extensive restoration. A bequest in 1980 provided the answer and, since 1983, the outside has resembled a building site.

Exterior

The west front features three doorways with Flamboyant Gothic gables. The central doorway bears a statue representing St Nicholas' miracle, believed to be the work of Claude Richier, brother of Ligier Richier. On the north side, note six basket-handled recesses in which traders used to set up shop at pilgrimage time

Interior

The interior stands out for its extremely tall nave (32m/105ft) and the tall pillars of the transept vaulting (28m/92ft high, the highest in France). The stained-glass windows of the apse, made by Nicole Droguet of Lyon in 1507 to 1510, are particularly remarkable; those of the aisle and chapels on the north side date from the same period and are the work of Valentin Bousch from Strasbourg. The Renaissance influence can already be seen in the decorative motifs.

The sanctuary that received St Nicholas' relic in the 11C was probably located where the **baptismal chapel** now stands. Several 16C painted wood panels illustrate scenes from the Life of St Nicholas. The **treasury** includes a silver gilt reliquary arm of St Nicholas (19C), the cardinal of Lorraine's ship (16C), a silver reliquary of the True Cross (15C) and Voltaire's ivory Crucifix.

For coin ranges, see the Legend on the cover flap.

WHERE TO EAT

Auberge de la Mirabelle – *6 rte de Nancy, 54210 Ferrières. 12km/7mi S of St-Nicolas-de-Port on D 115 and D 112. 03 83 26 62 14. www.auberge-mirabelle.com. Closed Mon & evenings except Sat.* As its name suggests, Léon's farm specialises in mirabelle plums. In the old cowshed which now serves as restaurant, the cooking is simple family fare, much appreciated locally.

Musée français de la Brasserie

62 r. Charles-Courtois. Guided tour (1hr 30min) mid-Apr–mid-Oct daily 2.30-6.30pm. Rest of the year Tue–Sun 2-6pm. Closed mid-Dec–early Jan. €4. 03 83 46 95 52, www.passionbrasserie.com. Brewing demonstrations on 1st and 3rd Sun of the month.

The museum is housed in an old brewery which closed in 1986. The visit of the Art Deco brewing tower takes in the laboratory, the malt loft, hops storeroom, the brewing room with its fine copper vats, the refrigerating equipment and the cold room with the fermentation vats.

Musée du Cinéma, de la Photographie et des Arts audiovisuels

10 rue Georges-Rémy. Open Thu-Sat 2-6pm, Sun 2.30-6.30pm (last admission 90min before closing). Closed public holidays. €4 (children €3). 03 83 45 18 32, www.museecinemaphoto.com

Kids Magic lanterns and other forgotten equipment illustrate the evolution of moving pictures and animation from the early 19C to the birth of the cinema.

R. Mattès/MICHELIN

The basilica from afar

STE-MENEHOULD

MARNE. POPULATION 5 410

MICHELIN LOCAL MAP 306: L-8

Ste-Menehould is famous for its speciality of pigs' trotters and as the town where Louis XVI stopped to dine when attempting to flee Paris during the French Revolution in June 1791. A young boy recognised the monarch and the king was arrested at Varennes *(see ARGONNE).*

- **Tourist office**: 5 place du Général-Leclerc, 51800 Ste-Menehould. ☎03 26 60 85 83.
- **Orient yourself**: Located near the A4 motorway, the town consists of a lower Ville Basse and the upper Ville Haute on the Butte du Château.

Sights

Place du Général-Leclerc

Split into two by the main road (N 3), the square is lined by fine pink-brick buildings, including the **town hall** (1730), designed by Philippe de la Force who rebuilt the city after the fire of 1719.

Butte du Château

The upper town has a villagey feel with its low timber-framed, flower-decked houses. The 13C-15C **Église Notre Dame** (also called Église du Château) sits in a cemetery.

Musée

Closed for restoration.

Housed in an 18C mansion, the museum contains various regional collections.

Excursion

Château de Braux-Ste-Cohière★

5.5km/3.4mi W by N3 and D384. Open mid-June–mid-Sept weekends 2-6pm. €8. ☎01 44 41 44 33.

The buildings were erected in the 16C and 17C by Philippe de Thomassin, governor of Châlons for the Household Cavalry. In 1792, General Dumouriez made his headquarters here to prepare for the Battle of Valmy against the Prussians. Today, the vast moated château is used for cultural events by the **Association culturelle Champagne-Argonne**. In the courtyard, the dovecote houses the **Musée régional d'Orientation** (geology, local history, popular art).

Address Book

For coin ranges, see the Legend on the cover flap.

WHERE TO EAT

Aux Berges de la Biesme – *RN 3, La Vignette, 8km/5mi E of Ste-Menehould on N 3 towards Verdun. ☎03 26 60 09 22. Closed Mon evening and Wed.* This white house with a flowered façade is conveniently located on the N3. Carefully prepared traditional dishes are served in a pleasant dining room, with panelled walls, parquet floors and a small fireplace.

WHERE TO STAY

L'Argonnais – *2 r. Florion. ☎03 26 60 70 84. 7 rooms. €5,50.* This small modern hotel is near the town centre and all the rooms are well sound-proofed and protected by digicode, while enjoying a pleasant view of the Aisne. Genial welcome and good value-for-money.

MONT STE-ODILE★★

BAS-RHIN. MICHELIN LOCAL MAP 315: I-6

ALSO SEE LE HOHWALD

Mont Ste-Odile (alt. 764m/2 507ft) is one of the most popular sights in Alsace, drawing both pilgrims and tourists for the spectacular setting and views, with its pink cliffs rising out of the forest.

- **Orient yourself**: The mountain is SW of Obernai.

A Bit of History

In the 7C, the mountain was the site of the Hohenburg Castle, summer residence of Duke Étichon. According to legend, he rejected his baby daughter Odile, who was born blind. Saved by her nurse, she miraculously recovered her sight on the day of her baptism and thereafter devoted her life to religion. Her father eventually made her a present of Hohenburg where she founded her convent. After St Odile's death, the convent became an important place of pilgrimage.

Sights

Convent

Pilgrims flock here all year round, in particular for the feast of St Odile. The porch, located beneath the former hostel, gives access to the main courtyard. On the right is the **monastery church**, rebuilt in 1692. Inside, it has richly carved 18C confessionals; a door on the left leads to the 11C **Chapelle de la Croix**★. Four groined vaults are supported by a single Romanesque pillar with a carved capital. A sarcophagus housed the remains of Duke Étichon, Odile's father. On the left, a low doorway decorated with Carolingian carvings leads to the small 12C Chapelle Ste-Odile, supposedly on the site of an earlier chapel where Odile died. An 8C sarcophagus contains the saints relics.

On the northeast corner of the terace, the **Chapelle des Larmes** is on the site of the Merovingian cemetery (several graves carved in the rock are visible outside). The mosaic (1935) represents the grave with Léon IX and Ste Eugénie round it; Christ and Christian virtues are depicted on the vaulting and Odile can be seen praying over the door.

On the edge of the precipice is another chapel, the **Chapelle des Anges**. According to a local lore, if a young

R. Mattès/MICHELIN

St Odile's convent

woman went round it nine times, she would be sure to find a husband before the end of the year!

Fontaine de Ste-Odile

The road leading down to St-Nabor *(D 33)* runs past the spring *(protected by a railing)* which is said to have gushed forth from the rock at St Odile's request to quench the thirst of an exhausted blind man. It is now a place of pilgrimage for people with eye complaints.

Mur païen

30min on foot there and back. Take the staircase on the left of the convent exit and follow the footpath at the bottom.
It would take four or five hours to walk round the remains of this mysterious wall running through forests and screes for more than 10km/6mi, but even seeing a part of it is an awe-inspiring experience: an average 1.7m/5.5ft thick and as much as 3m/10ft high in the best-preserved section. Some claim it dates from the 10C BC, others it is a 1CBC Germanic fort, others that it is Merovingian.

SARREBOURG

MOSELLE. POPULATION 13 330
MICHELIN LOCAL MAP 307: N-6

This city of Roman origin belonged to the bishops of Metz during the Middle Ages and then to the duchy of Lorraine before becoming part of France in the late 17C. Today Sarrebourg is the starting point of fine excursions along the River Sarre in an area renowned for its crystal works.

- **Tourist office**: Place des Cordeliers, 57400 Sarrebourg. ☎03 87 03 11 82, www.sarrebourg.fr
- **Orient yourself**: Sarrebourg is at the gateway to the Vosges, 73km/45mi. NE of Strasbourg.

Sights

Chapelle des Cordeliers

Open May–Sep daily 10am–noon, 2–6pm; Oct-Apr Mon–Sat 10am-noon, 2-5pm. Closed holidays Oct –1 May. €2.50 (combined ticket with Musée du Pays de Sarrebourg: €5). ☎03 87 03 11 82.
This deconsecrated Franciscan chapel houses the tourist office. Its west front is lit by a huge **stained-glass window**★ by Marc Chagall illustrating *"peace"*. In the centre, vivid blues, reds and greens symbolise the Tree of Life in Genesis with Adam and Eve surrounded by the Serpent, Christ's cross, the Prophet Isaiah, the Lamb, the Candelabra, Suffering and Death illustrate mankind.

Musée du Pays de Sarrebourg

Rue de la Paix. Open Mon & Wed–Sat 10am-noon, 2-6pm, Sun 2-6pm. Closed 1 Jan, Good Friday, Easter Sunday, 1 May, 25 and 26 Dec. €3.50 (combined ticket with Chapelle des Cordeliers: €5). ☎03 87 08 08 68.
The museum contains regional archaeological finds, medieval sculpture (beautiful 15C Crucifix) and 18C ceramics and porcelain from nearby Niderviller.

Cimetière national des Prisonniers

On the outskirts of town, on the right of rue de Verdun (D 27).
The cemetery contains some 13 000 First World War graves . The monument facing the gate, entitled Giant in chains, was sculpted by Stoll while he was a prisoner of war.

Excursions

St-Ulrich, Villa gallo-romaine

4km/2.5mi NW. Open Wed-Sun 10am-noon, 2-6pm. Closed major holidays. No charge. ☎03 87 08 08 68.

The 1C villa was the residence of a rich landowner. It was extended during the 2C to include more than 100 rooms, courtyards, galleries and even baths.

Fénétrange

15km/9mi N along D 43.
This small fortified town has several beautiful medieval houses, a fine largely 15C collegiate church and an elegant château.

SARREGUEMINES

MOSELLE. POPULATION 23 202
MICHELIN LOCAL MAP 307: N-4

This border town, situated at the confluence of the Sarre and the Blies, is often associated with the pottery manufacture that bears its name. Sarreguemines used to be the seat of a feudal domain guarding the borders of the duchy of Lorraine.

- **Tourist office**: 11 rue du Maire-Massing, 57203 Sarreguemines. ☎03 87 98 80 01, www.ot-sarreguemines.fr.
- **Orient yourself**: 70km. E of Metz, 91 km/mi. NE of Nancy.

A Bit of History

Pottery

The Sarreguemines manufacture, founded in 1790, developed in spite of financial difficulties and the annexation of Lorraine in 1870 thanks to the inspired management of the De Geiger family. Production reached its peak at the turn of the 20C: more than 3 000 workers produced majolica, porcelain, dinner sets and panels. Bought by the Lunéville-St-Clément group in 1979, the pottery now mainly produces floor tiles. In 1982, it was renamed Sarreguemines-Bâtiment.

Sights

Musée des Faïences de Sarreguemines

17 rue Poincaré. Open Jul-Sep daily 10am-noon, 2-6pm. Oct-Jun Wed–Mon 10am-noon, 2-6pm. Closed 1 Jan, Easter Sunday, 1 May, 25 Dec. €3, no charge 1st Sun of the month. ☎03 87 98 93 50. www.sarreguemines-museum.com.
Housed in the former residence of the manager of the earthenware manufacture, the ceramics **collection**★ retraces the history of Sarreguemines pottery over the past 200 years. The **winter garden**★★, designed by Paul de Geiger in 1882, is particularly remarkable, with its monumental Renaissance-style majolica fountain offering a shimmering display of yellows, greens, ochres and browns.

Musée des Techniques faïencières

Moulin de la Blies, 125 av. de la Blies. Same hours as museum above.
A living museum designed to explain the manufacture of earthenware. Authentic machinery and tools have been used in the reconstruction of a production unit on three levels: preparation, firing and decoration.

A. Mertz/Ville de Sarreguemines

The Earth

Circuit de la faïence de Sarreguemines

3km/1.9mi. with the leaflet from the Tourist office. A walking tour links the main sites connected with the manufacture of earthenware in Sarreguemines.

Excursion

Parc archéologique européen de Bliesbruck-Reinheim

9.5km/5.9mi E via Bliesbruck. Open mid-Mar–Oct daily 10am-6pm. €4.60. 03 87 02 25 79, www.archeo57.com.

Stretching either side of the Franco-Germain border lies the remains of an antique settlement, apparently going back to the Neolithic period, which became an important city after the arrival of the Celts. Replicas (the originals are in Sarrebruck museum) of gold jewellery and a wine service found in the grave of the "Reinheim Princess" (c 400 BC) are displayed in a reconstructed **tumulus** near the remains of a large villa. in Bliesbruck, the **public baths**★ are protected under a huge glass structure.

SAVERNE★

BAS-RHIN. POPULATION 11 201
MICHELIN LOCAL MAP 315: I-4

The 16C peasant rebellion ended tragically in Saverne when the Duke of Lorraine besieged the town; he promised to spare the lives of the 20 000 peasants if they came out unarmed, but when they did, they were massacred to the last one by the duke's soldiers. Today Saverne is a rather more peaceful town known for its annual rose festival and its marina.

- **Tourist office:** 37 Grand'Rue, 67700 Saverne. 03 88 91 80 47, www.ot-saverne.fr.
- **Orient yourself:** Situated on the Zorn river and the Marne-Rhine Canal, 45 km/28 mi. NW of Strasbourg.
- **Also See:** *Parc naturel régional des VOSGES DU NORD: The Hanau region.*

A Bit of History

From the 13C to the Revolution, Saverne belonged to the bishops of Strasbourg. These princes stayed in the castle and sometimes welcomed royal visitors (Louis XIV in 1681, Louis XV in 1744). Atfer being burnt down in 1779, it was rebuilt by **Louis de Rohan**, who lived there in lavish style.

Sights

Château★

The elegant red-sandstone château of the house of Rohan was rebuilt in the Louis XVI style and stands in a beautiful park bordered by the Marne-Rhine canal. It served as barracks between 1870 and 1944. The north **façade**★★, which is over 140m/153yd long is particularly impressive with fluted pilasters and a peristyle supported by eight Corinthian columns.

Musée

Open mid-Jun–mid-Sep Wed–Mon 10am-noon, 2-6pm. Rest of the year: Mon, Wed–Fri 2-6pm, weekends & holidays 10am-noon, 2-6pm. Closed Good Friday, 1 May, 1 Nov, 24-26 Dec. €2.65. 03 88 91 06 28.

The museum contains archaeological finds from the Gallo-Roman period, collections devoted to the town's history: medieval sculpture, pieces from nearby castles (Haut-Barr, Geroldseck, Wangenbourg) and mementoes of the House of Rohan, as well as the bequest of feminist politician Louise Weiss.

Address Book

For coin ranges, see the Legend on the cover flap.

WHERE TO EAT

Le Caveau de l'Escale – *10 quai du Canal – ☎03 88 91 12 23 – closed 27 June-10 Jul, 10 days at the end Oct, 21 Dec-6 Jan, Sat lunchtime, Tue evening and Wed.* A discreet-looking restaurant near the canal, where you can hire boats. Meals are served in the vaulted cellar, with regional cooking and *flammekueches* in the evening. Friendly atmosphere.

WHERE TO STAY

Chez Jean – *3 r. de la Gare – ☎03 88 91 10 19 – chez.jean@wanadoo.fr – closed 20 Dec-10 Jan – 25 rooms – €8.50 – restaurant* . A good place to stay in Saverne. The cosy, welcoming rooms have been renovated and have wood panelling. There is a choice of cuisine, between the regional dishes in the wine bar and a more elaborate menu in the restaurant.

Roseraie

Open Jun–mid-Sep daily 10am-6pm. Closed mid-Sep–May. €2.50. ☎03 88 71 83 33.

550 varieties of rose grow in this splendid park on the bank of the River Zorn.

Half-timbered houses★

Two particularly fine timber-framed houses (17C) stand on either side of the town hall. Others can be seen at No 96 Grand'Rue, on the corner of rue des Églises and rue des Pères and on the corner of rue des Pères and rue Poincaré.

Vieux château

The old castle, which was the former residence of the bishops, is now an administrative building. The stairtower has a beautiful Renaissance doorway.

Église paroissiale

Rebuilt in the 14C and 15C, the parish church has a 12C Romanesque belfry-porch. In the nave are a pulpit (1495) by Hans Hammer and a 16C high-relief marble sculpture representing Mary and John mourning Christ. The chapel of the Holy Sacrament in the north aisle is adorned with a 16C *Pietà* and a wooden bas-relief, depicting the Assumption. The 14C to 16C windows illustrate the Adoration of the Magi and scenes from the Passion. Gallo-Roman and Frankish gravestones can be seen in the garden adjacent to the church.

Ancien cloître des Récollets

The cloisters, built in 1303, have lovely red-sandstone Gothic arcades and nine murals (added in the 17C, restored) on the right of the entrance.

R. Mattès/MICHELIN

Château de Saverne

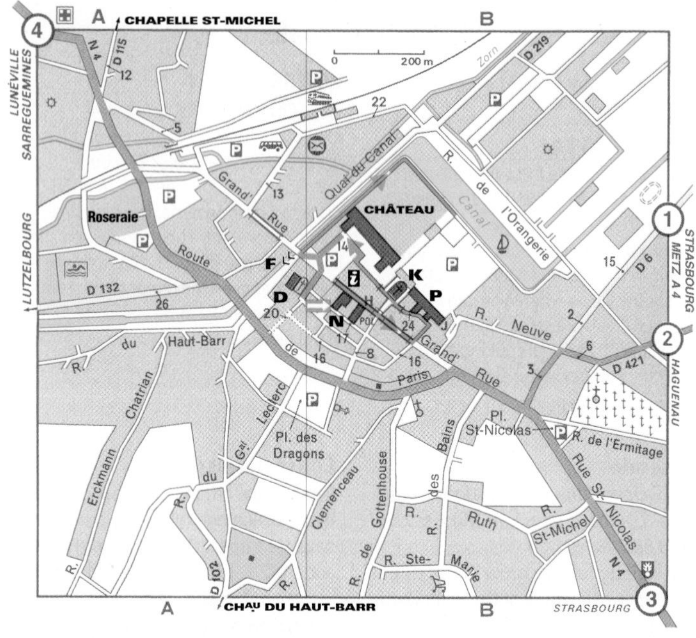

SAVERNE								
			Églises R. des	B	8	Murs R. des	AB	16
			Foch R. Mar.	A	12	Pères R. des	B	17
Bouxwiller R. de	B	2	Gare R. de la	A	13	Poincaré R.	A	20
Clés R. des	B	3	Gaulle Pl. Gén.-de	B	14	Poste R. de la	B	22
Côte R. de la	B	5	Grand'Rue	AB		Tribunal R. du	B	24
Dettwiller R. de	B	6	Joffre R. Mar.	B	15	19-Novembre R. du	A	26

Ancien cloître des Récollets	A	D	Maisons anciennes	B	N
Église paroissiale	A	K	Vieux château (sous-préfecture)	B	P
Écluse	A	F			

Excursions

Jardin botanique du col de Saverne

2.5km/1.5mi by N4 to car park, then 15min on foot there and back. Jul-Aug, 10am-noon, 2-6pm; May-Jun and early Sep to mid-Sep weekends & holidays 2-6pm. €2.50. 03 88 91 80 47.

Situated at an altitude of 335m/1 099ft, this botanical garden (2.3ha/5.7 acres) includes an arboretum, an Alpine garden, a small bog and numerous species of fern and orchid.

Saut du Prince Charles

Take forest track from botanical garden.

According to legend, a prince jumped over the red-sandstone cliff with his horse. There is a fine view of the foothills of the Vosges and the Plaine d'Alsace.

St-Jean-Saverne

5km/3mi N. The village **church** is all that remains of a Benedictine abbey founded in the early 12C. It has an 18C belfry over an interesting Romanesque doorway. At the entrance to the choir are Romanesque capitals carved with foliage. A road through the forest leads to the **Chapelle St-Michel** (*Open Jun-Sep daily 1-6pm. Rest of the year Sun 1-6pm. Closed Dec–Feb*), which dates from the same period as the abbey. Follow a path on the right of the chapel to the end of the rocky spur from where the **view**★ extends over the hills of Alsace to the Black Forest. The platform forms a circular hollow known as the **École des Sorcières** (witches' school). On the south side of the chapel, 57 steps lead down to a path on the left which leads to a cave known as the **Trou des Sorcières** (witches' hole).

SCHIRMECK

BAS-RHIN. POPULATION 2 177

MICHELIN LOCAL MAP 315: H-6

This lively small industrial town is the starting point for exploring the Bruche valley, with its forets and sawmills. A lovely west front and an octagonal tower are all that remains of the neo-Classical church (1754), while the Mémorial d'Alsace-Moselle gives an understanding of the region's more recent troubled history. of Alsace .

- **Tourist office** : 114 Grand'Rue, 67130 Schirmeck. ☎03 88 47 18 51.
- **Orient yourself**: On the N420 whicn follows the Left Bank of the Bruche; 53 km/33 mi.SW of Strasbourg.
- **Also See:** *MOLSHEIM.*

Sights

Mémorial d'Alsace-Moselle★

☎ 03 88 47 45 50, www.memorial-alsace-moselle.com. Open May–Sept Tue–Sat 10am-7pm. Rest of the year Tue–Sat 10am-6pm. Closed Mon & Jan. €10.
Inaugurated in 2005 on a hill facing the former Struthof concentration camp, the memorial gathers souvenirs of the suffering endured by the populations of Alsace and the Moselle from 1870 to the end of the Second World War. The area's annexation by Germany in 1940 is evoked, as are anti-semitism, the deportation and the concentration camp, the resistance and the postwar Franco-German reconciliation.

Excursions

Waldersbach

10 km/6.2 mi. by N420 and D57.
The old Protestant presbytery of this charming village houses the **Musée Oberlin** (*Open Wed–Mon 10am-noon, 2-6pm, weekends & holidays 2-6pm; Closed 1 Jan, Good Friday, Easter Sunday, 1 May, 24-25 and 31 Dec; €4; ☎03 88 97 30 27*), devoted to the philanthropist and amateur botanist Jean-Frédéric Oberlin (1740-1826), who created playschools and developed agriculture and crafts in the valley.

Mutzig

20km /12.4 mi. by N420.
This small garrison town has a lovely fountain and a 13C gate. The **Fort de Mutzig** (1893) was the first "modern" fort built by the German empire, with concrete defences and electricity (*guided tour Jul–mid-Sept daily 2pm, 3pm, May–June & mid–end Sept weekends 2pm, 3pm, €6*). The famous brewery founded in 1812 closed in 1990 but the town still hosts a beer festival on the first Sunday in September.
Antoine Chassepot, inventor of the Chassepot rifle, was born in Mutzig in 1833. In 1870, the French infantry was equipped with this rifle, which was far superior to its German counterpart and should have given the French a considerable advantage but a shortage of munitions made the Chassepot useless.
Near the river, the 17C **Château des Rohan** was converted into an arms factory after the Revolution. Today it houses a cultural centre and the **Musée régional des Armes** (*Open Jul-Aug, Wed-Sun 2-6pm; May-Jun and Sep-mid-Oct, Sat-Sun 2-6pm; Holidays except Sat-Sun; €2.50; ☎03 88 38 31 98)* (firearms – history of the Chassepot – swords, bayonets etc).

ARDENNES. POPULATION 20 548
MICHELIN LOCAL MAP 306: L-4

This frontier town sits beneath the largest fortress in Europe. South of the town, a 13ha/32-acre artificial lake is convenient for bathing and sailing. In addition to textiles, industrial activities include metalworks, chemicals and foodstuffs.

- **Tourist office**: Promenoir des Prêtres, 08200 Sedan. ☎03 24 27 73 73, www.sedan-bouillon.com
- **Orient yourself**: Near the Belgian frontier, 23km/14.3 mi. SE of Charleville-Mézières by A203.
- Kids **Specially for kids**: The huge fortress is a must for all would-be knights in armour.

A Bit of History

The name Sedan is mentioned for the first time in 997 as belonging to Mouzon Abbey. In 1594, it became the property of the La Tour d'Auvergne family. Henri de La Tour d'Auvergne, Viscount of **Turenne** and Marshal of France (1611-75), famed for his faithful service to Louis XIII and Louis XIV during the Thirty Years War and against the Fronde, was born in Sedan before the town was reunited with France in 1642.

The capitulation of Sedan on 2 September 1870, during the Franco-Prussian War, led to the proclamation of the Third Republic in Paris on 4 September. Seventy years later, in May 1940, another defeat at Sedan tolled the end of the Third Republic.

Sights

Château Fort★★

Kids *Place du Château.* *Open Jul-Aug daily 10am-6pm. Apr–Jun & school holidays daily 10am-noon, 1.30-6pm. Sept–Mar Tue–Fri 1.30-6pm, weekends & holidays 10am-noon, 1.30-6pm. €6.90 (children: €4.60). ☎03 24 27 73 73. www.sedan-bouillon.com.*

This fortress covering an area of 35 000m²/41 860sq yd on seven levels is the largest in Europe. It was built on a rocky spur on the site of a monastery. Work began in 1424; the **twin towers** and the **ramparts** date from that period. The latter (30m/98ft high), surrounded by ditches, were completed by bastions in the 16C. The **Château bas** was built in the 17C outside the walls (probably by Salomon de la Brosse who designed the Luxembourg Palace in Paris). Between 1642 and 1962, the stronghold was army property. The town then acquired it and undertook its restoration.

Historium

The tour of the castle *(audio-guides, explanatory panels)* includes reconstructed scenes with wax figures illustrating the lifestyle of princes, soldiers and servants in the past.

Musée du Château Fort

The twin towers house archaeological finds, ethnographic exhibits and documents relating to the town's history. One room is devoted to the Franco-Prussian War of 1870 and the First World War.

Sedan at the Height of the Cloth Industry

The heart of old Sedan, where many private mansions testify to the cloth industry's prosperity, is being carefully restored. The manufactures usually consisted of a large house along the street, workshops in the wings and a building closing off the courtyard at the back.

No 33 place de la Halle

This 18C mansion was probably both private house and warehouse. The main building has wings like the Dijonval.

No 1 rue du Mesnil

Built as a private mansion in 1629, the Hôtel de Lambermont became a royal

Address Book

For coin ranges, see the Legend on the cover flap.

WHERE TO STAY & EAT

Hôtellerie du Château – *in the castle, access by Porte de Princes. 03 24 26 11 00, www.hotelfp-sedan.com. 45 rooms. €15. Restaurant closed Sun dinner, Mon lunch.* The castle's 15C gunpowder store is now a comfortable, contemporary-styled hotel and restaurant. History-themed paintings adorn the bedrooms.

Château de Bazeilles – *3km/1.9 mi. from Sedan. 03 24 27 09 68. www.chateau-bazeilles.com. 20 rooms. €9. Restaurant . Closed two weeks Feb, Sun dinner, Mon lunch.* A hotel in the stables of an 18C château. L'Orangerie serves inventive cooking in an unusual vaulted dining room or on the terrace in summer.

manufacture in 1726. Note the heads above the windows in the first courtyard: they are believed to represent Elizabeth of Nassau, her family and friends. Opposite stands another draper's house dating from 1747.

No 3 rue Berchet
This dyer's workshop was acquired in 1823 by the owner of the royal manufacture.

No 8 rue de Bayle
A grand private mansion and cloth manufacture.

Église St-Charles
Henri de la Tour d'Auvergne had the church built for the Calvinist faith in 1593 . After the Revocation of the Edict of Nantes it became a Catholic church and Robert de Cotte added a vast rotunda-shaped chancel in 1688.

No 1 rue des Francs-Bourgeois
This 18C building with fine wrought-iron work was probably a draper's workshop.

No 1 place Turenne
An old cloth factory with an elaborate gateway in the courtyard.

No 1 rampe des Capucins
A former manufacture of fine cloth with an interesting staircase with wooden banisters at the rear of the courtyard.

Dijonval
Av. du Général-Margueritte.
This royal cloth manufacture founded in 1646 functioned until 1958. Its impo-

S. Sauvignier/MICHELIN

The Historium in the château of Sedan

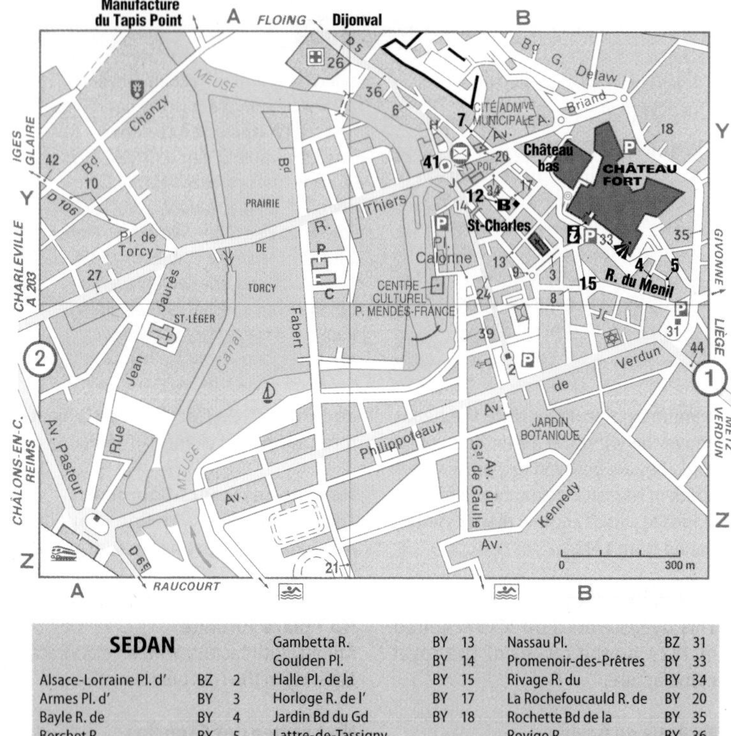

SEDAN			Gambetta R.	BY	13	Nassau Pl.	BZ	31
			Goulden Pl.	BY	14	Promenoir-des-Prêtres	BY	33
Alsace-Lorraine Pl. d'	BZ	2	Halle Pl. de la	BY	15	Rivage R. du	BY	34
Armes Pl. d'	BY	3	Horloge R. de l'	BY	17	La Rochefoucauld R. de	BY	20
Bayle R. de	BY	4	Jardin Bd du Gd	BY	18	Rochette Bd de la	BY	35
Berchet R.	BY	5	Lattre-de-Tassigny			Rovigo R.	BY	36
Blanpain R.	BY	6	Bd Mar.-de	AZ	21	Strasbourg R. de	BZ	39
Capucins Rampe	BY	7	Leclerc Av. du Mar.	BY	24	Turenne Pl.	BY	41
Carnot R.	BY	8	Margueritte Av. du G.	ABY	26	Vesseron-Lejay R.	AY	42
Crussy Pl.	BY	9	Martyrs-de-la-			Wuildet-Bizot R.	BZ	44
Fleuranges R. de	AY	10	Résistance Av. des	AY	27			
Francs-Bourgeois R. des	BY	12	Mesnil R. du	BY				

Ancien Hôtel de ville	BY	B

sing 18C façade extends either side of a pedimented central pavilion, flanked by curved wings prolonged by long straight ones.

Manufacture du Tapis Point de Sedan

13 bd. Gambetta. Open Mon–Tue, Thur–Sat 8am-noon, 2-6pm. €3. 03 24 29 04 60.

In this traditional carpet factory, weavers can be seen working on looms dating from 1878. The motif is drawn on squared paper and transcribed onto cardboard (each perforation represents one stitch). Several thousand spools of coloured wool are used and it takes five weavers three months to make a carpet (6m2/7.18sq yd).

Excursions

Bazeilles

3km/1.8mi SE along N 43.

Bitter fighting took place here on 31 August and 1 September 1870, before Sedan capitulated. The **Maison de la dernière cartouche** *(12 rue de la Dernière Cartouche. Open Apr–Sept daily 1.30–6pm. Rest of the year Wed–Sun 1/30-5pm. Closed 20 Dec-5 Jan. €3. 03 24 27 15 86)*, where a group of French soldiers resisted to their last round, is now a museum containing French and German items gathered on the battlefield. Nearby, an ossuary contains the remains of some 3 000 French and German soldiers.

SÉLESTAT★

BAS-RHIN. POPULATION 17 179

MICHELIN LOCAL MAP 315: I-7

This intimate historic city, lying on the west bank of the River Ill, has retained two fine churches and some interesting old houses. In the 15C and 16C, Sélestat was an important Humanist centre with one of the finest libraries in the world.

- **Tourist Office**: Commanderie St-Jean, boulevard du Général Leclerc, 67607 Sélestat. ☎03 88 58 87 20, www.selestat-tourisme.com.
- **Orient Yourself**: Halfway between Colmar and Strasbourg.
- **Don't Miss**: The Bibliothèque Humaniste.
- **Especially for Kids**: Watch breadmaking at the Maison du Pain, eagles at the Volerie des Aigles and Barbary apes roaming the Montagne des Singes.
- **See Also**: The Route des Vins.

Walking Tour★ *Allow 2hr*

From the tourist office, turn right onto rue du Vieux-Marché-aux-Vins. Cross place Gambetta and right on rue des Serruriers.

The **Ancienne Église des Récollets**, formerly part of a Franciscan monastery, is now a Protestant church.

Turn left onto rue de Verdun.

Maison de Stephan Ziegler

This 16C Renaissance house was built by one of the town's master builders.

Rue de Verdun leads to place de la Victoire.

Arsenal Ste-Barbe

The 14C former arsenal has a fine façade with a double-flight staircase. The roof is crowned by two storks' nests.

Continue on rue du 17-Novembre and turn right onto rue du 4e-Zouaves then left along boulevard du Maréchal-Joffre which leads to the ramparts.

Promenade des Remparts

There is a fine view from Vauban's fortifications.

Walk along boulevard de Verdun then rue Poincaré.

Tour de l'Horloge

The clock tower dates from the 14C, the upper part was restored in 1614.

Martin Bucer

Born in Sélestat in 1491, Martin Bucer entered a Dominican monastery after completing his studies. His meeting with Luther in Heidelberg in 1518 changed the course of his life.

He left his monastery, converted the town of Wissembourg to the ideas of the Reformation and settled in Strasbourg as pastor of Sainte-Aurélie. Influenced by Humanism, this open-minded thinker tried, through his writings and his actions, to restore a common doctrine among all Protestants. His spiritual influence spread throughout southern Germany and the state of Hesse.

After the defeat of the Schmalkaldic League opposed to the Habsburgs, Bucer was forced by Emperor Charles V to go into exile in 1549. He settled in Cambridge where he died in 1551.

Address Book

For coin ranges, see the Legend on the cover flap.

WHERE TO EAT

Auberge de l'Illwald – *67600 Le Schnellenbuhl, 8km/5mi SE of Sélestat on D 159 and D 424. 03 88 85 35 40. contact@illwald.com. 9 rooms . €10. Closed 22 Jun-7 Jul, 21 Dec-6 Jan, Tue and Wed.* A pleasant inn on the road towards Germany, run by a young couple who serve simple, well-presented local dishes. The dining room is decorated with murals. Also 9 comfortable rooms, some rustic chic, others more contemporary.

Les Deux Clefs – *72 r. du Gén.-Leclerc, 67600 Ebersmunster, 8km/5mi NE of Sélestat on N 83, Strasbourg direction, and D 210. 03 88 85 71 55. Closed Mon and Thu Jan-Mar. Booking advisable at weekends.* This typical Alsatian building opposite Ebersmunster's lovely church used to house the monastery abattoir. Today the restaurant serves *matelote* (freshwater fish stew) and fried fish, along with other classic regional dishes.

WHERE TO STAY

Hôtel Dontenville – *94 r. du Mar.-Foch, 67730 Châtenois, 5km/3mi W of Sélestat, St-Dié direction. 03 88 92 02 54. Closed Feb school holidays, Fri lunchtime and Tue. 13 rooms. €6. restaurant .* This 16C half-timbered hotel has retained the charm and simplicity of old Alsatian houses. The upper floor bedrooms are the best, with their exposed beams. Regional cuisine is served in the panelled dining room.

Chambre d'hôte La Romance – *17 rte de Neuve-Église, 67220 Dieffenbach-au-Val, 12km/7.5mi NW of Sélestat on N 59 and D 424, Villé direction. 03 88 85 67 09. 4 rooms.* Don't give up when looking for this house in the upper part of the village: it may not be easy to find, but it is quiet and comfortable. The modern rooms have been carefully decorated, the garden is pleasant and the sauna and jacuzzi ideal for relaxing.

Hostellerie Abbaye de la Pommeraie – *8 av. Mar. Foch. 03 88 92 07 84. www.pommeraie.fr. 14 rooms. €16. 2 restaurants and .* This plush hotel in a 17C aristocratic mansion in the old town has spacious bedrooms (either Louis XVI style or cosily beamed attics) and fanciful bathrooms. There are two restaurants: the gastronomic Le Prieuré and the homelier winstub Apfelstuebel.

SHOPPING

Local produce market – *Square Ehm, Sat morning.*

Kamm – *15 r. des Clefs. 03 88 92 11 04. Tue-Sat 8am-7pm, Sun 8am-2pm, holidays 9am-noon. Closed 19 Jan–1 Feb.* In summer, the terrace of this patisserie is extremely popular, but all year round regulars come here for its mousses, original chocolates and homemade ice creams and sorbets. Light meals are served at lunchtime.

Pâtisserie-chocolaterie Benoît Wach – *7 r. des Chevaliers. 03 88 92 12 80. Tue-Fri 7am-7pm, Sat-Sun 8am-6pm, holidays 7am-6pm. Closed one week in Jul-Aug and Sep.* In a lovely building decorated with *trompe-l'œil* mouldings, this cake shop and tearoom serves all kinds of regional specialities (to eat on the spot or take away): *oeufs de cigogne* ("storks' eggs"), gingerbread, *kougelhopf* and other Alsatian butter biscuits.

BICYCLE HIRE

Office du Tourisme – *Bd Leclerc. 03 88 58 87 23. May-Oct.* Sélestat has received an award for its 85km/53mi of cycle paths, and the tourist office can arrange the hire of new mountain bikes.

CALENDAR

Christmas Festivities – True to Alsatian tradition, Sélestat, birthplace of the Christmas tree, puts on numerous events at Christmas. As well as the giant Christmas trees of the Christmas market, guided musical tours with storytellers and costumed musicians, there are demonstrations of local specialities in the Maison du Pain and concerts in churches. *Enquire at the tourist office.*

Corso fleuri – On the second Saturday in August, floats decorated with 500 000 dahlias parade night and day in the town streets, accompanied by dancing and fireworks. *03 88 58 85 75.*

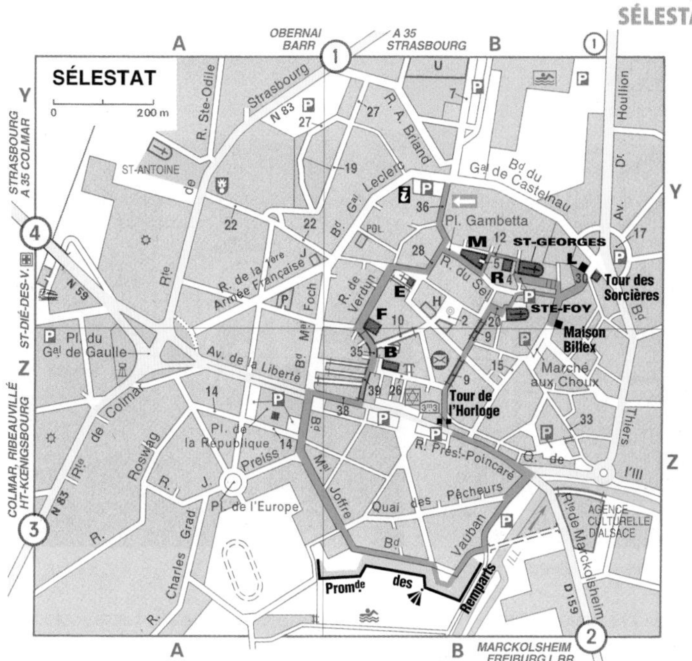

SÉLESTAT								
Armes Pl. d'	BY	2	Hôpital R. de l'	BZ	15	Serruriers R. des	BY	28
Babil R. du	BY	4	Lattre-de-Tassigny Pl. du Mar.de	BY	17	Strasbourg Pl. Pte-de	BY	30
Bibliothèque R. de la	BY	5	Maire-Knol Allée du	BY	19	Tanneurs Quai des	BZ	33
Charlemagne Bd	BY	7	Marché-Vert Pl. du	BY	20	Victoire Pl. de la	BZ	35
Chevaliers R. des	BYZ	9	Paix R. de la	AY	22	Vieux-Marché aux Vins R. du	BY	36
Clefs R. des	BYZ	10	Prés.-Poincaré R. du	BZ		17-Novembre R. du	BZ	39
Église R. de l'	BY	12	Sainte-Barbe R.	BZ	26	4e-Zouaves R. du	BZ	38
Gallieni R. du Gén.	AZ	14	Schweisguth Av.	ABY	27			

Ancien arsenal Ste-Barbe	BZ	B	Maison de Stephan Ziegler	BY	F
Ancienne église des Récollets	BY	E	Porte de Strasbourg	BY	L
Bibliothèque humaniste	BY	M	Résidence d'Ebersmunster	BY	R

Walk beneath the clock tower, then follow rue des Chevaliers straight ahead to place du Marché-Vert.

Église Ste-Foy★

This Romanesque church (12C), built of red sandstone and granite from the Vosges, was the church of a Benedictine priory. The capitals in the nave have beautiful floral motifs.

Leave the church by the small door behind the pulpit and take the narrow lane on the right to place du Marché-aux-Choux.

Maison Billex

In 1681, the city of Strasbourg signed its surrender to Louis XIV in this fine Renaissance house.

Walk to the Église St-Georges.

On the way, you will get a glimpse of the **Tour des Sorcières** on the right, part of the fortifications demolished by Louis XIV, and the Porte de Strasbourg, designed by Vauban in 1679.

Église St-Georges★

This imposing 13C to 15C Gothic church was considerably remodelled in the 19C. The nave is preceded by a wide narthex which spans the whole width of the west front and opens on the south side (place St-Georges) through an elegant doorway. The musician angels on the stained-glass of the west front date from the late 14C or early 15C; the rose-window (14C) above the south doorway of the narthex illustrates the Ten Commandments;

R. Mattès/MICHELIN

The Humanist Library

three 15C stained-glass windows in the chancel depict scenes from the lives of St Catherine, St Agnes and St Helena; the modern stained-glass in the east end and the chancel is by Max Ingrand.

▸ *Walk along rue de l'Église.*

Résidence d'Ebersmunster

No 8. Built in 1541, this was the town house of the Benedictine monks of Ebersmunster. The Renaissance doorway is decorated with Italian motifs.

▸ *A few yards farther on, turn left onto the narrow rue de la Bibliothèque.*

Bibliothèque humaniste★

Open Jul-Aug Mon, Wed–Fri 9am-noon, 2-6pm, weekends 2-5pm. Sep-Jun Mon, Wed–Fri 9am-noon, 2-6pm, Sat 9am-noon. Holidays. €3.60. ☎03 88 58 07 20.

Towards the middle of the 15C, Sélestat's Latin school flourished into a great Humanist school, which explains the extent of its splendid library now housed in the 19C grain exchange.

The library comprises two collections: the Latin library founded in 1452 and the private collection bequeathed by Beatus Rhenanus, a Humanist and close friend of Erasmus.

Among the precious manuscripts are the Merovingian Lectionary (late 7C), the oldest work still in Alsace, and the *Cosmographiæ Introductio* printed in St-Dié in 1507 (*see ST-DIÉ*).

▸ *Turn the corner to rue du Sél.*

La Maison du Pain

Open early Jan & end Jan–Nov Tue–Sun 9.30am–12.30pm, 2–6pm. Dec Tue–Sun 10am–7pm. Closed 16–30 Jan, 25 Dec–1 Jan. €4.60 (children under 16 no charge). ☎03 88 58 45 90, www.maison-dupain-d-alsace.com.

Kids Learn all about Alsace's countless types of bread in this unusual bakery, with its tempting smell of baking bread. After an introductory room explaining the history of breadmaking and flour-milling, there is ancient bakery adorned with all the tools that were used in the pre-industrial age, and a modern bakery, where you can see frequent demonstrations of break-making, as well as a tasting room and shop. Take a look also at the Zunft hall (1522) of the bakers' corporation.

Excursions

Château de Ramstein and Château d'Ortenbourg

7km/4.3mi W and then 1hr 15min on foot. Leave Sélestat by N 59, after 4.5km/2.8mi, turn right onto D 35 towards Scherwiller; 2km/1.2mi farther on, turn left

onto an unsurfaced path. Leave the car in Huhnelmuhl, near the inn and follow the footpath leading to two ruined castles 300m/328yd apart.
The ruins provide picturesque views of the Val de Villé and Plaine de Sélestat.

Volerie des Aigles

8.5km/5.3mi at Kintzheim by D 159, plus 30 min on foot there and back. Show (40min) Open Apr–mid-Nov enquire about times. Closed mid-Nov–Mar. €9 (children €5). ☎03 88 92 84 33. www.voleriedesaigles.com
Kids The courtyard of the ruined castle is home to about 80 birds of prey. Some of them take part in spectacular **training demonstrations**★ (except in bad weather).

Montagne des Singes

2km/mi. further on by forest road and D 159, and footpath to the electrified fence. Open Jul-Aug 10am-6pm. May-Jun & Sep 10am-noon, 1-6pm. Apr & Oct–11 Nov 10am-noon, 1-5pm. Closed 12 Nov–Mar. €7.50 (children €4.50). ☎03 88 92 11 05, www.montagnedessinges.com.
Kids 300 Barbary apes, well adapted to the Alsatian climate, live in total liberty in park on top of a hill. View of Haut-Kœnigsbourg Castle to the SW.

Benfeld

20km/12.4mi NE by N83.
The elegant 16C **town hall** has a lovely carved doorway and polygonal turret dating from 1617. The clock has three jacks striking the hours: Death, a Knight and Stubenhansel, a Traitor who, in 1331, sold the city to its enemies for a purse of gold, which he holds in his hand.

Ebersmunster

8km/5mi NE by N83.
A famous Benedictine abbey once stood in this peaceful village. It was believed to have been founded by St Odile's parents, Duke Étichon and his wife (*see Mont STE-ODILE*). Built c 1725, the **abbey church**★ can be seen from afar with its three onion-shaped steeples. The **interior**★★, with its stucco work and an imposing high altar with gilt carvings and a huge baldequin, is considered to be the finest example of early-18C Alsatian Baroque art. Organ and choral recitals, known as **"Les Heures musicales d'Ebersmunster,"** take place in the church every Sunday at 5pm in May (*☎03 88 85 78 32).*

SÉZANNE

MARNE. POPULATION 5 585

MICHELIN LOCAL MAP 306: E-10

Today peacefully settled on a hillside riddled with underground galleries and cellars, the lively small agricultural and industrial town of Sézanne was host to frequent trade fairs from medieval times onwards. The hillside vineyards produce still white wine.

- **Tourist Office**: Pl. de la République, 51120 Sézanne. ☎03 26 80 51 43.
- **Orient Yourself**: 45km/28mi. S of Épernay by D 951, from where there is a picturesque view of the town. A ring of broad avenues, which replaced the fortifications, surrounds the old town.

Sights

Église St-Denis

Place de la République.
This Flamboyant Gothic church is flanked by a massive Renaissance tower. The Flamboyant Gothic interior is very homogenous with fine star vaulting.

Mail des Cordeliers

Chestnut trees line the walkway along the former ramparts; the flattened

Address Book

For coin ranges, see the Legend on the cover flap.

WHERE TO STAY AND EAT

Hôtel de la Croix d'Or – *53 r. Notre-Dame. ☎03 26 80 61 10. Closed 2-12 Jan, Sun evenings and Wed. 12 rooms. €6. restaurant* . This hotel is situated on the town's main shopping street. The ivy-clad façade, rustic furniture in the living room, quaint dining room, traditional cooking and comfortable modernised rooms have a charmingly provincial atmosphere.

Hôtel Domaine de Montgivroux – *51120 Mondement-Montgivroux, 8km/5mi NE of Sézanne on D 39 and D 45. ☎03 26 42 06 93, www.audomainedemontgivroux.fr. 19 rooms.* This large 17C farmhouse nestled in the rolling hills of the Champagne countryside provides a warm welcome, with billiard table, swimming pool and mountain bikes on site. The bedrooms have recently been redecorated.

remains of two round towers recall the castle that once stood here.

Driving Tour

Forêt de Traconne

54km/34mi round tour – allow 2hr

The dense Traconne Forest, covering almost 3 000ha/7 413 acres, mainly consists of hornbeam thickets beneath tall oak trees. It is crisscrossed by numerous footpaths including a discovery trail.

Drive W out of Sézanne along D 239. In Launat, turn left towards Le Meix-St-Époing and, 500m/0.3mi farther on, right towards Bricot-la-Ville.

Bricot-la-Ville

This tiny village hidden in the heart of the forest has a charming little church, a lily-covered pond, and a manor house, which was home to Benedictine nuns from the 12C to the 16C.

Continue along the Grand Morin Valley to Châtillon-sur-Morin (fortified church), then turn left onto D 86 which joins D 48. In Essarts-le-Vicomte, turn left onto D 49.

L'Étoile

On the edge of this grass-covered roundabout, which has a column topped by an 18C iron cross in its centre, stands a twisted stunted birch from the Bois des Faux de Verzy (*see Parc naturel régional de la Montagne de REIMS*).

Follow D 49 to Barbonne-Fayel then turn right onto D 50.

Fontaine-Denis-Nuisy

A 13C fresco of the Last Judgement in the north transept of the **church**, depicts damned souls roasting in a vast cauldron.

Drive along D 350 towards St-Quentin-le-Verger.

Shortly after Nuisy, you will see a **dolmen** on the right.

In St-Quentin-le-Verger, turn left onto D 351 then right onto the Villeneuve-St-Vistre road, D 373, back to Sézanne.

SIERCK-LES-BAINS

MOSELLE. POPULATION 1872.
MICHELIN LOCAL MAP 307: J-2

Sierck lies in a picturesque setting on the banks of the River Moselle. The old village climbs up the hill crowned by a fortress. In the 12C, the duke of Lorraine and the archbishop of Trier fought over its ownership; it was ransacked and burned down by the Swedes during the Thirty Years War and by Turenne's army in 1661. The name alone recalls that Sierck was once a spa town with three springs, until the thermal establishment was replaced by the railway station.

- **Tourist Office**: Rue du Château, 57400 Sierck-les-Bains. ☎03 82 83 74 14.
- **Orient Yourself**: Near to the Luxembourg and German borders, 17km/10.6mi. NE of Thionville, Sierck is the starting point for boat trips on the Moselle.

Sights

Château des Ducs de Lorraine★

Open May–Sep Mon–Sat 10am-7pm, Sun & holidays 10am-8pm. Mar–Apr & Oct–Nov 10am–4pm, Sun & holidays 10am-5pm. Closed Dec–Feb. *€4.50. ☎03 82 83 67 97, www.chateau-sierck.com.* The castle, built on a rocky promontory, still has most of its 11C defensive system. The nearby **Chapelle de Marienfloss**, all that remains of a once flourishing Carthusian monastery, has been restored and extended.

For coin ranges, see the Legend on the cover flap.

WHERE TO EAT

Auberge de la Klauss – *57480 Montenach, 3.5 km/2mi SE of Sierck on D 956. ☎03 82 83 72 38. Closed 24 Dec-7 Jan & Mon.* There's a cheerful rural atmosphere in this country inn, where geese, ducks and pigs are raised. Regional cooking, good wines, game in season and above all home-made foie gras are a gourmet treat. Summer terrace.

Château de Malbrouck ★★

8km/5mi NE along N 153 then right along D 64. Open Apr–Dec Mon 2–6pm, Tue–Fri 10am–6pm, weekends 9&m–7pm. Closed Jan–Mar. €6.50 (children under 16 no charge). ☎03 82 82 42 92, www.chateau-malbrouck.com.

Kids The 15C fortress of the lords of Sierck has been restored by a clever modern restoration that doesn't attempt to imitate the original. In 1705, during the War of the Spanish Succession, John Churchill, Duke of Marlborough, used it as his headquarters.

R. Mattès/MICHELIN

Contz-les-Bains on the Moselle

COLLINE DE SION-VAUDÉMONT★★

MEURTHE-ET-MOSELLE. MICHELIN LOCAL MAP 307: H-8

The isolated horseshoe-shaped hill of Sion-Vaudémont is one of the most famous viewpoints in Lorraine. For 2 000 years, it has drawn pagan worshippers and later Christians. After the Franco-Prussian War of 1870, and after each of the two world wars, pilgrims came to pray on top of the hill. In 1973, a Peace monument was unveiled here.

Tourist Office: Rue Notre-Dame, 54330 Saxon-Sion. ☎03 83 25 14 85.

Orient Yourself: S of Nancy on the D50 near Vaudémont.

Sights

Basilique Notre-Dame de Sion★

The basilica dates mainly from the 18C, but the monumental 19C belfry sadly burnt down in 2003. In the apse (early 14C) is the statue of Notre-Dame-de-Sion, a 15C crowned Virgin Mary in gilt stone. There is a superb **panoramic view**★ by the Calvary.

Signal de Vaudémont★★

2.5km/1.5mi. S of Sion along D 53.

At the top of the Signal de Vaudémont (alt 541m/1 775ft) is the **Barrès Monument** (22m/72ft high) erected in 1928 in memory of writer and politician Maurice Barrès (1862-1923), a native of the area, who celebrated the hill, which he called the Colline inspiréé in one of his novels. There is a superb **panorama**★★ of the Lorraine plateau.

For coin ranges, see the Legend on the cover flap.

WHERE TO EAT

⊜⊜ **Domaine de Sion** – *R. de la Cense-Rouge, 54330 Saxon-Sion. ☎03 83 26 24 36. Booking essential.* This fruit-grower has a distillery that can be visited. In the simple restaurant you can sample home-grown fruit and vegetables in various guises. Pick up a few things for an afternoon snack!

Vaudémont

The Tour Brunehaut, last remnant of Vaudémont castle, **original seat of the House of the dukes of Lorraine**, stand near the church. The village remains largely unspoiled by modernisation. Grand'Rue is lined with semi-detached houses or farms with a rounded-archway giving access to the barn. The

R. Mattès/MICHELIN

Colline de Sion-Vaudémont

houses, built of rubble stone with little ornamentation, have just one storey, with a loft under the roof and a cellar accessible from the street.

SOULTZ-HAUT-RHIN

HAUT-RHIN. POPULATION 6 640

MICHELIN LOCAL MAP 315: H-9

This ancient town grew up around a vein of rock salt that still exists. Many old houses dating from the 16C to 18C, are adorned with oriels, stair turrets, porches bearing the construction date and inner courtyards which can be glimpsed through open doors.

- **Tourist Office**: 14 place de la République, 68360 Soultz-Haut-Rhin. ☎03 89 76 83 60.
- **Orient Yourself**: The town merges into neighbouring Guebwiller in a huge commercial zone, but the old town is well-preserved by partially conserved ramparts.

Sights

Old houses

Apart from the tourist office dating from 1575, there are several fine old houses in the historic centre: Maison Litty (1622) at No 15 rue des Sœurs; Maison Vigneronne (1656) at No 5 rue du Temple; Maison Horn (1588) at No 42 rue de Lattre-de-Tassigny; Maison Hubschwerlin (16C) with its lovely courtyard, at No 6 rue des Ouvriers. In rue Jean-Jaurès is the family mansion (1605) of the Heeckeren d'Anthès, a powerful Alsatian industrial dynasty; one of its members, Georges-Charles de Heeckeren, killed the Russian writer Pushkin in a dual near St-Petersburg in 1837.

Église St-Maurice

The church, which shows great unity of style, was built between 1270 and 1489. The tympanum of the south doorway bears a 14C representation of St Maurice on horseback. Inside, there is a fine early-17C pulpit, an organ by Silbermann (1750), a late-15C polychrome relief sculpture of St George slaying the dragon, and a mural of St Christopher.

Promenade de la citadelle

This walk, on the west side of town, follows a section of the ramparts, including the Tour des Sorcières (witches' tower).

La Nef des jouets

Open Apr-Dec Wed–Mon 2-6pm. Closed Jan–Mar, 1 May, 24–25 Dec, 31 Dec. €4.60 (children €1.50). ☎03 89 74 30 92.

Kids This eclectic toy collection gathered by two enthusiasts is displayed in the 12C former headquarters of the Order of the Knights of the Hospital of St John.

Musée du Bucheneck

Open 2 May-Oct Wed–Mon 2-6pm. €2.30. ☎03 89 76 02 22.

Address Book

For coin ranges, see the Legend on the cover flap.

WHERE TO EAT

Metzgerstuwa – *69 r. du Mar.-de-Lattre-de-Tassigny. ☎03 89 74 89 77. Closed 3 weeks end Jun–early Jul, 2 weeks Christmas–early Jan, Sat & Sun.* One part is a butcher's shop, the other, the restaurant, and the chef who runs both establishments makes everything himself: regional dishes, bread, *charcuterie, terrine, pieds farcis* and so on. A treat for those who love good food, and often packed.

The local history museum is housed in an 11C fortress, seat of the episcopal bailiff from 1289 to the Revolution.

STRASBOURG★★★

POPULATION 388 483
MICHELIN LOCAL MAP 315: K-5

With its busy river port and renowned university, Strasbourg is the intellectual and economic capital of Alsace. Built round its famous cathedral, Strasbourg is also a town rich in art treasures and one of the three "capitals" of Europe, for it is here that the European Parliament and the European Council are located. The city has proudly maintained its gastronomic tradition (foie gras, Alsatian wines, chocolate and liqueurs), which attract gourmets from all over the world. An important music festival takes place every year in June followed by the European Fair in early September. The historic centre of Strasbourg, which includes the cathedral, has been on UNESCO's World Heritage List since 1988.

- **Tourist Office:** 17 place de la Cathédrale, 67000 Strasbourg, ☎03 88 52 28 28, www.ot-strasbourg.fr
- **Orient Yourself:** Strasbourg is 156km/97mi east of Nancy on the A31 and A4, 165km/102mi east of Metz on the A4 and north of Mulhouse (116km/72mi) and Colmar 74km/46mi) on the A35.
- **Don't Miss:** Notre-Dame Cathedral and the picturesque Petite France district.
- **Especially for Kids:** Children (and adults) adore Strasbourg at Christmas time, and the challenge of climbing the cathedral spire.

A Bit of History

Famous oath

Argentoratum, which was but a small fishing and hunting village at the time of Julius Caesar, soon became a prosperous city and a major crossroads between Eastern and Western Europe: Strateburgum, the city of roads. This geographical position meant that Strasbourg found itself on the path of all invasions from across the Rhine and was destroyed, burnt down, ransacked and rebuilt many times throughout its history. In 842, it was chosen as a place of reconciliation by two of Charlemagne's grandsons, who swore an oath. This oath of fidelity is the first official text written both in a Romance and a Germanic language.

Gutenberg in Strasbourg

Born in Mainz in 1395, Gutenberg had to flee his native town for political reasons and came to settle in Strasbourg in 1434. He formed an association with three Alsatians to perfect a secret process which he had invented. But their association ended in a law suit in 1439 and this is how we know that the invention in question was the printing press. Gutenberg went back to Mainz in 1448 and, with his partner Johann Fust, he perfected the invention that deeply changed our society.

Rouget de Lisle's Marseillaise

On 24 April 1792, the mayor of Strasbourg, Frédéric de Dietrich, offered a farewell dinner to a group of volunteers from the Rhine army. The men talked about the necessity for the troops to have a song which would rouse their enthusiasm and the mayor asked one of the young officers named Rouget de Lisle, if he would write such a song. The next morning, the young man brought him his Chant de guerre pour l'Armée du Rhin (War song for the Rhine Army). Shortly afterwards, volunteers from Marseille on their way north adopted the song which then became known as the Marseillaise. It was designated the French national anthem in 1795. A plaque on the Banque de France building, at No 4 rue Broglie, recalls the memory of Rouget de Lisle.

1870-1918

On 27 September 1870, Strasbourg capitulated after being besieged and shelled by the Germans for 50 days. Under the terms of the Treaty of Frankfurt (10 May 1871), Strasbourg became a German city, which it remained until 11 November 1918.

European crossroads

Even before the end of the Second World War, major politicians (Winston Churchill, Robert Schuman, Konrad Adenauer, and Charles de Gaulle) agreed that Strasbourg should officially assume the role it had played throughout its history and become a European crossroads. Reconciliation between former enemies would have its roots in a city that had become a symbol, Strasbourg, lying alongside a mighty river once dotted with defensive works and now acting as a link between countries at the heart of Europe.

The **European Council** was created on 5 May 1949; it now has 41 member states. The Council, which has a purely consultative role, sends recommendations to governments and establishes conventions that commit the states signing the agreements, with the object of harmonising legislation in various fields of common interest. The most famous is the European Convention for the Safeguard of Human Rights (1950). It

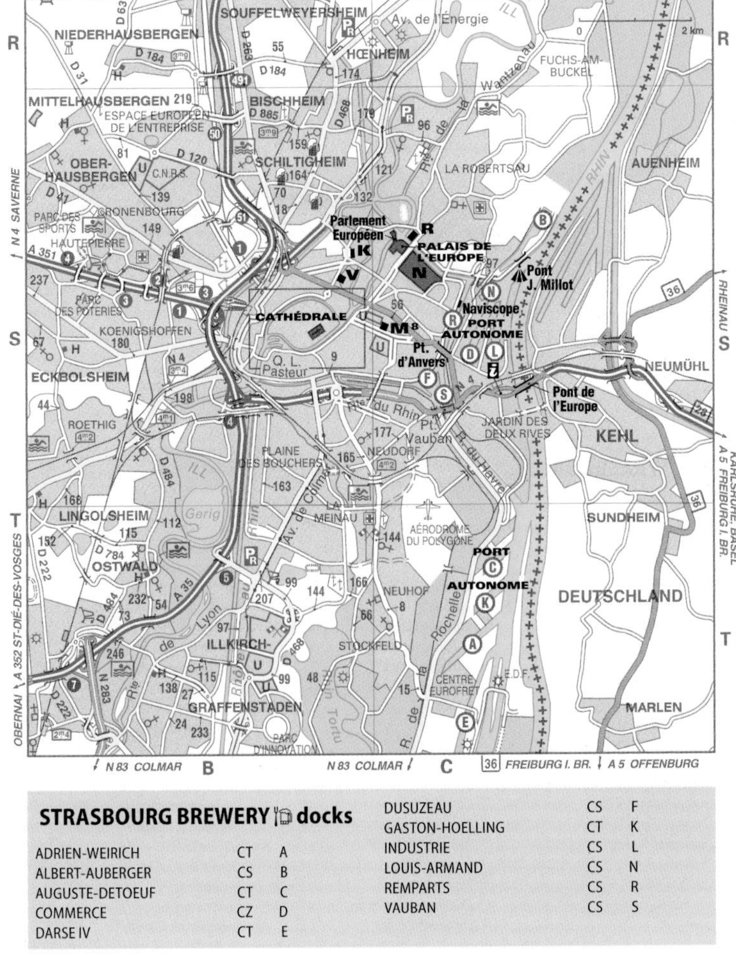

STRASBOURG BREWERY docks

ADRIEN-WEIRICH	CT	A
ALBERT-AUBERGER	CS	B
AUGUSTE-DETOEUF	CT	C
COMMERCE	CZ	D
DARSE IV	CT	E
DUSUZEAU	CS	F
GASTON-HOELLING	CT	K
INDUSTRIE	CS	L
LOUIS-ARMAND	CS	N
REMPARTS	CS	R
VAUBAN	CS	S

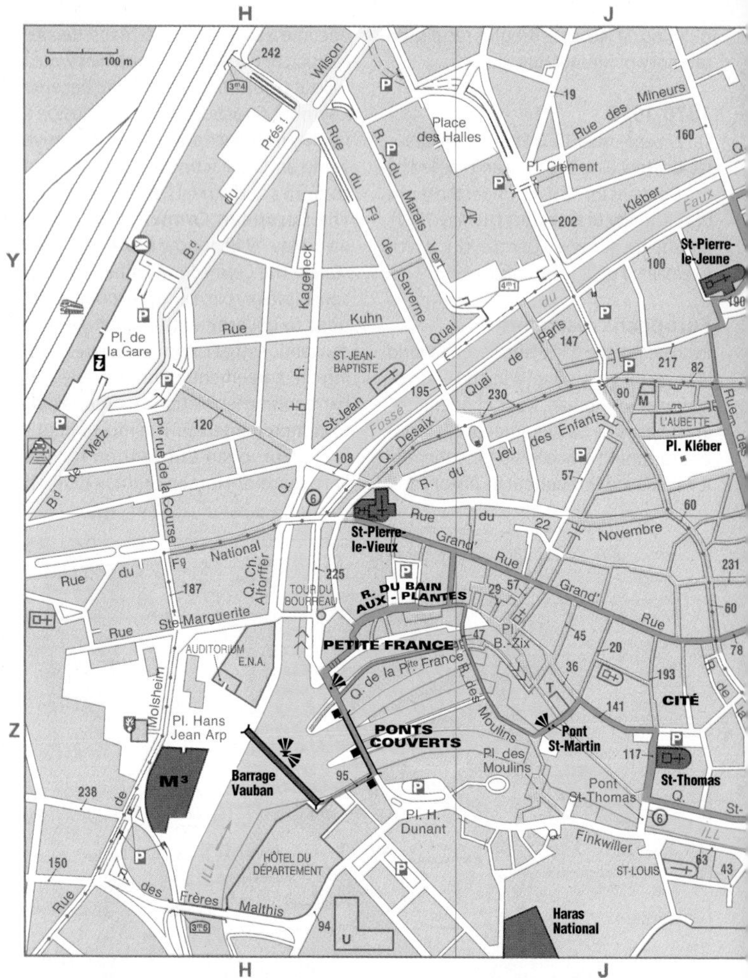

STRASBOURG

Street	Grid	No.
Abreuvoir R. de l'	LZ	3
Académie R. de l'	LZ	
Alsace Av. d'	LY	
Altorffer Quai Ch.	HZ	
Anvers Pont d'	CS	
Arc-en-Ciel R. de l'	KLY	7
Arcades R. Grandes	JKZ	
Atenheim Rte d'	CT	8
Austerlitz Pl. d'	KLZ	
Austerlitz Pont d'	BS	9
Austerlitz R. d'	KZ	10
Auvergne Pont d'	LY	12
Bain-aux-plantes R. du	HJZ	
Bateliers Quai des	KLZ	
Bateliers R. des	LZ	14
Bauerngrund R. de	CT	15
Bonnes-Gens R. des	JY	19
Bouchers R. des	KZ	
Bouclier R. du	JZ	20
Broglie Pl.	KY	
Brûlée R.	KY	
Calvin R.	LZ	
Castelnau R. Gén.-de	KY	25
Cathédrale Pl. de la	KZ	26
Château Pl. du	KZ	
Chaudron R. du	KY	28
Cheveux R. des	JZ	29
Clément Pl.	JY	
Colmar Av. de	BST	
Corbeau Cours du	KZ	
Corbeau Pl. du	KZ	31
Corbeau Pont du	KZ	
Cordiers R. des	KZ	32
Course Petite-rue-de la	HYZ	
Courtine R. de la	LY	34
Dentelles R. des	JZ	36
Desaix Quai	HY	
Dietrich Quai Marie	LY	
Division-Leclerc R.	JKZ	
Dôme R. du	KY	
Douane R. de la	KZ	
Dunant Pl. H.	KZ	
Écarlate R. de l'	JZ	43
Escarpée R.	JZ	45
Étudiants R. et Pl. des	KY	46
Europe Pont de l'	CS	
Faisan Pont du	JZ	47
Finkmatt Quai	JKY	
Finkwiller Quai	JZ	
Foin Pl. du	LZ	
Fonderie Pont de la	KY	52
Fonderie R. de la	KY	
Forêt-Noire Av. de la	CS	56
Fossé-des-Tanneurs R. du	JZ	57
Fossé-des-Treize R. du	KY	58
France Q. de la petite	HZ	
Francs-Bourgeois R. des	JZ	60
Frères R. des	KYZ	
Frères Malthis R. des	HZ	
Frey Quai Charles	JZ	63
Fritz R.	LZ	
Ganzau R. de la	BT	66
Gare Pl. de la	HY	
Gdes-Arcades R. des	JKY	
Grande-Boucherie Pl. de la	KZ	76
Grand'Rue	HJZ	
Gutenberg Pl.	KZ	
Gutenberg R.	JKZ	78
Hallebardes R. des	KZ	80

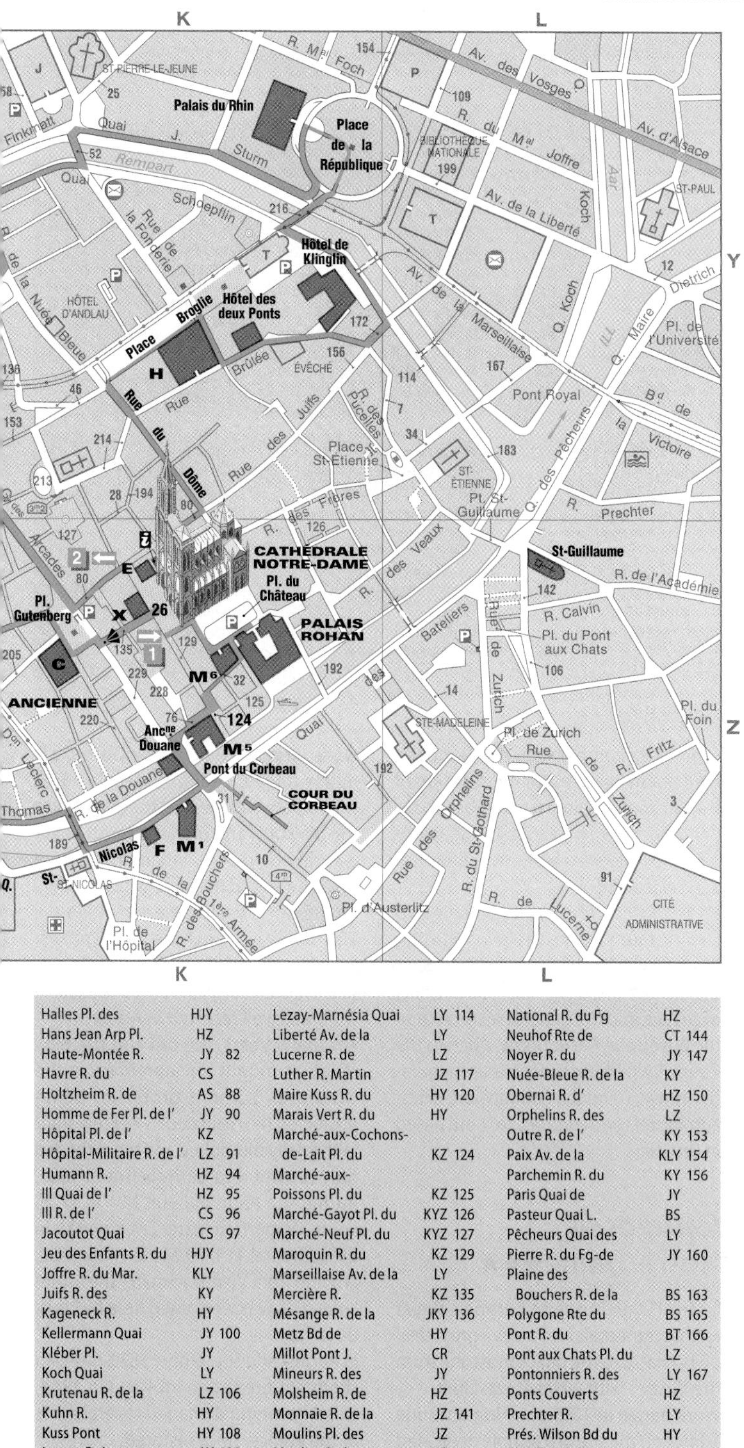

Street	Grid	No.
Halles Pl. des	HJY	
Hans Jean Arp Pl.	HZ	
Haute-Montée R.	JY	82
Havre R. du	CS	
Holtzheim R. de	AS	88
Homme de Fer Pl. de l'	JY	90
Hôpital Pl. de l'	KZ	
Hôpital-Militaire R. de l'	LZ	91
Humann R.	HZ	94
Ill Quai de l'	HZ	95
Ill R. de l'	CS	96
Jacoutot Quai	CS	97
Jeu des Enfants R. du	HJY	
Joffre R. du Mar.	KLY	
Juifs R. des	KY	
Kageneck R.	HY	
Kellermann Quai	JY	100
Kléber Pl.	JY	
Koch Quai	LY	
Krutenau R. de la	LZ	106
Kuhn R.	HY	
Kuss Pont	HY	108
Lamey R. Auguste	LY	109
Leclerc R. de la Don.	KZ	
Lezay-Marnésia Quai	LY	114
Liberté Av. de la	LY	
Lucerne R. de	LZ	
Luther R. Martin	JZ	117
Maire Kuss R. du	HY	120
Marais Vert R. du	HY	
Marché-aux-Cochons-de-Lait Pl. du	KZ	124
Marché-aux-Poissons Pl. du	KZ	125
Marché-Gayot Pl. du	KYZ	126
Marché-Neuf Pl. du	KYZ	127
Maroquin R. du	KZ	129
Marseillaise Av. de la	LY	
Mercière R.	KZ	135
Mésange R. de la	JKY	136
Metz Bd de	HY	
Millot Pont J.	CR	
Mineurs R. des	JY	
Molsheim R. de	HZ	
Monnaie R. de la	JZ	141
Moulins Pl. des	JZ	
Moulins R. des	JZ	
Munch R. Ernest	LZ	142
National R. du Fg	HZ	
Neuhof Rte de	CT	144
Noyer R. du	JY	147
Nuée-Bleue R. de la	KY	
Obernai R. d'	HZ	150
Orphelins R. des	LZ	
Outre R. de l'	KY	153
Paix Av. de la	KLY	154
Parchemin R. du	KY	156
Paris Quai de	JY	
Pasteur Quai L.	BS	
Pêcheurs Quai des	LY	
Pierre R. du Fg-de	JY	160
Plaine des Bouchers R. de la	BS	163
Polygone Rte du	BS	165
Pont R. du	BT	166
Pont aux Chats Pl. du	LZ	
Pontonniers R. des	LY	167
Ponts Couverts	HZ	
Prechter R.	LY	
Prés. Wilson Bd du	HY	
Pucelles R. des	KY	
Récollets R. des	KLY	172

Street	Grid	No.
République Pl. de la	KLY	
Rhin Rte du	CS	
Ribeauvillé R. de	CS	177
Rochelle R. de la	CT	
Romains Rte des	BS	180
Royal Pont	LY	
St-Étienne Pl.	KY	
St-Étienne Quai	LY	183
St-Gothard R. du	LZ	
St-Guillaume Pont	LY	
St-Jean Quai	HY	
St-Martin Pont	JZ	
St-Michel R.	HZ	187
St-Nicolas Pont	KZ	189
St-Nicolas Quai	KZ	
St-Pierre-le-Jeune Pl.	JKY	190
St-Thomas Pont	JZ	
St-Thomas Quai	JKZ	
Ste-Madeleine Pont et R.	KLZ	192
Ste-Marguerite R.	HZ	
Salzmann R.	JZ	193
Sanglier R. du	KY	194
Saverne Pont de	HY	195
Saverne R. du Fg-de	HY	
Schirmeck Rte de	BS	198
Schoelcher Av. Victor	LY	199
Schoepflin Quai	KY	
Sébastopol R. de	JY	202
Serruriers R. des	JKZ	205
Sturn Quai J.	KY	
Temple-Neuf Pl. du	KY	213
Temple-Neuf R. du	KY	214
Théâtre Pont du	KY	216
Thomann R. des	JY	217
Tonneliers R. des	KZ	220
Turckheim Quai	HZ	225
Université Pl. de l'	LY	
Vauban Pont	CS	
Veaux R. des	KLZ	
Victoire Bd de la	LY	
Vieil-Hôpital R. du	KZ	228
Vieux-Marché-aux-Poissons R. du	KZ	229
Vieux-Marché-aux-Vins R. et Pl. du	JY	230
Vieux-Seigle R. du	JZ	231
Vosges Av. des	LY	
Wantzenau Rte de la	CRS	
Wasselonne R.	HZ	238
Wodli R. Georges	HY	242
Zix Pl. B.	JZ	
Zurich Pl. de	LZ	
Zurich R. de	LZ	
1ère-Armée R. de la	KZ	
22-Novembre R. du	HJYZ	

Sight	Grid	Ref.
Ancienne Douane	KZ	
Barrage Vauban	HZ	
Cathédrale Notre-Dame	KZ	
Église St-Guillaume	LZ	
Église St-Pierre-le-Jeune	JY	
Église St-Pierre-le-Vieux	HYZ	
Église St-Thomas	JZ	
Haras National	JZ	
Hôtel de Klinglin	KY	
Hôtel de la Chambre de Commerce	KZ	C
Hôtel de ville	KY	H
Hôtel des deux Ponts	KY	
Maison Kammerzell	KZ	E
Maison de Pasteur	KZ	F
Maison de la Télévision de FR3 Alsace	BS	K
Musée alsacien	KZ	M1
Musée d'Art moderne et contemporain	HZ	M3
Musée de l'Œuvre Notre-Dame	KZ	M6
Musée historique	KZ	M5
Musée zoologique de l'université et de la ville	CS	M8
Naviscope	CS	
Orangerie	CS	N
Palais Rohan et ses musées	KZ	
Palais de l'Europe	CS	
Palais des droits de l'Homme	CS	R
Palais du Rhin	KY	
Parc des Contades	BS	V
Parlement Européen	CS	
Petite France	HZ	
Pharmacie du Cerf	KZ	X

shares its chamber with the European Parliament, an important institution of the European Union; its members have been elected by universal suffrage since 1979; its role is consultative, financial and restraining.
Strasbourg shares with Brussels and Luxembourg the privilege of housing the main institutions of the European Union. Luxembourg houses the Court of Justice and the general secretariat of the **European Parliament**, whereas the Council, which has executive and legislative powers, and the Commission, which administers and controls, are both based in Brussels.

Cathédrale Notre-Dame★★★

Notre-Dame is one of Europe's finest Gothic cathedrals and owes a great deal of its charm to the pink sandstone from the Vosges with which it was built.
Work began in 1015 on a Romanesque edifice on the site of a temple dedicated to Hercules. The cathedral architects were later influenced by Gothic art newly introduced in Alsace. In 1365, the towers were joined together up to the platform and then the north tower was raised. In 1439, Johann Hültz from Cologne added the spire which confers on the cathedral its amazing outline.
The Reformation whose main spokesman was Martin Bucer (1491-1551), settled in Strasbourg in 1523 (see *SÉLESTAT*), was well received in Alsace.
For many years, the old and the new religions fought for supremacy in the cathedral, Luther's proposals being posted on the main door. The Protestant faith finally triumphed and the cathedral only returned to Catholicism in 1681, during the reign of Louis XIV. In 1725, Louis XV married Marie Leszczynska in the cathedral. In 1770, Marie-Antoinette, arriving from Vienna to marry the future Louis XVI, was welcomed here by Louis de Rohan.
In August and September 1870, Prussian shells set fire to the roof and in 1944, allied bombing damaged several parts of the edifice, since restored.

Exterior

West front★★★

Erwin of Steinbach was the architect in charge of building to slightly above the Apostles' Gallery. The **central doorway** is the most richly decorated. The tympanum is made of four historiated bands: the first three, dating from the 13C, are remarkably realistic; the fourth is modern. They depict scenes from the Old and New Testaments. The decoration of the **right doorway** illustrating the parable of the Wise Virgins and the Foolish Virgins, includes several famous statues (some of them have been replaced by copies, originals in the Musée de l'Œuvre Notre-Dame). The 14C statues of the **left doorway** represent the graceful Virtues striking down the Vices.

Spire★★★

Kids 328 steps. Open Apr–Sep daily 9am-7.30pm (Jul–Aug Fri–Sat 9am–10pm). Oct–Mar daily 10am–5.30pm. Closed 1 Jan, 1 May, 25 Dec. €3 (children under 18 €1.50). ☏03 88 43 60 32.

The west-front platform is 66m/217ft high. The tower rises another 40m/131ft above the platform and is surmounted by Johann Hültz's graceful spire, whose tip is 142m/466ft above ground level. Octagonal at the base, it consists of six tiers of openwork turrets housing the stairs and is topped by a double cross. From the platform there is a fine **view**★ of the old town and the Rhine Valley.

South side

The beautiful 13C **clock doorway**, the cathedral's oldest doorway, consists of two adjacent Romanesque doors separated by a statue of Solomon on a pedestal which recalls his famous Judgement. On the left of Solomon's statue, the Church, wearing a crown and looking strong and proud, holds the cross in one hand and the chalice in the other. On the right of the statue, the Synagogue, looking tired and sad, bends over in an effort to catch the fragments of her lance and the Tables of the Law which are dropping out of her hands. The band that covers her eyes is the symbol of error. The tympanum of

B. Kaufmann/MICHELIN

The Foolish Virgins – right-hand doorway of the cathedral

the left-hand door depicts the **Death of the Virgin**★★.

The outside dial of the astronomical clock can be seen above the doors.

North side

The late 15C **St Laurence doorway**★ illustrates the martyrdom of St Laurence (restored 19C). On the left are the statues of the Virgin Mary, the three kings and a shepherd; on the right are five statues including St Laurence (originals in the Musée de l'Œuvre Notre-Dame).

Interior

Open Mon–Sat 7–11.40am, 12.40–7pm. Sun 12.40-7pm.

The 12C, 13C and 14C **stained-glass windows**★★★ are magnificent, even though they have suffered over the years.

Nave and south aisle

Work on the nave began in the 13C. The stained glass of the clerestory windows and that of the aisles date from the 13C and 14C. Note the 50 or so statuettes decorating the hexagonal **pulpit**★★ (**1**), in true Flamboyant Gothic style, designed by Hans Hammer for the Reformation preacher Geiler of Kaysersberg.

The **organ**★★ (**2**) has a magnificent polychrome organ case (14C and 15C) spanning the full width of a bay. The corbelled loft is carved with a representation of Samson with, on either side, a town herald and a pretzel seller. These articulated characters would

Address Book

For coin ranges, see the Legend on the cover flap.

PRACTICAL INFORMATION

Park & Ride – Eight car parks situated on the outskirts of town are at the disposal of visitors *(from €2.40 to €2.70; tram ticket offered)* who are invited to take a tramway into town. The car parks are indicated by a square panel with the letters P+R on a violet background.

Tramways – *CTS. ☏03 88 77 70 70.* 4 lines link many tourist sights in and around Strasbourg. *Lines A, B and C operate Mon-Sun 4.30am-0.30am; line D operates Mon-Sat 7am-7pm except during the summer school holidays.*

Buses – *CTS. ☏03 88 77 70 70.* 26 bus routes crisscross the Strasbourg conurbation; in addition, 11 intercity buses link the city with the most beautiful Alsatian villages.

Tickets – A **Unipass** *(€1.20)* is a single-journey ticket valid for an hour on the bus and tram network; A **Tourpass** *(€3.10)* is valid for 24 hours for an unlimited number of journeys. A **Familipass** *(€4.20)* is valid for 24 hours for an unlimited number of journeys, for a family of 2 to 5 persons travelling together *(minimum: 1 adult and 1 child).*

Strasbourg Pass – Issued by the Tourist office, this pass allows free or half-price admission to 10 sights and monuments. *Valid for 3 days, it is on sale in the Tourist office information centres (place de la Cathédrale, place de la Gare and Pont de l'Europe) and in some hotels. €10.60.*

Guided tours – The town organises guided tours (1hr 30min) by approved guides. *€6.80. Enquire at the tourist office.*

Audio-guided tours – The itinerary, meant to last 1hr 30min, enables visitors to discover the cathedral, the old town and the Petite France at their own speed. A leaflet is given with the Walkman *(deposit: €30). 24-hour hiring cost: €6. Apply at the Tourist office.*

Mini-train – *Apr to Oct.* Departure place du Château, next to the cathedral, every half-hour or every hour depending on time of year. *€4.80. ☏03 88 77 70 03. Guided tour of the old town (50min) with a stop at Barrage Vauban.*

Vélocation – *4 rue Maire-Kuss – ☏03 88 43 64 30.* Bike hire service. Strasbourg has an extensive network of cycle tracks (300km/186.4mi).

Taxi 13 – *☏03 88 36 13 13.* This association proposes tours by taxi of the main tourist sights.

Boat trips on the Ill – ♿ Guided trips (1hr 10min)along the River Ill *(departure from the Palais Rohan pier)* taking in the Petite France, past Barrage Vauban, then the Faux Rempart moat as far as Palais de l'Europe. *Apr to Oct: 1hr 10min, departure every half-hour 9.30am-9pm; Nov-Dec and Jan-Mar: 4 departures a day 10.30am, 1pm, 2.30pm and 4.30pm. €6.80 (children €3.40).*

Boat trips on the Rhine and tour of the **harbour** – ♿ Departure from the Promenade Dauphine pier. *Jul-Aug: guided trip (2hr 15min) at 2.30pm. €8 (children €4). ☏03 88 84 13 13, www.strasbourgport.fr.*

Flights – *Aéro-Club d'Alsace – aérodrome du Polygone (BX) – Strasbourg-Neudorf – ☏03 88 34 00 98.* Prices vary *(€34 – €82)* according to the length of the flight, between 15min and 45min. Around Strasbourg: Château du Haut-Kœnigsbourg and the Rhine Valley.

WHERE TO EAT

Pommes de Terre et Cie – *4 r. de l'Écurie. ☏03 88 22 36 82, www.pommes-de-terre-cie.com, booking advisable.* If you want a change from *choucroute*, this friendly restaurant specialises in jacket potatoes accompanied by meat, fish or cheese. Blue and yellow decor. Local produce.

Aux Fines Gourmandises – *5 pl. Corbeau. ☏03 88 36 09 92 – brm1@noos.fr, booking advisable in summer.* Internet enthusiasts will love this spacious restaurant-tea room with its internet café. Wide choice of dishes including *tartes flambées* and *choucroute* and a delicious selection of pastries.

Flam's – *29 r. des Frères. ☏03 88 36 36 90 – freres@flams.fr, booking advisable at weekends.* This half-timbered house very close to the cathedral houses a restaurant specialising in *flam-*

mekueches. The three dining rooms and two cellars have been redecorated in lovely bright colours. Note the superb 15C painted ceiling.

⊜ **Au Hanneton** – *5 r. Ste-Madeleine. ☎03 88 36 93 76. closed Tue lunchtime and Mon. booking advisable.* This tiny winstub is faithful to Alsace tradition with its warm, intimate rustic decor, its friendly atmosphere and regional specialities such as fish *choucroute* and Munster cordon bleu. Lovely terrace for sunny days.

⊜ **Pfifferbriader** – *6 pl. du Marché-aux-Cochons-de-Lait. ☎03 88 32 15 43. closed Sun.* You immediately feel at home in this low-beamed dining room, with windows decorated with wine-making scenes. Tasty regional dishes including käseknefples, choucroute and bäeckehoffe are served along with classic French cuisine. Good choice of regional wines.

⊜ **Le Pigeon** – *23 r. des Tonneliers☎03 88 23 31 30. Closed 3 weeks in Jan and 3 weeks in Jun.* This typical winstub owes its name to two pigeons sculpted on the facade of one of the oldest houses in Strasbourg. Traditional Alsatian cooking.

⊜ **Zum Strissel** – *5 pl. de la Grande-Boucherie. ☎03 88 32 14 73. closed 27 Jan-7 Feb, 3 Jul- 2 Aug, Sun & Mon.* An authentic wine bar, run by the same family since 1920. The much-loved decor consists of wood panelling, decorative wrought iron, stained-glass windows depicting Bacchus and a 14C wine press. Regional cooking accompanied by Alsace wines, including the famous *kaefferkopf d'Ammerschwihr.*

⊜⊜ **Art Café** – (at the Musée d'Art Moderne et Contemporain) – *1 pl. Hans-Jean-Arp. ☎03 88 22 18 88. artcafe@mames.com, closed Mon, holidays and according to museum opening times.* You will be hard pushed to find a lovelier view of Strasbourg than that afforded by the terrace of this restaurant on the first floor of the modern art museum. The high design interior matches the location and the trendy cooking. Brunch on Sunday and holidays.

⊜⊜ **La Choucrouterie** – *20 r. St-Louis. ☎03 88 36 52 87. Closed Aug, Sat and Sun lunchtimes.* This 18C coaching inn was the last place in Strasbourg to make pickled cabbage. Feast and have fun in a slightly chaotic setting, enlivened by music, cabaret or theatre. Alsace cuisine served with local white wine.

⊜⊜ **Caveau Gurtlerhoft** – *13 pl. de la Cathédrale – ☎03 88 75 00 75.* Sample regional and traditional cooking in the lovely cellars of this 14C canonical building near the cathedral, with their splendid vaulting and massive pillars. Mouth-watering menus and fixed-price lunch. Unhurried service.

⊜⊜ **La Coccinelle** – *22 r. Ste-Madeleine. ☎03 88 36 19 27. Closed 15 Jul-15 Aug, Sat lunchtime and Sun – booking advisable.* Wood panelling, beams, copperware, stained-glass and vintage photos lend this winstub its typical Alsace feel. Among the regional dishes are some house specialities: the classic choucroute, but also *quenelles de foie* (liver quenelles), *jambonneau rôti* (roast knuckle of ham) and *bœuf gros sel* (boiled beef). Good choice of wines served by the jug.

⊜⊜ **Pont St-Martin** – *13-15 r. des Moulins. ☎03 88 32 45 13, www.pont-saint-martin.com, booking advisable.* This ever-popular restaurant in a venerable half-timbered building is in the heart of the picturesque Petite France district, just above the water. Typical Alsace interior of panelling, wainscoting and checked tablecloths. Regional cooking and frequent musical entertainment.

⊜⊜ **La Taverne du Sommelier** – *Ruelle de la Bruche (Krutenau distict). ☎03 88 24 24 10. Closed fortnight in Aug, 1 Jan, 25 Dec, booking essential.* The type of little restaurant it's always a pleasure to discover. The decor of yellow walls and lithographs is perfect to set off the intimate atmosphere. The cooking follows the seasons, while the wine list features wines from the Languedoc and the Rhône Valley.

⊜⊜ **Petit Ours** – *3 r. de l'Écurie (quartier des Tonneliers). ☎03 88 32 13 21, booking advisable.* Great little restaurant decorated with Tuscany-inspired colours. Light floods through the bay windows of one room, and the cellar is also very pleasant. Each dish (mostly fish) is characterised by a particular herb or spice.

Au Renard Prêchant – *34 r. de Zürich. ☎03 88 35 62 87. Cosed lunchtime on Sat, Sun and public holidays.* A 16C chapel in a pedestrianised street, which takes its name from the murals decorating its walls telling the story of the preaching fox. Rustic dining room, pretty terrace in summer, and reasonable fixed-price lunches.

Brasserie Kirn – *6-8 r. l'Outre. ☎03 88 52 03 03. Closed Sun evening.* This restaurant set in what used to be a butcher's is reminiscent of the 1900s with its lovely central cupola and attractive stained-glass windows. For more intimacy, try the tables in the booths. Brasserie-style food.

Le Clou – *3 r. du Chaudron. ☎03 88 32 11 67. Closed Wed lunchtime, Sun and holidays.* This small wine bar in a little street near the cathedral is eternally popular, with its typical decor, friendly atmosphere and good Alsace cooking. Well-known locally.

La Maison des Tanneurs, known as "Gerwerstub" – *42 r. du Bain-aux-Plantes. ☎03 88 32 79 70, maison.des.tanneurs@wanadoo.fr. Closed 29 Dec-21 Jan, Sun & Mon.* A picture-postcard restaurant on the banks of the Ill, in a cobbled street in la Petite France district. Inside, the rooms have dark wood panelling and Alsatian furniture. Typical regional cuisine includes an excellent choucroute garnie.

Buerieshel – *in the Parc de 'Orangerie. ☎03 88 45 56 65, www.buerehiesel.fr. Closed 30 Jul–23 Aug, 31 Dec–17 Jan, Sun dinner, Tue dinner and weekday lunchtime.* Famous chef Antine Westermann has handed over to his son Eric in the kitchens but this remains one of Alsace's gastronomic temples. The setting is a beautiful half-timbered farmhouse in the Parc de l'Orangerie.

WHERE TO STAY

Patricia – *R. du Puits. ☎03 88 32 14 60, www.hotelpatricia.fr. – booking advisable. 22 rooms –* €5. Two small wooden printers are a reminder that this venerable residence (listed façade) was the home of the regional printer in the 19C. It is now a hotel with quiet, bright rooms where TV is banished and smoking not permitted.

Chambre d'hôte La Maison du Charron – *15 r. Principale, 67370 Pfettisheim; 13km/8mi NW of Strasbourg on D 31 – ☎03 88 69 60 35. www.maisonducharron.com. . 5 rooms.* The owner of this 1858 property has done up the rooms himself, making each one individual by using different woods, while his wife's hobby is patchwork. Small garden, stabling for horses and two holiday cottages.

Couvent du Franciscain – *18 r. du Fg-de-Pierre. ☎03 88 32 93 93, www.hotel-franciscain.com. Closed 24 Dec-9 Jan . 43 rooms.* €8. At the end of a cul-de-sac you will find these two buildings, which are joined by a pleasant hall. We recommend the rooms in the new wing. The breakfast room is in the cellar. A good option within walking distance of the old city.

Hôtel de L'Ill – *8 r. des Bâteliers. ☎03 88 36 20 01 - info@hotel-ill.com. Closed 29 Dec-6 Jan . 27 rooms.* *€6.50.* Renovated hotel with family atmosphere. The rooms of differing sizes are impeccably clean, while the old-fashioned breakfast room has a cuckoo clock. You can take a boat trip on the River Ill just nearby.

Hôtel Pax – *24 r. du Fg-National – ☎03 88 32 14 54 – info@paxhotel.com – closed 23 Dec-4 Jan – 106 rooms – €7 – restaurant* . A family hotel in a busy street on the edge of the city's old district. Its plain rooms are well kept, and its restaurant serves regional dishes. You can eat in the vine-shaded courtyard in summer.

Hôtel Beaucour – *5 r. des Bouchers. ☎03 88 76 72 00 . www.hotel-beaucour.com. 49 rooms. €11.* Those who like staying in lovely places will enjoy this elegant city-centre hotel spread out over two 18C houses. Attractions include the flower-decked courtyard, cosy rooms and regional furniture.

Hôtel Cardinal de Rohan – *17 r. Maroquin. ☎03 88 32 85 11. www.hotel-rohan.com. 36 rooms. €10.50.* Named after the nearby palais de Rohan, this little hotel is on a pedestrian street near the cathedral. Its quiet, pleasant rooms are furnished in Louis XV, Louis XVI or rustic style; those on the south side have air conditioning.

Hôtel du Dragon – *2 r. Écarlate. ☎03 88 35 79 80. hotel@dragon.fr. 32 rooms.* *€11.* A 17C residence with a resolutely contemporary interior: shades of grey, designer furniture, minimalist bedrooms and art exhibitions.

ON THE TOWN

Au Brasseur – *22 r. des Veaux. ☎03 88 36 12 13. daily 11.30am-1am. Closed 25 Dec, 1 Jan.* This micro-brasserie proposes a wide variety of beers brewed on the premises. Locals also come here to dine and for jazz, rock and blues concerts at weekends.

Bar à Champgane– *5 r. des Moulins. ☎03 88 76 43 43. www.regent-hotels.com – 5pm-2am.* This is the hotel bar of the luxurious Regent Petite France, which was a mill for 800 years and then an ice manufacturer until the late 1980s. No effort has been spared to ensure that you spend a relaxing evening here: the fine contemporary decor, the riverside terrace, discreet background jazz, a good choice of cocktails and the best champagnes.

Café de l'Opéra (in the opera house) – *Pl. Broglie. ☎ 03 88 75 48 26 .Mon-Sat 11am-1.30am, Sun 2-8pm. closed 25 Jul- 16 Aug, 24-26 Dec and 31 Dec.* The purple and gold decor in this theatre bar evokes the world of the stage. A classy setting for an intimate date over a glass of whisky or wine – or a hot chocolate with the family. Painting and photography exhibitions.

SHOWTIME

Demandez le programme! – To find out the programme of theatres, concerts, seminars, exhibitions and sporting events, get a copy of the monthy *Strasbourg actualités* or *Hebdoscope*, with weekly listings for arts and shows.

Opéra National du Rhin – *19 pl. Broglie. ☎03 88 75 48 23 – www.opera-national-du-rhin.com. Box office: Mon-Fri 11am-6pm, Sat 11am-4pm, and 45min before performance. Closed mid-Jul –mid-Aug. €5.50–€75.* The Rhine Opera was created in 1972 to manage the opera houses in Strasbourg, Mulhouse and Colmar. Apart from the classic opera repertoire, the programme includes high quality chamber music, dance and recitals. The auditorium can seat 1 142 people.

SHOPPING

Markets – Markets generally open from 7am-1pm. Traditional market Tue and Fri place Kléber, Wed rue Krutenau and rue de St-Gothard. Farmers' market on Sat, pl. du Marché-aux-Poissons. Flea market (9am-6pm) Wed and Sat, r. du Vieil-Hôpital and pl. de la Grande-Boucherie. Book market (9am-6pm) Wed and Sat, pl. and r. Gutenberg and r. des Hallebardes. Christmas market in Dec.

Un Noël en Alsace – *10 r. des Dentelles, Petite France. ☎ 03 88 32 32 32 – www.noelenalsace.fr. Mon–Sat 10am-12.30pm, 1.30-7pm (from Jul, Sun 2-6pm). closed Jan-Feb.* It's Christmas every day in this 16C building in the heart of the Petite France district. Tinsel, little wood figurines, twinkling stars and coloured baubles: you name it, they have it!

Au Paradis des Pains d'Epices – *14 r. des Dentelles, Petite France. ☎03 88 32 33 34 32 – www.paindesoleil.com – daily 9am-7pm except Mon mornings.* Scents of orange, honey, cinnamon and cardamom greet you as you enter this tiny shop located in a timber-framed house dating from 1643. Heaven on earth for gingerbread fans: soft or crunchy, sweet or savoury, even iced varieties to tempt you.

CALENDAR

European Fair – *Early Sep, Parc des Expositions du Wacken.* Over 1000 exhibitors representing a wide range of activities. *Enquiries: ☎03 88 37 21 21.*

Strasbourg, Christmas Capital - Countless events and shows all over town: Christmas market (Christkindelsmärik), illuminations, giant Christmas tree, exhibitions, nativity scene and concerts.

sometimes come to life during sermons to entertain the congregation. St Catherine's chapelcontains an epitaph of the Death of Mary (**3**), dating from 1480, and 14C stained glass.

South transept

The **Angels** or **Last Judgement**★★ pier (**4**), erected in the 13C, stands in the centre.

Astronomical Clock★ (5)

The cathedral's most popular feature was designed by mathematicians and built by Swiss clock-makers between 1550 and 1574, it stopped in 1780. Schwilgué, a native of Strasbourg, studied it for thirty years and then rebuilt it between 1838 to 1842.

The seven days of the week are represented by chariots led by gods, who appear through an opening beneath the dial: Diana on Mondays, then Mars, Mercury, Jupiter, Venus, Saturn and Apollo.

A series of automata strikes twice every quarter hour. The hours are struck by Death. On the last stroke, the second angel of the Lion's Gallery reverses his hourglass.

The astronomical clock is half an hour behind normal time. The midday chiming occurs at 12.30pm. As soon as it happens, a great parade takes place in the recess at the top of the clock. The Apostles pass in front of Christ and bow to him; Jesus blesses them as the cock, perched on the left-hand tower, flaps his wings and crows three times, a reminder of Peter's denial of Christ.

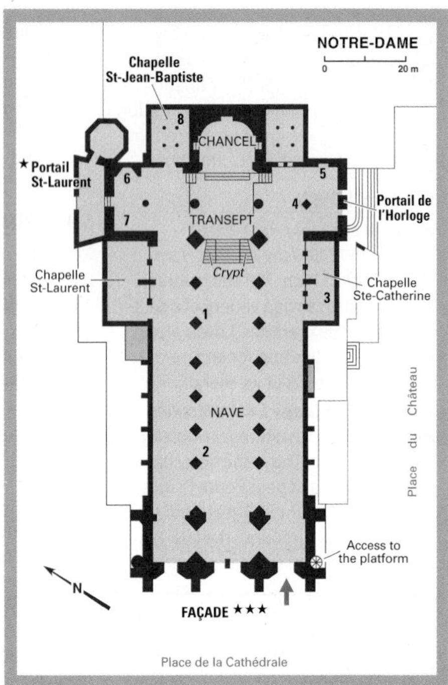

North transept

This contains splendid Flamboyant Gothic christening fonts (**6**). An unusual stone group represents Christ on the Mount of Olives (**7**). The 13C and 14C stained glass depicts emperors of the Holy Roman Empire.

Chapelle St-Jean-Baptiste

The 13C chapel, attributed to Erwin, contains the tomb of Bishop Conrad of Lichtenberg (**8**) who began the construction of the west front.

Tapestries★★

The cathedral owns 14 splendid 17C tapestries depicting scenes from the Life of the Virgin, designed by Philippe de Champaigne, Charles Poerson and Jacques Stella. They are hung in the nave on special occasions.

Palais de Rohan and its Museums

Palais de Rohan★

The beautiful classical bishop's palace was built in 1704 for Cardinal Armand de Rohan-Soubise by royal architect Robert de Cotte.

Musée des Arts décoratifs★★

Open Wed–Mon Tue 10am-6pm. Closed 1 Jan, Good Friday, 1 May, 1 and 11 Nov, 25 Dec. €4, no charge 1st Sun of the month. 03 88 52 50 00. www.musees-strasbourg.org.

The Decorative Arts Museum is housed on the ground floor and in the stables wing and Hans-Hang pavilions.

The **Grands Appartements** rank among the finest 18C French interiors. The synod room, the king's bedroom, the assembly room, the cardinals' library, the morning room and the emperor's bedroom are particularly remarkable for their decoration, ceremonial furniture, tapestries and 18C paintings.
The museum, which is devoted to the **arts and crafts of Strasbourg and eastern France** from the end of the 17C to the mid-19C, containsone of the most important **ceramics collections**★★ in France, including faience and porcelain from the Strasbourg and Haguenau manufacture, founded and run by the **Hannong** family from 1721 to 1781, and the Niderviller manufacture, founded in 1748 by the Baron of Beyerlé, the director of Strasbourg's royal mint.
Look for the "blue" period pieces, the transitional polychrome style, terrines shaped like animals or vegetables and above all magnificent crimson floral decorations which inspired many European manufactures after 1750.

Musée des Beaux-Arts★

Same conditions as the Musée des Arts décoratifs.
The Fine Art Museum is housed on the 1st and 2nd floors of the main building.
Italian painting (primitive and Renaissance works) is very well represented by Filippino Lippi, Botticelli, Cima da Conegliano (*St Sebastian*) and Correggio (*Judith and the Servant*).
The **Spanish School** includes works by Zurbarán, Murillo, Goya and above all a *Mater Dolorosa* by El Greco.
The collection of paintings from the 15C-17C **Dutch School** is particularly rich: fine *Christ of Mercy* by Simon Marmion, *Engaged Couple* by Lucas of Leyden, several works by Rubens, *St John* (portrait of the artist) by Van Dyck, and *Going for a Walk* by Pieter de Hooch.
The French and Alsatian schools of the 17C-19C are illustrated by several works including *The Beautiful Woman from Strasbourg* by N de Largillière (1703).
The museum also has a fine collection of **still-life paintings**, among them the **Bunch of Flowers** by Velvet Brueghel.

Musée archéologique★★

Same conditions as the Musée des Arts décoratifs. Located in the basement.
The archaeological collections concern the prehistory and early history of Alsace from 600 000 BC to AD 800. Numerous objects illustrate the Bronze-Age and Iron-Age civilisations: ceramics, weapons and tools, jewellery, ceremonial plates and dishes imported from Greece or Italy, and the Ohnenheim funeral chariot. The Roman section includes remarkable stone carvings and inscriptions, fine glassware and everyday objects. Among outstanding Merovingian items are the Baldenheim helmet and military decorations from Ittenheim.

Other Sights

Old Town★★★ 1

Allow one day
The old town nestles round the cathedral, on the island formed by the two branches of the River Ill.

Place de la Cathédrale★

The **Pharmacie du Cerf** on the corner of rue Mercière, which dates from 1268, was the oldest chemist's in France until it closed in 2000. On the north side of the cathedral, the **Maison Kammerzell**★ (1589), restored 1954 and now a restaurant, has splendid carved wood.

Place du Château

Here are the Musée de l'Œuvre Notre-Dame (see MUSEUMS) and the **Palais Rohan**★.

Follow rue de Rohan then turn right onto rue des Cordiers.

Musée des Arts Décoratifs
Dish from the Hannong manufacture

Place du Marché-aux-Cochons-de-Lait★

A charming square lined with old houses including a 16C house with wooden galleries. The adjacent place de la Grande-Boucherie looks typically Alsatian.

▶ *Turn left onto rue du Vieux-Marché-aux-Poissons.*

The **Ancienne Douane** (former customs house) is on the right; it was rebuilt in 1965 for temporary exhibitions.

Pont du Corbeau

This is the former "execution" bridge from which those condemned for infanticides and parricides, tied up in sacks, were plunged into the water.

▶ *A carriage entrance at No 1 quai des Bateliers leads to the Cour du Corbeau.*

Cour du Corbeau★

Once a fashionable inn, which welcomed illustrious guests, such as Turenne, King Johann-Casimir of Poland, Frederick the Great and Emperor Joseph II, the picturesque courtyard dates from the 14C.

Quai St-Nicolas

The embankment is lined with some fine old houses; three are now the Musée Alsacien: *see MUSEUMS*).
Louis Pasteur lived at No 18.

▶ *Cross the Pont St-Nicolas and take quai St-Thomas.*

Église St-Thomas

This five-naved church, rebuilt at the end of the 12C, became a Lutheran cathedral in 1529. It contains the 18C mausoleum of the **Maréchal de Saxe**★★ sculpted by Pigalle. The allegorical sculpture represents France weeping and holding the marshal's hand while trying to push Death aside. Strength, symbolised by Hercules, gives way to grief and Love can be seen crying as he puts out his torch. On the left, a lion (Holland), a leopard (England) and an eagle (Austria), are represented vanquished, next to crumpled flags.

▶ *Walk along rue de la Monnaie to the Pont St-Martin.*

The bridge offers a fine **view**★ of the tanners' district. The river divides into four branches (watermills, dams and locks can still be seen).

▶ *Walk along rue des Moulins then follow the edge of the island.*

La Petite France★★

Once the fishermen's, tanners' and millers' district, this is today one of the most interesting and best-preserved areas of the old town. Quai de la Petite France runs alongside the canal, offering a

R. Mattès/MICHELIN

La Petite France

romantic **view★** particularly at dusk of the old houses reflected in the water.

Ponts Couverts★

This is the name given to three successive bridges spanning the River Ill; each guarded by a massive square tower, remaining from the 14C fortifications. The bridges once had wooden roofs.

Turn right just before the last tower and walk along quai de l'Ill.

Barrage Vauban

60 steps to Panoramic terrace Open daily 9am-7.30pm. No charge. ☎03 88 60 90 90.

There's a striking **view★★** of the Ponts Couverts, la Petite France and the cathedral from the terrace of the casemate bridge (part of Vauban's fortifications).

Go back over the Ponts Couverts.

Rue du Bain-aux-Plantes★★

The street is lined with timber-framed corbelled houses dating from the Alsatian Renaissance (16C-17C). Note, the tanners' house (Gerwerstub, No 42), from 1572, and Nos 31, 33, 27 and 25 (1651).

Return to Grand'Rue.

Église St-Pierre-le-Vieux

This church consists of two adjacent churches: one Catholic and the other Protestant. The north transept of the Catholic church (rebuilt in 1866) contains 16C carved-wood panels by Veit Wagner, depicting scenes from the Life of St Peter and St Valerus. The **scenes★** from the Passion (late 15C-early 16C), at the end of the chancel, are believed to be by Henri Lutzelmann, a native of Strasbourg. The south transept contains **painted panels★** by members of the Schongauer School (15C).

Continue along Grand'Rue lined with 16C-18C houses then rue Gutenberg.

On **place Gutenberg** stand the Renaissance **Hôtel de la Chambre de Commerce** and Gutenberg's statue by David d'Angers. No 52 rue du Vieux-Marché-aux-Poissons is the birthplace of Jean Arp (1887-1966), a sculptor, painter, poet and major protagonist of modern art.

Return to the cathedral by rue Mercière.

Old Town via Place Broglie 2

Start in front of the cathedral and follow rue des Grandes Arcades.

Place Kléber

On the north side is an 18C building called "l'Aubette" because the garrison came here at dawn (*aube*) to get their orders. In the centre is a statue of Strasbourg native **Jean-Baptiste Kléber** (1753-1800), a brilliant general of the Revolutionary period, who is buried beneath it. Reliefs depict his victories at Altenkirchen and Heliopolis.

Église St-Pierre-le-Jeune

Open Palm Sunday–1 Nov Mon 1-6pm, Tue-Sat 10.30am-6pm, Sun 2.30-6pm. ☎03 88 32 41 61.

Three successive churches have stood on this site. All that remains of the first church is a tomb with five funeral recesses, believed to date from the end of the Roman occupation (4C AD); the lovely restored cloisters belonged to the church built in 1031. The present Protestant church (13C, restored 1900) contains a fine Gothic **rood screen** decorated with paintings from 1620.

Walk along quai Schoepfin.

Place Broglie

This square was laid out in the 18C. On the south side is the **town hall★** built by Massol, former residence of the counts of Hanau-Lichtenberg. At the eastern end are the municipal theatre (1820) and the **Hôtel de Klinglin** (1736).

Rue du Dôme and adjacent streets

The old aristocratic district adjoining place Broglie has guarded several 18C mansions, particularly rue Brûlée: the **Hôtel des Deux-Ponts** (1754) at No 13, the bishop's residence at No 16, and at No 9 the town hall's side entrance.

The 19C German Quarter

After 1870, the Germans erected a great number of monumental public buildings in neo-Gothic Renaissance style. They intended to transfer the town centre to the north-east, and include the orangery and the university. This district with its broad avenues is a rare example of Prussian architecture.

Place de la République

This vast square has a shady circular garden in the centre, with a war memorial by Drivier (1936). On the left is the Palais du Rhin, the former imperial palace (1883-88); on the right are the National Theatre, housed in the former Landtag Palace, and the National Library.

Parc des Contades

This park situated north of place de la République is named after the military governor of Alsace who had it laid out. On the edge of the park, the **Synagogue de la Paix** was built in 1955 to replace the synagogue destroyed in 1940.

Maison de la Télévision FR3-Alsace

This was built in 1961; a monumental (30x6m/98x20ft) ceramic by Lurçat, symbolising the Creation, decorates the concave façade of the auditorium.

R. Mattès/MICHELIN

Place Kléber

Capital of Europe

Palais de l'Europe★

Allée Spach, av de l'Europe. Guided tour (1hr) by reservation. Service des visites, Conseil de l'Europe, 67075 Strasbourg Cedex. ☎03 88 41 20 29.

The palace houses the **European Council**, including the council of ministers, the parliamentary assembly and the international secretariat. The buildings, inaugurated in 1977 were designed by the French architect Henri Bernard. The palace contains 1 350 offices, meeting rooms, a library and the largest parliamentary amphitheatre in Europe. The ceiling is supported by a 12-ribbed wooden fan, a symbol which is repeated in the palace's entrance hall.

Opposite, the **Parc de l'Orangerie**★ was laid out by Le Nôtre in 1692 and remodelled in 1804 for Empress Josephine's stay, it includes a lake, a waterfall and a zoo where storks are a familiar sight. The Josephine pavilion is used for temporary exhibitions, plays and concerts.

Palais des Droits de l'Homme

Nearby, on the banks of the River Ill, stands the futuristic new Palais des Droits de l'Homme, designed by Richard Rogers, which houses the European Court of Human Rights.

Other Museums

Musée alsacien★★

23-25 quai St-Nicolas. Jul–Aug & Jan–Mar Wed–Mon 10am-6pm. Apr–Jun & Sep–Dec Wed–Mon noon-6pm. Closed 1 Jan, Good Friday, 1 May, 1 & 11 Nov, 25 Dec. €4, no charge 1st Sun of the month. ☎ 03 88 52 50 01. www.musees-strasbourg.org.

This museum of popular art, located in a maze of quaint rooms in three 16C-17C houses, gives a good insight into the history, customs and traditions of Alsace. Displays include costumes, prints, toys, flour-spitting masks that used to decorate mills, and reconstructed interiors such as an apothecary's laboratory and bedrooms furnished with box beds, painted furniture and vast stoves.

Musée de l'Œuvre Notre-Dame★★

3 place du Château. Open Tue–Sun 10am-6pm. Closed 1 Jan, Good Friday, 1 May, 1 & 11 Nov, 25 Dec. €4, no charge 1st Sun of the month. ☎03 88 52 50 00. www.musees-strasbourg.org.

The **Œuvre Notre-Dame** is a unique institution founded to collect donations for the building, upkeep and renovation of the cathedral. The first recorded donation dates from 1205.

Medieval and Renaissance Alsatian art is displayed in the Maison de l'Œuvre (1347 and 1578-85), the Hôtellerie du Cerf (14C) and in a 17C house, surrounding four small courtyard. The Cour du Cerf is planted with vegetables and medicinal and ornamental plants to recreate the Paradisgärtlein depicted in medieval Alsatian paintings and prints.

The hall which contains pre-Romanesque sculpture leads to the Romanesque sculpture rooms and rooms displaying 12C and 13C stained glass, some of it from the Romanesque cathedral; note the cloisters of Eschau (12C) and the **Christ's Head**★★ from Wissembourg, the oldest representational stained glass known (c 1070).

From there, the Cour de l'Œuvre, with a partly Flamboyant Gothic and partly Renaissance decor, leads to the hall of the builders' and stone masons' guild, whose woodwork and ceiling date from 1582. Next comes the main room of the Hôtellerie du Cerf where 13C works originally decorating the cathedral are exhibited.

The first floor houses an important collection of 15C-17C gold plate from Strasbourg. The second floor is devoted to the evolution of Alsatian art in the 15C, including **paintings**★★ of the Alsatian School: Conrad Witz and Alsatian primitives, and Nicolas of Leyden.

A 1580 spiral staircase returns to the first floor **Renaissance wing**, where a room is devoted to Hans Baldung Grien (1484-1545), a pupil of Dürer, who was the main representative of the Renaissance in Strasbourg.

Musée d'Art Moderne et Contemporain★★

1 place Hans-Jean-Arp. ♿ Open Tue–Sun 11am-7pm, Thu noon-10pm, Sun 10am-6pm. Closed 1 Jan, Good Friday, 1 May, 1 & 11 Nov, 25 Dec. €5, no charge 1st Sun of the month. ☎03 88 23 31 31. www.musees-strasbourg.org.

Standing on the bank of the River Ill, this modern building was designed by Adrien Fainsilber, the architect of the Cité des Sciences et de l'Industrie at La Villette in Paris.

Modern art from 1850 to 1950

Ground floor. The display covers the diverse artistic strands, which have left their stamp on the history of modern art, from the academic works of William Bouguereau to abstract works by Kandinsky, Poliakoff and Magneli. Renoir, Sisley and Monet illustrate Impressionism, and post-Impressionist and Nabis paintings Signac, Gauguin, Vuillard and Denis. Art at the turn of the last century is represented by a group of Symbolist works, notably Klimt's *Plenitude*.

Several rooms are devoted to **Jean Arp** and his wife Sophie Taeuber-Arp, who, in collaboration with Theo Van Doesburg, made a series of stained-glass panels recreating the constructivist interiors (1926-28) of l'Aubette on place Kléber. There is a room of Arp's sculpture and items connected with the Bauhaus, the De Stijl movement and Modernism (furniture by Eileen Gray and Marcel Breuer, dining room designed by Kandinsky).

As a reaction against the First World War, the Dadaists signed derisory even absurd works (Janco, Schwitters). Following in their footsteps, the Surrealists Brauner, Ernst and Arp tried to introduce the world of dreams into their works.

Furniture by **Charles Spindler**, sculpture by François-Rupert Carabin, Ringel d'Illzach and Bugatti, and stained glass made in Strasbourg testify to the renewal of fine and decorative arts in Alsace around 1900.

The **Salle Doré** was specially designed for the huge painting by Gustave Doré (1869), depicting Christ leaving the prætorium.

Modern art from 1950 onwards

First floor. In the first room, works by Picasso, Richier, Pinot-Gallizio, Kudo and Baselitz reflect postwar uncertainty. The next room illustrates the Fluxus movement with Filliou and Brecht, and Italian Arte povera with Kounellis, Penone and Merz, using so-called poor materials. The 1960s and 1970s are represented by the experiments of Buren, Parmentier, Toroni, Rutault, Morellet and Lavier, and the 1980s and 1990s by Grand, Balka, Boltanski, Ramette, Blaussyld and Pérez. There are also installations by Colin-Thiébaut and Sarkis, both of whom have worked in Strasbourg.

Driving Tour

Port Autonome and the Rhine

25km/16mi circuit – allow 1hr 30min. Strasbourg is one of the most important ports along the River Rhine. Its impact on eastern France's economy equals that of a major maritime port because of the exceptionally good navigable conditions and the network of waterways, railway lines and roads linking the whole region with Western and Central Europe.

▸ *From Pont d'Austerlitz, follow N 4. Shortly before the Pont Vauban, turn right onto rue du Havre, which runs parallel to the René-Graff dock.*

Rue de la Rochelle, which prolongs it, leads to the southern, most modern part of the port, with its three main docks: Auguste-Detœuf (cereals), Gaston-Hælling and Adrien-Weirich (containers and heavy goods) and basin IV.

▸ *Turn back along rue de la Rochelle and rue du Havre. Then turn right and cross the Pont Vauban. Avenue du Pont de l'Europe leads to the Rhine.*

The river, which at this point is 250m/273yd wide, is spanned by the **Pont de l'Europe** (1960) consisting of two metal arches and linking Strasbourg with Kehl on the German side.

▸ *Turn back and bear right to follow rue Coulaux, then rue du Port-du-Rhin (view of the Bassin du Commerce).*

From the **Pont d'Anvers**, the view embraces several docks.

▸ *Drive over the bridge and turn right onto rue du Général-Picquart skirting the Bassin des Remparts where the Naviscope is moored at no.18.*

Kids This former barge-driver has been turned into a **Musée du Rhin et de la Navigation** (Rhine Museum). *Open Jul–Aug Mon, Thur–Sat 3–5pm, Tue, Wed, Sun & holidays 2.30-5.30pm. Rest of the year Tue, Wed, Sun & holidays 2.30-5.30pm. Closed 1 Jan, 1 May, 1 Nov, 25 Dec. €4 (children €2.50). ☎03 88 60 22 23.*

▸ *Take rue Boussingault then cross the Marne-Rhine canal and turn right along quai Jacoutot.*

From the **Pont Jean-Millot**, at the entrance of the Albert-Auberger dock, the view takes in the Rhine and the north entrance of the harbour. The Marne-Rhine canal and three docks open into the northern outer harbour.

THE SUNDGAU★

HAUT-RHIN. MICHELIN LOCAL MAP 315: H/I-11

The southernmost area of Alsace in the foothills of the Jura has been deeply carved by the tributaries of the upper Ill; the resulting hills and limestone cliffs are crowned by forests and the valleys are dotted with numerous lakes – full of carp, a local gastronomic speciality – pastures and rich crops. Flower-decked farmhouses often have timber-framed walls roughcast in an ochre colour or clad with wooden planks. Altkirch is the only town of any importance, but many prosperous villages are scattered along the rivers or across sunny hillsides.

- **Tourist Office**: Espace Mazarin, route de Lucelle, 68480 Ferrette. ☎03 89 08 23 88, www.jura-alsacien.net
- **Orient Yourself**: The southernmost area of Alsace forms a lozenge bordered by the Swiss frontier and the Mulhouse-Basle and Mulhouse-Belfort motorway.
- **Also See**: Altkirch and Mulhouse.

Excursion

Round Tour from Altkirch

117km/73mi – allow half a day

Altkirch – *See ALTKIRCH.*

Drive E out of Altkirch on the D 419 along the south bank of the River Ill.

St-Morand

This village is a place of pilgrimage. The **church** contains the beautiful 12C sarcophagus of saint, Morand, who converted the Sungdau to Christianity, and was reputed to cure headaches.

The road continues along the Thalbach Valley before reaching the plateau. It then runs down towards the Rhine offering views of the Jura mountains, the Basle depression and the Black Forest.

As you enter Ranspach-le-Bas, turn off D 419 to the right. On leaving Ranspach-le-Haut, turn left towards Folgensbourg, where you turn S onto D 473 then left onto D 21bis to St-Blaise. Then take D 9bis to Leymen.

Address Book

For coin ranges, see the Legend on the cover flap.

WHERE TO STAY AND EAT

À l'Arbre Vert – *17 r. Principale, 68560 Heimersdorf, 9km/5.5mi S of Altkirch towards Ferrette. ☎03 89 07 11 40. Closed Mon & Tue.* Fried carp is so famous in Sundgau that there is a route you can follow to discover more about it. This family restaurant is a good place to sample it in a friendly atmosphere.

Le Moulin Bas – *1 r. Raedersdorf, 68480 Ligsdorf, 4km/2.5mi S of Ferrette on D 41 and D 432. ☎03 89 40 31 25 – info@le-moulin-bas.fr Closed Sep-Apr and Tue.* This watermill near the Swiss border is a lovely place to stay, surrounded by a garden through which the Ill flows. Typical local cooking in a country decor on the ground floor, and slightly more refined cuisine upstairs. Very pleasant bedrooms.

Chambre d'hôte Moulin de Huttingue – *68480 Oltingue, 1.5km/1mi S of Oltingue on D 21B. ☎03 89 40 72 91. Closed Jan & Feb. – 4 rooms.* Beside the Ill, which is only a stream here, this former flourmill has combined part of its original interior, such as the lovely wooden pillars, with a modern decor. The superb loft room, with its roof timbers, is definitely worth booking. Pretty garden and terrace in summer. Holiday cottage.

Château du Landskron

30min on foot there and back.

This castle, believed to date from the 11C, is in ruins. Reinforced by Vauban in the 17C, it was besieged and destroyed in 1814. From its privileged position on a height overlooking the border, the view embraces the small town of Leymen below and, farther north, the forested Sundgau and Basle region.

Return to St-Blaise and continue along the upper Ill Valley.

Oltingue

In the centre of this pretty village, the **Maison du Sundgau** *(Open mid-Jun–Sep Tue, Thu, Sat 3-6pm, Sun & holidays 11am-noon, 3-6pm; Mar–mid-Jun & Oct-Dec Sun 2-5pm; Closed Jan–Feb, €2, 03 89 40 79 24)* highlights regional architectural styles and displays furniture, crockery and kitchen utensils illustrating rural life in the past, including kugelhopf tins appropriately shaped for different feast days.

In Rædersdorf, continue along D 21B towards Kiffis.

Hippoltskirch

The **chapel** *(Open Sun 11am-5pm, other days by appointment; 03 89 40 44 46)* has an unusual painted coffered ceiling and a painted-wood balustrade along the gallery. Naive ex-voto paintings on the walls are dedicated to a miracle-working statue of the Virgin, on the left of the nave.

Leave Kiffis on your left and follow the international road (D 21BIII) which skirts the Swiss border (and briefly crosses it beyond Moulin-Neuf) along the bottom of a wooded coomb.

Lucelle

This lakeside village at the southern tip of Alsace, once stood next to a wealthy Cistercian abbey.

Drive N along D 432.

Ferrette★

The former capital of the Sundgau area was, from the 10C onwards, the residence of independent counts whose authority extended over much of Alsace. This region became the property of the House of Austria in the 14C and was ceded to France in 1648 by the Treaty of Westphalia. The prince of Monaco is still entitled to be called Count of Ferrette. The small town, lying in a picturesque **site**★, is overlooked by the ruins of two castles built on an impressive rocky spur rising to an altitude of 612m/2008ft.

Drive to Bouxwiller along D 473.

Bouxwiller

This pretty village adorned with fountains is built on a hillside. The **Église St-Jacques** contains a lovely 18C gilt-wood pulpit, from the Luppach Monastery, and an elaborate Baroque altarpiece.

D 9bis follows the upper Ill Valley to Grentzingen.

Grentzingen★

The characteristic timber-framed houses of this flower-decked village are lined up at right angles to the road. A few still have their original ochre colour.

Turn left in Grentzingen and continue through the village or Riespach.

Feldbach

The restored 12C Romanesque **church** has two parts, one for the nuns and one for the congregation.

Return to Altkirch by the D 432.

THANN★

HAUT-RHIN. POPULATION 8 033

MICHELIN LOCAL MAP 315: G-10

This small southern town is renowned for having the most richly decorated Gothic church in the Alsace. The steep, south-facing vineyards and volcanic soils of the Rangen mountain produce one of the most reputed of all the Alsace wine appellations, celebrated since the 16C.

- **Tourist Office**: 7 rue de l'Armée, 68800 Thann. ☎03 89 37 96 20, www.ot-thann.fr
- **Orient Yourself**: 21km/13mi. E of Mulhouse on the N66.
- **Also See**: The Thur Valley and the Route des Vins.

A Bit of History

From legend to history

The foundation of Thann is steeped in legend. When Bishop Thiébaut (Theobald) of Gubbio in Umbria died in 1160, he bequeathed his episcopal ring to his most trusted servant who took it, together with the bishop's thumb, hid it inside his staff and arrived in Alsace the following year. One night, he went to sleep in a fir forest after having driven his staff into the ground. In the morning, he was unable to lift it out of the ground. At the same time, three bright lights appeared above three fir trees; the lord of the nearby castle of Engelbourg saw the lights and arriving promptly, decided to build a chapel on the very site where the miracle had occurred. The chapel soon became a popular place of pilgrimage and the town of Thann, meaning fire tree, grew up around it. Each June, three fir trees are burnt in front of the church in commemoration.

Sights

Collégiale St-Thiébaut★★

The Gothic architecture of the collegiate church (14C-early 16C) shows a continuous progression towards the Flamboyant Gothic style. The west front has a remarkable 15m/49ft high **doorway**★★ with an elegant tympanum; on the north side there is a Flamboyant Gothic doorway with fine 15C statues.

Inside, a polychrome wood statue of the wine-growers' Virgin, carved c 1510, is bonded to the central buttress pier of the pentagonal chapel (access from

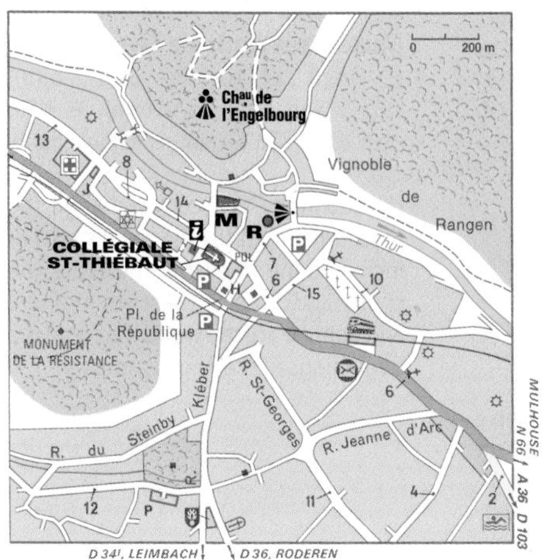

THANN	
Aspach R. d'	2
Clemenceau R.	4
Gaulle R. Gén.-de	6
Jacquot R. A.	7
Lattre-de-Tassigny Pl. de	8
Lebert R. H.	10
Paix R. de la	11
Poincaré Av.	12
St-Jacques R.	13
1ère-Armée R. de la	14
7-Août R. du	15

Musée des Amis de Thann	M
Tour des Sorcières	R

R. Mattès/MICHELIN

Under the gaze of the Witch's Eye

the south aisle). At the end of the aisle, in St-Thiébaut's Chapel, a polychrome wood statue of the saint dating from 1520 stands on the altar. The chancel is adorned with 15C statues of the 12 Apostles. However, the outstanding feature is the 15C oak **stalls**★★, which express all the fantasy of the Middle Ages in a profusion of carved foliage, gnomes and comic characters. The chancel is flooded with light pouring in through eight superb 15C **stained-glass windows**★.

For coin ranges, see the Legend on the cover flap.

WHERE TO STAY AND EAT

Le Moschenross – *42 r. du Gén. de Gaulle. 03 89 37 00 86, www.le-moschenross.com. Closed 1-20 Jul. 23 rooms .€6.50.* Dominated by the Rangon vineyard, this hotel-restaurant serves traditional cooking in a spacious dining room.

Hostellerie Alsacienne – *R. du Mar.-Foch, 68290 Masevaux, 15km/9.3mi SW of Thann. 03 89 82 45 25, philippe.battman@wanadoo.fr. Closed 25 Oct-8 Nov, 24 Dec-3 Jan and Mon. 8 rooms .* €7. Situated in a pedestrian street, this rustic inn serves appetising local dishes. Comfortable rooms. The menu is simple but there is enough choice, and the interior is interesting, with its carved wooden panelling. A few rooms are available.

L'Œil de la Sorcière

1hr on foot there and back.

Engelbourg Castle, built by the counts of Ferrette, became the property of the Habsburgs and, in 1648, of the king of France who, 10 years later, gave it to Cardinal Mazarin. In 1673, Louis XIV ordered its destruction. The lower part of the keep remained intact – its centre appears to be looking over the plain, hence its nickname, the "witch's eye."

A monument to the Alsatian Resistance stands on top of the Staufen, across the valley.

Musée des Amis de Thann

Open Jul-Aug Tue–Sun 2-6pm. Jun & Sep Fri–Sun 2-6pm. €2.50. 03 89 37 27 57, www.genealogiethann.org.

Housed in the 1519 corn exchange, the museum illustrates the town's history including the vineyards, the castle, the church and cult of St Theobald, furniture and popular art, the world wars, and the beginnings of the textile industry.

THIÉRACHE ARDENNAISE★

ARDENNES. MICHELIN LOCAL MAP 306: E/F/G-3/4

This area of forest and meadows southwest of Charleville-Mezières is good walking country and noted for its unusual fortified churches and farms, reflecting a history of constant invasion.

Tourist Office: Maison de la Thiérache, place de la Mairie, 08290 Liart. ☏03 24 54 48 33, www.ardennesmaisonnature.com.

A Bit of History

Churches were fortified during the late 16C and throughout the 17C in an effort to protect villages from the successive wars and hordes of plundering mercenaries that constantly invaded the region. Tall square keeps, round towers and bartizans were added not only to medieval churches, which were intended to shelter villagers in case of need, but also to farmhouses; extra accommodation was even added above the nave, which explains the presence of ceilings in most churches.

Excursion

Round Tour from Signy-l'Abbaye

116km/72mi – allow one day

Signy-l'Abbaye

This village in the Vaux Valley grew up near a famous Cistercian abbey founded in 1135 and destroyed in 1793. The parish church was built in 1900 on the site of the former sanctuary. The **Salle Guillaume-de-Saint-Thierry** (*Open Jul–mid-Sep weekends and holidays 3-7pm. No charge. ☏03 24 52 87 26*), named after St Bernard's biographer, houses an **exhibition** devoted to the former abbey and its grounds.

Forêt de Signy

Signy Forest, which extends over 3 535ha/8 735 acres, comprises two massifs separated by the Vaux Valley: the small forest (oak, beech) to the south-east and the damper large forest (oak, ash, maple) to the north-west.

Make a detour to the north-east, via the forest road, to admire the fine 18C covered market in **Saint-Jean-aux-Bois**.

Drive to Liart, NW of Signy by D 27.

The road passes the **Fontaine Rouge** (100m/110yd on right), a ferrous spring marking the start of a 4km/2.5mi footpath, then goes through the oak forest and reaches the path (parking area) leading down to the Gros Frêne. A stump and a slice of trunk are all that remain of this imposing ash tree, fallen in 1989 (45min there and back). Two other marked footpaths, 5km/3mi and 6km/3.7mi long, start from the parking area.

Liart

The medieval west front of the **Église Notre-Dame-de-Liart**★ was flanked in the 17C by a massive rectangular keep reinforced by brattices, crenels and loopholes whereas the east end was fortified by an octagonal tower with stairs leading to an attic above the chancel, used as a shelter in case of attack.

Continue along D 27.

Aouste

The **Église St-Rémi**★ (*Mar-Nov: 9am-7pm; Dec-Feb weekends and school holidays 9am-7pm; tour of the fortifications by appointment with Mme Deglaire, ☏03 24 54 40 32*) was built in the 17C on the ruins of a 15C church. The machicolated main doorway is reinforced by three brattices and a turret. The square tower, pierced with loopholes and strengthened by buttresses, was reached via a spiral staircase. This church had a bread oven in the nave and a well (now blocked) to feed the villagers in times of siege.

Turn left onto D 36 to La Férée then right onto D 236. In Blanchefosse, turn right onto D 10 to Mont-St-Jean, then right again onto D 977 to Rumigny.

Rumigny

As you enter the village, on the right admire the façade of the Renaissance **Château de la Cour des Prés** (*Jul-Aug, guided tour (1hr) Wed–Mon 3-7pm, Sat 3-5.30pm; Jun & Sep Sun and holidays 3-7pm; Apr–May & Sep ring for details. Closed Oct–Mar; €5; 03 24 35 52 66*) (1546), which was fortified at the request of François I. The ground floor consists of two halls with impressive fireplaces and drawing rooms with 18C panelling; upstairs, the bedrooms open onto the gallery decorated with family portraits. Concerts of Baroque music are organised in summer, followed by a meal in the candlelit Renaissance hall. The castle also provides bed and breakfast.

Continue along D 27.

Hannapes

Although it was not fortified, the **Église St-Jean-Baptiste** provided shelter to the villagers in case of invasion.

Turn right onto D 31.

Bossus-les-Rumigny

The church has two crenellated turrets; one of these is pierced with loopholes. The room located above the chancel is also pierced with loopholes.

Turn left onto D 10 to Fligny.

Fligny

Above the chancel of the **Église St-Étienne**, there is a room intended as a shelter, flanked with a round tower.

Continue along D 10.

Signy-le-Petit

The imposing 17C **church**★, fortified by brick-built corner towers, stands in the centre of a large square. The 18C château was remodelled in the 19C.

Kids The Étang de la Motte has a sand beach and supervised bathing in summer, as well as bike hire, a swimming pool and table tennis. *03 24 53 53 99.*

Drive towards Rocroi and Charleville then turn right onto D 34 to Tarzy.

Tarzy

A tower with canted corners pierced with loopholes was built to the left of the belfry of the hilltop **church**.

Antheny

Despite being destroyed by fire several times, the village still has some 16C and 17C fortified houses. The **Église St-Remy**, standing in the middle of the cemetery, features a buttressed square

Address Book

For coin ranges, see the Legend on the cover flap.

WHERE TO STAY AND EAT

Ferme-auberge de Gironval – *Gironval, 08460 Thin-le-Moutier, 10km/6.2mi NE of Signy-l'Abbaye on D 2. 03 24 54 74 40. Closed 16-30 Aug. Booking necessary. 5 rooms.* The inn housed in a former flour mill draws many regulars. The dining room with stone and wood decor offers a good view of the mill wheel. The cooking, using local farm produce, is a treat.

Auberge de l'Abbaye – *2 pl. Aristide-Briand, 08460 Signy-l'Abbaye. 03 24 52 81 27. Closed 10 Jan-5 Mar and Wed lunch. 7 rooms. €7.* This old stone posting inn set in a picturesque little village has a pleasant country feel. The cooking is simple and regional. Small, well-kept bedrooms and a welcoming atmosphere.

Chambre d'hôte La Cour des Prés – *08290 Rumigny, 03 24 35 52 66. Closed Nov-Mar and Tue Jul-Aug. 2 rooms.* A lovely welcome awaits you in this fortified house, built in 1546 by the provost of Rumigny. In summer there are candlelit dinner-concerts.

Th. Demont/MICHELIN

Fortified church in Signy-le-Petit

tower; the upper windows were blocked up in the 15C-16C for defence.

- *Continue along D 34 via Champlin and Estrebay.*

Prez

The church has an attic above the chancel, used for defence purposes. A round tower pierced with loopholes was added in the 16C. 18C stucco panels depicting Christ's life surround the chancel.

- *Continue along D 34 past Le Malpas, then left onto D32 towards La Cerleau, then right on D36 towards Flaignes.*

Flaignes-Havys

Clovis made a present of Flaignes to St Remi when he was baptised in Reims. The **Église St-Laurent**, fortified in the 16C-17C, has an unusually imposing chancel flanked by a round tower. In Havys, the **Église St-Gery** has a round tower pierced all round with loopholes used not only as look-outs but also to light the spiral staircase.

- *Continue along D 20 to Cernion then turn left to l'Échelle.*

L'Échelle

A fine **château** facing the church is framed by two 15C round towers. The bartizan in the north-west corner is

Launois, a Lively Tourist Centre

Third weekend in April: Festival of tourism in the Ardennes region
Last weekend in April: Regional heritage and rural dwellings fair
Weekend nearest 1 May: Ardennes' landscape gardening fair
Second weekend in May: Regional antiques fair
Whitsun weekend: North-east France gastronomic fair
Third weekend in June: Country Music Festival
Fourth weekend in June: Festival of arts and crafts in Champagne-Ardennes
Second weekend in August: Holidaymakers in Ardennes fair
Fourth weekend in September: Autumn flower show and rural market in Ardennes
First Sunday in October: Vintage car show
Third weekend in October: Gastronomic fair
First Sunday in December: St Nicholas and Christmas fair
Second Sunday of every month: Antiques market

known as the Massacre Tower in memory of the battle of Rocroi (1643). Opposite the castle is the Hôtel Beury, a former 18C coaching inn, now the **Centre d'art et de littérature** (*Open Jun–Aug Wed–Sun 2-7pm; Mar–May & Sep–Oct Fri–Sun 2-7pm; €2; 03 24 35 45 80*) with contemporary art exhibitions, a **literary café**, artists' residences and a sculpture garden.

Drive SE to Rouvroy-sur-Audry and cross D 978 to reach Servion.

Servion

The **Église St-Étienne** ★ has a remarkable fortified porch with slate-roofed turrets; now deconsecrated it is used for exhibitions *(Association des compagnons de St-Étienne, 06 82 20 55 00)*.

Continue along D 9. After Rémilly-les-Pothées, turn right onto D 39 towards Fagnon.

Ancienne Abbaye de Sept Fontaines

The former abbey, dating from the 17C, owes its name to the seven springs.

Take the D 34 to Évigny.

Évigny

Two **traditional houses** (*guided 1hr tour by appointment, mid-Jun-Aug Sun 2.30-6.30pm; €2; 03 24 58 21 41*) illustrate life in the past. The first one shows a reconstructed peasant home, the second has a **bakery** where you can buy traditionally baked loaves.

Turn back along D 34 then take D 3 left to Launois-sur-Vence.

Launois-sur-Vence

A 17C **posting inn** made communications between Amsterdam and Marseille easier. The buildings surrounding a vast courtyard include the postmaster's house, the timber-framed coach house, the stables, sheep pen and vaulted cider cellar. It is now occupied by the tourist office and a **cultural centre**.

Return to Signy-l'Abbaye by D27.

THIONVILLE

MOSELLE. POPULATION 40 907

MICHELIN LOCAL MAP 307: H-I 2

This old stronghold and iron town is the nerve centre of the whole industrial area which extends along the west bank of the River Moselle. The former convent of the Poor Clares' Order (1629), facing the river, now houses the town hall. Part of the town wall can be seen along the Moselle.

Tourist Office: 16 rue du Vieux-Collège, 57100 Thionville. 03 82 53 33 18, www.thionville.net

Orient Yourself: 30km N of Metz by the A31.

A Bit of History

The fortified town successively belonged to the counts of Luxembourg, the dukes of Burgundy, the Habsburgs, and the Low Countries then to the Spanish, who commissioned a Flemish engineer to rebuild the fortifications between 1590 and 1600. Thionville became French in 1659 by the Treaty of the Pyrenees.

Sights

Tour aux Puces

Cour du Château. Open mid-Jun–mid-Sep Tue–Sun 9.30-11.30am, 2-6pm; rest of the year Tue–Sun 2-6pm; €2.50, no charge 1st Sun of the month; Closed 1 Jan, Easter Sunday, 1 Nov, 25-26 Dec; 03 82 82 25 52.

This mighty 11C-12C keep, also known as the Tour au Puits (Well Tower), is the most important remnant of the feudal castle of the counts of Luxemburg. Inside, the **Musée du Pays thionvillois** retraces the history of Thionville from Palaeolithic times to the Middle Ages.

Beffroi

The 16C onion-domed belfry, situated near the market square, houses four bells including "Grosse Suzanne".

Château de la Grange★

Jul-Aug guided tour (45min) 2.30, 3.30, 4.30 and 5.30pm. mid-Mar–Jun & Sep–mid-Nov: weekends & holidays at the same times. Good Friday, 1 Nov. €5. 03 82 53 85 03.

Designed in 1731 by Robert de Cotte, the château was built over the foundations of a fortress. In the dining room, note the white and gold earthenware stove, almost 5m/16ft high, built for the marquis and the 17C Flemish tapestries in the entrance hall. The Empire-style bathroom contains a bath cut from a single block of marble, which belonged to Pauline Bonaparte (Napoleon's sister).

Excursions

Ecomusée des Mines de Fer de Neufchef★

13km/8mi. W. Guided tour (1hr 30min) Tue–Sat 2-6pm (last departure 4pm). Closed 1 Jan, 24-25 & 31 Dec. €6. 03 82 85 76 55. www.musee-minesde-fer-lorraine.com.

This hillside iron mine did not require the drilling of a shaft, which means it is now easily accessible to the public. Extracting processes of different periods since the 1820s have been recreated along a 1.5km/0.9mi-long stretch.

Ecomusée des Mines de Fer d'Aumetz

22km/13.67mi. NW. May-Sep guided tour (1hr 15min) Tue–Sun 2-6pm (last departure 4pm). €6. 03 82 91 96 26. www.musee-minesdefer-lorraine.com.

The former Bassompierre iron mine provides a valuable insight into miners' life in underground galleries. Above ground, the pithead frame has been preserved as have buildings housing the compressor room, the forge, etc.

THE THUR VALLEY★

HAUT-RHIN. MICHELIN LOCAL MAP 315: F-8 TO H-10

This large glaciated valley is a busy industrial area. While the upper Thur Valley and the Urbès Vale have remained rural with pasture- and forest-covered hillsides and varied flora and fauna, the lower Thur Valley is sprinkled with small towns that have a long-standing tradition in the textile industry.

- **Orient Yourself**: In the Vosges massif west of Mulhouse.
- **Also See:** Parc naturel régional des BALLONS DES VOSGES and the Route des CRÊTES

Driving Tours

Industrial Valley: From Thann to Husseren-Wesserling

12km/7.5mi – about 30min.

Thann★ – *See THANN.*

- *Drive NW out of Thann along N 66.*

Willer-sur-Thur

The D 13BVI branches off to join the scenic Route des Crêtes, leading to the Grand Ballon (alt 1424m/4 672ft), the highest summit in the Vosges.

Moosch

A cemetery on the eastern slope contains the graves of almost 1 000 French soldiers killed in the First World War.

St-Amarin

The **Musée Serret et de la vallée de St-Amarin** *(Open May-Sep Wed–Mon 2-6pm; €3.20 ; 03 89 38 24 66)* covers local history through prints and paintings, headdresses, weapons, wrought-iron and emblems of brotherhoods.

Ranspach

A pleasant botanic trail (2.5km/1.5mi), marked by a holly leaf, starts from the top of the village.

Husseren-Wesserling

The town is home to an important printed-fabric factory. The **Musée du Textile et des Costumes de Haute-Alsace** *(Kids Apr-Sep Tue–Sun (daily Jul–Aug) 10am-noon, 2-6pm; Oct-Mar Tue–Sun 10am-noon, 2-5pm; Mon (except Jul-Aug) and holidays Oct-Mar; €5, park and museum €6; 10-16 year olds: €2.50; 03 89 38 28 08, www.parc-wesserling.fr)* is housed in an old industrial building in the heart of a vast park. The museum deals with three main themes: from raw material to fabric, the history of the great industrial families, and the evolution of women's fashion.

Upper Valley: From Husseren-Wesserling to Grand Ventron★

46km/29mi – about 2hr.

The upper Thur Valley is dotted with granite knolls spared by glaciation. Three of these knolls overlook **Oderen**. From the southern approach to the village, there is a fine view of the escarpments of the Fellering woods. A fourth knoll, the forested Schlossberg, situated upstream, is crowned by the **ruins of Wildenstein Castle**.

In Kruth, turn left onto D 13B1.

Cascade St-Nicolas★

A succession of small waterfalls drop to the bottom of a lovely deep vale with densely forested slopes.

Return to Kruth.

Between Kruth and Wildenstein, the road runs to the right of Schlossberg through a narrow passage where the Thur once flowed.
Another road runs along the other side of Schlossberg and the **Kruth-Wildenstein dam**, one of the major elements of the Thur Valley's harnessing project *(this is a one-way road in the Wildenstein-Kruth direction; it is closed in winter)*.
Beyond Wildenstein, the road rises towards the Col de Bramont, offering a beautiful vista of the Thur Valley then runs through the forest.

Col de Bramont

Alt 956m/3 136ft. The pass is situated on the main ridge of the Vosges.

Lorraine's Iron and Steel Industry

The iron-ore deposits, located in the upper reaches of the Moselle, extend over a distance of 120km/75mi from the Haye Forest to Luxemburg. In just over 100 years, three billion tonnes of minette, a type of ore with a relatively low iron content (about 33%) have been extracted; peak production was reached in 1962 with 62 million tons. There was a subsequent decline owing to competition from imported ore, richer in iron content, and to a drop in traditional outlets. The mines closed down one after the other; the closure of the Roncourt mine in August 1993 put an end to the mining activity in the area, with the exception of the Bure-Tressange site (4km/2.5mi east of Aumetz), which exports its ore to Luxemburg via an underground route.

Having diversified its production and invested heavily in new technology, the steel industry has now regained a certain competitiveness. Thus the Usinor-Sacilor group ranks third in the world.

The area has also turned to other industries such as the car industry and nuclear energy.

R. Mattès/MICHELIN

Typical village in the Thur Valley

The access road branches off at the pass. Turn left onto the forest road (8km/5mi) via the Col de la Vierge on to the Chaume du Grand Ventron.

Grand Ventron★★

From the top (alt 1 204m/3 950ft), there is a vast **panorama**★★ of the valley and the Vosges summits, including Hohneck, Grand Ballon and Ballon d'Alsace.

Urbès Vale: From Husseren-Wesserling to the Col de Bussang

11km/7mi – about 30min .

The N 66 starts along the Thur Valley then enters the Urbès Vale.

See d'Urbès

Parking on the lake shore (signpost). The depression in which the lake (or see) is situated, was scooped out during the Quaternary Era by the glacier that carved the Thur Valley.

A marked path *(1hr 30min)*, dotted with explanatory panels about local flora, fauna and traditional activities, explains this remarkable landscape and its bogland vegetation.

The road then rises gently towards the Col de Bussang, affording lovely views.

Col de Bussang

From the pass, it is possible to drive down the upper Moselle Valley (*see REMIREMONT: Upriver from Remiremont*).

TOUL★

MEURTHE-ET-MOSELLE. POPULATION 16 945

MICHELIN LOCAL MAP 307: G-6

Situated on the banks of the River Moselle, the ancient bishopric of Toul occupies a strategic position at the intersection of several main roads and waterways.

Tourist Office: Parvis de la Cathédrale, 54203 Toul. ☎03 83 64 11 69.

Orient Yourself: Around 20km/12.4mi. W of Nancy by A31.

A Bit of History

The ancient city of Tullum, which was already a bishopric by the 4C AD, soon became so prosperous that it was granted its independence in 928 under the terms of the Mainz Charter.

In 1700, Vauban, Louis XIV's military engineer, built new ramparts round the city (the Porte de Metz is all that remains today). The fortifications were improved at regular intervals so that on the eve of the First World War, Toul was considered one of the best-defended strongholds in Europe.

Walking Tour

Old houses

There are Renaissance houses along rue du Général-Gengoult at Nos 30, 28 and 26, and one 14C house at No 8. The 17C is represented by Nos 6 and 6bis (former Pimodan mansion) and No 4; No 16 rue Michâtel has a fine Renaissance house decorated with gargoyles.

Cathédrale St-Étienne★★

Jun-Sep: 9am-noon, 1.30-6pm; Oct-May: daily except Sun 10am-noon, 2-4pm.

The cathedral's magnificent **west front**★★, built 1460-96, is a superb example of Flamboyant Gothic; the statues were destroyed during the Revolution.

The interior shows the influence of the Champagne Gothic style, with high and low galleries over the main arcades and the aisles, extremely pointed arches, and the absence of triforium. Note, on the right, the fine Renaissance chapel with a coffered cupola.

Numerous old tombstones pave the floor of the cathedral, particularly in the transept. Before leaving, have a look at the elegant Louis XV-style gallery supporting the monumental organ (1963) placed beneath the great rose-window.

Cloître

Entered through a small doorway on place des Clercs, the 13C-14C cloisters are some of the largest in France. Note the beautiful capitals with foliage motifs and interesting gargoyles on the walls.

Ancien palais épiscopal

The former bishop's palace, built between 1735 and 1743, is now the town hall. The imposing **façade**★ is adorned with colossal-order pilasters.

Additional Sights

Église St-Gengoult

Open Jul–mid-Sep daily 10am-noon, 2-5.30pm. Rest of the year Sun morning only. ☎03 83 64 11 69.

This former collegiate church, built in the 13C and 15C, is a fine example of Champagne Gothic architecture. The west front has an elegant 15C doorway. Inside, note the change in style between the last two bays and the first two which have to support the weight of the towers. The apsidal chapels open onto the chancel and the transept, typical of the Champagne school. The chapels are lit by fine 13C stained-glass windows.

Cloître St-Gengoult★★

These elegant 16C cloisters mix Flamboyant Gothic and Renaissance elements. The star vaulting has ornately worked keystones.

Musée d'Art et d'Histoire★

25 rue Gouvion-St-Cyr. Open Jul–Aug-Wed–Mon 9.30am–noon, 2-6.30pm. Jun & Sep Wed-Mon 10am-noon, 2-6pm. Oct–May Mon, Wed–Fri 9.30am–noon, 2-5.30pm, weekends 2-6pm. Closed 1 Jan, Easter Sun and Mon, 1 May, 1 Nov and 25 Dec. €3. ☎03 83 64 13 38.

Housed in the old Maison-Dieu (almshouse), the municipal museum contains collections of painting, sculpture, Flemish tapestries, ceramics (Toul-Bellevue manufacture), religious art, antique and medieval archaeology, folk art. Boucher's *The Enjoyable Lesson* hangs in a Louis XVI-style salon. The two world wars are illustrated by weapons, uniforms and mementoes. The 13C vaulted Gothic sick ward★, remodelled many times, was used both for worship and as hospital for all kinds of sick people.

Excursions

Vannes-le-Châtel

18km S by D 960 then D 113.

This village has a long-standing glass-making tradition (Daum Crystalworks). It therefore seems only natural that a European research and training centre, the **Plate-forme ver-**

rière (♿ 🕓 Guided tour (1hr30) *Wed–Mon 10am-noon, 1.30-5.30pm, Sat-Sun and holidays 1.30-5.30pm; €2.50; ☎03 83 25 47 44)* should be based here. Its aim is to encourage craftsmen to create their own collection. There is an exhibition of contemporary glass and a demonstration of various techniques including glass-blowing.

Cloisters of St Gencoult

B. Kaufmann/MICHELIN

Ensemble fortifié de Villey-le-Sec ★

7km/4.3mi E by N 4 then D 909; park outside village. 🕓 guided tour (2h 30min) mid-Jul–mid-Aug Tue–Sun 3pm. mid-Aug–Sep & May–mid-Jul Sun and holidays 3pm. €5. ☎03 83 63 90 09, www.villey-le-sec.com.

This village, on top of a ridge overlooking the east bank of the Moselle, is a unique example in France of a village integrated within late 19C fortifications. Put up after the 1870 Franco-Prussian War, the north battery with its armour-

Address Book

For coin ranges, see the Legend on the cover flap.

WHERE TO EAT

⊖⊖ **La Belle Époque** – *31 av. Victor-Hugo. ☎03 83 43 23 71. Closed early May, 24 Dec-5 Jan, Sat lunch, Mon evening & Sun.* This small restaurant near the station has an old-fashioned dining room with vintage zinc bar, old posters and tightly packed tables. The menu mixes regional dishes and French classics. Good-value lunch menu.

WHERE TO STAY

⊖⊖ **La Villa Lorraine** – *15 r. Gambetta. ☎03 83 43 08 95. 21 rooms.* ☕ *€6.50. Closed Nov school hols.* This small hotel in the heart of the fortified city has well soundproofed bedrooms with rustic furnishings and a pleasant breakfast room.

ON THE TOWN

Place des Trois-Évêchés – Most of the bars that are open in the evening are found in this central square. Sample the local speciality, *vin gris de Toul*, so named for its pink colour which is obtained from the combination of gamay, pinot noir and a third grape variety from the Auxerre region.

TOURING WINE CELLARS

A complete list of wine producers is available from the tourist office.

Vincent Laroppe – *253 r. de la République, 54200 Bruley. ☎03 83 43 11 04. www.laroppe.com. Mon-Sat 9am-noon, 2-6pm.* A lovely early 19C vaulted cellar with a wine-making museum. The owner makes an excellent red pinot noir as well as gris and Côtes de Toul. No charge for the tour and tasting.

Au Caveau "En Passant par la Lorraine" – *6 r. Victor-Hugo, 54200 Bruley. ☎03 83 64 55 09. Daily 10am-6pm.* This former boy's school is now a showcase for regional wines and produce.

Lelièvre – *3 r. de la Gare, 54200 Lucey. ☎03 83 63 81 36.* Tour of the cellars, vineyard and orchards. Tasting. The owners also sell organic produce and a farm-style "four o'clock" (light-meal).

M. Michel Vosgien – *24 r. St-Vincent, 54113 Bulligny. ☎03 83 62 50 55. Daily 9am-7pm, holidays by appointment.* Mr Vosgien's good gris, white and red Côtes de Toul wine, sparkling wine and mirabelle liqueur have won many prizes. Tastings, sales and visits.

Coopérative des vignerons du Toulois – *54113 Mont-le-Vignoble. ☎03 83 62 59 93. Tue-Sun 2-6pm.* Cellar tour. Tasting and sale of Côtes de Toul.

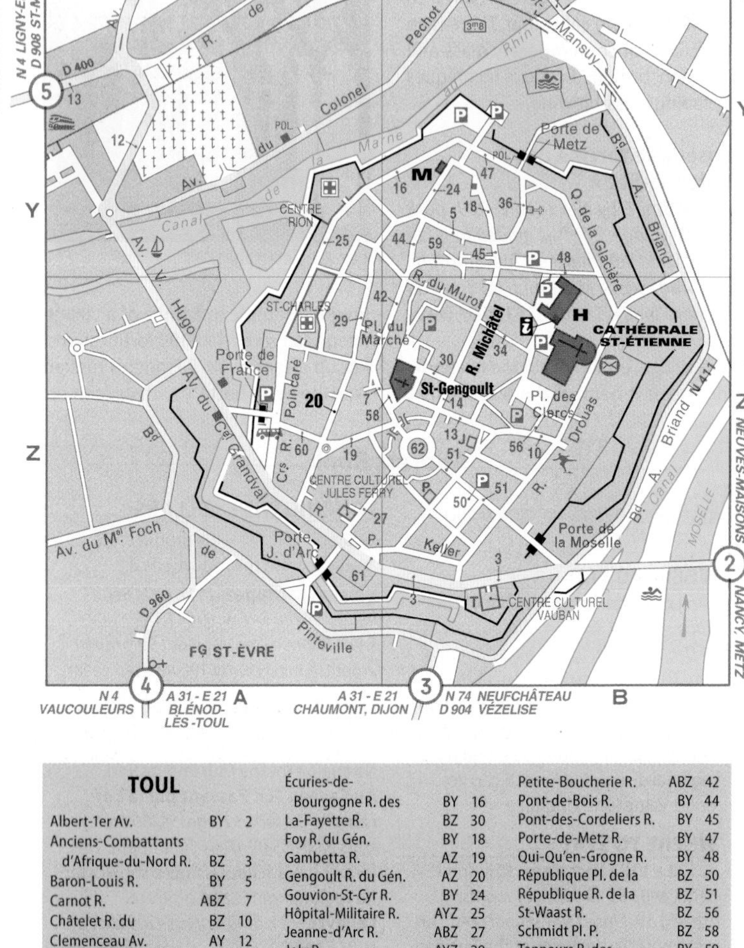

TOUL

Street	Grid	No.
Albert-1er Av.	BY	2
Anciens-Combattants d'Afrique-du-Nord R.	BZ	3
Baron-Louis R.	BY	5
Carnot R.	ABZ	7
Châtelet R. du	BZ	10
Clemenceau Av.	AY	12
Corne-de-Cerf R.	BZ	13
Dr-Chapuis R. du	BZ	14
Écuries-de-Bourgogne R. des	BY	16
La-Fayette R.	BZ	30
Foy R. du Gén.	BY	18
Gambetta R.	AZ	19
Gengoult R. du Gén.	AZ	20
Gouvion-St-Cyr R.	BY	24
Hôpital-Militaire R.	AYZ	25
Jeanne-d'Arc R.	ABZ	27
Joly R.	AYZ	29
Liouville R.	BZ	34
Ménin R. du	BY	36
Michâtel R.	BZ	
Petite-Boucherie R.	ABZ	42
Pont-de-Bois R.	BY	44
Pont-des-Cordeliers R.	BY	45
Porte-de-Metz R.	BY	47
Qui-Qu'en-Grogne R.	BY	48
République Pl. de la	BZ	50
République R. de la	BZ	51
St-Waast R.	BZ	56
Schmidt Pl. P.	BZ	58
Tanneurs R. des	BY	59
Thiers R.	AZ	60
Vauban R.	AZ	61
3-Évêchés Pl. des	BZ	62

Ancien palais épiscopal (Hôtel de ville)	BZ	H
Musée municipal	BY	M

plating, ditch, caponiers, observation cupolas, and cannon turret with three-storey shooting chamber is a forerunner of the later forts along the Maginot Line. A narrow-gauge railway carries visitors to the fort or redoute, which houses the ammunition stores and barracks, a museum and a memorial crypt.

TROYES★★★

POPULATION 128 945

MICHELIN LOCAL MAP 313: E-4

The former capital of Champagne became a prosperous commercial city through its famous annual fairs as well as an artistic centre with a wealth of churches, museums, old houses and mansions. The town has now expanded outside the ring of boulevards surrounding the centre, whose shape suggests a Champagne cork. Troyes remains France's main hosiery centre in a tradition going back to the 16C, though it is now equally famed for its factory outlets.

- **Tourist Office:** 16 boulevard Carnot, 10014 Troyes. ☎03 25 82 62 70, www.ot-troyes.fr
- **Orient Yourself:** Troyes lies on the A5, 179km/111mi from Paris and 125km/77mi from Reims.
- **Don't Miss:** Troyes's Gothic churches and cathedral and the Fauve paintings in the Musée d'Art Moderne.
- **Also See**: The Parc naturel régional de la FORÊT D'ORIENT.

A Bit of History

The counts of Champagne

In the 10C, Troyes came under the authority of the counts of Champagne. One of them, **Henri I 'the Liberal'** founded 13 churches and 13 hospitals. His grandson, **Thibaud II**, a knight-poet, founded the Champagne fairs and brought fame and fortune to the town. When the last heiress of the counts of Champagne, Jeanne, married the king of France, Philippe le Bel, in 1284, her dowry included the Champagne region.

The shameful Treaty of Troyes

During the strife between Burgundians and Armagnacs at the height of the Hundred Years War, **Isabeau of Bavaria**, wife of mad French king, Charles VI, signed the shameful Treaty of Troyes disowning the dauphin (heir to the French throne) and sealing the marriage of Catherine of France with Henry V of England who was proclaimed regent pending his accession to the French throne on the death of Charles VI. Burgundian and English troops then occupied Troyes, which was liberated by Joan of Arc in 1429.

Major artistic centre

The city's artistic activities multiplied from the Renaissance onwards. Ignoring Italian influence, artists continued to work along the lines of the great Gothic tradition. The school of sculpture was famous throughout Champagne and even in neighbouring Burgundy. Sculptors such as **Jean Gailde** and **Jacques Julyot** created a wealth of charming works. Stained-glass makers, such as **Jehan Soudain** and **Linard Gontier**, were also well established and, from the 14C to 17C, their workshops produced all the fine stained glass decorating the town's churches. The artistic tradition continued into the 17C with painter **Pierre Mignard** and sculptor **François Girardon**, both natives of Troyes.

Th. Demont/MICHELIN

Half-timbered houses

Address Book

For coin ranges, see the Legend on the cover flap.

PRACTICAL INFORMATION

Guided tours – Troyes, City of Art and History, organises 1hr 30min tours by approved guides of the town. *Early Jul-mid-Sep at 2.30pm, €5.50.* The rest of the year audioguides can be reserved and theme tours are organised from Oct to Jun. *Enquire at the tourist office or on www.tourisme-troyes.com.*

Pass'Troyes – *Enquire at the tourist offce.* The tourist pass €12 valid one year, includes a guided visit or audio guide, free museum entrance, reductions in the factory shops and a champagne tasting.

Tourist circuit – The city has created two well signposted tours of the city's most noteworthy sites. Brochure from the tourist office.

WHERE TO EAT

Aux Crieurs de Vin – *4-6 pl. Jean-Jaurès . ☎03 25 40 01 01. Closed Sun and Mon.* Wine connoisseurs will appreciate this establishment, which is part wine and spirits shop, part atmospheric pre-1940s style bistro. The cuisine is a pleasure too, with fresh market-inspired cooking and regional dishes.

Au Jardin Gourmand – *31 r. Paillot de Montabert. ☎03 25 73 36 13. Closed 2 weeks Mar, 2 weeks Sep, Mon lunch and Sun.* Andouillette reigns at this reataurant in old Troyes with its oak-panelled dining room and peaceful courtyard terrace.

Bistrot DuPont – *5 pl. Charles-de-Gaulle, 10150 Pont-Ste-Marie, 3km/1.8mi NE of Troyes on N 77. ☎03 25 80 90 99. Closed Sun evening and Mon.* Flowers and smiles from the staff provide a fine welcome. In a simple but carefully planned setting, the cheerful dishes suit the style of the bistro. Terrace in summer.

Auberge de la Cray'Othe – *31 Grande-Rue, 10190 Messon, 12km/7.5mi W of Troyes on N 60 and left on D 83. ☎03 25 70 31 12. Closed 2 weeks in Jan, 2 weeks in Sep; open from Thu-Sun lunchtime. Booking necessary.* This beautiful farm houses a pleasant restaurant decorated with paintings of the village and surrounding area. Connoisseurs will love the authentic local dishes such as *coq au cidre du pays d'Othe* and the tasty farmhouse terrines.

Le Bistroquet – *Pl. Langevin – ☎03 25 73 65 65 – closed Sun except lunchtimes from Sep-June.* This restaurant occupying an old cinema in the pedestrianised centre of Troyes, is reminiscent of a Parisian belle époque brasserie, with its large dining room, leather seats, old-style lights, plants and lively atmosphere. All dishes are based on fresh ingredients. Terrace with shrubs and garden lights.

WHERE TO STAY

Les Comtes de Champagne – *56 r. de la Monnaie. ☎03 25 73 11 70, www.comtesdechampagne.com. 36 rooms. €6.* It is said that the counts of Champagne used to mint coins in the four 12C houses which make up this hotel. Renovated rooms; those with kitchenettes are ideal for families. The huge fireplace in the breakfast room testifies to the age of the premises.

Hôtel de Troyes – *168 av. du Gén.-de-Gaulle. ☎03 25 71 23 45. 21 rooms. €7.40.* Rooms are spread over two buildings either side of a bright plant-filled veranda. Modish colour schemes are combined with modern furniture.

Champ des Oiseaux – *20 r. Linard Gonthier. ☎03 25 80 58 50, www.champdesoiseaux.com. 13 rooms. €15.* This is a truly stylish option cocooned in three corbelled 15C and 16C half-timbered houses. Charm, tranquillity and attentive service.

SHOPPING

Specialities – Above all Troyes is renowned for its *andouillettes* (chitterling sausages)– grilled, unaccompanied or drizzled with olive oil flavoured with browned *fines herbes* and garlic. Try them with *mustard au vin de champagne* or Meaux mustard, accompanied by mashed potatoes, kidney beans or fried onion rings.

Other specialities include Chaource cheese, cider or *champagne choucroute, rosé des Riceys*, and *cacibel* (aperitif made with cider, blackcurrant and honey).

Halle de l'Hötel-de-ville – *Tue-Thu 7.30am-12.45pm, 3.30-7pm, Fri-Sat 9.30am-7pm, Sun 9am-12.30pm.* Among the stalls inside the covered market, visit **La Boucherie Moderne** for *andouillettes* made by Gilbert Lemelle, the largest French manufacturer of these chitterling sausages, the **Charcuterie Audry Chantal**, for real homemade Troyes *andouillettes*, and **Jean-Pierre Ozérée** for his fine selection of cheeses, including Chaource, Mussy and Langres.

Market – As well as the Halles, there's another daily market in the Place St-Remy halls, especially on Saturdays. There is another in the Chartreux area on Wed and on Sun morning. A farmers market is held every third Wed of the month on Boulevard Jules-Guesde.

Patrick Maury – *28 r. du Gén.-de-Gaulle. ☎03 25 73 06 84 – Tue-Fri 8.30am-12.45pm, 2.45-7pm; Sat 7.30am-8pm.* Opposite the market is this tiny boutique prized for its *andouillette de Troyes*, black pudding and other homemade *charcuterie*.

Le Palais du Chocolat – *2 r. de la Monnaie. ☎03 25 73 35 73 – www.pascal-coffet.com – Tue-Fri 9am-12.15pm, 2-7.15pm; Sat 9am-7.15pm; Sun and public holidays 9am-1pm.* An emporium of chocolate, as well as ice cream, sorbets and pastries. Among the specialities are *tuiles chocolatées et aux amandes* (chocolate almond thins), *cristallines de Troyes* and liquorice ganache which taste all the better in this magnificent setting.

Domaine du Moulin d'Eguebaude – *10190 Estissac ☎03 25 40 42 18.* Guided visits of this fish farm. Rooms and table d'hôte.

Factory Outlets – Troyes is well known for its factory outlets on the outskirts of town (St-Julien-les-Villas and Pont-Ste-Marie sites), offering discount prices on numerous fashion labels.

Marques Avenue – *114 bd de Dijon – ☎03 25 82 00 72 – Mon 2-7pm, Tue-Fri from 10am, Sat from 9.30am.* With 80 boutiques, Marques Avenue is the biggest centre for fins de séries (end-of-line) discount fashion stores in Europe. Here you will find all the big brand names, both French and foreign.

Mc Arthur Glen – *Voie des Bois – 10150 Pont-Ste-Marie – ☎03 25 70 47 10 – Mon 2-7pm, Tue-Fri 10am-7pm, Sat 9.30am-7pm – closed 1 May.* Opened in 1995, the village includes 80 end-of-line shops along an outside covered gallery.

Marques City – Pont Ste-Marie. Mon 2_7pm,Tue-Fri 10am-7pm, Sat 9/30am-7pm. 30 shops of clothes, sportwear and shoes are known for their good price reductions all year round.

ON THE TOWN

La Chope – *64 av. du Gén.-de-Gaulle – ☎03 25 73 11 99.* Wide selection of beers, whiskies and cocktails.

La Cocktaileraie – *56 r. Jaillant-Deschainets – BP 4102 – ☎03 25 73 77 04 – Tue-Sat 5pm-3am.* The clientele of this smart bar ranges from businessmen discussing stock options to young lovers whispering sweet nothings. A hundred or so cocktails are on offer, around 45 whiskies and many prestigious champagnes, as well as ice cream.

Le Bougnat des Pouilles – *29 r. Paillot-de-Montabert. ☎03 25 73 59 85. Daily 6pm-3am.* The high-quality vintages in this wine bar are sought out by the young proprietor himself, among the smaller producers in the region. The walls are often hung with exhibitions of painting and photography. The atmosphere is very peaceful and the music an easygoing blend of jazz, blues and world music. Concerts twice a month.

Le Chihuahua – *8 r. Charbonnet – ☎03 25 73 33 53 – Mon-Sat 6pm-3am.* This fashionable cellar bar (try the Tex-Mex cocktails) also has dancing, with theme nights each Thursday and monthly rock concerts.

Le Tricasse – *16 r. Paillot-de-Montabert. ☎03 25 73 14 80. Mon-Sat 3pm-3am.* Troyes's most famousnightspot offers a glorious mix of music, from jazz to salsa to house (DJ every Saturday night). Rum, champagne, cocktails and wines are specialities.

Capital of hosiery

Troyes' tradition of hosiery making goes back to the early 16C, with a handful of manufacturers of hand-knitted bonnets and stockings. In 1745, the Trinity Hospital (Hôtel de Mauroy) introduced special looms so that poor children in its care could learn to make stockings. By 1774, the hosiers' guild counted no fewer than 40 members. The industry further developed in the 19C and today counts 150 firms employing 10 000 people.

Walking Tour

Historic Centre★★

Allow 4hr.

Medieval Troyes consisted of two separate districts: the Cité, the aristocratic and ecclesiastical centre surrounding the cathedral, and the Bourg of the commercial burghers where the Champagne fairs took place. In 1524, a fire swept through the town. The prosperous inhabitants took this opportunity to build the more opulent houses that are still visible today.

The timber-framed houses had pointed gables, cob walls and corbelled upper floors. More opulent houses had walls of limestone rubble and brick in the traditional Champagne style. The most elegant mansions were built of stone, an expensive material in the region owing to the absence of hard-stone quarries.

Start from place Alexandre-Israël.

Place Alexandre-Israël

The square is overlooked by the Louis XIII façade of the **town hall**. Note the motto over the porch, dating from the 1789 Revolution: Liberty, Equality, Fraternity or Death.

Rue Champeaux

This unusually wide 16C street was the district's main thoroughfare. On the corner of rue Paillot-de-Montabert stands the **Maison du Boulanger** which houses the Thibaud-de-Champagne cultural centre; opposite, you can see the **Tourelle de l'Orfèvre** which owes its name to its first owner, a goldsmith. Partly clad with slates forming a chequered pattern, it is supported by caryatids and a telamon with goat's feet.

Walk beside the church then take rue Mignard back to rue Champeaux.

Across the street is the 1526 **Hôtel Juvénal-des-Ursins.** The white-stone façade has a pedimented doorway and a charming Renaissance oratory.

Ruelle des Chats★

A medieval atmosphere pervades this narrow lane lined with houses whose gables are so close that a cat can jump from one side to the other. The bollards marking the entrance of the alleyway were to prevent carriage wheels from hitting the walls of the houses. The street was closed by a portcullis at night.

The road widens into rue des Chats.

On the left, a passageway leads to the **Cour du Mortier d'or**, a fine courtyard built with various ancient elements.

Turn left onto rue Charbonnet.

Hôtel de Marisy

Erected in 1531, this beautiful stone mansion has a Renaissance corner turret, decorated with figures and emblems.

Turn left onto rue des Quinze-Vingts then right onto rue de la Monnaie.

Rue de la Monnaie

The street is lined with fine timber-framed houses. At **No 34** stands the 16C Hôtel de l'Élection, clad with shingles, and at **Nos 32-36** the stone early-16C Hôtel de la Croix d'Or, former residence of one of the town's mayors.

Turn left onto rue des Ursins and walk towards place Audiffred.

Note the 18C former mansion of another of Troyes' mayors, now the Chamber of Commerce and Industry.

Retrace your steps and continue along rue de la Monnaie. Turn left onto rue Colbert and left onto rue de la Bonne-

terie. At place Jean Jaurès, turn right onto rue de Turenne.

On the corner, note the old house standing over a modern one-storey building (the main doorway is on the first floor).

Hôtel de Chapelaines

55 rue Turenne. Beautiful Renaissance façade dating from 1524 to 1536.
The house on the corner of rue de Vauluisant is a fine example of Champagne bond (brick and limestone rubble). The corbelled upper part rests on consoles decorated with carved heads; on the corner is a fine *Virgin of the Apocalypse*.

Follow rue du Général-Saussier, then turn left onto rue de la Trinité.

Hôtel de Mauroy★★

7 rue de la Trinité. See also Musée de l'Outil et de la pensée ouvrière.
This mansion was built by rich merchants in 1550. The street façade has a chequered bond typical of Champagne, whereas on the courtyard side (visible as part of the museum), the building features a polygonal turret surrounded by timberframing, bricks, chequered slate-cladding and string-courses. Note also the Corinthian columns supporting the wooden gallery. The building later became the Hôpital de la Trinité, a home for poor children. In 1745 special looms were brought in, marking the start of machine-made hosiery in Troyes.

Next door, on the corner of rue de la Trinité and rue Thérèse-Bordet, stands the Maison des Allemands.

Maison des Allemands

Built in the 16C and decorated in the 18C, this timber-framed house used to welcome German merchants in town for the fairs, hence its name.

Turn right onto rue Thérèse-Bordet, then right again onto rue Larivey leading to rue Général-Saussier.

Rue du Général-Saussier

The street is lined with fine old houses; **No 26**: Hôtel des Angoiselles with a pinnacled tower; **No 11**: 18C mansion where Napoleon stayed; **No 3**: fine stone-and-brick 17C house with glazed ceramic tiles.

Retrace your steps, turn right on rue de la Montée-des-Changes, which leads to place du Marché-au-Pain.

Place du Marché-au-Pain

There's a fine view of the clock tower of the Église St-Jean.

Rue Urbain IV leads to place de la Libération. Cross the canal and follow rue Roger-Salengro, then rue Linard-Gonthier.

At **no 22** stands the Hôtel du Petit Louvre, the former bishop's residence (14C), turned into a coaching inn in 1821.

Turn left towards place St-Pierre.

The **Musée d'Art Moderne** housed in the former bishop's palace and the **cathedral** are on the right.

Rue de la Cité

This street follows the old Roman road from Lyon to Boulogne, which intersected the road from Paris to Troyes.

Take a few steps along rue du Paon, with its timber-framed houses.

Across rue de la Cité is the 18C **Hôtel-Dieu**, now part of Reims University.

Cross the canal again and pass north of St-Urbain Basilica to return to place Alexandre-Israël.

Ph. Gajic/MICHELIN

Detail of the gate, Hôtel-Dieu

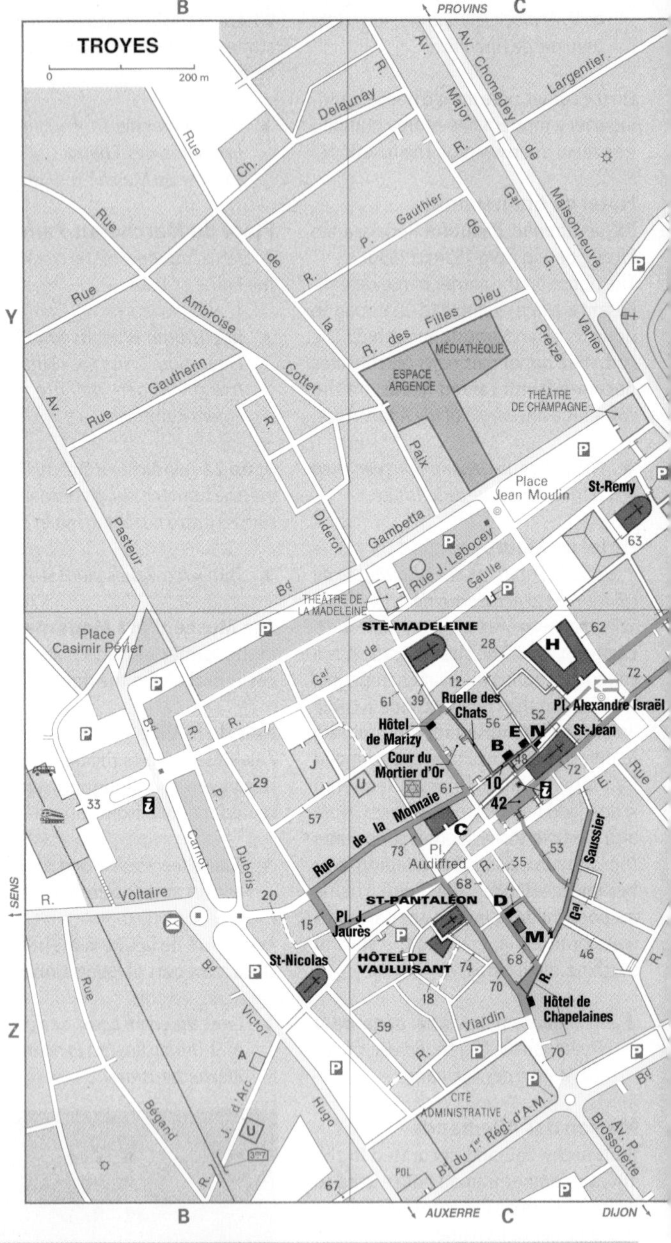

TROYES								
			Casimir-Périer Pl.	BZ		Comte-Henri Quai du	DZ	
			Champeaux R.	CZ	10	Comtes-de-Champagne		
Audiffred Pl.	CZ		Charbonnet R.	CZ	12	Quai des	DY	16
Barbusse Bd Henri	EYZ		Charmilles Mail des	EYZ		Cottet R. Ambroise	BY	
Bas-Trevois R. des	DZ		Charmilles Pl. des	EZ		Dampierre Quai	DY	17
Bégand R.	BZ		Chats Ruelle des	CZ		Danton Bd	DY	
Bordet R. Th.	CZ	4	Cité R. de la	DEY		Delaporte R. J.-L.	CDZ	
Boucherat R.	DY		Clemenceau R. G.	DY	13	Delaunay R. Ch.	BCY	
Bourgeoys R. M.	EYZ		Clément R. de la Planche	EYZ		Diderot R.	BY	
Brossolette Av. Pierre	CZ		Cloître-St-Étienne R. du	DEYZ		Dominique R.	CZ	18
Carnot Bd	BZ		Colbert R.	BZ	15	Driant R. Colonel	BZ	20

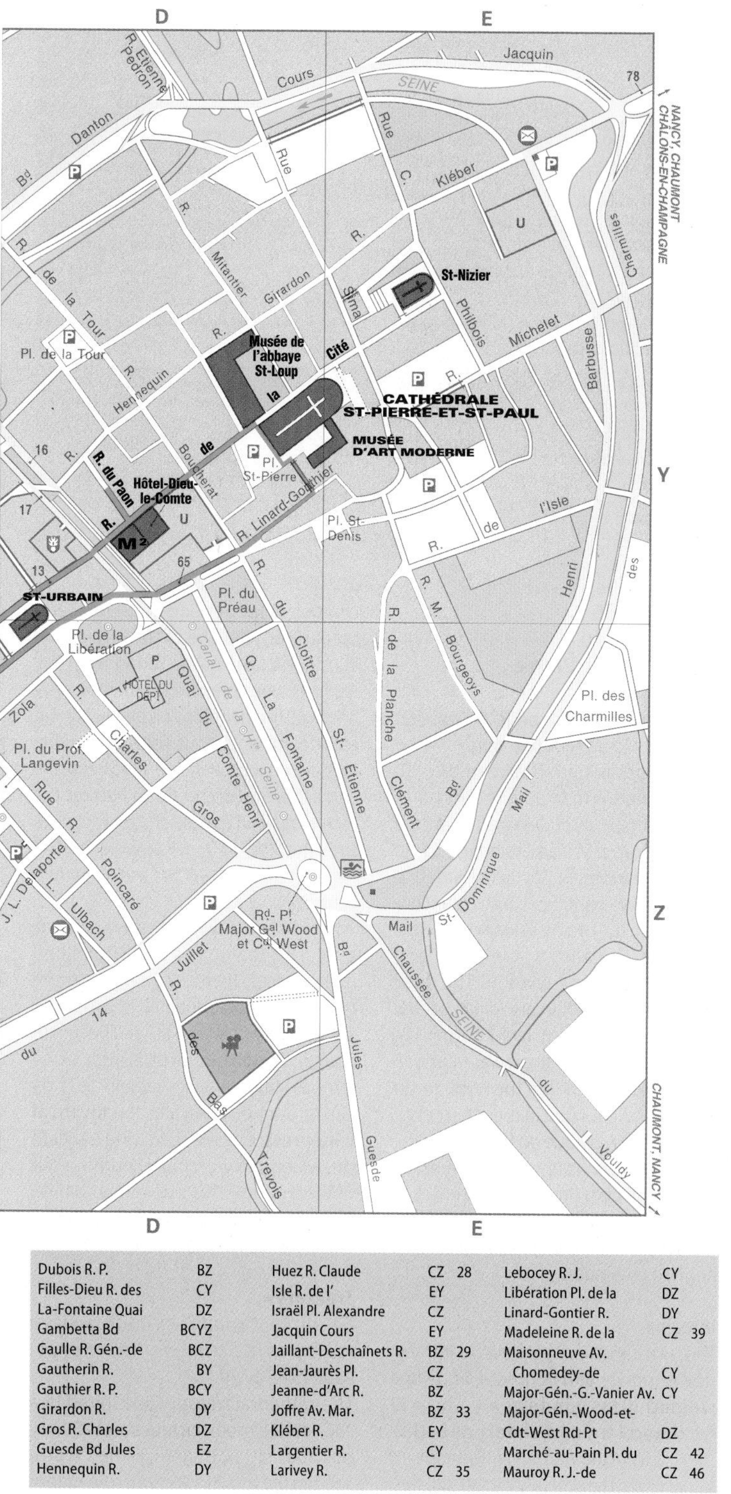

Dubois R. P.	BZ		Huez R. Claude	CZ	28	Lebocey R. J.	CY	
Filles-Dieu R. des	CY		Isle R. de l'	EY		Libération Pl. de la	DZ	
La-Fontaine Quai	DZ		Israël Pl. Alexandre	CZ		Linard-Gontier R.	DY	
Gambetta Bd	BCYZ		Jacquin Cours	EY		Madeleine R. de la	CZ	39
Gaulle R. Gén.-de	BCZ		Jaillant-Deschaînets R.	BZ	29	Maisonneuve Av. Chomedey-de	CY	
Gautherin R.	BY		Jean-Jaurès Pl.	CZ		Major-Gén.-G.-Vanier Av.	CY	
Gauthier R. P.	BCY		Jeanne-d'Arc R.	BZ		Major-Gén.-Wood-et-Cdt-West Rd-Pt	DZ	
Girardon R.	DY		Joffre Av. Mar.	BZ	33	Marché-au-Pain Pl. du	CZ	42
Gros R. Charles	DZ		Kléber R.	EY		Mauroy R. J.-de	CZ	46
Guesde Bd Jules	EZ		Largentier R.	CY				
Hennequin R.	DY		Larivey R.	CZ	35			

Michelet R.	EY	
Mignard R.	CZ	48
Mitantier R.	DY	
Molé R.	CZ	52
Monnaie R. de la	BCZ	
Montée-des-Changes	CZ	53
Mortier d'Or Cour du	CZ	
Moulin Pl. Jean	CY	
Paillot-de-Montabert R.	CZ	56
Paix R. de la	BCY	
Palais de Justice R. du	BZ	57
Paon R. du	DY	
Pasteur Av.	BY	
Pedron R. Étienne	DY	
Philbois R. C.	EY	
Pierre R. de la	CZ	59
Poincarré R. R.	DZ	
Préau Pl. du	DY	
Preize R. de	CY	
Professeur-Langevin Pl. du	DZ	
Quize-Vingts R. des	CZ	61
République R. de la	CZ	62
St-Denis Pl.	EY	
St-Dominique Mail	EZ	
St-Pierre Pl.	DY	
St-Rémy Pl.	CY	63
Salengro R. Roger	DY	65
Saussier R. Gén.	CZ	
Simart R.	DEY	
Siret R. Nicolas	CZ	79
Tour Pl. de la	DY	
Tour R. de la	DY	
Tour-Boileau R. de la	BZ	67
Trinité R. de la	CZ	68
Turenne R. de	CZ	70
Ulbach R. L.	CDZ	
Urbain-IV R.	CZ	72
Ursins R. des	CZ	73
Vauluisant R. de	CZ	74
Viardin R.	CZ	
Victor-Hugo Bd	BZ	
Voltaire R.	BZ	
Vouldy Chaussée du	EZ	
Zola R. E.	CDZ	
14-Juillet Bd du	CDZ	
1er-Mai Av. du	EY	78
1er-R.A.M. Bd du	CZ	

Apothicairerie	DY	M2
Basilique St-Urbain	DYZ	
Cathédrale St-Pierre-et-St-Paul	EY	
Chambre de Commerce	CZ	C
Église St-Jean	CZ	
Église St-Nicolas	BZ	
Église St-Nizier	EY	
Église St-Pantaléon	CZ	
Église St-Rémy	CY	
Église Ste-Madeleine	CZ	
Hôtel Juvénal-des-Ursins	CZ	B
Hôtel de Chapelaines	CZ	
Hôtel de Marisy	CZ	
Hôtel de Mauroy: Maison de l'Outil et de la Pensée ouvrière	CZ	M1
Hôtel de Vauluisant	CZ	
Hôtel de Ville	CZ	H
Hôtel-Dieu-le-Comte	DY	
Maison d'Art moderne	EY	
Maison des Allemands	CZ	D
Maison du Boulanger	CZ	E
Musée St-Loup	DY	
Tourelle de l'Orfèvre	CZ	N

Churches

Cathédrale St-Pierre-et-St-Paul★★

Open Tue–Sat 9am–noon, 1–5pm, Sun & holidays 10am–noon, 2–5pm.

The cathedral, built between the 13C and 17C, has remarkable proportions, exceptionally rich decoration and a beautiful nave. Martin Chambiges, who built the transept of Beauvais Cathedral and also worked on Sens Cathedral, contributed to the ornate **west front** (early 16C) adorned with a splendid Flamboyant Gothic rose-window. The three doorways have richly carved gables. The sculptures were destroyed during the Revolution. The cathedral was intended to have two towers, but the north tower alone was completed in the 17C (height: 66m/217ft). A plaque on the base of the tower reminds visitors that Joan of Arc stayed in Troyes on 10 July 1429.

On the north side, admire the **north-transept** doorway (13C) which has a huge rose-window.

Interior

This vast sanctuary conveys an impression of power and lightness, lit by fine **stained-glass windows**★★. Those of the **chancel** and **ambulatory** go back to the 13C. Note the warmth and intensity of the colours; they mainly depict isolated characters (popes and emperors) and scenes from the Life of the Virgin. The windows of the nave, dating from the early 16C, are completely different: they are more like paintings on glass with red as the dominant colour. The most remarkable are, on the north side, the *Story of the True Cross*, the *Legend of St Sebastian*, the *Story of Job* and that of *Toby*; on the south side, the *Story of Daniel* and *Joseph*, the *Parable of the Prodigal Son* and a magnificent *Tree of Jesse*.

The **rose-window of the west front** by Martin Chambiges, was completed in 1546 and decorated with stained glass by Jehan Soudain: the Patriarchs surrounding God the Father. The fourth chapel along the north aisle is lit by famous stained glass made in 1625 by Linard Gontier, known as the **mystical winepress:** Christ is seen lying beneath the winepress with blood pouring out of the wound in his side into a chalice. Out of his chest grows a vine whose branches support the 12 Apostles.

Treasury★

Jul–Aug, enquire at tourist office for opening times. No charge. 03 25 82 62 70.

The cathedral treasury, exhibited in a 13C vaulted room, includes an 11C ivory box, four 11C cloisonné enamels representing the four Evangelists, a 9C manuscript psalter, two missal covers inlaid with precious gems, the 12C reliquary of St Bernard, late-12C regional enamels, an embroidered 14C cope and gold plate from the 16C to 19C.

Basilique St-Urbain★

Open Mon–Sat 9.30am–12.3àpm, 2–5.30pm, Sun 2–5.30pm.

This is is a perfect example of Gothic architecture from the Champagne region. It was built 1262-86, by order of Pope Urban IV, a native of Troyes, on the site of his father's workshop.

Exterior

The **west front** is 19C but the doorway beneath the porch goes back to the 13C; the tympanum is decorated with the Last Judgement. However it is the east end that is most remarkable wth its graceful flying buttresses, elegant windows, delicate pinnacles, the gargoyles and profusion of decoration.

Interior

The chancel is almost entirely composed of stained-glass windows, a rare occurrence in Early Gothic architecture. The medallions of the low windows, the clerestory windows and high chancel windows, and the medallions of the Chapelle St-Joseph on the left of the chancel are all decorated with **13C stained-glass**. The chapel on the right of the chancel contains the statue of the smiling **Virgin with the Grapes**★.

Église Ste-Madeleine★

Open Mon–Sat 9.30am–12.3àpm, 2–5.30pm, Sun 2–5.30pm.

The nave contains a remarkable stone rood **screen**★★, carved in Flamboyant style in 1508-17 by Jean Gailde, a local sculptor and architect. It consists of three pointed arches underlined by delicate festoons and is decorated with a profusion of foliage and carved figures in Renaissance dress. On the top is a balustrade with fleur-de-lys motifs; on the chancel side, a staircase, lined with grotesques, leads to the gallery.

The east end is decorated with brightly coloured Renaissance **stained glass**★. In the south aisle, against a pillar of the nave, is a **statue** of **Martha**★, by the

B. Kaufmann/MICHELIN

Mystical winepress

Master of Chaource, one of the main exponents of 16C sculpture in Troyes.In the north aisle, note the wooden statue of saint Robert de Molesmes (early 15C), founder of the Cistercian Order.

As you come out of the church, note the Flamboyant doorway of the former charnel house (1525) decorated with a salamander, emblem of King François I.

Église St-Pantaléon★

Open Mon–Sat 9.30am–12.3àpm, 2–5.30pm, Sun 2–5.30pm.

This 16C church contains an important collection of **statues**★ brought here from churches and convents that were destroyed during the Revolution. Note, against the first pillar on the right, the statue of St James by **Dominique Florentin**, which is believed to be a self portrait and, opposite, the pulpit, a Gothic *Mater Dolorosa*; the pillars of the chancel are adorned with *Charity and Faith* also by Dominique Florentin, which reveal an Italian influence.

Église St-Jean

Enquire at tourist office for opening times.

It was in this church that the marriage of Catherine de France (daughter of Charles VI and Isabeau of Bavaria) and Henry V of England was celebrated in 1420. Above the altar are two paintings by Mignard. The tabernacle was made in 1692 after drawings by Girardon.

Église St-Nicolas

Enquire at tourist office for opening times.

Rebuilt after the fire of 1524, this church has a south doorway flanked by pilasters and statues by François Gentil.

Église St-Remy

Open Jul-Aug 10.30am-12.30pm. 03 25 82 62 70.

The restored 14C and 16C church has a delicate spiral steeple. The interior is adorned with 16C grisaille panels and bas-relief medallions and a bronze crucifix by Girardon, who was a parishioner.

Église St-Nizier

Jul-Aug open by appointment at the tourist office.

This 16C church roofed in brightly coloured glazed tiles can be seen from afar. It contains a beautiful *Entombment*, a 16C *Pietà* and a 16C *Christ Mocked* by artists from the Troyes School.

Museums

Musée d'Art moderne★★

Place St-Pierre. Open Tue–Sun 10am–1pm, 2–6pm. holidays. €5. 03 25 76 26 80.

In 1976, two local industrialists, Pierre and Denise Levy, donated to the State their rich collection of late 19C and early 20C art and African and Oceanic art, which is now housed in the former bishop's palace, a Renaissance edifice with a later 17C.

Fauvism★★ is particularly well represented. The fauves (wild beasts) were so-named for their pure, brilliant colours applied straight from the tube in what was qualified as an aggressive style. The Levy collection includes works by Derain (*Hyde Park, Big Ben*), Vlaminck (*Landscape in Chatou*), Braque (*Landscape at l'Estaque*) and Van Dongen.

The first few rooms contain paintings by Courbet, Degas, Seurat (*The Anglers*, a study which he used for his painting *The Grande Jatte*), Vallotton and Vuillard.

More recent works include paintings by Robert Delaunay before his abstract period, works by de la Fresnaye, Modigliani, Soutine, de Staël, Balthus and numerous post-fauvist paintings by **Derain**.

The collection of **African art**, which influenced many early 20C artists, includes statues, reliquary figures and headdresses in the form of antelopes.

Maison de l'Outil et de la Pensée ouvrière★★

7 rue de la Trinité. Open daily 10am-6pm. €6.50. Closed 1 Jan, 25 Dec. 03 25 73 28 26. www.Maison-de-l-outil.com

This museum is housed in the Hôtel de Mauroy restored by the **Compagnons du Devoir**. An itinerary enables visitors to admire a great number of 18C tools used for various crafts. A large room contains some of the impressive "master pieces" made by master craftsmen.

Musée de Vauluisant★

4 rue de Vauluisant. OpenJun–Sep Wed–Mon 10am-1pm, 2-6pm; Oct-May Wed–Sun 10am-noon, 2-6pm. Closed holidays. €3, no charge 1st Sun of the month (except during exhibitions). 03 25 73 05 85.

This Renaissance mansion contains two museums. The **Musée d'Art troyen**★ presents regional art from the Middle Ages to the 17C, including a Christ on the Cross sculpture believed to be by the Master of Chaource, as well as paintings and stained glass work. The **Musée de la Bonneterie** covers the history of hosiery and its manufacture, seen in embroidered stockings, looms, and a reconstruction of a 19C workshop.

Musées de l'Abbaye St-Loup

1 rue Chrétien-de-Troyes. Open Jun–Sep Wed–Mon 10am-1pm, 2-6pm. Oct-MayWed–Sun 10am-noon, 2-6pm. Closed holidays. €4; no charge 1st Sun of the month (except during exhibitions). 03 25 76 21 68. The former abbey, dating from the 17C and 18C and extended later, now house three museums. The **Musée d'Histoire naturelle** (Natural History Museum) contains a collection of mammals and birds from all over the world. Skeletons, rocks and meteorites are exhibited in the cloisters.

The **Musée d'Archéologie**★features regional archaeological finds from pre-

history to the Merovingian period are displayed in the abbey cellars. Highlights are the Apollo from Vaupoisson, a Gallo-Roman bronze statue, and the Pouan treasury, weapons and jewellery found in a 5C Merovingian grave.
The gallery of **medieval sculpture** testifies to the creative activity of the Champagne region from the 13C-15C.
On the first floor, the painting gallery of the **Musée des Beaux-Arts** covers all the major schools from the 15C to the 19C. The 17C is particularly well represented with paintings by Rubens, Van Dyck, Philippe de Champaigne, Le Brun and Mignard. Thereare also fine 18C works by Watteau Natoire, Boucher, Fragonard, Greuze (*Portrait of a Child with a Cat*), David and Elisabeth Vigée-Lebrun (*The Countess of Bossancourt*).

Excursions

Chaource★

29km/18mi S.
This village, which has given its name to a famous creamy cheese, has a 19C cast iron covered market and some 15C timber-framed houses.

Église St-Jean-Baptiste★

Open Apr-Oct daily 8.30am–7pm. Nov–May 9am–6pm).
The semi-underground chapel, left of the 13C chancel, contains a magnificent polychrome stone **Entombment**★★ carved in 1515 by the Master of Chaource; the facial expression of the Holy Women is extremely moving. Another chapel houses a 16C **gilt-wood crib**★ in the shape of a polyptych.

Musée du Fromage

Place de l'Église. Open Wed–Mon by appointment. €4. ☎03 25 40 10 67.
A collection of objects and tools connected with cheese-making from copper cauldrons to small huts once used by Pyrenean shepherds in summertime. The film shown is mainly devoted to Chaource, a cheeseswith an Appellation d'Origine Contrôlée (AOC) label, but other local cheeses such as Mussy, Ervy and Soumaintrain are also mentioned.

Musée des Voitures à Pedales

Place de l'Église. Guided tour (45min) Jun–Aug Thur–Tue 10am–noon, 2–6pm. Mar–May, Sep–Oct Thur–Tue 2–6pm. €4.50 (children €2). ☎06 10 04 69 66, www.voitures-a-pedales.net.
Kids An astonishing collection of over 200 pedal cars from the late 19C to today.

Ph. Gajic/MICHELIN

The Entombment, in St-Jean-Baptiste church

VAUCOULEURS

MEUSE. POPULATION 2 289

MICHELIN LOCAL MAP 307: E-7

Along with the nearby village of Domrémy-la-Pucelle, the peaceful little town of Vaucouleurs s associated with the hstory of Joan of Arc. It has retained part of its 13C fortifications and offers visitors boat trips on the Marne-to-Rhine canal and hikes through the forested Parc naturel régional de Lorraine.

- **Tourist Office**: 15 rue Jeanne d'Arc, 55140 Vaucouleurs. ☎03 29 89 51 82. www.otsi-vaucouleurs.com.
- **Orient Yourself**: 21km SW of Toul by the D960.

A Bit of History

In May 1428, a young shepherdess from Domrémy arrived in Vaucouleurs to see the governor and told him that God had sent her to save France. Robert de Baudricourt's first reaction was to send her back to her village but Joan of Arc persisted and after several months, urged by public enthusiasm, Baudricourt agreed to help. In February 1429, Joan left Vaucouleurs on her way to meet the king of France and her destiny which would eventually lead her to Rouen where she was burnt on 30 May 1431.

Sights

Site du château

The ruins of the castle where Joan was received by Baudricourt in 1428. The upper part of the **Porte de France** from where Joan of Arc left the town accompanied by a small escort remains, rebuilt in the 17C. The Chapelle castrale *(Open Jul–Aug 2-6pm; rest of the year: contact the Tourist office. ☎ 03 29 89 51 82)*, consisting of three chapels, was built over the 13C crypt of the castle chapel. In the central chapel is the statue of Notre-Dame-des-Voûtes before which Joan used to pray during her stay in Vaucouleurs.

Église

The 18C church has frescoes on the vault and an elaborately carved churchwardens' pew and the pulpit (1717).

Musée Jeanne d'Arc

Hôtel de Ville. May-Sep: 10am-noon, 2-6pm, Sat-Sun 2-6pm; rest of the year: by request at the Tourist office, daily except Sat-Sun 9am-noon, 2-6pm. 25 Dec-1 Jan, holidays except 14 Jul. €5. ☎03 29 89 51 82.

The highlight of this museum of local history and archaeology is the Christ de Septfonds, a magnificent oak crucifix from a nearby chapel where Joan of Arc went to pray for guidance.

Excursions

Domrémy-la-Pucelle★

19km/12mi S along D 964 then D 164.

This humble village is the birthplace of Joan of Arc (1412-31). An important pilgrimage takes place on the second Sunday in May, Joan of Arc's feast day, in Bois-Chenu Basilica (*see below*).

The **church** was remodelled in the 15C and extended in 1825. However, it has retained a few objects that were familiar to Joan of Arc: a stoup on the right of the entrance, a statue of St Margaret (14C) and the font over which she was christened.

Maison natale de Jeanne d'Arc★

Open Apr-Sep daily 9am-noon, 1.30-6.30pm. Oct-Mar Wed–Mon 10am-noon, 2-5pm. 1 Jan, 25 Dec. Interpretation centre closed 1-20 Jan. €3 ☎03 29 06 95 86.

The house where Joan of Arc was born is that of a comfortable peasant family; the walls are thick and there is the emblem of the family next to the arms of

R. Mattès/MICHELIN

Birthplace of Joan of Arc

France over the door. Behind the house, a modern **interpretation centre**★ has an exhibition about her life and times.

Basilique du Bois-Chenu

1.5km/0.9mi from Domrémy by D 53 towards Coussey.

The late-19C basilica stands on the site where Joan heard the voices of St Catherine, St Margaret and St Michael telling her about her mission. Start with the crypt (entrance on the left); statue of Notre-Dame-de-Bermont before which Joan prayed every Saturday. Inside the basilica contains frescoes and mosaics illustrating Joan's life.

Musée lorrain du Cheval

La Tour Ronde, Gondrecourt le Château, 20km/12.4mi S of Vaucouleurs by D 960 and D 966. Open Jun-Aug Wed–Mon 2-6pm. €2.50 (12-18 year olds: €1). 03 29 89 63 38.

Kids This museum, housed in a 15C tower, offers a lively account of the role played by horses throughout history.

VERDUN★★

MEUSE. POPULATION 19 624

MICHELIN LOCAL MAP 307: D-4

This ancient stronghold on a strategic position on the west bank of the Meuse has become the symbol of in France of the violence of the First World War.

- **Tourist Office**: Place de la Nation, 55160 Verdun. 03 29 86 14 18. www.verdun-tourisme.com.
- **Orient Yourself**: W of Metz by N3.
- **Don't Miss**: The battlefields and the Ossuaire de Douarmont.

A Bit of History

Verdun started out as a Gaulish fortress, then became a Roman fort under the name of Virodunum Castrum. In 843, the treaty splitting the Carolingian Empire into three kingdoms was signed in the city which was ceded to the kingdom of Lorraine. In 1552, Verdun was seized by Henri II and became part of the French kingdom.

Occupied briefly by the Prussians in 1792, it was liberated following the French victory at Valmy in the Argonne. In 1870,

the town was again besieged by the Prussians and was forced to capitulate. The occupation lasted three years.
At the start of the First World War, Verdun was, together with Toul, the most powerful stronghold in eastern France. The terrible Battle of Verdun took place all round the town between February 1916 and August 1917.

The Battle of Verdun

German troops had, since 1914, been trying in vain to skirt round Verdun and then to take it. Verdun nevertheless remained a formidable obstacle with its powerful citadel, its ring of forts and its gullied wooded plateaux. Yet this is where the German army, led by General von Falkenhayn, decided to strike a heavy blow in February 1916 in the hope of weakening the French army, lifting morale and thwarting the offensive which they suspected the Allies to be preparing (it actually came in July on the Somme). The Crown Prince, Emperor William II's own son, was entrusted with the operation.

German offensive (February-August 1916)

The German offensive took the French high command by surprise. It began on 21 February, 13km/8mi north of Verdun, with the heaviest concentration of shelling ever experienced. The resistance was stronger than expected but the Germans progressed slowly and the Fort de Douaumont soon fell, thus becoming a threat to the city. General Pétain, who was made commander in chief of the Verdun forces, began to organise the defence of the city. Reinforcements and supplies were brought in via the only available route, Bar-le-Duc to Verdun, nicknamed the **sacred way**.
The frontal attack was finally stopped on 26 February and, in March and April, German troops widened the front on both banks of the Meuse but failed to take several key positions.
There followed a savage war of attrition: forts, ruined villages or woods were taken over and over again at a terrible cost in human lives. On 11 July, German troops finally received the order to remain on the defensive.
The Russian offensive and the Franco-British offensive on the Somme put an end to any hope the Germans may have had of taking the advantage at Verdun.

French counter-offensive (October 1916-October 1917)

Three brilliant but costly offensives enabled French troops to take back all lost ground:

- the **Bataille de Douaumont-Vaux** (24 October-2 November 1916) on the east bank,
- the **Bataille de Louvemont-Bezonvaux** (15-18 December 1916), also on the east bank, which cleared the Vaux and Douaumont sectors once and for all.
- the **Bataille de la Cote 304 et du Mort-Homme** (20-24 August 1917) on the west bank; German troops were forced back to the positions they held on 22 February 1916 and tried in vain to counter-attack until well into October. The pressure on Verdun was released but it was only in September-October 1918, following the Franco-American offensive, that the front line was pushed back beyond its position of February 1916.

Ville Haute★

Allow 1hr 30min. Start from the tourist office. Walk across the bridge.

Porte Chaussée

This 16C gateway used to guard the entrance of the town and served as a prison; it is flanked by two round towers with crenellations and machicolations. It formed part of a thick wall surrounding the town and skirting the west bank of the River Meuse.

Take rue des Frères-Boulhaut on the right, walk round the left side of place Vauban to reach rue St-Paul.

Porte St-Paul

The two drawbridges can still be seen. This was the only way in and out for vehi-

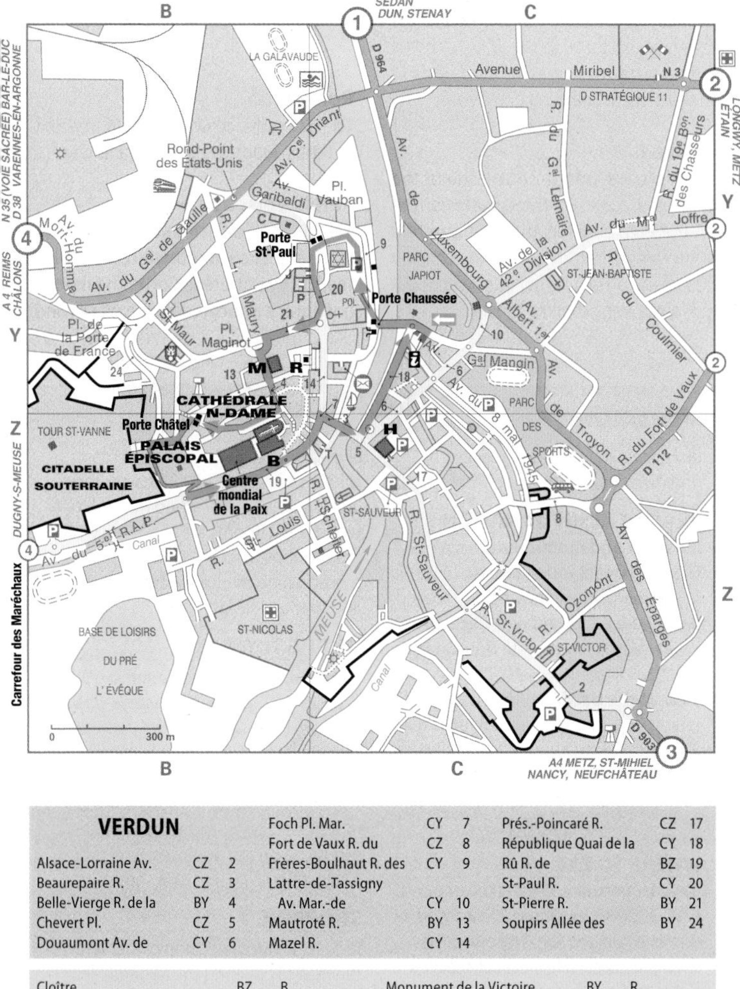

VERDUN

Alsace-Lorraine Av.	CZ	2	Foch Pl. Mar.	CY	7	Prés.-Poincaré R.	CZ	17
Beaurepaire R.	CZ	3	Fort de Vaux R. du	CZ	8	République Quai de la	CY	18
Belle-Vierge R. de la	BY	4	Frères-Boulhaut R. des	CY	9	Rû R. de	BZ	19
Chevert Pl.	CZ	5	Lattre-de-Tassigny Av. Mar.-de	CY	10	St-Paul R.	CY	20
Douaumont Av. de	CY	6	Mautroté R.	BY	13	St-Pierre R.	BY	21
			Mazel R.	CY	14	Soupirs Allée des	BY	24

Cloître	BZ	B	Monument de la Victoire	BY	R
Hôtel de ville	CZ	H	Musée de la Princerie	BY	M

cles before the ramparts disappeared in 1929. In front of the gate stands a bronze sculpture by Rodin (La Défense), offered to the town by the Netherlands.

Follow rue St-Paul then rue St-Pierre on the right to place Maginot and turn left towards the cathedral past the Musée de la Princerie (see below).

Cathédrale Notre-Dame★

Standing at the highest point of the town, the cathedral was built between 990 and 1024 in Rhenish style, with two chancels and two transepts. The west chancel is typically Rhenish, the east chancel (1130-40) shows Burgundian influence. The Gothic vaulting over the nave was added in the 14C.

After a fire in 1755 the Romanesque towers were replaced by two balustraded square Baroque towers. The nave was also transformed in Baroque style and an imposing baldaquin with twisted columns added over the high altar; the crypt was filled in and the Romanesque doorways concealed. The Romanesque part of the edifice was fortunately restored following the shelling of 1916. In the 12C crypt, note the beautiful capitals decorated with acanthus leaves along the aisles. Modern capitals are carved with scenes illustrating life in the trenches, *Suffering and Death*.

Cloître★

The cloisters, on the south side of the cathedral, consist of three galleries: that on the east side has three 14C arched openings which once led to the chapter house; the other two galleries were built in Flamboyant style in 1509-17.

Walk along the north side of the cathedral to place Châtel.

Porte Châtel

The 13C gate, crowned by 15C macchiolations, leads to place de la Roche.

Palais épiscopal★

The bishop's palace, set at the rear of a long semi-circular courtyard, was built in the 18C by Robert de Cotte. The municipal library is located in the west wing.

Address Book

For coin ranges, see the Legend on the cover flap.

PRACTICAL INFORMATION

Museum and monument pass – This pass treats you to at least 20% reduction on the following entrance fees: citadelle souterraine, forts (Vaux, Douaumont), ossuaire de Douaumont and Verdun memorial. *€17.50.*

Tour of the battle fields – Guided bus tour of Fort de Vaux, Verdun memorial, ossuaire de Douaumont, fort de Douaumont and Tranchée des baïonnettes. *May-Sep, departs from tourist office at 2pm, returns at 6pm. €25.50.*

WHERE TO EAT

Le Forum – *35 r. des Gros-Degrés. ☎03 29 86 46 88. Closed 22 Jul-5 Aug, Wed evening and Sun.* The owner has changed careers, from accountant to restaurateur and occasional painter. His wife does the cooking while he welcomes the customers in the two vaulted dining rooms, which are decorated with his work. A good place to eat, not far from the town centre.

WHERE TO STAY

Montaulbain – *4 r. Vieille-Prison. ☎03 29 86 00 47. 10 rooms. €5.50.* The rooms at this little hotel on a pedestrian street are rather cramped but recently renovated and very well kept. The cellars were the town prison in the 14C.

Chambre d'hôte Château de Labessière – *55320 Ancemont, 15km/9.3mi S of Verdun on D 34 (St-Mihiel road). ☎03 29 85 70 21. www.labessiere.com. Closed 25 Dec, 1 Jan. 4 rooms. Dinner.* This 18C château miraculously survived unscathed through two world wars. Rooms are charming with old furniture, and stylish dining room. A pretty garden and swimming pool add to the pleasure.

ON THE TOWN

L'Estaminet – *45 r. des Rouyers. ☎03 29 86 07 86. www.brasserie-de-verdun.com. Mon-Sat 2pm-3am.* A friendly pub, decorated with murals, old posters and dolls dressed as witches, who watch over the bar. A good choice of more than 250 beers includes three produced on the premises. Pool tables, a selection of cigars and a shop.

SHOPPING

In 1220, a hardware shop owner had the idea of covering the almonds that he used in making his cakes with a thin layer of sugar and honey, thus inventing the *dragée*. Soon christenings, communions and weddings became associated with this delicious sweet creation. *Dragées de Verdun.*

Dragées Braquier – *3 r. Pasteur – ☎03 29 86 05 02 – Tue-Sat 9am-noon, 2.30-7pm.* This old-fashioned little shop is the place to find the famous *dragées de Verdun*, the sweets that Goethe bought after the town was captured by the Prussians in 1792. Other regional specialities include madeleines from Commercy and the redcurrant jam from Bar-le-Duc, de-seeded with the help of a goose feather.

R. Mattès/MICHELIN

Palais épiscopal

The other part of the palace houses the Centre mondial de la Paix.

Return along rue de Rû to place du Maréchal-Foch.

Hôtel de ville

This 1623 mansion is a fine example of Louis XIII style.

Additional Sights

Musée de la Princerie

16 rue de la Belle-Vierge. Open Apr-Oct Wed–Mon 9.30am-noon, 2-6pm. €2. 03 29 86 10 62.

The museum is housed in an elegant 16C house built by two rich canons. Note the 12C carved-ivory comb, medieval statues, glazed earthenware from Argonne and paintings by local artists Jules Bastien Lepage and Louis Hector Leroux.

Citadelle souterraine★

Avenue de la 5e R.A.P. Open Apr-Sep daily 9am-6pm (Jul-Aug 7pm); Oct-Mar: daily 10am-noon, 2-5pm. Closed Jan. €6. 03 29 45 77 15. www.cg55.fr.

The citadel was built by Vauban on the site of the Abbaye de St-Vanne, of which only one 12C tower remains.

In 1916-17, the citadel was used as a rest area for troops during the Battle of Verdun. The 7km/4.3mi of galleries were equipped with an arsenal, telephone exchange, hospital with operating theatre, kitchens, bakery (nine ovens could turn out 28 000 rations of bread in 24 hours), butcher and cooperative.

A self-guided vehicle takes visitors on a **round-trip**★★ of the citadel where the soldiers' daily life during the Battle of Verdun is recreated through sound effects, lively scenes, virtual pictures (HQ, bakery) and reconstructed scenes of life in the trenches.

Centre mondial de la Paix

In the bishop's palace. Open Jul–Aug daily 9.30am-7pm; rest of the year daily 9.30am-noon, 2-6pm (last admission 1hr before closing). Closed mid-Dec–Jan. €3. 03 29 86 55 00. www.centremondialpaix.asso.fr.

The exhibition of the World Peace Centre has seven sections: war, the earth and its frontiers, from war to peace, Europe, the United Nations for peace, human rights, and peace concepts.

Monument de la Victoire

Open Apr mid-Nov daily 9.30am-noon, 2-6pm (Jul–Aug 9.30am–6.30pm). No charge. 03 29 87 24 29.

Seventy three steps lead to a terrace on which stands a high pyramid surmounted by the statue of a warrior wearing a helmet and leaning on his sword, as a symbol of Verdun's defence. The crypt beneath the monument bears the list of all the ex-servicemen who were awarded the medal of Verdun.

The Battlefields★★★

Almost a century on, the battlefields still bear the marks of the fierce fighting that took place from 21 February 1916 to 20 August 1917 in what is now known as the **Battle of Verdun**. In less than two years, this battle, which unfolded along a 200km/124mi front, involved several million soldiers and caused the death of 400 000 Frenchmen and almost as many Germans as well as several thousand American soldiers.

East Bank of the Meuse

21km/13mi – about 3hr. Michelin Local map 307: D-3.

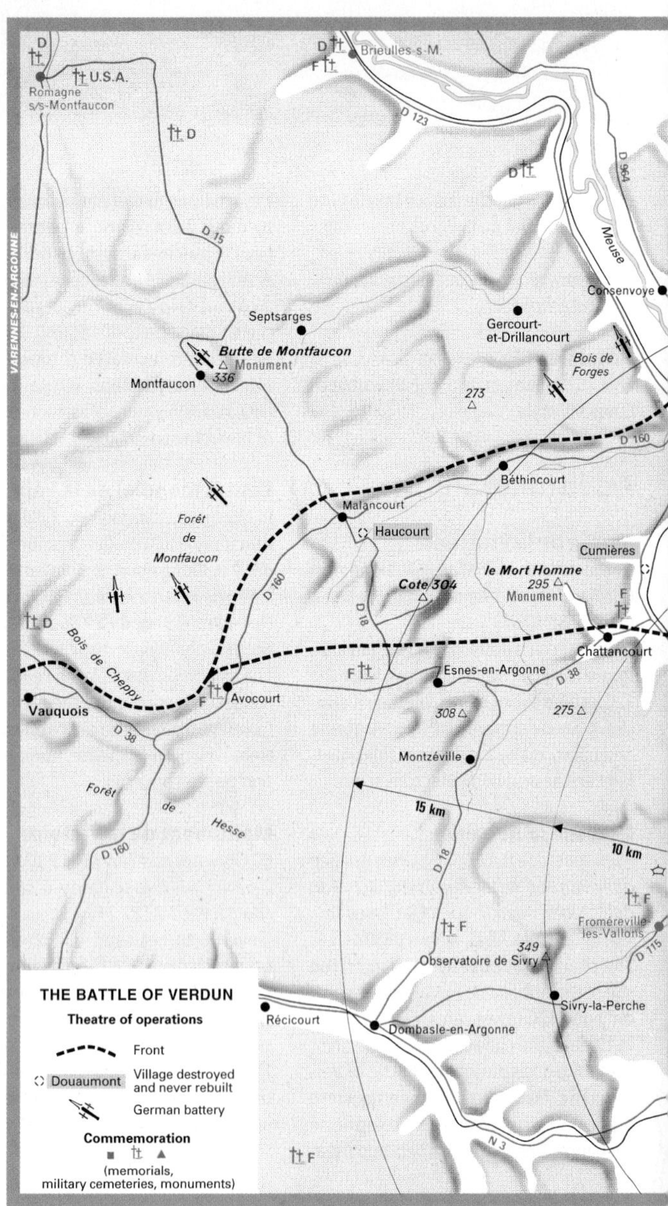

This was the main sector of the battle, where the decisive turning point occurred.

Drive E along avenue de la 42e-Division then avenue du Maréchal-Joffre and leave Verdun by ② on the town plan, N 3 towards Étain.

Cimetière militaire du Faubourg-Pavé

The cemetery contains the graves of 5 000 soldiers.

Turn left past the cemetery onto D 112 towards Mogeville.

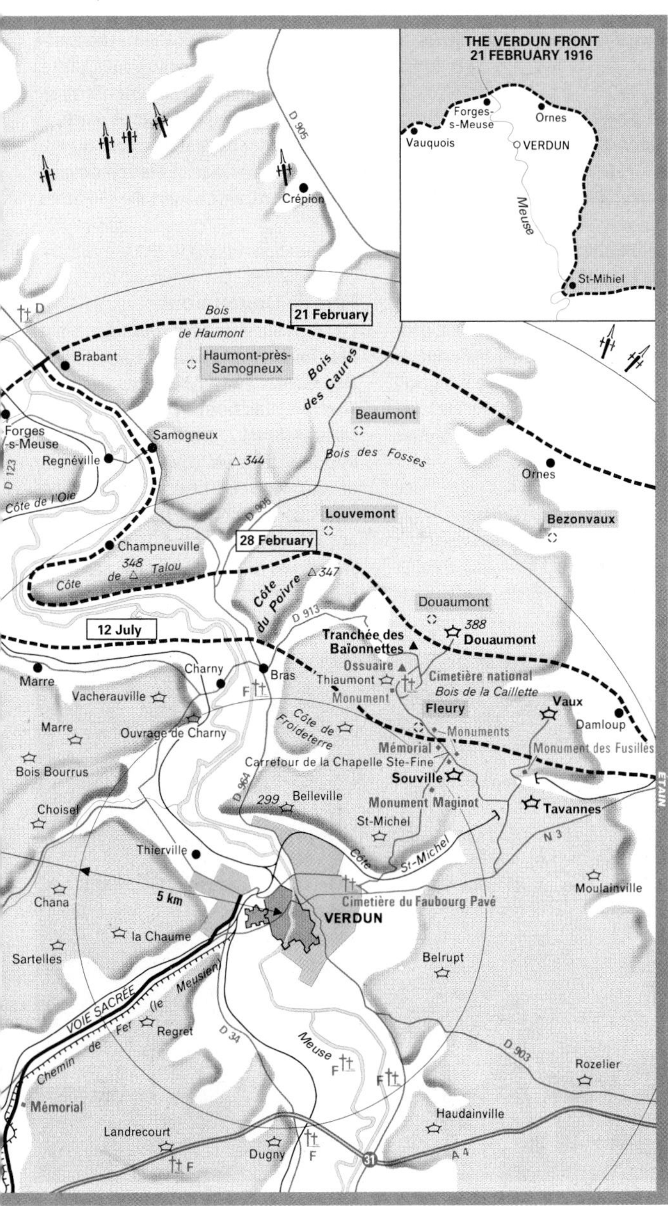

On the right, 6km/3.7mi farther on, stand the **Monument Maginot** and Souville Fort.

Turn right on D 913 towards Verdun then left on D 913A towards the Fort de Vaux.

The land remains profoundly marked by the war. On the right, slightly off the road, is the **Monument des Fusillés de Tavannes**, a reminder of an episode of the Second World War.

Fort de Vaux

Open Apr-Aug daily 9am-6pm; Sep-Oct & Feb–Mar 9am–noon, 1–5pm. Nov–Dec 10am-noon, 1-5pm. €3. 03 29 45 77 15.

Thirst drove the garrison to surrender on 7 June 1916 after two months' heroic resistance; the fort was reoccupied by the French five months later. The tour enables visitors to see a number of galleries. From the top, there is a good view of the ossuary, cemetery and fort of Douaumont, the Côtes de la Meuse and Plaine de la Woëvre.

Return to D 913 and turn right towards Fleury and Douaumont.

At the Chapelle Ste-Fine crossroads, the Monument du Lion marks the most forward position reached by the Germans.

Mémorial de Verdun

Open Apr-Sep daily 9am-6pm. Rest of the year 9am-noon, 2-6pm. Closed mid-Dec –Jan. €7. 03 29 84 35 34. www.memorial-14-18.com.

Videos, maps and slide shows explain the various stages of the battle and a collection of uniforms, weapons, pieces of equipment and documents illustrate the fierce fighting which took place.
A little farther on, a stele marks the site of the former village of **Fleury-devant-Douaumont**, which was taken 16 times.

Turn right onto D 913B.

Fort de Douaumont

Open Apr-Aug daily 10am-6pm. Sep-Mar 10am-1pm, 2-5pm. Jan & 25-26 Dec. €3. 03 29 45 77 55.

The fort was built in 1855 on a high point (388m/1 273ft), hence its strategic importance. It was covered with a layer of concrete 1m/3ft thick over a layer of sand also 1m/3ft thick. Taken by surprise at the beginning of the German offensive, it was recaptured by the French at the end of October.

R. Mattès/MICHELIN

Douaumont ossuary

The tour takes visitors through galleries, casemates and arsenals. A chapel marks the site of the walled-up gallery where 679 German soldiers, killed in the accidental explosion of an ammunition dump, were buried on 8 May 1916.
From the top of the fort, there is an view of the 1916 battlefield and the ossuary. Slightly farther on, to the right, a chapel stands on the site of the village church of **Douaumont** completely destroyed during the initial German attack.

Return to D 913 and turn right.

Ossuaire de Douaumont

Open May-Aug daily 9am-6.30pm. Sep daily 9am-noon, 2-6pm; Mar and Oct: 9am-noon, 2-5.30pm; Nov 9am-noon, 2-5pm; Dec & Feb school holidays: 2-5pm. €4. 03 29 84 54 81.
The ossuary, which was built to receive the unidentified remains of some 130 000 French and German soldiers killed during the battle, is the most important French monument of the First World War. It consists of a long gallery (137m/150yd) comprising 18 bays, each housing two granite sarcophagi. The chapel is located beneath the main vault. At the centre of the monument stands the Tour des Morts (Tower of the Dead), 46m/151ft high, shaped like a military shell and carved with four crosses. The first floor contains a small museum. At the top (204 steps), viewing tables enable visitors to spot the different sectors of the battlefield. The 15 000 crosses of the national cemetery are lined up in front of the ossuary.
A small path on the left of the car park, leads to the **Ouvrage de Thiaumont**, taken many times during the battle.

Tranchée des Baïonnettes

A massive door leads to the monument built over the trench where, on 10 June 1916, two companies of the 137 infantry regiment were buried following intense shelling. The tip of their rifles showing above ground was the only sign of their presence.

West Bank of the Meuse

40km/25mi – about 2hr. Michelin Local map 307: B/C-3

The fighting was just as fierce on the west bank. In September 1918, American troops led by General Pershing played a key role in this sector.

Drive out of Verdun NW along D 38 to Chattancourt and turn right towards Le Mort Homme, the site of fierce fighting. All the German attacks of March 1916 were halted on this ridge. Return to Chattancourt, turn right onto D 38 and right onto D 18 after Esnes-en-Argonne; 2km/1.2mi on, a path on the right leads to the Cote 304.

La Cote 304

For nearly 14 months the Germans met here unflinching resistance.

Butte de Montfaucon

This is the highest point of the area (336m/1 102ft); the village which stood at the top was fortified and used by the Germans as an observation point.
A **monument** (*Open Jul-Aug 9am-5pm; Sep-Jun, MonFri 9am-5pm. French and American public holidays; no charge; 03 29 85 14 18)* commemorates the victory of the 1st US army during the offensive of September-November 1918. A monumental staircase leads to a column (57m/187ft high, 235 steps) surmounted by a Statue of Liberty. From the top, there is a good **view**★ over the battlefield. The ruins of the village of Montfaucon can be seen near the monument; the village was totally destroyed and rebuilt 100m/110yd farther west.

Cimetière américain de Romagne-sous-Montfaucon

The American cemetery contains more than 14 000 graves in strict alignment amid shaded lawns, a pond and flower beds. In the centre stands the chapel and the side galleries bear the names of 954 missing soldiers; in the right-hand gallery, a map of the area of the battlefield has been engraved in the stone.

HAUTE-MARNE. POPULATION 307
MICHELIN LOCAL MAP 313: K-4

The picturesque village of Vigory, which is known for its Romanesque church, nestles under the ruins of a medieval castle..

- **Orient Yourself**: Situated between Chaumont and Joinville at the junction of the D40 and the N67.

Visit

Église St-Étienne★

Built c1000 by the lord of Vignory, this church is a rare example of mid-11C Romanesque architecture. The rectangular belfry is decorated with a storey of blind arcading beneath two storeys of twinned openings, topped by a stone cone with an octagonal roof.

Interior★

Although remodelled, the church has kept its original appearance with a nave extending over nine bays, separated from the aisles by three-storey elevations. The chancel has two parts: a front area with two-storey elevations and an oven-vaulted apse separated from the ambulatory by seven columns; some of which have capitals elaborately carved with lions, gazelles etc.

The church contains a wealth of sculpture from the 14C, 15C and 16C. Note the 14C monumental statue of the Virgin Mary carrying Jesus who is holding a bird in his hand. However, the most remarkable carvings are in the first chapel off the south aisle: an altarpiece and an altar front featuring the *Coronation of the Virgin* between St Peter and St Paul. The same regional workshop produced a series of small Nativity scenes to be found in the fourth chapel.

Castle ruins

The ruins are accessible by car up a narrow road leading to the keep.

From the esplanade laid out as a picnic area, there is a fine view of the town.

Ph. Gajic/ MICHELIN

An unusually decorative wash house

ROUTE DES VINS★★★

MICHELIN LOCAL MAP 315: I/G-5/10

The well-signposted 180km/112mi itinerary, known as the Route des Vins (Wine Road), winds its way along the foothills of the Vosges from Marlenheim to Thann, the northern and southern gateways to Alsace where there are information centres about Alsatian vineyards and wines. The numerous flower-decked villages along the route, nestling round their church and town hall, are one of the most charming aspects of the Alsace region, no doubt enhanced by convivial wine-tasting opportunities.

Tourist Office: **Dambach-la-Ville** Place du Marché, 67140 Dambach-la-Ville. 03 88 92 61 00, www.dambach-la-ville.fr. **Turckheim** Corps de Garde, 68230 Turckheim. 03 89 27 38 44, www.turckheim-alsace.com.

Alsatian Vineyards

Wine-growing in Alsace goes back to the 3C AD; since then, the region has been concerned with looking after its vineyards to the exclusion of any other form of agriculture. The landscape is characterised by terrace cultivation, with high stakes and low walls climbing the foothills of the Vosges. In the region entitled to the *appellation contrôlée* (label of origin), seven types of vines are grown: Riesling, Gewürztraminer, Sylvaner, Pinot Blanc, Tokay Pinot Gris, Muscat d'Alsace and Pinot Noir. These in turn give their name to the wines made from their grapes.

Driving Tours

Bas-Rhin Region — Marlenheim to Châtenois 1

68km/42mi – allow 4hr

Marlenheim

Renowned wine-growing centre *(information available about Alsatian wines)*.

Wangen

Wangen is a typical wine-growing village with twisting lanes lined with old houses and arched gates. Until 1830 the villagers had to pay St Stephen's Abbey in Strasbourg an annual tax calculated in litres of wine. The Fête de la Fontaine (Fountain Festival) is a reminder of this ancient custom: on the Sunday following 3 July, wine flows freely from Wangen's fountain.

Westhoffen

Wine-growing village with 16C and 17C houses and a Renaissance fountain.

Avolsheim – *See MOLSHEIM.*

Molsheim★ – *See MOLSHEIM.*

Rosheim★

See ROSHEIM.

Beyond Rosheim, the road runs through hills offering numerous viewpoints across the Plaine d'Alsace, with castles perched on promontories (Ottrott, Ortenbourg, Ramstein and Landsberg).

Boersch

This typical Alsatian village still has three ancient gateways and a picturesque **square**★ lined with old houses, the most remarkable being the town hall dating from the 16C. A Renaissance well marks the entrance of the square. Leave Boersch via the Porte du Haut (upper gate). Stop at the **Marquetry workshop** *(Open Mon-Sat 9am-noon, 2-6pm; Closed holidays; no charge; 03 88 95 80 17, www.spindler.tm.fr)* to see an exhibition and an audio-visual presentation of its work.

Ottrott

See Le HOHWALD: Drive 1.

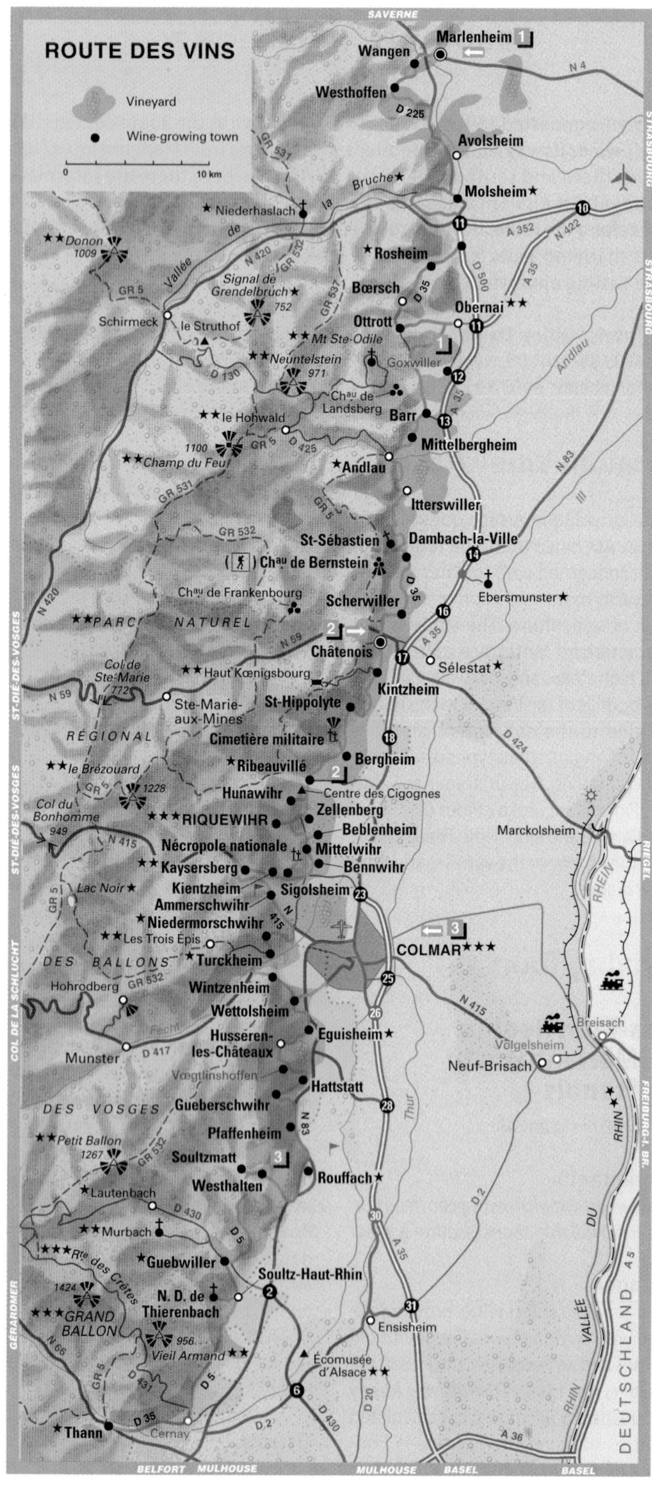
ROUTE DES VINS
Vineyard
Wine-growing town
0
10 km
SAVERNE
Marlenheim
Wangen
Westhoffen
Avolsheim
Molsheim
Rosheim
Bœrsch
Obernai
Ottrott
Goxwiller
Barr
Mittelbergheim
Andlau
Itterswiller
St-Sébastien
Dambach-la-Ville
Chau de Bernstein
Chau de Frankenbourg
Scherwiller
Ebersmunster
Châtenois
Sélestat
Kintzheim
Haut Kœnigsbourg
St-Hippolyte
Cimetière militaire
Bergheim
Ribeauvillé
Centre des Cigognes
Hunawihr
Zellenberg
Beblenheim
RIQUEWIHR
Nécropole nationale
Mittelwihr
Kaysersberg
Bennwihr
Kientzheim
Sigolsheim
Ammerschwihr
Niedermorschwihr
Les Trois Epis
Turckheim
COLMAR
Wintzenheim
Wettolsheim
Eguisheim
Husseren-les-Châteaux
Vœgtlinshoffen
Hattstatt
Gueberschwihr
Pfaffenheim
Soultzmatt
Westhalten
Rouffach
Lautenbach
Murbach
Guebwiller
Soultz-Haut-Rhin
N. D. de Thierenbach
Ensisheim
GRAND BALLON
Vieil Armand
Écomusée d'Alsace
Thann
Cernay
Niederhaslach
Donon 1009
Signal de Grendelbruch 752
Schirmeck
le Struthof
Mt Ste-Odile
Neuntelstein 971
Chau de Landsberg
le Hohwald
Champ du Feu
PARC NATUREL RÉGIONAL DES BALLONS DES VOSGES
Col de Ste-Marie 772
Ste-Marie-aux-Mines
le Brézouard
Col du Bonhomme 949
Lac Noir
Hohrodberg
Munster
Petit Ballon 1267
Rte des Crêtes
Marckolsheim
Breisach
Volgelsheim
Neuf-Brisach
Bruche
Andlau
Ill
Thur
Fecht
RHEIN
RHIN
VALLÉE DU RHIN
DEUTSCHLAND
STRASBOURG
ST-DIÉ-DES-VOSGES
COL DE LA SCHLUCHT
GÉRARDMER
RIEGEL
FREIBURG-I.-BR.
BELFORT
MULHOUSE
BASEL

Obernai★★ – *See OBERNAI.*

Barr

Barr is an industrial town (famous tanneries) as well as a wine-growing centre producing quality wines: Sylvaner, Riesling and above all Gewürztraminer. The annual wine fair is held in the town hall, a fine 17C building decorated with a loggia and a carved balcony; go into the courtyard to admire the rear part.

An 18C mansion, known as the **Folie Marco** (*Open Jul-Sep Wed–Mon 10am-noon, 2-6pm; May-Jun & Oct, weekends 10am-noon, 2-6pm; €3; ☎03 88 08 66 65)* houses 17C-19C furniture, porcelain, pewter and mementoes of local history.

Mittelbergheim

See Le HOHWALD.

Andlau★ – *See ANDLAU.*

Itterswiller

The flower-decked houses line the high street of this charming wine-growing village climbing up the hillside. Note the partly Gothic tower of the church which contains a 13C or 14C mural.

A footpath leads visitors on a tour of the vineyards *(about 1hr, viewpoint).*

Address Book

For coin ranges, see the Legend on the cover flap.

PRACTICAL INFORMATION

Maison des Vins d'Alsace, – *12 av. de la Foire-aux-Vins, 68012 Colmar, ☎03 89 20 16 20, www.vinsalsace.com*

WHERE TO EAT

À la Truite – *17 r. du 25 Jan, 68970 Illhaeusern. ☎03 89 71 83 51. Closed Tue evening, Thu lunch and Wed.* This 1950s waterfront restaurant has a colourful dining room and summer terrace by the river. Simple, no-frills cooking.

L'Auberge du Cabri – *67520 Nordheim, 3km/1.8mi N of Marlenheim on D 220. ☎03 88 87 56 87. Closed mid Dec-mid Jan, Wed evening, Thu evening, Mon and Tue.* Goats are raised on this farm, so goats' cheese and kid are on the menu, as well as charcuterie and other regional dishes.

Caveau Morakopf – *7 r. des Trois-Épis, 68230 Niedermorschwihr. ☎03 89 27 05 10 – caveau.morakopf@wanadoo.fr – closed 7-20 Jan, 23 Jun-7 Jul, Mon lunch and Sun.* In a charming little wine village, this cellar restaurant has a terraced garden where you can eat in fine weather. The cooking is rustic and typical of the region.

WHERE TO STAY

Vignoble – *67650 Dambach-la-Ville. ☎03 88 92 43 75 – closed 27 Jun-9 Jul, 24 Dec-12 Mar and Sun out of season. 7 rooms €6.* The bells of the nearby church remain silent throughout the night, so nothing will stop your enjoyment of the stylish little rooms in this converted Alsace barn built in 1765.

Domaine Bouxhof – *R. du Bouxhof, 68630 Mittelwhir – ☎03 89 47 93 67. Closed Jan. 3 rooms.* The owners will show you around the listed cellars of this lovely 17C house set among vines, and let you taste the wines made here. Breakfast in the 15C chapel is a must.

Hôtel Berceau du Vigneron – *Pl. de Turenne, 68230 Turckheim. ☎03 89 27 23 55 – hotel-berceau-du-vigneron@wanadoo.fr – closed Jan – 16 rooms – €8.* This traditional hotel in lovely place de Turenne has slightly old-fashioned but spacious and well-kept rooms, with old furniture. The breakfast room is typically Alsatian, with its wooden chairs and red-checked napkins.

Château d'Andlau – *2km from 67140 Barr, ☎03 88 08 96 78, hotelchateau-andlau@wanadoo.fr. 22 rooms. €8. Restaurant .* In a serene bucolic setting, this hotel proposes rustic bedrooms, traditional cooking and excellent wines.

CALENDAR

Advice – Grapes are harvested between late Sep and mid-Oct, during which time access to the wine paths is often restricted. Enquire on site.

R. Mattès/ MICHELIN

Dambach-la-Ville

Dambach-la-Ville

This renowned wine-growing centre (Frankstein vintages) lies in a picturesque setting overlooked by woods. The town centre with its timber-framed houses was once surrounded by ramparts, of which three town gates remain. A wine fair takes place on 14 and 15 August.

400m/437yd beyond the Porte Haute (upper gate) turn left for the path to the **Chapelle St-Sébastien**,which has a late-17C Baroque altar. The path continues *(2hr on foot there and back)* to the ruined **Château de Bernstein** (12C-13C), built on a granite ridge. There is a fine view of the Plaine d'Alsace.

Scherwiller

Lying at the foot of Ortenbourg and Ramstein castles, this village has retained its guardhouse,fine 18C timber-framed houses and old wash house along the River Aubach. Art, handicraft and Riesling fair during the third weekend in August.

Châtenois

Note the unusual Romanesque belfry, with a spire and four timber bartizans, and the picturesque 15C gatehouse known as the Tour des Sorcières (witches' tower) crowned by a stork's nest.

Haut-Rhin Region—From Châtenois to Colmar 2

54km/34mi – allow 5hr

As far south as Ribeauvillé, the road is overlooked by numerous castles: Haut-Kœnigsbourg, the ruins of Kintzheim, Frankenbourg, St-Ulrich, Girsberg and Haut-Ribeaupierre.

Kintzheim

See SÉLESTAT: Excursions.

St-Hippolyte – *See RIBEAUVILLÉ.*

Bergheim

The Porte Haute, a 14C fortified gate, leads into this wine-growing village shaded by an old lime tree believed to date back to 1300. The northern section of the medieval wall, which protected Bergheim from the Burgundians in 1470, is still standing with three of its original round towers. The village has many old houses and a picturesque market square. The red-sandstone **church** *(Open Jul-Sep; rest of the year, enquire at presbytery, 1 r. de l'Eglise; 03 89 73 63 20, www.eglise-bergheim.org)* has some 14C features; the rest dates from the 18C.

Cimetière militaire allemand

1.2km/0.7mi N of Bergheim along a road branching off D 1B on the left.

Built on a hillside, the cemetery contains the graves of German soldiers killed during the Second World War. Fine **view**★ from the cross at the top.

Ribeauvillé★

See RIBEAUVILLÉ. Beyond Ribeauvillé, the road rises half way up the hillsides offering a wider panorama of the Plaine d'Alsace. The heart of the Alsatian wine-growing centre is situated here, between Ribeauvillé and Colmar. Charming villages and famous wine-growing centres are scattered across the rolling hills lying on the edge of the Vosges.

Hunawihr

The square belfry of the church is as massive as a keep. The church is surrounded by a 14C wall which had only one entrance defended by a tower. The six bastions flanking the wall can still be seen. From the church, there is a good view of the three castles of Ribeauvillé and the Plaine d'Alsace.

The church is used for Catholic and Protestant church services. The chapel on the left of the chancel contains 15C-16C frescoes depicting the Life of St Nicholas, the miracles he accomplished and the canonisation of St Huna.

Kids A centre devoted to the return of storks **Centre de réintroduction des cigognes et des loutres** *(Open Jun-Aug: 10am-7pm (6.30pm Jul, 6pm Jun); Apr-Mar, depends on the weather; May & Sep-Oct: 10am-12.30pm, 2-6pm (5.30pm Apr, 5pm Oct), Sat-Sun and holidays all day; 1-11 Nov: Sat-Sun, holidays and school holidays 10am-12.30pm, 2-5pm; €7.50 (children: €5); 03 89 73 72 62; www.cigogne-loutre.com)* has been trying to encourage storks to remain in Alsace throughout the winter and to nest at the centre or in nearby villages. More than 200 storks are fed and looked after here. Every afternoon, there is a show involving various animals that are particularly clever at fishing: cormorants, penguins, sea-lions and otters. In 1991, a centre for the safeguard and reproduction of otters was created.

Kids The **Jardin des Papillons exotiques vivants** *(Open Jul-Aug: 10am-7pm; Apr-Jun & Sep: 10am-6pm; Oct & 1 Nov: 10am-5pm. €5.50 (children 5-14: €4); 03 89 73 33 33, www.jardinsdespapillons.fr)* includes more than 150 species of exotic butterflies, flying about freely inside a hothouse full of luxuriant vegetation.

A short distance from Hunawihr stands the small village of **Zellenberg**, at the top of a hill, overlooking Riqhewihr and the vineyards. A **historic trail** *(40min, booklet available from the town hall or the tourist offices of Ribeauvillé and Riquewihr)* indicates the most interesting old buildings.

Riquewihr★★★

See RIQUEWIHR.

Beblenheim – *See RIBEAUVILLÉ.*

Mittelwihr

At the southern end of the village is the Mur des Fleurs Martyres, a wall which, throughout the German occupation was decked with blue, white and red flowers as a token of Alsatian loyalty.

The hillsides all around enjoy a microclimate which causes almond trees to flower and yield fruit. The reputation of the Riesling and Gewürztraminer made in this area is steadily growing.

Bennwihr

This is another famous wine-growing village, with a monumental fountain in its centre. The modern **church** is brightly lit by a colourful stained-glass window stretching right across the south side. Note the soft tones of the stained glass decorating the chapel on the left.

Sigolsheim

This is supposed to be the place where, in 833, the sons of Louis the Meek, Charlemagne's son, met before capturing their father to have him imprisoned.

The Église St-Pierre-et-St-Paul dates from the 12C. The Romanesque doorway is adorned with a tympanum carved in a style similar to those of Kaysersberg and Andlau.

Follow rue de la 1re-Armée (the main street) beyond the Couvent des Capucins to the national necropolis.

Nécropole nationale de Sigolsheim

The necropolis, standing up 124 steps on top of a hill and surrounded by vines, contains the graves of 1 684 French soldiers killed in 1944. From the central platform, there is a splendid **panorama**★.

Kientzheim

This wine-growing village has several interesting medieval buildings, fortifications, squares, wells and sundials.

The **Porte Basse** is a fortified gate surmounted by a grinning head which was placed there as a warning to attackers that they did not stand a chance to get past this mighty tower. The medieval **castle** is the headquarters of St Stephen's Brotherhood, the official body controlling the quality of Alsatian wines. Housed in an outbuilding, the **Musée du Vignoble et des Vins d'Alsace** (*Open Jun-Oct: 10am-noon, 2-6pm; €3; 03 89 48 21 36)* is devoted to all aspects of wine-making from vineyard to wine. Inside the church, next to a 14C statue of the Virgin Mary, are the **tombstones**★ of Lazarus von Schwendi (d 1583), who brought Tokay vines back from Hungary, and of his son (see *KAYSERSBERG*).

The **Chapelle Sts-Felix-et-Régule** contains naive 'paintings on canvas and wood, dating from 1667 to 1865.

Kaysersberg★★

See KAYSERSBERG.

Ammerschwihr

Situated at the foot of vine-covered hills, Ammerschwihr was destroyed by fire following the bombings of December 1944 and January 1945. The town was rebuilt in traditional Alsatian style. All that remains from its past are the Gothic **Église St-Martin**, the Renaissance former town hall, two fortified towers, and the **Porte Haute**, on the western edge of the town. The gate's square tower, crowned by a stork's nest, is decorated with the arms of the town and a painted sundial.

Niedermorschwihr★

This lovely village set among vineyards has a modern church with a 13C spiral belfry. The high street is lined with old houses with oriels and balconies.

Turckheim★

This ancient fortified town is the last place in Alsace where a night watchman (May–Oct every evening at 10pm) walks through the streets carrying his lamp and horn; he stops and sings at every street corner. Admire the three fortified gateways, **Place de Turenne** with its 16C and 17 houses and the ornate **Hôtel des Deux-Clefs** on Grand'Rue.

R. Mattès/ MICHELIN

Vineyard and village of Ammerschwihr

Wintzenheim
This famous wine-growing centre (Hengst vintage) is a pleasant city, fortified in 1275. The old manor of the Knights of St John is now the town hall.

Colmar★★★ – See COLMAR.

From Colmar to Thann 3

59km/37mi – allow 3hr.

Colmar★★★ – See COLMAR..

Drive out of Colmar along D 417.

Wettolsheim
This village claims the honour of being the birthplace of Alsatian vine-growing, which was introduced here during the Roman occupation. A wine festival takes place during the last weekend in July.

Eguisheim★
See EGUISHEIM.

Husseren-les-Châteaux
This is the highest point of the Alsatian vineyards (alt 380m/1 247ft) and starting point of a tour of the five castles of Eguisheim (*see EGUISHEIM: Route des Cinq Châteaux*) above the village.

Hattstatt
This once-fortified village has an early-11C church with a 15C chancel containing a stone altar and 15C baptistery. Note the fine Renaissance calvary on the left of the nave. The 16C town hall stands next to fine old houses.

Gueberschwihr
A magnificent three-storey Romanesque belfry (all that remains of an early-12C church) overlooks this peaceful hillside village. Note the Merovingian sarcophagi nearby.

Pfaffenheim
See ROUFFACH: Excursion.

Rouffach★
See ROUFFACH. Shortly beyond Rouffach, Grand Ballon (*see Route des CRÊTES*) comes into view.

Westhalten
Picturesque village with two fountains and several old houses.

Soultzmatt
Charming city on the banks of the Ohmbach. The local Sylvaner, Riesling and Gewürztraminer are highly rated as are the mineral springs. There is a wine festival in early August. The **Château de Wagenbourg** stands nearby.

Guebwiller★ – See GUEBWILLER.

Soultz-Haut-Rhin
See SOULTZ-HAUT-RHIN.

Turn right onto D 51.

Basilique Notre-Dame de Thierenbach
The onion-shaped belfry can be seen from afar. The basilica was built in 1723 in the Austrian Baroque style by the architect Peter Thumb. An important pilgrimage, going back to the 8C and dedicated to Notre-Dame-de-l'Espérance takes place in the church. The basilica contains two Pietà: the miracle-working Virgin Mary dating from 1350 and the Mater Dolorosa dating from 1510.

Return to Soultz-Haut-Rhin and follow D 5 towards Cernay.

Cave vinicole du Vieil-Armand
This cooperative, on the outskirts of Soultz, groups 130 wine-growers and organses tastings. Two great wines are produced: Rangen, the most southern of Alsatian wines and Ollwiller, grown just beneath Vieil Armand. In the basement, a museum contains equipment used in the old days in vineyards and cellars.

Continue along D 5 then turn right onto D 35.

Thann★ – See THANN.

VITRY-LE-FRANÇOIS

MARNE. POPULATION 16 737

MICHELIN LOCAL MAP 306: J-10

Vitry-le-François is the capital of the Perthois area, a fertile plain extending from the River Marne to the Trois-Fontaines Forest. The town occupies a strategic position on the east bank of the Marne, at the foot of the Champagne limestone cliff and at the intersection of the Marne-Rhine and Marne-Saône canals.

- **Tourist Office**: Place Giraud, 51300 Vitry-le-François. ☎03 26 74 45 30.
- **Orient Yourself**: 29km NW of St-Dizier by N4.

A Bit of History

Vitry was built by King François I who gave it his name. He commissioned an engineer from Bologna who designed the grid plan, the fortifications and a citadel destroyed in the 17C. In 1940, the city was 90% destroyed by bombs and artillery fire. After the war, it was rebuilt along the lines of the original plan.

For coin ranges, see the Legend on the cover flap.

WHERE TO EAT

La Cloche – *34 r. Aristide-Briand. ☎03 26 74 03 84, www.hotel-de-la-cloche.fr. Closed 20 Dec-2 Jan, Sun evening Oct-May and Sat lunch.* Generous helpings of mouth-watering food based on good fresh produce make this a place definitely worth visiting. Two lovely old-fashioned buildings are separated by an inner courtyard, which serves as a terrace in summer. The rooms are plain and bright.

Sights

Collégiale Notre-Dame de l'Assomption

Place d'Armes. The 17C-18C church is an interesting example of the Classical style with a harmonious west front flanked by twinned towers adorned with scrolls and surmounted by flame vases. Inside, the imposing nave and transept are prolonged by a late-19C apse. The furniture includes a baldaquined altar, an organ case originally in the Abbaye de Trois-Fontaines and an 18C pulpit and carved churchwardens' pew. In the last chapel along the north aisle, there's a Crucifixion, painted in 1737 by Jean Restout.

Hôtel de ville

The town hall occupies a 17C convent.

Ph. Gajic/ MICHELIN

Church in St-Amand-sur-Fion

Porte du Pont

Fine triumphal arch (1748) erected in honour of Louis XIV. Taken down in 1938, it was only re-erected in 1984.

Excursions

St-Amand-sur-Fion★

10km/6mi N along N 44 then D 260.
Lying on the banks of the River Fion, the village has numerous timber-framed houses, five mills and a few wash-houses. The **church**★ is a successful mixture of Romanesque and Gothic styles. The beautiful arcaded porch dates from the 15C. Note the carved capitals and the 17C rood beam.

Ponthion

10km/6mi NE along D 982 then D 14.
Situated between the Marne-Rhine canal and the River Saulx, Ponthion has a medieval church with a lovely 12C porch. In 754, a meeting in this village between Pope Stephen II and Pepin the Short, the first Carolingian king, led to the creation of the Papal States.

VITTEL

VOSGES. POPULATION 6 117
MICHELIN LOCAL MAP 314: D-3

This renowned spa resort, which was highly fashionable during the Belle Epoque, owes its fame to the therapeutic qualities of its water and its situation at the heart of a picturesque wooded area.

- **Tourist Office**: 136 avenue Boulournié, 88800 Vittel. ☎03 29 08 08 88, www.vitteltourisme.com.
- **Orient Yourself**: 40km W of Epinal. The spa town is outside the town centre.

Sights

Parc★

This landscaped park has a bandstand where concerts take place in summer. Amid the greenery, discover the 1910 Grand Hôtel, the Casino and the new Palais de Congrès (inaugurated 1970). It is adjacent to vast sports grounds (horse racing, polo, golf, tennis etc).

Institut de l'eau Perrier Vittel

Open Apr–Oct 10am–noon, 2–6pm. €3.50. ☎03 29 08 77 29.
The exhibition "Water and Life" is housed in the former baths built by Charles Garnier (architect of the Paris opera) in 1884; it illustrates the scientific, technical and industrial aspects of water.

Excursions

Domjulien

8km/5mi NE along D 68. The 15C-16C church (considerably remodelled), contains some remarkable sculptures: an altarpiece (1541) of the Crucifixion and the 12 Apostles; an early-16C Entombment; statues of St George (16C) and St Julian and a fine 15C statue of the Virgin and Child playing with an angel.

Contrexéville

4km/2.5mi SW (see Introduction: Architecture and Art).
Known since the 18C, this popular spa town has five mineral springs used in the

R. Mattès/ MICHELIN

Vittel park

Address Book

For coin ranges, see the Legend on the cover flap.

WHERE TO EAT

César – *125 av. Châtillon. ☎03 29 08 61 73. Closed 23 Dec-16 Jan, Sun evening, Tue lunchtime & Mon.* Flavoursome modern cooking is served in an elegantly restored dining room with an agreeable bar lounge by the entrance.

WHERE TO STAY

Chambre d'hôte M. Breton Benoît – *74 r. des Récollets, 88140 Bulgnéville, 7.5km/4.6mi W of Contrexéville by D 164. ☎03 29 09 21 72 benoitbreton.chambresdhotes@wanadoo.fr. Closed 2 weeks in Jan. Booking necessary in winter. 4 rooms.* This lovely mansion dating from 1720 is shown to its best advantage... hardly surprising as the owner is an antique dealer. The rooms are modern but attractively furnished with antiques. Pleasant garden.

Hôtel d'Angleterre – *162 r. de Charmey. ☎03 29 08 08 42. www.abc-gesthotel.com. Closed 20 Dec-1 Jan. 55 rooms. Restaurant .* This grand early 20C hotel between the station and the thermal establishment has spacious comfortable rooms, a cosy bar and a shady garden. Traditional food served in the restaurant. Spa packages available.

ON THE TOWN

Casino de Vittel – *Parc Thermal. ☎03 29 08 12 35 – open daily from 10am. Gaming room from 9pm except Mon and Tue.* This is one of the main attractions of the spa resort, frequented by tourists, curists and local inhabitants Chance your luck with fruit machines, roulette, stud poker and blackjack. Tea dance on Sunday afternoon.

SHOPPING

Au Péché Mignon – *36 pl. du Gén.-de-Gaulle – ☎03 29 08 01 07 – Tue-Sat 7.45am-12.30pm, 2-7.30pm, Sun 7.30am-12.30pm, 3-7pm – closed 2 weeks in June.* Apart from a few classic local dishes (pâté from Lorraine or Vittel) this food shop sells chocolates: the "chocolate spa route" (four different chocolates, like the four Vosges spa towns), and creuchotte (a chocolate cream frog).

Délices Lorraines – *184 r. de Verdun – ☎03 29 08 03 30 – Mon-Sat 9am-12.30pm, 2.15-7.15pm, Sun 9am-12.30pm.* A wide variety of regional specialities includes honey, Lorraine wines (côte de Toul), aperitifs and liqueurs from the Vosges, wild fruit brandies and sweets (Vittel sweets, grès-rose des Vosges).

Brasserie-écomusée "La Vosgienne" – *48 r. de Mirecourt – 88270 Ville-sur-Illon. ☎03 29 36 58 05/03 29 36 53v18. mid Jun-early Oct Tue-Sun 2.30-6pm; rest of the year by appointment.* Ville-sur-Illon is renowned for the purety of its water, and produced beer from 1627. In 1887, Jacques Lobstein, an Alsatian brewer, built a Bavarian-style industrial brewery here, in operation until 1975. It is now an eco-museum, but some beer-lovers continue to produce a few beers using traditional methods, which can be tasted or bought on the premises.

SPORTS & RECREATION

Vittel St-Jean Golf Course – *1 av. Gilbert Trigano, ☎03 29 08 59 40.*

Thermes de Vittel – *Parc thermal – ☎03 29 08 76 54. Closed Jan.*The Vittel baths date from 1856: the mineral-water basin where the spring emerges results from a tectonic weakness south of town. The sulphated calcic or magnesian water is used to treat liver and kidney ailments, post-traumatic injuries, nutritional problems and rheumatic disorders. Revitalising treatments.

ENTERTAINMENT

All year round there are concerts, folk events and musicals, horse shows, tennis tournaments and fireworks.

Casino de Contrexéville – *R. du Gén.-Hirschauer-Parc thermal – ☎03 29 08 01 14 – daily from 11am.* As the resort's main leisure centre, the casino offers numerous activities: fruit machines, boule, cinema, nightclub and restaurant. Out of season, parties and tea with dancing (Sunday afternoons) are on the programme.

Spa – *☎03 29 08 03 24. Apr-Oct.* The 11°C/51.8°F waters of the five natural mineral springs are prescribed for obesity, renal, urinary and biliary infections, and gout. Package for dieters.

treatment of kidney and liver dieases, excess of cholesterol and obesity. In addition, the thermal establishment, built in 1912 in neo-Byzantine style, proposes slimming and fitness formulae.

PARC NATUREL RÉGIONAL DES VOSGES DU NORD★★

MOSELLE AND BAS-RHINE. MICHELIN LOCAL MAP 315: I TO J-3

The northern Vosges are relatively low yet often steep mountains which differ considerably from the rest of the massif. The sandstone cover has been torn open by deep valleys and shaped into horizontal plateaux or rolling hills generally less than 500m/1 640ft high. Erosion has carved the sandstone crust into isolated jagged rocks reminiscent of towers, mushrooms or arches. Numerous fortresses still stand on the densely forested heights.

Orient Yourself: The park extends from the north of the Lorraine plateau to the Plaine d'Alsace and from the German border to the A 4 Metz-Strasbourg motorway.

The Regional Park

Created in 1975, the regional park aims to safeguard the natural heritage and preserve the quality of life. Forests (beech, oak, pine, spruce) cover more than 60% of the area. Hikes, riding tours, bike tours and nature excursions enable visitors to discover local flora and fauna and get an insight into the lifestyle and economic activities of the region, with its charming Alsatian villages and their picturesque traditions, as well as crystal-works, technical and folk museums and, of course, old castles full of mystery.

The Parc naturel régional des Vosges du Nord has been designated by UNESCO as one of the biosphere's world reserves.

Driving Tours

Hanau Region: Round-trip from Saverne 1

125km/78mi – allow 4hr 30min

Saverne★

See SAVERNE.

Soon after leaving Saverne via Ottersthal, D 115 crosses the green Muhlbach Vale then passes beneath the motorway.

St-Jean-Saverne

See ST-JEAN-SAVERNE.

Just beyond St-Jean-Saverne, the ruins of **Haut-Barr Castle**★ (*see Château du HAUT-BARR*) can be seen on a wooded height,and soon after the ruins of Griffon Castle.

Turn left to Neuwiller-les-Saverne via Dossenheim-sur-Zinsel.

Neuwiller-lès-Saverne★

See NEUWILLER-LÈS-SAVERNE.

Bouxwiller

This small town was, until 1791, the capital of the county of Hanau-Lichtenberg, extending across the Rhine and the picturesque streets are lined with German Renaissance houses. Part of the ramparts have been restored. The **Protestant church** (*Open Jul–Aug Fri 3-6pm, Sat 10am-noon, 3-6pm, Sun 11am-noon, 3-6pm. 03 88 70 71 15*) contains a fine **pulpit**★ in sculpted stone and painted wood, an organ by Silbermann, and a seigneurial box pew with ornate stuccowork.

The **Musée du pays de Hanau** (*Open Jul–Sep Tue–Sun 2-6pm, Sat 2-5pm; Oct-Jun Tue–Sun 2-5pm. 1 Jan, Good Friday, 1 May, 24-26 & 31 Dec; €2; 03 88 70 99 15*) houses collections of painted furniture, glassware from Bouxwiller, and reconstructions of interiors. The former synagogue (1842) is now the **Musée judéo-alsacien** *(Open late Apr–mid-Sep Tue–Fri 2-5pm, Sun & holidays 2-6pm; €6; Closed Mon & Sat. 03 88 70 97 17, www.sdv.fr/judaisme)* which illustrates the history and culture of Alsace's Jewish community.

A 6km/3.7mi geological trail *(information from tourist office)*, extremely rich in fossils, leads to the summit of Bastberg. The summit is also accessible by car from Imbsheim (from Bouxwiller, follow D 6 then turn right just before Imbsheim).

From Bouxwiller, drive to Ingwiller via Niedersoultzbach, then take D 28, through Rothbach and Offwiller to Zinswiller and turn left onto D 141 along the north bank of the Zinsel between Offwiller Forest and Niederbronn Forest. Arnsbourg Castle is on the right, near the GR33.

Baerenthal

This charming village is situated on the north bank of the River **Zinsel**. It is possible to go round the Baerenthal Lake, a nature reserve with an exceptionally rich flora. An observation tower makes it possible watch birds, particularly migratory species in spring and autumn.

Between Baerenthal and Mouterhouse, the road follows the valley once dotted with metalworks belonging to the De Dietrich family, now almost all gone.

Continue along D 36 to Lemberg.

The narrow road winds along the Breitenbach stream. On the right is the Mouterhouse Forest.

St-Louis-lès-Bitche

This is the headquarters of the **cristalleries de St-Louis**, former royal crystal works founded in 1767. It today produces a variety of ornaments and tablewares *(shop open Mon–Sat 10am-noon, 1.30-5pm, 03 87 06 60 15)*.

Rejoin D 37 and turn right.

Goetzenbruck

Glass-making is the main activity here including an important factory producing glasses for spectacles.

Meisenthal

In the centre of the village, the old glassworks (closed 1970) house the **Maison du verre et du cristal** *(Open Easter–Oct Wed–Mon 2-6pm. €5, 03 87 96 91v51)* glass and crystal museum.

Soucht

2km/1.2mi from Meisenthal. A former workshop contains the **Musée du Sabot**, where you can watch clogs being made; *Open Jul-Aug guided tour only (40min) 2-6pm; Easter–Jun & Sep–Oct weekends & holidays 2-6pm. €2. 03 87 96 86 97).*

R. Mattès/ MICHELIN

Dwellings built into the cliffs in Graufthal

Return to D 37.

From the Colonne de Wingen, there is a fine view of the Meisenthal Valley.

Pierre des 12 apôtres

This ancient standing stone was only carved in the 18C following a vow. Under the cross, one can see the 12 Apostles. Lalique crystalworks are situated near **Wingen-sur-Moder**.

Turn left in Wimmenau onto D 157.

Reipertswiller

The **Église St-Jacques** overlooking the village has a 12C square belfry and a Gothic chancel built c 1480 by the last member of the Lichtenberg family.

Château de Lichtenberg

Follow the Lichtenberg high street prolonged by D 257 to the path leading to the castle and leave the car. Open Jun-Aug Mon 1.30-6pm, Tue–Sun 10am-6pm ; Apr-May & Sep-Oct: Mon 1.30-6pm, Tue–Sat 10am-noon, 1.30-6pm, Sun & holidays 10am-6pm; Mar & Nov: 1-4pm.

Address Book

For coin ranges, see the Legend on the cover flap.

THE PRACTICAL PARK

Maison du Parc – *Château de la Petite-Pierre, 67290 La Petite-Pierre, 03 88 01 49 59.*

Entertainment – The park is the venue of exhibitions and shows year-round: music, theatre, literary festival. Christmas markets liven up the area throughout December, notably at Bouxwiller. A free information brochure about activities and events taking place in the park between May and October, is available from the Maison du Parc.

Courses – From April to October, the Maison du Parc organises nature-discovery outings lasting a whole day and monitored by professionals or voluntary helpers.

Discovery trails – Brochures/guides containing information about discovery trails, the cultural heritage, the region's history and traditional villages, are available from the Maison du Parc.

WHERE TO STAY AND EAT

Auberge des Mésanges – *2 r. du Tiseur, 57960 Meisenthal. 03 87 96 92 28, hotel-restaurant. auberge-mesanges@wanadoo.fr. Closed 7-23 Feb and 22-26 Dec. 20 rooms. €6. Restaurant.* A good place to stay or eat after visiting the glass and crystal museum. The rooms are well equipped and impeccably kept. Simple, inexpensive meals, with *flammekueches* and pizzas starring at weekends.

La Cour du Tonnelier – *84 a Grand'rue, 67730 Bouxwiller. 03 88 70 72 57. www.courdutonnelier.com. Closed 9-31 Aug, Sun evening and Mon. 16 room. ; €6 . Restaurant.* This pale pink house near the town centre conceals an impeccably run hotel. The renovated rooms are decorated in warm colours, with lovely carpets and cherry wood furniture. The bathrooms are modern and functional. The small garden contains a swimming pool.

Le Cheval Blanc – *19 r. Principale, 67320 Graufthal. 03 88 70 17 11. Closed 6-23 Sep, 3-25 Jan, Mon evening, Wed evening & Tue.* This welcoming rustic inn remains faithful to regional cuisine. One dining rooms has a pretty faience stove.

Auberge du Cheval Blanc – *4 rte Wissembourg, 67510 Lembach. 03 88 94 41 86, www.au-cheval-blanc.fr. Closed 14 Jan-8 Feb, 20 Aug-7 Sep. 7 rooms.* This old coaching inn offers a grand dining experiences. Revisited Alsatian cuisine in the main restaurant with its fireplace and coffered ceiling, plus a simpler bistro.

ON THE TOWN

Le Royal Palace – *20 r. Hochfelden, 67330 Kirrwiller, 4km/2.5 E of Bouxwiller. 03 88 70 71 81. www.royal-palace.com. Times vary. Closed mid Jul-Aug.* This glitzy cabaret is the third biggest music hall in the country, pulling in the crowds from France and across the border.

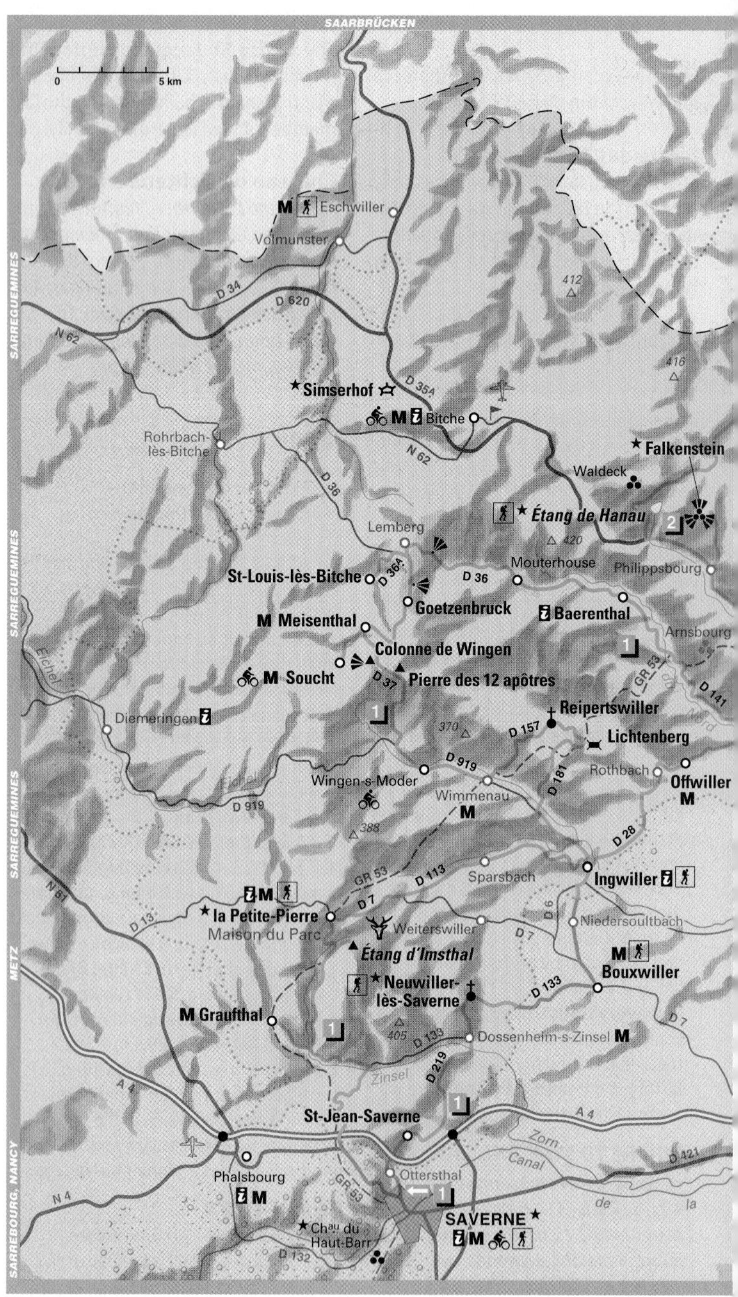

The castle, which has a 13C keep, was restored following shelling in the 1870 Franco-Prussian War.

Follow D 113 SW via Sparsbach.

La Petite-Pierre★

See La PETITE-PIERRE.

Graufthal

This hamlet of the Zinsel Valley has **troglodyte houses** dug into the red-sand-

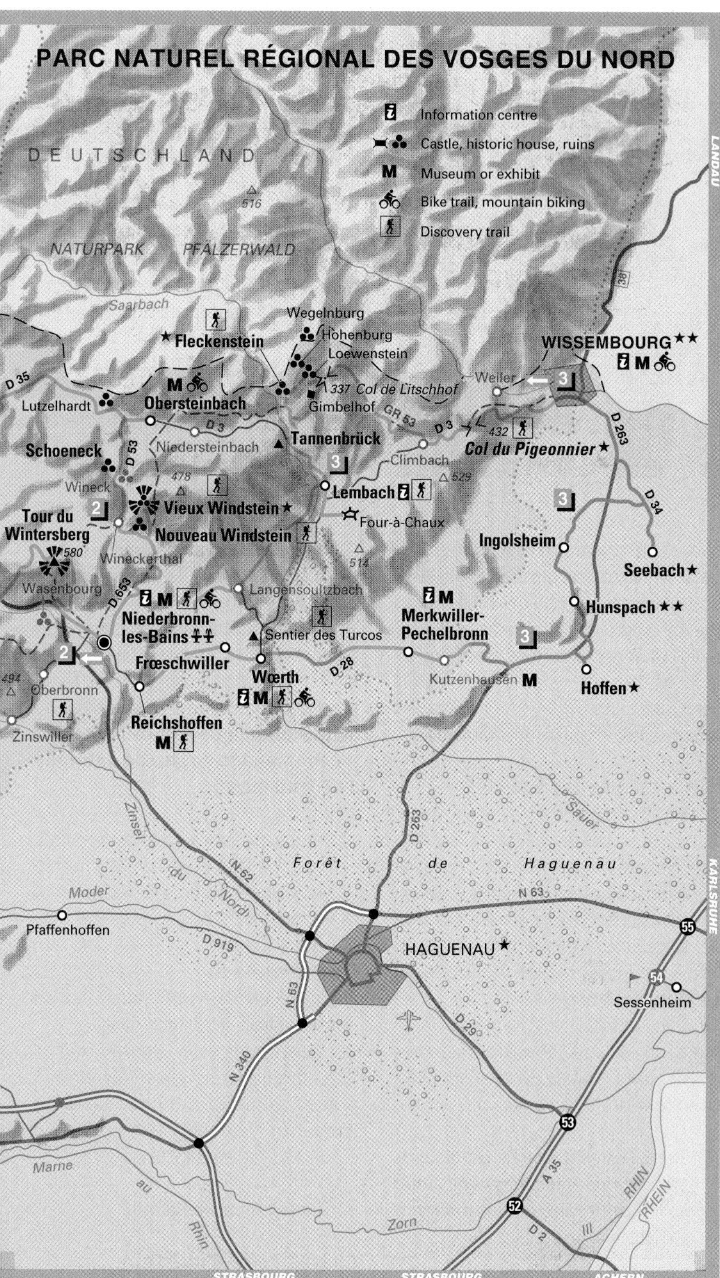

stone cliffs (70m/230ft high); they were inhabited until 1958 (*open Jul–Aug daily 2–6pm, Easter–Jun & Sep Sun & holidays 2–6pm, €2*).

Return to Saverne.

Castle Country: Round-trip from Niederbronn-les-Bains 2

54km/34mi – allow 2hr 30min.

R. Mattès/ MICHELIN

Fleckenstein Ruins

The area on the borders of the German palatinate, of Lorraine and Alsace is dotted with ruined castles built during the 12C and early 13C by the powerful dukes of Alsace, the Hohenstaufens, or by noble landowners who contested their authority. Today, their scattered ruins are full of romantic atmosphere.

Niederbronn-les-Bains

See NIEDERBRONN-LES-BAINS.

Leave Niederbronn towards Philippsbourg. Opposite the ruins of Wasenbourg Castle, turn right off N 62 then left onto a forest road.

Le Wintersberg

Alt 580m/1903ft. This is the highest summit of the Vosges du Nord. From the watch tower (112 steps), there is a fine panorama of the lower Vosges.

The 6.5km/4mi forest road rejoins N 62; turn right then right again onto D 87 just beyond Philippsbourg to Falkenstein Castle.

Château de Falkenstein★

45 min on foot there and back. Park at the crossroads and follow the second path on the left (marked with blue triangles) for 15min go up a few steps and turn left then right. Go through a doorway, turn left and walk round the peak on which the castle stands.

The castle, built in 1128, was struck by lightning and damaged by fire in 1564. Go through another door to find on your left, a vast cave carved into the rock, known as the Salle des Gardes (guardroom). Another small doorway leads to a flight of steps (with a handrail). You will notice several natural caves, where the rockface has been carved by streaming water, as well as several man-made caves. After a footbridge and stairs steps, you will reach the top of the castle,where there is a fine **panorama**★.

According to legend, the ghost of a cooper haunts the cellars at midnight and with a mallet, strikes a number of times corresponding to the number of casks of wine that will be produced during the year.

Rejoin N 62 and turn right 3km/1.9mi after Philippsbourg to Hanau Lake.

Étang de Hanau★

The lake, situated in marshland, has facilities for watersports (supervised bathing, pedalos, rowing boats). There are two waymarked footpaths: the **Sentier botanique de la tourbière** and the **Promenade de l'arche naturelle de Erbsenfelsen**.

Follow the forest road between the lake and Waldeck Castle to join D 35 which leads to Obersteinbach past the ruins of Lutzelhardt Castle.

Obersteinbach

Picturesque village with timber-framed houses on red-sandstone bases.

On the way out, D 53 is overlooked by several ruins which probably formed part of a line of defence guarding Haguenau's imperial castle at the end of the 12C (*see HAGUENAU*).

Turn left in Wineckerthal.

Châteaux de Windstein

Car park at the end of the left branch of the road by restaurant-hotel Aux Châteaux.

The two Windstein castles, standing 500m/547yd apart, were destroyed in 1676 by French troops commanded by Baron de Montclar. On the top of knoll **Vieux Windstein** (45 min on foot there and back) dates from the late 12C and is partly troglodyte. On another mound **Nouveau Windstein** (30 min on foot there and back) dates from 1340 and has some lovely Gothic arches.

Return to Niederbronn along D 653.

A Well-Guarded Border: Round-trip from Wissembourg 3

42km/26mi – allow half a day

Wissembourg★★

See WISSEMBOURG.

Château de Fleckenstein★

Open Jul-Aug daily 10am-6pm. Apr-Jun & Sep–mid-Oct daily 10am-5pm; late Mar & mid-Oct–early Nov 10am-4pm; rest of the year (except during snow or ice) weekends noon-4pm (daily 26-30 Dec). €9.50. ☎03 88 94 28 52, www.chateau-enigmes.com.

The castle was part of the 12C defences of the northern border of the duchy of Alsace. The castle was destroyed in 1680. The ruins occupy a remarkable position on a rock spur amid woods.

The walled lower courtyard is accessible through a fortified gateway. Note the impressive square tower built against the main rock. Inside, stairs lead to several rooms hewn out of the rock, including the amazing Salle des chevaliers (Knights' Hall) with its central monolithic pillar, and then onto the platform (8m/26ft wide) where the seigneurial residence stood.

Lembach

This charming small town has some fine old houses, wash-houses, inns. Viewpoints around the village have explanatory panels on themes such as urbanism, geology and botany.

1km/0.6mi along the road to Woerth is the entrance of the **Ouvrage du Four à Chaux** (*see Ligne MAGINOT*).

In Lembach, take the minor road along the Sauer to Reichshoffen.

The road goes through villages caught up in the 1870 Franco-Prussian War. Numerous roadside monuments commemorate the sacrifice of French and German soldiers killed in the fighting.

Reichshoffen

The village witnessed the heroic cavalry charge (6 August 1870) which ended in a massacre in Morsbronn-les-Bains nearby. The **Musée du Fer** illustrates the history of local mines and ironworks since the 14C (*Open Jun-Sep Wed–Mon 2-6pm; €2.50 ; ☎03 88 80 34 49*) .

Woerth

In the castle, the **Musée de la Bataille du 6 août 1870** contains uniforms, weapons, documents and pictures and a large diorama of the battle. *Open*

R. Mattes/ MICHELIN

Seebach typifies the beauty of an Alsatian village

mid-Jun–mid-Sep & Easter & Nov school holidays Wed–Mon 10am-noon, 2-6pm; Apr-May and Sep-Oct Wed–Mon 2–5pm; Feb-Mar & Nov-Dec weekends 2-5pm. *Jan. €3. ☎03 88 09 30 21.*

The **Sentier des Turcos** (starting just after the Alko France factory, on the left, on the way out of Woerth towards Lembach) is a history trail (2km/1.2mi) explains the main stages of the battle.

Merkwiller-Pechelbronn

This was the main centre of the oil fields of northern Alsace. All extracting operations stopped in 1970 but the small **Musée français du Pétrole** (*open Apr–Oct Thu, Sun & holidays 2.30-6pm, €4, ☎03 88 80 91 08, www.musee-du-petrole.com*) illustrates the main aspects of the industry. The town is now essentially a spa resort.

Hoffen★

This traditional village nestles round its church and its strange town hall supported by three wooden pillars. A lime tree planted during the Revolution stands next to the old public well.

Hunspach★★

White timber-framed houses with canopied façades line the streets of this agricultural village, ranking as one of the the most beautiful in France.

Seebach★

This flower-decked village has typical Alsatian timber-framed houses.

VOUZIERS

ARDENNES. POPULATION 4 742

MICHELIN LOCAL MAP 306: K-6

From a simple medieval village, Vouziers became in the 12C the rallying point of pilgrims with sick children seeking a cure from St Maurille, a 4C archbishop of Reims. Vouziers later developed into an important trading centre following the creation in 1516 by King François I of an annual fair.

- **Tourist Office**: 58 rue Chanzy, 08400 Vouziers. ☎03 24 71 97 57, www.ville-vouziers.fr
- **Orient Yourself**: 22km/13.7mi. E of Rethel by D946 on a branch of the Ardennes Canal.

Visit

Église St-Maurille

The west front has an interesting Renaissance triple **doorway**★, the first part of a new church whose construction was interrupted by the Wars of Religion. For over 200 years, the doorway stood isolated. In 1764, it was joined to the existing edifice by means of two additional bays. The

Ph. Gajic/ MICHELIN

St-Maurille church

WHERE TO STAY AND EAT

Chambre d'hôte Auberge du Pied des Monts – *08400 Grivy-Loisy, 7km/4.3mi NW of Vouziers on D 946 and D 21. ☎03 24 71 92 38, auberge-du-pied-des-monts@wanadoo.fr. Closed Jan. 5 rooms. €5.50. Evening meal* An inn in the centre of a quiet rural village. The rooms, four of which are huge with mezzanines, are in the converted stables of an old farm.

statues of the four evangelists are placed in recesses separating the three portals. The tympanum of the left door represents a skeleton, whereas the right one shows the risen Christ. A series of pendants representing the Good Shepherd and six Apostles decorate the central doorway. The tympanum depicts the Annunciation.

Excursions

Forêt de Croix-aux-Bois

The **Bois de Ham footpath** *(5.5km/3.5mi)* winds through the forest, planted with chestnuts, beeches and oaks, to the Étang de la Demoiselle; along the way, panels provide information on the forest biotope.

Canal des Ardennes

The canal which was dug during the reign of Louis-Philippe (1830-48), links the River Meuse to the River Aisne and to the waterways of the Seine Basin. There are 27 locks between Semuy and Le Chesne, over a distance of just 9km/5.6mi; the most interesting is in Montgon. North-east of Le Chesne, the canal follows the fertile valley of the River Bar.

Lac de Bairon

This lake (4km/2.5mi wide), set in hilly surroundings, is used as a reservoir of the Canal des Ardennes. It is divided into two by a causeway. There is a fine view of it from D 991. A section has been set aside as a bird sanctuary. The lake offers various activities including fishing, canoeing and walking.

Nocturnia à Olizy

11km by D946. Open Jul–Aug 10am–7.30pm. Apr–Jun & Nov school holidays–Feb Tue–Sun 10am–6pm. Mar, Sep–Oct Wed & weekends 2–6pm. P8.50 (children P6). 03 24 71 07 38.

Kids Opened in 2006, this centre is devoted to nocturnal species: birds of prey, bats, insects. In a dark room, an informative interactive route recreates the night-time environment.

WANGENBOURG

BAS-RHIN. POPULATION 1 182

MICHELIN LOCAL MAP 315: H-5

This charming summer resort is set amid meadows dotted with chalets and forests overlooked by the Schneeberg summit. A tree-felling competition takes place on the Sunday following the 14 July celebrations.

- **Tourist Office**: 32 avenue du Général de Gaulle, 67710 Wangenbourg-Engerthal. 03 88 87 33 50. www.suisse-alsace.com.
- **Orient Yourself**: 40km/25mi. W of Strasbourg by N4 and D224.

Visit

Castle ruins

The ruins are accessible on foot *(15min there and back; leave the car in the parking area, 200m/220yd beyond the church; walk past a huge lime tree and follow a path which prolongs the main street)*. The 13C and 14C castle belonged to Andlau Abbey. The pentagonal keep and important sections of walls are still visible. A path, which partly runs along the castle moat, takes you round the huge sandstone outcrop crowned by the ruins.

Excursions

The picturesque **Dabo-Wangenbourg Region**★★ lies on the border of Alsace and Lorraine. Its austere sandstone massifs are separated by green valleys and calm sandy rivers.

Forêt de Saverne

78km/48.5mi round-trip N of Wangenbourg – allow 3hr 30min

R. Mattès/ MICHELIN

The falls at Nideck

Obersteigen

This is a pleasant summer resort. The church marks the transition between the Romanesque and Gothic styles.

Follow D 45 to Dabo.

The winding road enters a splendid forest and offers fine glimpses of the Rocher de Dabo, the fertile Kochersberg plateau and of the Plaine d'Alsace.

Rocher de Dabo★

Signposted Rocher St-Léon. Open May–Oct daily 9am-6pm, mid-Apr–end Apr 1–6pm. €2. 03 87 07 40 12.

This sandstone rock is crowned by two viewing tables and a chapel dedicated to St Léon (Leo IX). Beneath the tower, to the left of the doorway giving access to the chapel, a small door opens onto a staircase (92 steps). The **panorama**★ from the top of the tower includes the main summits of the Vosges and the X-shaped village of Dabo.

For coin ranges, see the Legend on the cover flap.

WHERE TO EAT

Auberge des Randonneurs – *3 pl. de l'Église, 57850 Dabo, 15km/mi NW of Wangenbourg on D 218, D 143 then D 45. 03 87 07 47 48. Closed 24-25 Dec.* This simple inn, in a small alley in the village, serves unpretentious regional food. The dining room is decorated with the owner's wood carvings and pictures. Shady terrace and delicious home-made pâté.

Dabo

This summer resort lies in a very pleasant **setting**★ in a forested area.

Beyond Schaeferhof, bear left along D 45 and turn left again onto D 96 5km/3mi farther on.

On approaching Schaeferhof, one can see the hilltop village of Haselbourg.

Cristallerie de Vallerysthal

Open daily 10am–noon, 1–5pm. Closed 1 Jan, 25 Dec. No charge. 03 87 25 62 04.

In 1838, Baron Klinglin transferred the Plaine-de-Walsch glassworks here; the new works prospered during the second half of the 19C, employing up to 1 300 workers in 1914. Nearly 40 000 pieces, displayed on the premises, illustrate the production from the 18C to today.

Return to D 98C.

Rocher du Nutzkopf★

Accessible by D 98D from Sparsbrod then a forest track on the left and finally a footpath signposted on the left (45min on foot there and back).

From the top (alt 515m/1 690ft) of this strange tabular rock, the **view★** extends to the Rocher de Dabo, the village of La Hoube and Grossthal Valley.

Return to D 98C then turn right onto D 98 which follows the Zorn Valley.

Plan incliné de St-Louis-Arzviller★

Guided tour with boat lift (1hr 30min), Jul-Aug 10.30am-5.30pm (8 departures); May-Jun and Sep: 10am-5pm (6 departures). Enquire. €7. Guided tour only (45min). €3. 03 87 25 30 69. www.plan-incline.com.fr.

It is best seen from D 98C. Inaugurated in 1969, this boat elevator is equipped with an inclined plane 108.65m/356.46ft long in order to clear the 44.55m/146ft drop. It replaced 17 locks previously spread over a distance of 4km/2.5mi alongside the railway, which took a whole day to negotiate. Now, a 43m/141ft long ferry truck going up sideways on rails along a concrete ramp by a system of counterbalance, transfers barges from one level to the other in 20min.

Vallée de la Zorn★

This pleasant wooded valley is the busiest route through the northern Vosges mountains. The ruins of the medieval **Château de Lutzelbourg** stand on a promontory; overlooking D 38-D 132.

Château du Haut-Barr★

See Château du HAUT-BARR.

Saverne★ – *See SAVERNE.*

Marmoutier★★ – *See MARMOUTIER.*

Forêt de Haslach

44km/27mi round-trip S of Wangenbourg – allow 2hr 30min

Beyond Wolfsthal, D 218 climbs up to the beautiful **Haslach Forest**. A pleasant drive leads to the forest lodge then past a stele on the left, which commemorates the building of the road. Farther on (500m/547yd), the road starts winding down towards Oberhaslach.

Château and Cascade du Nideck★★

Park in the car park below the forest lodge and follow signposted footpath (1hr 15min on foot there and back).

A 13C tower and 14C keep, standing in a romantic **setting★★**, are all that remains of two castles destroyed by fire in 1636. The German-speaking poet Chamisso de Boncourt, known as Adalbert von Chamisso, celebrated this site in his poems. From the top of the tower and the keep, there are fine views.

Walk to the right of the keep and follow a path on the left to the waterfall. Bear right beyond a wooden shelter and a small bridge to the viewpoint (very dangerous in spite of the railing).

From the belvedere, there is a splendid **view★★** of the glacial valley and the wooded chasm into which the waterfall drops from the top of a porphyry wall. To see the waterfall, continue past the viewpoint along a marked path *(30min there and back).*

Return to D 218.

Oberhaslach

This village is particularly lively on the Sunday following 7 November, when pilgrims come to pray to St Florent who, in the 7C, was believed to have the power to tame wild animals. Today, he still protects domestic animals but he also intervenes on behalf of pilgrims. Numerous grateful acknowledgements testify to his efficiency. The Baroque chapel, built in 1750 and restored in 1987, stands on the spot where the saint lived as a hermit before he became the seventh bishop of Strasbourg.

Église de Niederhaslach★

The village once had an abbey said to have been founded by St Florent in rather comic circumstances: for having cured his daughter, King Dagobert granted St Florent as much land as his donkey could delimit during the time the king spent washing and dressing; on the day in question, the king spent more time than he usually did and the donkey went galloping off, so that St Florent was given a considerable amount of land. The Gothic church, stands on the site of the former abbey. The doorway is framed by small statues and decorated with a tympanum illustrating the legend of St Florent curing King Dagobert's daughter. Note the beautiful 14C-15C stained-glass **windows**★.

▸ *Follow D 75.*

Wasselonne

An old tower is the only part left of the castle overlooking this former stronghold whose houses are scattered on the slopes of the last foothill of the Kochersberg. The Wasselonne fair (last Sun and Mon in August) sees an impressive procession of floral floats.

▸ *Drive W along D 224.*

Vallée de la Mossig

Strange projecting sandstone rocks overlook the River Mossig. Strasbourg Cathedral is built of sandstone from here.

WASSY

HAUTE-MARNE. POPULATION 3 294

MICHELIN LOCAL MAP 313: J 2-3

This quiet little town, at the heart of "wet Champagne," has retained the traditional ironworks which brought prosperity at a time when, before the First World War, Wassy was one of the main centres of iron-ore mining and metalwork in France. In 1562, Wassy was the setting for a massacre that marked the start of the Wars of Religion.

Tourist Office: Square Eppingen, 52130 Wassy. ☎03 25 07 64 47.

▸ **Orient Yourself**: On the River Blaise, 19km from St-Dizier by D2.

Sights

Église Notre-Dame

The late 12C church has both Romanesque and Gothic features.

Musée Protestant

Open mid-Jun–mid-Sep Tue–Sun 2-6pm. Rest of the year by appointment. holidays. No charge. ☎03 25 07 64 47.

Ph. Gajic/ MICHELIN

Château of Cirey-sur-Blaise

The Wassy Massacre

In 1562, François de Guise returned to Wassy one Sunday when the Protestant community was assembled in a vast barn. The duke's men began quarrelling with some of the Protestants and, having entered the barn, they massacred all those they could lay their hands on. The duke later disavowed the massacre although he had done nothing to stop it. This event deeply stirred the growing Protestant population of France and was one of the causes of the Wars of Religion which tore the country apart until 1598 when the Edict of Nantes was signed, granting religious freedom to all French subjects.

The Protestant museum illustrates the history of the reformed church of Wassy in the 16C and 17C and is located in a Protestant church, built on the site of the barn where the massacre took place. **Paul and Camille Claudel** lived opposite with their parents. Paul later became a poet and playwright and his sister Camille a talented sculptor and close friend of Rodin.

Driving Tour

Vallée de la Blaise

34km/21mi from Wassy to Cirey-sur-Blaise.

As early as 1157, monks from Clairvaux founded the first industrial forge in Wassy and smelting works and workshops gradually settled along the river, using wood from the nearby forests, water power and local iron ore.

In 1840, Osne-le-Val was the birthplace of ornamental cast iron. In 1900, Hector Guimard chose St-Dizier for his Art Nouveau creations. Today, the area produces urban furniture for many towns throughout the world. In addition, some 100 highly specialised metalworks supply the aeronautical industry, the car industry and the chemical industry.

An unmarked road, known as the Route du Fer, links the main sites which testify to this ancient metalworking tradition.

Drive S along D 2 to Dommartin-le-Franc.

Dommartin-le-Franc

The former **smelting works** built in 1834 are now used for exhibitions about metalwork and ornamental cast iron (*open mid-Jul–Aug Tue–Sun 2.30–6pm. Sept weekends 2.30-6pm. €3.50. 06 15 38 48 90, www.fontesdart.org*).

Continue S along D 60 and turn right 2km/1.2mi farther on.

Sommevoire

In the 19C this village specialised in the production of ornamental cast iron (fountains, lamps, vases, religious statues) initiated by Antoine Durenne. The **Paradis** (*open mid-Jul–mid-Sep Tue–Sun 2.30-6pm, rest of the year by request, 03 25 94 22 05*) houses a collection of his models, monumental plaster casts, some of them by eminent artists such as Bartholdi. The **Église St-Pierre** (*Same conditions as the Paradis above*), deconsecrated, is used as an exhibition hall for cast-iron creations.

From Sommevoire drive SE along D 229 and rejoin the River Blaise in the iron town of Doulevant-le-Château. Then continue S along the river.

Cirey-sur-Blaise

From 1733 to 1749, Voltaire stayed for long periods in the **château** (*guided tour (1hr) Jul–Aug 2.30-6.30pm; May-Jun and Sep, Sun and holidays, 2.30-6.30pm; €7; 03 25 955 43 04*) of his friend the Marquise du Châtelet, whom he called the "divine Émilie." He wrote several works here, including two tragedies: Alzire and Mahomet. The château consists of a 17C pavilion and an 18C wing built by Madame du Châtelet and Voltaire. Note the doorway in the Rocaille style designed by Voltaire.

WISSEMBOURG★★

BAS-RHIN. POPULATION 8 170

MICHELIN LOCAL MAP 315: L-2

Wissembourg grew up beside a prosperous Benedictine abbey; the city became a member of Decapolis (*see MULHOUSE*) in 1354. Today, it still has a considerable part of its fortifications. The River Lauter splits into several arms here, giving character to the town, especially the Schlupf district known as the Little Venice of Wissembourg. The annual fair on Whit Monday offers visitors the opportunity to see many Alsatian costumes.

- **Tourist Office**: 9 place de la République, 67160 Wissembourg, ☎03 88 94 10 11, www.ot-wissembourg.fr.
- **Orient Yourself**: On the German border, 33km N or Haguenau by D263.

A Bit of History

Stanislas Leszczynski, deposed king of Poland (*see NANCY*), having lost his fortune, settled in Wissembourg with his daughter Maria and a few loyal friends. In 1725, Duc d'Antin arrived from Paris and announced that King Louis XV had decided to marry his daughter. The royal couple was married by proxy in Strasbourg Cathedral; Louis XV was 15 years old, Maria 22.

Sights

Hôtel de ville

Place de la République.

Built of pink sandstone with pediment, small tower and clock (1741-52).

Église St-Pierre-et-St-Paul★

rue du Châpitre.

This 13C largely Gothic church has an interesting 15C fresco, depicting St Christopher holding Jesus in his arms: the largest painted character known in France (11m/36ft). The chancel is lit by 13C stained-glass windows, however, the oldest stained glass is the late 12C little rose of the Virgin and Child on the gable of the north transept. On the north side of the church, a gallery and two bays are all that remain of a splendid yet never completed **cloister**. A door leads to an 11C Romanesque chapel.

Ancien Hôpital

This was the residence of Stanislas Leszczinski from 1719 to 1725, when his daughter married Louis XV.

R. Mattès/ MICHELIN

The remarkable roof of the Maison du Sel, in the centre of town

WISSEMBOURG			Chapitre R. du	A	3	République Pl. et R.	B	7
			Marché-aux-Choux Pl. du	B	5	Saumon Pl. du	A	8
24-Novembre Q. du	A	13	Nationale R.	B		Sous-Préfecture Av. de la	A	9
Anselman Quai	A	2	Ordre-Teutonique R. de l'	A	6	Stanislas R.	A	10

Ancien hôpital	A	B	Maison du sel	A	K
Grange dîmière	A	F	Musée Westercamp	A	M
Hôtel de ville	B	H	Sous-Préfecture	A	P
Maison Vogelsberger	A	L	Ancienne Couronne	A	N

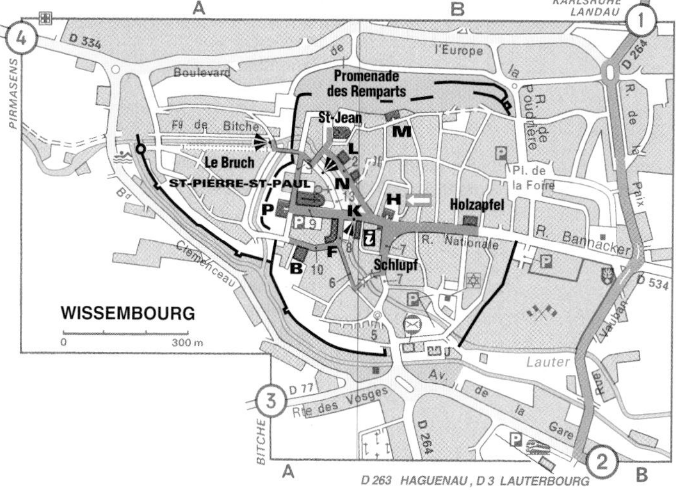

Address Book

For coin ranges, see the Legend on the cover flap.

PRACTICAL INFORMATION

Mini-train touristique – Tour with commentary in French, English or German (45min). Leaves from Place de la République. *Info. from the Tourist Office. Apr-Oct €5 (children: €2.50).*

WHERE TO EAT

Le Carrousel Bleu – *17 r. Nationale. ☎03 88 54 33 10. Closed 1-15 Aug, Wed evening, Sun evening & Mon.* This agreeable restaurant on the main street seres original recipes that transport you miles from the "Little Venice".

Auberge du Pfaffenschlick – *Col de Pfaffenschlick, 67510 Climbach, 12km/7.5mi SW of Wissembourg on D 3, Lembach direction, and the mountain road on D 51. ☎03 88 54 28v84 www.restaurant-du-pfaffenschlick. Closed 15 Jan-15 Feb, Mon and Tue.* A restaurant in the middle of the forest, just opposite a cabin used as a canteen during the construction of the Maginot Line. Long frequented by walkers, it continues to serve homely local fare.

WHERE TO STAY

Moulin de la Walk – *2 r. Walk. ☎03 88 94 06 44. www.moulin-walk.com. Closed 2-23 Jan. 25 rooms. €7.50. Restaurant* . On the remains of an old water mill beside the Lauter, rooms here are functional and fresh.

SHOPPING

Cave vinicole de Cleebourg – *Rte du Vin, 67160 Cleebourg. ☎03 88 94 50 33. www.cave-cleebourg.com. Mon-Sat 8am-noon, 2-6pm, Sun and holidays from 10am. Closed 1 Jan, Easter, 25 Dec.* Free wine tasting and sales.

Pâtisserie Rebert – *7 pl. du Marché-aux-Choux. ☎03 88 94 01 66. danielrebert@wanadoo.fr. Tue-Sat 7am-6.30pm (Sun 8am); tearoom: Oct-Apr. Closed 26 Dec.* The speciality in this chocolate shop is the pavés de Wissembourg, little chocolate creams.

D

Driving Tours

E

F

G

H

N

O

P

R

S

WHERE TO EAT

WHERE TO STAY

LIST OF MAPS

THEMATIC MAPS

MONUMENTS

LOCAL MAPS FOR TOURING

TOWN PLANS

MAPS AND PLANS

COMPANION PUBLICATIONS

REGIONAL AND LOCAL MAPS

To make the most of your journey, travel with Michelin Regional maps nos 514 and 515, and the Local maps at a scale of 1:150 000, which are illustrated on the map of France opposite.
And remember to travel with the latest edition of the map of France no 721 (1:1 000 000), also available in atlas format: spiral bound, hard back and mini-atlas – perfect for your glove compartment.

Michelin is pleased to offer a route-planning service on the Internet: www.ViaMichelin.com
Choose the shortest route, a route without tolls, or the Michelin recommended route to your destination; you can also access information about hotels and restaurants from the Michelin Guide, and tourist sites from The Green Guide.
Bon voyage!

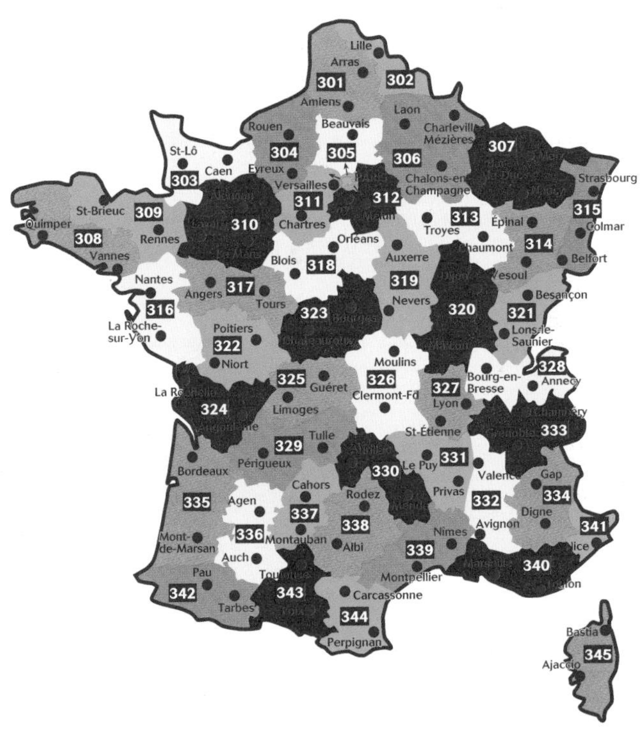

Abbreviations

A	Agricultural office (Chambre d'agriculture)
C	Chamber of Commerce (Chambre de commerce)
H	Town hall (Hôtel de ville)
J	Law courts (Palais de justice)
M	Museum (Musée)
P	Local authority offices (Préfecture, sous-préfecture)
POL.	Police station (Police)
	Police station (Gendarmerie)
T	Theatre (Théâtre)
U	University (Université)

Selected monuments and sights

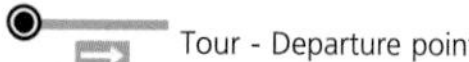
Tour - Departure point

Catholic church

Protestant church, other temple

Synagogue - Mosque

Building

Statue, small building

Calvary, wayside cross

Fountain

Rampart - Tower - Gate

Château, castle, historic house

Ruins

Dam

Factory, power plant

Fort

Cave

Troglodyte dwelling

Prehistoric site

Viewing table

Viewpoint

Other place of interest

LEGEND

	Sight	Seaside resort	Winter sports resort	Spa
Highly recommended	★★★			
Recommended	★★			
Interesting	★			

Additional symbols

	Tourist information
	Motorway or other primary route
	Junction: complete, limited
	Pedestrian street
	Unsuitable for traffic, street subject to restrictions
	Steps – Footpath
	Train station – Auto-train station
S.N.C.F.	Coach (bus) station
	Tram
	Metro, underground
	Park-and-Ride
	Access for the disabled
	Post office
	Telephone
	Covered market
	Barracks
	Drawbridge
	Quarry
	Mine
B F	Car ferry (river or lake)
	Ferry service: cars and passengers
	Foot passengers only
③	Access route number common to Michelin maps and town plans
Bert (R.)...	Main shopping street
AZ **B**	Map co-ordinates

Sports and recreation

	Racecourse
	Skating rink
	Outdoor, indoor swimming pool
	Multiplex Cinema
	Marina, sailing centre
	Trail refuge hut
	Cable cars, gondolas
	Funicular, rack railway
	Tourist train
	Recreation area, park
	Theme, amusement park
	Wildlife park, zoo
	Gardens, park, arboretum
	Bird sanctuary, aviary
	Walking tour, footpath
	Of special interest to children

Michelin Apa Publications Ltd

A joint venture between Michelin and Langenscheidt

Suite 6, Tulip House, 70 Borough High Street, London SE1 1XF, United Kingdom

ISBN 978-1-906261-04-7

Printed: September 2007

Printed and bound in Germany

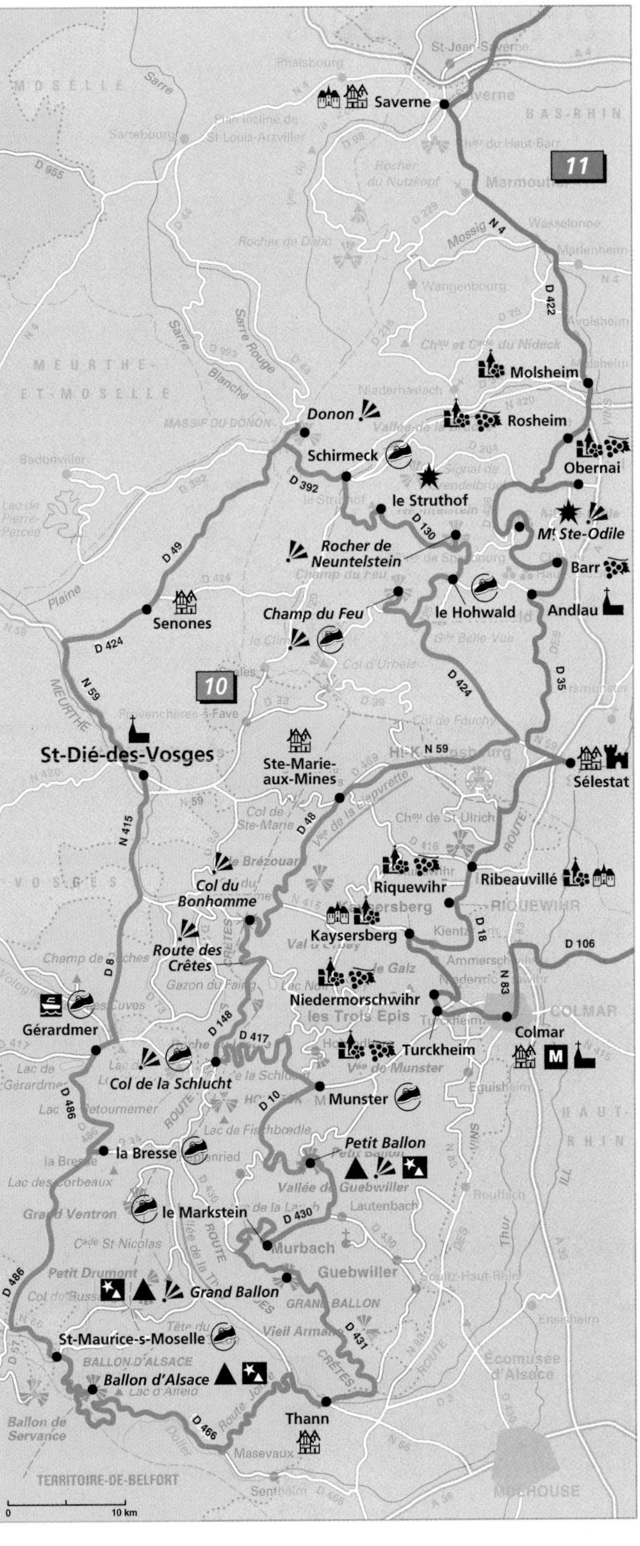

11
10
Saverne
Molsheim
Donon
Rosheim
Obernai
Schirmeck
le Struthof
Mt Ste-Odile
Rocher de Neuntelstein
Barr
Champ du Feu
le Hohwald
Andlau
Senones
St-Dié-des-Vosges
Ste-Marie-aux-Mines
Sélestat
Ribeauvillé
Riquewihr
Col du Bonhomme
Kaysersberg
Route des Crêtes
Niedermorschwihr
Gérardmer
Colmar
Turckheim
Col de la Schlucht
Munster
Petit Ballon
la Bresse
le Markstein
Murbach
Grand Ballon
St-Maurice-s-Moselle
Ballon d'Alsace
Thann
D 392
D 130
D 49
D 424
N 59
N 415
D 48
D 8
D 148
D 417
D 10
D 486
D 430
D 431
D 466
D 18
N 83
D 106
D 35
D 422
N 4
0
10 km

Driving tours

For descriptions of these tours, turn to the *Planning Your Trip* section following.

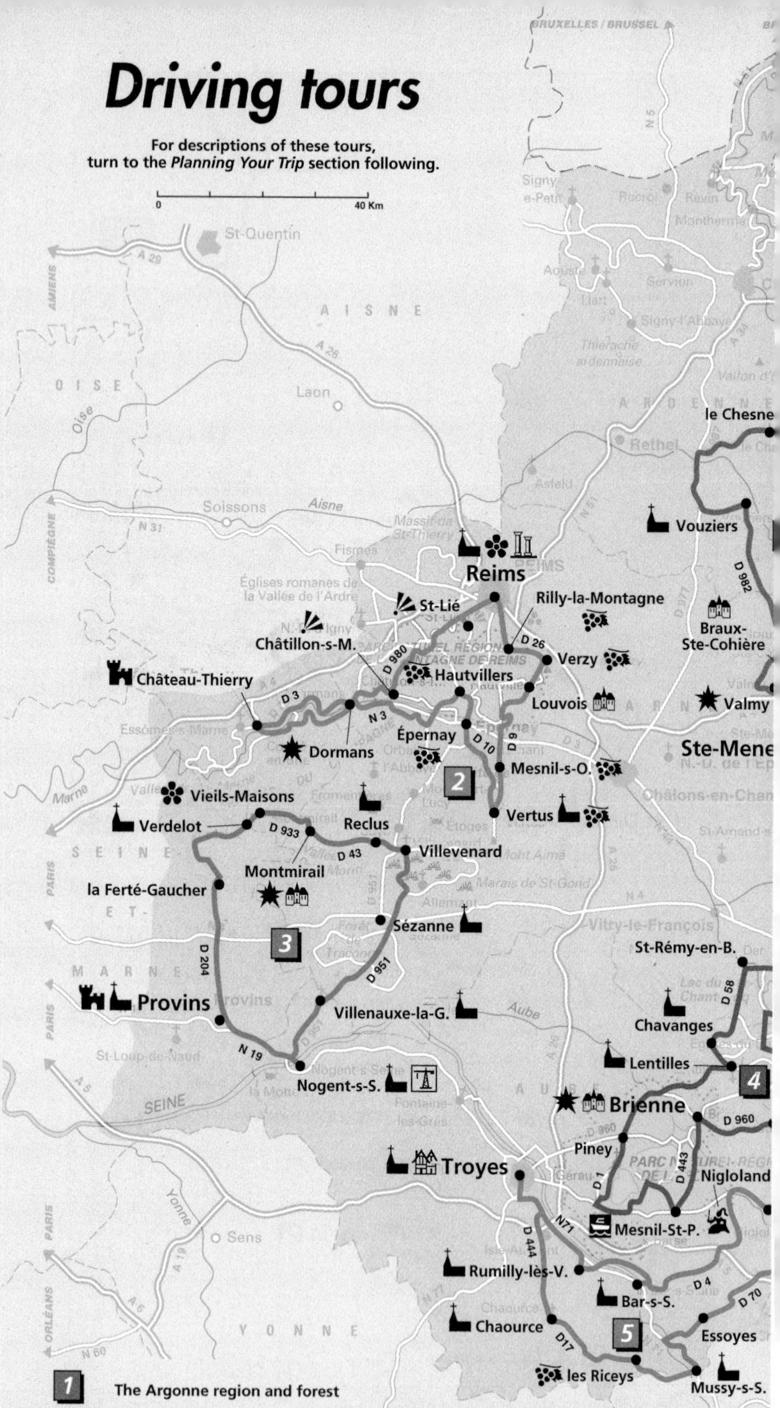

1 The Argonne region and forest

2 The Golden Triangle

3 Brie champenoise

4 The lakes of the Der region

5 Champagne: from Bar to Bar

6 Arts and crafts in Haute-Marne

7 Remembering two World Wars

8 Between Meuse and Moselle

9 Spa resorts in the Vosges

10 The Vosges forest

11 The Alsatian Wine Road